MW00786936

Turfgrass Maintenance Reduction Handbook:

Sports, Lawns, and Golf

by

DOUG BREDE, PH.D.

ANN ARBOR PRESS
CHELSEA, MICHIGAN

Library of Congress Cataloging-in-Publication Data

Brede, Doug.
Turfgrass maintenance reduction handbook : sports, lawns, and golf: research-proven strategies for maintaining your lawn, park, sports field, or golf course with less water, fertilizer, mowing, pesticide, and effort / by Doug Brede.
p. cm.
Includes bibliographical references (p.).
ISBN 1-57504-106-5
1. Turf management—Handbooks, manuals, etc. I. Title.

SB433 .B74 2000
635.9'642—dc21 99-08778

ISBN 1-57504-106-5

Direct all inquiries to Sleeping Bear Press, 310 North Main Street, P.O. Box 20, Chelsea, MI 48118.

PRINTED IN THE UNITED STATES OF AMERICA
10 9 8 7 6 5 4 3 2 1

ABOUT THE AUTHOR

Doug Brede has had a lifelong interest in lowering maintenance, starting with his first job as a teenager, mowing yards for spending money. "I think it was all those trips back and forth to the clippings pile at Mrs. Fernstead's house that first convinced me there's got to be an easier way to do the things we do," he says, referring to one of his early lawn care clients (see introduction to Chapter 9).

Brede attended Penn State University as an agronomy major, discovering turf management as a career during his sophomore year. He spent summers during college maintaining a 2-hole golf course. (The other 16 holes were under construction.) "I did it single-handedly and without a lot of equipment. That's probably where I acquired my experience at improvising," he says.

After graduation, Brede worked as an assistant superintendent for Valley Brook Country Club, a 27-hole course south of Pittsburgh, PA. He discusses some of his learning experiences as an assistant superintendent in Chapters 6 and 10. While at the course, he became interested in turf research, putting out plot trials on the fairways and greens.

After two years at the golf course, he reenrolled at Penn State University to pursue an MS and Ph.D. degree under the direction of Joe Duich, a leading turfgrass expert and breeder of the Penn-series of grasses. Brede's thesis projects dealt with turf establishment and grass seed mixtures. He worked half-time during school, planting, harvesting, and rating the breeding plots at Penn State.

After graduation in 1982, Brede took a job as an assistant professor at Oklahoma State University, replacing Wayne Huffine, a noted roadside turf researcher. He continued two of Huffine's long-term grants on roadside research, as well as pursuing a variety of interests on fine turf. He was awarded tenure and promoted to associate professor after four years. Shortly after that, he took the job of research director at Simplot Turf & Horticulture in Post Falls, ID, where he works today.

Brede's research department has released over 50 improved cultivars of Kentucky bluegrass, creeping bentgrass, tall fescue, fine fescue, perennial ryegrass, zoysiagrass, and bermudagrass. He has personally developed the PVP patents on many of these varieties, and holds utility patents in plant breeding. Brede breeds the bluegrasses and bentgrasses himself, and supervises two breeders for the other species. His grasses have been planted in more than 50 countries worldwide. Brede is a popular speaker at turf conferences, and was the organizer of the first turf conference in the Peoples Republic of China in 1990.

Brede currently serves as associate editor for *Agronomy Journal*, the most widely circulated periodical in the agronomic sciences. He has published over 100 articles in journal and popular trade magazines on turf and related subjects. He has served on research committees for the Golf Course Superintendents Association, the Lawn Institute, the Turfgrass Breeders Association, the National Turfgrass Evaluation Program, the National Grass Variety Review Board, the Idaho State Grasscycling Board, and the Crop Science Society of Agronomy.

Brede lives with his wife, Linda, and children, Lori, Amanda, and Michael, in their home in Washington State.

"I want to stress that the story of low maintenance turf does not end here," he says. "If you have ideas, tips, suggestions for new maintenance-saving ideas, please write to me and let me know. Brede can be contacted by email at *dbrede@jacklin.com* or at his office at W. 5300 Riverbend Avenue, Post Falls, ID 83854.

PREFACE

Anyone who's sweated away a long, hot summer afternoon pushing a lawn mower might view "low maintenance turfgrass" as a contradiction of terms. Most people consider turf upkeep a lot of hard work. To attain the perfect lawn—or it seems even a borderline acceptable turf—requires time, money, muscle power, and a whole lot of artificial ingredients.

But things are changing. People are taking another look at turf, trying to decide if there are easier ways to do the things we do. Even the President of the United States has gotten into the act. In a 1994 Executive Memorandum, President Bill Clinton mandated a reduced maintenance approach to all future federal landscaping projects (McRoland, 1995). Henceforth, all new government buildings and federally-funded roadways will have to seek lower maintenance landscaping solutions. And of course, a majority of these changes will involve the turf.

Turfgrass in the United States is big business. It encompasses a land area equivalent to the five New England states put together. Worldwide, there's probably more money socked into turf than the total national GNP of many third-world countries. With all this land area and billions of dollars tied up in turf culture, the potential exists for tremendous savings by using maintenance-cutting techniques. If every turf facility could trim their maintenance budget by just a few dollars a year, the net savings worldwide would be immense.

Another big reason to seek lower maintenance is environmental concern. In turfgrass—perhaps more than in any other crop—the potential exists for the misuse or overapplication of fertilizers and pesticides. That's because with turf, unlike other crops, fertilizers and chemicals are applied by millions of unlicensed, untrained homeowners whose philosophy seems to be: "If a little bit works, a lot should work even better."

According to U.S. Department of Agriculture statistics, each acre of agricultural land is doused with an average of 5.8 lb of pesticide and 52 lb of fertilizer per year (Wagner, 1994). Groundwater pollution from fertilizers and pesticides is escalating in many regions of the country, particularly the Midwest and Gulf Coast. Chemical residues have been detected in drinking water supplies in at least 26 states (Wagner, 1994).

Aside from the presidential mandates and environmental concerns, there are also some very personal reasons to trim your maintenance. Turf care is expensive, time-consuming, and, just plain boring. Reduced turf maintenance translates directly into money savings and more leisure time—not to mention less reliance on valuable natural resources.

As I see it, cutting your maintenance is not a passive process but an *active* one. Neglect is passive. Cutting your maintenance, on the other hand, involves a proactive approach—planning and constructing a lawn or sports turf that will demand less care *for perpetuity*.

Simply neglecting your lawn won't work. For example, if today you started mowing your turf one fewer time per month, you'd probably cut your mowing expenses. But at what cost? The result would be a taller, shaggier, unsightly turf. You may have saved a mowing, but you sacrificed the quality, aesthetics, and playability.

Maintenance reduction involves an amalgamation of tools and practices. It may require changes in your grass species or variety, your soil, fertilizer, mowing, watering, or pest control practices. It involves preparation and design. It takes concerted effort with all of the changes working together to produce a tough, attractive turf capable of withstanding less care. But it can be done.

Of course, the single most important ingredient for cutting maintenance isn't bioinsecticides, natural fertilizers, native grass species, or high-tech irrigation systems. The most important ingredient is YOU. Lower maintenance calls for a new way of thinking about grass. It involves questioning your present practices and developing new ones. Seldom is one adjustment sufficient.

In this book, I'll share with you some of the secrets for !owering your maintenance, along with some new, innovative techniques pioneered by top turf researchers. Many of these research findings are so new, they've not yet found their way into scientific journals.

This book is laid out to build on a concept of developing a healthy foundation for your turf. Chapter 1 describes the prerequisites for a durable, low maintenance turf. It's all too easy to shut the water faucet or apply one less bag of fertilizer. But if your turf suffers, what have you gained? An effective turf foundation will allow you to reduce maintenance without sacrificing quality.

Chapters 2, 3, and 4 show you how to the choose the right grass for your space. One of the secrets of low maintenance turf care is to select the grass best adapted for your location. These chapters provide timely data on turfgrass species and varieties. Included is one of the most comprehensive catalogs of unusual and unconventional turfgrasses ever assembled. Chapter 5 assists you in picking the ideal grass for your unique location, whether your lawn is in Tacoma or Timbuktu. World maps pinpoint your site and offer grassing options.

Chapters 6 and 7 guide you through the process of installing turfgrasses, including new construction and renovation of tired, old turf. Chapter 8 digs into the vital building block of *turf soil*—the essential but often neglected component of a successful low maintenance turf. Soil modification, drainage, and remediation of wear, compaction, and thatch are detailed.

Chapters 9, 10, and 11 offer practical how-to tips for trimming fertilizer, water, and mowing. After a solid low maintenance foundation is in place, your turf is ready to withstand fewer inputs. Professional turf managers and turf scientists share their pointers *that really work*.

The last chapter, Chapter 12, confronts pest control. Time-tested methods offer effective pest control with less reliance on pesticides. A balanced discussion highlights how and when cultural changes can be substituted for chemicals.

CONTENTS

Turfgrass Maintenance Reduction Handbook:

Sports, Lawns, and Golf

Chapter 1

Strategies of Lower Maintenance Turf

EVERYONE CAN BENEFIT FROM LOWER MAINTENANCE

Ask a dozen people what their idea of "low maintenance turf" is, and you'll get a dozen interesting answers. To many people, low maintenance turf is the brown, thin, clumpy stand of grass you find on some old roadside or abandoned right-of-way. Yes, those turf stands are indeed low maintenance—about as low in maintenance as you can go. Nearly zero, in fact.

But low maintenance turf has another meaning—one that applies equally well to all turfs, including home lawns and premium golf courses. Sometimes the highest maintenance turf sites stand to reap the greatest rewards from maintenance-reducing techniques. The tips and techniques detailed in this book can benefit every situation, from the basic home lawn to a championship pro sports field.

Here's a story to illustrate the point: Consider two houses side by side. Both houses are poorly insulated against the cold, wasting a lot of heat during the winter. House A averages $400 per month in winter heating bills, while smaller House B pays $200. Homeowners in both houses decide to add insulation to help cut their heating costs. The installation contractor says the additional insulation will cut their heating bills in half. Which of the two houses—A or B—will save more money?

Of course the answer is that *both* houses stand to gain from added insulation. But House A with the higher heating bills will reap the greatest reward: House A will save $200 per month while house B pockets $100.

This same concept applies to turf (Figure 1.1). The more money, labor, and products you currently expend on your turf, the more you stand to gain from lower maintenance. A golf course or sports field with a beefy maintenance budget can save far more by trimming maintenance than can a park or cemetery. A turf facility that's already spending rock bottom maintenance-wise stands little to gain by additional reductions. It's already nearly zero. However, even this type of turf can be improved in quality and appearance by the techniques outlined in this book.

Before you charge out to cut your maintenance, it's important to define exactly what you're saving. Maintenance reductions come in many forms. In the house analogy, money savings was the key issue. The homeowners saved money by insulating their houses. But other things can be conserved as well, such as your time and valuable natural resources. It's a good idea to develop a priorities list for your turf site, and then use this book to solve your high priority issues.

This chapter examines various turf maintenance practices and puts them into perspective against other landscaping practices. You'll discover that turf can be quite thrifty if you design it that way from the start.

Is turf really a maintenance hog?

If you believed all the media hype you hear about turf these days, you'd swear that turf was a maintenance hog. However, a recent study in California has dispelled the popular hype by comparing turfgrass to other landscape plant materials. The researchers quantified the labor involved in upkeeping various types of turf, flower, and ornamental ground covers (Table 1.1). Amazing as it may seem, turf was not the high-

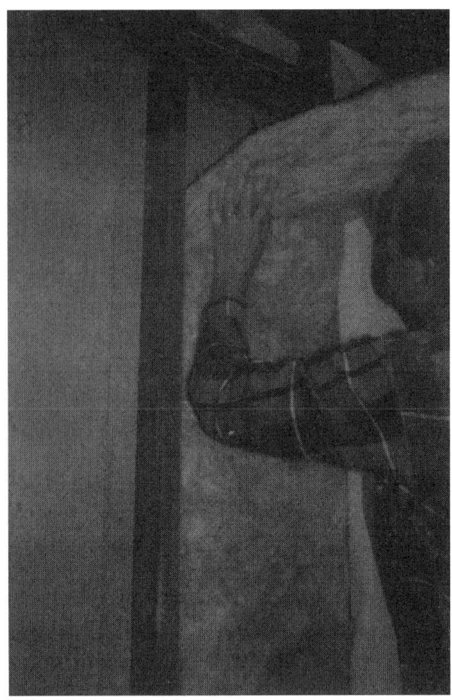

Figure 1.1. Turf maintenance can be reduced simply by *turning down the thermostat*—or in other words, by directly reducing inputs of water, fertilizer, mowing, and pesticides. Today, for instance, you could simply decide to water your turf less often. Unfortunately, unless the turf is *prepared* for these reductions, its performance will suffer—just as surely as you'd suffer in a cold, uninsulated house. The approach of *adding more insulation* makes more sense. With turf, the process of "adding insulation" against adversity may involve soil improvements, selection of adapted grass varieties, and other cultural changes. Once a good low maintenance foundation is in place, you can safely reduce inputs without sacrificing quality.

est maintenance ground cover. It didn't even come in second.

Ground covers have generally been viewed as a low maintenance replacement for grass. But many of the ground covers in this study guzzled more maintenance time and dollars than turf—a lot more. Of the ground covers tested, creeping fig was the most labor-intensive plant material, requiring 47 hours of labor per year to upkeep 1000 ft^2. Considering that a typical home lawn averages 5000 ft^2 (540 m^2), yearly upkeep of a whole yard of creeping fig would be nearly a full-time job.

Flowering annuals ranked second in maintenance needs, requiring an average of 25 hours per 1000 ft^2 per year. Annuals demand a lot of manual maintenance: planting, weeding, and watering.

Turf ranked 5th and 8th place in overall maintenance, depending on which grass was chosen. Turf consumed between 4 and 8 hours of maintenance per 1000 ft^2 per year. The difference from one grass to the next amounted to a surprising *50% savings* in labor according to the study. In other words, switching from a high maintenance grass to a lower maintenance one could cut upkeep by half. Keep that in mind when reading the following chapters on grass selection.

"Contrary to what many people think, getting rid of mowed grass and replacing it with ground covers, mulches and wildflowers will not reduce landscape maintenance," echoes Don Williams, who performed a similar study at the University of Tennessee (Anonymous, 1995e).

Williams observed workers performing their routine maintenance tasks on turf and other ground covers. He then tallied the yearly upkeep for each type of landscape, turf included.

"My extensive studies document that mowed grass does not deserve its 'high maintenance' label," he says. "In fact, other forms of ground cover will almost always require more maintenance than lawns."

According to Williams, a 1-acre park would require only *1 second of maintenance* per square foot per year when mowed with a 60-in. mower 15 times per year. Other ground covers require as much as *60 times* more yearly tending on a square-foot basis. "What other type of landscape maintenance can be done at 1 second per square foot per year?" he asks.

Thus, while turfgrass is by no means free of upkeep, it does compare favorably to other landscaping options. Turf is not the total maintenance hog it's often portrayed to be. And blindly

Figure 1.2. No doubt about it, turfgrass installation and care takes a lot of hard work. Mowing, watering, fertilizing, and pest control require considerable time and effort, not to mention the cost involved and the depletion of natural resources. Deciding to lower maintenance is the first step in reducing your workload.

Table 1.1. Labor inputs required per year for several types of ground cover and turfgrasses in California (Cockerham and Van Dam, 1992). The number values indicate the hours of work needed per year to maintain turf and nonturf ground covers.

Ground Covers	Hours per 100 m^2	Hours per 1000 ft^2
Creeping fig (*Ficus pumila* L.)	51	47
Annuals	26	25
Baby tears (*Helxine soleirolii*)	20	18
Iris (*Iris* spp.)	9	8
African daisy (*Arctotis* spp.)	9	8
Algerian ivy (*Hedera canariensis* L.)	5	5
Gazania (*Gazania ringens*)	4	4
Jasmine (*Jasminum* spp.)	4	3
Lily-of-the-Nile (*Agapanathus africanus* L.)	2	2
Bellflower (*Campanula* spp.)	2	2
Cissus (*Cissus* spp.)	2	1
Turfgrasses		
Perennial ryegrass	9	8
Bermudagrass	7	7
Kentucky bluegrass	5	4
General turf	4	4

switching from turf to other landscape options is not the automatic solution to lowering maintenance. If fact, many can end up costing far more in upkeep than turf.

ENVIRONMENTAL IMPACTS OF TURF MAINTENANCE

Conventional wisdom today says that turfgrass is a major waste of natural resources. As a result, turf has become a perpetual target of environmental groups. To many, turf epitomizes mankind's careless disregard of irreplaceable resources for the sake of unnecessary aesthetics.

But how does turf harm the environment? And what exactly are we saving when we reduce turf maintenance to aid the environment?

To answer these questions, let's confront the ways turf is accused of negatively impacting the environment:

- *Generating solid waste*—Grass clippings and yard waste comprise over one-third of the solid material deposited in landfills.
- *Surface water pollution*—Fertilizers and pesticides applied to turf can wash away during heavy rain and wind up in lakes and streams.
- *Groundwater pollution*—Fertilizers and pesticides applied to turf can leach through the soil and end up in the underground drinking water supply.
- *Polluting the air*—Volatilization (evaporation) of fertilizers and pesticides can release pollutants into the air. Exhaust fumes from turf machinery contribute to air pollution.
- *Loss of habitat*—Soil erosion, stream siltation, and destruction of wildlands can take place during turf construction. Converting woodlands and wetlands to turf deprives wildlife of natural habitat.
- *Lack of genetic diversity*—To most people, turf is viewed as a **monoculture**, meaning it is comprised of a single species, rather than the vast diversity of species normally found in nature. Of course this is not true, as the chapter on mixtures explains (Chapter 6).
- *Injury to wildlife and pets*—Benign organisms (birds, pets, worms, etc.) can be harmed by machinery or pesticides.
- *Depletion of natural resources*—Mining minerals to make fertilizer, refining oil to manufacture pesticides, and pumping fresh water to irrigate turf wastes resources that could be used to produce food and fiber.
- *Other impacts*—If you cogitate long enough you could come up with a laundry list of abstract impacts of turf culture on the environment, such as the pollution generated by the rubber plant that manufactures tires for your lawn mower. But going that far just confuses the issue. After all, everything we do—short of staying in bed—affects the environment directly or indirectly.

Many of the negative impacts of turf are offset by the benefits turf has to offer. The following section demonstrates how the positive often outweighs the negative. Furthermore, many of the negative impacts of turf maintenance can be reduced or eliminated by switching to a regimen of reduced maintenance.

BENEFICIAL ASPECTS OF TURF

Turf does have its good points. In addition to providing natural beauty, turf serves many practical functions—functions no other commodity can do quite as well.

The real function of turf is utilitarian. Turf serves a purpose. It provides a resilient, wear resistant surface for sports, leisure, and a wealth of human activities. Listed below are some of the other benefits of turf:

Minimizes erosion. Turf is nature's solution to soil erosion. Turf can literally stop erosion in its tracks, as demonstrated by numerous research studies.

Jim Baird and his associates at Oklahoma State University (Baird, 1995) showed that turf reduces water runoff after a rainstorm to essentially nil. That's no small accomplishment, seeing as Baird's research was located in "thunderstorm alley" of central Oklahoma, where a 5-in. (125 mm) pelting of rain is not that uncommon.

Mark Welterlen and his coworkers at the University of Maryland (Gross et al., 1991) also studied erosive water flow from turf. They determined that 200 lb (90 kg) of soil per acre could be eroded from bare soil during a 30-minute, 3-in. (75 mm) rainstorm. However, when the ground was covered with a vigorous tall fescue turf, minimal topsoil was lost—only 9 to 54 lb (4 to 25 kg) of soil per acre, depending on the age and density of the turf.

Dust trapping. Turfgrass traps and retains an estimated 12 million tons of dust and dirt each year in America (Anonymous, 1989b). This trapped dust aids in the continual soil-building process. With time, dust and dirt become entombed, causing the surface elevation of turf to actually rise slightly.

Binding and storage of carbon dioxide. Turf absorbs quantities of carbon dioxide, the so-called greenhouse gas. Grass converts CO_2 into structural carbohydrates of leaves and stems. With time, plant parts slough off and die, forming the mat and thatch layers underneath a stand.

Detractors argue that a climax stand of trees entombs far more CO_2 than grass, which is true. On the other hand, the contribution of grass is not trivial either.

Furnishes oxygen. It's been said many times that a 50-by-50 ft (230 m^2) patch of turf generates enough oxygen to meet the ongoing needs of a family of four (Anonymous, 1989b). Grass releases pure oxygen while removing CO_2 from the air.

Filters and purifies water. Turf, as it turns out, is one of nature's best absorbers of impurities in water. Many golf courses throughout the desert region of the United States irrigate using reclaimed sewage effluent water. The thatch under a turf stand is a vital, living zone, chock full of bacteria and fungi that rapidly absorb and degrade impurities and turn effluent back into pure water. Turf performs the same vital filtering function when pesticides and fertilizers are applied. Virtually none of them leach through the grass profile unabsorbed (Hull et al., 1993).

Because of turf's remarkable filtering ability, many landscape planners are now turning to **grassy swales** in their designs as a way to eliminate pollution from roads and parking lots. Surface runoff is filtered through a bed of grass. Purified water is returned to the aquifer and not shunted into overloaded storm drains. Some state and municipal governments have issued mandates for grass swales in new construction, as a way to minimize storm runoff and replenish the aquifer (see Figure 1.3).

Temperature moderation. In a north Phoenix, Arizona, neighborhood, scientists have found that turf outside a residence makes a big difference on the environment *inside*. In a large, real-life experiment, four suburban homes were connected to a monitoring system one summer to determine their water usage. Baseline utility bills, particularly monthly cooling costs, were collected before and after installing landscaping. Landscapes of two of the four homes were modified, one to a bermudagrass lawn and the other to mesquite trees.

"We found between 10 and 17% reduction in actual measured cooling energy use in the house with the new turf. We did also notice a reduction in air temperature outside the building where the grass was planted," says project leader Jim Simpson, landscape architect at the University of Arizona (Dale, 1993).

Contrary to what the researchers expected, the house planted to mesquite showed *less* total cost savings than the house with the grass. The turf paid for itself in energy savings.

In terms of its actual "air conditioning equivalent," the front lawn of a typical residential house provides the cooling equivalent of a 9-ton air conditioner (Anonymous, 1989b). By compari-

Figure 1.3. Instead of routing surface water into storm drains, many municipalities are now mandating grassy swales. On-site grass swales capture surface runoff water from parking lots and downspouts, filter it, and return it to the aquifer without overloading the city's storm sewers. The concept of grassy swales illustrates the unique ability of grasses to cleanse the environment.

son, a typical home-size central air conditioning unit rates only in the 3- to 4-ton capacity.

To provide a balanced view of the issue, however, it's important to remember where the cooling effect of turf originates. Grass generates cooling by actively pumping water through its vascular system, much like a swamp cooler. Applied irrigation provides the cooling, albeit indirectly. However, with grass—as opposed to commercial air conditioning units—sunlight and photosynthesis power the cooling, not fossil fuel.

Controls unwanted animals. Mowed residential lawns help minimize the risk of unwanted pests around the home, such as snakes, rats, mice, mosquitoes, ticks, and chiggers (Beard and Green, 1994).

A cushion for human safety. We humans spend a lot of our leisure and recreational time on turf. Anthropologists speculate that this may spring from the fact that humans evolved on the grassy savannas of Africa (Coppens, 1994). Early humans were drawn to the safety and comfort of grass, often dwelling within the shadowy interface between grass and trees. Predators were easier to spot on grass flats than in the jungle. Some scientists believe this may have even encouraged early humans to stand upright from their previous four-legged posture. Without grass, some say that the human species as such might never have evolved.

Today, grass still hosts a multitude of human activities. Real grass—unlike advanced, synthetic playing surfaces—has a desirable, nonabrasive, cushioning effect that helps minimize sports injuries.

Researchers Trey Rogers and Don Waddington (Beard and Green, 1994) quantified the injury-reducing properties of turf. They studied the cushioning effect of turf using a **decelerometer**, a device that measures how hard an object hits the ground. A decelerometer spits out numbers in terms of gravity G-forces—the same G-forces used by jet pilots. The researchers found that a well-maintained turf exhibits only 2.5% of the G-force that a solid sports track does.

Here's an experiment that maybe easier to relate to than G-forces: A dozen raw eggs were dropped from a height of 11 ft (3.3 m) onto a natural grass athletic field. None broke. But when dropped from a height of only 18 in. (0.4 m) onto an all-weather sports track, all of them broke (Anonymous, 1989b; Macik, 1987).

Turf is active even when it's resting. Turf can have a beneficial effect on the environment even when it's in a dry, brown, dormant state. Erosion control, mud and dust stabilization, water entrapment, organic chemical degradation, carbon storage, and a human safety cushion all remain intact when turf is dry and dormant (Beard, 1993).

Encourages exercise. For many people, yard work is about the only aerobic exercise they get. In a recent Gallop Poll, over half of Americans surveyed indicated they regularly participate in lawn upkeep (Anonymous, 1992a). In fact, more people participate in turf care than in any other landscape or gardening activity (Figure 1.4). Regular exercise has a number of health benefits, most notably to the cardiovascular system. Professor Bormann of Yale (Hair, 1993; Jones, 1993) suggests a return to the *manually propelled* (motorless) lawn mower. It gives an outstanding cardiovascular workout and doesn't pollute the air.

Increases your investment. For most folks, their house is their biggest single investment. An attractive lawn not only improves the visual appeal of a house but boosts its real estate value. Money spent on landscaping compares favorably to other home improvements, providing one of the highest net returns to the homeowner (Anonymous, 1993a):

- *Pool*—20 to 50% of the invested value is returned at the sale of the home
- *Deck*—40 to 70%
- *Bath*—80 to 120%
- *Kitchen*—75 to 125%
- *Turf and landscaping*—100 to 200%

A better quality of life. Turf does more for us than just improve our investments. It adds aesthetics and environmental beauty to our surroundings. In a recent study, homeowners surveyed about their lawns responded that an attractive turf was important, because it sets a positive reflection on the neighborhood, provides elegance and comfort, and enhances their living environment.

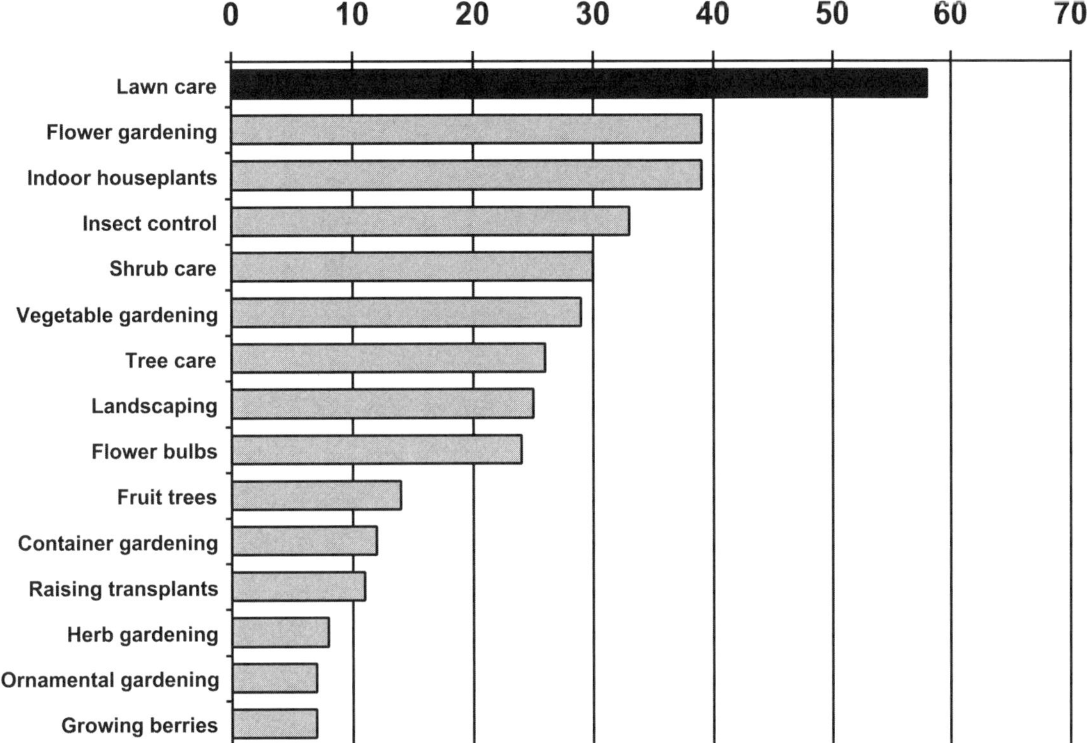

Figure 1.4. More Americans participate in lawn care than in any other aspect of landscaping or gardening, according to a survey by the Gallup Organization for the National Gardening Association (National Gardening Survey, 1991–1992, Burlington, Vermont [Anonymous, 1992a]).

Turf also benefits the workplace. Rachel Kaplan, a psychologist specializing in natural resources at the University of Michigan, found that workers who had a view of grass lawns had "more enthusiasm for their jobs, less frustration, more patience, and fewer physical ailments."

Kaplan found that even when work stations were modern and well lit, employees without a window to the outside were more "vulnerable to distractions, less flexible in their thinking, more impulsive, less able to solve problems, and more irritable." She attributed the differences to workers being able to rest their eyes on a natural landscape, offsetting **directed attention fatigue**, a mental condition caused by steady focusing on job tasks. Working conditions and attitudes of 783 employees were surveyed (Kaplan et al., 1998).

Just Because Something Feels Right Doesn't Mean It Will Cut Your Maintenance

Margaret Glessner was bound and determined to reduce her yard work. Glessner, a homeowner and lifelong resident of Long Island, New York, decided she was sick of endlessly mowing, watering, and weeding her lawn. No matter what the cost, she was going to make a change.

"I'd been reading in gardening magazines about how 'zero-scaping' was the wave of the future," she says. "You rip out your grass lawn and you put in plants that take less work."

With the help of a local contractor, Glessner proceeded to excavate her attractive yard of bluegrass and fescue and in its place, installed a yard of gravel, cactus, and prairiegrass. To say the least, the conversion was costly. But as the work progressed, Glessner looked forward to the day when she could spend time enjoying her yard, instead of being enslaved by it.

But to her dismay, two years after the conversion, Glessner was putting just as much elbow grease into her yard as before.

"Right away I lost my cactus. I mean, it got some sort of a white mold and collapsed. Then I started getting weeds popping up all over my gravel. I've had to have the lawn man spray the gravel three times now. And the prairiegrass I planted got overrun with bluegrass. So I had the contractor come back and put new bluegrass sod over top of the prairiegrass."

What went wrong here?

Some might argue that Glessner jumped ship a little too fast in converting back to a traditional lawn. Or that she should have used a different contractor. But her conversion to a lower maintenance yard was less than successful. Her plight illustrates three significant points about lower maintenance:

- Decisions on plant materials should be based on local growing conditions, not on a picture in a magazine somewhere from a different climatic zone,
- Choosing something different just because it's different is not a good idea, and
- Modifications that promise lower maintenance should be verified by science to indeed save time and resources.

Before attempting to Cut Your Maintenance, it's paramount that your decisions be based on fact, not intuition. When eliminating a vital maintenance practice, it's important to know whether that cut will translate into savings. If it won't, what good is it?

Switching to lower maintenance is not choosing something different simply because it's different. It's not bucking an established cultural practice just because it's established. Instead, each cultural change we make needs to be weighed to determine its actual value. A change can only be justified if its savings are real. There are a lot of changes you can make that will do nothing. Or worse yet, they may end up costing you *more* overall maintenance later on.

A good example of intuition overpowering reality is the Xeriscape® craze. Xeriscape® was one of the first attempts by the green industry to buck the flow of maintenance, and for that it should be commended. Xeriscape® was conceived by Douglas Welsh, a professor in the trees and shrubs department at Texas A&M University, as a way of "sensibly" using less water (see sidebar). Trouble was, guidelines of how to conserve maintenance were promoted before they could be tested by science.

One of the downfalls of the now-defunct National Xeriscape® Council was its reliance on (and I quote from their position paper) "the *seemingly logical* approach to reducing landscape water consumption." As it turns out, their *seemingly logical* approach was "to reduce the incidence of water-intensive turf." Get rid of the turf and install trees and gravel! Welsh quickly became a folk hero to those in the nursery tree industry who stood to benefit from his campaign.

But what seems logical on the surface can sometimes turn out quite the opposite when scientifically tested. Consider *The Cactus Principle*:

The Cactus Principle

Everyone knows that a cactus is about the most water efficient plant around. After all, if you go to the depths of Death Valley where only a few inches of rain precipitate each year, what do you find growing? Cactus, of course. Certainly not large expanses of turf.

But what happens to a cactus in the desert when that paltry inch of rain falls? The cactus voraciously sucks up as much water as it can hold and hordes it inside the plant. Dryland plants are water thrifty *only* when there's no water to absorb. When water's available, sometimes they're gluttons.

If you transfer a desert plant into a domestic landscape, it responds just like in the desert. Given water, desert plants can be gluttonous consumers. And not just cacti: trees, shrubs, and even turfgrasses, can exhibit *The Cactus Principle*. Sometimes the plants that seem the most logical choice for conservation, turn out just the opposite.

Dale Devitt, horticulturist at the University of Nevada (Devitt et al., 1995), was one of the first

"Plants don't waste water, people do!"

The Xeriscape® controversy

Adapting a catchphrase from the National Rifle Association as their slogan, the National Xeriscape® Council, Inc., was formed in 1981 to promote water savings in the landscape. The word Xeriscape® (trademarked by the Council) is derived from the Greek word, xeri, meaning dry. Though the council itself disbanded in 1993, the term, Xeriscape® lives on in our vernacular. It has found its way into the everyday language of a number of landscapers, environmentalists, journalists, and homeowners.

The Council's goals were well-intentioned: To find ways to limit water use in the landscape. Droughts in the Southwest in the late 1980s and fears of global warming transformed Xeriscaping® into a modern buzzword.

But as time passed, the concept of Xeriscape® began to drift and evolve as one journalist quoted another. No longer was Xeriscaping® the *practical reduction* of watering. Now it was the *complete cessation* of landscape watering. Xeriscape® became synonymous with a front yard of gravel, cacti, and perhaps one tree. Turf was taboo.

Turfgrass was always a core focus of the Xeriscape® craze because of "the tremendous opportunity for abusive use of irrigation water in the name of maintaining turfgrasses." No one ever questioned the possible abuse of water by the mesquite trees and cacti the Council was promoting (see text).

It wasn't until years later that reason prevailed, as Professors Jim Beard and Dick Duble, physiologists from Texas A&M University, were added to the Council's board of directors. The Council issued a revised position paper stating its moderated guidelines for reducing landscape watering—guidelines that were reasonable and well thought out (*Source*: D.F. Welsh, position paper from the National Xeriscape® Council, Inc.). In fact, many of these recommendations are even mirrored here in this book.

1. Planning and design
   - Placement of turf species into landscape zones based on their water requirements
   - Use of irrigated turf in areas that provide essential functions (i.e., recreation, aesthetic, foot traffic, dust and noise abatement, glare reduction, temperature mitigation)
   - Use of nonirrigated turf areas as appropriate
2. Soil improvement
3. Selection of appropriate plants
   - Adapted, low-water turf species and varieties
4. Practical turf areas
5. Efficient irrigation
   - Irrigation based on the turf's true water needs
6. Mulching
7. Appropriate maintenance
   - Increased mowing heights to decrease evaporation
   - Decreased fertilizer rates and proper scheduling of fertilization

Unfortunately these new guidelines came too late. By then, the damage was done; the moderated guidelines were largely ignored. The valuable place for turfgrasses in the landscape was forgotten. And the Xeriscape® phenomenon served as fodder for angry journalists in the controversy over lawns and landscapes.

to scientifically test the water use differences among landscape plants. Using side-by-side comparative studies in the arid Nevada desert, he found that trees transpire *3 to 4 times* the amount of water per square foot as a low fertility bermudagrass/perennial ryegrass turf. One single oak tree had the equivalent evapotranspiration (water use) as an entire 2000 ft^2 (215 m^2) lawn. Desert tree species such as mesquite that were seen by Xeriscapers as water scrooges, turned out to be even *less* efficient water users than willow or oak.

Among turfgrasses there was also an enormous difference in water use. Devitt determined that tall fescue consumes 87 in. (221 cm) of irrigation water per year compared to 45 in. (116 cm) for a low fertility bermudagrass/perennial ryegrass turf. The implications were profound: Water use could be cut in half just by planting a different kind of grass (details in Chapter 10).

A great deal can be learned about water use by where grass and trees naturally occur in nature. Great native stands of trees can be found along the two coasts of the United States, in regions of abundant natural rainfall. Across the drier Great Plains where annual rainfall dips to 15 in. (380 mm), grasses make up the bulk of the native vegetation.

Another misconception about trees is that because of their deep roots, they can locate and extract "free" water somewhere down in the soil. While this strategy may be beneficial in rainier climates, in areas with a finite aquifer, deep rooted trees may actually compete with humans for groundwater. In Australia, one municipality planted trees over the top of its aquifer in an effort to conserve water (Beard, 1992a). As the trees grew, they plunged roots into the groundwater 20 to 30 ft (6 to 9 m) below, consuming greater and greater volumes of water, placing the city's drinking water supply in peril. City officials are considering whether to remove the trees and replace them with turf. A similar problem is taking place over Edward's aquifer in San Antonio, Texas. Water authorities there are considering paying ranchers to remove desert shrubs and mesquite trees from over the aquifer, substituting grass in their place (Beard, 1992a).

In conclusion, woody ornamentals are not the water-saving salvation they were once thought to be. Like the cactus, they too have their own water-wasting shortcomings. But it took years of hard research data to dispel this popular notion.

You Can Fool Yourself with Grasses, too

Taming the maintenance genie takes a number of adjustments in turf culture, all of them working together to create the desired result (see Figure 1.5). Rarely will a single change make a difference. Sometimes it can even backfire.

Turf management has its roots in the world's second oldest profession: Agriculture. Because grass management and agriculture have been around for so many centuries, there are not a lot of new things that haven't already been tried a hundred times before. In short, there are no fast miracle cures. Advances are incremental. But the increments *do* add up. And by combining the techniques of advanced grass species, better soils, improved establishment, renovation, mowing, watering, fertilizing, and pest control, it is possible to grow grass with less overall maintenance.

A singular approach to maintenance savings, on the other hand, is rarely successful. A singular approach means simply changing to a different fertilizer or grass variety. Altering only one factor may even backfire. An example of this is: *The Miracle Grasses of Canada*.

The Miracle Grasses of Canada. If you saw *Time* or *Life* magazine in the late 1980s, you might have noticed a story about the upcoming revolution in lawn maintenance: "*Grasses that never need mowing.*" These articles described a collection of innovative, low-growing grasses from Canada that were so short they never needed cutting. Imagine, you could throw away your lawn mower. Reportedly, lawn equipment manufacturers were getting nervous at the mere thought.

But there's more. These grasses were not only short-growing, they reportedly also gave off natural herbicides, controlling lawn weeds all by themselves. No longer would a homeowner have to hire a lawn service to rid their yard of weeds. The grasses would do it themselves. Rumor was that an unnamed multinational agrochemical

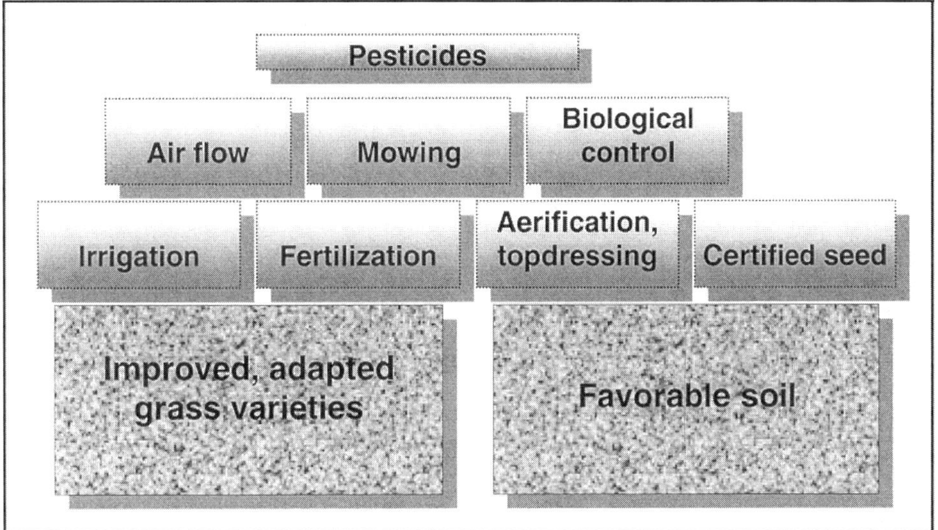

Figure 1.5. Developing sustainable low maintenance turf means first establishing a solid foundation of improved, adapted grass varieties growing in a favorable soil. Turf varieties should be chosen which offer proven adaptation and performance to your particular climate. Attempting to "stretch" a species beyond its natural range of adaptation is a recipe for disaster. Before planting, the soil should be examined for underlying problems that may compromise growth, such as waterlogging, saltiness, layering, or a tendency to compact. Problem soils should be rectified by incorporating compost or other soil amendments as detailed in Chapter 8. Some soil problems such as sandiness or stones are really no problem at all for most turf applications, if they're managed appropriately. After the two key elements—variety and soil—are in place, other resources such as irrigation, fertilization, mowing, and pesticides can be safely trimmed. Adequate air flow over the turf, soil aerification, use of certified seed, and biological pest control measures also help lower the turf's dependency on pesticides.

corporation was trying to buy up the discovery and bury the grasses.

And there's more: Because these grasses originated from the arid Canadian Rockies and could grow on dry, gravely soils, they would need no irrigation or fertilizer to maintain a luxurious playing surface.

Sound too good to be true?

Well in agriculture as in life, when something sounds too good to be true, it usually is.

Where are these Miracle Grasses today? A corporation was formed by the developer and some U.S. investors to bring the Miracle Grasses to market. Six years later, the company folded, and the major stockholders split the coffers (more details in Chapter 4).

A conspiracy, you say? The multinationals got to them? No, the reason the Miracle Grasses flopped was performance. An incidental ingredient the developers forgot was seed yield. I guess you're somewhat preoccupied when your head's spinning with the possibility of putting an end to lawn mowers, agrochemicals, irrigation, and turf maintenance as we know it.

The Miracle Grasses produced few seed. Furthermore, some of the grasses, because of their alpine adaptation, developed all sorts of new diseases when faced with the "harsh" climate of Newark, New Jersey, for instance.

Where are the Miracle Grasses today? Believe it or not, many of the Miracle Grass species are included in the Appendix. Some of the same grass species as the Miracle Grasses are regularly bought and sold as commodities in the land reclamation trade. A few are quite low-growing, with leaves no taller than a toadstool. Others can survive on as little as 8 in. (20 cm) of precipitation per year, making them competitive even with mesquite and cacti.

Are these grasses going to revolutionize turfgrass management as we know it? No. Or they would have done so already. Low maintenance grasses are only a small part of the holistic approach to low maintenance turf. When combined with other tips and techniques, they hold promise for cutting maintenance. But they alone are not a miracle.

The Eco-Lawn:

One Example of a Maintenance Saving Idea Gone Awry

Remember when I said that everything "new" in turfgrass management has probably been tried before? Here's a prime example:

Over the last few years an idea has been gaining momentum: *The Ecology Lawn*. The eco-lawn concept is rooted in the theory of **species diversification**, which states that a multitude of species can exploit an ecosystem better than one. Lawn detractors argue that grass is a monostand of a single species (this is certainly not true; see Chapter 6 for tips on mixing turfgrasses). A diversity of plants *in theory* should be able to provide a lower maintenance, more sustainable landscape ecology than just one species. The eco-lawn sounds like the right thing to do. But is it?

Sowing an eco-lawn. To create an eco-lawn, you first start with a grass—preferably a weak one. Tom Cook, the turfgrass scientist at Oregon State University who pioneered the eco-lawn concept, says that weaker grasses work best (Cline, 1993b). Grasses that are too aggressive, such as Chewings fescue, hard fescue, or bentgrass, eventually push out their weaker companions. Red or tall fescue are acceptable, but Kentucky bluegrass and perennial ryegrass are preferred because they are less aggressive against the eco-lawn's other components (Cook, 1994b).

"My goal [in developing the eco-lawn] has been to combine grasses with selected broadleaf plants in an attempt to produce an ecologically stable mixture of plants that would persist with fewer inputs than the typical lawn," says Cook (1994b) (Figure 1.6).

Next, add some clover. After selecting a grass base, the next step in creating an eco-lawn is to add clover. Clover is a member of the legume family, a group of plants with one unique feature: Bacterial nodules in their roots. Most plants lack the ability to absorb nitrogen from the air and convert it into a form they can use. Air is made of 78% nitrogen, but unfortunately most plants can't absorb it. Along the lines of evolution plants somehow lost the ability to fix nitrogen. **Nitrogen fixation** is the conversion of inert, atmospheric nitrogen into a form plants can use. Only primitive single-cell bacteria still retain this unique ability. That's why some plants—the legumes—have formed a strategic alliance with rhizobium bacteria. The clover provides energy to the bacteria from the sunlight it absorbs, and the rhizobium takes that energy and manufactures **fixed nitrogen** for the plant. The fixed nitrogen may also end up leaking to nearby grass plants in the lawn. A vigorous stand of clover can add 100 lb of fixed nitrogen to the soil per acre per year (11 g/m^2) (Wheeler and Hill, 1957).

"We started off with common white clover but [it was] too vigorous and produced more dry matter [clippings] than I wanted. Strawberry clover is slightly less vigorous so all current mixes contain only it," says Cook. Researchers at other universities (Gibeault and Leanard, 1987) have also tested strawberry clover for lawns.

Even strawberry clover, Cook admits, produces more growth than he would like to see in a low maintenance lawn. In other words, it yields too many clippings, too much foliage.

"If I could I would replace both of these [clovers] with less vigorous legumes. As we move on we'll be testing other clovers for that purpose. The goal is to find a good nitrogen fixer that doesn't grow much."

Add deep-rooted flowering perennials. The last step in designing an eco-lawn is to add perennial plants that can ferret water from deep in the soil profile—water unavailable to the grass. Cook has tested strongly taprooted broadleaf species such as Roman chamomile (*Chamaemelum nobile*) and yarrow (*Achillea millifolium*), which root to great depths while providing flowering beauty (Cline, 1993b). Other species have included baby blue eyes (*Nemophila menjiesii*) and English lawn daisy (*Bellis perennis*) (Simon, 1988).

The History of the Lawn Repeats Itself

The eco-lawn is an exciting innovation in turf management. But is it really new?

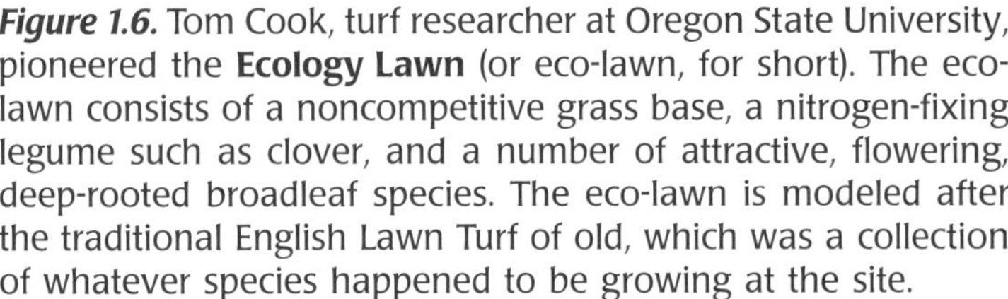

Figure 1.6. Tom Cook, turf researcher at Oregon State University, pioneered the **Ecology Lawn** (or eco-lawn, for short). The eco-lawn consists of a noncompetitive grass base, a nitrogen-fixing legume such as clover, and a number of attractive, flowering, deep-rooted broadleaf species. The eco-lawn is modeled after the traditional English Lawn Turf of old, which was a collection of whatever species happened to be growing at the site.

Well, it may be exciting, but the eco-lawn certainly isn't new. Eco-lawns trace their heritage to the English herbal lawns of old (Simon, 1988). During the colonial period, the classic British lawn was a mixture of native grasses and forbs. Whatever vegetation happened to be growing was clipped down to lawn height (Haldane, 1934). Because of the timely and abundant rainfall in the British Isles, the range of suitable species was expansive. The British at the time also utilized another remarkable concept in low maintenance turf: *The Organic Lawn Mower* (sheep and goats).

During that same period of history, two new sports were emerging: Golf and soccer (fute ball). Young Brits at the time were becoming enamored with these new sports and were neglecting their State-mandated archery practice. As a result, England's King James (of Bible fame) banned both sports because he believed they interfered with archery, the common national defense at the time:

> "Decreed and ordained... that fute ball and golfe must be utterly cryitdune."
> — *King James II, March 6, 1457.*

James's decree was largely ignored by his subjects, who continued to play their sports in spite of the threat of royal punishment. Even the King's wife, Mary Queen of Scots, resumed playing golf immediately after her husband's death, claiming it eased her sorrow (Connolly, 1995).

Later in 1603, King James's successor decreed that golf could once again be openly played, as long as Sunday church attendance was regularly observed.

Golf in its infancy was played in farm pastures on whatever vegetation happened to be growing there. The playing surface was contiguous from beginning to end. The tee, fairway, and putting green as such did not exist as separate structures. At the finish of each hole was the flag stick; the concept of a golf *hole* didn't come until later.

When the Royal & Ancient Golf Society of St. Andrews was founded in 1754, the game of golf was played on traditional English lawn turf, and mowed with the traditional English *Organic Lawn Mowers* (Organic Lawn Mowers also doubled as *Organic Fertilizer Spreaders*). The first mechanical lawn mowing machine wasn't conceived until 1830. Curiously, the reel mower was invented

Shortcomings of the Eco-Lawn

Lack of soil binding. A key feature of grass is its fine, fibrous root system which binds the soil into a tight, interconnected fabric. When you tread on turf, your weight is widely dispersed, similar to the way snowshoes work. The soil binding keeps your ankles from sinking into the mud.

Broadleaf plants for the most part lack significant soil-binding ability compared to grasses. Most broadleaf plants are taprooted. Mixing broadleaf plants with grasses only reduces the turf's overall binding strength.

Poor wear tolerance. **Wear tolerance** is the ability of a plant to withstand repeated traffic abrasion and still maintain a solid stand. As early golf superintendents discovered, broadleaf plants have minimal wear tolerance. Their wide, papery leaves are easily torn and shredded. More importantly, their growing point is *above* ground, not safely tucked underground like grasses. If the growing point of a broadleaf plant is destroyed by abrasion, the whole plant dies. A belowground growing point is what makes grass so tolerant of foot traffic. (A few broadleaf plants *can* regenerate from buds below ground, which is what makes these plants notorious lawn weeds.)

Poor cutting tolerance. Broadleaf plants have problems with mowing. Broadleaf plants grow by extending a stem vertically. Grasses, on the other hand, maintain their stems below ground. The only part of the grass plant that protrudes into the air is leaves. (Seed stalks and stolons are grass's only aboveground stems, but from the plant's perspective, they're expendable.)

Bees. People who have sown an eco-lawn remark on "the diversity of pollinators" attracted to their lawn (Bormann et al., 1993). "In a small plot of eco-turf we've counted as many as 25 bees," says Cook.

Don't get me wrong, wildflowers and flowering herbs have a definite place in the landscape. But if you manage a park where people come to play, it's best to stick to nonflowering plants underneath the beach blankets.

Fast vertical growth rate. Broadleaf plants by their very nature grow mainly in one direction: Up. Broadleaf plants are competitive in the wilds because of their ability to grow taller than nearby plants, shading them out. In turf, fast vertical growth is a detriment. It means your lawn gets taller and needs mowing more often. Cook (Cline, 1993b; Simon, 1988) is still working out the bugs of how to prevent eco-clippings from plugging up a lawn mower.

"Since clippings are normally returned, growth has increased over time, possibly due to nitrogen loading," Cook postulates.

No thatch cushion. Turf textbooks of the 1970s often decried the evils of thatch. And true, too much of anything is bad. But today we've learned to appreciate thatch. Thatch provides a resilient cushion between the plant and the soil. It reduces sports injuries. It absorbs and denatures organic contaminants.

"I'd brag about a field of dandelions and crabgrass if it provided a safe, sure footing and it cushioned falls," says one recreational director of a small Florida town (Kieffer, 1995). Only grasses provide the cushion and secure footing needed for sports. Broadleaf plants do not form a thatch layer and offer none of the benefits of grass thatch (see Chapter 8 for additional facts on thatch).

Bare spots. One of the miracles of grass is its ability to fill bare spots all by itself. Grasses with rhizomes or stolons send runners along the soil surface, searching for a sunny place to peg down. When these runners find a bare spot, they root and produce a **daughter plant.** As the daughter plant grows, it neatly fills the bare spot.

Some grasses like tall fescue or perennial ryegrass lack lateral runners. As a result, they're not as effective at filling bare spots. Grasses without runners are termed **bunch type**. Their growth habit is **tufted**, but when grown in mass they form a smooth, uniform surface.

Most broadleaf plants lack the ability to fill in bare spots. A few have the ability to run—clover, for example. Broadleaf plants with rhizomes or stolons can be competitive weeds.

For the most part, though, holes in an eco-lawn remain holes—unless crabgrass germinates to fill the void.

The unstable balance of nature. Plant competition is an ugly thing. It's true: Plants do compete with one another. They don't compete as actively as people do, in the Olympics for instance. But they are constantly grinding and straining under the competition from nearby plants, searching for nutrients, sunlight, and moisture.

And plants aren't out just to elbow each other around a little. At heart, each would like to dominate the world, wiping out all other species in their wake.

But because there are so many plant species all vying for world domination, no single plant ever wins. The result is an incessant struggle between diverse plant groups. In a turf composed of divergent species, mixtures seldom stay mixed. Pretty soon the lawn becomes a swirling patchwork of species, each with its own dominion.

On one hand you might say they're adapting to their own little niche environments. On the other hand, the swirling, patchy populations present an unattractive, poorly blended appearance. Furthermore, if one plant species is killed by insects or disease, that part of the turf is lost—or at least takes quite a while to recover. In the meantime, you're left with bare ground.

Allergy problems. Grasses, with a few exceptions, do not normally produce seed stalks in mowed turf. They may *try* to put them up out of genetic obligation, but they're usually nipped off before flowering. Thus mowed turfgrasses never get the chance to flower and produce pollen, except under unusual occasions.

Many broadleaf plants—otherwise known as turf weeds—have the ability to flower, pollinate, and set seed at mowed turf heights. The pretty flowers come with a price: Pollen and allergies. Not everyone is bothered by weed pollen. But if you are, then minimizing the pollinating plants in your environs is important. And a flowering lawn is not for you.

A reservoir of weed seed. Landscape designers have only scratched the surface of possible uses of native flowers and forbs in the landscape. Flowers are a tremendous source of beauty in our surrounding environment.

But what's one person's flower is another person's weed. The cute, perky yarrow in your eco-lawn is considered a noxious weed by a number of states and countries. The flowering chamomile in your eco-lawn can't even be killed with Roundup® herbicide. Turned loose, chamomile can be a serious agricultural weed.

An eco-lawn can serve as a weed-seed source for an entire neighborhood. Birds and wind pick up seed and carry it from lawn to lawn. Real economic damage can be done by planting an eco-lawn adjacent to cropland. Attractive broadleaf lawn plants can escape and become nasty farm weeds. Take a lesson from the poor guy who first thought kudzu would make an attractive ground cover. Today, kudzu blankets miles of cropland across the southeastern United States, smothering fields, forests, and even a few houses.

No selective herbicides. One purpose of an eco-lawn is to reduce reliance on chemical pesticides. The natural, ecological aspects of an eco-lawn are among its most appealing features.

But what do you do when your eco-lawn gets dandelions? Okay, well maybe you can pass them off as part of the ecosystem. But how about Russian thistle? Or poison ivy? Or kudzu? Now you've got a problem.

If your eco-lawn is just a small patch behind your patio, no problem. You can don protective gloves and yank those suckers out of the ground. But what if your eco-lawn is a 50-acre park? Big problem. The cost to hand pull all those weeds might exceed the cost of the real estate. No labeled herbicides exist for weed control in eco-lawns.

"Unless you really know what you're doing, herbicides have no place on [eco-] lawns," he cautions (Cook, 1994b). With turfgrass lawns, however, there are herbicides to control most weed outbreaks (see Chapter 12 for pesticide-saving tips).

Real ecological benefits? An eco-lawn is indeed capable of reducing the need for nitrogen fertilizer, though it still requires potassium and phosphorous fertilization and correction of any errant pH levels in the soil. Similarly, it is not immune to other soil problems such as compaction or waterlogging.

One fascinating study of "environmental seed mixtures" (a concept similar to the eco-lawn) was done by Jack Fry and Jack Butler at Colorado State University (Fry and Butler, 1989a). Researchers examined water-use rates of turf, clover, and a few weed species (Figure 1.7). They wanted to compare the water use of "Merion" Kentucky bluegrass, one of the *least* water-efficient turfgrasses, against white clover, yellow foxtail, barnyardgrass, and smooth crabgrass—weeds that sometimes make up substantial proportions of turf.

The Colorado researchers used **mini-lysimeters** to measure water use. A minilysimeter is simply a bucket of soil implanted in the turf with grass or clover growing in it. As strange as it sounds, this is a useful way to get a representative water-use rate of turf or ground covers.

During a particularly dry week in midsummer, all five species in the experiment drank about the same quantity of water. *The Cactus Principle* comes into play here: If water is unavailable, plants are very thrifty. Clover had a somewhat higher water use than the others, but not substantially.

Later when moisture was available, however, clover consumed almost *twice* as much water as Merion Kentucky bluegrass. Interestingly, the three grassy weed species were slightly more water efficient than the bluegrass. The reason lies in the physiological difference between these grasses. Grass plants come in two kinds, based on their type of photosynthesis: C_3 or C_4. Over the millennia, na-

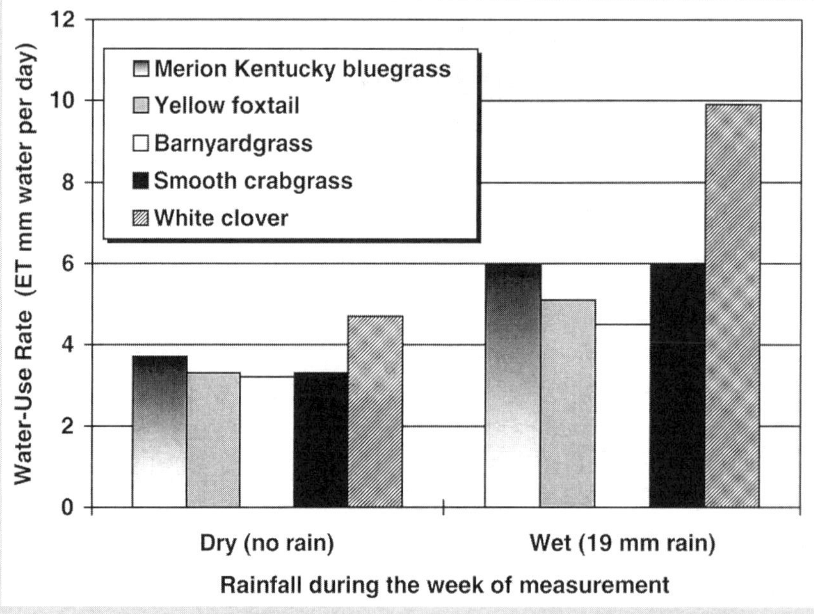

Figure 1.7. Research at Colorado State University by Jack Fry and Jack Butler (Fry and Butler, 1989a) demonstrated the water-use of five lawn plants. All five plants used water relatively efficiently when water was scarce (left bars). When water was plentiful (3/4 in. of rain), all species increased their uptake (right bars). White clover was a less efficient water user than Kentucky bluegrass under high or low moisture conditions. Using clover in a lawn compromises the overall water-use efficiency of the turf. The benefits of the "fixed nitrogen" provided by the clover are offset by water inefficiency. Maintenance savings are sometimes a matter of trade-offs.

ture evolved two distinctly different ways of tapping sunlight energy. In C_3 plants, carbon dioxide (CO_2) is captured from the air and stuck onto a 2-carbon receptor molecule. In C_4 plants, a 3-carbon molecule does the receiving, forming a 4-carbon sugar, hence the name, C_4.

Though the difference sounds academic, the implications to turf management are profound. C_4 photosynthesis is more efficient under bright light than C_3. In the sun, C_4 plants can literally outgrow C_3 plants. Under low light, the reverse is true. Fortunately there's room in the world for both types of grasses.

Another advantage of C_4 photosynthesis is that it is more water efficient. That's why you'll find C_4 plants growing throughout the warmer and drier parts of the world. Another name for a C_4 grass is a **warm-season grass**; C_3 grasses are called **cool-season grasses**. The three grassy weed species in the Colorado experiment were all C_4 grasses. That's why they were water efficient. A C_4 *turf* species would also be highly water efficient. Bermudagrass, zoysiagrass, and centipedegrass are examples of C_4 turf species (see Chapter 2).

Conclusions. You may have thought I was picking on the eco-lawn in the above discussion, since much of the discourse was admittedly one-sided. Actually I chose the eco-lawn as an example to illustrate two important points:

1. The eco-lawn concept emphasizes the need to scrutinize everything you hear or read that promises environmental friendliness, to make sure it lives up to its goals, and
2. It helped bring to life some of the basic terms and concepts used in turfgrass management, rather than as stiff, dry definitions.

In the future, it's unlikely that the eco-lawn will supplant large acreages of turfgrass around the world. The eco-lawn will probably find its niche among people who want to try something radically different than their friends and neighbors. The concept *does* open up some interesting avenues for thought and discussion about the future of lawns. But as mentioned in the text, many of the principles on which the eco-lawn is based have been tried and discarded decades earlier.

prior to the rotary mower. The reel mower, patented by Edwin Budding of Stroud, Gloucestershire, England, was an offshoot of a similar machine used in factories for trimming the pile of carpets.

As the popularity of golf grew, early golf course superintendents (pasture farmers) became faced with a dilemma: The players were wearing out the course. Of course, this is also a chronic complaint of modern golf course superintendents. But the damage to the courses back then was caused by a few hundred rounds of golf, compared to the tens of thousands of rounds played on today's courses.

The traditional English lawn turf was giving way, leaving bare soil on which to play. Coupled with the incessant English precipitation, the bare soil turned to mud.

As early as 1665, observant turf managers began noticing that some plants held up better under foot traffic than others (Rea, 1665). These early turf pioneers took plugs and cuttings from these enduring patches and propagated them across the course, particularly into the heavy wear areas—the greens and tees—which later became well defined. As it turned out, all of these tough plants were grasses. Early superintendents shared knowledge of the best plants for golf. Golf courses abandoned the traditional English lawn turf in favor of wear tolerant grasses.

* * *

Therefore, the concept of the eco-lawn is exciting but it's hardly new. It is what turf management evolved from. It is our roots.

Maintenance Savings Begins with Good Design

The landscape designer, architect, or contractor plays a key role in holding down long-term maintenance costs of a new turf planting. A landscape built with conservation in mind will save money, labor, and resources over the life of the stand.

On the flip side, bad design begets higher maintenance. Take for example a poorly designed sports field. A field built so that surrounding surface water drains directly onto the field is a design flaw that will perpetually require higher upkeep. Whenever it rains, surface water washes onto the field, adding to compaction, wear, and upkeep. A problem like this is best solved in the design phase.

In Table 1.2 are a few design measures for conserving resources and saving maintenance, adapted from an article by Phil Busey and Terry Riordan (Riordan and Busey, 1993):

Table 1.2. Tips for conserving maintenance and resources by good design.

Design Elements to Help Conserve Resources	Pros (What is actually saved)	Cons (Problems that may need to be overcome)
Minimize the use of unnecessary mounds and berms in the landscape. Eliminate short, narrow turf strips that are tough to maintain.	Reduces the need for specialized irrigation and expensive mowing of slopes.	This limits the designer's need for topographic diversity and the client's need for visual privacy.
Anticipate the future growth of trees and shrubs. Use slower growing woody plants.	Excessive shade can damage turf or contribute to disease. Tree removal at a later date adds to upkeep.	Clients prefer an "instant" landscape, with enough trees and shrubs to create a mature appearance.
Provide paved paths and roadways to take wear pressure off the turf.	Reduced turf wear means less need for aerification of compacted areas, fewer weed and mud problems.	Concrete and asphalt detract from the natural surroundings.
Install mulched beds around trees and shrubs.	Conserves water by allowing the tree to grow without competing with the grass. Cuts down on "weed-whacker injury" to the tree. Reduces trimming work.	Added installation costs. A "disconnected" look between the turf and trees.
Cluster vegetation types into coherent groups, based on their maintenance needs.	Helps cut down on spot maintenance of individual plantings which can be labor intensive.	Groupings are difficult to implement on smaller landscapes due to size restrictions.
Anticipate drainage problems. Provide surface and subsurface drainage.	Drainage improves plant growth and vigor by minimizing waterlogging. Mud and compaction are reduced. Future turf disease problems may be averted.	Added costs. Anticipating future drainage problems is not always possible when a great deal of soil moving takes place.

Design Elements to Help Conserve Resources	Pros (What is actually saved)	Cons (Problems that may need to be overcome)
Diversify the landscape with a broad spectrum of plant materials.	Allows specialized needs to be addressed with the right plant materials. Avoids "cookie cutter" landscapes.	Availability, delivery, and inventory problems can complicate a project.
Specify plant materials that are deliverable.	Assures that specified materials can be delivered to the job. Minimizes delays in constructions.	Limits diversity in the landscape.
Use specs that are high quality but realistic.	Specifying quality seed and plant materials helps cut down on weeds, diseases, and insects later on.	Added costs may be involved. Requires more information and searching on the part of the designer.
Allow for nonmaintained or minimal maintenance areas where appropriate.	Areas that are out of the normal traffic pattern should be relegated to minimal maintenance turfgrasses or other vegetation.	The look of a nonmaintained area may clash with the manicured appearance of a high class landscape.
Modify soils that are prone to compaction or poor drainage.	Soil modification provides a better growing medium for turf and ornamentals and may reduce pest problems later on.	Added cost and time is required to obtain sand, peat, or compost and incorporate it uniformly.

There *is* a place today for the eco-lawn—in situations traffic and wear are not a factor. But the eco-lawn is by no means the salvation for everyone. Nor is it what turf is evolving into. In spite of its low maintenance implications and attractive flowers, eco-lawns suffer from some of the same basic problems as its ancestor, the English lawn turf. These problems illustrate why diversity for its own sake is not always ideal, and why grass is such a valuable playing surface.

Putting the Pieces Together

Margaret Glessner, the Long Island homeowner, found out the hard way that making changes in the landscape without first verifying their fitness can spell disaster (see section, *Just Because Something Feels Right*). Glessner and others have discovered by trial and error that installing untested innovations in the landscape can sometimes lead to even higher upkeep.

The best way to develop a lower maintenance turf is by designing and building it right from the start. The sidebar, *Maintenance Savings Begins with Good Design,* offers interesting insights to consider as you begin your new landscaping project, to make sure all the maintenance-wasting aspects are ironed out in the design phase.

But even if you're nursing along a maintenance-hungry turf that's already established, there are ways to fight back. Over time, improvements can be made in the grass species, the soil, and other cultural practices, transforming your turf into one with fewer needs. Many of these transformations are virtually invisible and can even be made while sports play continues. Chapter 7 provides a wealth of tips for partially or fully retrofitting your turf with modern, resource-friendly varieties.

Chapter 2

Performance of the "Traditional" Turf Species under Reduced Maintenance

A lot of people believe that the "traditional" turfgrass species—bluegrass, bermudagrass, ryegrass, fescue, and the like—are maintenance hogs. And if you check out the grasses growing on the highest maintenance golf courses and pro sports fields worldwide, you'd probably come to the same conclusion. Because those are the grasses you'll find planted there.

In the last chapter, I showed why the traditional turfgrass species have tended to dominate heavy play turf. Under close mowing and high wear, many plant species simply fall apart. Only a select few grasses can survive the daily pounding of foot traffic and mowing and still reward you with a resilient playing surface. When it comes to grassing a golf course putting green or a daily-use athletic field, turf managers have few options other than the traditional turf species.

You might be surprised to learn that among the traditional turf species, there's an enormous, untapped potential for low maintenance. These grasses can withstand considerable cuts in water, fertilizer, mowing, and pesticides, as long as the right varieties are selected.

To a large extent, this capacity for low maintenance endurance has gone unnoticed. Here's an example: Among all the grasses in the world—exotic or domestic—one of the best, most efficient water-users can be found within the everyday lawngrasses. It's true. Sheep fescue, bermudagrass, and zoysiagrass are among the most water-thrifty grasses in existence. Of course, not every variety of every species is resource friendly. Some are just the opposite. So it's important to know the right ones to pick.

In this chapter, I'll compare the performance of the traditional turfgrass species with the trendy native and range grasses, as they adapt to restricted maintenance. This chapter delves into current research to help explain the real structural differences between "high maintenance" grasses versus grasses that adapt to lower upkeep. The first section in this chapter illustrates the inherent differences between low and high maintenance grasses. Later in the chapter, I compare performance of these grasses in several climatic regions. At the conclusion of the chapter is a section listing the advantages and disadvantages of each grass for low maintenance conditions.

RESEARCH UPDATE: BUILDING A BETTER GRASS PLANT

Nick Christians was one of the first to recognize the low maintenance potential among the traditional turf species. His studies at Iowa State University (Burt and Christians, 1990; Christians, 1989a, 1989b; Christians and Burt, 1989) uncovered varieties that perform *better* as maintenance levels are reduced. Christians' interest in these grasses was kindled in 1980 when he observed side-by-side plantings of Kentucky bluegrass varieties at two levels of management:

- *High maintenance plots*—Irrigated freely as needed to prevent moisture stress; 4 lb nitrogen fertilization per 1000 ft^2 (20 g/m^2) annually.
- *Low maintenance plots*—No irrigation; 1 lb nitrogen per 1000 ft^2 (5 g/m^2) annually.

Christians monitored both trials over four growing seasons. After a particularly grueling

Table 2.1. The turfgrass species described in Chapter 2, including their Latin name and authority.

Cool-Season Grasses	Warm-Season Grasses
Colonial bentgrass • *Agrostis capillaris* L. Creeping bentgrass • *Agrostis stolonifera* L. Tall fescue • *Festuca arundinacea* Schreb. Sheep fescue • *Festuca ovina* L. Strong creeping red fescue • *Festuca rubra* L. Chewings fescue • *Festuca rubra* L. ssp. *falax* Thuill. Slender creeping fescue • *Festuca rubra* ssp. *litoralis* (G.F.W. Meyer) Auquier Hard fescue • *Festuca trachyphylla* (Hack.) Krajina Perennial ryegrass • *Lolium perenne* L. Kentucky bluegrass • *Poa pratensis* L.	Bermudagrass • *Cynodon dactylon* (L.) Pers. • *C. dactylon x C. transvaalensis* Burtt-Davy St. Augustinegrass • *Stenotaphrum secundatum* (Walt.) Kuntze Zoysiagrass • *Zoysia japonica* Steud. • *Z. matrella* (L.) Merr. • *Z. tenuifolia* Willd. ex Trin.

summer, it became apparent to him that the top varieties in one test were not the same top varieties in the other. Some varieties were adapting better to reduced maintenance than others. The names of the varieties in this particular trial are not important because most are now obsolete. But what's important is that a new concept was identified: *The low maintenance turf variety*.

Follow-up studies. Christians went on to do additional studies, selecting the top five varieties from each trial (high and low maintenance) to study their growth habits. He wanted to know what makes a low maintenance grass tick. What special features or adaptations do they have that make them able to withstand neglect?

If you think about it, the answers to these questions have far-reaching implications. By pinpointing the characteristics that impart low maintenance tolerance, a person could then judge a low maintenance grass just by looking at it—like judging a book by its cover. Plant breeders would have a map for choosing grasses for low upkeep. That alone would speed the development of new low maintenance grasses considerably.

In three experiments Christians and his colleagues monitored rooting depth and clipping yield of grasses among the high and low maintenance groups. Three-week-old seedlings were transplanted into the greenhouse and were grown in soil media deficient in nutrients. He found significant differences between groups in rooting and shoot growth, even though the trial was run for a scant 10 weeks (Burt and Christians, 1990).

As a group, the lower maintenance varieties had several characteristics in common:

- *12% deeper rooting*—deep rooting aids in ferreting moisture from the soil
- *56% more root mass*—a greater distribution of the plant's weight was in its roots (more root weight per unit of shoot weight)
- *Narrower blades and a more vertical leaf orientation*—finer, more upright blades help curtail water wastage
- *More leaf folding*—folding of leaves is a mechanism plants use to "close the shutters" and stifle evaporative loss during drought

- *27% longer sheaths and 13% fewer leaves per shoot*—an upright architecture helps rid the stand of excess heat buildup
- *More clippings*—oh well, you can't have everything

The architecture of grass. Grasses in the two groups—high and low maintenance varieties—had strikingly different **plant architectures**. Plant architecture can be thought of like building a house. Plants are built a certain way to help withstand environmental stresses. Instead of lumber and concrete, plants are built from fiber and physiology to withstanding whatever nature dishes out. Plants have specialized survival structures, just as a house has a roof to keep out rain and windows to let in light and air.

Architects use a catch phrase: *"Form follows function."* This simply means that the *purpose* of a structure determines its form and appearance. A solar home for example might feature large glass windows or an active heat collection panel on the roof. The architecture is there to serve a purpose.

Plant architecture works the same way. Scientists can decipher the purpose of a particular plant architecture by using reverse technology: The form or appearance of a plant part tells you its function.

In the Iowa study, the vertical leaf orientation and fewer leaves per plant of low maintenance varieties point to an architecture that benefits heating, cooling, and water use. Upright leaves are more efficient at dispersing heat without resorting to water to cool the plant. In fact if you look at them, vertical grass leaves resemble the vertical cooling fins used by engineers on the backs of some electronic equipment—a case of engineering mimicking nature.

High maintenance varieties possess other specialized adaptations and structures for withstanding the rigors of high wear and close cut. As a group, high maintenance varieties in the ISU study had more leaves per plant, less topgrowth, and nearly horizontal leaves. This type of architecture is efficient for surviving close mowing. Horizontal leaves are able to grow longer before they're cut.

Both types of varieties—high *and* low maintenance—have a valuable place within the realm of turfgrass management. High maintenance varieties are best suited to close-cut turf. Low maintenance varieties are best where upkeep is limited. By blending these two groups of grasses together you can incorporate both attributes into your turf (see Chapter 6 for blending instructions).

Grasses that tolerate both. Recently, a new class of turfgrass has been identified: Varieties that excel under *both* high and low maintenance. Christians initially recognized that one of the Kentucky bluegrass varieties in his test, "Ram I," performed well regardless of maintenance. This was his first hint of a new class of grass.

In 1990, Christians and 20 other researchers across the country embarked on a test to verify Christians's earlier observations. A new national Kentucky bluegrass test was established, and unlike earlier tests, this one was planted as separate high and low maintenance trials, similar to the Iowa State study.

Sixty-two Kentucky bluegrass varieties were established in the low maintenance test and 125 in the high maintenance test. After five years of evaluation, 11 commercial varieties rose to the top half of entries in both trials. These 11 unique varieties show superior growth and performance under diverse sets of maintenance conditions.

- *Varieties that excelled under both high and low maintenance conditions*—Bartitia, Caliber, Cobalt, Haga, Liberty, Livingston, Midnight, NuStar, SR2000, Unique, Washington
- *Varieties that performed better under low maintenance than high maintenance*—Belmont, Baron, Crest, Freedom, Merit, Monopoly, Opal, Ram I
- *Varieties that performed better under high maintenance than low maintenance*—NuBlue, Cynthia
- *Varieties that performed below average under both high and low maintenance*—Barzan, Chelsea, Destiny, Fortuna, Gnome, Kenblue, Merion, Miracle, South Dakota Common, Suffolk

These dual-purpose varieties give the turf manager added flexibility under diverse grow-

Performance of Kentucky bluegrass varieties under high vs. low maintenance, according to rankings from the National Turfgrass Evaluation Program 1993 report

How the groups were determined. Beginning in 1990, the National Turfgrass Evaluation Program (NTEP) began performing varietal performance trials on Kentucky bluegrasses under high maintenance (simulating a golf-course fairway) and low maintenance (simulating a low maintenance home lawn) conditions. Varietal performance in these trials was recorded for five years at 20 or more locations across North America (Figure 2.1).

To obtain the groups of varieties noted in the text, the following method was used. If a variety ranked in the top half of the trial for both tests, it appeared in my "high-and-low" list. A variety was placed in the "low maintenance only" list if it ranked in the top half of the low maintenance list but the bottom half of the high maintenance list. A variety that ranked in the top half of the high maintenance test but the bottom half of the low maintenance test, was placed in the "high maintenance only" list. Varieties that ranked in the bottom half of both trials were so noted.

The lists contain only commercial varieties; unnamed, experimental entries were omitted. Also, not all varieties appeared in both trials. Only varieties present in both trials were included.

Current, up-to-the-minute varietal performance results of bluegrasses and all the other popular turf species can be obtained online, by accessing the web site of the NTEP at: *http://www.ntep.org*

ing conditions. Even on a high maintenance golf course, for example, there're bound to be spots with good and bad soil. A turf needs to be able to withstand both.

As a whole, common-type varieties (such as "Kenblue" or "South Dakota common") bombed in both the high and low maintenance national tests. In the past, common-type varieties were promoted as the best choice for low maintenance conditions. Common varieties lack resistance to leafspot and other important diseases. They also possess an upright growth habit, limiting their usefulness under highly managed conditions (Keeley and Koski, 1995; Riordan et al., 1979).

The popular belief that common-type varieties were well suited to low maintenance may have been fostered by the sellers of common seed who had something to gain. Based on results of this test, I would recommend *against* using common varieties of the traditional turf species, regardless of the level of maintenance chosen.

Outside of the bluegrasses, little work has been focused on identifying dual-purpose varieties. Tall fescue is the exception. Research has shown that good tall fescue varieties under high maintenance also tend to be good varieties under low maintenance. In an Illinois study (Figure 2.2) and others like it, improved cultivars performed well regardless of fertility or irrigation. Older, common varieties like "Kentucky-31" (a forage tall fescue) gave a poor showing at any maintenance level (Anonymous, 1991a; Portz, 1986).

Warm-season grasses. Like bluegrass, the warm-season grasses also differ in plant architecture. Dave Casnoff and Jim Beard at Texas A&M University (Casnoff and Beard, 1986) studied the rooting of warm-season turf species in a greenhouse trial similar to the one at Iowa State. They found turfgrasses with roots approaching 7 ft (2 m) in depth (Figure 2.3). Bermudagrass was the hands-down winner with the deepest roots of all. Bahiagrass, St. Augustinegrass, seashore paspalum, and "Emerald" zoysia rooted half as deep as bermudagrass. Buffalograss, centipedegrass, and "Meyer" zoysia roots were half again as deep.

The Texas study indicated a strong relationship between rooting depth and drought toler-

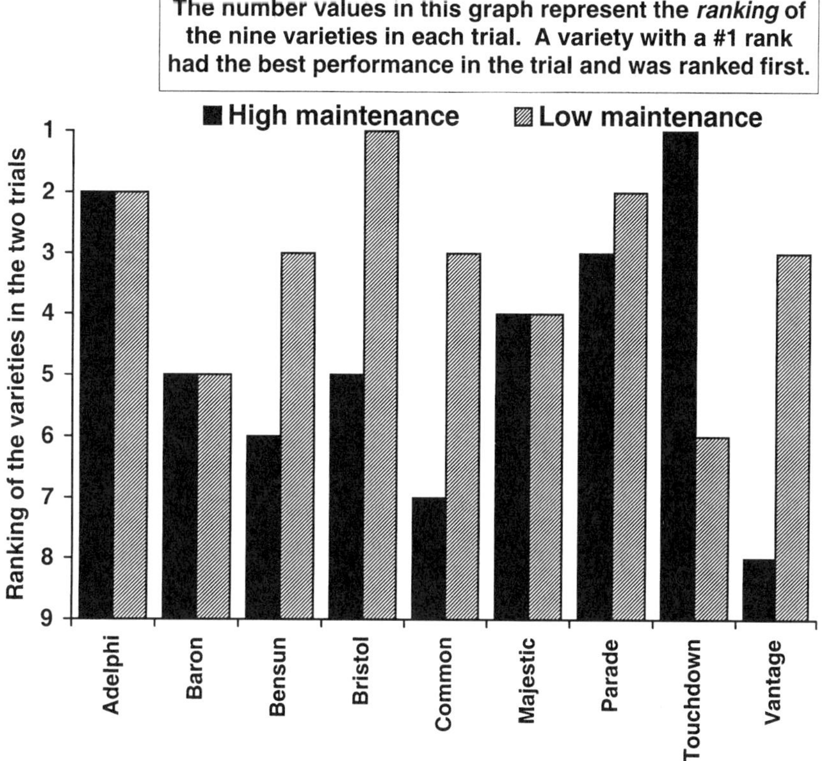

Figure 2.1. Most Kentucky bluegrass varieties respond quite differently to high versus low maintenance. High maintenance performance is not necessarily a good predictor of low maintenance performance. Some varieties are better suited to high maintenance; others to low. A few (examples: "Adelphi," "Baron," "Majestic") bridge the gap and are well suited to either. "Common" Kentucky bluegrass performed acceptably in this trial under low maintenance but fell apart under high. "Touchdown" did just the opposite, making it a better choice for higher maintenance (Portz, 1986). *High maintenance*–1 1/4-in. (32 mm) cutting height; irrigated. *Low maintenance*–2 1/4-in. (57 mm) cutting height; unirrigated.

ance. Deeper rooted grasses endured drought with less discoloration and stand loss. Their findings also verified that Christians's earlier observations on low maintenance plant architecture applied to other grasses as well.

I would expect that in general, bermudagrass and zoysiagrass varieties would exhibit the same highly specific maintenance preference as does bluegrass, where high maintenance performance does not *automatically* infer low maintenance performance. These species propagate vegetatively and clonally. Entire stands of bermuda or zoysia are comprised of a single genetic clone.

I would venture to guess that the fine fescues, bentgrasses, ryegrasses, and seeded warm-season grasses would respond similar to tall fescue in regard to their maintenance preference: Superior high maintenance varieties would also be the better low maintenance ones. But more research needs to be done to confirm my hypothesis.

THE TRADITIONAL TURFGRASSES:

How They Compare with the Unconventional, Low Maintenance Grasses

Believe it or not, some of the traditional turfgrass species actually stand toe-to-toe with the unconventional, ultra-low maintenance grasses (i.e., the ones listed in Chapters 3 and 4).

I'm sure at this point you're thinking: *"That's not what I've heard!"*

But in fact it's true. Some traditional turfgrasses stack up well against the prairie and rangegrasses when it comes to low maintenance. The great equalizer of course is: *Mowing*. Many of the low

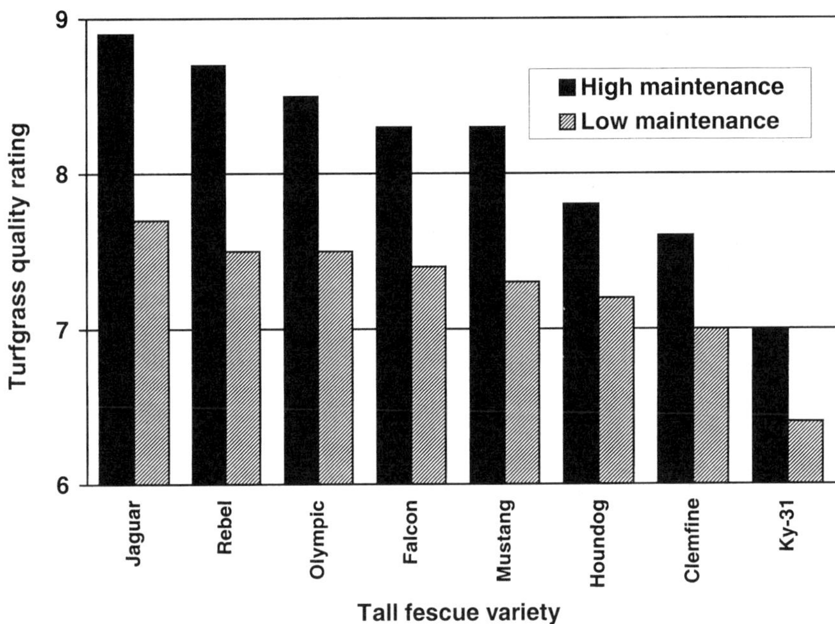

Figure 2.2. A University of Illinois–Urbana turf trial (Portz, 1986) found a nice, orderly correlation between high and low maintenance performance of tall fescues. Results support the theory that a superior tall fescue variety will perform comparatively well regardless of the maintenance level provided.

High maintenance–4 lb nitrogen fertilizer per 1000 ft^2 (20 g/m^2) in 1983 and 1984, 2 lb (10 g/m^2) in 1985; irrigated as often as needed.

Low maintenance–1 lb nitrogen fertilizer (5 g/m^2) in 1983 and 1984, and none in 1985; no irrigation.

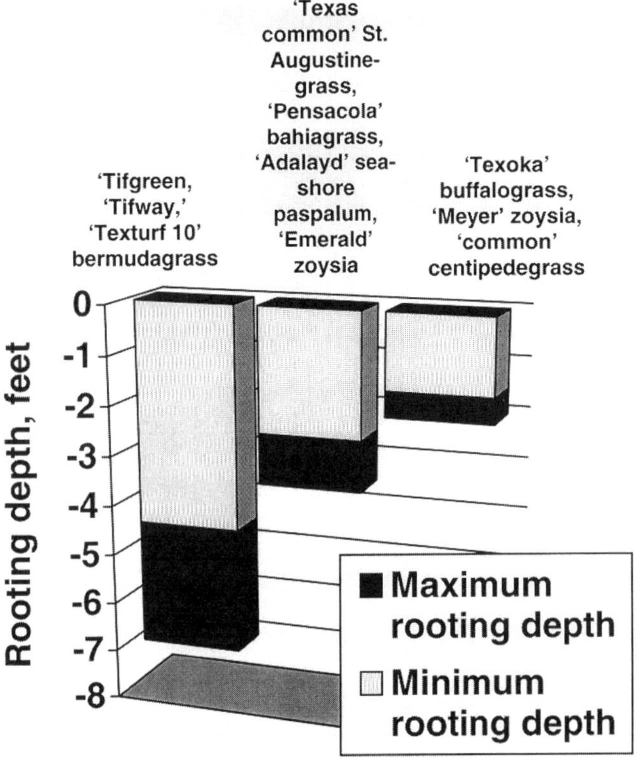

Figure 2.3. Grasses with deeper roots are able to extract moisture from a greater soil volume. The rooting differences shown here, from a greenhouse study at Texas A&M University (Casnoff and Beard, 1986), do not automatically infer that deeper roots are more *efficient* at absorbing water. But when moisture is short, deeper rooted turfgrasses can be expected to pull water from a greater depth. (Metric conversion: 7 ft = 2.1 m).

maintenance prairiegrasses won't tolerate mowing. Mowing *height* is also a determining factor. Few low maintenance grasses can survive below a 2-in. (50-mm) cut. At 4 in. (100 mm) they stand a chance. And under *unmowed* conditions, the unconventional species do exceptionally well.

Good as they may be, the traditional turf species aren't suited to *all* low maintenance tasks. There are conditions where other grasses are far better, such as:

- *Wet conditions*—waterlogged soils, flooding, or standing water
- *Highly acidic or alkaline soils*—pHs below 4.5 or above 9
- *Contaminated soils*—high salt concentrations, heavy metals, or pollutants
- *Extremely droughty conditions*—less than 15 in. (380 mm) of annual precipitation with no irrigation
- *Excessive heat*—above 100°F (38°C) for months at a time

Under these extremes, the traditional turf species fade away. They may be useful as a "nurse" crop to temporarily nurse along a slower germinating grass, but it's doubtful they'll persist long term. Under extreme conditions, alternative species are needed. Alternative grasses are listed in the next two chapters, indexed by the special problems they're known to tolerate.

RESEARCH UPDATE: HEAD-TO-HEAD COMPARISON TRIALS OF THE TRADITIONAL VS. UNCONVENTIONAL GRASSES

Trials comparing the traditional turf species against the unconventional grass species are scarce—especially under maintained turf conditions. Only within the last few years have a handful of these trials been run. Comparative trials provide insight into how the traditional turf species stack up against their subsistence cousins.

Below I've summarized several trials, grouped by their climatic region. This grouping was done to allow extrapolation of results to similar climates worldwide. Chapter 5 will assist you in determining which region is most comparable to your local conditions.

Cool, mountain climate

Over the last decade, I've conducted two field trials in northern Idaho comparing turfgrasses with their wild counterparts. Northern Idaho is classed as Zone 1 in the climate charts in Chapter 5. Zone 1 encompasses a broad swath of the temperate region of the world, including notable cities of New York, Chicago, Beijing, and Berlin.

Annual precipitation at the test site averages 18 in. (450 mm) and humidity during summer is low. Thus, high-humidity diseases such as brown patch are not a factor. On the other hand, cool-weather diseases such as leaf spot, necrotic ring spot, and snow mold can be oppressive. Icy winters with temperatures to −25°F (−31°C) limit the growth of all but the most hardy warm-season grasses. Hot summers up to 100°F (38°C) stress alpine species.

Persistence trial. The first trial was planted in 1982 by Arden Jacklin and Leah Brilman. I evaluated survival of the plots after five growing seasons of virtually no maintenance except for occasional mowing (Table 2.2).

All plots were initially fertilized and irrigated to ensure a uniform establishment. After 2 months of growth, maintenance was slashed.

As a rule, turf researchers generally irrigate and fertilize test trials during establishment to bring all plots up to an equal footing. From a test standpoint this practice is controversial because:

- *Pro*—It gets all varieties to the same level of establishment before treatments are imposed. Otherwise, years later you might still be seeing the effects of sluggish establishment on one or more grasses.
- *Con*—In the real world of low maintenance, uniform water and fertilizer are not always available. Rainfall is often used to bring up a stand. If a grass establishes poorly with natural rainfall, it may be of little value. Also, ample water and fertilizer during establishment do little to harden off plants for surviving the

Table 2.2. Endurance of the traditional turf species versus several unconventional lawngrasses in a mowed (2 in. [50 mm]), nonirrigated, nonfertilized persistence trial in Northern Idaho. Plots were established on gravel soil in 1982 and were evaluated after five growing seasons. Annual precipitation at the site averages 18 in. (450 mm); plots were irrigated for establishment.

Turf Coverage	"Traditional" Turf Species	"Low Maintenance" Species
Complete ground coverage (75–100% cover)	Hard fescue, 'Durar' Tall fescue, 'Fawn'	Bulbous bluegrass Canby bluegrass, 'Canbar'
Satisfactory coverage (40–75% cover)	Chewings fescue, 'Baruba,' 'Checker' Kentucky bluegrass, 'S-21' Perennial ryegrass, 'All*Star' Tall fescue, 'Arid,' 'Falcon,' 'Galway,' 'Ky-31,' 'Mesa,' 'Olympic,' 'Rebel' Sheep fescue, 'Covar'	Big bluegrass, 'Sherman' Canada bluegrass, 'Reubens' Crested hairgrass, 'Barkoel' Crested wheatgrass, 'Fairway' Meadow bromegrass, 'Regar' Redtop, 'Streaker' Streambank wheatgrass, 'Critana,' 'Sodar' Upland bluegrass
Thin coverage (25–40% cover)	Kentucky bluegrass, 'Banjo,' 'Huntsville,' 'Kenblue,' 'Nassau,' 'Wabash' Hard fescue, 'Biljart,' 'Reliant,' 'Scaldis' Strong creeping red fescue, 'Center,' 'Ceres,' 'Pennlawn,' 'Ensylva' Slender creeping fescue, 'Logro' Tall fescue, 'Houndog' Perennial ryegrass, 'Manhattan'	Alkali sacaton Arizona fescue Blue grama Crested wheatgrass, 'Ephraim,' 'Ruff' Idaho fescue Intermediate wheatgrass, 'Greenar,' 'Oahe,' 'Tegmar' Lemmons alkaligrass Little bluestem Siberian wheatgrass, 'P-27' Smooth bromegrass, 'Manchar' Standard wheatgrass, 'Nordan' Timothy, 'Liam' Upland bluegrass, 'Tundra' Western wheatgrass, 'Rosanna,' 'Common' Wood meadowgrass, 'Barnemo'
Bare ground (0–25% cover)	Kentucky bluegrass, 'Argyle,' 'Fylking,' 'Glade,' 'South Dakota common,' 'Troy,' 'Vantage' Roughstalk bluegrass, 'Sabre'	Alkaligrass, 'Fults' Deertonguegrass, 'Tioga' Meadow fescue, 'First,' 'Common' Smooth bromegrass, 'Bromar' Timothy, 'Climax'

rigors of low maintenance. If anything, they may predispose it to failure.

During the first year of growth, the traditional turf species of bluegrass and ryegrass provided the densest, most attractive turf cover. One reason the traditional turf species perform well initially is that they all have good seedling vigor and few seed dormancy problems. Later in the experiment when the maintenance faucet was shut, many of the bluegrasses plummeted from 100% ground coverage to less than 25%. The common-type bluegrasses ("Argyle," "South Dakota common," "Troy") dropped the most.

Improved bluegrasses with superior disease and stress tolerance fared better.

Of all the grasses in the trial, hard and tall fescue survived low maintenance the best. Some fescue varieties survived better than others. "Durar" hard fescue, a variety developed by the Soil Conservation Service for extreme soil conditions, had the highest ground coverage after five years.

Among the unconventional grasses, bulbous and Canby bluegrass provided the greatest ground coverage at the conclusion of the trial. Part of the reason bulbous and Canby bluegrass excelled in this trial was due to the date of the final rating: October. Grasses like bulbous and Canby bluegrass escape harsh summers by going dormant. In the fall they vigorously bounce back to life. Dormant turf is hardly attractive, but it does provide the grass an option for surviving extreme conditions.

Home lawn trial. My second trial had a different purpose than the first. In the first trial, the grasses were established and then—except for mowing—given over to Mother Nature. In the second trial, the grasses were planted and managed like a home lawn, with:

- *Weekly mowing*—1 1/4 in. (3 cm)
- *Some irrigation*—only enough to keep the grasses from turning completely brown
- *Fertilization*—a once-a-year shot in the spring
- *No pesticides*—except for an annual broadleaf weed cleanup

In this test, visual ratings of turf performance were recorded every month, just as they are with the U.S. National tests. To excel, grasses had to produce an attractive turf 12 months of the year.

Results again showed hard and tall fescue topping the chart (Table 2.3). Kentucky bluegrass fared better in this trial than in the earlier persistence trial.

Among the unconventional species, Kentucky bluegrass's relatives (big, Canada, and upland bluegrass) provided satisfactory to excellent turf cover. Crested hairgrass also prospered. Canby bluegrass and the wheatgrasses showed fair to poor performance, unlike in the persistence trial.

In conclusion, under low maintenance the traditional turf species provided remarkable performance. Varietal selection is critical because some varieties are ill suited to low upkeep.

Mediterranean climate

The inland valleys of California enjoy a warm, Mediterranean climate, with mild winters and hot, dry summers. Mediterranean climates are found worldwide, in southern Europe and the Middle East, South Africa, southwestern South America, and most of Australia. Irrigation is essential for turf survival in this region. Water costs are usually high and watering bans are sometimes an annual event.

Warm-season grasses provide nearly flawless summer performance for this region. Warm-season grasses go dormant in winter but are seldom

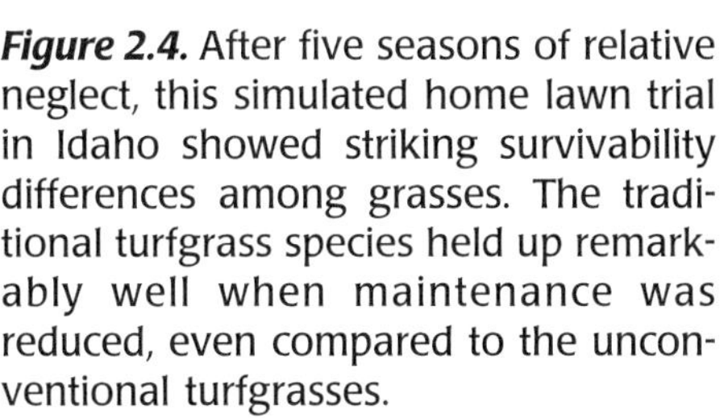

Figure 2.4. After five seasons of relative neglect, this simulated home lawn trial in Idaho showed striking survivability differences among grasses. The traditional turfgrass species held up remarkably well when maintenance was reduced, even compared to the unconventional turfgrasses.

Table 2.3. A simulated home-lawn trial comparing the turf quality of the traditional turf species with several unconventional lawngrasses (see Figure 2.4). Plots were established on gravelly silt loam soil in Northern Idaho and were evaluated for turfgrass quality monthly for three years. Plots were given supplemental irrigation to prevent drought dormancy and were fertilized with a 4-1-2 ratio fertilizer at 1 lb nitrogen per 1000 ft^2 per year (5 g/m^2) each spring. Mowing was weekly at $1\frac{1}{4}$ in. (32 mm).

Turfgrass Quality	"Traditional" Turf Species	"Low Maintenance" Species
Excellent quality (6 to 7 average rating)	Hard fescue, 'ST-1679' Kentucky bluegrass, 'Columbia,' 'Wabash' Tall fescue, 'Arid,' 'Gremlin,' 'Taurus'	Big bluegrass Canada bluegrass, 'Reubens' Crested hairgrass, 'Barkoel'
Satisfactory quality (5 to 6 average rating)	Hard fescue, 'EcoStar' Sheep fescue, 'Mecklenburger,' 'Common' Tall fescue, 'Safe'	Redtop, 'Streaker' Smooth bromegrass, 'Arly' Upland bluegrass, 'Draylar'
Unsatisfactory quality (4 to 5 average rating)	Chewings fescue, 'Countess'	Alkaligrass Alpine bluegrass Canby bluegrass, 'Canbar' Tufted hairgrass Wood meadowgrass, 'Barnemo,' 'Common'
Poor quality (3 to 4 average rating)	Chewings fescue, 'Highlight'	Blue grama, 'W.6' Green needlegrass, 'Lodorm' Idaho fescue, 'Nezpers,' 'Herbs' Siberian wheatgrass, 'P-27' Streambank wheatgrass, 'Sodar' Upland bluegrass, 'Tundra'

injured by the mild temperatures. Cool-season grasses can be grown satisfactorily but at the expense of a lot of water.

Because of the low humidity, diseases are infrequent. However, summer irrigation can inflame brown patch and pythium disease outbreaks and certain insects.

Coastal California enjoys an even milder climate, with moderate summers and very mild winters. Cool-season grasses prosper under these conditions, with turf disease prevalent during foggy periods.

California research. Lin Wu and Ali Harivandi, turf professors at the University of California (Wu and Harivandi, 1988), studied 2 traditional turf species and 10 unconventional ones at a dual-site experiment in the two areas described above. One experiment was located in the inland desert near Davis and the other at the UC coastal station near San Francisco.

The researchers provided limited irrigation to the grasses, gauged at 50% of open-pan evaporation. Open-pan evaporation can be thought of as follows: If an open pail of water evaporates 1 in. of water in a week, the researchers would apply $\frac{1}{2}$ in. of water to the turf. This method of metering water has become a standard in the irrigation business, as described in Chapter 10.

Wu and Harivandi reported that "among the 12 species evaluated, western and crested wheatgrass, weeping and lemmons alkaligrass, smooth brome, perennial ryegrass, and saltgrass performed very poorly." These grasses either failed to establish a solid turf cover or rapidly declined in density, allowing weed invasion.

Tall fescue showed excellent performance at the coastal location (Table 2.4). Tall fescue "is now the front-runner of low-maintenance turfgrasses. It possesses most of the quality components of traditional turfgrasses, such as Ken-

Table 2.4. A low maintenance comparison trial in Davis and Santa Clara County, California (Wu and Harivandi, 1988). Plots were irrigated at 50% of net evaporation, fertilized at 1 to 1.5 lb nitrogen per 1000 ft^2 per year (5 to 7.5 g/m^2), and mowed at 1.5 to 2 in. (38 to 51 mm). Plots were maintained without thatch, disease, insect, and weed control. The plots were evaluated by the researchers for their potential use as low maintenance turf.

Potential for Use Under Low Maintenance*	"Traditional" Turf Species	"Low Maintenance" Species
High potential	Tall fescue	Buffalograss Torgrass
Medium potential		Blue grama Sideoats grama
Low potential	Perennial ryegrass	Alkaligrass Crested wheatgrass Lemmons alkaligrass Seashore saltgrass Smooth bromegrass Western wheatgrass

tucky bluegrass and perennial ryegrass, while requiring much less care," they wrote.

Among the less conventional species, buffalograss and tor grass showed promise. Buffalograss excelled at both test sites, and tor grass showed potential at the Davis location (Figure 2.5). Buffalograss is a stoloniferous, warm-season grass native to the American Great Plains. Tor grass is a cool-season perennial from Europe. Both grasses demonstrated superior heat and drought tolerance. Buffalograss is discussed in Chapter 3 and tor grass in Chapter 4.

Cool, continental climate

A turf manager in a cold climate has few choices when it comes to grassing for minimal maintenance. Warm-season grasses as a whole are efficient under reduced maintenance, but they're out of the question as you progress into the colder regions of the world. Even the most cold hardy lines succumb to the long, hard winters. Your choices are restricted to cool-season grasses, and sometimes to the few among them that can tolerate the winters.

Research in central Canada. Jim Ross and his coworkers at Olds College (McKernan et al., 1996) established a pair of grass comparison

Figure 2.5. Researchers at the University of California found that tor grass, a little known turf species from Europe, performed remarkably well in a low maintenance trial there. They rated it as having "high potential" for low maintenance, along with tall fescue and buffalograss. Additional characteristics of tor grass are listed in Chapter 4.

trials in two contrasting regions of Alberta, Canada:

- *Lethbridge*—in the shadow of the Livingston Range of the Rocky Mountains
- *Medicine Hat*—in the heart of the vast Canadian prairie

The trials were planted in May 1993 and were evaluated three times per year for ground coverage, clumping, height between mowings, and weeds. Twenty-three varieties were included in the test, including 13 traditional turf species and 10 lower maintenance grasses (Table 2.5). Plots were mowed weekly and were not watered or fertilized.

Tall fescue and perennial ryegrass jumped to the fastest start initially, due to excellent seedling vigor. Rapid initial establishment helped crowd out weed invasion. Rough fescue, junegrass, and blue grama were slow establishing, in spite of unusually favorable rainfall during the 1993 season.

No single species had ideal responses in all measured categories. In general, the fescues, ryegrasses, and wheatgrasses provided the fullest cover and fewest weeds. Hard, sheep, and tall fescue outperformed their cousins, strong creeping red and chewings fescue.

The researchers found that crested wheatgrass may not be the ideal grass species to choose if reduced mowing is your goal. In Alberta, the wheatgrasses—particularly crested or "Fairway" wheatgrass—have become an icon of low maintenance turf. But perhaps their reputation is undeserving.

"Generally, the wheatgrasses were the tallest in height. If elimination of mowing is one of the goals, then the wheatgrasses would receive a low rating."

But the wheatgrasses had other redeeming features. "Drought stress was very evident in 1994 and 1995 in southern Alberta. The grasses which showed the greatest drought tolerance during these periods were the wheatgrasses (intermediate, western, and northern) and the Canada bluegrass. One of the Kentucky bluegrasses, 'Washington,' also showed good drought stress tolerance. This was unexpected, as Kentucky bluegrass is not considered drought tolerant," says Ross (McKernan et al., 1996).

Sheep and hard fescue produced the least topgrowth between mowings. Among the unconventional grasses, rough fescue and junegrass had the least topgrowth. This brings up an interesting point: Ideally, we'd like a low maintenance grass to cover the ground *horizontally* as much as possible but grow *vertically* as little as possible. Having both attributes in a single package is rarely possible. Rough fescue and junegrass grew vertically very little because there was not much of them to grow. But they fell short when it came to filling the ground with dense foliage. A true low maintenance grass needs to have robust lateral growth but slow vertical growth.

As in the Idaho test, the fescue family—particularly sheep, hard, and tall fescue—were best adapted for reduced maintenance, flying in the face of the long-held beliefs that native prairiegrasses were automatically best for prairie turf. Crested and northern wheatgrass performed well but others fell completely apart. "The worst performers included rough fescue, junegrass, slender wheatgrass, and alkaligrass," the researchers concluded.

A temperate, continental climate

One of the most extensive grass comparison trials ever undertaken was performed by the North Central Work Group, a collaboration of university turf researchers from Ohio to Iowa. In 1988, they teamed up to plant an 8-site experiment, comparing 5 traditional turf species with 11 less traditional ones (Voigt and Haley, 1990). Each site had three separate experiments, comparing the grasses under three different mowing regimes:

- $1^{1}/2$-in. (38 mm) mowing height
- 3-in. (76 mm) mowing height
- Unmowed

When averaged over the 3 heights of cut, the 8 locations, and the 4 years of study, the results were (drumroll, please): The traditional turf species came out on top (Table 2.6). As in the above

Table 2.5. Results of a turf trial comparing the "traditional" turf species to several low maintenance alternative grasses, under a cool, continental climate. Plots at two sites in Alberta, Canada, were given no supplemental irrigation, fertilizer, or disease, insect, or weed control. The box shading on the graphic below was adapted from actual plot rating numbers (McKernan and Ross, 1993).

- ***Ground coverage*** **ratings included such factors as winter-hardiness, spring recovery, and shoot density.**
- ***Freedom from clumping*** **was the ability to maintain an even stand without clumps.**
- ***Height between mowings*** **was a measure of the leaf growth (cm) in between mowings, including seedheads when present. A low height was most desirable.**
- ***Freedom from weeds*** **was a measure of actual weed counts. As you'd expect, it tended to be correlated with the other factors: A tight, dense stand excluded weeds.**

Grass species	Ground Coverage	Freedom from Clumps	Height Between Mowings	Freedom from Weeds
"Traditional" turfgrass species				
Kentucky bluegrass, 'Washington'	Below average	Below average	Above average	Above average
Kentucky bluegrass, 'Midnight'	Poor performance	Below average	Superior performance	Below average
Strong creeping fescue, 'Shadow'	Above average	Below average	Above average	Above average
Strong creeping fescue, 'Boreal'	Above average	Below average	Above average	Poor performance
Chewings fescue, 'Victory'	Above average	Poor performance	Above average	Above average
Hard fescue, 'Aurora'	Below average	Below average	Superior performance	Above average
Hard fescue, 'Spartan'	Above average	Below average	Superior performance	Above average
Hard fescue, 'Warwick'	Below average	Poor performance	Above average	Below average
Sheep fescue, 'Nakiska'	Above average	Above average	Superior performance	Above average
Tall fescue, 'Arid'	Superior performance	Below average	Below average	Superior performance
Tall fescue, 'Mustang'	Above average	Below average	Below average	Superior performance
Perennial ryegrass, 'Blazer'	Superior performance	Superior performance	Below average	Superior performance
Perennial ryegrass, 'Fiesta'	Superior performance	Above average	Above average	Superior performance
"Low maintenance" turf species				
Alkaligrass, 'Fults'	Poor performance	Below average	Above average	Above average
Blue grama	Above average	Superior performance	Above average	Above average
Crested wheatgrass, 'Fairway'	Superior performance	Superior performance	Poor performance	Superior performance
Intermediate wheatgrass, 'Clarke'	Above average	Poor performance	Below average	Superior performance
Prairie junegrass	Poor performance	Poor performance	Superior performance	Poor performance
Rough fescue	Poor performance	Poor performance	Superior performance	Below average
Russian wildrye, 'Swift'	Below average	Superior performance	Poor performance	Superior performance
Slender wheatgrass, 'Elbee'	Above average	Above average	Poor performance	Above average
Slender wheatgrass, 'Highlander'	Poor performance	Poor performance	Above average	Above average
Streambank wheatgrass, 'Sodar'	Above average	Superior performance	Poor performance	Superior performance

Shading	Turf desirability
White	Superior performance
Light hatching	Above average
Cross-hatching	Below average
Black	Poor performance

studies, tall, sheep, and hard fescue were the best all-around grasses for low maintenance conditions across the Northcentral region. Redtop, Canada bluegrass, and buffalograss were the most promising among the unconventional group.

CONCLUSIONS

The traditional turf species have gotten a bum rap when it comes to reduced maintenance. In head-to-head tests under diverse climatic conditions, they hold up respectably, sometimes even topping the charts (Table 2.7). Tall fescue in particular has been praised by a number of researchers for its adaptation to low maintenance.

More research work needs to be done around the world to confirm the effectiveness of the traditional turfgrasses under a variety of climates. Data from tropical and subtropical climates is particularly lacking. Over time as more information is amassed, the same conclusion may be reached: That traditional turf species should not be overlooked when considering the switch to lower maintenance.

A GUIDE TO THE GRASSES

Rule #1 for reducing your maintenance is to *pick the right grass for your location*. Turf fails when a less-than-perfect grass is substituted for a truly adapted one. Grass selection should be based on hard science, not what's in vogue. I've devoted an entire chapter (Chapter 5) to selecting the right grass for your location. As you will see, there is a science to selecting grasses.

The other part of the equation is to know your grasses—specifically, their limitations. In this Guide to Grasses, I've pointed out the drawbacks of each grass, as well as their virtues. When you're considering the switch to lower maintenance, a grass's limiting factors can become far more critical than its attributes.

In your search for the right grass, you may find several that match your criteria. That's when a mixture should be considered. A combination of grasses is always better at living off the land than one. Turfgrass mixtures are discussed in Chapter 6.

What's in a variety?

To the untrained eye, grass is grass. Yes, there may be subtle differences in appearance, but they're all basically green and carpet-like. Some grasses are a little coarser, some a little finer. However all mowed turfgrasses look pretty much alike—especially when growing under favorable conditions.

The difference occurs when stress or disease hits. Some grasses are almost totally immune to heat stress, to drought stress, to certain diseases. Others aren't. Under adverse conditions, grasses sometimes differ from 100% green to 100% dead.

But before we charge into varietal selection, an explanation is necessary as to what exactly constitutes a variety.

Cultivated variety. A **variety** is a plant line that breeds true-to-type. It's unique, identifiable, and sustainable. Agronomists use the moniker, **cultivar**, in place of variety. Cultivar means **cultivated variety** or simply a variety that's in use or cultivation. The word **cultivar** differentiates a cultivated variety from a wild or native-ecotype one.

In the years before turfgrass breeding, all turf seed originated from native pastures or wild populations of grass. Wild seed harvested from these environments was termed **common**, as in common bermudagrass seed. Thus, Arizona common bermudagrass seed was whatever landrace happened to be growing in a field in Arizona when someone decided to harvest. Often, it was a pasture or forage-type variety, poorly suited to mowed turf.

The problem with common seed is that it gives no assurance of varietal purity. One lot of common can be strikingly different from another. This dilemma is what paved the way to the development of improved turf cultivars through plant breeding.

Turf breeding began in the 1930s, but it wasn't until the 1950s that the first improved cultivars became widely available. Early varieties were **public releases**. They were bred by public institutions—usually state universities—and distributed freely to anyone who wanted to grow them.

Proprietary varieties. In 1970 the United States Congress passed the Plant Variety Protection (PVP) Act, which allowed for protection and

Table 2.6. Performance of the traditional versus the less conventional turfgrass species in a test trial conducted under a temperate, continental climate across the Northcentral region of the United States. Turf quality ratings were averaged across mowing heights and locations. Quality ratings were based upon a scale of 1 to 9, with 1 equal to complete absence of turf, and 9 equal to complete and uniform cover (Voigt and Haley, 1990).

Species	Iowa	Michigan	Ohio	Indiana	South Illinois	Central Illinois	Missouri	Wisconsin	Average
				Turfgrass quality ratings, 9=best					
				"Traditional" turf species					
Tall fescue, 'Alta'	5.4	4.5	5.6	4.1	4.9	4.3	5.5	5.3	4.9
Sheep fescue, 'Common'	6.1	5.0	6.0	4.1	4.2	4.5	3.4	5.3	4.8
Hard fescue, 'Durar'	6.0	3.7	3.7	4.1	4.0	3.7	2.4	3.7	3.9
Colonial bentgrass, 'Exeter'	3.0	4.0	3.3	2.8	4.1	3.7	5.6	3.8	3.8
Sheep fescue, 'Covar'	5.6	3.6	5.7	2.5	2.0	3.5	2.0	3.0	3.5
				"Low maintenance" turf species					
Redtop, 'Reton'	3.3	2.9	2.7	1.7	2.8	3.7	5.0	5.3	3.4
Canada bluegrass, 'Reubens'	4.9	3.8	3.7	1.6	3.3	3.7	2.1	3.0	3.2
Buffalograss, 'Texoka'	3.7	2.0	6.0	2.2	5.2	3.0	1.0	1.0	3.0
Buffalograss, 'NE 315'	3.7	2.1	7.0	2.6	5.4	3.0	1.0	1.0	2.7
Crested wheatgrass, 'Fairway'	4.9	2.9	3.7	1.9	1.2	2.8	1.0	1.0	2.4
Roughstalk bluegrass, 'Common'	1.2	1.9	1.3	1.2	1.1	3.3	3.9	4.0	2.2
Streambank wheatgrass, 'Sodar'	3.9	3.2	2.0	1.8	1.1	3.5	1.0	1.0	2.2
Crested wheatgrass, 'Ephraim'	4.3	2.5	2.3	1.6	1.2	3.0	1.0	1.0	2.1
Alpine bluegrass	2.3	2.0	2.7	1.1	1.1	2.9	1.0	3.3	2.0
Bulbous bluegrass	3.4	1.3	1.0	1.4	1.4	2.7	1.0	2.0	1.8
Crested wheatgrass, 'Ruff'	3.8	2.7	1.0	1.9	1.3	1.0	1.0	1.3	1.8
$LSD_{0.05}$				0.8					1.1

Table 2.7. Performance differences among the "traditional" turf species. No one species has all the advantages. To choose the best species for your location, start by analyzing the limiting factors at your site and listing them by order of importance. Then select a grass (or grasses) that best matches your limitations. Box color indicates relative performance ranking (references: Dudeck, 1994; Harivandi, 1993; Harivandi et al., 1992; Harivandi et al., 1984; Peacock, 1986).

Species	Establishment rate	N requirements	Mowing requirements	Close mowing tolerance	Wear resistance	Wear recovery	Water use rate	Drought tolerance	Rooting depth	Thatch accumulation	Shade tolerance	Cold tolerance	Heat tolerance	Salt tolerance
Kentucky bluegrass														
Perennial ryegrass														
Tall fescue														
Strong creeping fescue														
Chewings fescue														
Slender creeping fescue														
Hard fescue														
Sheep fescue														
Colonial bentgrass														
Creeping bentgrass														
Roughstalk bluegrass														
Bermudagrass														
Zoysiagrass														
Buffalograss														
Bahiagrass														
St. Augustinegrass														
Centipedegrass														
Seashore paspalum														

Species	Varieties with low maintenance adaptation	Rapid breeding (&obsolescence) of varieties (black=slow)	Flooding tolerance	Invasive nature (creeping into other areas) (black=invasive)	Mixing ability with other turfgrasses	Relative seed cost	Leaf width (white=narrow) (black=wide)	Seedheads produced in mowed turf (black=many)	Seed size (white=large) (black=small)	Bunch, Rhiz-omes, Stolons
Kentucky bluegrass										*R*
Perennial ryegrass										*B*
Tall fescue										*B*
Strong creeping fescue										*R*
Chewings fescue										*B*
Slender creeping fescue										*R*
Hard fescue										*B*
Sheep fescue										*B*
Colonial bentgrass										*R*
Creeping bentgrass										*S*
Roughstalk bluegrass										*S*
Bermudagrass										*RS*
Zoysiagrass										*RS*
Buffalograss										*S*
Bahiagrass										*RS*
St. Augustinegrass										*S*
Centipedegrass										*S*
Seashore paspalum										*S*

	Favorable performance
	Moderate
	Fair
	Unfavorable performance

enforcement of proprietary varieties, in the same way as patents are used to protect inventions. Later, other countries joined in, adopting breeders' rights laws of their own.

The PVP law allows for private, protectable ownership of a variety for 20 years. The law encourages investment in research and development, since companies could now recoup their R&D investment by selling exclusive varieties.

Today, millions of dollars annually are poured into the development of new turf cultivars. Of course companies make a profit. But the net winner is the consumer, who benefits from the enormous investment in state-of-the-art technology.

But public and common varieties have not disappeared from the landscape. A few public varieties still persist, especially among the warm-season grasses: "Tifway" bermudagrass and "Meyer" zoysiagrass are public varieties still in extensive service. As varieties age and their patents run out, more proprietary varieties will enter the public realm.

Landrace varieties. Today, the production of **common** turf seed from naturally-occurring landraces has almost vanished. Instead, nearly all of the common seed sold today is seed of an unnamed, proprietary variety. **Variety-Not-Stated (VNS)** seed has become synonymous with common. It has replaced landrace seed as the primary source of common. Therefore, if you're buying common turfgrass seed with the idea of getting a natural landrace, you're in for a rude awakening. Nine times out of ten, you're getting seed of an established variety that someone couldn't sell, due to overproduction or under-quality. You are *not* getting a broad-based, landrace ecotype.

With the traditional turf species, it's important to take the time to seek out improved varieties. Common and VNS seed should be avoided for low maintenance plantings. Only with the unconventional grasses do landraces still rule the roost.

THE WARM-SEASON GRASSES

It is no coincidence that I begin the Guide to Grasses with the warm-season species. Where they're adapted, warm-season grasses unequivocally outperform their cool-season counterparts when it comes to low maintenance endurance (Fry and Butler, 1989a; Youngner et al., 1981). Warm-season grasses, as explained in Chapter 1, possess a more efficient form of photosynthesis under intense sunlight and heat and drought stress. Photosynthesis of cool-season grasses is more efficient under shade and in cool, moist conditions. The maintenance-wise turf manager makes use of both types of grass in the landscape: Warm-season grasses for parched full-sun areas and cool-season grasses under the trees. Of course, a lot depends on your climate and location. But where they're adapted, warm-season species should be preferentially chosen over cool-seasons because of their superior low maintenance performance.

Bermudagrass

Bermudagrass is legendary for its adaptation to poor soils, adverse climates, and minimal maintenance. *The Guinness Book of Records* (Matthews et al., 1993) touts bermudagrass as the most common grass in the world. Bermudagrass is found on all continents except Antarctica. It has followed mankind's footsteps throughout the world. Bermudagrass was introduced into the Americas in the 1700s and has since blanketed much of the southern landscape.

Bermudagrass's invasiveness is legendary. Bermudagrass propagates by rhizomes, stolons, and seed. Its efficient C_4 photosynthesis allows it to literally grow over the top of other grasses. Ornamental gardeners loathe bermudagrass for it aggressiveness in blanketing anything in its path. It's no coincidence that *The Guinness Book of Records* also classifies bermudagrass as one of the 10 most serious *weeds* in the world. As a weed it impacts 40 crops in 80 countries, with stolons growing up to 6 in. (15 cm) per day and extending to 18 ft (5.5 m) in length (Matthews et al., 1993).

There are three types of turf bermudagrass in popular culture:

- *Cynodon dactylon* L.—Known as common or American bermudagrass

- *Cynodon transvaalensis* Burtt-Davy—African or *transvaalensis* bermudagrass
- *Hybrid bermudagrass*—A cross between the two

Common bermudagrass can be found throughout the world. African bermudagrass is confined mostly to South Africa and has been used sparingly on golf putting greens in warmer climates. Hybrid bermuda is an interspecific cross between the two species, combining the better characteristics of both. A few naturally occurring hybrids can be found in the wilds, but most hybrids have been created by plant breeders.

The majority of the elite turf bermudagrasses are hybrids. They are vegetatively propagated, lacking the ability to set seed. Hybrid bermuda is bred in the same way as seedless watermelon: A plant with the normal 2 sets of chromosomes (African bermuda) is crossed with a plant with 4 sets (common bermuda) to form a sterile plant with 3 sets. These hybrids go through all the motions of reproduction like putting up seedheads, etc., but set no seed. Hybrid bermudas are propagated by sprigging, plugging, or sodding.

Advantages of bermudagrass for low maintenance

- *Superior water-use efficiency*—Bermudagrass is one of the most water stingy turf plants, requiring half the water of some cool-seasons (Beard, 1988; Garrot and Mancino, 1994).
- *Excellent drought tolerance*—A deep, spreading root system helps it survive intense drought (see Figure 2.3).
- *Aggressive growth*—Bermuda rapidly colonizes bare spots and weak lawn areas, forming a dense sod mat that chokes out weeds.
- *Salt tolerant*—Bermuda is one of the more salt-tolerant turf species.
- *Low growth habit*—For most varieties, unmowed height is about 12 in. (30 cm). Some forage bermudas are taller, some hybrids shorter. In general, the plant height is acceptable for unmowed roadsides and utility turf.
- *Rapid vegetative establishment*—It establishes quickly from sprigs, relative to other grasses.
- *Close mowing tolerance*—Some hybrids can be mowed to putting green height.
- *Tolerant to traffic*—Bermudagrass wears well and recuperates quickly from injury.

Disadvantages of bermudagrass for low maintenance

- *High nitrogen fertilizer requirement*—For optimal turf performance, bermudagrass needs regular fertilization—as much as twice the nitrogen as cool-season grasses. It can survive on less, but the turf becomes open and stemmy. On gravelly or sandy soils, or soils devoid of organic matter, bermudagrass has been known to disappear entirely when unfertilized.
- *No shade tolerance*—Bermudagrass will grow up to the dripline of trees and no further; that's one of the drawbacks of C_4 photosynthesis.
- *Poor winter-hardiness*—Bermudagrass varieties differ in their tolerance to cold temperature. Fine textured strains generally lack cold-hardiness and will injure or kill at temperatures below −10 °F (−23 °C). Some wild strains have fairly good cold tolerance. Naturalized patches of winter-hardy bermudagrass can be found growing throughout the U.S. Rocky Mountains, Holland, Germany, and northern Asia.
- *Winter dormancy*—Nearly all warm-season grasses go dormant in winter. When night temperatures dip below 60 °F (15 °C), bermuda starts to go dormant. Dormancy is a response to dropping soil temperature, frost, and decreasing daylength. Dormancy is probably a protective mechanism to guard against winter injury. Interestingly, winter-hardy bermudas are the ones with the *longest* dormant periods.
- *Invasive*—Aggressive lateral growth is a bonus unless there's a shrub, flower, or sidewalk nearby.

- *Most varieties are vegetatively propagated*—Vegetative planting of grasses is a routine procedure for many turf specialists. With bermuda it's particularly easy because it propagates readily. But some areas of the world lack uncontaminated sources of planting stock. Seed-propagated bermuda offers an alternative. Seeded varieties have been introduced only within the last decade, and their turf quality is not yet at a par with the best vegetative cultivars. Vegetative hybrids tend not to be as drought tolerant as their seeded cousins and require more frequent close mowing for best results (Kneebone, 1981).
- *Poor mixability*—Bermuda's aggressiveness limits its use in turf mixtures. Bermuda literally outruns the competition. Recently, **blends**—combinations of several *varieties* mixed together—have been tested using some of the newer seeded bermudas. Long-term studies have yet to confirm whether these blends will stay blended in the long run.
- *Disease susceptibility*—In tropical climates, bermudagrass suffers from a foliar disease which limits its use on fine turf. It becomes spindly under foggy or dark overcast skies in some tropical locales such as Hong Kong or Singapore. In colder climates, bermudagrass can be injured by spring dead spot, a root-devouring, fungal disease that's active in winter.

St. Augustinegrass

"Snowbirds" from the northern United States are often shocked when first they travel to the deep South and lay their eyes on a lawn of St. Augustinegrass. "You call this a lawn?" is a common remark. St. Augustinegrass is so broad bladed that it resembles closely cropped bamboo. Walking on it with your bare feet is akin to walking on stubble. But locals who've grown up with it swear there's nothing quite as nice as a St. Augustinegrass lawn.

St. Augustinegrass is generally a high maintenance grass. Insects are a constant battle, and fungal diseases and even a virus are common. Dethatching is an annual ritual. Yet in the tropical regions of the world, St. Augustinegrass fills a vital niche.

St. Augustinegrass is native to the West Indies and can be found in mild, tropical climates in the southern United States, the Mediterranean, Africa, Australia, Singapore, and Malaysia. St. Augustinegrass adapts well to sandy, infertile seashore soils in areas with adequate rainfall.

Planting St. Augustinegrass is also a high maintenance affair. The species produces virtually no seed, though a few hundred pounds are bought and traded annually worldwide. Even sprigs are hard to harvest. Lawns are established either by plugs, prerooted plugs (grown like nursery stock), or sod. Establishment from plugs is rapid, due to vigorous runners.

Plant breeding over the last two decades has resulted in the release of varieties with improved low maintenance characteristics over earlier strains. Chinch bug resistance, drought tolerance, and resistance to Panicum Mosaic Virus, the cause of St. Augustinegrass Decline (SAD), have been accomplished by selective breeding. Future releases promise even more adaptations for low maintenance. With St. Augustinegrass it's important to select only the improved cultivars if you have low maintenance in mind.

Advantages of St. Augustinegrass for low maintenance

- *Tolerates a rainy, tropical climate*—The list of turfgrasses that can tolerate damp, tropical conditions is disgustingly short. St. Augustinegrass survives these conditions well, as long as the soil is well drained and not compacted.
- *Survives nonmaintained conditions*—St. Augustinegrass can be used as a roadside or utility turf provided the soil is fertile and rain is abundant. However, it may not develop the density necessary to crowd out weeds in some climates.
- *Good shade tolerance*—St. Augustinegrass is one of the most shade tolerant of the warm-season grasses. With selective tree pruning, it can grow clear up to the trunk.

- *Salt tolerant*—It is not one of the most salt tolerant turfgrass, but it can survive salt air and mild saline soil.

Disadvantages of St. Augustinegrass for low maintenance

- *Thatch*—St. Augustinegrass produces copious amounts of thatch, even under moderate fertility, requiring annual dethatching usually in the spring of the year.
- *Little drought tolerance*—You rarely see St. Augustinegrass growing in the desert. Its water-use rate is intermediate, but its drought tolerance is poor.
- *Winter tender*—Adaptation is limited to areas where winter temperatures rarely drop below freezing.
- *Long dormant period*—St. Augustinegrass goes dormant in the fall earlier than other warm-season grasses. Its fall color is rather unattractive and spring greenup is slow.
- *Poor wear tolerance*—St. Augustinegrass's inferior wear tolerance limits its use on sports fields. Recovery from wear is fairly rapid, though.
- *Iron chlorosis*—St. Augustinegrass gets a peculiar chlorotic yellowing from high soil pH, sandy soils, or soils lacking in iron. Foliar sprays with chelated iron or iron sulfate remedy the situation.
- *Insect susceptibility*—Bugs in the tropics are notorious. Without a winter season to thin their ranks, insects can grow unencumbered in warm climates. St. Augustinegrass tolerates insects better than many other grasses, but it can be obliterated by occasional unattended flare-ups. Some cultivars are more resistant than others.

Zoysiagrass

Zoysiagrass comes as close to the *ideal* low maintenance turfgrass as you can get. Zoysia typifies many of the standards of a low maintenance lawngrass, providing a luxurious, weed-free cover with virtually no upkeep. Were it not for a few minor flaws (notably its slow establishment and tendency to thatch) zoysia would be perfect.

Zoysiagrass is the name for a *family* of related grasses, comprised of two major zoysia species and three minor ones. Japanese lawngrass (*Z. japonica*) is the most common of the five zoysia species. It has the most cold tolerance and the most seed yielding ability. In nature its range of spread extends from the northern Japanese island of Hokkaido, through the Philippines, Malaysia, China, Australia, as far west as Madagascar. The species is most common along the Pacific shores from Seoul, Korea, to Qingdao, China, suggesting it may have evolved there.

Zoysia matrella is known as Korean lawngrass, korai in Japan, Manilagrass, or simply as matrella. It is a fine-bladed relative of Japanese zoysia, native to the tropics. Research by J.S. Choi (1993, personal communications) indicates that matrella is not a Korean native at all, but evolved on offshore islands further south. Matrella is a low growing, sod forming grass, capable of providing a carpet-like lawn with *no need for mowing*. Parks in China routinely use unmowed, unwatered, unfertilized matrella as a durable ground cover. Unmowed matrella rarely exceeds 3 in. (7.5 cm) in height. Under unmowed conditions, matrella forms a somewhat puffy, rolling surface. Its vigor crowds out weeds. A lack of cold tolerance restricts matrella to regions where bermudagrass is adapted.

Zoysia tenuifolia, *Z. sinica*, and *Z. machrostaycha* are minor zoysia species (Engleke and Murray, 1982). None have been used to any major extent as turf, outside of a curious planting of *tenuifolia* at the Disney theme parks (Johns and Beard, 1978). However, each has unique qualifications awaiting commercial use.

Zoysia sinica and *Z. machrostaycha* are unexploited zoysia species with desirable low maintenance adaptations. Both are highly salt tolerant, with *Z. machrostaycha* able to grow with seawater washing its roots. *Z. machrostaycha* is rather upright and stemmy, but it could serve as a vegetative cover on otherwise unusable saline land. Some scientists believe it to be a true **halophyte**—a plant that *requires* salt as part of its metabolism (Christians and Engleke, 1994; Engleke and Murray, 1982).

Zoysia sinica, or seashore zoysiagrass, closely resembles *Z. japonica.* It produces larger, almost ryegrass-size seed, which possess more seedling vigor than *japonica.* No improved cultivars have been bred from the three minor zoysia species, although an experimental *sinica,* "J-14," is currently making its way through the U.S. National tests.

Establishment limits zoysia from becoming the panacea of low maintenance turf. *Zoysia japonica* bears a small, hard, waxy seed. Left untreated, seed has less than 10% germination. Full germination requires a month or more.

Years ago several Korean companies developed a treatment process that bathes zoysia seed in a caustic chemical base, etching the seed coat and exposing small pores for water absorption. Herb Portz at Southern Illinois University (Diesburg and Portz, 1993) studied the process and added refinements. Today, germination rates as high as 90% can be attained with treated seedlots.

But seed treatment does not solve all of the establishment problems. Seedling vigor is still weak, requiring 3 to 4 weeks for emergence. Seed will not germinate unless soil temperatures are just right, preferably above 70 °F (21 °C). The soil surface must be kept *constantly* moist. Adequate moisture during grow-in cannot be overemphasized. This is the main cause of establishment failure in zoysia.

Some golf courses in America and Korea have gone so far as to cover their newly seeded zoysia fairways with clear plastic sheets to increase soil temperature, hold moisture, and encourage sprouting. Occasional holes are cut in the plastic for watering and heat dissipation. The plastic generates intense temperatures in sunlight. But even temperatures as high as 120 °F (49 °C) do not seem to harm zoysia seedlings as long as moisture is present. I've personally seen weeds wilting away like limp lettuce under the clear plastic while young zoysia seedlings grow unencumbered (Figure 2.6).

Vegetative establishment of zoysia is sluggish too. Sprigging can be done, but only if sprigs are fresh and the soil is kept constantly moist. In Japan, sprigging is more prevalent than in America where plugging and sodding of zoysia are the norm.

Zoysia stolons creep quite slowly, relative to other warm-season grasses. As a result, zoysia sod takes a long time to mature. This makes prices for zoysia sod among the highest in the industry. Some golf courses have used **strip sodding** in place of solid sodding, since solid sodding of 18 fairways to zoysia may cost $500,000. Strip sodding involves laying sod strips several inches apart, letting the zoysia fill the bare areas with stolons. Unfortunately, this creates a washboard effect for mowers.

Zoysia's notoriously slow creeping rate has opened the door for some innovative uses of zoysia in the landscape. Zoysia strips can be used as buffers, placed around sand bunkers or flower beds on golf courses to keep invasive species like bermuda out. Sod buffer strips minimize en-

Figure 2.6. Were it not for its sluggish establishment, zoysiagrass would be the ideal low maintenance turfgrass. Here, Joon Soo Choi of Dankook University (r.) is inspecting a fairway seeded to common zoysiagrass at the Gold Country Club in Seoul, Korea. After seeding, the fairway was covered with polyethylene plastic sheets to help retain moisture and temperature. Holes cut in the plastic allow water and fertilizer infiltration. Strangely enough, the zoysia seedlings seem unfazed by the high temperature induced from the plastic.

The Nearly Perfect Low Maintenance Turfgrass: Questions and Answers about Zoysiagrass

Q: What is zoysiagrass?

A: Zoysiagrass is actually a *family* of warm-season, creeping perennial grasses native to the Far East. Zoysiagrass creeps by means of underground rhizomes and slow-growing aboveground stolons. It has been cultivated in the United States since the 1920s, when it was introduced from Japan and China.

Q: I've seen some zoysiagrass lawns that were extremely fine textured—with leaves almost as fine as needles—and other zoysia lawns that were quite coarse bladed, like tall fescue. Are these all zoysiagrass?

A: There are three major species of zoysiagrass: *Zoysia japonica* (Japanese lawngrass), *Z. matrella* (matrella or Manilagrass), and *Z. tenuifolia*. Of these, only Japanese lawngrass is available from seed. *Zoysia japonica* is fairly broad-bladed while the others are fine bladed. As a rule, the finer the texture of a zoysia, the poorer its winter-hardiness.

Q: I've seen zoysia advertised in garden magazines for years as a "miracle grass." What gives?

A: One sod dealer on the U.S. East Coast has been advertising zoysia to homeowners through newspaper and magazine ads for years. For a price, he will provide you with a number of plugs with which you can plant zoysia in your lawn. The dealer obtains these plugs by coring an established "Meyer" zoysia sod with an aerifier and collecting the plugs. Some of the plugs are not viable. Homeowners become discouraged when their new lawngrass spreads so slowly. Twenty plugs (the normal amount shipped) will require 10 to 15 years to spread out and cover a lawn. Most people are not willing to wait that long, even for a miracle grass.

Q: Do all zoysias spread that slowly?

A: Most strains of zoysia are slow spreaders, creeping only about 6 in. (20 cm) laterally per year (Figure 2.7). Contrast that with bermudagrass that can creep 6 in. in a weekend! The slow spreading of zoysia limits its establishment via sprigs. Sprigging is the

Figure 2.7. The Little Rock (AR) Country Club uses a strip of "Meyer" zoysia to keep bermudagrass from straying into their sand bunkers. Zoysiagrass makes a good buffer grass because it creeps laterally slowly yet keeps bermudagrass at bay.

most common way of establishing bermudagrass, but it works poorly with zoysia because of its slow growth. This slow creeping also makes for expensive sod prices. "El Toro" zoysia is a vegetative *japonica* noted for its rapid spreading ability.

Q: Will seeding help?
A: Tests at Southern Illinois University have shown that seeded zoysia can be established in as little as 8 weeks. Compare this to the 1 to 2 years needed for sprigging or plugging.

Q: Are there any seeded zoysias on the market?
A: "Zenith" was the first commercial seeded zoysia. Varieties in the "Cathay" series are also becoming available. Seedlots of common zoysia are regularly imported from China where it's grown, harvested, and cleaned by hand.

Q: What about vegetatively propagated zoysias?
A: Meyer zoysia has been a mainstay variety since it was released by the U.S. Golf Association Green Section in 1951. Meyer is medium dark green, quite dense, and relatively broad-bladed. The high density tends to compensate for its broad blades, making it an attractive lawngrass. El Toro, a release from the University of California, has been gaining acceptance because of its rapid stolon growth.

Q: What does zoysia sod cost?
A: Because of zoysia's slow spreading ability, it takes 1 to 2 years to produce a sod crop. Bermudagrass, on the other hand, can sometimes yield 2 to 4 sod crops per year. Therefore, there's quite a difference in price. Zoysia sod sells for \$0.20 to \$1.00 per ft^2—sometimes more than the real estate it's planted on!

Q: Is zoysia a delicate grass?
A: Quite the contrary. In wear trials, Jim Beard and Bob Shearman (Gaussoin, 1994b) found that zoysiagrass was highly wear tolerant. Researchers developed a wheel device that continuously rolls around in circles, wearing the grass out. They timed the roller to see how many revolutions it took to wear out each species of grass. Most cool-season grasses bit the dust in a few hours or days. Bermudagrass lasted even longer. With zoysiagrass, however, the wheel just kept turning and turning. Of course, eventually any turf will wear out if given enough traffic. Recovery rate (also called **recuperative potential**) of zoysia is only moderate. Faster creeping species such as bermudagrass recover from wear damage more easily than zoysia.

Q: Does zoysiagrass require a lot of maintenance?
A: Zoysiagrass is one of the lowest maintenance turfgrasses available. Zoysia evolved in Asia where until recently, lawn care was unheard of. Zoysia provides a beautiful, scenic lawn with minimal care. Zoysia natively grows only about 6 in. (20 cm) tall, so mowings are sometimes unnecessary for vista-type turfs. Zoysia needs little or no fertilizer after establishment to maintain a thick, green appearance. One application every year or two is usually ample. During the establishment phase, zoysia does benefit from ample nitrogen fertilization. After the turf fills in, though, fertilization should be cut. Recent university studies have shown zoysia to be one of the most drought tolerant turfgrass species in existence (Green et al., 1991; White et al., 1993). Only *Cynodon dactylon* bermudagrass has a better water-use efficiency. Zoysia's incredible drought tolerance allows it to survive on minimal water in most areas.

Q: What about weeds?

A: The dense habit of zoysia helps crowd out weeds. An established zoysiagrass lawn remains weed-free for years, with minimal care. If weeds ever do encroach, herbicidal control is no problem. Zoysia tolerates a wide array of selective herbicides. One application of Roundup® combined with a preemergence herbicide in late winter (when the turf is dormant) will keep the turf weed-free all year.

Q: Does zoysia get any lawn diseases?

A: Until a few years ago, there were no known diseases of zoysiagrass. Now we know that zoysia will get some of the same diseases as other warm-season species when it's pushed with too much maintenance. High temperature and humidity occasionally bring on disease. Backing off on the fertilization and watering generally takes care of the situation. Zoysia patch is a newly identified disease of zoysia: Its symptoms are large, round patches of thin turf, 1 to 20 ft (0.3 to 6 m) in diameter. Zoysia patch does not kill the turf but disfigures it and thins it out. In most areas, however, zoysia lawns experience no disease problems at all.

Q: When is the best time to plant zoysia?

A: In most areas, zoysia can be planted anytime *with the exception of late summer*. Late summer plantings do not allow enough time for establishment before the onset of winter. The ideal planting time is spring, when soil temperatures reach 70°F (21°C). In cooler areas, golf courses have tried spreading clear plastic sheets over their newly seeded zoysia fairways to enable establishment earlier in the spring.

Q: Is zoysia hard to mow?

A: Meyer and "Emerald" zoysia have the reputation for being hard to mow, because of their dense, stiff leaves. Reel mowers seem to encounter more of a problem on these varieties than rotaries. Keeping the mower blades sharp seems to help. I personally have stalled a reel mower when mowing across a plot of Meyer. Other zoysias such as Chinese common or El Toro have a moderate density and little or no mower problems.

Q: How should zoysia turf be mowed?

A: Turf managers familiar with the maintenance of common bermudagrass can mow zoysia similarly. Zoysia has been successfully maintained at 3/8 in. (1 cm) on golf tee boxes but survives best at a 1/2 to 1 1/2 in. (12 to 38 mm) cutting height. Mowing frequency will depend upon the rate of nitrogen fertilization.

Q: Does zoysia have a thatch problem?

A: Given enough water and fertilizer, aggressive zoysias like Meyer and Emerald can be notorious thatch-formers. Golf courses that have tried Meyer as a collar around putting greens found this out the hard way. With the spill-over of water and fertilizer from the green, the Meyer collars got thatchy in a hurry. Zoysia does best and develops the least thatch when watered and fertilized very little. Less aggressive varieties seem to have the fewest thatch problems.

croachment by other grasses. Buffer-zone sodding is a cost-effective low maintenance technique. Use of zoysia as a buffer around putting greens, however, has met with limited success (see Q&A sidebar).

Breeding for low maintenance. Plant breeding is just now beginning to produce improvements in zoysia. New matrellas have been released to the sod industry from breeding at Texas A&M University. The late Jack Murray at the USDA introduced a number of seeded *japonica* varieties (Murray, 1985), some of which are only now reaching the market. Zoysia is slow to propagate and even slower to breed (Samudio, 1996). "El

Figure 2.8. Common zoysiagrass seed from China is hand harvested mostly by children and housewives. The seed is collected from mountainsides, ocean shores, and dry stream beds where cultivated crops can't be grown. The children sell the seed to merchants to help pay for their school textbooks, which are not free in China.

Toro," a *japonica* developed by Vic Youngner at the University of California, solves the problem of sluggish vegetative establishment by an accelerated creeping ability—its main claim to fame.

Common zoysia seed. Even as the improved varieties slowly reach the market, a steady supply of Chinese common zoysia seed is filling the void. Originally, common zoysia seed was produced in Japan. Later as the Japanese economy grew, production shifted to neighboring Korea, and eventually to China (Figure 2.8). In Asia, zoysia seed is harvested by hand from native patches, usually in mountainous areas where productive crops can't be grown. Some consumers still use the misnomer **Korean common** for all zoysia seed, even though seed has not been harvested from that country in years (Gordon, 1986).

Chinese common zoysia seed is sold under several **brand** names, such as Sunrise® and Zen® (Diesburg and Portz, 1993). A brand name is different than a variety name, giving no assurance of breeding or background. It's simply a company's marketing identification for their product. It is used by companies to identify supplies of common seed with a more consistent level of purity and germination.

Advantages of zoysiagrass for low maintenance

- *Tolerates zero maintenance*—Few grasses can make this claim. After it's established, zoysia can be totally neglected and still maintain a decent turf. Ancient turfs surrounding medieval temples and cemeteries in Asia attest to the staying power of zoysia under zero maintenance.
- *Crowds out weeds*—Zoysia requires virtually no herbicides. It forms a tight cover that excludes weeds. The only weed control required might be during establishment or as a yearly cleanup for winter annuals.
- *Low fertility requirement*—Zoysia can persist without fertilizing and still maintain a complete ground cover (Dunn et al., 1993; Henry, 1991). There are few other grasses that can do this. During grow-in, zoysia benefits from frequent nitrogen fertilization. But after a tight sod is formed, heavy fertilizer applications can be detrimental, causing excessive thatch. Some golf courses reportedly use as little as 1 lb N per 1000 ft^2 (5 g/m^2) per year on mature zoysia fairways.
- *Can be left unmowed*—Japanese zoysia grows to about 6 in. (15 cm). *Z. matrella* grows even shorter. Both can be used on unmowed golf course roughs, utility lawns, parks, and roadsides.
- *Winter-hardy*—*Zoysia japonica* is one of the most winter-hardy warm-season turfgrasses. It survives cold temperatures in basically the same range as perennial

ryegrass or tall fescue. Zoysias other than *japonica* are not as hardy.

- *Early greenup*—Zoysia greens up in the spring several weeks before bermudagrass. Its fall color may persist longer than bermuda. The winter color of zoysia is a pleasing straw yellow; some people prefer it to the muddy brown of other dormant grasses.
- *Drought tolerant*—Research has shown that zoysia is one of the most drought tolerant, water efficient turf species (Green et al., 1991; White et al., 1993). However, given a steady high maintenance diet, close-cut zoysia fairways will use just as much water as other grasses.
- *Heat tolerant*—Zoysia is capable of withstanding high temperatures with little injury. Yet seldom do you see zoysia used in desert areas. While zoysia may persist in arid climates, it does not form the same luxurious growth as it does in wetter areas.
- *Some shade tolerance*—Zoysia has more shade tolerance than bermudagrass. Zoysia can persist clear up to the trunk with selective tree pruning.
- *Extremely salt tolerant*—The unexploited *Z. sinica* and *Z. machrostaycha* species offer the best possibilities when it comes to salt, but *Z. japonica* is no slouch.
- *Adapts to a wide range of soils*—Zoysia persists on everything from sands to clays.
- *Tolerates wet, tropical climates*—Zoysia survives the overcast, drizzly weather of many tropical areas, conditions that incite a general unthriftiness in bermuda. As a result, zoysia is seeing more use as sports turf in Hong Kong, Singapore, and in similar overcast climates.
- *Wear tolerant*—Studies by Bob Shearman at the University of Nebraska (Gaussoin, 1994b) indicate that zoysia is one of the most wear tolerant turfgrasses. Unfortunately, zoysia's *recovery* from wear is slow, limiting its usefulness on football and soccer fields.

Disadvantages of zoysiagrass for low maintenance

- *Really slow establishment*—Zoysia is horribly slow to establish from seed or sprigs. It can be plugged, provided the plugs are of sufficient diameter. Ads in American newspapers regularly advertise zoysia plugs for sale by mail. These plugs are usually derived from aerifier cores, many of which do not even contain enough plant to be viable. Full coverage of a typical yard from a handful of plugs can take decades.
- *Thatch prone*—Zoysia can spawn so much thatch that it literally drowns itself (Soper et al., 1988). The best advice is: Back off on the nitrogen rate.
- *Winter dormant*—Like all warm-season grasses, zoysia is winter dormant. And in colder climates, dormancy can last for as long as 9 months of the year. Winter annual weeds are a problem if dormancy is long.
- *Hard to mow*—"Meyer" zoysia in particular generates such a high plant density that it's been known to stall a mower. Reel mowing at *regular* intervals helps maintain its attractive surface.
- *Puffy growth habit*—Matrella develops a peculiar puffy habit resembling ocean waves. Vertical mowing corrects the problem but may open up and damage the stand. This puffiness has limited matrella's usefulness on golf fairways.
- *Expensive*—Because it takes so long to produce, zoysia sod can be expensive. Seed costs are usually higher than for an improved seeded bermudagrass.
- *Disruptive rhizomes*—Zoysia has powerful rhizomes that tunnel under asphalt pavement in the spring and poke right through. Zoysia rhizomes can chew an inch or two off asphalt roads or cart paths each year.
- *Light green color*—Zoysia at best can be considered a medium green. Nitrogen fertilizer turns it dark green but at the

expense of overgrowth. Applications of foliar iron darken it without the growth problem.

THE COOL-SEASON GRASSES

Many people prefer the cool-season turfgrasses for lawns and sports turf because they're softer, less bristly, richer green, and generally more luxurious than the warm-season grasses. Moreover, cool-season grasses stay green all year, permitting sports play during winter when warm seasons would be dormant brown.

As a result, the turf industry has quietly pushed the use of cool-season grasses into areas where warm-season grasses are better adapted. Sometimes these attempts have been successful, but often successes have come at the expense of additional applications of water and pesticides—additions that would not have been required by an adapted warm-season grass.

In warmer climates, cool-season grasses should be used *sparingly* if low maintenance is the goal. Winter overseeding of a cool-season grass into a dormant warm-season grass can combine the best characteristics of both, but at added expense.

Tall fescue

Fescue should be #1 on anyone's list when considering the traditional cool-season turfgrasses for low maintenance. Tall, hard, and sheep fescue are the three premier cool-season turfgrasses for reduced maintenance conditions.

Fescue's strength lies in its drought tolerance. Tall fescue has more roots in the lower soil quadrant than other cool-season turfgrasses, allowing it to extract water and stay green long after others have gone brown (Branham, 1989). In many climates tall fescue can be maintained through the summer without irrigation. In a particularly hot and dry climate, tall fescue may be thinned by summer heat. Rejuvenating the stand may require overseeding to replenish the plant population. Fescue, lacking runners, has no way to repopulate bare spots by itself. In Tulsa, Oklahoma, for example, homeowners routinely reseed their lawns every September to fill in spots thinned from summer damage.

Yet in spite of its legendary drought prowess, tall fescue can be a water glutton when ample water is available. Its water-use efficiency during times of plentiful water is dismal (Beard, 1985a; Fry and Butler, 1989c). In desert climates where a turf receives virtually all of its water from irrigation, it makes sense to choose grasses with better water efficiency.

Breeding for low maintenance. Originally, tall fescue was used *exclusively* for low maintenance. That's because no one would have ever considered this stiff, yellow, open, broad-bladed grass for fine turf. It served a utilitarian function on roadsides or industrial turf but never on a golf course and rarely on home lawns.

Then plant breeders changed everything. In the late 1970s, "Rebel" tall fescue was released and the term **turf-type tall fescue** was coined. Rebel and subsequent improved varieties offered advantages in denser and darker green turf to the point where today's tall fescues are even darker than the darkest bluegrasses.

In about 1980, something unusual happened: Breeders began observing curious, miniature plants in their breeding nurseries. Soon the concept of **dwarf tall fescue** caught fire. These Lilliputian plants were tapped as a solution to the perpetual downfall of the species: *Tall fescue didn't earn the name "tall" for nothing.*

Vertical growth rate of tall fescue is faster than many other turfgrasses. From a low-maintenance standpoint this is a real drawback, necessitating frequent mowing. These dwarf plants were viewed as a way to throttle back fescue's runaway growth.

The dwarf revolution was short-lived because many of the early dwarfs also had dwarf roots. But dwarfs did have some interesting implications for turf culture. In climates like Southern California where disease pressure was minimal, the dwarf fescues were breathtaking. You would wonder why anyone would plant anything else. But in a humid climate with disease pressure, the dwarfs got clobbered. Scientists theorize that the dense, tightly packed plants provide an ideal growing medium for fungus, similar to the smooth fertile surface of a laboratory petri dish.

The fungus spreads easily across the turf, unimpeded as it jumps from plant to plant.

It wasn't until the 1990s that the trend towards dwarfs reversed. Later fescue varieties were beefier than their predecessors, yet maintaining a rich color and high density. Breeders have even reestablished a reliable disease profile and deeper rooting in the newer varieties.

Endophyte. **Endophyte** is one of the most remarkable advances in turf varieties since the dawn of breeding. Endophyte offers natural control against several important turf insects without the need for pesticide. It is a low maintenance dream come true.

Fescue and ryegrass varieties are the only turfgrasses to presently contain this valuable component although scientists are scrambling to move them into other turf species as well. It is *definitely* worth the time to seek out endophyte-enhanced varieties of fescue and ryegrass.

An endophyte is a beneficial organism that lives in between cells in the sheath of certain grasses. In exchange for its shared home, endophytes give off alkaloids that are toxic to insects. The alkaloids remain in the plants and do not rinse into the environment. The toxins harm only insects, or animals that make their sole diet on lawngrass. Cats and other occasional nibblers are unharmed. Chapter 12 offers more detail on endophytes and their role in biological pest control.

Tall fescue varieties vary in endophyte content from 0 to 100% (Saha and Johnson-Cicalese, 1988). Some researchers feel a minimum infection level of 35% in tall fescue is needed to convey the benefits of endophyte. With a 35% infection rate, 35 seeds out of 100 in the seed bag would contain a viable endophyte. That's enough to fend off most insects. The higher the percentage the better, though. Research has shown that a 35% infection level at establishment will eventually climb to 50% and above as insects selectively destroy uninfected plants. With ryegrass, 80% endophyte is considered a desirable minimum.

Unfortunately, there are no laws requiring labeling of endophyte content in seed. You've got to do some digging in the literature to find the value listed.

Advantages of tall fescue for low maintenance

- *Wear tolerant*—You'll find tall fescue on many high-wear athletic fields, because it tolerates daily pounding better than other grasses.
- *Shade tolerant*—Fescues are among the most shade tolerant turfgrasses. Tall fescue ranks behind only its fine fescue relatives in shade tolerance.
- *Rapid establishment*—Tall fescue establishes rapidly and reliably. It is slower than ryegrass but faster than bluegrass. Because of its large seed and vigorous germination, tall fescue can be reseeded into existing turf to thicken it up (consult Chapter 7 for tips).
- *Inexpensive seed price*—Tall fescue seed fields yield more per acre than other turfgrasses, making seed prices inexpensive. Moreover, improved varieties have been bred which outyield common by twice. There is still considerable production of cheap "K-31" seed, primarily from the U.S. Midwest. K-31 seed prices are low, as are its seed quality, genetic purity, and freedom from grassy weeds. Little if any *certified* K-31 seed is produced.
- *Adapted well into the warm-season belt*—Tall fescue survives warm summers in areas where other cool-season grasses wilt. It does not tolerate tropical conditions, however.
- *Drought tolerant*—Research has shown that tall fescue can survive on every-other-day irrigation at a paltry 50% of evapotranspiration with only a minor reduction in visual quality (Fry and Butler, 1989b). That level of watering severely damages other grasses, even hard fescue.
- *Improved disease resistance*—Newer varieties are more resistant to brown patch and net blotch disease than their predecessors.
- *May contain an endophyte*—Biological control of insects.

Disadvantages of tall fescue for low maintenance

- *Somewhat cold tender*—Tall fescue can be damaged by a cold, open winter. Tall fescue is winter-hardy in all U.S. states but Alaska, North Dakota, Minnesota, and parts of Wisconsin, Maine, Wyoming, and Montana. Its use in Canada is restricted to the most southerly parts. Tall fescue is rarely used in northern Europe and Scandinavia.
- *Stiff, coarse texture*—The dwarf fescues overcame this deficit but at the expense of disease susceptibility. Newer varieties offer disease resistance and mask the coarseness by a proliferation of leaves.
- *Frequent mowing requirements*—Newer, slower-growing varieties have throttled fescue's compulsion for frequent mowing somewhat. But in general, you can still plan to mow your fescue turf more often than other species—one of the trade-offs in the switch to lower maintenance.
- *A bunch grass*—Fescue needs help (i.e., overseeding) to fill in large bare spots.

Fine fescue

There's an old story about a farmer who had two horses he couldn't tell apart. Both horses measured 15 hands high. Both weighed the same. Both had identical spots in identical places. It seemed no matter how hard he tried, the farmer just couldn't tell the black horse from the white one.

Fine fescues are the same way. They all look alike. All five of the fine fescue species have delicate, needle-like leaves that produce an unmistakable, fine textured lawn turf. Even career turf people have a tough time telling them apart. When handed a clump of grass, you'll hear them say: "That's, red... Er, I mean, strong, red, hard, ... Er, it's fine fescue!"

So what's the real difference between the fine fescues?

The difference is performance. The five fine fescue species that look quite alike perform radically differently in turf situations (see Table 2.8). Knowing which one to pick can help ensure maximum performance.

The five fine fescue species are chewings, strong creeping red, slender creeping, hard, and sheep. For low maintenance conditions, hard and sheep hold the most promise. But each species has its own unique niche where it excels.

Chewings fescue. Of the five fine fescue species, plant breeders have put their most effort into chewings fescue. And it's paid off. New varieties of chewings are dense and fine bladed, with a good degree of disease resistance built in (Skogley, 1984). Many chewings varieties are quite aggressive. In seed mixtures they should be used at no more than 10 to 20% by weight. Otherwise, they'll dominate the stand, forcing out other mixture components.

Characteristics of chewings fescue:

- Bunch-type growth habit
- Extensive tillering
- Tolerant of close mowing, clear down to golf course fairway height (some chewings varieties have even been used on putting greens for winter overseeding or even as permanent turf)
- Excellent shade tolerance
- Lower fertility requirement
- Tolerant of acid pH
- Improved density, disease resistance, seed yield
- May dominate mixtures

Strong creeping red fescue. In spite of long-term breeding efforts on strong creeping red fescue, new varieties have changed little from older varieties of "Pennlawn" or Canadian common. Improved varieties do offer better uniformity and seed quality than common red fescue. And some improved red fescue varieties boast an endophyte.

Part of the lack of breeding in this species stems from the seemingly limitless supply of dirt cheap red fescue seed from the Peace River region of Alberta, Canada. With the base price of strong creeping red fescue set so low, production companies have little incentive to invest R&D money in this species.

Table 2.8. The five species of turf fine fescue and their characteristics.

	Chewings	Strong creeping red	Slender creeping	Hard	Sheep
Species	*F. rubra* L. subsp. *commutata*	*F. rubra* L. subsp. *rubra*	*F. rubra* L. subsp. *litoralis*	*F. longifolia*	*F. ovina* L. subsp. *ovina*
Spreading	Very little	Strong	Little	Very little	Very little
Height	Moderately low	Moderately tall	Medium	Low	Low
Leaf texture	Fine	Broad (almost like Kentucky bluegrass)	Medium	Fine	Fine and wiry
Leaf color	Light to medium green	Medium green	Light to medium green	Dark grayish green	Powdery blue-green
Usefulness in low maintenance	Limited to cool, moist climates. Useful under adverse fertility, pH.	Limited to cool, moist climates. Useful under adverse fertility, pH.	Limited to cool, moist climates. Useful under adverse fertility, pH.	Drought and heat tolerant. Adapted in transition zone areas.	Drought and heat tolerant. Adapted in transition zone areas.
Typical varieties	Highlight, Jamestown II, Dover	Audubon, Revere, Pennlawn	Marker, Dawson	Biljart, Rescue 911, Scaldis	Azay, MX-86 AE, Bighorn

Strong creeping red fescue is the best mixer of the five fine fescue species. Its extensive rhizome system and comparatively broad blades make it compatible with Kentucky bluegrass or perennial ryegrass. Strong creeping red fescue is also not overly aggressive. It can be used at up to 50% in mixtures without dominating the stand.

Characteristics of strong creeping red fescue:

- Good uniformity and quality in modern cultivars
- Larger seed, better seedling vigor than other fine fescues
- An aggressive rhizome system that fills bare spots
- Improved disease resistance and seed yield in the newer varieties

Slender creeping fescue. Depending on who you talk to, slender creeping fescue is either heaven or hell. Europeans love it. For them, slender creeping fescue produces a dense, fine-leafed stand with a compact growth habit.

In America, however, the National Turfgrass Evaluation Program (NTEP) trial has been ruthless to the slender creepers. Varieties of slender creeping fescue inevitably end up near the bottom of the trial results. About 10 years ago, my company submitted "Logro," a European-bred slender creeping fescue into the NTEP trials. Logro had long been a top European performer. But for all five years of the NTEP trial, it held a stranglehold on last place.

The slender creepers prosper under a cool, moist European climate. In Canada, slender creepers perform best in coastal areas.

Characteristics of slender creeping fescue:

- Short, slender rhizomes
- Fine, dense, compact growth
- Resistant to heavy metals

Hard fescue. Hard fescue has been a recent innovation to turf. Not that the species itself is new—it's been around for decades with minor use in low maintenance and reclamation. It's only been within the last ten years that hard fescue has received the attention it deserves. In the 1989 NTEP fine fescue trial, a predominance of the top scorers were hard fescues. Hard fescues perform better than the strong creeping reds and slenders under the continental climate prevalent at most of the NTEP testing sites.

Because of its recent development, little information exists in textbooks concerning the care and feeding of hard fescue. Some texts actually discourage its use, saying that it becomes too bunchy to use as turf. But when mowed as turf, hard fescue produces a pleasing, consistent growth habit. I've never seen hard fescue exhibit the negative qualities described in older textbooks unless it is severely neglected.

Several recent turf research studies have extolled the virtues of hard fescue for low maintenance. Joe Neal (Neal et al., 1994b) and his coworkers put out field trials in Ithaca and Long Island, New York, to test the hypothesis that certain grasses exclude weeds better than others under low maintenance. In Neal's trial under zero nitrogen fertilization, hard fescue had the greatest density with little or no weed encroachment after 3 years. Hard fescue was followed by tall fescue, perennial ryegrass, and Kentucky bluegrass, in order of decreasing grass density. Clover was the prevailing weed under these unfertilized conditions, which being a legume manufactures its own nitrogen.

Pete Dernoeden at the University of Maryland reached a conclusion similar to Neal's while evaluating smooth crabgrass invasion into low maintenance turf (Dernoeden et al., 1994). A mix of hard and sheep fescue eliminated crabgrass from the turf as effectively as herbicide. Tall fescue, by comparison, contained as much as 30% crabgrass invasion.

Characteristics of hard fescue:

- Extensive root system
- Very drought tolerant
- Good shoot density
- Gray-green leaves; newer varieties have a deeper green leaf color
- Improved low growth and disease resistance
- Newer varieties are endophyte infected
- An *excellent* choice for low maintenance

Sheep fescue. If you believed everything you read, you'd never plant sheep fescue. Jim Beard in his classic textbook on turfgrass science, stated that sheep fescue, "forms a relatively low quality turf. It seldom forms a turf of uniform shoot density and appearance."

But a recent North American NTEP trial found otherwise. The two sheep fescue entries, "MX-86" and "Bighorn," were among the top performers, besting many popular chewings and strong creeping red fescues. As with hard fescue, the heat and drought tolerance of sheep fescue helped it through harsh summers.

Turf water researchers have classified sheep fescue as *the most* water efficient of the cool-season turfgrasses. In fact, they placed it in a category among the most water-thrifty *warm-season* grasses:

Species	Drought Tolerance	Degree of drought the species can tolerate
Sheep	Excellent	Frequent, severe
Hard	Good	Occasional, long-term
Chewings	Medium	Frequent, moderate
Strong creeping red	Medium	Frequent, moderate
Slender creeping	Poor	Infrequent, short duration

Colorado State University data (Butler and Fry, 1987)

In a similar study, Wade Albrecht (Albrecht, 1993) of the Flagstaff, Arizona, arboretum, tested the evapotranspiration of four turfgrasses. He found that sheep fescue had the lowest water use through the hot Arizona midsummer period of June through August. Hard fescue finished second to sheep fescue in water-use efficiency, tall fescue third, and Kentucky bluegrass fourth (Figure 2.9).

Sheep fescue is often used as unmowed, vista turf. It has a beautiful blue color and short foliage if unmowed. I have 2 acres of "MX-86" sheep fescue in my backyard that provides an attractive, meadow-like appearance. Golf courses use sheep fescue on unmowed rough areas, particularly on slopes, where it creates a cascading waterfall appearance.

Characteristics of sheep fescue:

- Ornamental, dusty blue appearance
- Fine texture with stiff leaves
- Tufted growth habit
- Attractive reddish seedheads during flowering
- A bunch grass with some minor creeping (rhizome) ability
- Can survive on as little as 10 in. (250 mm) of annual precipitation with no irrigation
- Very tolerant of acid pH and drought
- Can be maintained with only monthly mowings (even unmown, it rarely exceeds 1 ft [30 cm] tall)
- Endophyte has been introduced into a couple of the newer varieties
- Subcategorizes: Blue fescue, fine-leafed sheep fescue

Advantages of fine fescue for low maintenance

- *Excellent drought tolerance*—Sheep and hard fescue are particularly noteworthy (Fry and Butler, 1989b).
- *Lower fertility requirement*—Maintains a full turf with less fertilizer.
- *Superior shade tolerance*—The fine fescues are unmatched in shade tolerance. If the shade is so intense fine fescue can't survive, try bark mulch.
- *Low growing*—Fine fescue has a slow vertical growth rate that requires fewer mowings.
- *Winter-hardy*—It is cold tolerant well into Canada and Scandinavia.
- *Attractive cool-weather color*—Good winter and early spring growth and color.
- *Quick germination*—Seeds are relatively large. Germination is slightly faster than tall fescue but slower than ryegrass.
- *Fine bladed*—Delicate, needle-like leaves
- *May contain an endophyte to help fight insects*—Older fine fescue varieties such as "Reliant" are now being retrofitted with endophyte. The endophyte enhancement adds insect resistance with-

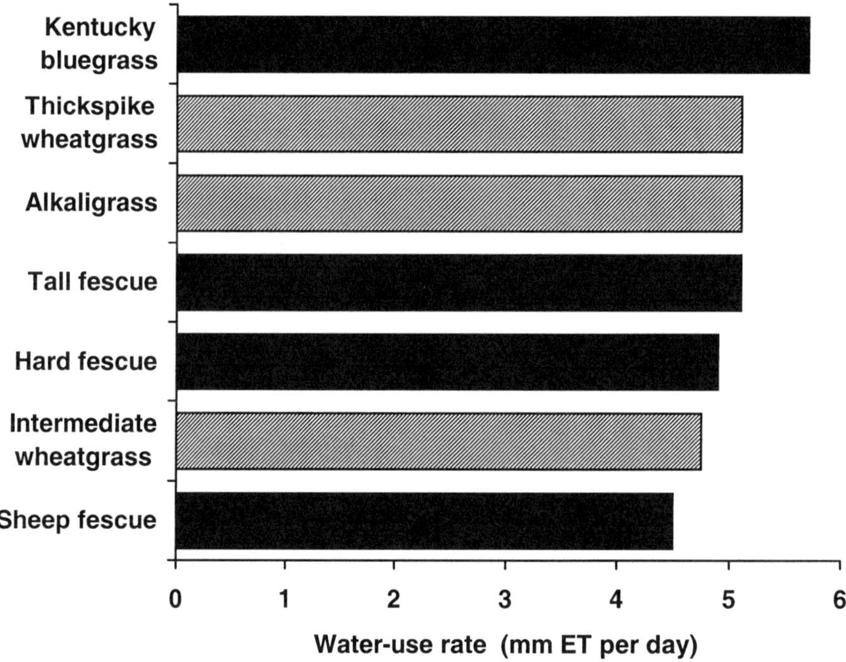

Figure 2.9. Water-use rates of 4 turf species and 3 prairiegrass species, averaged over a 12-week summer period in northern Arizona (Albrecht, 1993). Kentucky bluegrass (a blend of bluegrass varieties: "Baron," "Fylking," "Nugget," "Ram I," "Park") consumed the most water. Other traditional turf species were more water thrifty. "Critana" thickspike wheatgrass and "Fults" alkaligrass—two supposed low maintenance prairiegrasses—were equivalent in water-use to tall fescue. Sheep fescue was the most water-efficient grass of all.

out changing the desirable characteristics of a variety.

Disadvantages of fine fescue for low maintenance

- *Summer dormant*—Fine fescues go to sleep when daytime temperatures get too warm. Even a cold splash with irrigation water can't wake them out if it. Dormancy is most pronounced in slender creeping, strong creeping red, and chewings (Branham, 1989). Hard and sheep manage to avoid it.
- *Higher water requirement*—Fine fescues are pretty water thrifty, unless you're trying to keep them from going summer dormant. Avoiding dormancy requires added irrigation. Again, hard and sheep fescue are more drought tolerant than the others.
- *Restricted geographical range*—Slender creeping, strong creeping, and chewings fescue have little usefulness outside of Zone 2 (see Chapter 5 for zone classification).
- *Little wear tolerance*—Fine fescue is easily worn out on athletic fields except in the most cool, drizzly climates.

Kentucky Bluegrass

Kentucky bluegrass has long been the whipping boy when it comes to maintenance complaints. Everyone points to bluegrass as a prime example of landscape wastage. Xeriscape® promoters recite the inferior water-use efficiency of bluegrass as an example of why lawns should be banned.

But in spite of its notorious reputation, Kentucky bluegrass offers some promise for use as a low maintenance grass. Part of the misconception with Kentucky bluegrass stems from the enormous differences from variety to variety. The species is so diverse that some botanists recognize distinct species and subspecies within Kentucky bluegrass (example: *Poa angustifolia*).

Therefore, when a research trial draws a conclusion about Kentucky bluegrass based on a single variety, it is missing the enormous diversity within the bluegrass species (Figure 2.10). Often an antique, water-hungry variety like "Merion" is held up as the representative for the entire species (Beard, 1985a; Feldhake et al., 1983).

Breeding for low maintenance. Drought tolerance and winter performance have been bred into many new varieties of bluegrass. But the most important improvements have been in disease and insect resistance (Keeley and Koski, 1995). Bluegrass varieties now offer resistance to virtually every known disease or insect pest. This genetic resistance reduces or eliminates the need for costly pesticide applications, cutting maintenance costs considerably.

Better shade tolerance of bluegrasses has also been achieved. "Glade" Kentucky bluegrass, once recognized as superior in shade tolerance, is now mid-ranked in shade tolerance. Newer bluegrasses such as "NuGlade" and "Absolute" have eclipsed even the shade tolerance of Glade. Shade tolerance is a complex physiological response combining such things as: photosynthesis under low light, tree root competition, and resistance to shade diseases like powdery mildew.

Some bluegrasses can be grown with less fertilizer. The low maintenance NTEP trial of 1990 screened varieties using little or no fertilizer. The goal was to find varieties that efficiently ferret out soil minerals and require less input. Top varieties in this trial are capable of maintaining a thick, full turf with little added fertilizer.

A second issue in fertilizer management is turf color. It stands to reason that varieties with a naturally dark, rich genetic color would require fewer applications of fertilizer to keep them green (Shank, 1991). Some varieties are so naturally dark—even under low maintenance conditions—that they rarely appear hungry for fertilizer.

Advantages of Kentucky bluegrass for low maintenance

- *Good recuperative potential*—Bluegrass, because of its strong rhizome system, rebounds readily from stress or wear, making it valuable as athletic turf. Its rhizomes fill in bare spots.
- *Drought tolerant*—Good drought dormancy mechanisms and rapid and reliable drought recovery ensure survival of the turf. Drought tolerance of bluegrass is classed between that of tall fescue and strong creeping red fescue.
- *Cold tolerant*—Kentucky bluegrass can be grown in much of Canada, Scandinavia, and Russia, in areas where tall fescue and perennial ryegrass winterkill (Beard, 1986).
- *Good mixing ability*—Bluegrass mixes well with other cool-season grasses without dominating them or shrinking away.
- *Thatch cushion*—A carpet installer once told me that the pad under the carpet is more important to wear than the carpet itself. On sports turf, a buoyant blue-

Figure 2.10. Kentucky bluegrass has come a long way in recent years, thanks to immense breeding efforts like this one in Idaho. Bluegrass is **apomictic** in nature, meaning it reproduces genetically identical offspring through seed. It takes thousands of progeny to find a handful that are true hybrids, and not just carbon-copies of the mother.

grass thatch helps cushion injuries and reduce wear.

- *Improved resistance to diseases, insects, and shade*—Newer varieties offer considerable improvements in pest and stress tolerance, allowing them to be managed with fewer chemicals.

Disadvantages of Kentucky bluegrass for low maintenance

- *Comparatively poor water-use rate*—When water is available, bluegrass will use it. When it's all used up, bluegrass goes dormant. Some varieties handle this situation better than others.
- *Shallow root system*—Bluegrass roots primarily in the top 6 in. (15 cm) (Stetson et al., 1993). It cannot draw water from greater depths like fescue can. Mid-Atlantic ecotype varieties seem deeper rooted and better able to withstand drought (Keeley and Koski, 1995; McKernan and Ross, 1993; Murphy et al., 1993).
- *Dormancy in summer*—Dormancy is a *plus* when it comes to survivability but a *minus* for aesthetics. Summer dormancy can be avoided (unlike in strong creeping red fescue where it's virtually unavoidable) but at the expense of added irrigation water.
- *Slow to establish*—Kentucky bluegrass is one of the slowest cool-season turfgrasses to establish, requiring about twice the time of ryegrass. Seed establishment speed is similar to the seeded warm-season grasses.
- *Not as shade tolerant as fescue*—Bluegrass varieties vary considerably in shade tolerance but none are as shade tolerant as fine fescue.
- *Poor adaptation to warmer climates*—It cannot be grown in Zone 4 as tall fescue can (see Chapter 5).
- *No endophyte*—Researchers are now attempting to move endophytes from neighboring *Poa* species into Kentucky bluegrass. Varieties with endophyte may be available in a couple of years.
- *Intolerant of close mowing*—Older varieties faded away below 1-in. (25 mm) cut. Newer varieties offer better close-cutting tolerance, even down to $^1/_2$ in. (12 mm). Densely aggressive varieties are most tolerate to close cut.
- *Thatch buildup*—The "flip side" of aggressive varieties is that they thatch too quickly. Thatch can be kept in check by using less aggressive varieties, reducing nitrogen fertilization, and by aerification.

Perennial ryegrass

Perennial ryegrass is not the ideal low maintenance grass. Modern perennial ryegrass varieties were bred for higher maintenance tasks such as golf fairways or premium home lawns. But ryegrass has one remarkable attribute that makes it difficult to ignore: *An overwhelmingly fast establishment rate.* Perennial ryegrass can establish with more ease and less skill than any other turfgrass. That single attribute has endeared it to legions of turf managers who rely on ryegrass for quick establishment and repairs, even under adverse conditions.

Its quick establishment has earned ryegrass the nickname of Band-Aid grass. Perennial rye is one of the few turfgrasses that can be successfully sown directly into a living stand of grass and have it sprout and grow. This remarkable ability has paved the way for an entire renovation industry involving slit seeders, overseeding chemicals, and custom services. Given six weeks, a renovation crew can kill your existing lawn, replant it to perennial ryegrass, and have it ready to use. Only sodding rivals the turnaround time of perennial ryegrass seed.

Breeding for low maintenance. In the beginning there was "Linn." Linn is an antiquated variety of common perennial ryegrass originating from Linn County, Oregon. It is valuable as cow fodder but has no place in fine turf. Linn produces large, clumpy, stemmy plants not unlike K-31 tall fescue. Linn perennial ryegrass is still in production today; some even makes its way into supermarket turf mixtures. But since enormously better varieties are available today, Linn should be avoided at all costs.

In the 1960s, breeders in New Jersey and Pennsylvania independently developed the first improved, turf-type ryegrass varieties, "Manhattan" and "Pennfine." Virtually all of today's popular varieties trace their origins to these early releases. Each breeding generation since then has been an improvement, a refinement on the one before.

Breeding of perennial ryegrass has progressed so rapidly over the last three decades that past varieties are only a shadow of present ones. The bright, clean, uniform appearance of ryegrass has attracted a lot of top breeders. As a result, breeding efforts have been highly competitive, with few breeders willing to stray from the path toward turfgrass perfection. Little effort has been invested in low maintenance characteristics, with exception of improvements in disease resistance, drought tolerance, and endophyte. Color has been vastly improved, so modern varieties should require less nitrogen solely for color.

Advantages of perennial ryegrass for low maintenance

- *Rapid establishment*—It's not unusual to have perennial ryegrass seedlings emerge 4 days after sowing, under optimal conditions. With good care, expect to begin mowing newly planted rye within 3 weeks and playing on it in 6 to 8. The rapid establishment also lends itself to rapid reestablishment (overseeding) of worn or aging turf (see Chapter 7 for renovation tips).
- *Mixes well with other grasses*—Newer varieties have a growth habit that blends well with Kentucky bluegrass, tall fescue, or fine fescue. Although perennial ryegrass is not an ideal low maintenance grass, its presence in a mixture does extend the genetic diversity of a stand.
- *Endophyte*—Most perennial ryegrass varieties contain an endophyte to help cut the use of insecticide. Research has shown that the endophyte may even improve the disease resistance and stress tolerance of ryegrass. Newer varieties have near 100% endophyte levels.
- *Traffic tolerant*—The rapid tillering of ryegrass helps it wear well. Perennial ryegrass is somewhat slow to recover from wear. Because it is a bunch grass, it has limited ability to refill bare spots.
- *No thatch*—Ryegrass produces no thatch, even when prodded by fertilizer.
- *Summer stress tolerant*—Adaptation of perennial ryegrass to warm climates is better than Kentucky bluegrass but not as good as tall fescue. Newer varieties offer improvements in heat, drought, and disease tolerance. Perennial ryegrass does not have the summer dormancy tendency (or advantages!) of Kentucky bluegrass and strong creeping red fescue. It will go dormant, however, if drought persists.
- *Dark genetic color*—Modern varieties have intensely dark color, requiring fewer fertilizer applications to maintain color.
- *Shade tolerant*—Perennial ryegrass is about equal to Kentucky bluegrass in shade tolerance but not as good as the fescues.
- *Close cutting tolerance*—Ryegrass can be maintained below 1 in. (25 mm), even down to putting green height for temporary winter overseeding. Optimal height for "permanent" turf is $1^1/2$ in. (38 mm).
- *Useful in winter overseeding*—Winter overseeding of dormant warm-season turf is *not* a low maintenance practice. Winter overseeding is reserved for high profile lawns, golf courses, and sports fields. Nonetheless, perennial ryegrass serves a vital function here.

Disadvantages of perennial ryegrass for low maintenance

- *Winter tender*—Perennial ryegrass has been known to winterkill even in locations like State College, Pennsylvania, and New Brunswick, New Jersey, where the first ryegrass turf varieties were developed. Winter injury tends to be erratic, favoring years with an open winter. Ryegrass should be mixed with Kentucky bluegrass where winter temperatures dip below -10°F (-23°C) to ensure stand survival.

- *Pythium blight susceptible*—Perennial ryegrass is *the* most susceptible turfgrass to pythium. When conditions are ripe (hot and moist), whole stands can be obliterated overnight. Systemic fungicides offer protection against the disease for up to 21 days at a shot, but are expensive to apply. Red thread and gray leaf spot are also nagging ailments.
- *Added mowing requirements*—The vertical growth rate of the newer ryes has been throttled back considerably from older varieties. Even so, plan to mow perennial ryegrass turf more often than fine fescue or bluegrass.
- *No sod knitting*—Perennial ryegrass requires nylon netting for sod production, or at least the addition of a rhizome-forming companion grass. The lack of knitting also means slow refilling of bare spots.
- *"Touchy" seed mixtures*—Ryegrass's explosive seedling growth can literally overwhelm a mixture component (Howard and McConnell, 1989). Mix perennial ryegrass seed at a *maximum* of 10 to 20% by weight—any higher and you'll end up with a 100% ryegrass stand.
- *Sluggish greenup*—Under cool soil conditions, perennial ryegrass can be slow to green up in the spring. Greening commences as soon as the soil warms.

Bentgrass

Creeping bentgrass has the honor of being the grass most tolerant to extremely close clipping. Bentgrass can be maintained at a lower cutting height than any other grass—as close as 1/8 or even 1/10 in. (2.5 to 3 mm). No other grass can make this claim. Chewings fescue, bermudagrass, matrella, perennial ryegrass, and rough bluegrass can be mowed to putting green height but they do not persist like bentgrass does under ultra-close cuts. As a result, bentgrass is invaluable for golf greens and tees, bowling greens, and grass tennis courts.

The bentgrass family is comprised of about 100 species worldwide. Some bentgrasses like creeping bentgrass are maintenance-intensive, while others hold low maintenance potential.

Two bentgrass species are discussed here in Chapter 2: creeping bentgrass and colonial bentgrass. Other bentgrasses are covered in the next two chapters. Creeping and colonial bent are discussed together here because many of their characteristics overlap. They are also somewhat "mixable" with one another and have been known to cross-pollinate in nature.

Creeping bentgrass is strongly stoloniferous, spreading readily into voids or over the top of other grasses. Colonial bent spreads more slowly by weak rhizomes and occasional stolons. A few strains of colonial bentgrass have been discovered in nature with strong stolons or rhizomes but these have never entered the trade. Colonial bent is not as tolerant to close mowing as creeping bent. Its practical limit extends to about 3/8 in. (9.5 mm).

Creeping and colonial bentgrass can be cultivated as low maintenance grasses in Zone 2 (Chapter 5). There, they can serve as a ground cover with little need for mowing. Bentgrass is persistent under cool, damp conditions and can be managed with minimal upkeep (Richardson and Evans, 1986). Its flowing growth habit forms an attractive hillside cover. On seashores, bent will grow nearly to water's edge, indicating good salt and moisture tolerance (Wu and Harivandi, 1988).

Advantages of bentgrass for low maintenance

- *Low maintenance in Zone 2*—A good rule of thumb: A grass is truly low maintenance when it's grown in its area of adaptation.
- *Rapid stolon growth*—Bentgrass spreads quickly to heal itself.
- *Heat tolerant*—While it's no match for a warm-season grass, creeping bentgrass can withstand summer temperatures in any of the world's deserts—provided ample irrigation is provided (Wu and Harivandi, 1988). Colonial bentgrass is not as tolerant.

- *Cold tolerant*—Bentgrass is highly cold tolerant. Only in parts of New England (U.S.), Canada, and Scandinavia has it been known to regularly winterkill. Many times, bent's winterkill can be traced to ice cover, rather than temperature extremes.
- *Shade tolerant*—Bent tolerates partial shade. Its shade tolerance is equal to Kentucky bluegrass but not as good as fescue. Closer-cut bent tends to be less shade tolerant.
- *Close-mowing tolerant*—Creeping bentgrass is one of the only grasses that can be mowed as close as moss. In fact, moss is one of bent's main competitors at close-cut.
- *Very fine bladed (when mowed)*—Bent's blade density per square inch is higher than any other grass. Interestingly, when unmowed the blades are fairly broad.

Disadvantages of bentgrass for low maintenance

- *Disease-prone*—Creeping and colonial bent seem to get every disease in the book under closer cutting heights. Dollar spot is the "common cold" of bentgrass.
- *Requires modified soil*—Managing bentgrass below 3/16 in. (5 mm) on native, unmodified soil is nearly pointless. Sand modification is required to open drainage and minimize compaction.
- *High N requirements*—A steady dose of nitrogen is needed to keep bent growing, at about 1 lb N per growing season month (5 g/m^2).
- *Thatching tendency*—Nitrogen rate should be balanced against wear. Bentgrass is unforgiving if given too much N.
- *High irrigation requirement*—Water-use rate is not outrageously high compared to other cool-season grasses. However, the tiny plants and corresponding tiny root system mandate regular sprinkling. Drought tolerance is not bentgrass's strong suit.
- *Forms false crowns, puffiness*—When mowed above 3/4 in. (19 mm), bentgrass elongates, forming stemmy **false crowns** at the top of the leaf canopy. Mowing trims the false crowns unevenly, leaving brown streaks. Colonial bentgrass is particularly prone to this irregularity.
- *Cannot be mixed with other grasses*—Creeping and colonial bent can sometimes be seeded with each other but rarely mix well *long term* with other grasses. Segregation results.
- *Can become an unwanted weed*—Creeping bentgrass creeps readily via stolons and can escape and invade other grasses or ornamental plantings. Mowers propagate bent patches from one area to another.
- *Slow seedling establishment*—Germination rate is about equal to Kentucky bluegrass. However, bent seedlings are extremely small and initially frail until they establish.
- *Slow spring greenup*—Bentgrass likes cool weather but it really needs a warm spell in the spring before it rebounds from winter. It tends to stagnate when soil temperatures are cold.

Chapter 3

Grasses That Demand Less Maintenance

Would you like to grow a lawn that never needed fertilizing? How about a turf that demanded 30 to 50% less irrigation water? Or what about a grass that grew no taller than your ankles and rarely needed mowing? If you answered yes to any of these questions, then you're probably as lazy as I am. And you're ready to explore the world of alternative turfgrasses.

Turfgrasses that require substantially less input of water, fertilizer, pesticides, and mowing are not some futuristic vision. You don't have to wait around for years hoping some high-powered biotechnology lab will conjure them up. These grasses are available *today*, from a sod grower or seed supplier near you. And for the most part, the supply of their seed, sprigs, or sod is stable from year to year.

You may be asking: *"Then why haven't I heard about these grasses?"*

There are two reasons:

- *Lack of technical data*—Earlier turf textbooks gave only passing mention to these grasses. Prior to 1990, little was known about their care and feeding.
- *Limited range*—Some of these grasses have a more restricted use-range than other turfgrasses. For example, tall fescue—one of the "traditional" lawngrasses—can be grown in perhaps 40 of the 50 United States. By comparison, kikuyu grass—an alternative species—might find application in only a handful of states. But if you're lucky enough to live in one of those states, you'll find it a terrific lawngrass.

WARM-SEASON GRASSES

Carpetgrass

Two species of carpetgrass are used for turf: **narrow leaf carpetgrass** and **broadleaf carpetgrass**. Narrow leaf carpetgrass is native to the Americas, while broadleaf hails from Malaysia, Indonesia, the Philippines, and Southeast Asia (Beard, 1991). Both carpetgrasses are comparatively wide bladed, although there's considerable variation within each species. Broadleaf carpetgrass is so coarse it is often mistaken for a dicot weed. Yet in spite of their broad blades, both carpetgrasses are aggressive turfgrasses well suited to low maintenance conditions in warm climates.

Carpetgrass produces a distinctively dense, low growing, medium to light green turf. It is quite tolerant of close-mowing—an ability rivaled only by bermudagrass. Its basal growth allows for close-cutting without total defoliation of the plant. When in flower, carpetgrass plants resemble crabgrass (*Digitaria*) with stolons. The seedhead of narrow leaf carpetgrass is strikingly similar to crabgrass (Judd, 1979).

Carpetgrass is grown as **volunteer turf** in many parts of the world, as opposed to turf that's intentionally planted (Burbidge, 1966). *Poa annua* (annual bluegrass) is another example of a volunteer turf used on a large scale. Carpetgrass is found typically on old lawns or golf courses in tropical climates where the local vegetation was simply mowed down to turf height. What persisted was usually the indigenous carpetgrass. Better golf courses often try to eradicate the carpetgrass and substitute zoysia or bermuda

Table 3.1. Grasses that demand less maintenance: The turfgrass species described in Chapter 3, including their Latin name and authority.

Common Name	Latin Name	Typical Varieties
	Warm-Season Grasses	
Narrow leaf carpetgrass	*Axonopus affinis* Chase.	
Broadleaf carpetgrass	*Axonopus fissifolius* (Raddi) Kuhlm.	
Buffalograss	*Buchloe dactyloides* (Nutt.) Engelm.	609, Bison, Cody, Mesa, Plains, Tatanka, Texoka, Topgun
Centipede grass	*Eremochloa ophiuroides* (Munro) Hack.	Au-Centennial, Oklawn, Tennessee Hardy, Tennessee Tuff
Bahia grass	*Paspalum notatum* Flugge.	Argentine, Nan-ou, Nanpu, Paraguay, Paraguay 22, Pensacola, Riba, Tifhy 1, Tifton 9, Wilmington
Seashore paspalum	*Paspalum vaginatum* Swartz	Adelaide (Excalibre), Tropical Shore
Kikuyu grass	*Pennisetum clandestinum* Hochst. ex Chiov.	Breakwell, Hosaka, Kabete, Molo, Noonan, Rongai, Whittet
	Cool-Season Grasses	
Velvet bentgrass	*Agrostis canina* L. ssp. canina	Barbella, Kingstown, Piper, Kernwood, Raritan, Silver Needles, SR7200, Vesper
Highland bentgrass	*Agrostis castellana* Boiss. & Reuter	Highland
Redtop	*Agrostis gigantea* Roth	Freja, Gosta, Karmos, Kita, Listra, Reton, Streaker, Zygma
Canada bluegrass	*Poa compressa* L.	Canon, Reubens
Supine bluegrass	*Poa supina* Schrader	Supranova, Supra
Roughstalk bluegrass	*Poa trivialis* L.	Colt, Cypress, Dasas, Darkhorse, Laser, Omega, Otofte, Polder, Polis, Sabre II, Stevens, Tritana
Alkaligrass	*Puccinellia distans* (L.) Parl.	Fults, Salty

Figure 3.1. Broadleaf carpetgrass has leaves so incredibly wide they almost resemble buckhorn plantain. Golfers complain that hitting off a carpetgrass fairway is akin to hitting from a jute mat. Taller carpetgrass in roughs grows so bushy that it's been known to swallow golf balls.

(Beard, 1991). Carpetgrass offers a poor, flat golf ball lie according to tropical superintendents—especially the broadleaf species (Figure 3.1).

Yet in spite of its shortcomings, carpetgrass is well suited to low maintenance. Its occurrence as a volunteer turfgrass on old turfs is a testimonial to its rigorous adaptation. Carpetgrass won't provide the dense, plush appearance of zoysia or bermuda, but it can sustain a green, playable ground cover under some pretty harsh soil conditions.

Advantages of carpetgrass for low maintenance

- *Tolerates low cultural intensity*—Mowing is required but little else. The preferred mowing height is 1 to 2 in. (2.5 to 5 cm), but it can tolerate heights as low as 1/4 in. (6 mm) on fairways. When mowed above 2 in., a mowing frequency of once or twice a month can be applied. One application of a slow-release fertilizer per year is sufficient to keep it growing, even under golf course conditions.
- *Relatively pest free*—Heavy fertilization may bring on foliar diseases such as brown patch. But overall, carpetgrass is free of most pests.
- *Moderate shade tolerance*—Its shade tolerance is intermediate between St. Augustinegrass and bermudagrass.
- *Tolerates adverse soil*—Carpetgrass flourishes on heavy, wet or acid soils (to pH 4.5). It persists on rocky, infertile soils and slopes.
- *Rapid establishment*—Establishment is rapid from seed or sprigs. Seed supplies are usually available but because seed volume of this species is limited, only the more specialized dealers carry it.

Disadvantages of carpetgrass for low maintenance

- *Coarse, yellow appearance*—Carpetgrass is not the most attractive turfgrass species, that's for sure. But it fills the bill for reduced maintenance programs.
- *Problems with golf ball lie*—If cut short, broadleaf carpetgrass gives no support to a golf ball. Golfers say it's akin to hitting off a jute mat. Another more serious problem occurs if it's allowed to grow too tall. Three-inch (8 cm) carpetgrass has been known to "swallow up" golf balls. Golfers can't even find their ball if they're standing right above it. Regular mowing is critical to the game of golf.
- *No salt tolerance*—Carpetgrass is one of the poorer warm-season grasses when it comes to salt.
- *Poor drought tolerance*—Carpetgrass flourishes in moist, tropical climates. It shrivels and browns in drought and returns only slowly.
- *Not cold-hardy*—Carpetgrass has no mechanism for withstanding winter. You'll never find carpetgrass and freezing temperatures in the same location.
- *Produces seedheads in the turf stand*—Rotary mowing is required during flowering season to keep the heads at bay.
- *No improved varieties available*—In spite of its low maintenance potential, breeders have ignored these species.

BUFFALOGRASS

Buffalograss is a good grass with a bad name. The very thought of "buffalograss" brings to mind a tall, stemmy forage grass growing among the tumbleweeds. Other grasses, like Kentucky bluegrass, bermudagrass, or seashore paspalum have interesting, almost romantic monikers. Perhaps that's one reason why acceptance of this native U.S. prairie turfgrass has been sluggish for so many years.

Now its popularity is taking off. Buffalograss—hailed as the "grass of the future"—was featured on the front page of the November 20, 1995, *Wall Street Journal.* "Buffalograss is the hottest thing on the market," claims the *Journal.* However, to put things into perspective, the entire acreage of *all* varieties of buffalograss sod being grown in the United States today is still less than that of a *single* successful Kentucky bluegrass variety.

Buffalograss certainly isn't a new grass. According to University of California researcher, Ali Harivandi (Harivandi and Wu, 1995), it's been kicking around the Kansas prairie for 7 million years. Buffalograss is the classical grass of the short-grass prairie. Botanists believe buffalograss originated in the deserts of central Mexico, in an area receiving 15 to 25 in. (380 to 630 mm) of rainfall (Riordan et al., 1993). As it spread through the Great Plains, buffalograss adapted to the cold. One of the adaptations was a tripling of the cell chromosome number. No one knows why this occurred, only that it conveyed cold-hardiness, winter dormancy, and a general slower growth to the plant. Today, native stands of buffalograss can be found as far north as Saskatchewan, Canada (Riordan et al., 1993).

Buffalograss has two adaptations valuable for low maintenance: It's water-thrifty (Beard and Kim, 1989; Harivandi and Wu, 1995), and it's short-growing. Buffalograss ranks with bermudagrass and zoysia in water-use efficiency and drought tolerance, though its roots tend to be shallower (Figure 2.3). Under optimal conditions, buffalograss consumes less than $^1/_4$ in. (6 mm) of water per day (Riordan et al., 1993). It can survive unirrigated in areas with as little as 15 in. (380 mm) of annual precipitation. However, under these bone-dry conditions buffalograss is dormant much of the year, which comes as quite a shock to the uninitiated grower. Greenup occurs in mid to late spring. Flowering takes place shortly thereafter. By early summer the color fades to a straw brown as drought dormancy sets in. Under dry, nonirrigated conditions, buffalograss can be dormant brown for up to 10 months a year. For lawns, summer irrigation with 1 in. (25 mm) of water every 2 to 4 weeks is enough to keep buffalograss from going brown (Borland and Butler, 1982). However, nothing can be done to avoid its winter dormancy.

Mowing is another highlight of buffalograss. Buffalograss grows only 3 to 5 in. tall (7 to 13 cm). It rarely exceeds 10 in. (25 cm) even when pushed with water and fertilizer (Borland and Butler, 1982). Thus, buffalograss can be used under *unmowed* turf conditions. This ability to provide a turfy appearance without the need for mowing is rare among grasses. Only zoysia, centipedegrass, and alpine bluegrass rival it. The concept of a mow-free lawn is certainly appealing to many.

In reality, an unmowed buffalograss lawn looks "interesting" and prairie-like but somewhat shaggy and unkempt (Brammer and Rondon, 1982). Grass blades do not elongate evenly to the same height. Nature is approximate. But that may be a suitable compromise for those who want to sell the old John Deere.

Breeding for low maintenance. State universities in Texas and Oklahoma led the way in buffalograss breeding, developing "Texoka," an early turf/forage/reclamation release some 30 years ago. Texoka (and varieties bred from it) (Anonymous, 1995d) found limited application on lawns in the southern Great Plains and, curiously, in Beijing, China.

Ed Kinbacher of the University of Nebraska in 1984 began scouring his state for turf-adapted buffalograsses (Riordan et al., 1993). Kinbacher's small project turned into a major breeding operation when Terry Riordan at the University stepped into the picture funded by a grant from the U.S. Golf Association. By 1991 the first commercial varieties of improved turf-type buffalograss were being test marketed.

The present buffalograss releases from the Nebraska program were southern-adapted types, lacking the cold tolerance even for Nebraska. They were developed from plants collected on old turf sites in southern Texas (Riordan, 1994). Later releases offered improved winter-hardiness.

This latest wave of buffalograss varieties are **vegetatively propagated**. Vegetative establishment is not a new concept for warm-season grasses, but it was a bold step for a prairie grass. Today, buffalograss varieties are available as seed, sod, sprigs, or plugs (Figure 3.2). **Prerooted plugs** are arguably the easiest method of establishment. Prerooted plugs are made from soil cores taken from a turf stand. The plugs are allowed time to stabilize and regrow roots prior to sale. Establishment time is shorter than with traditional plugs but cost is higher.

Using buffalograss sod for the first time can be a shocking experience. Buffalograss sod exhibits a curious shock-response not seen in other

Figure 3.2. Seeded buffalograss (bottom half of photo) flowers in mid-season by extruding a tan spike a few inches above the grass canopy. Vegetative cultivars (top plot) are comprised of a single female clone. Because the female flower is located down in the foliage, its presence isn't apparent.

turfgrasses. Shortly after sod is laid, it goes into shock. The grass wilts, turns brown, and appears to die. This has prompted many an angry call back to the sod farmer. The affected homeowner assumes their new lawn has died from poor handling. However, buffalograss is responding to sodding the same way it responds to drought—with a rapid shutting down of the machinery. Buffalograss bounces back after transplant shock by regrowing new foliage, which may take several weeks. The fresher the sod, the less the shock response. Although even very fresh sod still exhibits *some* browning.

Advantages of buffalograss for low maintenance

- *Unsurpassed drought tolerance*—It doesn't get any better than this, folks. Buffalograss can produce a dense turf stand in arid areas where other grasses fail (McIver, 1992). Water-use efficiency is excellent, but when ample water is available, buffalograss *will* use it. Some studies suggest that buffalograss is not particularly efficient under "nonlimiting" water conditions. Thus if you switch your turf from ryegrass to buffalograss but forget to reset the sprinkler timers, your turf will use exactly the same amount of water. Curious how that works.
- *Low growing*—Buffalograss lends itself to unmowed, turf conditions. It can be used on a golf course rough with mowing only once or twice a season (Borland and Butler, 1982).
- *Salt tolerant*—Growth reduction takes place at the 50 mM salt level in the soil (Harivandi and Wu, 1995). Most cool-season turfgrasses are dead at that point. It is not as salt tolerant as zoysia or bermudagrass.
- *Low fertilizer requirement*—Only one or two applications of fertilizer per year are necessary to maintain buffalograss. Apply 1 lb N per 1000 ft^2 (5 g N/m^2) once in the spring and possibly once in the summer. *Overapplying* fertilizer is a bigger problem than underapplying. With too much fertilizer, buffalograss loses its competitive edge against weeds and grasses. Taller growing plants shade out buffalograss and eventually stifle its growth.
- *Improved turf quality and stolon vigor*—New, vegetative varieties produce a more attractive turf than common buffalograss (Riordan, 1994). They also creep faster, making sprigging and plugging feasible.
- *Low mowing tolerance*—Buffalograss likes to be clipped at 1 1/2 to 2 in. (3 to 5 cm). It can be shaved down to 2/3 in. (1.6 cm) for golf course fairways and pre-

mium lawns (Riordan, 1994). At that height it is virtually indistinguishable from common bermudagrass.

- *Wide soil adaptation*—Buffalograss excels on heavy, alkaline soils. It tolerates a pH range of 4.7 to 8.3.

Disadvantages of buffalograss for low maintenance

- *Long dormant period*—Nothing is perfect. If a grass uses substantially less water, you can bet it does so by going dormant for part of the year. Summer dormancy in buffalograss can be avoided by weekly or monthly irrigation. Winter dormancy of buffalograss is similar to other warm-season grasses, occurring whenever temperatures dip below freezing.
- *Not competitive in high rainfall areas*—The jury is still out on whether buffalograss can be successfully moved into areas with higher rainfall. It certainly presents some interesting possibilities for surviving that occasional, parched-dry summer. In moist climates crabgrass and other summer annuals overrun buffalograss. Winter annual broadleaf weeds and even cool-season turfgrasses dominate during its winter dormant period.
- *Winter weed control may be required*—Buffalograss requires herbicides when managed above subsistence levels. It outcompetes weeds only when it's left alone. When pushed with water and fertilizer, it rewards you with *more* weeds rather than fewer.
- *Slow establishment by seed*—Buffalograss reproduces by **burs**—a type of seed encasement about the size of a pea, containing 2 or 3 actual seeds (Fry et al., 1993). The burs are formed deep in the leaf axle down in the turf stand. Seed harvest is tedious and yields are low. Establishment of burs requires a relatively high seeding rate, upward of 7 lb per 1000 ft^2 (35 g/m^2) (Borland and Butler, 1982). Scarification, dehulling, and pretreatment can enhance germination. Planting of deburred (naked) seed at a rate of 2 lb per 1000 ft^2 (35 g/m^2) when soil temperatures are above 60°F (15°C) can bring a stand ready for mowing in as little as 6 weeks. Unfortunately, deburred seed is rather uncommon in the trade.
- *Marginal wear tolerance*—Buffalograss does remarkably well in wear tolerance, considering it's a low water grass. It resists wearout even while dormant. But beyond a certain point, buffalograss simply vanishes (Borland and Butler, 1982; Christians and Engleke, 1994). Regrowth occurs only from surface stolons. That's why you'll rarely find buffalograss growing on athletic fields.
- *Flowering at turf height*—Buffalograss is **dioecious**, meaning it has separate male and female plants (Christians and Engleke, 1994). Most grasses are **monoecious**, meaning they have male and female parts on the same plant. Male buffalograss plants put up a tan, shaggy flower in early summer. This male flower is objectionable only when turf is maintained in an unmowed or infrequently mowed condition, since mowing nips them off. Seeded buffalograsses contain about 50% male plants. Vegetative buffalograss varieties are all female and don't put up a flower stem.
- *Poor shade tolerance*—Buffalograss has shade tolerance similar to bermudagrass—essentially nil. Ali Harivandi (Harivandi and Wu, 1995) discovered that some of his buffalograss breeding selections survive 50% shade but concludes, "buffalograss is basically intolerant of shade."
- *Variable cold tolerance*—As time goes by, buffalograss varieties are shaking down into cold types and warm types (Riordan et al., 1993). Cold types survive winters virtually anywhere tall fescue can. Warm types have an adaptation similar to centipedegrass. Before you plant, make sure you're getting the right one for *your* area.

- *Pest problems*—Whenever any new grass species is introduced into the trade, it has a 5 to 10 year "honeymoon" period where nothing seems to bother it. Merion Kentucky bluegrass enjoyed such a success in the 1960s. Then everything changes. Insects and diseases breed and mutate with time. When a new grass enters widespread use, it opens the door for a host of new insects and fungi to work on it until one finally cracks the grass's defenses and proliferates. Merion's downfall was leaf spot. For buffalograss, mealybug may prove to be its Waterloo (Riordan et al., 1993). More predators will undoubtedly surface with time.

CENTIPEDEGRASS

If you were to visit an old cemetery in Georgia or northern Florida, you'd swear that centipedegrass was the ultimate low maintenance grass. Georgia cemeteries are often covered fence to fence with a thick, lush carpet of centipedegrass, with not one weed in sight. Centipedegrass thoroughly crowds out weeds while requiring little care other than occasional mowing or watering. Within its rather narrow range of adaptation, centipedegrass comes close to low maintenance perfection.

Centipedegrass was introduced into the western world in 1919 by Frank Meyer, a noted USDA plant explorer in Asia. Meyer was one of the first to identify the species, although earlier explorers to China had observed it. Plants and seed of centipedegrass were found in Meyer's steamer trunk after his final visit to Asia. The plants survived the trip; Meyer did not. He died in China of unknown causes. Foul play was suspected but never confirmed.

After its introduction into the United States, centipedegrass was planted in trial grounds in Oklahoma and Georgia (Featherly, 1946). Later, sod and seed farms in Georgia grew the first vegetative stock and sold scraps to local cemetery operators. Before then, Georgia cemeteries had been bare red clay. Centipedegrass blanketed the clay with a plush green, low maintenance cover.

Breeding for low maintenance. No active breeding of centipedegrass has taken place in the past 20 to 30 years, aside from a minor program at one southern college. Earlier releases of "Oklawn" from Oklahoma Agriculture Experiment Station (Featherly, 1946) and "Tennessee Hardy" from the Tennessee Agriculture Experiment Station were improvements primarily in cold-hardiness. These varieties successfully extended the range of centipedegrass several hundred miles north into the transition zone. In the United States, centipedegrass winterkills north of Oklahoma, Tennessee, and North Carolina. Worldwide, it is primarily a subtropical (Zone 4) grass, with some adaptation in the tropics (Zone 5). Plant explorers at China Agricultural University have discovered centipedegrass plants growing in northern China, in an area far removed from its normal range of adaptation. This find suggests the possibility of breeding centipedegrass with cold tolerance equal to zoysia.

One reason for the few breeding advances is that virtually all the centipedegrass in the West traces to the original clones Meyer and his contemporaries brought back in the early 1900s, which is far too narrow a population to mount a successful breeding effort. I believe there is potential—through additional germplasm collection and breeding—to develop centipedegrass into a turfgrass equally as attractive and widely adapted as zoysia. But that will have to wait until breeders rediscover the species.

Advantages of centipedegrass for low maintenance

- *Demands little or no fertilizer after establishment*—Once a stand of centipedegrass has filled in, you can back off on the fertilizer (Johnson and Carrow, 1988). Too-heavy fertilization brings unwanted pests and thatch. No fertilizer is really required—perhaps only a once-a-year shot of slow-release fertilizer. Too much nitrogen fertilizer sometimes has a backward effect on centipedegrass, turning it yellow from iron chlorosis rather than green. The grass literally grows faster than its roots can take up iron.

- *Minimal mowing*—Unmowed centipedegrass will grow ankle-deep and stop. In early summer, single-spiked seedheads appear a couple of inches above the stand. The seedheads are prolific and objectionable only on fertile soils or with heavier fertilization. Monthly mowing is usually sufficient to trim the heads and tidy up the stand. Preferred mowing height is 1 to 2 in. (2.5 to 5 cm) although I've seen centipedegrass maintained beautifully at fairway height (1/2 in. [12 mm]) in Hong Kong.
- *Crowds out weeds*—Centipedegrass forms a dense, weed-free carpet even under minimal maintenance. In drier climates its turf is more open, requiring preventive herbicides for summer annual weeds. Preemergence herbicides are preferred, because postemergence arsenical herbicides injure or kill centipedegrass.
- *Relatively pest-free*—Centipedegrass is pest-free at lower levels of maintenance. Ground pearl (a root insect), mole cricket, nematodes, brown patch, or dollar spot may leave an occasional blemish but rarely devastate the stand.
- *Adapted to poorer soils*—Centipedegrass grows equally well on red, acidic, clay soils as it does on sandy prairie soils. It can tolerate a soil pH as low as 4.5. Alkaline pH tolerance is limited, because high pH accentuates iron chlorosis.
- *Moderate drought tolerance*—In areas with plentiful rainfall, centipedegrass can tolerate the occasional summer drought with no problems. Under drier prairie climates, centipedegrass benefits from a monthly sprinkling during summer drought. You'll rarely find centipedegrass used in desert areas. The published literature recommends centipedegrass in areas with at least 35 in. (880 mm) of precipitation. However, my experience in Oklahoma is that centipedegrass can withstand perhaps as little as 20 in. (500 mm) of annual rainfall, though it does not form the same dense, plush carpet.

Disadvantages of centipedegrass for low maintenance

- *Slow establishment*—It's safe to say that any grass that grows slowly and seldom needs mowing, also establishes slowly. Centipedegrass can be established from sod, sprigs, plugs, or seed. Establishment (except for sodding) usually requires *one full growing season* or more. Stolons creep slowly. Seed requires 10 to 14 days to emerge. During grow-in, centipedegrass is readily outcompeted by crabgrass and other summer weeds. Herbicides can be used to throttle weeds and speed establishment. Centipedegrass responds well to fertilization during grow-in.
- *High seed prices*—Establishment from seed is complicated by high seed prices. Centipedegrass is a low seed yielder commanding a higher seed price. Centipedegrass produces only about 150 lb per acre of clean seed versus 1500 lb for perennial ryegrass. As a result, some people have planted centipedegrass at a fraction of its recommended seeding rate, making grow-in even more time-consuming.
- *Slow recovery from injury*—Slow regrowth limits centipedegrass's use on sports turf. It is best suited to areas with little traffic, like cemeteries, roadsides, and parks.
- *Not salt tolerant*—Centipedegrass isn't a great seashore grass because it lacks salt tolerance compared to other warm-season grasses (Smith, 1975). Centipedegrass evolved inland, away from salt spray.
- *Susceptible to iron chlorosis*—Iron chlorosis rarely damages centipedegrass but it does disfigure it. Foliar iron applications green the turf back up.
- *Lack of improved varieties*—"Tennessee Hardy," "Tennessee Tuff," "AU Centennial," and "Oklawn" are the only improved varieties of centipedegrass. None are substantial advances over Georgia

common or "red" centipedegrass as it's called, except in winter-hardiness. Georgia red got that name because of its red seedheads. Other Georgia strains have green or yellowish heads and are said to be inferior to red.

- *Coarse textured*—Centipedegrass has broad leaves intermediate between St. Augustinegrass and zoysia. Leaf orientation is horizontal, making the broad leaves appear slightly more attractive.

BAHIAGRASS

Bahiagrass has a lot going for it: It tolerates zero maintenance. It is seed propagated. Seed supplies are good, prices moderate. And when maintained, bahiagrass forms a moderately attractive turf (Smith, 1975).

But bahiagrass is considered a second-class citizen in the turf world. In the tropical zone (Zone 5) where it's adapted, bahiagrass is considered inferior to St. Augustinegrass for lawns and inferior to bermudagrass for golf. Bahiagrass is relegated to roadsides or rough areas. In Florida, bahiagrass blankets an estimated 2.5-million acres of land (1 million ha), serving multiple functions of animal feed, soil conservation, reclamation, and turf (Chambliss, 1991).

John Piersol, turf instructor at Florida's Lake City Community College (Piersol, 1994) says bahia "gets no respect." Piersol was determined to bring out the best in bahiagrass by planting it around two homes he purchased in 1974 and 1987. He discovered that with correct care—focusing on reduced maintenance—bahiagrass could be equally attractive as other grasses.

Piersol found that using a higher cutting height capitalizes on the toughness of the species. "Most people try to mow bahia at one to two inches," he says (2.5 to 5 cm). "It will tolerate such abuse, but it is a battle keeping the grass that low when it is actively growing." He found that 3 in. (7.6 cm) was a better compromise height. A sharp rotary mower blade at a 3-in. cut keeps the grass quite attractive, Piersol says.

Bahiagrass spreads by means of short, stout rhizomes and stolons. It has a rather upright, leafy appearance, in contrast to the horizontal, lanky appearance of other warm-season grasses with their long, wiry stolons (Judd, 1979). The root system of bahia is deep and extensive, making it drought tolerant even on sandy coastal soils. In extreme drought bahiagrass turns as brown as a paper bag. But it bounces back once rain arrives.

Bahiagrass and zoysiagrass have opposite responses when it comes to fertilization. When zoysia is fertilized heavily, it grows thatch. When bahia is fertilized, it grows leaves. Both grasses benefit from lesser fertilization. Heavily fertilized bahiagrass requires twice-weekly mowing, versus monthly mowing if unfertilized. Color will suffer if it isn't fertilized, but the grass will survive, as Piersol discovered.

Breeding for low maintenance. Bahiagrass, like centipedegrass, has been largely ignored by turf breeders. No varietal improvement work has been accomplished on the species since 1944 when "Argentine" was released from the Florida Agricultural Experiment Station. Earlier varieties, "Paraguay," "Pensacola," and "Wilmington," are less attractive and are more suited to animal agriculture than turf.

Advantages of bahiagrass for low maintenance

- *Tolerates minimal maintenance*—Bahiagrass can withstand little or no watering, fertilizing, and pesticides. Because of its vertical growth, bahia needs periodic mowing for best results.
- *Drought tolerant*—Bahiagrass is adapted to coastal, tropical climates with adequate rainfall. Under these conditions, it is tolerant of drought and recovers rapidly if stressed into dormancy. Bahia is occasionally used in desert areas, though supplemental irrigation is required. It is not as hardy under sustained drought as prairie grasses.
- *Easily seed propagated*—Bahiagrass is one of the few warm-season turfgrasses that is readily seeded (Anonymous, 1993c). Vegetative propagation of bahia is uncommon. Seedheads are abundant (even

in mowed turf, unfortunately) and seed yields are high. Seeds have a tough outer coat that benefits from chemical or mechanical scarification (scratching). Germination is prolonged but reliable.

- *Wear tolerant*—Bahiagrass tolerates foot traffic and recovers quickly.
- *Retains color during winter*—Bahiagrass hangs onto its green color longer than St. Augustinegrass or centipedegrass through winter. In milder climates, it avoids dormancy altogether.
- *Broad soil adaptation*—It grows on coarse sands or heavy, poorly drained, low pH clays.
- *Some shade tolerance*—Bahiagrass tolerates a little more shade than bermudagrass, but not as much as St. Augustinegrass.
- *Relatively pest-free*—Bahia resists most damaging insects and diseases, except for the ubiquitous mole cricket (Chambliss, 1991).

Disadvantages of bahiagrass for low maintenance

- *Erect growth habit*—Bahiagrass has an upright, almost tufted growth habit. Leaf blades are rather coarse and erect, similar to tall fescue. A sharp mower is required to keep the foliage in check, especially during heading season. Heavy fertilization only makes it worse.
- *No turf-type varieties available*—Varieties are 50 years out of date. Argentine is more turfy than the others. All varieties suffer from low shoot density and rapid vertical growth. Plant breeders could fix this if a serious effort was mounted. Rumor has it that one Oregon seed company is now trying to breed a variety for turf.
- *Seedheads in the stand*—The wiry, spiked heads emerge quickly and make the turf look untidy. Mowing remedies the problem temporarily but more grow back. Argentine reportedly produces fewer heads in the turf than Pensacola (Chambliss, 1991).
- *Sensitive to the "usual" warm-season herbicides*—Avoid triazine or arsenical herbicides on bahiagrass. They cause substantial thinning.

SEASHORE PASPALUM

Seashore paspalum has only recently been recognized as a valuable turf species. That's because for years, it existed incognito on seaside lawns and golf courses, mistaken by many for bermudagrass.

Seashore paspalum is found natively along the Georgia and Florida coast, throughout the Caribbean islands, in Argentina, Brazil, the Mediterranean-African coast, and along the Pacific rim. It is most common from 35° N to 35° S latitude, in areas where temperatures dip no lower than 17°F (–8°C) (Duncan, 1996).

Seashore paspalum is often confused with other grasses. Wild-type seashore paspalum may appear as broad bladed as St. Augustinegrass or as narrow leafed as a premium hybrid bermuda. The characteristic identifying seashore paspalum is its bermuda-like seedhead. Bermuda has 3 or more spikes on its seedhead—most commonly 4 to 5. Seashore paspalum has only 2. Seashore paspalum can also be identified by its hairier leaf collar and leaf edge. In mowed turf, it can be spotted in the early morning when the dew makes it stand out from surrounding grasses. Seashore paspalum glistens less in the dew than bermuda.

Seashore paspalum is largely unexploited for its low maintenance potential. Only one variety is currently in use in the United States: "Adelaide" was introduced into southern California from Australia by Pacific Sod, a major West Coast sod company.

Seashore paspalum has many adaptations favorable to low maintenance culture. Ronny Duncan (Duncan, 1996), grass breeder at the University of Georgia, believes seashore paspalum can be managed with few pesticides, 20 to 40% of the fertilizer required for bermudagrass, and water requirements equal to bermuda or centipede.

Duncan has tested seashore paspalum ecotypes under a number of adverse soil conditions. He found that seashore paspalum tolerates up to 14,000 ppm salt concentration, a wide soil pH range, and even recycled irrigation water (treated sewage effluent).

As with many of the low maintenance grasses, problems arise when it's given *too much* care. When pampered like bermuda, seashore paspalum produces a thatchy, shallow rooted, easily scalped, unappealing turf with limited traffic tolerance. Backing off on the maintenance solves this problem, the same way it does with centipedegrass or zoysia.

Advantages of seashore paspalum for low maintenance

- *Salt tolerant*—Seashore paspalum can grow in or near seawater saltiness. It prospers on sandy dunes with frequent salt mist. One Texas golf course even irrigates its paspalum with water drawn directly from a brackish estuary.
- *Withstands cloudy, rainy tropical weather*—Seashore paspalum seems to tolerate gray, tropical skies better than bermuda. Bermudagrass—particularly the hybrid bermudas—has a tough time when the sun ducks behind the clouds.
- *Demands less fertilizer*—Seashore paspalum performs poorly if it gets *too much* fertilizer.
- *Drought tolerant*—Seashore paspalum tops the charts in drought tolerance and water efficiency, matching bermuda and centipedegrass.
- *Fine texture*—Some plant lines of seashore paspalum rival the hybrid bermudas in their fine leaves and low growth habit.
- *Wide pH tolerance*—It withstands pHs from 4 to 9.8
- *Longer fall green period*—Seashore paspalum stays green about 2 to 3 weeks later in the fall than other warm-season grasses. Unfortunately, in the spring it takes 2 to 3 weeks longer to green up.
- *Moderate shade tolerance*—It can withstand up to 35% shade, somewhat more than bermuda.
- *Wide soil adaptation*—Grows on sandy, clay, or muck soils.

Disadvantages of seashore paspalum for low maintenance

- *Lack of cold tolerance*—Present sources of seashore paspalum lack cold tolerance. In general, it is less cold tolerant than the better bermudas but more cold tolerant than some others. A few of Duncan's breeding lines have survived an arctic blast of –3°F (–19°C).
- *Can be easily overmanaged*—Seashore paspalum should be managed like zoysia or centipedegrass: ease up on the water and fertilizer.
- *Few improved varieties*—Only one variety is presently available, and in limiting quantities. Duncan's breeding program may change things. The chances of seeing a seeded variety are slim due to paspalum's scant seeding ability.
- *Susceptible to the "usual" tropical insects and diseases*—Fall armyworm, mole cricket, spittlebug, dollar spot, pythium blight, and curvularia cause concern.

KIKUYU GRASS

Kikuyu is one of the most aggressive, invasive turfgrasses known. Its lack of cold tolerance is the only reason kikuyu has not enveloped the entire world. Kikuyu rarely survives temperatures below freezing. It is found mainly in areas where the temperatures remain above 60°F (15°C) (Hathaway, 1979).

Kikuyu grass originated in Africa and was introduced into Australia in 1919 and later into Mexico and the United States in the 1930s and 1940s (Cudney et al., 1994). From there it spread throughout regions with a mild, coastal, Mediterranean climate. It is common in pastures and turf in Australia, New Zealand, Mexico, and Southern California, as far north as the San Francisco bay (Youngner, 1961). Kikuyu tolerates heat and drought but is not competitive where droughts are frequent. Thus, you rarely find kikuyu growing in the desert (Khan et al., 1995). Unlike bermudagrass, it does not need hot temperatures to proliferate. Kikuyu does just fine with mild daytime temperatures in the 70s °F (>20 °C), provided the overall nighttime minimums stay above 60 °F (15 °C).

Kikuyu offers tremendous advantages for low maintenance. But it also has a couple of whopping drawbacks. One of its main advantages is its overwhelmingly vigorous growth habit. Kikuyu smothers the ground so aggressively it totally excludes weeds, even when minimally maintained. Weed control after establishment is seldom required.

Kikuyu's vigor is undiminished even at zero fertilization. Once kikuyu has formed a solid cover, it requires little fertilization to maintain. Experience has shown that 1 or 2 lb N per 1000 ft^2 per year (5 to 10 g N/m^2) is the most you'd want to apply. And even then, the turf should be fertilized only during the off-season, and only using slow-release fertilizers. Some golf courses in Mexico successfully maintain kikuyu fairways without any fertilizer at all.

Higher N rates lead to one of kikuyu's downfalls: Thatch. Even modest fertilization piles up large, woody stolons and rhizomes, forming a thick, fibrous mat. Vertical mowing and traffic help control the mat. Khan (Khan et al., 1995) and his coworkers found that kikuyu can tolerate up to 3 vertical mowings per year. More frequent vertical mowing causes diminished turf quality. With minimal fertilization, however, it *is* possible to maintain kikuyu without the need for vertical mowing.

Another of kikuyu's drawbacks is its need for almost daily mowing. Mower blades should be kept sharp and the cutting height low, commonly $^1/_2$ in. (12 mm). At lower fertility levels, kikuyu can get by with as few as 2 to 3 mowings per week. Still, that's a lot of mowing.

Kikuyu grass finds its best low maintenance applications on golf and sports turf, roadsides and parks, and nonmaintained erosion-control plantings in areas where climates are mild. It can be maintained with minimal machinery other than a tractor and pull-behind reel mower. That trait alone has made kikuyu a favorite in developing countries, where irrigation, pesticides, fertilizers, and maintenance equipment are not always available.

Advantages of kikuyu grass for low maintenance

- *Extremely aggressive*—Kikuyu crowds out weeds. It spreads readily by rhizomes, stolons, and seed.
- *Drought tolerant*—A deep root system (to 5 ft. [1.5 m] depth) and coarse rhizomes help resist drought with little need for irrigation. It survives unirrigated in areas with 35 in. (880 mm) of rainfall.
- *Little or no need for fertilizer*—Kikuyu responds to fertilizer during the grow-in phase. After that, it needs virtually no fertilizer. Foliar-applied iron can be used in place of nitrogen for color.
- *Good winter color retention*—In mild climates kikuyu retains its color even when bermuda or St. Augustinegrass have faded.
- *Tolerant of close mowing*—Kikuyu performs best when closely mowed. Close, frequent mowing keeps its vigor in check.

Disadvantages of kikuyu grass for low maintenance

- *Can be overly aggressive*—Kikuyu readily escapes from where it's planted. If you choose to plant a kikuyu lawn, plan on your neighbors' lawn and *their* neighbors' lawn eventually becoming kikuyu too. Propagation occurs by mowers and even birds. Aggressive stolons up to 9 ft. (3 m) in length can invade golf course putting greens, sand bunkers, and just about everything else.
- *Frequent mowing required*—Mowing is a definite drawback to kikuyu.
- *Thatch-prone*—Aerification, vertical mowing, reduced fertility, and traffic help minimize the thatching potential.
- *No cold tolerance*—Kikuyu won't grow in areas with freezing weather. Period.
- *Light green color*—Iron applications can darken its color, but in general this is a pale green grass.

- *Produces flowers in the turf*—During the active growing season, kikuyu shoots a strange, whitish blossom an inch or so about the turf. The blossom is actually a male flower; the female is tucked within the leaves at the base of the stem (Judd, 1979). Flowering occurs so quickly that even daily mowing does not eliminate the blossoms. Uninformed observers mistake the flowers for weeds.
- *Not easily overseeded*—Kikuyu never really goes winter dormant within its range of adaptation. And being a dense, competitive grass, it is not easily overseeded. Vertical mowing (during overseeding) damages the stand. Some success has been had overseeding it with tall fescue.
- *No improved varieties*—A breeding program at the University of California may someday remedy the lack of improved varieties. At present, the few named varieties are scarcely available and barely improved.

COOL-SEASON GRASSES

The *Agrostis* species: Highland bentgrass, velvet bentgrass, and redtop

Creeping and colonial bentgrass, the two most common *Agrostis* species of fine turf, were covered in the last chapter. Creeping and colonial bentgrass are best suited to higher maintenance golf turf. Three other *Agrostis* species—Highland bentgrass, velvet bentgrass, and redtop—are more suited to low maintenance. All are members of a broad family encompassing some 125 *Agrostis* species worldwide (Christians and Engleke, 1994).

Highland bentgrass

Highland bentgrass—also known as dryland bent—was for years lumped into the same species category as colonial bentgrass. And it's easy to see why: Both grasses have nearly identical botanical characteristics (Hubbard, 1984). Highland and colonial bent both are fine bladed with a dense, slowly creeping habit. Both perform best with closer (1/2 to 1 in. [12 to 25 mm]) mowing, since higher cuts bring out their stemminess. Neither Highland nor colonial bent does particularly well at putting green height, although this may change with time and breeding. And both grasses attract a host of diseases and insects.

The attribute that differentiates Highland bent from colonial bent is its drought tolerance. Colonial bentgrass persists only in climates with steady moisture. Highland bent thrives in drier climes. Highland bentgrass is common throughout the foothills of the Cascade Mountains in Oregon, where summer precipitation is virtually nonexistent.

As with other bents, thatch can also plague Highland. Regular aerification, vertical mowing, and topdressing are needed to keep its growth in check. This adds to maintenance costs.

A lot of problems can be avoided simply by reducing maintenance. Maintaining it a little dry and a little hungry is a good rule of thumb. As a matter of fact, that's a good rule of thumb for other turfgrasses as well.

Highland bentgrass can be used on non-maintained golf course roughs, by itself or in mixtures. On hillsides it provides an attractive, cascading appearance with visible, golden brown seedheads in summer. It's adapted to a drier, cool, marine environment (Zone 2) but it can also be used in milder parts of Zone 1.

Velvet bentgrass

Velvet bentgrass has a notable distinction: It is the finest bladed turfgrass in the world, bar none. Grown under putting green conditions, velvet bentgrass does indeed resemble green velvet.

Velvet bentgrass was first recognized back in 1932 for its superior putting qualities. Ten professional golfers were brought to the Arlington Turf Gardens in Virginia (now the site of the Pentagon) to help pick the best putting green grass. Plots included four well-known creeping bentgrasses, one colonial bent, South German mixed bent, and velvet bent. Ten out of 10 pros chose the velvet bent as the most luxurious putting surface.

Howard Sprague (Sprague, 1940), a noted turf specialist of the era, commented on the low

Successful Velvet Bentgrass Management: A Case Study

Velvet bentgrass has a lot to offer the golf course superintendent seeking a lower maintenance alternative for putting greens. Trouble is, no one outside of a few, select superintendents in Massachusetts know how to manage this grass without it "blowing up." Jim Connolly, senior technical agronomist for JacklinGolf® and former U.S. Golf Association agronomist for New England, shares some of his personal findings and experiences below, based on his visits to one of New England's premier velvet bent golf courses.

Golf course: Spring Valley Country Club, Sharon, Massachusetts
Superintendent: John Adamonis
Architect: Geoff Cornish
Built: 1961
Greens planted to: Stolonized with "Vesper" velvet bentgrass
Greens currently: 70% velvet, 30% creeping bentgrass and *Poa annua*
Soil base: 4 in. (10 cm) of topdressed sand over a sandy loam soil
Topdressing: 3 to 4 *light* sand applications per year
Aerification: Deep tine aerification, performed 6 times since the course was built
Vertical mowing: 2 to 3 times per year to a depth of 2 in. (5 cm), known locally as "ripping," in spring
Cutting height: 1/8 in. (3 mm) bench setting, riding triplex
Fertilization: 3 lb of actual nitrogen per 1000 ft^2 per year (15 g N/m^2)
Superintendent's complaints: Localized dry spots, thatch, nematodes, thin turf in shade, *Poa annua*, moss, different management than for creeping bent
Golfer's complaints: Greens too fast, ball marks, spongy to walk on when wet
Low maintenance advantages of the velvet bent: Fewer fungicide applications, generally healthy greens except where poorly drained, finer texture than creeping bent

maintenance adaptation of velvet bentgrass in his 1940 textbook:

"The species has the widest range of usefulness of any [bent] species. It thrives under close mowing as well as creeping bent, but is also well suited for use on lawns. It is one of the most drought-tolerant grasses for temperate regions and is tolerant of heat and cold. Unlike other bents, it is well adapted for use in shady locations as well as in the sun. Velvet bent is rather tolerant of infertile soils, but does not thrive on soils that are poorly drained."

So why hasn't velvet bentgrass dominated golf course turf? The trouble with velvet bentgrass is that it's almost too fine bladed—like moss—making it hard to manage. Its use outside of a few select courses in New England is virtually nil. That's because only a handful of superintendents know how to culture velvet bent. The secret of managing velvet bent is low maintenance. Anything you try to do to aid velvet bentgrass inevitably backfires. If you fertilize it, it puffs up. If you verticut or aerify it, it heals poorly, allowing annual bluegrass to invade. It also doesn't like a lot of water or herbicides either.

Yale Country Club in Connecticut has successfully managed a mixed stand of velvet bentgrass and *Poa annua* for years. Their success comes from not disturbing or poking at it. Over the years, a dense thatch has accumulated resembling balsa wood. But the velvet bent is happy and healthy.

"Kingstown" was the first improved seeded variety of velvet bent. It was released from the Rhode Island Agricultural Experiment Station in 1962. "SR7200," released by Rhode Island in 1994, is a darker, more uniform variety. SR7200 has been racking up some remarkable accolades recently at higher cutting heights, from 1/2 to 2 in. Velvet bentgrass may have an overlooked potential for roadside and utility turf, particularly in Zone 2.

I predict velvet bentgrass will see relatively little turf usage until the knowledge spreads of how to manage it. With velvet bentgrass, it's low maintenance or nothing.

Redtop

Once upon a time redtop was prescribed for every turf planting (Sprague, 1940). It wasn't until the late 1960s that turf specialists realized redtop was causing more problems than it was solving. Redtop establishes quickly and reliably. In warm soils, it pops out of the ground even faster than perennial ryegrass.

Redtop, like the other *Agrostis* species, has extremely small seeds with 5 million seed per lb (11 million seed/kg). Seedlings are tiny but vigorous. They emerge quickly but are so small that they take time to form a solid cover.

In the past, redtop was used as a **nurse grass**, nursing desirable species (usually Kentucky bluegrass) until it was big enough to fend for itself. But then the trouble began: Redtop didn't go away once its nursing duties were through. Mature redtop plants become large, broad-bladed, and stemmy—and are particularly noticeable in mixtures.

Redtop can be grown acceptably as a **monostand** (by itself). When planted alone and cut above 3 in. (8 cm), it produces an acceptable low maintenance turf.

Redtop's service as a nurse grass is over. Today it is used in occasional roadside mixtures or for reclamation of problem soils. It has desirable attributes for surviving adverse conditions, such as acid pH or heavy metal contamination.

The *Other* Bluegrass Species: Canada bluegrass, roughstalk bluegrass, supine bluegrass

Roughstalk, Canada, and supine bluegrass are less widely known than their cousin, Kentucky bluegrass. Nonetheless they pack some valuable credentials for low maintenance. All are presently in production and seed supplies are favorable. Many of the growth characteristics of these

Highland bentgrass	Velvet bentgrass	Redtop
	Advantages for low maintenance	
• Fine bladed, dark green foliage	• Low fertility requirement	• Quick establishment
• Drought tolerant	• Shade tolerant	• Tolerates acid soil and heavy metal contamination
• Wide soil adaptation including acid soils	• Aggressive against annual bluegrass (if undisturbed by aerification)	• Withstands infertile, waterlogged soils
• Useful in mixtures with other turfgrass species	• Finest texture of any *Agrostis* species	• Useful as a mixture component in winter overseeding of dormant bermudagrass
• Can be used to create a "links-look" golf course	• Adapted to a wide range of soils	• Prized in meadow plantings for its brilliant red summer seedheads
	Disadvantages for low maintenance	
• Disease susceptible	• Won't tolerate drying out	• Broad, stemmy leaves
• Not heat tolerant	• Very light green color	• Not heat tolerant
• Poor wear tolerance	• Hard to manage—few people have the expertise to grow it	• Poor wear tolerance
• Stemmy, puffy growth habit	• Intolerant of poor or waterlogged soils	• Forms unattractive patches when used in mixtures

grasses are similar to Kentucky bluegrass. Notable differences are pointed out below.

Canada bluegrass

Canada bluegrass, as its name implies, is a cool-weather grass. Canada bluegrass offers excellent cold tolerance and can be grown in Scandinavia, Siberia, Alaska, and of course, Canada. Its U.S. adaptation extends southward into Minnesota, Michigan, New York, the Rocky Mountain states, and other sites with a cool climate (Campbell et al., 1956; Voigt and Haley, 1990). In warmer areas, disease pressures restrict its growth (Gover et al., 1989).

Just as Kentucky bluegrass is not actually native to Kentucky, neither is Canada bluegrass native to Canada. Both bluegrasses originate in Eurasia.

Canada bluegrass is most useful as non-irrigated turf. It survives infertile, acidic, and droughty soils better than Kentucky bluegrass. Canada bluegrass has been successfully put to task on slopes and high elevation (Cuany, 1982).

Canada bluegrass's main drawback is its poor mowability. If you mow it at 1 1/2 in. (4 cm), Canada bluegrass turns into stubble. It performs best above 2 in. (5 cm)—the higher the better.

Roughstalk bluegrass

Roughstalk bluegrass (a.k.a. rough bluegrass, or *triv*) gets its name from the scratchy feel to its seedstalk—a characteristic that differentiates it from Kentucky bluegrass. Rough bluegrass is a niche grass with two valuable assets:

- It thrives in damp, shady conditions under trees
- It serves as a useful grass for winter overseeding of dormant golf greens, providing a fine bladed, true putting surface.

Roughstalk bluegrass is a soft bladed, fine textured, yellowish-green turfgrass. It spreads by weak stolons and can develop a remarkably high shoot density if well managed. Its root system is shallow, and drought and heat tolerance are poor. Under cool, moist, shady conditions roughstalk bluegrass outperforms many other turf species.

In recent years, roughstalk bluegrass has found a second niche: Winter overseeding of dormant bermudagrass putting greens. The fine texture of roughstalk bluegrass is preferred by golfers over the coarser blades of perennial ryegrass. However, its use is limited to golf courses with light winter play, since its wear tolerance is poor and it can easily be trampled out. Rarely do you find roughstalk bluegrass overseeded on public courses.

The booming overseeding business has sparked new breeding of rough bluegrass varieties. The principal improvement has been a darker leaf color. Some of the newer varieties are approaching (but not attaining) the color of Kentucky bluegrass. None yet match the color of creeping bentgrass.

Breeding and production of new rough bluegrass varieties has brought out a new problem for the seed industry: Contamination. Rough bluegrass has become a contaminant in cool-season turf seed. Roughstalk bluegrass seed is grown in the same region as perennial ryegrass and Kentucky bluegrass. Seed is then cleaned with the same cleaning machines. Contaminated seed has found its way onto sod farms and ultimately to golf courses and home lawns. Improved, vigorous roughstalk varieties have exacerbated the problem. Newer, more aggressive varieties form persistent, spreading patches.

As a result, seed growers have taken steps to restrict roughstalk bluegrass's production to select counties. Further, rough bluegrass is now being cleaned by many companies on dedicated seed cleaning machines, to keep contamination to a minimum. Lawsuits from impacted sod farms have underscored the seriousness of the problem.

Supine bluegrass

Annual bluegrass (*Poa annua)* and supine bluegrass (*Poa supina)* are closely related—so closely in fact that botanists believe annual bluegrass originated eons ago when supine bluegrass naturally hybridized with *Poa infirma* (Lundell, 1994).

Annual bluegrass is technically a turf weed. It volunteers in turf stands and is hard to eradicate. But it also has many desirable characteristics. Worldwide, more golf is probably played on annual bluegrass than on any other turf. And it's all volunteer—no one seeds it. Annual bluegrass offers superior putting qualities and is quite forgiving, reseeding itself to repair divots and blemishes.

Unfortunately, annual bluegrass seed is generally unavailable to those who appreciate it. You can't buy seed of it to overseed bare spots. Many states still consider it a noxious weed and prohibit annual bluegrass seed to be sold. The small quantities that are available are screened out of perennial ryegrass seedlots in Oregon. The annual bluegrass obtained this way is an obligate annual that flowers and dies within a year after planting. The principal golf course *Poa annua* ecotype is actually a perennial, classified as *P. annua* ssp. *reptans*.

That's where supine bluegrass steps in. Supine bluegrass has all the good characteristics of annual bluegrass, but it isn't *Poa annua*. Therefore seed can be sold though normal channels.

Supine bluegrass has the same light green color, aggressive spreading qualities, and indiscriminate seedhead production as its cousin. Supine bluegrass has a dormant winter color—browner than *Poa annua*—but rapidly greens up in the spring. It is best used as a monostand, because being mildly stoloniferous, it forms circular patches in mixtures with other grasses.

Seed is expensive due to the fact that seedheads trickle up throughout the year (versus the "flush" of seedheads with most turf species). Supine bluegrass can be sown at a low seeding rate with hopes that with natural reseeding and spreading it will fill in over time.

Of course, just as with annual bluegrass, supine bluegrass can become a weed out of control. Its aggressive growth and seed setting ability—even at close cut—can result in the unleashing of a potential weed onto your property (Figure 3.3). But if annual bluegrass is already abundant at your site, why worry?

ALKALIGRASS

Salt is becoming an increasing concern in turf management. In the Canadian province of Alberta, for instance, government officials estimate that 600,000 acres (250,000 ha) of the province are presently being affected by salt and alkali seeps. They estimate that the area impacted by salt is swelling at a rate of 10% per year (Weijer, 1989).

Salt can come from many sources (Allison et al., 1954):

- Inherent salty soils at the site
- Application of saline irrigation water
- Intrusion of salt from subsurface water or ocean spray
- Use of saline effluent irrigation water

Figure 3.3. Supine bluegrass has weak stolons, and it sets seed in the turf, allowing it to creep away from where it's planted. In this photo, a test plot of supine bluegrass has expanded to 3 times its original size.

Canada bluegrass	Rough bluegrass	Supine bluegrass
Advantages for low maintenance		
• Bluish green foliage	• Thrives on perennially damp soil	• Very aggressive
• Drought tolerant	• Shade tolerant	• Withstands compacted, water-logged soils
• Wide soil adaptation, including infertile or acid soils, from clays to gravel	• Aggressive, with a high shoot density	• Has all the good qualities of *Poa annua* with a few less of the bad
• Useful in alpine areas or high elevation	• Very winter-hardy	• Excellent recovery from wear
Disadvantages for low maintenance		
• Intolerant of mowing much below 3 in. (7 cm)	• Poor drought tolerance	• Invasive; can escape and become a weed
• Sensitive to heat	• Does not mix well with other grasses (patch-forming)	• Mixes poorly with other grasses
• Disease susceptible in warmer climates	• Light green color	• Light green summer color and brown winter color
	• Soft leaf tissue does not tolerate wear	• Does not tolerate putting green heights (Neal et al., 1994a)
	• Shallow rooted	• Shallow rooted

- Runoff from roadways where deicing salts are used
- Repeated use of salty fertilizers

A number of grasses are noteworthy for their salt tolerance. Most are warm-season grasses. Seashore paspalum, bermudagrass, and zoysiagrass are able to grow in soil with near seawater saltiness. Few cool-season grasses have this ability. And far fewer have the ability to produce a dense turf stand at the same time.

Alkaligrass is a specialty grass known for its outstanding tolerance to salt and alkali (Kinbacher et al., 1981). It is a fine textured, bunchgrass similar in appearance to fine fescue. It performs well at cutting heights above 1 1/2 in. (4 cm). Under close mowing it becomes stemmy and brown. "Fults" and "Salty" are improved varieties with better turf than common.

Alkaligrass is useful in mixtures where salt is a problem, or as a preventive where salt *may become* a problem in the future: along sidewalks, driveways, roadsides, and parking lots (Figure 3.4). Alkaligrass is competitive and persistent under salty conditions, crowding out grasses like perennial ryegrass or Kentucky bluegrass. However, it lacks competitiveness on normal soils with no salt and a neutral pH. Adding a bit of alkaligrass to a seed mixture helps incorporate some insurance against future salt problems.

Advantages of alkaligrass for low maintenance

- *Persistent under adverse soil conditions*—Alkaligrass tolerates high salt and high pH.
- *Good color and density*—Leaf texture is similar to fine fescue.
- *Low growing*—Mature, unmowed height is 12 to 16 in. (about 40 cm). Alkaligrass will tolerate mowing to 1 1/2 in. (4 cm), although 3 in. (8 cm) suits it better.
- *Drought tolerant*—Alkaligrass can be grown unirrigated in areas receiving as little as 20 in. (500 mm) of rainfall.

Figure 3.4. Harborside Golf Club in Chicago uses alkaligrass in their roughs as a hedge against salt. Several golf clubs in the Chicago area have salty soil or irrigate with high sodium irrigation water. Alkaligrass is a cool-season turfgrass with exceptional tolerance to salt and alkali. Unmowed, it grows to a height of 12 to 16 in. (about 40 cm).

Disadvantages of alkaligrass for low maintenance

- *Rather stemmy*—Stemminess is accentuated by close-cutting.
- *Noncompetitive at neutral pH, low salt*—Alkaligrass is crowded out by other grasses on soils that are fertile and well balanced.
- *Not heat tolerant*—Its range is restricted by summer stress.

Chapter 4

Unconventional Grasses and Grass-Like Plants

The grasses listed in the last two chapters should satisfy most people's everyday needs for a low maintenance lawn. The grasses listed in Chapters 2 and 3 offer tremendous diversity and potential for reducing upkeep.

But if you're adventuresome, Chapter 4 offers you even more possibilities. In this chapter I've cataloged perhaps the most comprehensive list of unconventional grasses and grass-like plants available anywhere, and scored them according to their turf suitability. Information was gleaned from over 500 research sources.

Many of the grasses listed in this chapter are in use today as turfgrasses. And many can be obtained from local or regional suppliers of seed or sprigs. Oftentimes the *primary* use of these grasses is not for turf but for some related function. In this chapter are range grasses, alpine grasses, forage grasses, ornamental grasses, reclamation grasses, pasture grasses, tropical grasses, and even a section on plants that look like grass but really aren't. All of these grasses have application to turf—anywhere from a golf course fairway to an unmowed, vista turf area. The possibilities are nearly endless for grassing low maintenance landscapes the world over, using the grasses presented here.

FIRST, A FEW SURPRISES

The grasses listed in this chapter and the Appendix have the potential of saving you a lot of maintenance and upkeep. But planting them for the first time can be a real eye-opening experience. If you're accustomed to the easy germination and smooth performance produced by the traditional species, you're bound to find these unconventional grasses a bit unsettling, as I'll explain below. However, for people willing to weather some of the customary difficulties with these grasses, you'll be rewarded with reduced maintenance later on.

Surprise #1—Locating planting stock. Don't expect to trot down to your neighborhood grocery and find bags of these grasses lying on the shelf. It'll take some dedicated searching to locate seed or sprigs of some of these grasses. And try as you may, you won't find every one available in every single year. Their availability fluctuates dramatically from season to season—a lot more than you're accustomed to with traditional turfgrasses.

Here's how things work with these grasses: A new set of grasses becomes available each time a new government land project or major reclamation venture begins. Growers start growing seed or planting stock in response to a major need or contract. Any unsold seed later becomes available to the public through the usual seed outlets (see the sidebar on how to locate unconventional grasses).

To make locating these unconventional grasses a bit easier, I've included a column in the Appendix that scores the grasses by how simple they are to locate. I've also included the names of several mail-order seed houses in the references.

Some of the unconventional species can be obtained rather easily. They are regularly bought and sold as commodities. You'll find them stocked by the larger specialty seed houses.

Surprise #2—Sticker shock. Don't be surprised to pay more for seed or sprigs of these unconventional grasses than you would for traditional

How to Locate the Seed You Want

Finding seed or planting stock of the grass you want is sometimes a challenge, especially if it's one of the unconventional grasses listed in the Appendix. Except for 30 or 40 of the more common species, most of the unconventional grasses are not "off the shelf" items. Seed is sometimes grown or harvested only *after* an order is placed. One of the goals of this book is to help create a demand for the low maintenance grasses by explaining their uses and applications. Perhaps if more people start asking for these grasses, suppliers will start carrying them.

Bob Vilotti is a low maintenance seed guru for Arkansas Valley Seed Company in Denver. Vilotti's company has long been a supplier of low maintenance and native grass seed to all facets of the turf industry—from reclamation projects to golf courses. In the following interview, Vilotti provides tips for finding seed of unconventional grasses.

Cut Your Maintenance: Where does low maintenance grass seed come from?

Vilotti: There're three basic acquisition processes we go through to get seed: First, there's the open market, if it's a commercially produced item. This includes grasses that are in higher demand, such as crested wheatgrass. Secondly, we can contract with a farmer to grow seed for you. Thirdly, with most of these obscure grasses, we have to rely on someone hand-collecting them from nature. There isn't a big enough demand for many of these grasses to have a farmer grow it. Take for example prairie junegrass. For the last 10 years nobody ever had any seed of it, nobody got it, nobody collected it, nobody grew it. Then maybe 100 lb would pop up somewhere so I'd buy it. Then it might take 10 years for me to sell that 100 lb. Without a good consistent demand for a product, you have a very difficult time locating it, if ever.

Cut: Let's say I'm a seed buyer for a landscape project that's going to be built two years from now. What should I do to ensure the seed I need is ready for planting?

Vilotti: First you'll want to determine if the items are readily available: Are they generally obtainable 365 days a year? Or are they something nobody's ever heard of? Typically, if they're something that will have to be grown specifically for the project, then two years may not be enough. Whoever is writing the specifications needs to contact someone in the seed industry to find out whether these grasses are commercially and consistently available. That way, you won't run into a supply problem when it comes to planting your project. We get a lot of calls from architects. Most of them want us to design mixes for them, so obviously we're going to use grasses that we know are more common and available, rather than pick one no one's ever heard of.

Cut: Let's say I'm a homeowner, and I've read about these grasses in this book, and I want to plant them in my yard. How should I proceed in getting seed?

Vilotti: It's a matter of finding a company that, (1) deals with these types of grasses, and (2) that sells in small quantities. Our company and a few others do sell seed in small amounts.

Cut: Do you sell by mail order?

Vilotti: Well, not officially. But if somebody calls us, and they're in New Mexico, and they want to buy a few pounds of these native grasses, we will send them out UPS. I don't know of anybody doing a regular mail order business in the low maintenance grasses. There are all kinds of mail order catalogs on flowers and forbs, but none really offer the native-type grasses. The overall demand is so small at this point.

Cut: When specifying seed of low maintenance grasses, what types of specs are unreasonable?

Vilotti: We see this kind of thing with federal government specs all the time—they call for certified seed. And of course you can't have certified seed unless you've got a cultivar. They'll also put a geographical restriction on where the seed is to come from. For example, here in Colorado, the specs might call for certified annual ryegrass produced in the state of Colorado. Well, you can't do it. You can't get that specific. No one that I know of is producing certified annual ryegrass seed in Colorado. If you want locally produced seed, then you have to be familiar with what's being produced in the area. Here's an interesting twist: There are states that are closing their borders to any native grass seed coming in from out of state. While at the same time, these states don't have a native grass seed production industry of their own.

Cut: Hasn't AOSCA (Young et al., 1995), the seed certification people, recently begun a certification program for wildland seed?

Vilotti: They have a program right now dealing primarily with the shrub and forb seeds, where they **source identify** a particular genotype—for example, big sage brush or rabbit brush. They identify the state, the county, the elevation where it was collected, to give people a better idea of what might be adapted for their site. For example, the seed has been collected from a 10,000 ft. elevation, and your site's at 5000 ft., you might want to get a source from another elevation. The Department of Agriculture will issue a certified tag—a gold tag, not blue—as a source identification. In terms of grasses, I guess you can do the same thing, but grasses are more of a cultivated-field crop that probably wouldn't justify wildland certification.

Cut: Some of the native grasses need seed treatment or scarification for best germination. When I'm buying grass seed, how do I know if these grasses have been pretreated or not?

Vilotti: Typically, there are not a lot of grass species that *need* to be scarified—there're a few where it's *recommended.* Indian ricegrass is a good example. Most of the Indian ricegrass that gets planted never gets scarified. Scarification has to be done just prior to planting. Scarified seed has a short shelf life. Not a lot of people have the type of equipment to scarify. Occasionally we get a set of specs where scarified seed is required, but very infrequently. So we just rely on Mother Nature to break the dormancy, and if it takes 10 years, so be it. Usually you'll want to plant other grasses in mixtures with these, so you'll have something to hold the stand together. Eventually the seed *will* come up. Scarification is not the standard practice in the industry.

Cut: In your opinion, what kinds of grasses work best for low maintenance lawns?

Vilotti: If they're sod forming or stoloniferous, typically they'll work better for lawns. If they're not, they'll thin out and eventually get too clumpy for turf. If you seed bunchgrasses extremely heavy, then you're back to the same situation where you have to water them like bluegrass to keep them dense—even if they are a low maintenance native-type grass.

Cut: What would be your picks for undiscovered, unconventional grasses with lawn adaptation?

Vilotti: Streambank wheatgrass, tufted hairgrass, crested wheatgrass.

lawngrasses—sometimes a lot more. Most unconventional turfgrasses retail in the range of $5 to $30 per lb. Traditional turfgrasses by comparison retail for $1 to $10 per lb. Depending on supply and demand, a few native grasses have even commanded a whopping $900 per lb (Harper-Lore, 1995). The *Wall Street Journal* calls the business of selling native grass seeds "an emerging growth industry" (Harper-Lore, 1995).

Surprise #3—Dead seed. To add insult to injury, some of the seed you'll buy is going to be nonviable. It's dead. Germination rates of the unconventional turfgrasses typically range from 40 to 60%—compared to 80 to 95% for traditional turfgrasses. If you buy a bag of seed with 50% germination, only *half* of the seed in the bag is alive. The rest is dead inert. This effectively doubles the cost of a pound of seed. But that's the nature of these grasses—they haven't been refined and selected over the centuries into high seed-yielding varieties like the traditional turfgrasses have.

Unconventional grass seed is generally sold by percent **Pure Live Seed (PLS)**. Pure Live Seed indicates the weight of actual, viable seed in the bag versus how much is inert. Often, dealers quote their price per pound of PLS. That allows you to comparison shop across diverse seedlots and sources, while holding viability constant. As a rule of thumb, it's always a good idea to at least *ask* the seed supplier what the PLS level of a seedlot is.

One more warning about seed: Seed of these unconventional grasses oftentimes has trouble germinating—even if the germination rate listed on the bag is satisfactory. Laboratory seed inspectors who measure germination do it under ideal growing conditions. The germination rate listed on the bag might not be the germination rate you find in the field. In most cases field germination is half (Gifford, 1984).

"Uneducated consumers, not knowing what to expect from a native grass lawn are disappointed to say the least," says Tom Voges, low maintenance seed specialist at Arkansas Valley Seed Company in Denver (Whitmore, 1989). "Blue grama and buffalograss are about ten times harder to establish than bluegrass. Also, once they begin growing, they look a little rougher." Voges has counseled many a disappointed homeowner on what they can realistically expect from native grass lawns (Figure 4.1).

A seed supplier is usually aware of potential germination problems with a seedlot and may take steps to **pretreat** the seed. Chemical baths, **scarification** (mechanical surface scratching), and **dehulling** (removal of the seed hulls) can be used to boost emergence of tough-to-germinate lots (Fry et al., 1993). It's always a good idea to ask your supplier whether the seed has been pretreated for enhanced germination.

Surprise #4—After the honeymoon. You've successfully located your new grass seed, you've waded through the pricing and PLS statistics, and

Figure 4.1. One of the biggest shocks a person encounters when planting the unconventional turfgrasses, is their difficulty in establishment. In this low maintenance home lawn trial, a plot of redtop (*Agrostis gigantea*) establishes readily (lower left) compared to a plot of streambank wheatgrass (*Elymus lanceolatus*) (lower right). Idaho fescue (*Festuca idahoensis*) is also particularly slow to establish (top right). For some unconventional grasses, establishment may take one or two entire growing seasons. This photo is from the Idaho home lawn trial referenced in Chapter 2.

Picks and Pans of the Unconventional Grasses

Picks

Choosing grasses that hold promise for the future is never simple. For one thing, not every grass is adapted everywhere. So by recommending one particular grass as upcoming and desirable, someone in a distant zone may find it's anything but.

Secondly, not all grasses are suited to turf without human intervention. Take perennial ryegrass for example. The ryegrass that's found in nature is not exactly what you'd call a turfgrass. It's stemmy, bunchy, and fraught with stress and disease problems. Only after repeated cycles of plant breeding was perennial ryegrass developed into a grass capable of withstanding close-cut golf fairways. Raw ryegrass harvested directly from nature could never have survived fairway mowing. Any new unconventional species will require the same—perhaps five years of selection and breeding—before it can stand toe-to-toe with even a moderate turf variety.

With those disclaimers in mind, I will attempt to pick a few grasses that are "diamonds in the rough" for low maintenance turf. True, these grasses may not be ready for prime time, but they hold potential for development into desirable turfgrasses, just as perennial ryegrass was honed into a remarkable grass. Particular species that show potential for turf include: Curly mesquite (Ralowicz, 1991), *Panicum laxum*, serangoon grass (Beard, 1991), Australian weeping grass, seashore zoysiagrass (Murray, 1985), Idaho bentgrass, prairie junegrass, alpine bluegrass, crested dog's tail, orchardgrass, sweet vernal grass, tor grass (Wu and Harivandi, 1988), tufted hairgrass, and blue fescue.

Pans

There's no such thing as a *bad* grass. Every grass has its good and bad points. A grass will flourish as long as it's planted into the correct environment where it is well suited and happy.

Now let me remove my rose-colored glasses. Yes, there are widely used low maintenance grasses that are disappointing. These grasses are widely grown for a couple of reasons: (1) their seed is inexpensive and readily available, or (2) their name is permanently imprinted on the seeding specs of a number of organizations and government agencies.

"Many of our highway departments, fire rehabilitation agencies, agricultural universities, and soil conservation offices are still recommending these [undesirable] plants," says Craig Dremann of Redwood City Seed Company. Dremann laments the fact that better adapted grasses are not spec'ed in many plantings because of outdated recommendations. He has compiled a list of desirable and undesirable low maintenance grasses from his customers' experiences. His top-ten list of "not-wanted plants" can be found on the internet at *http://www.batnet.com/rwc-seed/grasses.html.* They include: "Blando" brome, crested wheatgrass, fountain grass, intermediate wheatgrass, orchardgrass, perennial ryegrass, red brome, smooth brome, tall oatgrass, yellow clover, and "Zorro" annual fescue.

you've planted your long-awaited low maintenance lawn. But what now comes out of the ground is not exactly what you expected.

Most unconventional grasses are not as attractive as bermudagrass or bluegrass. They're not nearly as dense or handsome. Some are coarse textured with broad, upright blades. And their color ranges from a dismal olive green to a disappointing yellow gray. But remember, these grasses have virtues *other* than color.

Mowing is often at the root of the problem (see the Appendix). Many of the unconventional grasses are notoriously intolerant of close mowing. Mowing tolerance is less of a concern if you're establishing an unmowed or infrequently mowed meadow turf. But if you intend to keep these grasses manicured as tight as bermudagrass or Kentucky bluegrass, you'd better choose only those ones listed with a favorable (✪) mowing rating.

Tall grasses, as you'd expect, adapt poorly to mowing. Shorter grasses fare much better. The 10-ft-tall wildrye listed here won't persist under frequent mowing. Eventually it'll thin out and disappear. Certain grasses are better suited to unmowed vista or meadow turf. Other times the easiest solution to mowing problems is to simply raise your height of cut.

Figure 4.2. Blue grama is a superior grass for drought tolerance and efficient use of water. Unfortunately under mowed turf conditions, blue grama, like so many of the unconventional grasses, can become overrun with other plants.

THE TROUBLE WITH MIRACLES

In Chapter 1, I told the tale of the Miracle Grasses of Canada, a collection of low growing, drought-loving grasses that were supposed to revolutionize turf management as we know it today. The Miracle Grasses promised the elimination of mowing, watering, and herbicides. But unfortunately these grasses never revolutionized anything. We're still mowing and tending turf pretty much the way it's always been done.

A handful of the grasses listed here in Chapter 4 are the exact same species as The Miracle Grass collection—they encompass the species of *Agropyron, Deschampsia, Festuca, Koeleria, Phleum, Poa,* and *Trisetum.* No, they're not the exact same *plants* brought forth by the eccentric Canadian professor. But seed of these species is regularly traded as a commodity in the land reclamation business. Over the years, they've been tentatively tested for lawns, often with mixed results.

The shortcomings of The Miracle Grasses serve as a lesson on how to adapt prairie, range, and reclamation grasses to lawn turf. I use them here to help illustrate several key points about using unconventional grasses for lawns. The mistake people often make with these grasses is to expect something unrealistic from them. If these grasses could single-handedly revolutionize lawn maintenance as we know it, they would have already done so. Their benefits should be examined with a level head.

Throw away your lawn mower?

You may have noticed that when left unmowed, all grasses grow to slightly different natural heights. Some grasses mature to a scant few inches tall; others tower overhead at 10 ft (3 m) or more (consult the *Unmowed Height* column in the Appendix for specific details). The shorter growing grasses hold the most promise for mowed turf. Some grasses are so tiny that they never even grow tall enough to touch a mower blade. These very tiny grasses can be adapted for use as a no-mow lawn (Sadasivaiah and Weijer, 1981). Unfortunately they also pose some drawbacks.

Dwarf grasses evolved in nature under stress. Stresses such as restricted rainfall or a brief growing season restricted these grasses to no more than a few inches tall. Taller grasses evolved where rainfall was abundant and the growing season long. For the most part, tall grasses need moisture and a long season to generate foliage several feet in the air. Grasses from the shortgrass prairie—where moisture is limiting—are naturally shorter than those from the higher precipitation tall grass prairie.

Alpine grasses are also basically dwarf. These unique grasses are suited to completing their life cycle as quickly as possible before cold temperatures return. They accomplish this feat by producing as little foliar topgrowth as possible.

It stands to reason that anything that's slow to grow will be slow to establish. These miniature grasses are usually tough to establish. Seed dormancy may be the culprit. In the wilds, seed dormancy postpones emergence until favorable conditions arrive. In turf, seed dormancy delays fill-in, allowing weeds to encroach. Short growing grasses can sometimes take months or even years to fully knit a turf.

Slow, miniature growth also translates into distinct problems with wear recovery. For if a grass is growing slowly, it will regrow scuff marks and divots so slowly that it may take a year or more to heal—too long for practical lawn or sports use. These grasses find their best application on untrafficked turf areas.

Throw away your weed killers?

Some plants secrete chemicals that alter the growth of nearby plants. This process of natural herbicides is called **allelopathy**. Quackgrass, a particularly nasty turf weed, has been found to secrete chemicals from its underground rootstocks, thereby impacting nearby plants. This makes quackgrass an even tougher competitor. Scientists have speculated that some unconventional grasses may possess allelopathy and have the ability to "self weed."

But research has shown that in turf, allelopathy plays a minor role at best. Though scientists have documented a case or two of turf allelopathy (Rice, 1984), the phenomenon remains more of a scientific curiosity than a replacement for herbicides (Brede, 1991a). It's really the vigorous vegetative growth of turfgrasses—not allelopathy—that drives weeds from a lawn.

Throw away your sprinkler?

Grasses differ drastically in their water needs. Choosing the right grass species can cut your watering by as much as 50%. But if you're expecting to grow turf in the desert without irrigation, forget it. At best, an unconventional grass can *reduce* watering but never eliminate it. Sometimes they reduce watering by going to sleep and turning dormant brown (Hook et al., 1992). Dormancy works well to conserve plant moisture, but it robs the turf of aesthetics.

Conclusions

I hope I haven't discouraged you from these unconventional lawngrasses. Each has something unique to offer. But none will eliminate all need for watering, fertilizing, mowing, and pesticides. Your best approach is to choose the maintenance operation you'd most like to reduce and then seek the grass that best fills your need. For example, if less watering is your goal, pick a drought tolerant, water-efficient grass. Don't try to find one grass that will solve all your problems.

OTHER JOBS FOR UNCONVENTIONAL GRASSES IN THE LANDSCAPE

The grasses in the Appendix serve a multitude of functions in the landscape other than just lawn. The definition of low maintenance turf is broad enough to encompass a whole host of possible applications. Here are some creative uses for unconventional grasses in the landscape (Booth, 1995):

Table 4.1. Unconventional grasses and grass-like plants that excel under special conditions.

• **Grasses for tropical climates (Zone 5)**	Boer lovegrass, buffel grass, California fescue, creeping bluegrass, creeping bluestem, curly mesquite, dallis grass, desert saltgrass, flaccid grass, giant bermudagrass, green sprangletop, inland saltgrass, Lehmann lovegrass, natal grass, palm grass, pangola grass, *Panicum laxum,* prickly couch grass, purple needlegrass, red grass, rhodes grass, saltmeadow cordgrass, seashore zoysiagrass, serangoon grass, signal grass, silver beardgrass, spike muhly, torpedo grass, wallaby grass, Wilman lovegrass
• **Drought tolerant grasses that can be mowed as lawn turf (less than 18 in. or 450 mm of annual precipitation)**	Arizona fescue, big bluegrass, blue grama, Boer lovegrass, bottlebrush squirreltail, buffel grass, bulbous bluegrass, Canby bluegrass, crested wheatgrass, curly mesquite, desert saltgrass, galleta, giant bermudagrass, green sprangletop, Idaho fescue, Indian ricegrass, Lehmann lovegrass, natal grass, Nuttal alkaligrass, prairie june grass, prairie sandreed, purple three awn, red grama, sand dropseed, Sandberg bluegrass, Siberian wheatgrass, sideoats grama, spike muhly, standard crested wheatgrass, streambank wheatgrass, timothy, Western wheatgrass, Wilman lovegrass
• **Mowable grasses for shady locations**	Alpine bluegrass, Arizona fescue, autumn moor grass, bear skin fescue, big bluegrass, big squirreltail, blue fescue, bluejoint reedgrass, bottlebrush squirreltail, broomsedge bluestem, bulbous bluegrass, California fescue, Canby bluegrass, common hairgrass, creeping foxtail, crested dog's-tail, crested hair grass, crested wheatgrass, deer tongue grass, forest bluegrass, foul bluegrass, green moor grass, hair fescue, Idaho bentgrass, Idaho fescue, Indian ricegrass, inland bluegrass, Lemmons alkaligrass, mat muhly, meadow fescue, meadow foxtail, moor grass, nimblewill, Nuttal alkaligrass, orchardgrass, *Panicum laxum,* pine bluegrass, polargrass, prairie june grass, Sandberg bluegrass, Siberian wheatgrass, signal grass, slender fescue, smooth brome, soft grass, squirrel's tail grass, standard crested wheatgrass, streambank wheatgrass, sweet vernal grass, sweetgrass, Texas bluegrass, ticklegrass, timothy, tor grass, tufted hairgrass, upland bluegrass, velvet grass, wallaby grass, weeping grass, Western fescue, Western wheatgrass
• **Short-growing grasses that may be maintained without mowing**	Alpine bluegrass, alpine hairgrass, amethyst blue fescue, annual bluegrass, bear skin fescue, blue fescue, blue hair grass, bottlebrush squirreltail, bulbous bluegrass, California barley, crested hair grass, curly mesquite, desert saltgrass, foxtail fescue, galleta grass, hair fescue, Idaho bentgrass, inland bluegrass, Lemmons alkaligrass, mat muhly, needle grama, nimblewill, polargrass, prickly couch grass, red grama, salt marsh grass, Sandberg bluegrass, seashore zoysiagrass, slender fescue, upland bluegrass, wallaby grass, Wallis fescue, weeping grass
• **Lower growing, mowable sedges and rushes for wetlands**	Big headed sedge, bird's foot sedge, black sedge, blue sedge, broad-leaved sedge, brown sedge, dwarf sedge, elk sedge, finger sedge, green sedge, hairy woodrush, inland sedge, low sedge, miniature sedge, mountain sedge, New Zealand hair, Pennsylvania sedge, purple woodrush, velebit sedge
• **Taller growing ornamental specimen and hedge grasses (4 ft or 1.2 m or taller)**	Bamboo muhly, basin wildrye, beardless wildrye, big bluestem, Eastern gamagrass, eulalia, flaccid grass, giant Chinese silver grass, indiangrass, mammoth wildrye, manna grass, palm grass, pampas grass, pheasant grass, plume grass, prairie cordgrass, purple pampas grass, sea oats, silver banner grass, switchgrass, tall wheatgrass, vetiver grass, vine reed
• **Annual grasses for quick cover or for use as a temporary or "nurse" grass**	American sloughgrass, annual bluegrass, big quaking grass, California brome, cloud grass, foxtail fescue, hare's tail, Italian ryegrass, Mediterranean grass, needle grama, red brome, rescue grass, soft chess

Wildlife habitat

Some of the taller growing grasses are valuable for providing shelter for wildlife. Wildlife areas, planted adjacent to manicured turf, provide an interesting and ever-changing backdrop. Many grasses produce grain-like seed that attract birds (USGA, 1994). Virtually any unmowed grass can serve as nesting material and shelter for wild birds and mammals. Don't overlook the traditional turfgrass species for this purpose either. Tall fescue—especially the newer, upright cultivars—produces colorful bunch plants with abundant seed when used in unmowed, naturalized wildlife areas.

Watershed protection

The U.S. Environmental Protection Agency reports that **nonpoint-source pollution** is now becoming an even greater pollution menace than point-source pollution (Wagner, 1994). Point-source polluters are those factories and businesses that dump waste and pollution into rivers and lakes through a discharge pipe. They're relatively easy to spot and regulate. The EPA has made great strides in identifying them and mitigating their discharge.

Nonpoint-source pollution is harder to detect and correct. It results from runoff and erosion of soil, fertilizers, pesticides, and other pollutants from agricultural, construction, and barren lands into adjacent waterways and wetlands. Dislodged soil particles ferry away fertilizers and pesticides.

Grasses—particularly the sod forming type—planted around streams and lakes can trap and retain runoff and pollutants. Grass berms and buffer strips reduce runoff to nearly zero (Baird, 1995) (see Chapters 9 and 12 for research details).

To serve as an effective waterside buffer, grasses must be able to withstand wet feet. Many grasses can do this but not all. Under perpetually wet soils, reeds and sedges may be a better choice (Catling et al., 1994) (Table 4.2).

Moisture-loving plants are particularly useful in wetland restoration and the creation of artificial wetlands. An increasing number of turf construction projects are now required by government regulators to create artificial wetlands as part of the project.

Roadside stabilization

Lady Bird Johnson's roadside beautification program of 1964 drew attention to the charm and function of America's roadsides. Low maintenance grasses have long played a critical role in roadside beautification (Huffine et al., 1982).

From an engineering standpoint, grasses serve a vital stabilization function (Huffine et al., 1974; Huffine et al., 1977). Imagine what would happen to all those pedestaled overpasses and underpasses if grass wasn't there to retain the soil.

Reclaiming disturbed, barren, and abandoned lands

The vital role of grass in land stabilization was illustrated by a 1960s ecological disaster: China during the reign of Mao Tse Tung learned what happens to a country devoid of grass. Mao ordered the Red Army to eradicate (hand-pull) grass from the landscape, to rid the countryside of what he saw as a Capitalist symbol. Millions of square miles of grassland were laid bare from eradication and overgrazing. These barren lands quickly turned to dust.

For the last three decades, Beijing has received a daily powdering of topsoil, eroded by wind from the barren Chinese countryside. The government first tried to quell the dust with an aggressive tree planting program. But in spite of planting millions of saplings, the daily blanketing continued.

Today, the Chinese government has reassessed their tree-planting policy and has embarked on an ambitious program to reseed barren lands to grass. They hope to finally stabilize and restore these shifting lands using grasses like the wheatgrasses (*Agropyron*) and others listed here.

Fire rehabilitation

Recent mega-fires in California, Wyoming, and Australia laid waste to vast regions of federal and private forest lands. Restoration of these fire-ravaged lands was essential to preventing mudslides and wind erosion later on. Locally adapted grasses were brought in and planted in a massive restoration effort.

Quick germinating grasses are critical to the function of fire rehabilitation, because they help stabilize the soil as rapidly as possible. A *mixture* of grasses is usually sown, combining quick germinating annuals with slower establishing perennials. This mixture helps knit the soil rapidly while eventually returning the land to more enduring perennials.

Ornamental value

Increasingly, grasses are being sought for their ornamental value. Grasses can function as a specimen plant, similar to a shrub or flower. They can add beauty to a flower or rock garden. They can be used in mass as a background screen or property-line hedge. Or they can be sown into large open spaces where a landowner wants reduced maintenance and enhanced beauty.

Pampasgrass, miscanthus, and perhaps blue fescue are the grasses that most readily come to mind when discussing ornamental grasses. However, there are literally *hundreds* of grasses with bona fide ornamental value. Even some of the traditional turf species hold ornamental potential. The fescues and bentgrasses have a particularly attractive seedhead when in flower.

Nearly all grasses flower. Flower colors range from yellowish green to deep red to purple, depending on species (Oakes, 1990). After flowering, seedheads generally remain in place, creating an interesting textural contrast with shrubs or flowers throughout the winter season (Steinegger et al., 1979). Some even have spikes that protrude through the snow (see comments in the species table).

By tradition, most ornamental grasses are vegetatively established, purchased in pots like flowers or nursery stock. But nearly all grasses set seed. Seed planting is a viable way of establishing ornamental grasses. Seeding is more cost-effective especially for larger areas.

But be aware that seed reproduction—as opposed to **cloning** (taking cuttings)—does not ensure a uniform appearance to the resulting plants. Any unusual color or leaf striping may be lost through seed propagation.

Upkeep of ornamental grass beds. Many people in search of a low maintenance alternative to lawns have tried ornamental grasses, only to find that beds of ornamental grass can sometimes be a maintenance nightmare. Often they require more care and maintenance than even a flower garden. Virgil Robinson, golf course superintendent at the PGA West in California planted 65 to 70 acres of ornamental grass beds on his golf course, thinking of course that it would reduce his maintenance. Instead, the beds ended up costing *more* maintenance than even his closely shaven fairways.

"Ornamental grasses were supposed to be less maintenance. But let me tell you, they are not," says Robinson (Cline, 1995).

Here's the problem: Grasses grow in clumps. As a clump matures it spreads outward. The older shoots in the center of the clump die out, leaving a brown, dead looking core.

Rejuvenation of ornamental grass beds is an annual affair. It involves mowing, chopping, or burning the plants in early spring to remove the dead tissue and reinvigorate the clumps. Nearly all ornamental grasses benefit from this practice.

Robinson had to rework his whole management and irrigation scheme to accommodate the grass beds before he was finally able to reduce maintenance. "We learned you cannot irrigate them with the same system that irrigates the grass. All you do is blow weed seeds into them and cause more problems. Drip irrigation had to be used," he says. Adjustments in fertilization and weed control were also required before the beds became truly low maintenance.

Even though grasses planted as clumps are attractive, the open spaces between plants invites weed invasion. Solid plantings—as opposed to spaced plantings—are one way to minimize weeds in ornamental grass beds. The grasses' natural competitive ability is tapped to fight the weeds. Solid plantings lack the attractive mounded appearance of spaced plants, but they require a whole lot less maintenance. Landscape managers who have tried this technique report that the beds can be kept virtually weed free using only a single yearly application of herbicide.

THE MAJOR GRASS FAMILIES

The Bentgrasses

The bentgrass (*Agrostis*) family is comprised of high and low maintenance members used for turf throughout the cool, temperate region of the world. Bentgrasses are cool-season, fine-textured, coastal grasses, many with a vigorous creeping habit. Because of their origins in damp regions of Europe (Zone 2), bentgrasses tend to be shallow rooted, lacking significant drought tolerance. Dryland, Highland, and Idaho bentgrass are notable exceptions, persisting on as little as 16 in. (400 mm) of rainfall per year. Several bentgrass species tolerate salt, heavy metals, or adverse soil pH.

American and European **agrostologists** (grass specialists) disagree over the classification of several of the bents (Hitchcock, 1951; Hubbard, 1984). Europeans call creeping bentgrass *A. stolonifera*, while Americans call it *A. palustris*. Redtop is *A. gigantea* in Europe and *A. alba* in America. Colonial and dryland bents are also under dispute. But the European system seems to be winning out. Therefore, I've listed the *Agrostis* grasses in the Appendix by their European-style Latin names.

The bentgrasses as a whole have a couple of prime attributes: They are shade tolerant and capable of withstanding close, regular mowing. Unmowed, most grow to heights of 1 to 3 ft (0.3 to 1 m). Their seedheads are airy, finely branched, and reddish purple when flowering. Bentgrasses are useful for creating a "Scottish links" landscape appearance, with rolling green mounds of soft, finely textured foliage. Their limitations are their moisture needs, disease susceptibility, and a tendency to get puffy with excessive vegetative growth.

Idaho bentgrass. Idaho bentgrass is a native bentgrass found throughout the western United States, from New Mexico to Fairbanks, Alaska. Botanically, it is distinct from creeping and colonial bentgrass. It is a species that has never before been used for turf—or for anything else, for that matter. Now Idaho bentgrass is set to make its turf debut.

Idaho bentgrass is a bunch-type bent, unlike other turf bents that creep with rhizomes and stolons. Although creeping runners help fill in bare spots, they also create the grain and false crowns in fine turf. The vertical mower was invented just to correct this deficiency in bentgrass. Idaho bentgrass, being a bunch-type bent, does not have this shortcoming.

The bunch habit allows it to be mixed with other turf species such as fine fescue, to create a sustainable links-appearance golf course or landscape. Mixtures of creeping bent with fine fescue, on the other hand, eventually become 100% bent in most locations as the aggressive bent stolons drive out the fescue.

I discovered the turf possibilities of Idaho bentgrass several years ago when one of my as-

The Controversy over Native vs. Exotic Grasses

Are native grasses really better than grasses introduced from abroad? Some people think so. Surprisingly few of our traditionally cultivated turfgrasses are native to North America. Most originated from Europe, Africa, or Asia.

Reed Barker, research geneticist at Oregon State University, makes a living studying introduced and native grasses. He summarized his thoughts on the subject at the 26th Grass Breeders Work Planning Conference in Logan, Utah (Anonymous, 1981).

"The word 'native' somehow stirs the inner feelings associated with motherhood and/or loyalty to country, while words like 'introduced' or 'naturalized' conjure feelings of invasion by exotics or abnormals," says Barker.

Attitudes toward this issue are highly polarized, with strong emotional sentiment toward native species over exotics. A common belief is that a native grass is somehow better than an introduced one.

Ray Brown, plant pathologist at the Forest Service's Intermountain Forest and Range Experiment Station in Logan, echoes Barkers thoughts (Anonymous, 1981). "Although species selection should ideally be linked to ecological principles, it is often tainted with human attributes such as relative 'goodness' or 'badness' that have little or no relationship to biological fact. Perhaps most unfortunate of all, many of these attitudes have influenced some recent revegetation guidelines and laws handed down by regulatory agencies and legislatures," says Brown.

Logical arguments exist on both sides of the issue:

Pro: Native grasses. For years wildlife biologists have criticized the practice of using introduced species because it threatens the loss of diversity in the local animal ecosystem. Wildlife populations depend on the balance of natural vegetation. Introduced species that dominate or supplant native grasses may shift wildlife populations.

Secondly, it is logical to assume that a species that evolved in a given locale has had eons of time to refine its ability to survive in that niche. One might theorize that a native plant would be far better adapted to grow in a particular spot than one that's been brought in from oceans away.

Some government regulators have taken this issue one step further by specifying that all plant materials used in construction of government projects must originate from native stands within 300 miles of a project (Booth, 1995; Harper-Lore, 1995). A recent memorandum by the President of the United States has mandated this policy on all new federal government installations.

Thirdly, proponents argue that introduced species may not have the necessary immunity to local insects and diseases. Native grasses, it is assumed, have had ample opportunity to evolve resistance schemes toward local pests. Introduced species may also possess such resistance by default, but they need to be screened first before they're planted.

Pro: Exotic grasses. Arguing in favor of introduced grasses is kind of like arguing in favor of child abuse. No one is in favor of using strictly introduced grasses. Most agriculturists believe in a balanced approach—considering the value of both native and introduced species. Here's their argument: In a given locale there might exist a few dozen native grass species. But around the world there are tens of thousands of species. Nature has had a much larger pallet to work the wonders of evolution and come up with fit grasses with unique qualifications. If we limit our search to grasses native within a few hundred miles of one location, we are really limiting our options.

Strikingly similar climatic regions occur throughout large regions of the world. For example, conditions in the American Rockies are similar to those of the Russian Steppes. Why not then use an introduced grass from a similar zone elsewhere?

Secondly, among grasses it's not clear what's really native and what isn't. Even after centuries of exploration and classification, scientists are still discovering plants in places they shouldn't be. Kevin Jensen, research geneticist at the USDA in Logan, recently found a wildrye plant in Asia that was thought to occur only in North America. As our knowledge of the world expands, the dividing line between what's native and what's not has become blurred.

Researchers believe that at one point in history, all of the world's continents were joined in a type of supercontinent. **Plate tectonics**, the movement of continents atop a sea of molten magma, relocated them into their present locations. That's how, it is believed, bermudagrass jumped from its birthplace in Africa to colonize South America.

Selection of grasses should be based on scientific merit, and not on merely where they originated. If an introduced grass is best suited to your application, proponents argue that you should use it.

"Distinctions between groups of species based on location alone, without concern for relative adaptability, are not warranted," says Brown.

sociates brought me what he though was a dwarf redtop plant. I later identified the specimen as *Agrostis idahoensis,* Idaho bentgrass.

My early work with the species showed that Idaho bent plants taken from the wilds had a turf quality potential only slightly better than that of redtop. It produced a stemmy turf with a distinctively brown summer color. But by selectively breeding over successive generations, turf performance jumped dramatically. First commercial seed of an improved Idaho bentgrass cultivar, "GolfStar," was released in 1999. GolfStar is America's first native bentgrass variety.

The Bluegrasses

The bluegrasses—or meadowgrasses as they're called in Europe—comprise an extensive family of cool-season, temperate-zone turfgrasses suited to high or low maintenance. Kentucky bluegrass, the best known of the *Poa* species, exhibits enormous diversity in growth habit, from small, dense, fine-leafed plants to upright forage types. Scientists speculate that *Poa*'s diversity may stem from its ability to "absorb" genes from other grasses. *Poa* species have been known to hybridize with each other and produce intergrade offspring.

Controversy exists among botanists in the classification of *Poas.* Studies in the U.S. Northwest have indicated that *P. secunda, P. glauca, P. ampla, P. canbyi* and possibly others, are virtually indistinguishable. Researchers have lumped them all into a single species: *P. secunda* (Campbell et al., 1956; Cronquist et al., 1977; Munshower, 1994; Spackeen, 1993). The lack of distinctive features may be a result of *Poa*'s lax genetics and tendency to swap genes.

Some *Poas* are so dwarf they can be used as unmowed lawn turf (Oakes, 1990). Alpine bluegrass (*P. alpina*) grows no taller than 3 to 6 in. (8 to 15 cm) and can be maintained *without a lawn mower* (Figure 4.3). Actually, you might need to mow it once or twice a year in early summer to nip off the seedheads. Other *Poas,* such as inland bluegrass (*P. interior*), annual bluegrass (*P. annua*), and supine bluegrass (*P. supina*), share this ability and can be maintained ankle deep without mowing (Lundell, 1994).

For the most part, *Poas* grow best in moist climates with timely rainfall. A few dryland species (*P. secunda,* etc.) can survive on as little as 10 in. (250 mm) of rain. However, these dryland *Poas* tolerate drought by entering a prolonged summer dormancy period. Growth resumes when moisture arrives and temperatures cool.

The Bluestems

The bluestems—or beardgrasses—are a group of warm-season bunchgrasses native to the prairies of North America and Asia (Spackeen, 1993; Wiesner and Brown, 1984). Recent botanical reclassification has split the bluestems into several genera, making things more complicated for the layman. It's tough enough to remember one Latin name, let alone an old one and a new one. Originally, most bluestems were classed as *Andropogon*—big bluestem (*A. gerardii*) and sand

Figure 4.3. Alpine bluegrass (*Poa alpina*) is one of the few grasses that can be grown at lawn height without the need for mowing. In its natural state, the leaves of alpine bluegrass grow only 3 in. (7.5 cm) tall. Seedheads, which appear in late spring, extend to about 6 in. (15 cm).

bluestem (*A. hallii*) still are. Caucasian, yellow, and silver bluestem were split off into the *Bothriochloa*, while little bluestem was moved to the *Schizachyrium*. The updated Latin names appear in the Appendix along with their former names for reference purposes.

The bluestems share some valuable attributes for low rainfall areas. These grasses are the classic grass of the tall-grass prairie (Campbell et al., 1956). They are unmatched for creating a natural-looking prairie landscape. The bluestems are winter dormant, yet possess remarkable cold tolerance for a warm-season grass. They are deeply rooted and universally drought tolerant.

As their name implies, bluestem/beardgrass has an appealing bluish-green leaf color and showy, whitish flower plumage. Ornamental cultivars have been bred with interesting steely foliage or colorful heads.

For the most part, the bluestems tolerate mowing fairly well, with the exception of a few taller growing species. Under mowing they perform best at a higher, 3- to 4-in. (7 to 10 cm) cut. Or they can be maintained unmowed for an interesting prairie appearance.

The bluestems become generally noncompetitive in the humid tropics, being crowded out by more aggressive plants. In high rainfall areas, foliar diseases limit their growth.

The Cordgrasses

The cordgrasses (*Spartina* spp.) are a family of taller-growing, tough, wiry, salt-loving seashore grasses. These cool-season grasses grow on salt flats where other grasses wither and die. Their strong creeping rhizomes are useful for knitting droughty or sandy soils. Cordgrass's main claim to fame is its use in restoration of disturbed coastal marsh flats. Cordgrass finds turf application on high salt and alkaline soils where less tolerant grasses won't persist.

The cordgrasses are not particularly attractive under mowed turf conditions, but they can be maintained with infrequent "brush-hog" clipping. Seed production is spotty and seed availability fluctuates from year to year. Vegetative reproduction (harvesting and sprigging of rhizomes) is an alternative planting method.

The Fescues

There are two basic groups of fescue grasses: The taller growing (3 to 6 ft [1–2 m]), coarse-leafed types characterized by tall (*F. arundinacea*) and meadow fescue (*F. pratensis*), and the shorter growing (1 to 2 ft [30 to 60 cm]), needle-leafed species, like sheep fescue (*F. ovina*) and hair fescue (*F. capillata*). Most fescues fall into one or the other of these two groups.

The fescue family comprises a broad range of drought tolerant, cool-season turfgrasses found from the arctic to the subtropics (White et al., 1993). Most of the species yield a good deal of seed, making seed prices reasonable and availability dependable. A notable exception is Idaho fescue (*F. idahoensis*), a valuable low maintenance grass that has been held back in popularity by its poor seed set (Figure 4.4).

Some fescues are cultivated for their ornamental value. Amethyst blue fescue (*F. amethystin*), bear skin fescue (*F. scoparia*), Maires fescue (*F. mairei*), and Wallis fescue (*F. valesiaca*) are used in ornamental plantings and are usually propagated vegetatively (Darke et al., 1994). Ornamental blue fescue cultivars such as "Elija Blue" are clonally propagated to retain their unique colors and tufted growth habit (Steinegger et al., 1979).

All fescues—even the ornamental ones—yield some seed, making seeding possible when supplies can be located. Some farmers specialize in supplying seed of unique grasses on demand. Given enough notice (and a favorable contract) they will grow seed of unusual species for special purposes.

Fountaingrass, Pampas Grass, and Miscanthus

The fountaingrasses (*Pennisetum* spp.) are among the world's best known ornamental grasses. Along with pampas grass (*Cortaderia*) and Eulalia (*Miscanthus*), they comprise most people's ideal of what an ornamental grass should be. These three genera of tall, plumey ornamentals have a lot in common. For one thing, there exists an enormous array of curious vegetative cultivars of each, with head colors from white to purple and unique vertical or hori-

Figure 4.4. Idaho fescue (*Festuca idahoensis*) is a fine-bladed fescue native to North America. Idaho fescue is similar in appearance to sheep fescue. It provides excellent long-term soil stabilization of highway slopes in arid regions, such as in the desert region of Washington State, shown here.

zontal leaf striping of white or yellow (Greenlee and Fell, 1992).

Seed of these grasses is regularly traded, but prices are usually high and quality low. Ornamental colors and textures do not reproduce through seed; vegetative cloning is needed to maintain the unique colors. Sometimes unique striped leaf patterns arise spontaneously from seed. If you're lucky enough to find one, you've discovered your own personal cultivar. Name it after yourself and start a business.

Fountaingrass, pampas grass, and Eulalia are warm-season grasses with minimal adaptation to the temperate zone (Zone 1 and 6). They are better suited to warmer climates and are particularly dependable in Mediterranean or coastal areas with mild winters, where they can grow unencumbered in terms of height and plumage. They are generally intolerant of mowing (regular mowing defeats the purpose of having a large, plumey ornamental grass, as you might expect), but are revitalized by an annual clip at the beginning of the growing season to force new shoots. These large bunchgrasses can be grown in attractive meadow plantings, mixed with other low maintenance grasses planted by seed. The combination of heights, colors, and textures creates an exciting backdrop.

The Lovegrasses

The lovegrasses (*Eragrostis* spp.) are a huge clan of moderately low growing, drought tolerant, warm-season prairie grasses native to North America and nearly everywhere else (Archer and Sellers, 1956; Spackeen, 1993; Stubbendieck et al., 1991; Troeh et al., 1991). The lovegrasses are the ideal Zone 3 grass. In colder climates lovegrasses winter-kill. In the tropics, they persist but turn into a maintenance nightmare; the jungle vegetation literally overruns them. The lovegrasses are most competitive under dryland conditions (20 to 30 in. [50–75 cm] annual rainfall), with or without supplemental irrigation.

Weeping lovegrass (*E. curvula*)—and many other lovegrass species—are valued for their wispy, cascading, waterfall appearance on slopes. They tolerate poor soil with no added fertility or irrigation. Mowing is no problem as long as the height is above 4 in. (10 cm).

Seeds are small but germination is remarkably fast and reliable. Weeping lovegrass has become a mainstay of roadside and golf course slopes throughout the warm-temperate zone and, if anything, has been a bit overused. Other grasses in the lovegrass family can be used in lieu of weeping lovegrass for an interesting contrast.

The Needlegrasses

The needlegrasses get their name from the long, curious, needle-like awns protruding from their seedheads. Depending upon the species, these needles can be up to several inches long. The needlegrasses belong to the cool-season *Stipa* genus and are medium-tall, desert bunchgrasses, with excellent drought hardiness and an attractive slender appearance. Green needlegrass, a cold-loving cousin, was recently reclassified from *Stipa* to the *Nassella* genus. Green, Columbia, and Letterman needlegrass have the most coldhardiness of the needlegrasses. Others are better adapted for the transition zone (Zones 3 and 4).

The needlegrasses are prized for their unmowed, ornamental appeal in meadow mixtures with other drought tolerant, medium-tall prairie grasses. They tolerant infrequent mowing and should not be clipped below 4 in. (10 cm).

"Mandan" is a natural interspecific hybrid between *Stipa* and drought-hardy Indian ricegrass (*Oryzopsis hymenoides*), with characteristics most similar to the latter. It is useful as a conservation grass in semiarid areas (Alderson and Sharp, 1994).

Sedges, Rushes, and Reeds

Normally, turf specialists shy away from the sedges, rushes, and reeds. Or we treat them like weeds and dream up ways to eradicate them. The color and appearance of sedges, rushes, and reeds when mowed is similar to grass. But in premium turf their presence can be disruptive, so they are usually killed with selective herbicides.

Fortunately under low maintenance, anything goes. Grasses (with a few exceptions) cannot tolerate perpetual wet feet or standing water. And as more construction projects include wetland restorations, these grass-like plants are finding increasing value. Many states and municipalities now have laws mandating the conservation of wetland areas during landscape construction. These grass alternatives are being used along stream banks to stabilize the soil and prevent runoff. They can be sown directly into damp, marshy, and even submerged areas for soil stabilization.

A surprising number of the sedges, rushes, and reeds have bona fide ornamental value, with interesting, often twisting foliage bearing colors from deep green to blue to bright orange. A number of sedge (*Carex*) species are also tolerant of mowing and can persist when clipped as close as 1 in. (2.5 cm) (Catling et al., 1994).

The principal shortcoming of the sedges, rushes, and reeds is that they can become invasive—some more than others. Particularly aggressive species are noted in Table 4.2. These species should be used with caution, as they may escape and become serious turf or waterway weeds. However, aggressiveness can also be an asset when it comes to revegetating particularly tough sites (Figure 4.5).

The Gramas

One of the more important groups of drought-hardy, warm-season prairie grasses is the gramas (*Bouteloua* spp.). The gramas are native North American prairiegrasses that can persist in deserts with as little as 9 to 12 in. (225 to 300 mm) of rain. This amount of rainfall is near the practical limit for the growth of *any* grass species. Below this level of rainfall only waxy-leafed desert shrubs and cacti can persist. Unlike grass, however, shrubs and cacti don't contribute to knitting the soil and preventing erosion. That's why gramas are such crucial dryland plants.

Blue grama (*B. gracilis*) is the most popular of the gramas for turf. Its creeping, bunch-type growth habit produces a moderately dense sod when mowed at 2 to 4 in. (5 to 10 cm). It can be mixed with other low maintenance grasses such as buffalograss and wheatgrass to add diversity. However, from what I've seen, grama adds little to buffalograss from a turf standpoint. Buffalograss is better used alone.

The gramas are not competitive in high rainfall areas or under irrigation. Under these conditions grama segregates into unappealing clumps of hairy, blue turf (Figure 4.2). A breeding program at Colorado State University is developing improved turf-type blue gramas with higher density and better mowing tolerance. Adding turf credentials to this already drought-hardy grass will bring a valuable new commodity to low maintenance turf.

The Wildryes

The wildrye grasses, like the wheatgrasses, have endured a major reorganization in recent years. Originally the wildryes were classed among the *Elymus* species. Now they have been split among

Table 4.2. Sedges, reeds, and rushes with adaptation for wetland turf use. Some of the plants listed here are tolerant of mowing and can be planted on seasonally wet or submerged turf sites. The taller species listed here find application for ornamental purposes or restoration of disturbed wetlands. The column on the right, marked "*Seed?*," designates whether seed is available for sale (* = yes).

Latin Name	Common Name	Seed?
Sedges with a growth height of 2 ft (0.6 m) or less		
Carex bebbii Olney	Beautiful sedge	*
C. brunnea Thunb.	Sedge	
C. buchananii C.B. Clarke	Leatherleaf sedge	
C. comans Bergg.	New Zealand hair sedge	
C. communis L.H. Bailey	Sedge	
C. conica F. Boott	Miniature sedge	
C. crinita Lam. var crinita	Caterpillar sedge	*
C. digitata L.	Finger sedge	
C. eleocharis Bailey	Low sedge	
C. *firma* Host.	Dwarf sedge	
C. flacca Schreber non Carey ex Boon.	Blue sedge	
C. flagellifera Colenso.	Weeping brown New Zealand sedge	
C. flava L.	Yellow sedge	
C. geyeri Boott	Elk sedge	
C. gracilis Mack.	Graceful sedge	
C. grayi Carey	Gray's sedge	
C. humilis Leysser	Velebit sedge	
C. interior L.H. Bailey	Inland sedge	
C. macrocephala Willd.	Big headed sedge	*
C. morrowii F. Boott	Japanese sedge	
C. nigra (L.) Reichard	Black sedge	
C. ornithopoda Willd.	Bird's foot sedge	
C. pensylvanica Lam.	Pennsylvania sedge	
C. petriei Cheesem.	Brown sedge	
C. phyllocephala T. Koyama	Sedge	
C. plantaginea Lam.	Wide leaf sedge	
C. podocarpa R. Brown	Mountain sedge	
C. siderosticha Hance.	Broad-leaved sedge	
C. stricta Lam.	Tussock sedge	*
C. sylvatica Hudson	Forest sedge	
C. tumuicola Mack.	Berkeley sedge	
C. viridula Michx.	Green sedge	
C. vulpinoidea Michx.	Fox sedge	*
Sedges with a growth height of greater than 2 ft (0.6 m)		
C. aquatilis Wahlenb.	Water sedge	*
C. bicknellii Britt.	Bicknell's sedge	*
C. comosa Boott.	Bristly sedge	*
C. elata All.	Golden sedge	
C. hystricina Muhl.	Bottlebrush sedge	*
C. intumescens Rudge	Bladder sedge	*
C. lacustris Willd.	Lake sedge	*
C. lupuliformis Sartwell	Hoplike sedge	
C. lupulina Muhl. ex Willd.	Hop sedge	*
C. lurida Wahl.	Bottlebrush sedge	
C. muskingumensis Schwein.	Palm beach sedge	
C. nebraskensis Dewey	Nebraska sedge	*
C. obnupta L.H. Bailey	Slough sedge	*
C. pendula Hudson	Weeping sedge	

Table 4.2. Sedges, reeds, and rushes with adaptation for wetland turf use. Some of the plants listed here are tolerant of mowing and can be planted on seasonally wet or submerged turf sites. The taller species listed here find application for ornamental purposes or restoration of disturbed wetlands. The column on the right, marked *"Seed?,"* designates whether seed is available for sale (* = yes) (continued).

Latin Name	Common Name	Seed?
Sedges with a growth height of greater than 2 ft (0.6 m) (continued)		
C. polysticha Bockeler	Cyperus-like sedge	
C. retrorsa Schwein.	Retrorsa sedge	
C. rostrata Stokes	Beaked sedge	*
C. scoparia Schkuhr. ex Willd.	Pointed broom sedge	*
C. stipata Muhl.	Sawbeak sedge	*
C. tuckermanii Boott ex Dewey	Tuckerman's sedge	
C. vesicaria L.	Inflated sedge	*
Rushes and reeds with a growth height of 2 ft. (0.6 m) or less		
Juncus alpinoarticulatus Chaix	Northern rush	
Juncus balticus Willd.	Baltic rush	*
Juncus ensifolius Wiks.	Swordleaf rush	
Juncus tenuis Willd.	Slender rush	*
Luzula elegans Lowe	Purple woodrush	
Luzula nivea (L.) DC	Snowy woodrush	
Luzula pilosa (L.) Willd.	Hairy woodrush	
Luzula sylvatica (Huds.) Gaud.	Greater woodrush	
Scirpus cernuus Vahl.	Fiber optics grass	
Typha minima Funck	Japanese cattail	
Rushes and reeds with a growth height of greater than 2 ft (0.6 m)		
Arundo donax L.	Giant reed	*
Eleocharis palustris (L.) Roem. & Schult.	Spike rush	*
Gynerium sagittatum (aubl.) Beauv.	Pink uva grass	
Juncus effusus L.	Soft rush	*
Juncus torreyi Cov.	Torrey's rush	*
Junicus inflexus L.	Blue rush	
Phragmites australis (Cav.) trin. ex Steud.	Common reed	*
Scirpus acutus Muhl.	Hardstem bulrush	*
Scirpus atrovirens Willd.	Dark green rush	*
Scirpus cyperinus (L.) Kunth	Wool grass	*
Scirpus fluviatilis (Torr.) Gray	River bulrush	
Scirpus maritimus L.	Alkali bulrush	*
Scirpus microcarpus Presl.	Small-fruited bulrush	*
Scripus tabernaemontani C.C. Gmel.	Soft stem bulrush	*
Typha angustifolia L.	Narrow-leaf cattail	*
Typha latifolia L.	Common cattail	*

the *Psathyrostachys, Elymus,* and *Leymus*. This reclassification has not yet found its way into many seed catalogs and extension bulletins (Anonymous, 1993f). Thus, you may need to specify wildryes by their former as well as present Latin names, to make certain you're getting the grass you want.

The wildryes are mostly tall-growing (3 to 9 ft [1–3 m]), perennial, cool-season grasses, useful for forage, rangeland, and ornamental purposes throughout the temperate region. They represent a valuable source of graze and seed for wildlife. Wildryes are prized for their upright, arching leaves and often striking blue color, as well as their ability to withstand extremes in salinity, cold, and drought (rainfall to 15 in. [370 mm]). They adapt poorly to mowing and should rarely be cut below 6 in. (15 cm). They are useful in the

Figure 4.5. Tiannamen Square, Beijing, China—one of the most notorious patches of turf in the world. This small swatch of green on the expansive concrete square is under constant guard, because it houses the focal point of the square, the nation's flag. The turf was originally planted to Kentucky bluegrass many years ago, but because the site alternates from bone dry to flooded, the Chinese government overseeded it with sedge (*Carex*). The sedge is maintained as mowed turf, and from all practical standpoints, it is indistinguishable from a normal lawn.

landscape to provide a simulated tall-grass-prairie look, or as a hedge or background planting.

The most prominent of the North American wildryes are Great Basin wildrye (*L. cinereus*), blue wildrye (*E. glaucus*), and Canada wildrye (*E. canadensis*). Russian wildrye (*P. juncea*), Altai wildrye (*L. angustus*), and Dahurian wildrye (*E. dahuricus*) are wildryes introduced from Eastern Russia.

The major drawback of the wildryes is their meager seed yield, slow seed germination rate, and tendency toward **seed shattering** (dropping seed at harvest). As you can imagine, seed prices are generally high. Canada wildrye is the one exception. It yields ample quantities of quality seed without shattering (Berdahl and Baker, 1980). Still, time required from establishment to full-height maturity can take two or more years.

The Wheatgrasses

For many people, the wheatgrasses—perhaps more than any other grass—are the grasses that come to mind when discussing low maintenance turf. The wheatgrasses are a ubiquitous group of low-input, cool-season prairiegrasses used throughout much of the semiarid temperate world. The wheatgrass family is comprised of 100 Eurasian species and 22 to 30 North American species. They are a fractured clan of grasses all distantly related to cultivated wheat grain (Asay and Jensen, 1996). This connection to wheat has led contemporary wheat breeders to the wheatgrasses in hopes of creating interspecies crosses. Their goal is to develop the elusive **perennial wheat**. Currently, cereal wheat is an annual crop that has to be resown each year. Perennial wheat, if developed, could be planted once and would yield grain each summer without repeated tillage and resowing.

Originally plant taxonomists lumped all the wheatgrasses together under the collective genus of *Agropyron*. But recent work at Utah State University (Asay and Jensen, 1996) has regrouped these grasses into other genera. Only crested wheatgrass has remained among the *Agropyron*.

While this reclassification of species may be botanically correct, it has created confusion in the marketplace. Some wheatgrasses were switched to *Pascopyrum*, others to *Thinopyrum*, and a few to the new *Pseudoroegneria* genera. This reclassification was not merely a Latin name change. No, it went so far as to take *varieties of the same species* and split them into distinctly separate species. As a result, you'll find confused buyers and sellers clinging to the old Latin names in their business transactions. Both the old and new Latin names are used almost interchangeably in seed catalogs. The most current Latin names appear in the Appendix, along with their older synonyms.

Crested wheatgrass. Crested wheatgrass, the most turfworthy member of the wheatgrass clan, is native to the Steppe region of Russia. It was introduced into North America in 1892 and 1906 by early plant explorers (Asay and Jensen, 1996). Crested wheatgrass is well suited to the semiarid climate of the Great Plains and has become one of its prime rangegrasses (Figure 4.6).

Crested wheatgrass has even been credited with salvaging America from one of its worst ecological disasters. During the Depression era, vast areas of prairie land were laid waste by overtillage, drought, and wind erosion. The resulting dust bowl of the 1930s drove many early settlers from their homes as farms and fields turned to powder. These ravaged areas were later reclaimed by planting wheatgrass to stabilize the blowing soil.

"Fairway" was the first cultivated variety of crested wheatgrass, released from the University of Saskatchewan in 1927 (Asay and Jensen, 1996). Fairway found use in a number of turf applications, including roadside, lawn, park, and even a few golf fairway plantings. It is persistent and competitive against weeds, as long as the cutting height is not too short and it's not given too much irrigation. Wheatgrass—like many prairiegrasses—loses its competitive edge against weeds when supplied with too much irrigation.

Steady supplies of relatively inexpensive crested wheatgrass seed have launched this species into a number of mowed and unmowed turf applications. Detractors argue that crested wheatgrass is overused, and that other grasses would be better suited. They lament that wheatgrass is used in solid plantings rather than in mixed stands, limiting the genetic diversity of the turf. They cite the fact that crested wheatgrass is an introduced grass, not one native to North America.

Yet in spite of its criticism, the value of crested wheatgrass is unmistakable. Crested wheatgrass's water-use efficiency, relatively good mowing tolerance, resistance to salinity, and ability to crowd out noxious weeds has made it a valuable lawn and conservation grass for the drier, cooler parts of the world.

Other wheatgrasses. Tall wheatgrass, as its name implies, is a taller growing member of the wheatgrass clan, used mainly for ornamental plantings, soil stabilization, vista turf, and as a wind or snow break. Its natural bluish-green color intensifies as it undergoes drought or alkaline stress. Its main point of interest is its tremendous salt tolerance—few grasses can rival the tolerance of tall wheatgrass to salty soils. Seeds of tall wheatgrass are large and plump, and they germinate well to produce a stand relatively quickly. Its main downside is its coarse, vertical growth and tendency to vanish if mowed too close or too often. Eight inches (20 cm) is its lowest practical cutting height.

Bluebunch and beardless are two wheatgrasses that have now been classified into "varieties" of the same species. Bluebunch wheatgrass has awns or whiskers attached to its seed, while beardless does not. These are not "varieties" in the usual sense, but **botanical varieties**. They're

Figure 4.6. Crested wheatgrass breeding at Utah State University in Logan. Breeders with the USDA there have developed a variety of crested wheatgrass with strong rhizomes, named "Road Crest," to improve its turf knitting. Normal crested wheatgrass has little or no rhizome activity. Crested wheatgrass is one of the premier low maintenance lawngrasses throughout the semiarid region.

different enough to see a visible difference between them but close enough that they'll intercross in the field. The ability to intercross is the criterion botanists use to judge whether two species are different or not.

Bluebunch wheatgrass has a whitish-green, upright foliage with a unique spiky seedhead with twisted whiskers. Seed spikes are slender and 3 to 6 in. (8 to 15 cm) long. Beardless wheatgrass looks similar to bluebunch but minus the twisted whiskers. Bluebunch and beardless wheatgrasses are used primarily for their ornamental and vista value, since they are readily thinned by repeated close mowing. Left unmowed, though, they can form a dense stand in most areas with no supplemental irrigation.

Streambank, western, slender, bluebunch, and beardless wheatgrass are the only wheatgrasses native to North America. All other wheatgrass species have been introduced from abroad, most often from northern Asia.

Western wheatgrass is a tough, rhizomatous native grass. Though it offers the advantage of native adaptation, it has serious limitations compared to other wheatgrasses. Western wheatgrass is an inferior seed producer. When it does yield seed, the seeds have a problem with dormancy and poor seedling vigor (Asay and Jensen, 1996). Then as it grows, it becomes coarse and stemmy through summer. Its water-use efficiency is also substantially below other native prairie grasses.

Western wheatgrass does have a few saving graces: It tolerates alkali and salty soils better than any other native wheatgrass (Asay and Jensen, 1996). It also withstands continuous mowing better than many prairiegrasses, often dominating mixed stands when mowed.

Future prospects. To date, breeding of the wheatgrasses has focused on increasing their forage yield. This of course is counterproductive to their turf applications. Only Fairway crested wheatgrass was selected specifically for its lower, more turfy growth.

The wheatgrasses hold potential for development into turf-type varieties through selective breeding. Recent efforts at universities in Colorado and Utah hold the promise for attractive, water efficient, sod-forming turfgrasses from this family of rugged, arid rangegrasses.

Chapter 5

Choosing the Best Grass for Your Location

One question I'm asked a lot is, "What's the best grass for me to plant in my location?" And I can understand why. Contemporary turf textbooks offer little or no practical guidance for placing the right grass in the right location, which seems strange considering grass selection is at the cornerstone of Integrated Pest Management. At best, textbooks provide lip-service, instructing you to plant warm-season grasses in areas that are warm and cool-season grasses where it's cool. Other than that, you're on your own. Some even direct you to your local county extension agent for advice.

As a result, seed companies have been filling the void with their own brochures describing where grasses grow worldwide (Anonymous, 1993f; Anonymous, 1995c; Brede, 1993b; Schaff, 1994). Some brochures slice the globe into as many as 23 distinct zones of turf adaptation. But if you read the fine print, you realize that the same varieties are being recommended in 15 of those 23 zones. What's the point of having 23?

Instead, I've used the KISS (keep it simple, stupid) method for determining zones, dividing the world into six basic growing regions for turfgrasses (Figure 5.1). Why 6 and not 23? Turfgrasses have a broad range of adaptation, often spanning several USDA-plant zones in a single bound. Not only that, but fewer zones means easier interpretation.

How the zones were determined. Temperature dictates turf adaptation more than any other factor. If it's too cold, certain grasses won't survive—likewise, if it's too hot.

Irrigation is the great equalizer when it comes to zones. In arid areas, it is assumed some irrigation will be used for turf culture. If you don't plan to irrigate at all, there are unconventional turf species (Chapter 4) that can be grown without irrigation. It's unlikely that the traditional turf species will persist as unirrigated lawns in areas with less than 20 in. (500 mm) of annual rainfall.

CHOOSING THE RIGHT GRASS

Step by Step

Below, I've presented a basic four-step plan for selecting the best grasses for your site. It starts by pinpointing your turf zone on the world map, exploring possible grassing options, examining your local microclimate, and finally, picking the best varieties. The charts and sidebars in this chapter will guide you along the selection process.

Step #1—Locate your zone

I've divided the world into six turf adaptation zones, from the very cold to the very warm. Within this range of climates, there are grasses to fill just about any requirement. The first step in selecting the right grass for your site is to identify your zone in Figure 5.1.

Zone 1—Cool temperate. Much of the northern United States, Europe, and Asia fall into Zone 1. This zone enjoys a temperate, continental climate. Summers are typically warm, and temperatures over 100°F (38°C) are the exception. Winters can be long and cold, limiting the adaptation of warm-season grasses to only the most winter-hardy ones. Precipitation throughout the zone varies from about 8 to over 40 in. (200 to 1000 mm). Irrigation is practiced in the drier parts of this zone to minimize summer dor-

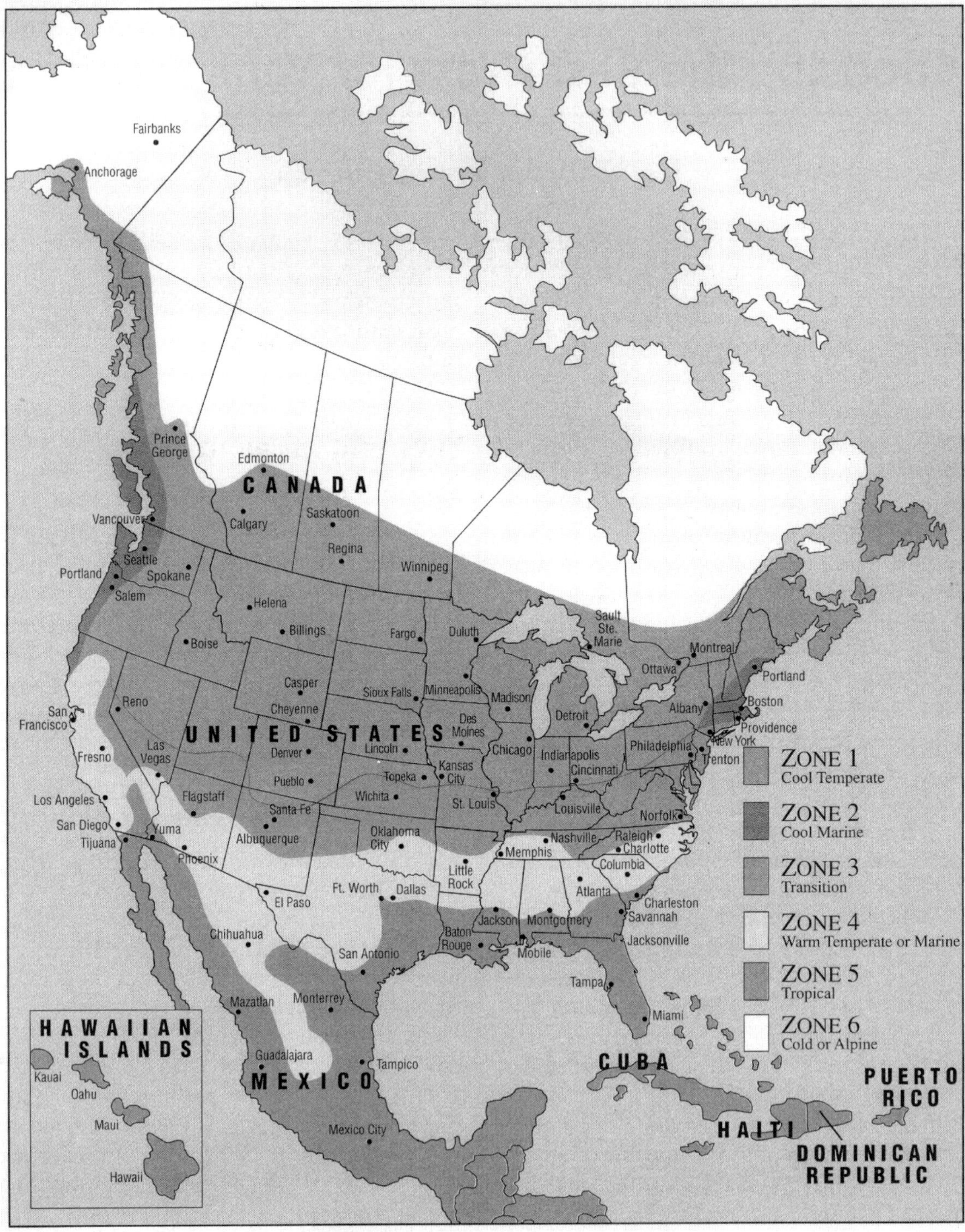

Figure 5.1. Zone maps of the world. To use the maps, locate your site on the chart, noting the color of the surrounding area. The color designates the zone of adaptation. The zone number can then be used in charts and tables in this chapter to determine your best adapted grasses.

CENTRAL AND SOUTH AMERICA

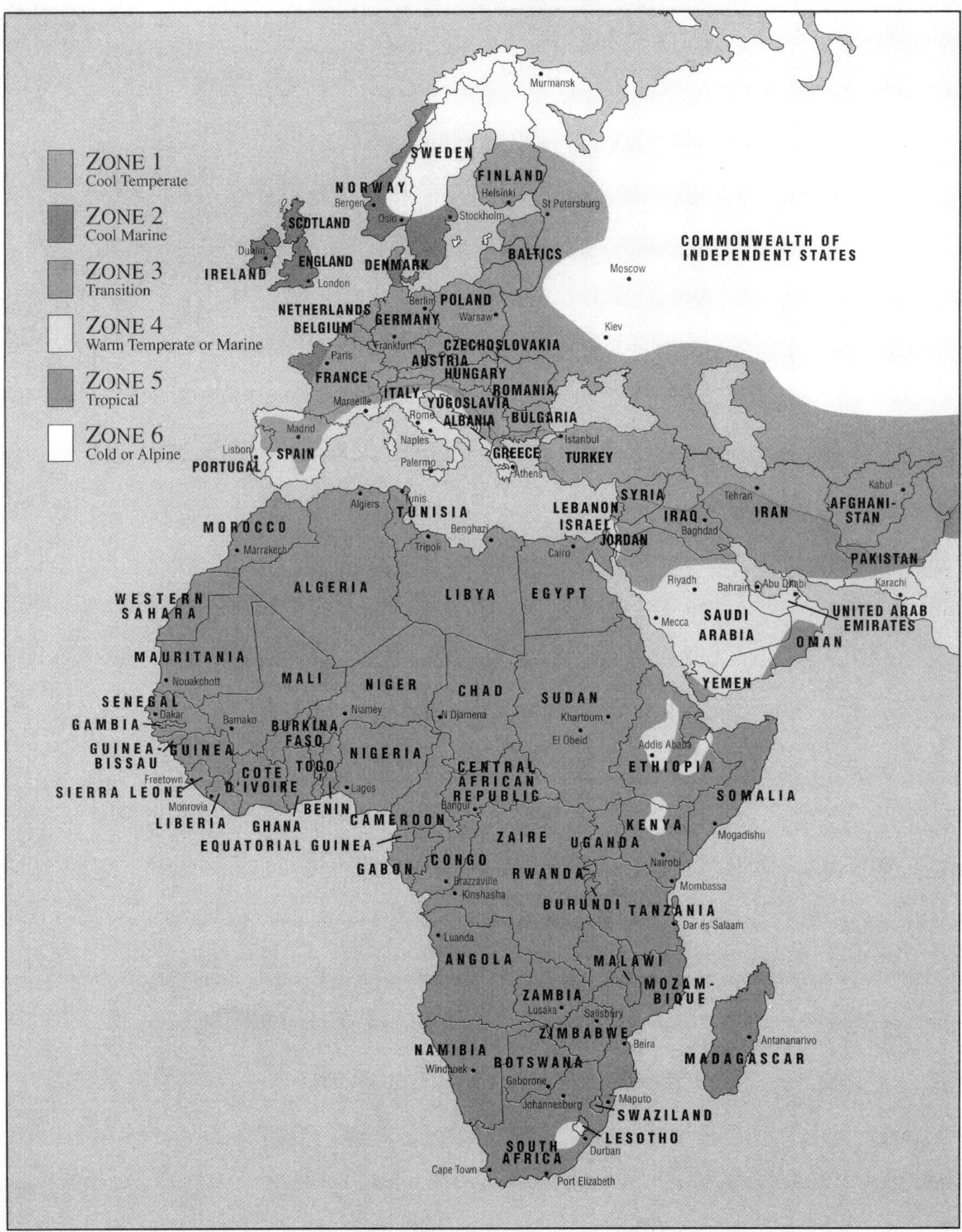

Figure 5.1. Zone maps of the world. To use the maps, locate your site on the chart, noting the color of the surrounding area. The color designates the zone of adaptation. The zone number can then be used in charts and tables in this chapter to determine your best adapted grasses (continued).

PACIFIC RIM AND FAR EAST ASIA

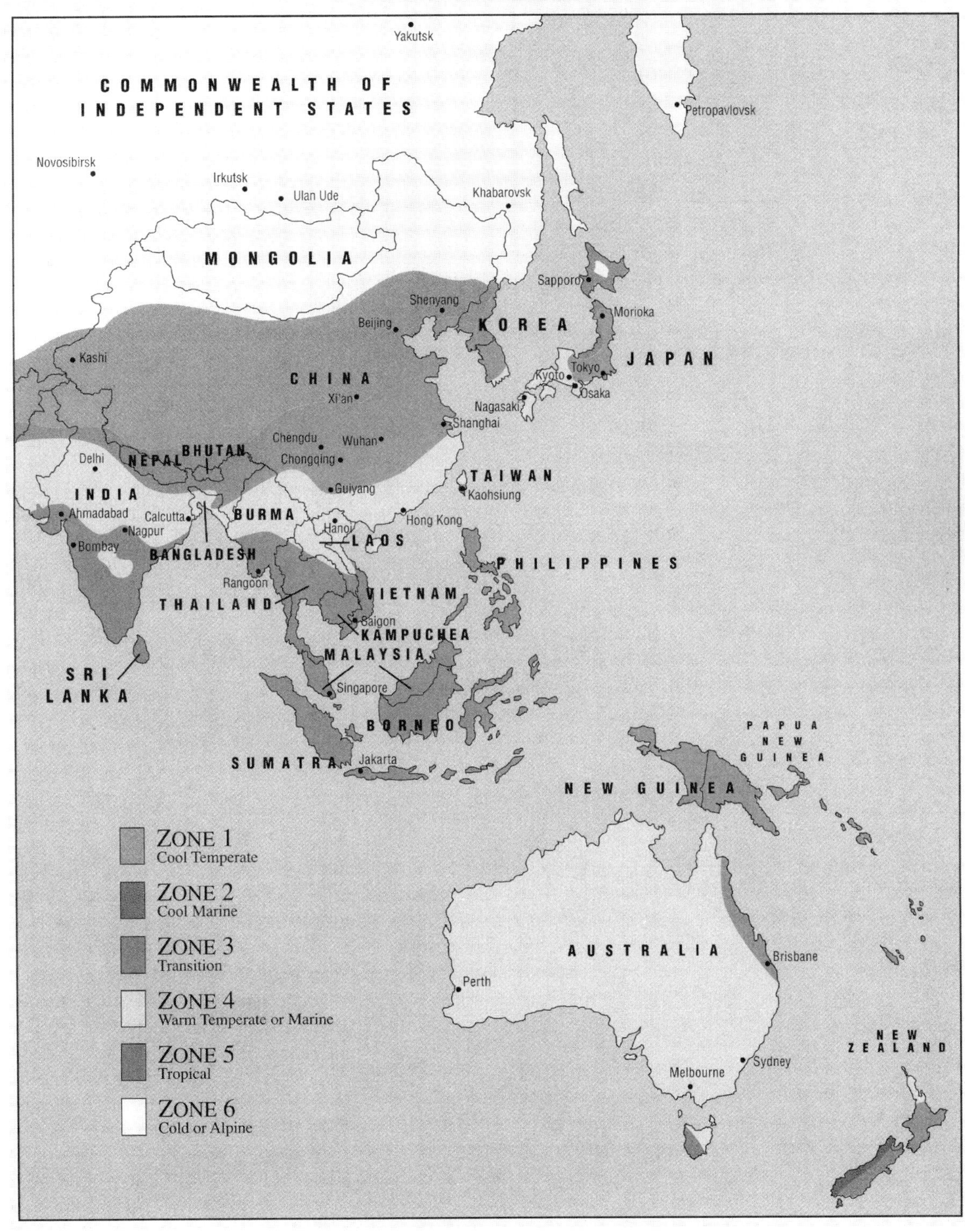

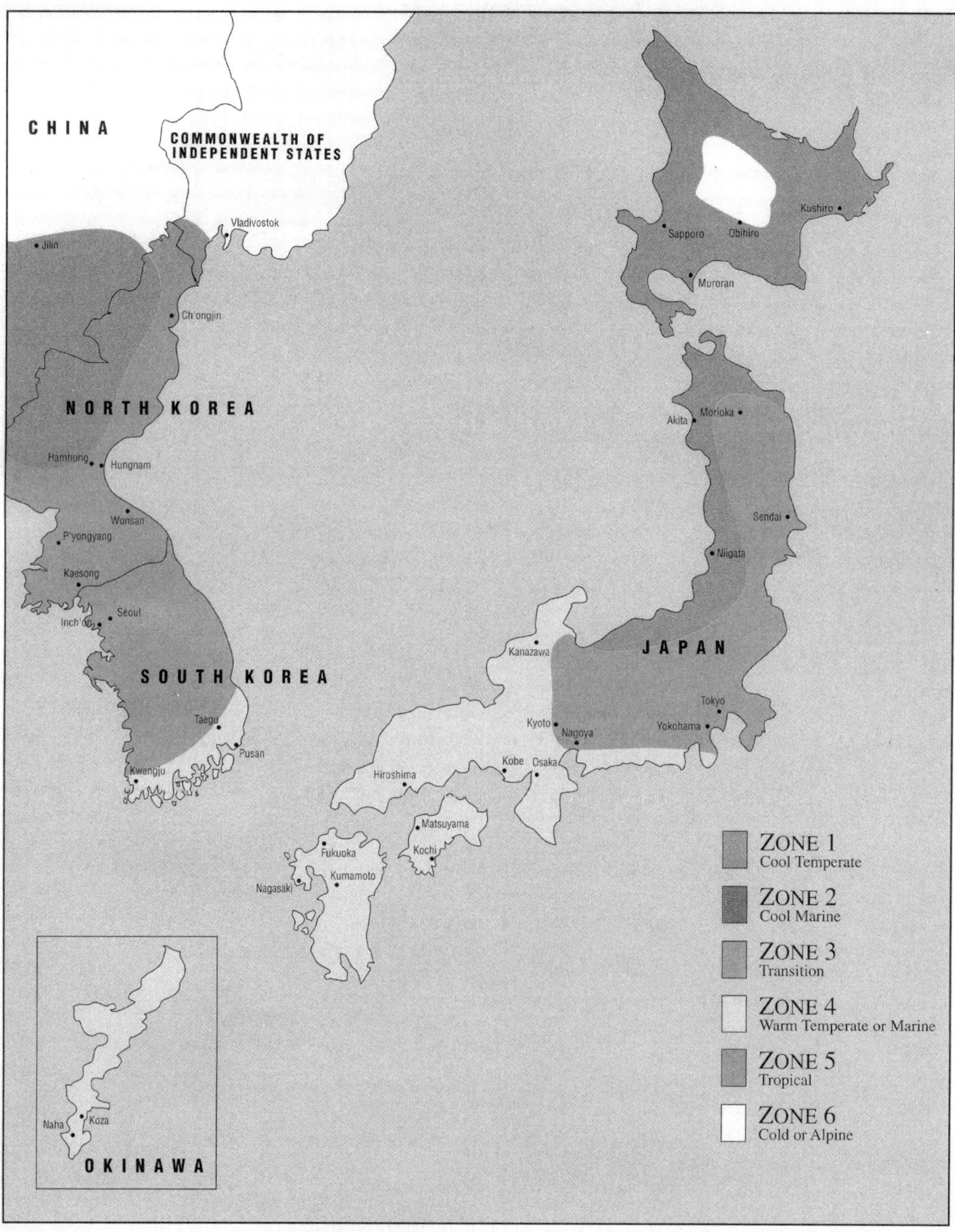

Figure 5.1. Zone maps of the world. To use the maps, locate your site on the chart, noting the color of the surrounding area. The color designates the zone of adaptation. The zone number can then be used in charts and tables in this chapter to determine your best adapted grasses (continued).

mancy. Cool-season grasses are best adapted to Zone 1, although zoysia (a warm-season grass) can also be reliably grown.

Zone 2—Cool marine. For the most part, temperatures in Zone 2 differ little from Zone 1. What makes Zone 2's climate—and choice of grasses—unique is its prominent ocean influence. Summers may be warm, but winters in Zone 2 are generally milder than Zone 1, often with rain instead of snow. Rain tends to precipitate in small increments, rather than in a few pounding thundershowers, making growing conditions ideal for shallow rooted grasses like *Poa annua* (annual bluegrass). Annual bluegrass dominates close-cut golf turf, easily outcompeting bentgrass. Perennial ryegrass and fine fescue fare far better in this zone than Kentucky bluegrass and tall fescue. Many warm-season grasses persist in this zone but tend to languish from lack of heat.

Zone 3—Transition. The **Transition Zone** is so named because it represents the transition from cool- to warm-season grasses. Neither group flourishes in this region. Warm-season grasses are damaged by the chilly winters of the continental climate. Cool-season grasses suffer the sweltering summers. Summer annual grassy weeds often predominate, because these opportunistic warm-season weeds can sit out the cold winters as seed.

Bermudagrass and zoysia hold up best in this zone, provided you use cold-tolerant varieties. Tall fescue fills the bill for the best all-around, cool-season grass for lawns, particularly in the shade.

Zone 4—Warm temperate or marine. Zone 4 spans both the warm marine and warm continental regions. There was no need to split Zone 4 into separate marine and continental zones, because the same grasses adapt to both. Zone 4 is prime bermudagrass territory. Tall fescue is used to a limited extent here, mostly in the shade. Zone 4 winters distress St. Augustinegrass and other tropical grasses. In the more arid part of Zone 4, cool-season grasses flourish, but at the expense of a lot of irrigation. Warm-season grasses are usually a better choice because of their efficient water use.

Zone 5—Tropical. Tropical grasses possess little if any cold tolerance. The little cold tolerance they do have can be attributed to the fact that the growing point of grass is naturally tucked below ground, providing some shelter from the cold. This negligible amount of cold tolerance allows tropical grasses to be stretched into subtropical locales like Orlando or Phoenix where winter frosts occur. But tropical grasses can't endure freezing temperatures for long without stand loss.

For the most part, tropical grasses are large, robust, aggressive grasses, better suited to forage than turf. A few tropical grasses (seashore paspalum, kikuyu, zoysia, carpetgrass) are shorter, sod-forming species. Insect resistance is a major issue in this zone, because insects flourish unchecked in the tropics. Disease can also be a determining factor.

Zone 6—Cold or alpine. Winter survival and snow mold resistance are prominent issues in Zone 6. Not all cool-season grasses can survive these cold conditions. Tall fescue and perennial ryegrass frequently winter-kill. Even bentgrass bites the dust occasionally.

Alpine grasses fill a vital niche because of their cold tolerance and ability to tolerate a short growing season. As a bonus, these alpine grasses are naturally low growing, demanding less mowing.

Step #2–Analyze your local climate

Each turf site is unique. Before you can choose the best adapted grasses, you need to carefully investigate your local **microclimate**. Your site may be a little higher or lower in elevation than another just a few miles away. It may have a southern exposure or towering shade trees. It may be on a lake or in the shadow of a mountain range.

Local meteorological data can be gleaned from a nearby weather station or airport. Yearly averages and extremes in temperature and rainfall will give you an idea of climatic extremes. Worldwide meteorological data are also available on the Internet and on CD-ROM databases. One such CD-ROM database is produced by the U.S. Navy. These databases are a source of detailed climate data, averaged over years, from primary and even secondary weather stations and airports.

If your site differs by more than 1000 ft (300 m) in elevation from a nearby weather station or is located some distance away, you may want to chart your own local weather. Consider investing in a recording **hygrothermograph** to record daily highs and lows of temperature and humidity at the site. A hygrothermograph can provide you with a monthly temperature and humidity chart of the actual conditions at your site (Figure 5.2).

Once you've accumulated local weather data, you are ready to see how it affects turf selection. Begin by inserting your data into the chart in Table 5.1. This chart was designed to illustrate *why* certain grasses are best adapted for a particular location.

Exceptions to the rule. The Zone Maps (Figure 5.1) suffice for the majority of turf sites. But every now and then the local microclimate of a site defies the maps, such as when a site is shadowed by a nearby mountain. That's why it's important to use your *local* microclimate data in the grass adaptation chart (Table 5.1) in place of the broader Zone Maps.

Below, I've detailed four sites that defied the Zone Maps. These are actual examples of grassing recommendations I've made that have run amok. They illustrate why it's important to examine your *local* growing conditions:

- *A golf course near Bogota, Columbia, South America*—A new golf club in Columbia really wanted to plant cool-season grasses, but the Zone Charts said tropical. On close examination, I found that the site was at 5000 ft (1500 m) elevation where frosts are a yearly occurrence. Summer temperatures above 80°F (27°C) were rare. This course is now the only cool-season grass golf course in northern South America.
- *A soccer field in Lisbon, Portugal*—Lisbon is bathed in a mild, Mediterranean climate which—if you look solely at minimum temperatures—should be ideal for bermudagrass. Well, it's not. A mild, prevailing ocean breeze keeps daytime temperatures too cool for bermudagrass. The bermudagrass I recommended for a soccer field sat there and refused to grow. Cool-season grasses later proved a wiser choice.
- *A hotel and golf complex on Cheju Island, South Korea*—On the map, Cheju island, off the southern coast of Korea, looks like a tropical paradise. Even the USDA-hardiness zone indicates a mild, subtropical climate, warm enough to sustain groves of native nutmeg trees. But as with Lisbon, the ocean was the key. Ocean breezes from the 60°F (15°C) Siberian currents create a unique microclimate. Zoysiagrass, though native to Korea, languishes in this mild microclimate. Cool-season grasses proved a better choice, even though summer diseases

Figure 5.2. A recording hygrothermograph is an inexpensive way to map the local weather of your turf site. Electronic versions are also available.

Table 5.1. The climate at your turf site dictates which grasses are best adapted. Weather data can be obtained from a nearby weather station or from worldwide climate databases. However, each turf site is unique, with its own particular topography and microclimate. To choose the right grass, begin by asking yourself the questions listed here. Remember, local conditions may vary from that of a weather station just a few miles away.

Climate at your turf site	How your climate affects your recommended grasses:
What is the maximum temperature in the summer? **______degrees**	• Most turfgrasses can tolerate a few days of hot temperature now and then. But prolonged heat can spawn disease, drought, or stress problems in many turfgrasses. • If the maximum temperature exceeds 100°F (38°C) you can forget about using fine fescue or the alpine grasses. • If temperatures spike above 115°F (46°C) warm-season grasses are *strongly* advised. • On the other hand, without adequate heat, warm-season grasses become noncompetitive. If your summer temperatures rarely exceed 80°F (27°C), warm-season grasses may grow too slowly to be of value.
How many days per year does the temperature exceed 90°F (32°C)? **______days above 90°F**	• *Prolonged* heat is one of the great dividing lines among grasses. • Most cool-season grasses can endure 20 to 30 days per year above 90°F (32°C). But when there are more than 30 days, the only suitable cool-season alternatives among the traditional species are tall, hard, and sheep fescue. • Beyond 60 days of high temperature, the warm-season grasses are strongly preferred. Cool-season grasses can still be used in shaded conditions, away from direct sunlight. • Bentgrass can withstand up to about 90 days of high temperature per year, provided the soil has been modified (sand) and humidity is low.
What is the minimum temperature in winter? **______degrees**	• Fine fescue, bentgrass, and most bluegrasses are hardy to about −40°F (−40°C). • Perennial ryegrass and tall fescue survive temperatures to about −15°F (−26°C). Colder temperatures—especially with an ice pack or no snow cover—can cause damage. • Zoysia, buffalograss, and bermuda are reliable in areas with minimum temperatures above 5°F (−15°C). Certain cold-tolerant varieties can withstand temperatures to −15°F (−26°C). • Centipedegrass, St. Augustinegrass, bahiagrass, and seashore paspalum are limited to regions with temperatures generally above 20°F (−7°C), with some differences among varieties.
How many months of frost-free growing season? **______months**	• A short frost-free season curtails the use of warm-season grasses. Even if your winters are mild and warm-season grasses can *survive,* short summers will not allow enough time for the *warm-season* grass to flourish. They will be dormant for most of the year. • Cool-season grasses are preferable in areas with less than 6 months of frost-free growing season.
Does the area ever receive frost? **______yes/no**	• Tropical climates (Zone 5), where frosts are rare, can maintain warm-season grasses year-round with little or no loss of color. • In the Transition (Zone 3) and subtropical (Zone 4) regions, dormant turf may need winter overseeding with a cool-season grass to maintain playability and color.
What is the average daytime relative humidity during summer? **______% humidity**	• Humidity is a major limiting factor of cool-season grasses. Humidity combined with warm temperature brings on disease. A good rule of thumb: If your temperature (in Fahrenheit) added to your relative humidity (%) regularly exceeds 150, expect diseases to be a problem. • Arid areas with low humidity can grow almost any grass provided water is applied to allow the grass to cool itself by evapotranspiration. Evaporative cooling is stifled as humidity rises.

Table 5.1. The climate at your turf site dictates which grasses are best adapted. Weather data can be obtained from a nearby weather station or from worldwide climate databases. However, each turf site is unique, with its own particular topography and microclimate. To choose the right grass, begin by asking yourself the questions listed here. Remember, local conditions may vary from that of a weather station just a few miles away (continued).

Climate at your turf site	How your climate affects your recommended grasses:
Does the area receive prolonged periods of heavy overcast? During what time of year? **_____yes/no**	• Some climates—especially locations with an ocean nearby—can experience months of dark, overcast skies, even though temperatures are moderate. This condition limits the growth of sun-loving grasses such as bermuda, buffalograss, and the prairie grasses. • Grasses with shade tolerance are preferable under overcast skies. Zoysia and St. Augustinegrass will remain dense and playable while bermuda becomes thin and stemmy.
How many total inches (mm) of snowfall does the site receive per year? **_____inches of snow**	• Snow does little harm to grasses and is not a major factor in itself. Snow cover often *protects* grasses from blistering winter winds and low temperatures. • Rarely are warm-season grasses used in areas receiving more than 60 in. (1.5 m) of annual snowfall.
Does the snow remain on the ground for months at a time? Or does it generally melt away after a few days? **_____yes/no**	• Prolonged snow cover can shelter grasses from winter temperatures. But it also serves as a breeding ground for snow mold. • If snow blankets the ground for more than a month during winter, you should consider snow-mold-resistant species or varieties, or the use of preventive fungicides. • Warm-season grasses have no particular problem withstanding snow cover. In fact, winter damage to warm-season grass usually occurs when snow cover *is not* present, from direct low temperature kill of the crown.
What is the average annual rainfall? **_____inches or mm**	• Annual rainfall amount is important in grass selection for unirrigated or infrequently irrigated sites. • On irrigated sites in arid regions, some turf managers claim they *prefer* less rain because it gives them more control over water application in their management scheme with fewer unexpected disease outbreaks. • It takes at least 30 in. (760 mm) of timely rainfall per year to sustain mowed traditional turfgrasses without irrigation. • Unirrigated sites with less than 30 in. of rain should consider using the prairie and range grasses listed in Chapter 4. • Sites with greater than 60 in. (1500 mm) of rain or with seasonal flooding might consider the moisture-loving grasses listed in the Appendix, or grass alternatives such as sedge (Table 4.2).
Is there a distinct rainy season? Or is rainfall evenly distributed through the year? Are summer droughts common? **_____yes/no**	• *Timeliness* of rainfall is as important than quantity. Climates with a reliable, weekly dose of rain can maintain turfgrasses without irrigation more effectively than areas where rain comes as a seasonal monsoon. • Choose a drought tolerant grass if your climate includes a yearly dry period.
Will irrigation be available? For establishment? For maintenance? Automatic or manual irrigation? **_____yes/no**	• Irrigation during establishment is not absolutely essential for turf. But it is valuable in bringing up a stand evenly and quickly and should be used whenever possible, even if you don't plan to water the mature turf. Irrigated seedlings develop quickly and uniformly and compete effectively against weeds and erosion. • Close-cut turf and turf grown on sand-modified soil will require irrigation even in moist environments.
Are there any problems with the irrigation: Watering restrictions? Salinity? Adverse water pH? Use of effluent water? **_____yes/no**	• Present *and future* problems with irrigation water should be considered prior to planting. Municipal watering restrictions imposed during a drought year can result in stand loss if a drought-sensitive grass is used. • Irrigating with salty or poor quality water will lead to deteriorating growing conditions with time. Plan to incorporate into your seed mixture a grass with salt or pH tolerance such as *Puccinellia*.

Climate at your turf site	How your climate affects your recommended grasses:
Is dew frequent? ______**yes/no**	• Fungi creep in dew. You find the most disease problems in areas with a regular morning dew. If dew is a frequent occurrence, you should definitely seek disease resistant species and varieties. • In certain mild, humid sites (such as Seoul, Korea), night and day temperatures may differ by only a degree or two. Dew formed at night may not evaporate during the day, leaving the turf vulnerable to disease attack even in the afternoon. • Warm-season grasses have better disease tolerance under these conditions, particularly the zoysias. • Areas blessed with low humidity or a steady nighttime breeze seldom experience dew. In these areas you can plan on substantially less need for fungicide for disease control.
Is the site windy or exposed? ______**yes/no**	• Windy, exposed sites in cool climates put the turf at risk for winter injury. Cold-hardy species such as Canada or alpine bluegrass can be added to the seed mix where injury is anticipated. • In other areas, wind is a bonus to turf management. It accelerates drying of dew and moisture, reducing disease pressure.
Is it level or hilly? ______**yes/no**	• Steep slopes require special care to minimize erosion. Fast establishing grasses such as perennial ryegrass can be added to the seed mix to stabilize the soil as quickly as possible. Perennial ryegrass is preferred over annual grasses because it does not later become a chronic weed problem. • Cereal rye grain can be sown to secure extremely erosive soils. It germinates rapidly and vigorously even under cold soil temperatures and later can be mowed or sprayed out. • Long-term stabilization of slopes calls for a sod-forming grass. Rhizomatous species are best for knitting the soil and preventing rain washing.
Are there adverse soils: Alkaline, acid, salty, rocky, erosive, etc.? ______**yes/no**	• Be certain to check the attributes of the grass you're planting to be sure it will tolerate existing soil conditions. Good advice is to add an "insurance" grass to the seed mixture to help tolerate the local soil problems. Several such grasses are listed in Chapter 4.
What is the elevation at the site? ______**feet or meters**	• If your site is more than 2000 ft (600 m) higher or lower than a local weather station, its climate may substantially differ. You may want to select grasses from the next cooler zone.
Is there an ocean influence on the climate? For instance, a Mediterranean climate? ______**yes/no**	• Oceans moderate local temperature extremes and provide a generally mild growing environment. As a result, a wide array of grass species often can be grown. Under these conditions, you should choose a grass based upon its water-use efficiency or other low maintenance attribute, rather than on its tolerance to temperature.
Are there any drainage problems? Seasonal standing water? ______**yes/no**	• High traffic, low cutting height, and soil drainage problems combine to produce a condition known as mud. No grass, just mud. Even moisture-loving grasses thin out on poorly drained soils. It's been said that grasses may "tolerate" wet feet, but they don't "like" them. • Moisture-loving grasses and sedges can be planted in perennially wet areas. A better solution is to install subsurface drainage to remove water pockets.

Table 5.1. The climate at your turf site dictates which grasses are best adapted. Weather data can be obtained from a nearby weather station or from worldwide climate databases. However, each turf site is unique, with its own particular topography and microclimate. To choose the right grass, begin by asking yourself the questions listed here. Remember, local conditions may vary from that of a weather station just a few miles away (continued).

Climate at your turf site	How your climate affects your recommended grasses:
Soil texture: Sand, silt, clay? Does it vary from one area to another? **______yes/no**	• A lot has been written on which soils grasses prefer: sand, silt, and clay. However, as long as drainage is favorable, there's really little practical difference in the adaptation of grass species to soil texture. • Sandy soils hold comparatively little moisture and tend to be droughty. An automatic sprinkling system can grow grass even on pure sand by metering out small amounts of water. Many golf course putting greens are, in fact, made of sand. • Clay soils tend to retain *too much* water. Moreover, they are prone to compaction. Chapter 8 deals with methods for remedying poorly drained, clay soils. • On sites with varying soils from one area to another, seed mixtures and blends are advised. Mixtures ensure a wider range of adaptation to soil.
Are there any local restrictions on the use of pesticides? **______yes/no**	• A few areas worldwide have restricted or banned the use of chemical pesticides on turf. Chiba Prefecture in Japan, for example, has banned use of pesticides on all new golf course construction. In many third-world countries, the availability of pesticides is limited due to import restrictions. Even in areas like California, turf managers are often prevented from using the latest products due to local regulations. • If pesticide use is restricted, an enormous emphasis will have to be placed on cultural control measures. Cultural pest controls can work successfully with low maintenance turf on roadsides, home lawns, or parks. Whether they work with golf courses is debatable. • Consult Chapter 12 for suggestions on controlling pests without pesticides.
What time of year will you be planting the grass? **______month**	• In the tropics (Zone 5), plant grass any time you'd like. Try coinciding planting with the end of the dry season, before the beginning of the rainy season, to provide adequate moisture for growth. • In areas with a distinct summer and winter season, *timing* of planting is critical. Plant warm-season grasses in the spring after the last frost date. Plant cool-season grasses in late summer and early autumn. • In colder regions (Zone 6 and cooler parts of Zone 1), spring plantings are preferred over fall to allow adequate time for establishment. • Of course, not all construction projects fit neatly into these agronomic recommendations. Sodding and dormant seeding can help stretch the season in many must-plant situations.
What is the desired height of cut? **______inches or mm**	• If you feel you *must* mow at 1 in. (2.5 cm) or below, you've restricted yourself to using perhaps 5% of available grasses, mostly the traditional turf species. • A few low maintenance grasses can be grown at 1 in. You'll find them among the *Agrostis, Axonopus, Digitaria, Cynodon, Poa,* and *Zoysia* species (see Appendix). • Low maintenance grasses are best at a cutting height of 3 in. (7.5 cm) or more.
Overall level of maintenance: High, medium, low, none? **______level**	• The traditional turf species can be tapped for lower maintenance sites if the right varieties are chosen (see Chapter 2). • The unconventional grasses are at their best under low (or zero) maintenance. Many perform admirably even up to medium maintenance levels (see Chapter 2).

Climate at your turf site	How your climate affects your recommended grasses:
Overall level of wear/traffic: High, medium, low, none? **______level**	• Maintenance compensates for wear. Water and fertilizer are used to outgrow damage from too many feet. Don't plan to skimp on maintenance where thousands of people tread. Lightly trafficked or vista turfs are ideally suited to low maintenance solutions. • For high wear projects, stick with the traditional turf species.
Will the turf be played on all 12 months of the year? Or just seasonally? **______all year/seasonal**	• Twelve-month play presents a dilemma to any turfgrass. Whether it's a warm- or cool-season grass, the turf will be dormant or sluggish in at least one season of the year. • Mixtures between warm- and cool-season grasses have been tested. For example, tall fescue–zoysia mixtures persist in the Transition Zone (Zone 3). Sometimes permanent cool/warm-season mixtures can be used in Mediterranean climates (in Zones 3 or 4). Additional mixture information is presented in Chapter 6. • Winter overseeding of perennial ryegrass into a dormant warm-season stand is another way to extend play to 12 months.
Is the site heavily shaded, full sun, or something in between? **______yes/no**	• Warm-season grasses perform poorly in the shade. Cool-seasons are preferred where adapted. Species and varieties within the two groups vary considerably in shade performance, as described in earlier chapters.

can occasionally hit during particularly balmy periods.

- *A home lawn in Oklahoma, USA*—I believe that ladies at garden clubs *live* to prove experts wrong. After speaking to a local garden club on the best lawn choices for Oklahoma, one frail, older woman came up to me and said, "young man, you're full of crap!" She went on to explain—contrary to what I'd just preached—that St. Augustinegrass could indeed be grown in northern Oklahoma. She had moved there years ago from Houston, Texas, bringing her beloved St. Augustinegrass with her. Her south-facing backyard was sandwiched between taller buildings. The southern exposure and the shelter of the buildings created a microclimate pocket conducive to St. Augustinegrass. I ate my words, although she sheepishly admitted she had to occasionally resprig areas that winterkilled.

Step #3—Determine your species options

Your grassing options depend on how you intend to *use* the grass. For instance, you'd never use creeping bentgrass on a football field even if it were adapted to your zone. Judgment is called for.

Table 5.2 helps determine the best grassing options based on your climatic zone. One of the first things you'll notice is that the unconventional turfgrass species (Chapter 4) are not suited to every turf application. In many cases, they won't take the pounding of daily wear. But for less demanding situations, they are definitely an option to explore.

Folks who live on a zone fringe or in a unique microclimate that differs in elevation or exposure from its surroundings, may want to explore additional grassing options from the chart in Table 5.3. If you're fortunate enough to live near one of the cities listed in Table 5.3 you can get a direct readout of the best grasses for your particular location.

Step #4—Select the best possible varieties

Now that you've settled on the best grass species for your site, your next task is to choose varieties. Rather than list variety suggestions here—which would quickly become out of date—I will refer you to the latest variety recommendations from the National Turfgrass Evaluation Program (NTEP) (Morris, 1995a; 1995b). NTEP is a coalition of university test sites that performs field trials on the latest turfgrass releases. It provides yearly updates of current variety performance. Data are available by mail for

Table 5.2. Popular grassing options for the six climatic zones described on the world maps. Suggested options are arranged somewhat in order of desirability within the zone. Of course, a lot depends on the desired maintenance level, the intended use of the facility, and the available budget.

Uses	Grassing options
Zone 1 – Cool Temperate	
Golf Course	
Putting green	• Creeping bentgrass • Velvet bentgrass
Fairway	• Creeping bentgrass blend • Kentucky bluegrass/perennial ryegrass mixture • Colonial/Highland bentgrass mixture
Tee ground	• Perennial ryegrass • Kentucky bluegrass/perennial ryegrass mixture • Creeping bentgrass blend • Colonial/ Highland bentgrass mixture
Roughs	• Tall fescue/Kentucky bluegrass mixture • Low maintenance grass mixture
Out-of-play	• Fine fescue/Kentucky bluegrass mixture • Low maintenance grass mixture
Other turf facilities	
Athletic field	• Tall fescue/Kentucky bluegrass mixture • Kentucky bluegrass/perennial ryegrass mixture
Home lawn **Parks** **School yards**	• Kentucky bluegrass/perennial ryegrass mixture • Tall fescue/Kentucky bluegrass mixture • Fine fescue/Kentucky bluegrass mixture • Low maintenance grass mixture • *Zoysia japonica*
Roadsides **Vista turf** **Cemeteries**	• Low maintenance grass mixture • Tall fescue/Kentucky bluegrass mixture • Fine fescue/Kentucky bluegrass mixture • Kentucky bluegrass/perennial ryegrass mixture
Shade	• Fine fescue/Kentucky bluegrass mixture • Tall fescue/Kentucky bluegrass mixture • Low maintenance grass mixture
Zone 2 – Cool Marine	
Golf Course	
Putting green	• Creeping bentgrass • Velvet bentgrass • Chewings fescue
Fairway	• Perennial ryegrass • Fine fescue/Kentucky bluegrass mixture • Perennial ryegrass/Kentucky bluegrass mixture • Creeping bentgrass blend • Colonial/Highland bentgrass mixture • Colonial bentgrass/chewings fescue mixture
Tee ground	• Perennial ryegrass • Perennial ryegrass/Kentucky bluegrass mixture • Creeping bentgrass blend • Colonial/Highland bentgrass mixture

Uses	Grassing options
	Zone 2 – Cool Marine (continued)
	Golf Course
Roughs	• Perennial ryegrass • Perennial ryegrass/Kentucky bluegrass mixture • Fine fescue/Kentucky bluegrass mixture • Tall fescue/Kentucky bluegrass mixture • Low maintenance grass mixture
Out-of-play	• Low maintenance grass mixture • Fine fescue/Kentucky bluegrass mixture
	Other turf facilities
Athletic field	• Perennial ryegrass/Kentucky bluegrass mixture • Tall fescue/Kentucky bluegrass mixture
Home lawn **Parks** **School yards**	• Perennial ryegrass/Kentucky bluegrass mixture • Tall fescue/Kentucky bluegrass mixture • Fine fescue/Kentucky bluegrass mixture • Low maintenance grass mixture
Roadsides **Vista turf** **Cemeteries**	• Low maintenance grass mixture • Tall fescue/Kentucky bluegrass mixture • Fine fescue/Kentucky bluegrass mixture • Kentucky bluegrass/perennial ryegrass mixture
Shade	• Fine fescue • Low maintenance grass mixture
	Zone 3 – Transition
	Golf Course
Putting green	• Creeping bentgrass
Fairway	• Perennial ryegrass • Creeping bentgrass blend • *Zoysia japonica* • Cold-tolerant bermudagrass variety • Kentucky bluegrass/perennial ryegrass mixture
Tee ground	• Perennial ryegrass • Kentucky bluegrass/perennial ryegrass mixture • Creeping bentgrass blend • *Zoysia japonica*
Roughs	• Tall fescue/Kentucky bluegrass mixture • Cold-tolerant bermudagrass variety • Low maintenance grass mixture • *Zoysia japonica*
Out-of-play	• Tall fescue/Kentucky bluegrass mixture • Buffalograss • Weeping lovegrass • Low maintenance grass mixture
	Other turf facilities
Athletic field	• Tall fescue/Kentucky bluegrass mixture • *Zoysia japonica* • Cold-tolerant bermudagrass variety
Home lawn **Parks** **School yards**	• Tall fescue/Kentucky bluegrass mixture • *Zoysia japonica* • Cold-tolerant bermudagrass variety • Low maintenance grass mixture

Table 5.2. Popular grassing options for the six climatic zones described on the world maps. Suggested options are arranged somewhat in order of desirability within the zone. Of course, a lot depends on the desired maintenance level, the intended use of the facility, and the available budget (continued).

Uses	Grassing options
	Zone 3 – Transition (continued)
	Other turf facilities
Roadsides **Vista turf** **Cemeteries**	• Tall fescue/Kentucky bluegrass mixture • Low maintenance grass mixture
Shade	• Tall fescue/Kentucky bluegrass mixture • Hard/sheep fescue mixture • Low maintenance grass mixture
	Zone 4 – Warm Temperate or Marine
	Golf Course
Putting green	• Hybrid bermudagrass • *Zoysia matrella*
Fairway	• Hybrid bermudagrass • Improved seeded bermudagrass • *Zoysia japonica* • Kikuyu grass • Seashore paspalum
Tee ground	• Hybrid bermudagrass • Improved seeded bermudagrass • *Zoysia japonica*
Roughs	• Improved seeded bermudagrass • Low maintenance grass mixture • *Zoysia japonica*
Out-of-play	• Improved seeded bermudagrass • Bahiagrass • Low maintenance grass mixture
	Other turf facilities
Athletic field	• Improved seeded bermudagrass • Hybrid bermudagrass
Home lawn **Parks** **School yards**	• Improved seeded bermudagrass • Hybrid bermudagrass • *Zoysia japonica* • St. Augustinegrass • Tall fescue mixture • Low maintenance grass mixture
Roadsides **Vista turf** **Cemeteries**	• Low maintenance grass mixture • Tall fescue mixture • Centipedegrass • Bahiagrass
Shade	• Tall fescue mixture • St. Augustinegrass
	Zone 5 – Tropical
	Golf Course
Putting green	• Hybrid bermudagrass • *Zoysia matrella*

Uses	Grassing options
	Zone 5 – Tropical (continued)
Fairway	• Hybrid bermudagrass • *Zoysia japonica* • Improved seeded bermudagrass • Kikuyu grass • Seashore paspalum
Tee ground	• Hybrid bermudagrass • Improved seeded bermudagrass • *Zoysia japonica*
Roughs	• Improved seeded bermudagrass • Low maintenance grass mixture • *Zoysia japonica* • Carpetgrass • Centipedegrass
Out-of-play	• Improved seeded bermudagrass • Bahiagrass • Low maintenance grass mixture
	Other turf facilities
Athletic field	• Improved seeded bermudagrass • Hybrid bermudagrass
Home lawn **Parks** **School yards**	• Improved seeded bermudagrass • Hybrid bermudagrass • *Zoysia japonica* • St. Augustinegrass • Narrow leaf carpet grass • Low maintenance grass mixture
Roadsides **Vista turf** **Cemeteries**	• Low maintenance grass mixture • Bahiagrass
Shade	• St. Augustinegrass
	Zone 6 – Cold or Alpine
	Golf Course
Putting green	• Creeping bentgrass • Velvet bentgrass
Fairway	• Kentucky bluegrass/perennial ryegrass mixture • Creeping bentgrass blend • Colonial bentgrass/chewings fescue mixture • Fine fescue/Kentucky bluegrass mixture • Colonial/Highland bentgrass mixture
Tee ground	• Kentucky bluegrass • Creeping bentgrass blend • Colonial/Highland bentgrass mixture
Roughs	• Fine fescue/Kentucky bluegrass mixture • Canada bluegrass/Kentucky bluegrass mixture • Low maintenance grass mixture
Out-of-play	• Fine fescue/Kentucky bluegrass mixture • Low maintenance grass mixture

Table 5.2. Popular grassing options for the six climatic zones described on the world maps. Suggested options are arranged somewhat in order of desirability within the zone. Of course, a lot depends on the desired maintenance level, the intended use of the facility, and the available budget (continued).

Zone 6 – Cold or Alpine (continued)	
Other turf facilities	
Athletic field	• Kentucky bluegrass
Home lawn **Parks** **School yards**	• Kentucky bluegrass • Fine fescue/Kentucky bluegrass mixture • Low maintenance grass mixture
Roadsides **Vista turf** **Cemeteries**	• Low maintenance grass mixture • Fine fescue/Kentucky bluegrass mixture • Kentucky bluegrass
Shade	• Fine fescue • Fine fescue/Kentucky bluegrass mixture

a nominal fee or online via the World Wide Web at *http://www.ntep.org*

Unfortunately, variety testing of the unconventional grasses (Chapter 4) is still in its infancy. NTEP has discussed hosting such a trial, but it's still years away from reality.

Finding good varieties. Varietal selection can be complicated by many unforeseen factors. Before getting your heart set on a particular variety, consider this:

- *Everybody, it seems, wants to buy and plant the #1 variety in the trials.* Some people jokingly call the national trials "beauty contests," because they feel the trials are biased toward showing off the prettiest entries rather than the toughest ones. Personally, I think a better analogy is a "dog show." The real purpose of the national trial is *not* to pick the prettiest variety but to weed out the dogs. Varieties in the top half of the trial generally do as well as the #1. These midranged varieties are more readily available and sometimes at a cheaper price.
- *Not every grass variety is available for sale in every given year.* Production is geared to demand. If no one (but you) is asking for sod or seed of a particular variety, you can bet it will be hard to find. Sometimes varieties go *out of production* without notifying anyone. There is no central repository of information regarding which varieties are in production at a given time. A pity.
- *If you've found more than one grassing option, you may want to consider a mixture.* Mixing turfgrasses combines the best characteristics of each. But not all turfgrasses mix well together. Some combinations grow ugly and patchy with time. Chapter 6 points the way to tried-and-true mixtures.

THE ETERNAL CHALLENGE: GROWING TURF IN THE SHADE

Turf management would be a snap if it weren't for trees. Trees are those immovable objects in the middle of a lawn that can all but obliterate our stylish, straight-as-an-arrow mower stripes. Trees challenge even the best of turf managers, who when spraying herbicides, are constantly looking over their shoulders trying to avoid driplines.

But seriously, trees are an integral part of nearly every landscape. Lawns without trees lack character. Furthermore, trees provide beneficial cooling to houses and their surroundings. By optimizing the growth of lawngrasses in shade, it *is* possible for turf and trees to peacefully coexist.

"Turfgrasses really don't do well in shade," wrote Stephen Cockerham, University of California–Riverside turf researcher, in *Western Landscaping News*. "The most obvious problem with

Table 5.3. Adaptation of 29 turfgrass species to cities around the world. Additional information on these grasses can be found in Chapters 2 and 3. (Note: The adaptation of creeping bentgrass into Zones 3 and 4 is for putting green use only. A modified rootzone mixture is strongly recommended in these zones.)

Species	Bahiagrass	Bermudagrass	Buffalograss	Broad leaf carpet grass	Narrow leaf carpet grass	Centipedegrass	Kikuyu grass	Seashore paspalum	St. Augustinegrass	*Zoysia japonica*	*Zoysia matrella*	*Zoysia tenuifolia*	Alkaligrass, distans	Colonial bentgrass	Creeping bentgrass	Highland bentgrass	Velvet bentgrass	Canada bluegrass	Kentucky bluegrass	Roughstalk bluegrass	Supine bluegrass	Chewings fescue	Hard fescue	Sheep fescue	Slender creeping fescue	Strong creeping fescue	Tall fescue	Perennial ryegrass	Redtop
Auckland																													
Brisbane																													
Sydney																													
Hong Kong																													
Tokyo																													
Johannesburg																													
Cairo																													
Stockholm																													
Athens																													
Lisbon																													
Rome																													
Madrid																													
Berlin																													
London																													
Vancouver																													
Edmonton																													
Toronto																													
Seattle																													
Los Angeles																													
Phoenix																													
Denver																													
Chicago																													
St. Louis																													
Dallas																													
Miami																													
Atlanta																													
Washington, DC																													
New York																													
Boston																													
Can be used in the cooler parts of zone			5			5				5			3,4	3	4			1,2	3				4	4	1	3	4	4	2,3
Can be used in the warmer parts of zone		1,3	1	4		3			4	2	3	4	6	6			6						6	6					
Ideal zone	4,5	4,5	3,4	5	4,5	4	4,5	4,5	5	1,3,4	4,5	5	1,2	1,2	1,2,3,6	1,2,3,6	1,2	6	1,2,6	1,2,6	1,2	1,2,6	1,2,3	1,2,3	2,6	1,2,6	1,2,3	1,2,3	1,6

Table 5.3. Continued

Key to table color codes.

Adaptation	
Ideally suited to the location	(white)
Not the top pick, but adaptable	(light shading)
Medium to low performance	(dark shading)
Not adapted, probably won't survive	(black)

shade is the fact that there isn't enough light—that not being a particularly illuminating conclusion."

Light affects nearly every facet of grass growth. Particularly hard hit are the warm-season grasses, which evolved under high temperatures and bright light intensities. Bermudagrass, for instance, will grow only up to the dripline of a tree. It seldom persists under shade for very long.

Sunlight fuels growth of plants. Reduced light spells reduced **carbohydrate** levels (Blake, 1982). Just as with human beings, carbohydrates give plants the energy to grow, develop, and resist stress.

Grasses respond to reduced light with,

- *Smaller root systems*—less tolerance of drought
- *Thinner cuticles*—cuticles are the waxy coverings on grass leaves that help fend off disease organisms
- *A poorly developed vascular system*—this translates into an increased tendency to wilt
- *Increased succulence*—**succulence** is the turf word for water-weight gain; succulence makes plants more susceptible to wear, drought, and temperature stress, and to attack from insects and disease
- *More disease*—trees restrict air flow, leading to the buildup of humidity, dew, and disease
- *Weak, stemmy, upright growth*—shade induces an upright growth in grasses and grass plants suffer more from defoliation.

The culprit: Tree roots

Competition between tree roots and grass roots can be intense. Most people visualize tree roots as a single subterranean branch extending straight downward. But in fact most tree roots mingle in the same surface soil profile as grass roots. Trees go head-to-head with grasses exploring for water and nutrients.

Carl Whitcomb, author of *Know It and Grow It*, has seen many a stately shade tree killed when a turf manager got the brilliant idea to rototill the soil underneath a tree. This fact illustrates that tree roots are *right there*—intertwined with grass roots, competing with them for water and minerals (Whitcomb and Roberts, 1973). Furthermore, contrary to popular belief, tree roots do not stop at the tree's dripline. They venture out sometimes twice the dripline-diameter of the tree. Anyone who's dug sprinkler trenches knows that tree roots can be found in just about any part of a yard, often a long distance from the trunk. Tree roots compete with grasses even in the full sun, out away from the tree.

Allelopathy may also play a role in tree-turf interaction. Allelopathy is the phenomenon in plants whereby one plant exudes a chemical that harms another (see Chapter 4 for more details). It's a type of defense mechanism, carving out a niche for a plant by chemical warfare (Rice, 1984). Whitcomb has long felt that tree roots excrete allelopathic chemicals that are toxic to grasses (Whitcomb and Roberts, 1973). His doctoral thesis centered on tree root competition with turfgrasses. Evidently the trees won, as Whitcomb later became a noted tree expert.

Turf shade research

Turf researchers have been studying shade and its effect on turf for many years. And while no treatment short of a chainsaw can completely eliminate the problems of shade, there are several options open to the turf manager.

"Obviously, the first step to successful turf shade culture is to make every effort to reduce the problem by pruning, thinning, and removal of excess trees and shrubs," says Cockerham. Golf course superintendents are well acquainted with the practice of tree trimming as a means of in-

Questions and Answers about the Six Zones

Q: From what I can determine, I live right on the border between two zones. Which one do I choose?

A: You have the advantage of being able to pick grasses from *either* zone. If your site tends to be on the warm side, select from the warmer of the two zones. If your site is exposed, shaded, north-facing, or at a higher elevation, choose from the cooler zone.

Q: I live in a sheltered valley in Zone 1. Can I try some of the warm-season grasses recommended for Zone 3?

A: Your local microclimate may be quite different from the surrounding region. Check the chart in Table 5.3, under the column labeled, "Can be used in the warmer parts of zone," for options.

Q: I live in Zone 4 at an elevation of 4000 ft (1200 m). Should I readjust my selections?

A: Yes. A 4000-ft elevation is enough to place you in the next cooler zone. Consult local weather charts and plug your local data into the analysis chart (Table 5.1).

Q: I live in Mexico City (Zone 5) where grasses like perennial ryegrass persist year round. Your charts tell me to plant tropical grasses. What gives?

A: Places like Mexico City with a warm, mild climate have broad options when it comes to grassing. In such a location, cool-season grasses persist but tropical grasses are the more efficient users of water. Where maintenance is at issue, I'd stick with the warm-season grasses.

Q: Are the zones described in this book similar to the USDA's plant hardiness zones?

A: To a large extent, both sets of zones are comparable. For example, Grass Zone #1 is analogous to USDA zones 2-3-4-5. The reason there are fewer grass zones is that grasses tolerate a broader temperature spectrum. Adding additional zones to the grass maps would only make them unnecessarily complicated, without adding anything beneficial.

Q: How many grass adaptation zones did you say there were again?

A: Six.

creasing air flow. Other turf managers don't always have this luxury. Alternative solutions are needed.

To the rescue comes Bob Duell, Rutgers University shade researcher, who along with other scientists, is performing controlled experiments on shaded turf. More importantly, they're examining what can be done to combat shade effects on grass.

Duell and his students set up a large experiment to compare the performance of turfgrasses under

- natural chestnut shade,
- artificial shade cloth, and
- unshaded, full sun conditions.

Duell constructed two shade houses—similar in appearance to greenhouses—except that they were covered with two grades of artificial shade cloth instead of glass. "The two shade meshes we tested excluded 92 and 76% of the solar energy. Under the artificial shade, of course, the only stress was the reduction of solar energy," he says. Duell's shade houses are analogous to the type of shade found around buildings and other inanimate objects, devoid of tree roots.

"In the natural shade treatment (chestnut trees), there was the additional stress for moisture and nutrients. We tried to maintain the artificial shade plots so that these stresses were not a factor," he says.

Between the two shade treatments—artificial and natural—Duell got differing responses from the grass. "In full sunlight, moisture stresses in midsummer browned the grass off. In the tree shade in spite of occasional irrigation, the turf didn't do so well either," he says.

Turf under the 76% shade cloth was soft, uniform, somewhat long bladed, and only a slight bit thin (see Figure 5.3). "To look at it, it looked like really nice turf, even across all six grass species that we tested," he says.

Hard and chewings fescues performed the best in Duell's variety trials, followed closely by tall fescue. Even ryegrass looked good, which surprised Duell, since perennial ryegrass is not known for its shade tolerance. Kentucky bluegrass's shade performance was variety dependent: Kentucky bluegrass cultivars noted for their shade tolerance from earlier trials also performed well in Duell's trials (see recommendations below).

Establishing turf in the shade

Have you ever noticed that establishing turf in the shade seems to take more water, more tending, and more time than in the sun? Research has proved this fact to be true. When planting turf in the shade, existing tree roots draw water and nutrients away from young grass seedlings, complicating establishment.

Duell observed this phenomenon firsthand on the Rutgers campus. "On campus, the grounds maintenance people have been trying for years to reestablish a grass cover under the red oaks. Each spring they'll seed, get a showing of green for graduation, and then by midsummer all the seedlings die back. We were making no progress in spite of adding lime and fertilizer in place of sunlight. It just didn't work," he says.

After years of prodding by Duell, the maintenance crew finally switched their seeding to autumn. By seeding in the fall, the grass could establish while the leaves were off the deciduous trees. The establishment project proved successful.

"There's one essential proviso," cautions Duell. "Don't let fallen leaves accumulate under the trees during grass establishment." Leaf blowers and vacuums are preferred to raking, because they're less disruptive to the seedlings.

Shade varieties

Varieties like "Glade" Kentucky bluegrass were identified early in their development for their ability to perform in the shade and establish quickly. Shade varieties utilize the limited available light to the highest degree. Keith Karnok, University of Georgia turf professor, discovered that varieties like Glade exhibit a higher net rate of photosynthesis under low light than non-shade-tolerant varieties (Karnok, 1981).

Joe DiPaola, former North Carolina State University turf researcher, recommends the following list of varieties for shade (Blake, 1982; DiPaola, 1994):

- *Kentucky bluegrass*—Glade, A-34, Georgetown (Glade has been superseded by NuGlade, which has even more shade tolerance)
- *Perennial ryegrass*—All*Star, Birdie II, Cowboy, Elka
- *Fine fescue*—Aurora, Biljart, Reliant, Scaldis, Sparta, SR3000, Waldina
- *Roughstalk bluegrass*—Laser
- *Tall fescue*—Arid, Adventure, Apache, Trident
- *St. Augustinegrass*—Common, Roselawn, Bitterblue, Floralawn, Floratine, Raleigh
- *Zoysiagrass*—Belaire
- *Centipedegrass*—Common, Oklawn, Tennessee Hardy, Centennial
- *Bahiagrass*—Argentine, Pensacola
- *Bermudagrass*—(forget it)

Solutions to shade problems

Mowing. Grass in shade changes its plant form, becoming more upright. Leaves point skyward, as opposed to their near horizontal orientation in full sun. One quick fix is to raise your mowing height to compensate. Grasses grown in shade become **etiolated**—the same leggy, light green growth you get from house plants grown in a dark corner. A higher cut allows the etiolated grass to grow without severing too many of its

Figure 5.3. Bob Duell (foreground, left of center), Rutgers University turf researcher, is demonstrating his artificial shade house to fellow scientists. The artificial shade created by the shade cloth is analogous to the inanimate shade created by buildings or hills.

leaves. Typical recommendations are for a 1/2 to 1 in. (12 to 25 mm) higher cut in shade than in sun (Augustin, n.d.). This may or may not be practical, depending on how many mowers you have on hand and whether their height is easily adjustable (Figure 5.4).

A tricky mowing challenge arises in Transition Zone landscapes (Zones 3 and 4), where bermudagrass is grown in the sunny part of a lawn and tall fescue is grown in the shade. One or the other of the grasses has to *take it on the chin* when it comes to mowing height (Burns, 1976; Haley et al., 1985). It's quite unusual for a homeowner to set the mower to 3/4 in. (2 cm) for the bermuda and then *readjust* it to 2 1/2 in. (6 cm) for the fescue. Usually it's the shade grass that gets cut at the wrong height. Tall fescue ends up getting shaved at 3/4 in. in the shade, leaving the homeowner wondering why it didn't survive.

Disease. Long-term shade success of a grass is linked to its powdery mildew resistance. Powdery mildew is a parasitic disease seldom seen in full sun. Perhaps the fungus is destroyed by UV light and needs reduced light to survive. Perhaps it thrives on the higher leaf moistures and thinner cuticles found in shade. Or maybe it's some unknown factor. Whatever the reason, some turf varieties perform better in the shade than others, and powdery mildew resistance seems to be at the root of it all.

"Even in moderate shade, powdery mildew really knocks out certain Kentucky bluegrasses," says Karl Danneberger, Ohio State University turf professor. "If you're maintaining a high quality lawn, bluegrass varieties resistant to powdery mildew and melting out are essential. Some cultivars can be resistant to melting out in full sun, but you put them in the shade, and they're not." Danneberger advises turf managers to choose varieties for shade that have proved disease resistance.

Danneberger finds that perennial ryegrass performs poorly in shade. "The ryegrasses look good when you first establish them, but then they get blotchy and die out in areas. I don't think ryegrass is a option for shade right now," he says.

Irrigation. During establishment of shade turf, the seedbed needs ample water, applied in many light applications. Don't stop irrigating prematurely just because you haven't yet seen green. Seedlings planted in shade can take 2 to 4 weeks *longer* to emerge than seedlings in full sun. Even after emergence, watch the seedlings for signs of drying out—moisture stress strikes fast in shade due to those tree roots.

After the turf is mature, irrigate the turf so that the grass blades are not left damp for prolonged periods of time. This will help cut down on disease. Water during the early morning hours so the turf can dry before evening.

Fertilization. Scotts, the lawn fertilizer people, recommend increasing the "feeding rates for a shaded lawn to compensate for the needs of the tree and grass." On the flip side, Cockerham believes that "shaded turf areas should receive *much less fertilizer* than sunny areas." He theorizes that reduced fertilizer "helps to inhibit the develop-

Figure 5.4. Southern Hills Country Club in Tulsa, Oklahoma, grows bermudagrass in the sun and Kentucky bluegrass in the shade. This photo, taken in winter, illustrates the natural patterning of grasses as a result of tree shade. This combination of warm and cool-season grasses is a valuable low maintenance solution in Zones 3 and 4, but also presents a mowing height dilemma (see text).

ment of succulent tissue which is more prone to injury from disease and wear."

Applying extra nitrogen fertilizer to feed both the grass and the trees only serves to make the grass grow taller and leggier. A better solution is to apply only enough nitrogen to keep the turf green and growing. Turf needs a certain amount of nitrogen to outgrow the effects of powdery mildew (Cook, 1994a). As long as turf is producing fresh tissue, powdery mildew can't keep up.

One management practice that has met with mixed success is **fertilizer tree spikes**. Fertilizer spikes are applied by pounding them into the ground. Presumably down there, the tree can use them and the grass can't. Well, nice theory. In practice, they overstimulate the grass above the spike, leaving a dog-drop appearance to the turf. Whitcomb and other tree specialists instead recommend a simple over-the-top, slow release, granular fertilizer applied uniformly across the turf. Potassium fertilization is particularly beneficial to turf in shade. It strengthens the plant without producing unneeded foliage (Carroll and Petrovic, 1991).

Weed control. Shade brings with it its own gentry of weeds. Weeds that are rare in full sun can be a real problem in the shade—ground ivy, for example.

Shade weed control can be complicated by the limits of certain herbicides. Water-soluble herbicides like dicamba applied under the driplines can injure trees (Blake, 1982). The number of suitable herbicide options is painfully few. But on the plus side, there are some weeds you seldom see in shade. "Many turf weeds are eliminated by shade. For example, you seldom if ever see crabgrass under trees," says Duell.

Chapter 6

Mixing Turfgrasses

MIXING THE OLD-FASHIONED WAY: THE SHOTGUN APPROACH

Turf mixtures have been around as long as lawns have. The historic example of a turf mixture is the **shotgun mixture**. In the early days of turfgrass management, little was known about the performance of grasses under different growing conditions. The common strategy was to throw in as many components into a mixture as you could think of, in hopes that "survival of the fittest" would prevail. In other words, nature selected your grasses rather than you.

The shotgun approach was actually a carryover from the fact that early seed harvests were anything but pure. Turf seed a century ago was a amalgamation of whatever happened to be growing in a pasture at the time it was harvested. The resulting turf contained a number of grasses, including taller, unfit ones, which presumably would be mowed away, leaving the finer, more compact grasses to persist in your lawn.

The theory of the shotgun mixture was basically sound: Plant a lot of grasses and one or more should survive. Grass diversification has numerous advantages (as described in the next section). Different components in the mixture would prosper depending upon whether a spot was too wet, too dry, in full sun, or full shade.

But over time the shortcomings of the shotgun mixture became apparent. Survival of the fittest has one big flaw: Fit plants are never able to *completely* push out the less fit. As a result, taller, bunchy grasses such as redtop, tall fescue, and smooth bromegrass persisted in the turf, albeit at low populations, leaving a clumpy cluster of colors and textures. Between mowings the taller clumps may grow several inches higher than the surrounding turf, leading to a mounded appearance.

Burt Musser's classic book on turf management in the 1950s (Musser, 1950) recommended shotgun-style mixtures for virtually every purpose. Redtop and other coarse grasses were in vogue as **companion crops**—a concept borrowed from forage management (Brede, 1988b). Many of the early turf management professors were in fact transplanted forage scientists.

A companion crop is a vigorous, fast germinating grass that is added to a weaker one to nurse it along during establishment. These grasses were also called **nurse crops**. It wasn't until the late 1960s and early 1970s that the disadvantages of nurse crops were seen to outweigh their advantages, and researchers began recommending against them.

Even today, a segment of the turf industry still clings to a shotgun approach in mixing. Many discount-store turf seed products still contain a range of undesirable grasses including annual ryegrass (see the following section on junk mixtures). The low cost of annual ryegrass seed makes for an inexpensive package price. Trouble arises later, though, when these undesirable grasses turn ugly (see Table 6.4).

THE BENEFITS OF BIODIVERSITY IN MIXTURES

The main advantage of mixtures is **biodiversity**. By combining two or more turfgrasses, you bring together the desirable characteristics of each while masking their shortcomings. For example, if grass A has drought tolerance, grass B has shade tolerance, and grass C has early spring greenup, then turf planted to A+B+C would have good drought and shade tolerance, and would green up early in spring. What a deal.

Turf researchers have discovered other reasons to mix:

- *Higher shoot density*—Studies have shown that a mixture of two grasses can generate a slightly higher **tiller density** than either grass by itself (Brede, 1984a). In theory, two grasses should be able to mine the soil better than one, allowing them to produce a thicker, denser lawn. Tiller density is measured in shoots per square inch of ground surface.
- *Enhanced disease resistance*—Combining grasses broadens the disease resistance spectrum of the turf. Vic Gibeault, University of California–Riverside researcher and extension specialist, found better resistance to dollar spot and summer patch disease in mixtures, over and above that of either component used alone (Gibeault et al., 1980). Researchers at the Sports Turf Research Institute in Bingley, England, came to the same conclusion (Raikes et al., 1996). They found that red thread and fusarium patch could be minimized by mixing Kentucky bluegrass and perennial ryegrass together. Optimal disease suppression was found at the midpoint of the mixtures: 50% bluegrass and 50% ryegrass shoots.
- *Better shade tolerance*—A turf's shade tolerance can be improved by including a shade-loving grass such as fescue in the mix (Karnok, 1981; Roberts and Roberts, 1993). That way, the turf will have good shade tolerance no matter where the shadows fall.
- *Improved insect resistance*—Combining an endophyte-containing grass with one lacking endophyte adds insect resistance (Saha and Johnson-Cicalese, 1988). Chapter 12 describes the benefits of endophyte to turf management.
- *Earlier spring greenup*—A mixture of two grasses can green up earlier in the spring: In an experiment using Kentucky bluegrass/perennial ryegrass mixtures, I found that a mixed stand greened up earlier in the spring than either of its components alone (Brede, 1984a).
- *Better tolerance to low maintenance*—Having two or more grasses broadens the chances of surviving drought, infrequent mowing, or reduced fertilizer and pesticide use.
- *Better looking turf*—Michigan State University researchers (Krick et al., 1995) found that under the wear and tear of heavy foot traffic, mixtures of perennial ryegrass and Kentucky bluegrass were more attractive than either grass grown alone.

GRASSES THAT MIX, AND GRASSES THAT DON'T

It would be easy to mix grasses together if they all were "mixable." Trouble is, they're not. Some grasses mix with relative ease, while others will fight anything they're combined with; they result in an uneven, patchy stand, with swirls of colors and textures—not the uniform green carpet we've come to expect from turfgrasses (Figure 6.1).

So, how do you tell in advance if a particular mixture will work? It's not easy. Think about all the grasses mentioned in this book—over 300 of them. Now consider the number of possible mixtures you could concoct with them. Why, just the 2-way mixtures would top 100,000 possible combinations—not counting the 3, 4, and ***n***-way mixtures. Of the 100,000 possible combinations, turfgrass researchers have performed practical field testing on about 10 or 20 different mixtures. For the remaining 99,980 combinations, it's only an educated guess whether or not they'll work.

Fortunately, there are some guidelines to follow in creating successful mixtures. These guidelines were developed using the traditional turf species (Table 6.1), but the theories are sound and should extrapolate to the unconventional grasses as well.

Successful mixing. The best mixing grasses are either **bunch-type** or **rhizomatous** (Chapter 1 explains these growth habits). Across the board,

Table 6.1. Compatibility of turfgrasses in mixtures. This table compares pairs of grasses in 2-way combinations. To check for compatibility of a given pair, locate the box where the horizontal row of one grass intersects with the vertical column of another. The color of that box indicates the level of compatibility, as shown on the key. Most of the grass combinations in this table *have not* been tested by practical field research for their positive compatibility. Relatively few pairs of grasses have undergone extensive research evaluation (see text).

Species	Bahiagrass	Bermudagrass	Buffalograss	Broad leaf carpet grass	Narrcw leaf carpet grass	Centipede grass	Kikuyu grass	Seashore paspalum	St. Augustinegrass	*Zoysia japonica*	*Zoysia matrella*	*Zoysia tenuifolia*
Bermudagrass												
Buffalograss												
Broad leaf carpet grass												
Narrow leaf carpet grass												
Centipede grass												
Kikuyu grass												
Seashore paspalum												
St. Augustinegrass												
Zoysia japonica												
Zoysia matrella												
Zoysia tenuifolia												
Alkaligrass, distans												
Colonial bentgrass												
Creeping bentgrass												
Highland bentgrass												
Velvet bentgrass												
Canada bluegrass												
Kentucky bluegrass												
Roughstalk bluegrass												
Supine bluegrass												
Chewings fescue												
Hard fescue												
Sheep fescue												
Slender creeping fescue												
Strong creeping red												
Tall fescue												
Perennial ryegrass												
Redtop												

Table 6.1. Compatibility of turfgrasses in mixtures. This table compares pairs of grasses in 2-way combinations. To check for compatibility of a given pair, locate the box where the horizontal row of one grass intersects with the vertical column of another. The color of that box indicates the level of compatibility, as shown on the key. Most of the grass combinations in this table *have not* been tested by practical field research for their positive compatibility. Relatively few pairs of grasses have undergone extensive research evaluation (see text) (continued).

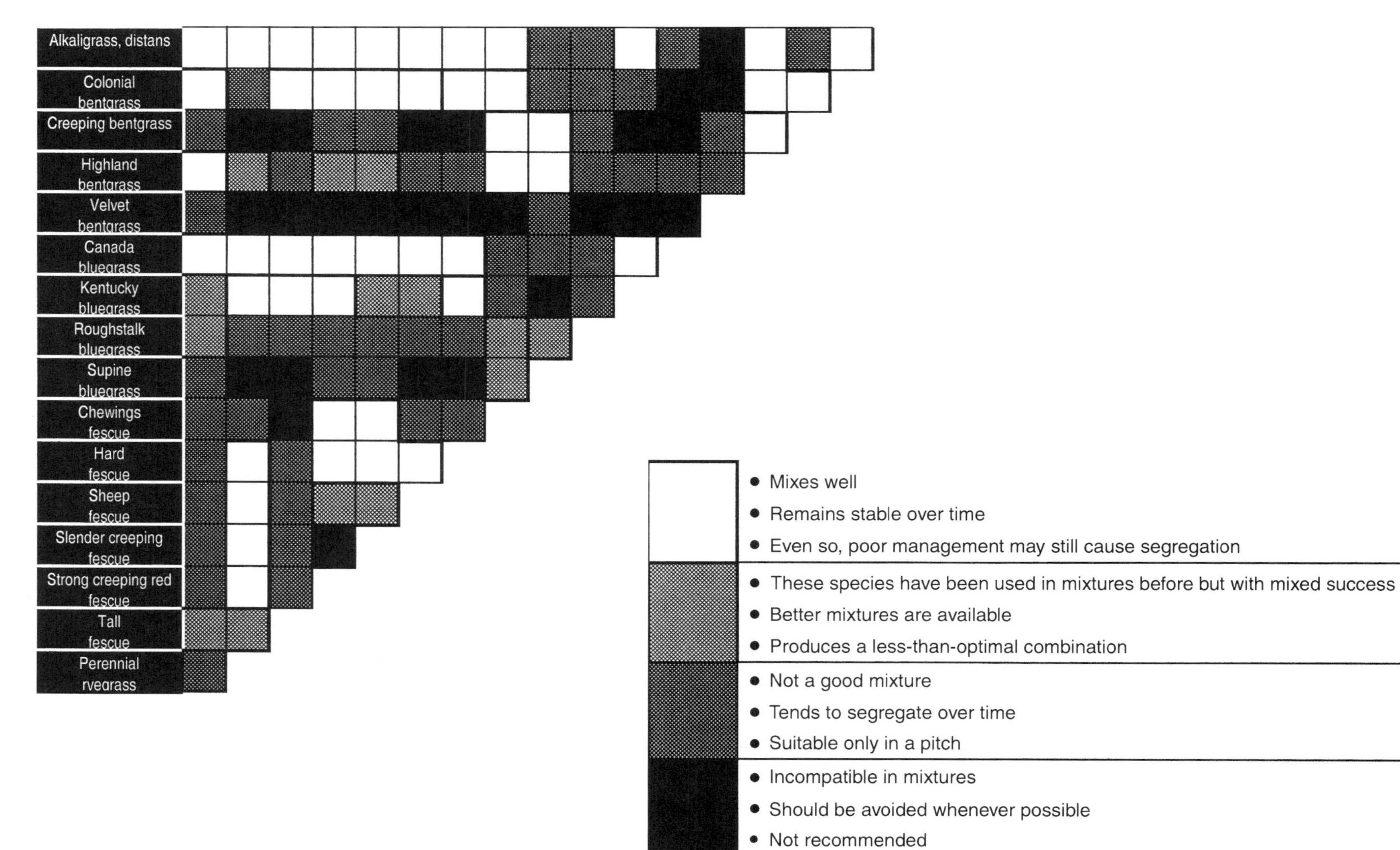

Table 6.2. Compatibility of turfgrass growth habits in mixtures. Turf species with a rhizome growth habit, for example, are compatible in mixtures with bunch-type grasses (see top line in table). For an explanation of these growth habits, consult Chapter 1.

	Rhizomes and stolons	Stolons	Rhizomes	Bunch
Bunch				
Rhizomes				
Stolons				
Rhizomes and stolons				

- Mixes well
- Remains stable over time

- In general these mixtures are fairly unstable
- Some mixtures have been created with these combinations, but success usually depends on matching up the right varieties

- Plants tend to crawl all over each other resulting in patches
- Not recommended; should be avoided

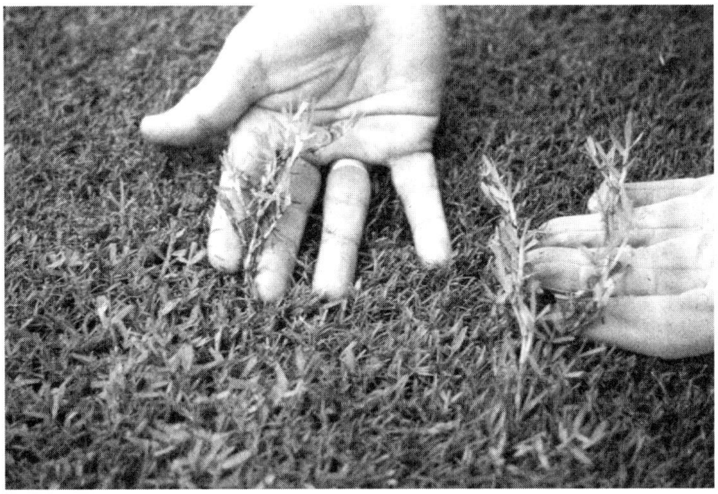

Figure 6.1. Stoloniferous grasses are notoriously poor mixers. At Laguna National Golf Course in Singapore (shown here), plants of volunteer common bermudagrass are overriding the "Tifway 419" planted on the fairways. The coarser stolons of common bermudagrass create unattractive patches by literally crawling over top of its competition.

Figure 6.2. Extremely broad and fine bladed grasses should be avoided in mixtures. This St. Augustinegrass lawn in Orlando, Florida, was overseeded with fine fescue, creating a cacophony of wide and narrow blades.

bunch-type and rhizomatous grasses mix fairly well with each other or with others of the same category. Problems arise when you attempt to mix anything with **stoloniferous** grasses (Table 6.2). Stoloniferous grasses creep over the top of their competitors, forming large, unsightly patches. Over time, a stoloniferous grass may force out its companion. Therefore, stoloniferous grasses are best planted by themselves. This same rule applies to grasses that have *both* stolons and rhizomes.

Although growth habit (bunch/rhizomes/stolons) is the key issue in successful mixing, other factors contribute to a good mixture. Here are a few things to watch for when choosing mixture components:

- *Plant height and vertical growth rate*—When picking grasses for a mixture, select species that are similar in their mature (unclipped) plant heights. Mature height is a good indicator of the vertical growth rate of grasses—how much they're obliged to pile on the topgrowth. For example, if you're trying to create a "prairie landscape," combine grasses of all about 3 to 4 ft (1 to 1.5 m) tall. On the other hand, if you're trying to create a reduced-mowing lawn mixture, match together several shorter growing species.
- *Blade width*—Tall fescue and hard fescue are two grasses you'd rarely want to mix. Why? Although these grasses are both bunch-type (and Table 6.2 says bunch types are generally compatible), they differ vastly in blade width. The mixed turf would appear as a swirl of broad and needle-like blades (Figure 6.2). The same goes for other pairs of wide and narrow-bladed grasses.
- *Leaf color*—Many references caution about combining grasses with dissimilar tints. Grasses vary in hue from a rich bluish-green to a pale apple yellow. However, for the most part, I haven't found color differences to be a big stumbling block in creating mixtures—provided you avoid the extremes. For example, the yellow-green of annual bluegrass combines poorly with the dark blue-green of creeping bentgrass. But beyond these extremes, all's fair.

EXAMPLES OF SUCCESSFUL AND UNSUCCESSFUL MIXTURES AND BLENDS

A lot can be learned from the successes and failures of others. This section details experiments and experiences of researchers and managers who have tried various turf mixtures. Their problems and triumphs point the way to creating desirable combinations of grasses.

Many of these examples are based on the traditional turf species, where much of the research information lies. The final section in this chap-

Terminology

- **Mixture**—the combination of two or more turf *species* together
- **Blend**—a combination of two or more *varieties* of the same grass species

ter attempts to extrapolate this information to the unconventional grasses, using the basic concepts learned with the traditional grasses.

Blending bluegrass varieties together

Blending varieties is important with Kentucky bluegrass. Unlike other turf species, Kentucky bluegrass is **apomictic**, meaning all the seeds of a given variety are genetically identical. As explained in Chapter 2, bluegrass clones itself through seed. Other turfgrasses contain a genetically diverse **population** within each variety. Thus, blending is not as critical as with bluegrass. Blending of bluegrasses is necessary to broaden the genetic base and offer additional disease and adaptation options not offered in a single variety.

Reed Funk, Rutgers University turf breeder, is the father to many of the bluegrass varieties on the market. As part of his breeding work, Funk regularly observes thousands of breeding plots in a given year. When you look at as many plots as Funk does, you can't help but notice patterns.

Over the years, Funk began seeing a pattern among his Kentucky bluegrass varieties: Some varieties greened up early in the spring, while others took their own sweet time. Some varieties became stemmy during flowering season, others didn't. After years of observation, Funk and his colleagues began grouping these grasses, based on their performance characteristics. Their groupings, they later discovered, were valuable in formulating blends.

"We made an attempt to classify the varieties. It's something you always have reluctance to do, because next time you'd probably do it a little differently," says Funk.

Funk's system of blending is based on performance groupings and parentage (Murphy et al., 1993). It makes sense to combine varieties that offer *additional* performance features. After all, the main idea of mixing grasses is to extend their adaptation. Combining grasses with identical performance would add nothing to the turf.

One day Funk asked Jim Murphy, Rutgers turf extension specialist, to look over the plots. "I went out to the plots one day in mid January and put wooden stakes facing one direction in all the ones I called 'Bellevue' types and stakes facing the other direction in the 'BVMG' types," says Funk. "Jim couldn't see any differences between them. I mean, you could see great differences between the two types but no differences within the types." Varieties within the Bellevue grouping all had similar disease responses. All BVMG types also reacted similar to one another. But the Bellevue types as a whole resisted a *different* spectrum of diseases than the BVMG types.

Recommendations. Funk recommends combining 3 to 4 bluegrasses, each originating from a different performance group. That way, you create the broadest possible range of adaptation. For example, since the winter color, spring greenup, and disease resistance patterns of the Bellevue types are all similar, there would be little sense to blend together more than one Bellevue type.

"If you want a Bellevue type in there, just pick the best Bellevue type that performs best for you. There's no point in adding more than one," says Funk.

Funk's seven groupings of bluegrasses are listed in Table 6.3. Sample varieties are provided with each group. To choose a good blend, pick one variety from within each group. Select the 3 or 4 groupings that have the characteristics you're seeking in a grass, such as early green up or wear tolerance. You don't need to choose varieties from all 7 categories.

Benefits of mixing Kentucky bluegrass with other grasses

Where adapted, Kentucky bluegrass has many desirable features to offer heavy-play turf. Even in low maintenance settings, bluegrass adds wear-resisting properties to turf mixtures.

Table 6.3. Kentucky bluegrass varieties can be categorized into seven distinct groups based on their performance profile as turf, according to Reed Funk, turf breeding professor at Rutgers University. These categories become important when blending varieties together. Combining varieties from the same category into a blend adds little to the genetic diversity of the stand. The best recommendation is to choose one variety from each of 3 to 4 categories.

Group	Characteristics	Sample Varieties
Aggressive types	• High shoot density • Creeps by rhizomes into neighboring areas • Tend to dominate in blends and mixtures	Bensun A-34, Limousine, P-104, Touchdown
Baron types (BVMG)	• Medium, good turf characteristics • Excellent seed yield • Susceptible to stripe smut	Abbey, Baron, Bluestar, Crest, Fortuna, Gnome, Kelly, Marquis, Merit, Raven, Viva
Bellevue types	• Medium, good turf characteristics • Excellent winter color and spring greenup • Little or no cool-temperature purpling or browning	Banff, Classic, Dawn, Freedom, Georgetown, Haga, Suffolk, Trenton
Midwest ecotypes	• Erect growth habit • Narrow leaves • Early seed maturity • Susceptible to leaf spot • Responds to drought by quickly going dormant	Alene, Ginger, Greenley, Huntsville, Kenblue, Ronde, South Dakota
Mid-Atlantic ecotypes	• Medium, high density • Deep, extensive rhizome system • Excellent summer stress tolerance	SR 2000, Eagleton, Huntsville, Livingston, Monopoly, Preakness, Wabash
North Latitude Compact types	• Elite turf performance • Low, compact growth habit • Late spring greenup • Excellent leaf spot resistance	Able I, Alpine, Amazon, America, Apex, Award, Barsweet, Blacksburg, Conni, Eva, Glade, Indigo, Midnight, Nugget, NuGlade, Opal, Platini, Trampas, Unique
Other types	• These varieties possess characteristics of two or more different groups • They defy classification (for now)	Allure, Ampellia, Ascot, Aspen, Barblue, Caliber, Cardiff, Challenger, Chelsea, Cheri, Cobalt, Coventry, Eclipse, Estate, Fylking, Julia, Liberty, NuBlue, NuStar, Ram I, Shamrock, Washington

Here are some benefits for including Kentucky bluegrass in a turf mixture:

- *A buoyant cushion*—A carpet installer once told me that the *pad* underneath is more important to the longevity of a carpet than the carpet itself. The same applies to turf. Bluegrass thatch provides a resilient cushion to sports turf and other high wear applications. Without thatch, heavy traffic can grind out the grass crowns, injuring the stand. Sports turf managers also report that ripping or tearing of turf is less severe with bluegrass turf because of its rugged rhizome system (Brede, 1994b).
- *An even surface*—Mixing Kentucky bluegrass with a broader bladed grass like

tall fescue helps even out the somewhat rough texture of the fescue. Bluegrass mixes well with tall fescue. Recent studies have shown that the newer fescue cultivars are better mixers than the older ones (Brede, 1993a).

- *Added shade tolerance*—In warmer regions, bluegrass can be introduced into a turf to enhance shade tolerance. If you sow a mixture of bluegrass and bermudagrass seed, eventually you'll end up with bermudagrass in the sun and bluegrass in the shade (see Figure 5.4).
- *Winter insurance*—Winter injury to bluegrass is rare, occurring only under special circumstances such as ice or arctic cold. Other cool-season grasses (tall fescue, perennial ryegrass) do not persist in Zone 6 or even in cooler parts of Zone 1 (Raikes et al., 1996). Adding bluegrass to a mixture increases the winter-hardiness of your turf. "In our area [of New York state], bluegrass is the grass of choice," says Norm Hummel, former turfgrass extension specialist at Cornell University. "If you look at our national test trials, after 10 years the bluegrasses look the same as a year or so after they were put in. The ryegrasses and tall fescues are not nearly as persistent after 4 years. If you don't overseed them, they're heavily infested with other grasses."
- *It bounces back*—Kentucky bluegrass has good recuperative potential. Because of its rhizomes, it can repopulate a thinned stand (Carroll and Petrovic, 1991). Bunch grasses, on the other hand, may require periodic reseeding to maintain their density, especially on sports fields.
- *Broader disease resistance*—Bluegrass mixtures offer the potential for pesticide savings even on high maintenance turfs like golf courses. "Last year in New England I saw golf courses spend perhaps $3500 for one pythium (fungicide) application," says Jim Connolly, former USGA Northeastern Regional Agronomist. "If these courses had had some bluegrass in there, they might not have been as concerned. The negative with 100% ryegrass is that every year you have to reseed 300 lb to the acre (35 g/m^2). And with that, you end up getting your density so high you end up with more disease."

Blending bentgrass varieties on a golf course

Blending bentgrass varieties on putting greens has never been popular in the past. The main reason, of course, was that up until about 1985, there was really only one major bent variety in existence: "Penncross." Today there are 20 and counting.

Golf superintendents were initially skeptical about blending grasses on a green. Grass segregation on a putting green can be disfiguring. Penncross itself has been known to segregate into genetically different, circular patches after about 20 years of growth. Adding a second or third bent variety panicked even the more progressive superintendents.

"Segregation is not strictly cosmetic," says Ken Mangum of the Atlanta Athletic Club, Duluth, Georgia. Mangum finds that differences in leaf texture and density among segregating bent patches can affect the game of golf. "You can see a different putting speed and a different grain in some of these older segregated patches," he says.

After years of uneasiness, the golf course industry finally has begun to embrace putting green blends. Today, they're seen as a means of diversifying the grass population in hopes of fighting a broader range of diseases and stress.

But until recently, no one knew for sure if bentgrass blends really *did* good or whether they just sounded like a good idea. A series of studies by Yue-lan Chen, a graduate student at the University of Guelph, Ontario, Canada, has helped resolve this speculation. Chen and her advisors studied mixtures of "Emerald" and "Cobra" creeping bentgrass and "Astoria" colonial bentgrass (Chen et al., 1996).

Chen's three bent varieties differed in color. Yet in spite of these differences, the blended stand appeared uniform and well mixed. The study was run only 2 years, thus it remains unclear whether segregation will still occur 20 years down the road. However, university trials are seldom set up to answer these long-term questions.

Chen's study also showed desirable blending effects on disease resistance. Dollar spot susceptibility was masked by the addition of a resistant companion. One grass' strengths compensated for another's weakness.

Competitiveness against weeds was also bolstered by blending. Annual bluegrass encroachment was less in the blended plots than in straight-variety plots. Furthermore, the annual bluegrass plants in blended plots had fewer tillers and shorter roots than in the single-variety plots. Chen concluded that, "mixture populations are significantly superior to monocultures in competitive ability against annual bluegrass. This may be due to enhanced vigor of the bentgrass mixtures."

Tall fescue mixtures

There was a time in the not-too-distant past when mixing tall fescue with any other grass was taboo. Career turf managers would quietly snicker as they saw newbies attempting to combine tall fescue with Kentucky bluegrass, for example. They knew from years of trial and error that the resulting turf would be a bunchy mess. Jack Harper, retired extension specialist at Penn State University, was not alone when he cautioned turf managers in a 1984 fact sheet (Harper and Landschoot, 1991) that "under no circumstances should other grass species be seeded with tall fescue."

The tall fescue of yesteryear was a broad bladed, stemmy, upright-growing bunch grass. "Kentucky 31," the popular variety at the time, was actually a forage grass, selected for its high foliage yields. Kentucky-31 also suffers from orchardgrass contamination in many of its seedlots, which introduces yet another broad bladed grass.

Improved varieties mix better. The newer tall fescues are so strikingly different from Kentucky-31 that trained botanists might mistake them for a different species. "Essentially, we've taken a species that natively matures its seedheads at nose height and changed it into a dense, dark, compact grass that sets seed at waist height or below," says Mark Sellmann, tall fescue breeder for Simplot Turf & Hort.

Other innovations in tall fescue have been a slower vertical growth rate, darker green color, better disease resistance, and a generally more leafy and less stemmy growth habit. Furthermore, unlike Kentucky-31, the new fescue varieties are available as certified seed. Today, nearly all new fescue varieties are grown in Oregon, where orchardgrass-contaminated seedlots are a thing of the past.

With such a dramatic evolution in tall fescue, I decided it was time to reexamine the old taboo of mixing tall fescue with Kentucky bluegrass. Had plant breeding progressed far enough that tall fescue was now a good mixer? The best way to answer that question was with an experiment.

Ratio research results. In my study, results indicated that seed ratio was more flexible with the newer fescue cultivars than with the older, common types. The standard 90% fescue—10% bluegrass ratio of old seemed to be essential only when common tall fescue was used, not with the improved varieties. A broader range of ratios—extending from 50 to 95% fescue seed—could be used with the newer fescues.

Many uses of tall fescue/Kentucky bluegrass mixtures. Sod producers were the first to discover the benefits of a tall fescue/Kentucky bluegrass mixture. To harvest sod of tall fescue (a bunch grass), they use **nylon netting** to bind the sod together. The netting is laid down before planting and the roots intertwine with it, knitting the grass as it's cut and harvested.

One day a rather clever sod grower once got the idea to try Kentucky bluegrass rhizomes to bind tall fescue sod, instead of netting. The idea worked. Mixing bluegrass with fescue to bind the sod caught on among sod producers across the nation.

Later, other segments of the turf industry learned of the advantages of mixing these two grasses together. Athletic field managers liked the combination. The fescue was tough and deep rooted. The bluegrass knitted the turf together and helped fill bare spots. Mixtures of the two species formed a compatible combination for a diversity of uses.

Perennial ryegrass/Kentucky bluegrass mixtures

As explained in Chapter 2, perennial ryegrass is notoriously vigorous in the seedbed. Its explosive seedling growth can literally wipe out other components mixed with it. Perennial ryegrass plants have been shown to generate 4 times the shoots, 10 times the leaves, 15 times the roots, and 33 times the overall plant weight as Kentucky bluegrass during the first weeks of establishment (Brede, 1984b).

Over the years, I have performed a number of experiments on perennial ryegrass/Kentucky bluegrass mixtures. These experiments have led me to believe—contrary to earlier thought—that ryegrass/bluegrass mixtures can indeed be tamed.

Timing is everything. Competition between these two grasses depends on *when* they are planted. I found that the planting season makes a big difference, swinging the competition one way or the other.

In one experiment, I seeded plots of ryegrass and bluegrass twice a month from April through November. I then monitored the growth of the seedlings for six weeks of establishment—the *critical period* for determining a balanced mix with ryegrass. What I found was two totally different growth patterns throughout the year. Bluegrass's growth rate stayed fairly constant, producing about two shoots for every one seedling that emerged—regardless of when it was planted.

Ryegrass was different. In spring and fall, ryegrass produced a number of shoots equal to bluegrass. But in midsummer (June and July) when days were long and the sun was bright, ryegrass generated five times as many shoots as Kentucky bluegrass. Thus spring or fall would be preferable to a midseason planting for constructing a balanced blend.

Mow your way to a balanced blend. Another handy tool for shifting competition is your mower. Mowing has a profound impact on the balance of a mixture, especially during the critical establishment phase.

When establishing grass, a manager might typically begin mowing 4 to 6 weeks after planting. In a series of establishment mowing studies, I discovered that mowing sooner after sowing—rather than later—shifted the competition toward the slower establishing grass (Brede, 1984b). Earlier mowing (as soon as one or two weeks after planting) nipped off the emerging ryegrass, allowing more bluegrass plants to establish (Figure 6.3). The same trick was later tried on annual ryegrass/tall fescue mixtures and was found to work just as effectively (Brede, 1988b). Thus this technique appears to be a valuable and inexpensive tool for throttling the growth of a faster establishing grass to keep it from obliterating its slower sprouting companion.

Bentgrass/annual bluegrass mixtures

Mixtures of bentgrass and annual bluegrass on golf course greens, tees, and fairways are not intentional mixtures. They result from the invasion of annual bluegrass over time as a weed. Annual bluegrass prospers under moist, closely trimmed, compacted conditions. Bentgrass doesn't.

This mixture of grasses has created more heated debate—with fewer solutions—than any other subject in golf course management. The story that follows illustrates one of my own experiences with bentgrass/annual bluegrass mixtures, including research work I later performed to help understand the problem.

A golf course experience. My first turf job after graduating with my undergraduate degree was as assistant superintendent for a 27-hole country club outside Pittsburgh. The course boasted three 9-hole courses with "Highland" and "Astoria" bentgrass fairways. Needless to say, annual bluegrass was wall to wall.

After a few months on the job, my boss suggested that we add some "Penncross" creeping bentgrass seed into the fairways to increase the bent population and stem the spread of annual bluegrass. At the time the fairways were 30 to 40% annual bluegrass.

I instructed our crew to vertically mow the fairways and slit seed 2 lb per 1000 ft^2 (10 g/m^2) of Penncross into the slits. After two weeks of careful planting and watering, lo and behold, we had slivers of grass emerging. Another week brought still more seedlings, until after 4 weeks, we had a stand to be proud of.

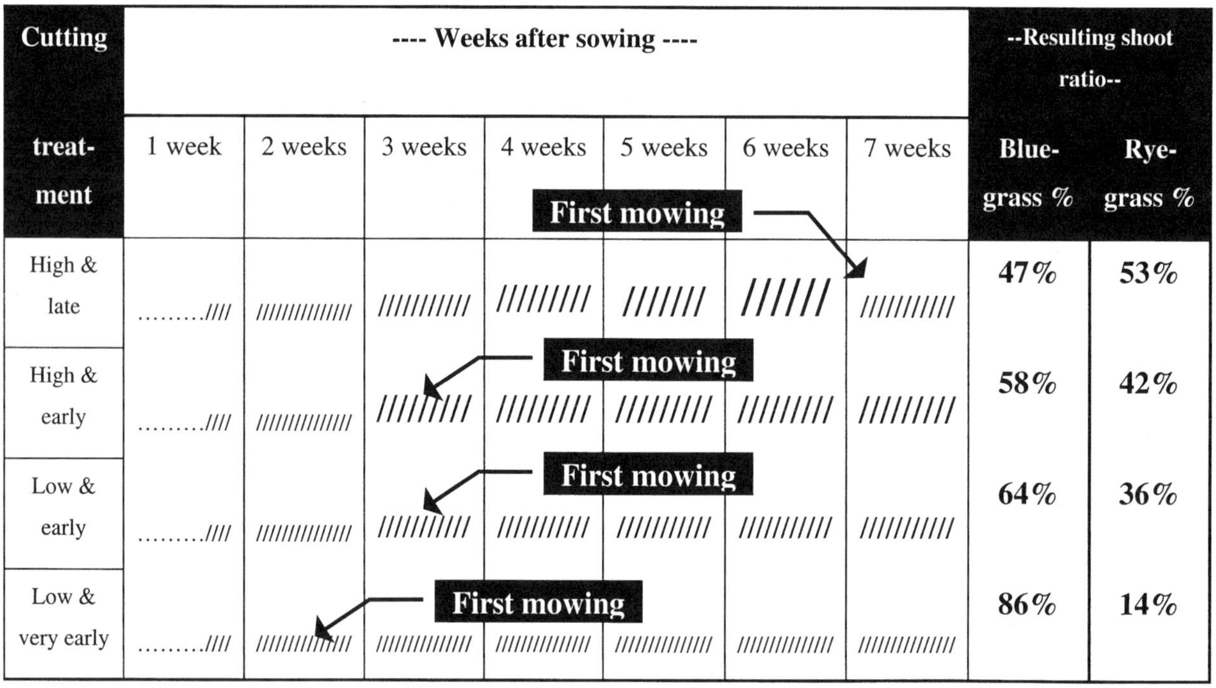

Cutting treat-ment	---- Weeks after sowing ----							--Resulting shoot ratio--	
	1 week	2 weeks	3 weeks	4 weeks	5 weeks	6 weeks	7 weeks	Blue-grass %	Rye-grass %
High & late	.........////	//////////////	//////////	////////	///////	//////	First mowing → //////////	47%	53%
High & early	.........////	//////////////	First mowing → //////////	/////////	/////////	/////////	/////////	58%	42%
Low & early	.........////	//////////////	First mowing → //////////	//////////	//////////	//////////	//////////	64%	36%
Low & very early	.........////	First mowing → //////////////	/////////////	/////////////	/////////////	/////////////	/////////////	86%	14%

Figure 6.3. Dramatic shifts in mixtures can be induced by initial mowing practices. The simple choice of *when* you start mowing can shift populations from one species to another. In this Pennsylvania study, mowing treatments were begun on different dates and at one of two heights: "Low"=$^1/2$ in. (13 mm) or "High"=1 $^1/2$ in. (38 mm). All plots were seeded to the same mix of 95% Kentucky bluegrass and 5% perennial ryegrass seed. Population percentage readings were taken after 2 months by actual tiller counting. An early (2 to 3 weeks after sowing) and close ($^1/2$ in.) initial mow strongly favored the slower establishing bluegrass, by nipping off the quicker sprouting ryegrass. This technique also works with other mixtures of slow/fast establishing grasses.

By 5 weeks the individual seedlings were starting to tiller. My boss was so proud, he invited a number of local golf superintendents over to view our successful battle against annual bluegrass. While showing off the plants, I took a closer look at our new seedlings. To my horror I discovered that nearly every of them was annual bluegrass! It's times like this that keeps a person humble. "What happened to the bentgrass seedlings?" I wondered. I had originally seen a good number of genuine bentgrass seedlings coming up. A few weeks later, they were gone.

Research to the rescue. Years passed and I earned a doctorate degree and took a research job at Oklahoma State University, but I never forgot about my experience with bentgrass overseeding, and wondered why my golf course overseeding attempt of years earlier had failed. To answer that question, I conducted four years of lab and field studies on a rather large scale to find an answer.

I learned that annual bluegrass comes in several forms. Researchers have long noted the diversity in annual bluegrass. Some strains of annual bluegrass are true annuals while others have creeping stolons and a perennial growth habit. No wonder annual bluegrass is hard to control. This enormous diversity adds to the difficulty in taming this tough weed.

My first series of studies examined the seedling growth of annual bluegrass versus creeping bentgrass. On a bare seedbed, I planted seeds of annual bluegrass and bentgrass; both established rapidly. By 5 weeks, bentgrass had a slight advantage over annual bluegrass in shoot numbers.

Next I tried interplanting seeds into an established sod. In a competitive environment—interseeding bentgrass into a mature sod of

Figure 6.4. In this experiment at Oklahoma State University, creeping bentgrass and annual bluegrass seedlings reacted strikingly different when overseeded. Nearly all of the annual bluegrass seed introduced into this aerifier hole in a mature annual bluegrass sod emerged to form an adult plant (l.). However, virtually none of the overseeded bentgrass seedlings persisted (r.).

annual bluegrass—the opposite occurred: Annual bluegrass flourished and bent withered. Results mirrored my failed fairway overseeding attempt of years earlier.

In my experiment, bentgrass seeds were sown into aerifier holes punched in an annual bluegrass sod. The seeds germinated rapidly. In fact, seedlings in the sod actually sprouted a few days quicker than seedlings on the bare seedbed (probably due to the sheltering effect of the surrounding sod, which moderates the microclimate around the sprouts).

But shortly after emergence, the bentgrass seedlings in the sod began to turn spindly and wither. The frail bentgrass seedlings were unable to reach the sunlight.

To make a long story short, annual bluegrass proved a more fearsome competitor than bentgrass in an interseeded situation (Figure 6.4). The data even suggest that annual bluegrass may be using chemical weapons against bentgrass, releasing natural herbicides to control its opponent (Brede, 1991a). However if such chemicals do exist, they appear to be short-range weapons, affecting only the very plant next door.

In conclusion, *Poa annua* is a tough competitor against bentgrass. When an ample pool of annual bluegrass seed exists in the soil, *Poa* will normally have the edge over tiny-seeded bent. Herbicides and growth regulators can be used to favor bent establishment. Some handy tips are offered in Chapters 7 and 12.

Zoysiagrass/tall fescue mixtures

In theory, mixtures of cool- and warm-season grasses should be a godsend for Transition Zone turf. If only the right combination of grasses could be found. In theory, the warm-season grass would withstand the grueling summer temperatures, then in the autumn, the cool-season would kick in and grow throughout the winter. Such a mixture would provide a green playing surface in all four seasons, suggesting the name **four-season turf**.

In reality, a true four-season turf mixture has been elusive. Part of the problem traces to the stoloniferous growth of warm-season grasses—a trait incompatible in mixtures (Table 6.2). Some warm/cool-season combinations have been tried: Kentucky bluegrass with bermudagrass, creeping bentgrass with bermudagrass, and tall fescue with bahiagrass, to name a few (Brede, 1992a; Dunn et al., 1994). But none had the staying power for a true four-season mixture. Usually, the cool-season grass requires periodic reseeding to prevent its disappearance.

Research at the U.S. Department of Agriculture (USDA) at Beltsville in the early 1980s (Murray, 1985) suggested that mixtures of *Zoy-*

sia japonica and tall fescue might stand a chance for four-season success, if the technology could be mastered. Zoysia and tall fescue are both well adapted to the Transition Zone. Both have similar blade width and general appearance. Both are tough, wear-resistant grasses, suitable for sports fields. It seemed like a match made in heaven.

But mastering the technology was more complicated than it first appeared. To maintain a *stable* mixture, several factors had to be fine tuned: The right seeding rate, planting date, species ratio, varieties, cutting height, and fertility schedule had to be worked out. Also, there was the question of whether this mixture would work *outside* the narrow geographic window in which it was developed. In cooler regions, the tall fescue might become too aggressive and force out the zoysia. In warmer regions, just the opposite might occur. Questions remained to be answered.

USDA research. A pilot study proved successful (Murray, 1985). Jack Murray, the USDA turf researcher who pioneered the four-season mixture, concluded: "Results indicate that zoysiagrass can be successfully established with tall fescue, perennial rye, or Kentucky bluegrass, if seeded during the summer when temperatures are high enough (80°F [25°C] or above) for rapid zoysiagrass germination. Establishment was best where one to two pounds of tall fescue (5 to 10 g/m^2) and one pound of zoysiagrass (5 g/m^2) were seeded per 1000 ft^2. Perennial ryegrass and Kentucky bluegrass establishment have not been as good as tall fescue."

Later, the difficulty of establishing tall fescue and zoysiagrass *simultaneously* became apparent. Simple factors like seeding date became a major complication. A midsummer planting would get the zoysia growing, but it would be hard on the fescue. A fall planting would compromise the zoysia establishment, but the fescue would like it.

In later research, a concession was reached: The best results were obtained by dividing the planting in two—planting the zoysia by itself in early summer, allowing time for it to establish, and then overseeding in the fall with tall fescue. Thus, both grasses could be sown at their optimal season.

Kevin Morris followed up on Murray's work and continued several of his experiments (Morris, 1995a; Morris, 1995b). In a later series of tests under simulated sports-field wear, Morris concluded:

- A *lower* cutting height provided better overall performance than cutting heights over 3 in. (7.5 cm). Zoysia was unduly favored above 3 in.—a result that was totally unexpected.
- Applications of nitrogen fertilizer should be timed to favor the tall fescue (in early spring and late autumn). This helps overcome the tendency for zoysiagrass to dominate.
- Annual fall overseeding with tall fescue seed helps maintain its density.
- Traffic can have a big impact on the success or failure of the mixture.

Foot traffic was simulated on the plots using a differential-slip wear machine developed in England (Morris, 1995a). Fifteen passes per week were made over the plots using the wear machine, scuffing up the turf like a squad of linemen. After 8 weeks, the results were tallied.

Unlike in the earlier trials, the four-season mix performed poorly under heavy wear. The zoysiagrass/tall fescue mixture had the *second poorest* endurance of all the plots in the trial. Kentucky bluegrass—by itself or in combinations with other cool-season grasses—had the best traffic tolerance. (More information on wear tolerance and wear simulators can be found in Chapter 8.)

Therefore it's back to the drawing board for this four-season mixture, at least in terms of its athletic field applications. Other warm/cool-season combinations may be developed in the future. But because the growth habit and growing season differ so drastically between warm- and cool-season grasses, they may never be truly compatible in mixtures (Table 6.1).

Winter overseeding with a cool-season grass into a dormant warm-season grass

Technically, overseeding a cool-season grass into a dormant warm-season grass is a type of mixture. Both the cool- and warm-season grass are coexisting in the same space at the same time. However, this combination does not typify a stable, well-blended mixture. In the spring, the warm-season grass wakes up and pushes out the cool-season. By fall, all semblance of cool-season grass is gone and it must be overseeded again. Nonetheless, these are indeed mixtures, and this chapter is the place to discuss them.

Several grasses have been tested for winter overseeding with varying degrees of success. Only summary mention will be devoted to these mixtures in this book, because they constitute relatively high maintenance options.

Grasses commonly used in winter overseeding:

Warm-season grasses

- *Bermudagrass*—Bermuda has become the universal grass of the overseeding business. It recovers reliably in the springtime.
- *Zoysiagrass*—Overseeding of dormant *Zoysia japonica* fairways in Asia has been tried with mixed results. If the soil is scratched or vertically mowed too deeply, the zoysia rhizomes and crowns are injured, leading to spotty recovery in the spring.
- *St. Augustinegrass*—Where it's adapted, St. Augustinegrass may not always go completely dormant in a given year. Thus it may not require overseeding to maintain color. Furthermore, the textural difference between the broad St. Augustinegrass blades and anything else is a concern. That's why you'll seldom see overseeded St. Augustinegrass lawns.

Cool-season grasses

- *Perennial ryegrass*—Perennial ryegrass has become the gold standard of winter overseeding. It establishes quickly and easily and forms a dense, wear resistant surface. Ryegrass's main deficits are its relatively coarse leaves and rapid vertical growth.
- *Annual ryegrass*—Annual ryegrass is used mainly for low budget overseeding applications. Its yellow color and vigorous upright growth limit its application to second-rate lawns.
- *Roughstalk bluegrass*—Roughstalk bluegrass has caught on for putting green overseeding in recent years, because of its fine texture and easy spring transition. It is slower to establish than perennial ryegrass and lighter green in color. Roughstalk bluegrass is best suited to private golf courses, because it has too little wear tolerance to withstand resort or public course abuse.
- *Chewings and strong creeping red fescue*—Fine fescue has met with some success in winter overseeding. Fescue grasses are slower to establish than perennial ryegrass and lighter green in color. They are used mostly in 2- and 3-way combinations with perennial ryegrass and other grasses.
- *Creeping, colonial, Highland, and Idaho bentgrass*—The bentgrass family has application to putting green overseeding only. In general, bentgrass is too slow to establish and too slow to transition. But when it's growing, golfers love its fine texture and dark, blue-green color. Idaho bentgrass, a new turf species native to North America, promises faster germination and an easier spring transition (see Chapter 4).
- *Redtop*—Redtop's use in overseeding is limited to 2- and 3-way mixtures. A mixture ratio of 85% perennial ryegrass and 15% redtop is typical. Redtop can convey the fine texture and blue-green color of bentgrass. It is slower to establish than ryegrass especially under cold soil temperatures, but it readily transitions back to the warm-season grass.
- *Kentucky bluegrass*—Bluegrass's use in winter overseeding has waned to nearly zip. It is too slow to establish.
- *Annual, bulbous, and supine bluegrass*—Bluegrasses other than Kentucky bluegrass have been tested on winter greens. Their color is apple green and their germination is slow. However, once estab-

Figure 6.5. "Junk" or discount store grass seed mixtures seldom produce a quality turf. The reason traces to the quantities of annual ryegrass used as diluent in these products to make them inexpensive. This field trial at the Sports Turf Research Institute in Bingley, England, shows that junk mixtures (the light, stemmy plots) are no bargain.

lished, putting quality is good and spring transition is nearly ideal. High seed prices have limited their use.

"Junk" mixtures

Low cost is not necessarily synonymous with low maintenance. Sometimes it's better to spend a little extra up front than to pay a lot more later in added maintenance. It's like the old mechanics adage about changing your motor oil: "You can pay me now or you can pay me later...."

Junk seed mixtures represent a cheap alternative aimed at the uneducated consumer. These mixtures are concocted not on agronomics but on price. Components are added simply to bring the cost down as low as possible. Many people are suckered in by these inferior products (Figure 6.5).

The primary "cheapening agent" used in junk seed mixtures is annual ryegrass. Annual ryegrass is low-priced because it grows in the fertile seed fields of Oregon's Willamette Valley without even being planted or watered. A typical consumer mixture might contain as much as 88% annual ryegrass (Meyer, 1993). With a mixture like that, there's not much grass left to persist beyond the first growing season.

In the early 1990s, Bill Rose of Turf Seed, Inc., Hubbard, Oregon, had his staff locate and plant junk mixtures collected from local discount department stores (Meyer, 1993). Similar studies have since been conducted at Oregon State University and at International Seeds, Inc., Halsey, OR. In each case, the conclusion was the same: Junk seed performed like junk. High quality mixtures containing improved varieties always topped the trials (Table 6.4). Some of the discount-store mixtures without annual ryegrass performed acceptably, but still not as well as mixtures containing improved varieties. As more annual ryegrass was added, quality plummeted.

Junk seed is no bargain when it comes to long-term turf performance. Annual ryegrass crowds out the desirable grasses. Then it dies.

It's better to pay a little more to get quality planting stock than to later have to redo your turf. Junk seed does not fit into a low maintenance program.

Mixtures of low maintenance grasses

Hopefully, the foregoing sections have shed some light on the intricacies of turfgrass mixtures, because unfortunately, there's not much definitive information about how to concoct mixtures of low maintenance or unconventional grasses. The limited research that exists was accomplished by the late Wayne Huffine (Huffine et al., 1982; Huffine et al., 1977; Huffine et al., 1974), professor of agronomy at Oklahoma State University, a noted roadside turf investigator.

The mixing ability of a low maintenance grass is critically dependent on where and how it's going to be used. Even within his home state of Oklahoma, Huffine found that some mixtures

Table 6.4. "Junk" seed mixtures available from Oregon discount department stores, versus three commercial blends of improved cultivars. This study was conducted at Turf Seed, Inc., in Hubbard, Oregon (Meyer, 1993). Three improved blends were tested against several "supermarket" seed mixtures. Mixtures containing inferior varieties or annual ryegrass, performed poorly. Ratings (in parentheses in right column) were based on a 1 to 9 evaluation scale, with 9 equal to ideal turf, and 1 equal to very poor turf. Component percentages were rounded to the nearest 1% and may not total 100.

	–Components in the mixture–					
Mixture name and source	**Perennial ryegrass**	**Kentucky bluegrass**	**Tall fescue**	**Fine fescue**	**Annual ryegrass**	**Turfgrass quality**
Alliance perennial ryegrass blend ***(a blend of improved cultivars)***	25% 'BrightStar' 25% 'Saturn' 25% 'Charger' 25% 'Quickstart'					✪✪✪✪ (7.7)
Mowless tall fescue blend ***(a blend of improved cultivars)***			33% 'Silverado' 33% 'Eldorado' 33% 'Coronado'			✪✪✪ (6.0)
Confederate tall fescue blend ***(a blend of improved cultivars)***			33% 'Safari' 33% 'Toma-hawk' 33% 'Eldorado'			✪✪✪ (6.0)
Scotts Spirit Mix **K-Mart**		10% 'Abbey'	56% 'Wrangler' 32% 'Titan'			✪✪ (5.5)
Estate **Coastal Farm Store**	36% 'Premier'	19% 'Park' 10% 'Barzan'		14% fescue 14% 'Bridgeport' chewings		✪✪ (5.5)
Shade & Sun Mix **Fred Meyer**	49% 'Dandy'			29% 'Pennlawn' red 19.67% 'Cascade' chewings		✪✪ (5.5)
Scotts Family Favorite **K-Mart**	49% 'Pennant'	25% 'Abbey'		24% 'Molinda' chewings		✪ (4.5)

Table 6.4. "Junk" seed mixtures available from Oregon discount department stores, versus three commercial blends of improved cultivars. This study was conducted at Turf Seed, Inc., in Hubbard, Oregon (Meyer, 1993). Three improved blends were tested against several "supermarket" seed mixtures. Mixtures containing inferior varieties or annual ryegrass, performed poorly. Ratings (in parentheses in right column) were based on a 1 to 9 evaluation scale, with 9 equal to ideal turf, and 1 equal to very poor turf. Component percentages were rounded to the nearest 1% and may not total 100 (continued).

	–Components in the mixture–					
Mixture name and source	**Perennial ryegrass**	**Kentucky bluegrass**	**Tall fescue**	**Fine fescue**	**Annual ryegrass**	**Turfgrass quality**
Wonderlawn Playgreen Mix **Fred Meyer**	39.23% 'Pennant' 29.65% 'Competitor'				30% 'Gulf'	✪ (4.3)
Ed Humes Reseedit	35% 'Pennant' 30% 'Belle'	5% 'Haga'		29%		✪ (4.0)
Pennington Kentucky bluegrass **Walmart**		95% 'South Dakota'				☹ (3.7)
Lawn Master Playground Mix **Wilco**	49% 'Vantage'			14%	34%	☹ (3.5)
Green Meadow Sun & Shade **Lofts**	73% "Prelude"				24%	☹ (3.0)
Wonderlawn Fast Grown Perennial ryegrass mix	8%				42% 'Gulf' 42% ryegrass	☹☹ (1.7)
Speedy Green perennial ryegrass **Coastal Farm Store**	0.05% 'Linn'				88%	☹☹☹ (1.0)

preferred south-facing slopes, some favored north-facing slopes, and others were suited to east/west slopes, fill slopes, or upland areas (Huffine et al., 1974). Moreover, he discovered that the **aftercare** given a mixture eventually determines its composition (Chapter 7 discusses aftercare in detail). Fertilization, soil pH, seed quality, mixture ratio, mowing height, mowing frequency, erosion repair, growth regulators, and herbicides all affected the persistence of the mixture components.

Huffine felt that a shotgun mixture containing several diverse grasses was often the safest bet for low maintenance roadsides. With a shotgun mixture, the most fit species would survive on each individual site. In one particularly exhaustive study using nine mixture combinations, he found that plant populations three years later spanned the scale from 0% to 100% coverage for a given species (Huffine et al., 1982). Many plots ended up composed of a 50:50 mix of sideoats grama and switchgrass plants, regardless of which grass or which ratio he planted. Botanists call this phenomenon, **convergence**—population changes over time toward a common ratio.

Therefore, since low maintenance mixtures are so site-dependent, the best solution may be to include a greater number of grasses together. But as stated earlier, not all grasses are compatible with all others. Several considerations should be observed when concocting low maintenance mixtures:

- *Stoloniferous grasses don't combine well*—Use stoloniferous grasses alone rather than in mixtures (see Table 6.2). They'll crawl all over other grasses.
- *Nurse grasses can crowd out desirable ones*—Annual grasses can be added to mixtures to ensure faster establishment and less erosion. But then you're stuck with them. Annual nurse grasses outcompete desirable grasses and later die away, leaving large, blank spaces in the stand. If erosion is a problem, mulches or faster germinating perennial grasses should be used in place of annuals (Anonymous, 1993d).
- *Choose the optimal seeding date*—It's not always possible to plant grasses when the agronomic calendar dictates. More often, it's a matter of when construction is finished and is ready to go. But given the choice, warm-season grass mixtures should be planted in late spring and cool-season mixtures in late summer. Planting cool- and warm-season grasses simultaneously compromises at least one of the components.
- *Don't delay your first mow*—Begin mowing mixtures as soon as the blades exceed the intended cutting height or as soon as the soil is stable enough to support a mower. Waiting too long allows the faster germinating species to overwhelm the slow.
- *Match the seeding rate to the intended purpose*—A turf that's expected to withstand wear and mowing should be planted in the range of 1 to 10 lb of seed per 1000 ft^2 (5 to 50 g/m^2). Reclamation, roadside, or untrafficked vista turf can be sown at much lower rates, typically from 1 to 10 lb per acre (0.1 to 1 g/m^2) (Roybal, 1977). The following chapter on establishment provides pointers.
- *Match the mature plant heights*—Use grasses with similar, unmowed, mature plant heights. Grasses with similar heights tend to have similar growth rates, meaning they'll all need mowing at the same time. Consult the *Unmowed Height* column in the Appendix.
- *Don't mix cool-season grasses with warm*—For the most part, mixtures of cool- and warm-season grasses are unstable. One or the other will dominate. The only place this type of mixture seems to work is in the Transition Zone (Zone 3).
- *Avoid the "capture" effect*—A **capture effect** occurs when one component in a mixture is used in too small quantities. Grasses at ratios below about 10% exert little if any influence on performance. The predominant species is said to "capture" them. The turf performs just like a 100% stand of the stronger species, even

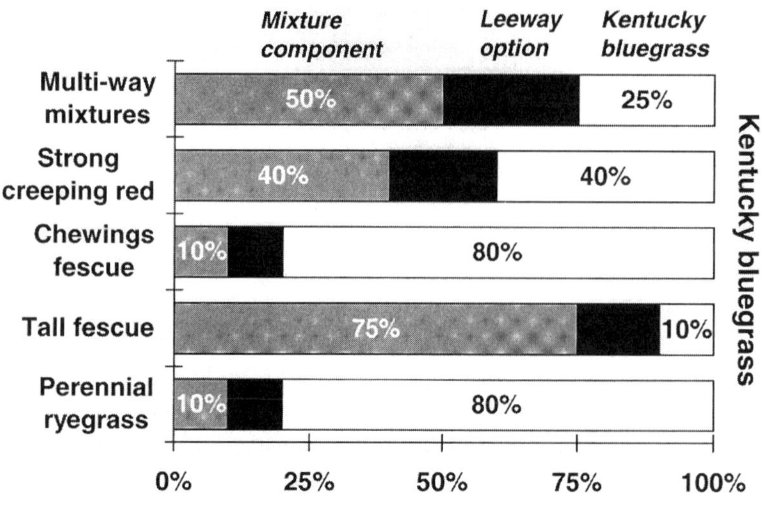

Figure 6.6. Recommended seed ratios for Kentucky bluegrass mixtures, by weight. Here's how to interpret this graph (see bottom bar): Mixtures of perennial ryegrass with Kentucky bluegrass require 90% bluegrass seed to create an balanced population of shoots in the turf. There is a 10% leeway, meaning that you can use 80% bluegrass instead of 90% if you wish.

though the weaker one may still be there in small numbers. When a population drops below a critical level, the influence of that component is lost—and so is the reason for having it there in the first place.

- *Blend varieties to add diversity*—Combining several varieties of the same species adds genetic diversity to a stand. Blending is touchy with stoloniferous, warm-season grasses such as vegetative bermudagrass (Uhring, 1995). Generally they'll segregate over time.
- *Use recommended seed ratios when available*—Few grass mixtures have been actually tested by research. Most have been concocted through seat-of-the-pants observation. But when research information exists, use it. Figure 6.6 shows recommended ratios for mixtures containing Kentucky bluegrass.
- *Match blade widths and colors for aesthetics*—In mowed turf, broad bladed grasses don't mix well with fine blades. Stick with a common texture and color theme for mowed turf. On the other hand, *unmowed* grasses look more interesting if a variety of colors and textures are interplayed. Bringing together grasses with a range of flowering dates ensures a continual display of attractive seedheads through the season.
- *Remember, what you see is **not** what you get*—Just because you mix 50 lb of grass A with 50 lb of grass B in the seeder hopper, doesn't mean you'll later get a 50:50 mix of *shoots* in the eventual turf. It's not that simple. Seed size, seedling vigor, seeding rate, and establishment date complicate the calculation. That's why it's best to rely on time-tested ratios, such as those listed in Figure 6.6. Or else buy your seed **preformulated** from a reputable dealer, who presumably knows how to merge them.
- *Use management tools of water, fertilizer, and mowing to keep a mixture mixed*—Management factors play a key role in retaining the components in a mixture. Too much or too little of a given resource can drive out one or more grasses from your mixture entirely. If you notice a decline over time in one component, you might consider adjusting your maintenance to compensate. Sometimes a simple switch of mowing heights or fertilization dates can snap a grass back from the brink of elimination.

Chapter 7

Turf Establishment and Renovation

Some people have the strange impression that with low maintenance turf, you ought to be able to cut corners when planting. Let me tell you, nothing could be further from the truth. Even roadside or vista turf needs adequate preplant preparation. Otherwise, a multitude of maintenance problems—weeds, unevenness of the soil, spotty establishment, erosion, etc.—will haunt you for years to come, resulting in a net *higher* maintenance over the life of the stand.

This chapter on turf establishment is divided into three sections: The first part is a step-by-step guide for planting new turf. It covers land acquisition, soil preparation, sowing, and aftercare. The second part deals with specific planting issues. After all, all plantings are not alike. You might be planting sod, sprigs, plugs, or seed of a hundred different species. You might be planting a cool-season grass or warm. You might be trying to quickly germinate a stand before next week's football game, or you might not care if it takes a year or more to fill in. Each situation is unique. Each is important.

The third part of this chapter covers turf renovation—the process of renewing tired, old grass. Techniques, from a light makeover to total reconstruction, are discussed.

PLANTING TURFGRASSES STEP BY STEP

Site Selection

Choosing a site for a new turf facility is a luxury and a curse. It's a luxury because you get to select among different locations, securing the spot best suited to serving your turf's needs.

But choosing a site can also be a curse. You never know if the peaceful expanse of meadow you're purchasing might have been a WWII waste dump. Or whether your new land is the sole home of the endangered blue-faced fig hopper.

If you're in the market for a piece of land for a new turf facility, there are some important aspects to consider beforehand. In this modern age, property liens and boundary disputes are only a fraction of the problems you're likely to encounter when acquiring a piece of land. Two factors are important in site selection: The ability of the land to serve the needs of the turf and the ability of the facility to peacefully coexist within the local ecology.

Rushing into the purchase of a new piece of property without first judging the good versus the bad is a recipe for disaster. Headaches can be avoided with good prepurchase planning.

The checklist below can help you avoid problems in the acquisition of land. This list was based on an article by Ross Campbell and Brad Rogers in *Landmark* magazine (Campbell and Rogers, 1996):

- *Adequate size*—Be certain there's enough usable land to meet the physical requirements of your project. Don't underestimate. Some portions of the land (slopes, lakes, wetlands) may be unplantable which will limit the usable size. When estimating size, remember that turf facilities can be a drawing card for neighbors. The real estate value of surrounding land soars whenever a new golf course, school, or park is built. You should consider buying extra land around your facility and selling it off yourself at a profit. Or perhaps retain the surrounding land in its native state as a green buffer against civilization. Many a pristine golf course has been spoiled by neighbors moving in next door.

- *Development of prime agricultural land*—Laws in some locales prohibit development of prime agricultural land. Zoning changes may be necessary before you begin your project. Other regulations may limit development of forest or grassland.
- *Take an ecological inventory*—Before you develop the land (or preferably before you buy) determine whether all or a portion of the land is considered an environmentally sensitive area which may require special government approvals. An impact statement may be needed concerning the effect of the proposed facility on habitats and ecological functions. Negative impacts may have to be assessed and mitigated. Check whether any endangered species live on the property.
- *Adequate irrigation supply*—Estimate in advance the quantity of water needed for the proposed facility. Well yields and potential sites for pumps should be matched with demand. If existing supplies are inadequate, and new sources can't be tapped, then obviously the site won't work. A hydrogeological analysis may help pinpoint water sources and quality. Check to see who your upstream neighbors are and what their water rights are.
- *Good soil drainage*—Inadequate soil drainage can cause two serious problems: (a) Poorly drained areas might not be suitable for turf. A larger-than-expected piece of land might be needed to compensate for unusable pieces. (b) In some regions, poorly drained soils are considered wetlands and require special governmental approvals.
- *Topography*—An engineering analysis of the property should include water drainage patterns, floodplains, watersheds and impoundments such as lakes, ponds, and reservoirs. Excessively steep slopes may be unstable and erosive. They limit the land available for turf functions. Excessively flat land (<2% slope) can also present a problem if surface water does not flow off the site.
- *Geology of the site*—The soils and overburden should be satisfactory for constructing building foundations, sanitary septic fields, roads, and other developments. The architect's cut and fill plans should be matched with the existing bedrock depth and topsoil thickness.
- *Other skeletons in the closet*—Although you can never anticipate every hidden obstacle with a new piece of land, some problems are avoidable. Before construction starts—or preferably before land is purchased—determine:

  ⇛ Road access and traffic patterns
  ⇛ Zoning, covenants, and deed restrictions
  ⇛ Easements
  ⇛ Availability of utilities
  ⇛ Visibility, views, and vistas
  ⇛ Prior uses of the land that may have led to soil contamination from chemicals or minerals
  ⇛ Salt in the soil or irrigation water
  ⇛ Periodic flooding
  ⇛ Local restrictions on pesticide use
  ⇛ Archaeological, historical, or cultural significance of the site—no buried bones!
  ⇛ Negative impacts on neighboring real estate
  ⇛ Suitable climate and microclimate

PLANTING TURF

Regardless of whether you're seeding, sprigging, plugging, stolonizing, or sodding, all turf plantings require the same basic soil preparation steps. Soil should be readied into a smooth yet firm surface for planting. Ideally soil should "footprint" no deeper than $^{1}/_{2}$ in. (1 cm). Sloppy preparation can lead to a myriad of maintenance problems: weeds remaining from preexisting vegetation, exposed stone, buried wood or stumps, water drainage problems, mowers bouncing from an uneven surface, and scalp.

Preplant preparation

1. *Control of preexisting weeds*—Weeds are easier to control *before* planting than after. Perennial weeds with thick rootstocks are difficult to selectively control. Nonselective herbicides can be used before tillage to knock down existing vegetation. Systemic herbicides translocate into the roots, killing the rootstocks of perennial weeds.

   Annual weeds might also present a problem. Annual weeds are prolific seed producers. Over the years they may have deposited millions of seed into the soil, all awaiting favorable conditions to sprout. Soil sterilization using a fumigant chemical can kill weed seed. However, the number of prospective herbicides for this purpose grows shorter each year.

   Fortunately, many weeds require no herbicidal controls at all. They're destroyed merely by tillage or mowing. Tall, upright, dicot weeds seldom persist in mowed turf.
2. *Grading and shaping*—Stumps, stones, and buried wood should be removed. Leaving buried wood in the ground invites fairy ring fungus to colonize the turf. Where major cuts and fills are anticipated, topsoil should be stockpiled and later redistributed. Deep cultivation by use of a ripping bar or **subsoiler** can help repair areas compacted from heavy construction equipment.
3. *Drainage and irrigation installation*—Surface shaping and crowning should be sculpted to allow surface water to drain off the playing surface and onto less trafficked areas. Subsurface drainage should be installed to remedy soils with slow water percolation or puddling tendencies. Drainpipe, dry wells, culverts, and waterways should be installed concurrently with irrigation.
4. *Adding sand or compost*—Soil modification is detailed in Chapter 8.

Final soil preparation and planting

5. *Corrective fertilizer*—A soil test for phosphorus (P), potassium (K), and pH is an inexpensive way to spot imbalances. Agricultural limestone or sulfur can be incorporated to compensate for errant pH levels, as recommended on the soil test report (McGinnies and Crofts, 1986).

   Deficiencies in P and K are best corrected *before* final tillage, so nutrients can be incorporated down to plow depth. Ignore the nitrogen requirement on the soil test. Starter and maintenance fertilizer will supply needed N.
6. *Surface smoothing and firming*—Nothing is worse than planting into soil that's too fluffy. Rototillers work great for gardens but poorly for turf. They pulverize the soil, destroying its **soil structure**, turning it into concrete. Rototilled soil settles unevenly, leaving a lumpy surface that can cause a mower to bounce (see sidebar on diagnosing establishment problems). If the prepared soil is too dry and fluffy—from whatever tillage equipment you happen to be using—prewatering can help settle it. Dampen the soil 2 to 3 weeks before planting. Bring the underlying soil moisture up to sufficiency. Then allow the surface to dry. Smooth it with a drag unit composed of an I-beam or a section of cyclone fence pulled behind a tractor. **Dragging** is a more effective method for final smoothing than even hand raking, and it is more labor efficient.
7. *Starter fertilizer*—**Starter fertilizer**, applied right before or during sowing, helps get the stand growing. Starter fertilizer is used *in addition* to the corrective fertilizer mentioned above. A starter fertilizer is a complete fertilizer applied at a rate of 1 to 2 lb of nitrogen per

1000 ft^2 (5 to 10 g N/m^2) of quick release 10-10-10 or similar. Heavier rates may cause leaching and nutrient runoff. Rates up to 2 lb of nitrogen per 1000 ft^2 (10 g N/m^2) are usually safe from foliar burning, even with tender, young turf plants.

8. *Planting the grass*—Each method of planting has its own advantages and disadvantages (see Table 7.1). Choose the method that best fits (a) your time frame for establishment, (b) your price range, and (c) the grass species and variety you've selected. For a larger turf facility, consider a **mixed-mode planting**. For example, rather than plant all the turf using one technique, you might consider hydroseeding the slopes, sodding around buildings and sprinklers, stolonizing high wear areas, and seeding the rest.
9. *Rolling and firming*—All new turf plantings benefit from good contact between the plant roots and the soil. Air pockets in loose or fluffy soil causes drying of tender, young plants. A weighted roller or packer should be used immediately after sowing to press the seed or sprigs into firm contact with the soil. **Cultipacker** seeders are one popular way to seed and firm in the same pass.

Aftercare

10. *Startup watering*—All new turf plantings benefit from irrigation, whether or not you're planning to irrigate the mature stand later on (Fry and Butler, 1989c). Irrigation helps bring up the plants evenly, ensuring complete coverage in the shortest possible time. Why is this important? Faster coverage means fewer weed problems.

    In many cases, startup irrigation can take place even before the entire site is planted. Speedy watering is essential to vegetative plantings, because they can dry out and die if not watered the day of planting. Don't wait until you've planted the whole property to turn on the sprinklers. Water as you go.

    Seed is more forgiving than sprigs. Seed can sit in dry soil and wait for water without being harmed. But once you start watering, you'll have to keep it up until the seedlings are stooling out.

    Initial watering should be done carefully with an eye on washing and runoff. Movable hand-line pipes with leaky joints may cause washing and should be avoided. Pop-up sprinklers can wash soil around each head. A square of sod placed around each sprinkler solves the problem (Figure 7.1).
11. *Watering during grow-in*—For seeded plantings, the first week after sowing is not as critical as the second and third. During the first week, sprinklers should be run preferably 5 days a week, putting down many light applications rather than one heavy one. During weeks 2 and 3, sprinklers should be run for brief periods every day, including weekends. Seedlings are breaking ground and are most vulnerable to wilt.

    With a vegetative planting, the *first* week after planting is most critical. Each day thereafter becomes progressively less critical.

    After 4 to 6 weeks of shallow, frequent irrigation, you can switch to a normal watering cycle. Turf can be gradually weaned of water after its first mow.
12. *Follow-up fertilization*—At about 3 weeks after emergence, seedlings may begin to turn yellow, indicating that the starter fertilizer is wearing off. Stony or sandy soil looses nitrogen quickly and may need a follow-up shot of N at about 3 weeks. Yellowing begins in low-lying areas and progresses outward. Light applications of quick-release fertilizer can be reapplied as needed—even on a weekly basis if the young plants seem sluggish or starved. Bruce Branham and his students at Michigan State Univer-

Figure 7.1. Irrigating new turf is problematic because sprinklers tend to puddle and wash away soil near the heads. An inexpensive solution to this perennial puzzle is to install a sod square around each sprinkler.

sity found less nitrogen leaching losses from repeated light shots of fertilizer on a weekly basis, compared with a single larger dose (Branham et al., 1995). The first shot of slow-release **maintenance fertilizer** should come at about 6 weeks.

13. *Weed control*—Almost every new planting has weeds. For the most part, herbicides are not safe on turf until 4 weeks after sowing. Only a few products are safe for seedling turf. Broadleaf weeds can be controlled by using a half label-rate of phenoxy herbicide after 4 weeks. Mowing will also destroy many weeds.
14. *The first mow*—Mowing new turf is tricky, because you have to wait until the seedlings reach a "critical mass" sufficient to support the weight of the mower. Otherwise, the mower will sink into the mud. This point occurs somewhere around 4 weeks. If you have the option, spray a herbicide to clean up weeds, wait 4 days, and then give the turf its first mow. That way the weeds take up the herbicide and the mowing gets rid of them. Mowing alone controls a number of weed species without the need for chemicals (see Chapter 12).

Waiting too long before the first mowing can be harmful to the grass. Young turf should be mowed as soon as their blades exceed the intended cutting height. Clipping signals the grass to begin *horizontal* growth rather than vertical. If the young stand gets too tall before its first mow, a large part of the green leaf area is removed, killing young seedlings. Furthermore, turf mixtures are particularly sensitive to their first cut. Research has shown that quicker germinating grasses can obliterate slower germinating ones if they get too tall before their first cutting (see Chapter 6).

THE SPECIFICS OF TURF ESTABLISHMENT

The section above outlined the basic establishment steps common to all turfgrass plantings. These tried-and-true procedures work with virtually every turf species. They serve equally well with seed, sprigs, plugs, or sod.

The issues addressed in the present section deal with the peculiarities of each planting job. Sprigging a vegetative grass in the tropics will have slightly different procedures than seeding an alpine grass in the cool-temperate zone.

ESTABLISHING UNCONVENTIONAL GRASSES

Before planting a low maintenance grass, you should first consider how that turf is going to be used. Is it going to be maintained as mowed turf, similar to the traditional home lawn, park, or golf course? Or will it be treated as unmowed

Diagnosing Establishment Problems:

"I planted the grass just like you said, and it didn't come up."

Whatever the cause of an establishment failure, the symptoms are always the same: *No grass.*

The natural tendency when faced with an establishment problem is to blame the planting stock. But statistics of establishment failures show that poor seed or weak sprigs are to blame in only a fraction of the failures.

Establishment failures can be prevented by examining their root causes. Of course, more than one factor may be at work, making diagnosis difficult. But by understanding the factors involved in successful and unsuccessful establishment, one can take the necessary steps to minimize problems.

Listed below are some common causes of establishment failures. A rating symbol appears in front of each cause, indicating how important and widespread it is: Four stars (★★★★) indicates a common, widespread problem, while one star (★) designates a relatively infrequent one.

★★★★ *Water problems*

Everyone knows that seeds and sprigs need water to grow. In spite of that, a majority of establishment failures can be traced to watering problems. With water, *timing* is just as critical as quantity. While mature turf survives best with deep, infrequent watering, seedlings prefer *shallow, frequent* watering. The sprig or seedling has only a tiny root in the top 2 mm of soil. We need to keep that top 2 mm moist at all times during establishment. There's little room for error, because the seedling cannot import water from deeper in the soil profile like mature turf can.

An important point in the life of a young plant comes when its shoot just emerges from the soil. That's the make-or-break time in its growth. Even though the seedling may look "well along to maturity," it is in fact very vulnerable to drying. Keep the top 2 mm well moistened until the seedling begins to tiller.

Too much water can also be a problem. Waterlogging is a major cause of seed dormancy. Once dormancy is triggered by waterlogging, it takes days of optimal moisture before the trigger switches back. Also, too much water can lead to seed washing and soil erosion.

★★★ *Seasonal problems*

Planting when soil temperatures are too cold can delay emergence by a factor of 2 or 3: A grass that normally emerges in 14 days may take a month and a half to come up. During that time, the seedbed is open to erosion, weed problems, and rotting of the seed or sprigs. The obvious answer is to wait until favorable temperatures arrive.

Planting when temperatures are too hot is the flip side of the coin. Although seed can be established under high temperatures, irrigation timings and disease control become so critical that even the most skilled turf managers have fits. Warm-season grasses can be established more readily during high temperatures than cool-season grasses.

★★ *Planting too deeply*

In the trade, there are countless horror stories of novice turf managers who incorporated seed or sprigs too deeply. I've even heard of one unfortunate homeowner who excavated 4 in. of his front lawn, spread the seed, and then replaced the soil. Needless to say, there were no survivors.

When planting too deeply, seedlings run out of fuel and die before they ever emerge. Optimally, turf seed likes to be buried 2 mm or less in the soil. Seed needs to "see" the sun, while being covered with only enough soil to keep it supplied with moisture. Some species—particularly the warm-season grasses—like to be seeded directly on top of the seedbed, and not covered with soil very much at all (see Figure 7.2). A light hand raking—without downward pressure on the rake—is the best tool for incorporating seed into soil. Never use large implements like an agricultural disk.

Sprigs should be planted with about one-third of the sprig showing and two-thirds below ground. Deeper sprigging is beneficial in situations where irrigation is unavailable for establishment. Burying the sprig entirely, though, reduces viability.

★★ *Fluffy soil*

Loose, powdery soil is a frequently overlooked cause of seeding failure. Before the advent of the rototiller, fluffy soil problems were virtually unheard of. Today, overtilled soil is one of the leading causes of patchy establishment. The reason fluffy soil is bad is that seeds become buried irregularly. Also, loose soil settles unevenly, causing scalping problems where the turf is later mowed.

Depending on the soil type, nearly any tillage tool can potentially cause a fluffy seedbed. Rolling with a packer wheel does only a meager job to alleviate the problem. The best solution is to lightly prewater the seedbed after tillage, allowing it to settle before planting. A final raking or finish dragging prior to planting will smooth the seedbed into a firm surface with a light dusting of soil on top. That's ideal for most grasses.

★ *Using untreated seed*

Some seeds, such as zoysiagrass or buffalograss, are virtually nonviable as they're picked from nature. The seed has a hard coating that inhibits or delays germination. Other species, such as bermudagrass, benefit from—but do not require—the removal of the seed hull for germination. Many of the unconventional grasses benefit from scratching or removing their hard seed coats.

Some unconventional grasses suffer from another seed malady: Heavy beards. Seed whiskers make seed a real devil to plant. For one thing, the light, fluffy seed consumes a lot of storage space. And then when you try to force it through a drop or whirlybird seeder, the equipment jams. Hydroseeding is often the only answer. Some seed dealers use **debearders**—machines designed to remove the fuzz—to trim the beards and make planting easier.

The best advice if you're using a grass that needs pretreatment for enhanced germination, is to check with your seed supplier before you buy.

★ *Other causes of establishment failures*

- Omitting an important planting step, such as rolling or starter fertilizer
- Soil crusting
- Damage from insects or diseases
- Saline, alkaline, or acid soil conditions
- Toxicity from fertilizers or pesticides
- Weak planting stock

(or seldom mowed) vista turf, such as you'd find on a roadside, prairie, or land reclamation project? Each type of turf has its advantages and disadvantages. But the decision needs to be made *before* planting as to what type of turf you're intending.

Preplanning is necessary because the procedures for establishing and maintaining each type of turf are different. And your expectations for each should be different too. You cannot expect a turf seeded to only a few pounds of seed per acre (<1 g/m^2) to perform like dense lawn. Establishment and aftercare are distinctly different for low versus high maintenance lawns.

Your choices are:

1. *Establish a low maintenance grass just as you would a* ***regular lawngrass***—This would involve:
   a) A heavier seeding rate—measured in lb per 1000 ft^2 rather than lb per acre
   b) Irrigation to establish
   c) Less weed competition during establishment
   d) A shorter grow-in period
   e) Less overall drought tolerance of the stand

2. *—or—Establish them like a* ***meadow or prairie***—This would involve:
   a) A lower seeding rate (Harlan et al., 1952)
   b) No irrigation
   c) Significant weed invasion in the first 2 years
   d) A prolonged grow-in period of a year or more
   e) Less overall maintenance after establishment.

Establishing low maintenance grasses using meadow planting techniques creates the "prairie look"—the appearance of a native grassland. It saves maintenance. But the tall, unkempt ap-

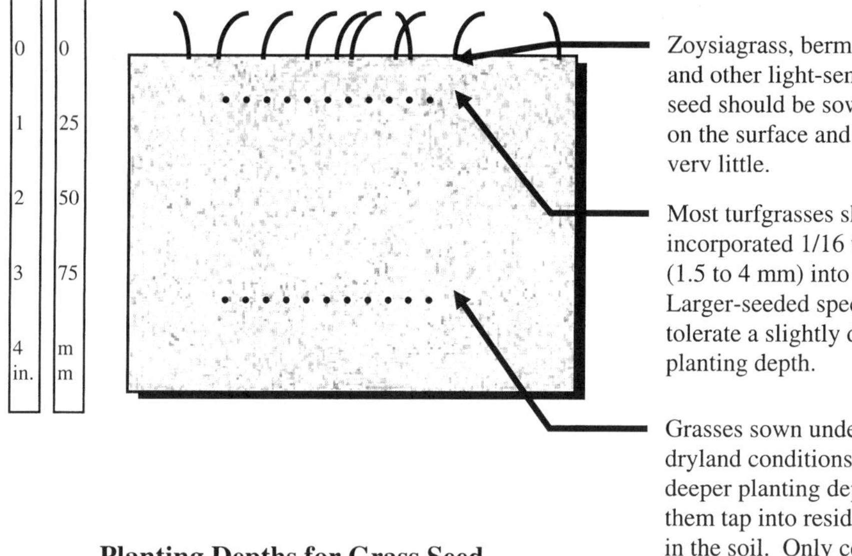

Figure 7.2. Grasses planted under unirrigated, dryland conditions benefit from a deeper sowing depth than traditional irrigated plantings. Deep planting helps put the seedling in contact with available soil moisture. However, with most grasses, planting deeply will bury the seed and drastically reduce establishment. Small seeded grasses possess only enough stored energy to emerge from planting depths of 1/4 inches (6 mm) or so. Doug Johnson and Kay Asay, range physiologists at USDA's Agricultural Research Service in Logan, Utah, have selected and bred varieties of crested wheatgrass and Russian wildrye for the ability to emerge from greater depths. "Two traits—weight of individual seeds and ability to emerge from a deep planting depth—most determine the success," says Asay. Scientists in Utah, North Dakota, and Canada jointly developed "Hycrest" crested wheatgrass and "Bozoisky-Select," "Mankota," and "Swift" Russian wildryes. These low maintenance grasses have the desired ability to sprout from deep, dryland plantings.

pearance is not suitable for every landscape. If you've never grown grasses this way before, it can be an eye opening experience.

Dave and Linda Stock, proprietors of Stock Seed Farms and marketers of wildland grasses and flowers, caution first-time growers about expecting too much from low maintenance grasses, especially when using meadow establishment techniques.

"Prairiegrasses grow down, not up, during the establishment year. The topgrowth normally amounts to a narrow, straight leaf until late in summer. These seedlings can be hard to see even for the experienced grower. Most of the time they actually have a good stand," says Stock. Patience is a virtue.

Mixing grasses. Meadow or vista turf is best established as a mixture of grasses. Mixed stands can be created simply by combining seed of various grasses in the hopper of the seeder. However, a better idea is to deliberately plant the grasses *separately* in patches and swirls, simulating what nature might create.

Here are some suggestions for establishing a landscape with a native grassland appearance (Anonymous, 1986):

- *Sow plants as nature might*—Avoid straight lines of drill rows from planting equipment.
- *Make a deliberate "statement" with your planting*—Develop a theme and carry it through your planting: Do you want a back-to-nature appearance or something artistic?
- *Adjust your starter fertilizer*—Some studies (McGinnies and Crofts, 1986) have shown little or no effect of nitrogen on stand establishment of low maintenance grasses. Phosphorus, on the other hand, aids seedling establishment (McGinnies and Crofts, 1986) especially when incorporated to a depth of 2 to 6 in. (5 to 15 cm) (Murphy and Zaurov, 1994).
- *Place taller grasses in back of shorter ones*—Use taller grasses as a backdrop or hedge.
- *Combine grasses to provide continuous blooming throughout the year*—Mix early and late maturing species together to provide season-long color.
- *A native grassland usually has one or two dominant grasses*—Don't add too many grasses to your mix or it will lose its native appeal.
- *Choose equally aggressive species*—Grasses that are too aggressive will push out weaker ones.
- *Leave a firebreak*—Fire is a natural component of grasslands, even ones we create. Tall, dry vegetation can pose a distinct fire hazard. Be sure to leave a green, mowed zone between dry vegetation and building structures.

METHODS OF VEGETATIVE ESTABLISHMENT

Vegetative propagation is the process of moving a live plant part from one area to another. *How* that plant is harvested and resown differentiates the various methods of vegetative propagation. Vegetative propagation is more common with warm-season grasses than cool-season, because of the vigorous, stoloniferous growth of warm-season grasses. Certain cool-season grasses in the past have been vegetatively planted, but today the practice is virtually extinct, owing to superior seeded varieties.

There are four basic methods of vegetative propagation—sodding, plugging, sprigging and stolonizing—each with their own unique variations:

Sodding

Turfgrass sod production has grown from a specialty crop into a major worldwide agribusiness. Sod has become a mainstay of the housing construction industry (Anonymous, 1993g). Builders can landscape a new home and have it ready for occupancy, complete with a lush green lawn, in short order.

Sodding is also becoming a common practice on many golf courses and sports fields. The additional cost for sod can be justified by quicker playability. For example, a new golf course might be able to open in half the time with sodding versus seeding. Revenues generated by an earlier opening date can sometimes offset the expense of sodding.

Table 7.1. Turf can be established by a variety of methods, each with its own set of requirements and costs. Stoloniferous warm-season grasses are by tradition established vegetatively, although recent innovations in seeded varieties offer options. This table was adapted and expanded from a publication by the Turfgrass Producers International.

Factors to consider	Seed	Hydroseeding	Sprigging and stolonizing	Plugging	Sodding
Time of year to install	Best done during the active growing season. Dormant planting can be done during winter.		Only during active growing months.	Best done during the growing season. Winter planting can be done if large plugs are used.	Virtually year-round, as long as the ground isn't frozen so sod can be cut.
Soil preparation	Good soil preparation is important regardless of your planting method. Sodding and hydroseeding are a little more "forgiving" in soil prep, but not much.				
Quality of planting stock	Certified seed should be specified for varietal assurance.		Certified sprigs, plugs, and sod are available in many areas. Uncertified sprigs may be subject to contamination with undesirable grasses or common-type varieties.		
Weed control	One or more herbicide applications are usually needed to clean up weeds that emerge with the seedlings.			With plugging, a large portion of the soil surface is bare, allowing weed invasion unless herbicides or a companion grass are used.	Sodding smothers emerging weed seedlings. Occasionally weeds emerge in the cracks between sod requiring herbicide attention.
Initial watering	After planting, seed can remain in the soil unwatered without harm. But once the seedlings start to sprout, consistent moisture is essential for full establishment.		Bare sprigs are very susceptible to drying, since they lack roots. Water is needed within hours of planting.	Grass plugs have an intact root system and can tolerate some watering abuse. But too much abuse and the soil-to-plug contact is broken by drying and shrinkage.	Sod covers and seals the soil surface, reducing evaporation from soil. Sod can be watered heavily, in contrast with other planting methods, which require frequent light waterings.

Erosion	Mulch is desirable on nearly all types of seed plantings to reduce erosion and limit evaporation.	Hydroseeding with mulch fiber reduces erosion. Steep slopes are still susceptible to erosion (see Mulch section for tips).	Sprigged plantings are susceptible to erosion because mulches are generally not used.	Erosion between plugs can be severe, especially on steep or erosive sites. A companion grass can be sown with the plugs to minimize runoff.	Virtually none occurs.
Time period for establishment	3 to 6 weeks before the first mow, depending on species.		4 to 6 weeks to first mow. Heavier sprigging rates provide faster establishment.	Slow growing grasses like zoysia may require an entire growing season to fill in. Faster growing grasses like bermuda cover and are ready to mow in 4 to 6 weeks.	Immediate coverage. Mowing can begin in 1 to 2 weeks, as soon as the soil firms up.
Time period until full traffic	4 to 6 months with most grasses. Slower growing species can take a full year or more to become dense enough to withstand heavy traffic.				Light traffic immediately. Full traffic within 3 to 4 weeks.
Installation cost*	$	$$	$$	$$$	$$$$

*For relative comparison purposes only. This does not imply that sodding is four times as expensive as seeding.

Transporting sod. Traditionally, sod has been sold in widths from 12 to 24 in. (30 to 60 cm). More recently, technology has developed the **jumbo roll**, a mega-roll of sod up to 3 to 4 ft across (1 to 1.2 m) that's harvested *and reestablished* mechanically. Jumbo rolls are useful for sodding large acreages like golf course fairways, athletic fields, and road medians (Figure 7.3).

Sod should be installed immediately after delivery, or at least within 24 to 48 hours of harvest. Microbial respiration in the sod generates heat that can damage stored sod. Temperatures escalate so high that the grass becomes burned and blackened. Watering of rolled sod does little to relieve the heating. Your best option if you're unable to plant sod immediately, is to roll it out onto a parking lot (keeping it watered, of course) until needed. Sod can be "stored" this way for a week or more. Some sod producers use refrigerated trucks to ship sod long distances. The refrigeration buys a few extra days of shelf life by offsetting the heating effects.

Laying sod. Most sod is still installed by hand, much like indoor carpeting. New technology is promising to mechanize the process, but the equipment is not yet available in most areas.

Lay sod starting along the longest straight edge available, like the side of a building, sidewalk, or road. Butt and push (never pull) sod pieces into tight contact. Avoid gaps, overlaps, and stretching. Stagger the rows in brickwork fashion to minimize seams. Sod is most susceptible to damage and drying at the seams. Some golf courses routinely add topsoil along the seams to minimize drying—a lesson that other facets of the turf industry could learn as well.

Use a machete, saw, or straight shovel to trim sod to fit corners. Wooden pegs can be used to anchor sod on slopes. Run sod strips *across* a slope, rather than up and down, to minimize stretching.

Water as you go. Apply 1 in. (25 mm) of water immediately after installation. You might use sheets of plywood to make it easier to carry sod across previously watered areas. Heavy plywood sheets can even be driven over by small fork trucks.

The same basic steps in turf establishment (outlined previously) apply to sod. Don't cut corners just because you're installing a product that hides your soil mistakes. Omitting a step such as soil smoothing, rolling, or aftercare can lead to spotty establishment.

Strip sodding. **Strip sodding** is a sodding variation where strips of sod are laid with a soil gap in between. Strip sodding is done to lower sodding costs, especially with expensive products like zoysia. The lateral runners of the grass are expected to fill over time. Mowing of strip-sodded turf can be a nuisance, reminiscent of riding a horse. Strip sodding does not create the smoothest surface. The barren strips also invite weeds.

Plugging

Plugging is a labor-intensive way to propagate vegetative turfgrasses. Although recent innova-

Figure 7.3. The jumbo roll—a wider-than-normal sod width—is becoming an increasingly popular way to sod, because it allows for the mechanical harvest and *laying* of sod. The wider width speeds installation and offers fewer seams to dry out.

tions in plugging machinery have been developed, most plugging is still done by hand. Plugs are commonly 2 to 8 in. across (5 to 20 cm). Plugs are usually cut from grass sod. Installation is typically on 6 to 24 in. centers (15 to 60 cm). Stolon and rhizome growth fills the voids over time. Closer spacing and larger plugs mean faster coverage (Table 7.2).

Grasses differ in how long they take to achieve complete ground coverage from plugs. Bermudagrass and buffalograss spread readily and cover the ground within 4 to 6 months (Fry et al., 1993; Ruemmele et al., 1993). St. Augustinegrass, centipedegrass, and zoysiagrass are more sluggish, taking a year or more for complete coverage (Gordon, 1986). *Zoysia tenuifolia*, an extremely slow growing grass, may take considerably more than a year to fully fill from plugs (Johns and Beard, 1978).

Plug size and plug spacing dictates coverage time. Coarse textured grasses like St. Augustinegrass and centipedegrass need bigger plugs. Small plugs (smaller than 4 in. [10 cm]) of coarse grasses can contain too little plant material to viably propagate.

Weed competition can hamper plugged grasses, since there's a lot of bare soil showing. Erosion can also take place in between plugs, leading to a lumpy surface. A companion grass (usually perennial ryegrass) may be seeded to hold the soil in place until the plugs fill.

Prerooted plugs. **Prerooted plugs** are a recent innovation. Plugs are cut from a sod field in the traditional manner. Then the plugs are placed on plastic sheeting (and sometimes in trays) to allow the roots to regrow. Growers report quicker, more vigorous establishment using prerooted plugs. Cost is higher than with conventional plugs due to the extra handling. Prerooted plots are sold in flats, and are particularly popular in the garden store market.

Sprigging

Sprigging is a popular method of vegetative propagation because handling is largely mechanized. Sprig harvesters and planters are available in both forage (wider spacing) and turf configurations.

Sprigging is the process of planting stolons or rhizomes in rows. It differs from plugging in that no soil is carried along with the plant. Depending on the row width and application rate, ground coverage from sprigging can be faster than from plugging. But plugging has advantages over sprigging:

- Plugs are forgiving of drying out. If sprigs dry out, they're dead.
- Plugs can be planted in any season of the year. Sprigs can be propagated only during active growth months. Naked sprigs are susceptible to damage from cold temperature.

Sprigs can be harvested by a number of methods (Figure 7.4). Sod can be cut with a sod harvester and fed into a **soil shredder**. Or a rototiller can be used to bring sprigs to the surface where a tractor can rake and windrow them. Or an all-in-one sprig harvester can cut, shred, haul, and load the sprigs.

When planting sprigs, tighter row spacing accelerates the coverage rate, particularly with slow creeping grasses (Table 7.2). A sprig planter is merely a modified agricultural disk that slices the sprigs into the soil. **Double sprigging**—sprigging twice in perpendicular directions—can be used for even faster coverage.

Bunch-grass sprigging. Bunch grasses can also be sprigged. Beachgrass and other low maintenance bunch grasses may be planted as sprigs for sand stabilization. Some of the sand-stabilizing grasses and ornamental grasses readily adapt to mechanical planting methods. This is important for grasses which set few seed, or ornamental grasses that lose their unique colors and textures through seed.

Stolonizing

Stolonizing is the fastest—and often the riskiest—method of vegetative planting. A good stolonizing job can establish turf in about *half* the time as other methods. A bad stolonizing job can result in dead sprigs. With stolonizing there is less room for error in planting and aftercare than with other methods.

Figure 7.4. Sprigging in many parts of the world is largely unmechanized. In this photo, workers in Shandong, China are harvesting sprigs of matrella for shipment to a new golf course. In North America, harvesting and planting of sprigs is done by specialized equipment capable of establishing several acres a day.

To stolonize, stolons and rhizomes are harvested as described for sprigging. But instead of row planting, the stolons are *broadcast* over the entire soil surface. The sprigs are distributed either by hand, with a straw blower, or through a mechanical hydroplanter.

If the stolons are not incorporated into the soil right away, they'll dry out and quickly die. Stolons can be incorporated by one of three methods:

- *Pressing them firmly into the soil with a cultipacker*—A cultipacker is a machine with a pair of offset, ridged rollers. Cultipacker establishment runs into problems with grasses that have long, wiry stolons which tend to pop back out of the ground after packing.
- *Disking them lightly with an agricultural disk*—Light disking is followed by rolling with a weighted packer wheel. Unfortunately, unless the disking job is precise, this technique can produce an uneven surface.
- *Topdressing the stolons with a thin layer of soil*—Stolons are broadcast on the soil surface and then buried with 15 to 25% of the sprig left exposed. This is the preferred technique for stolonizing putting greens and other close-cut applications.

Soil stolonizing. A common stolonizing variation used in road construction is for a contractor to load topsoil and stolons from a nearby farmer's pasture and redistribute them over the planting site. The advantages of this technique are: (a) low planting cost, (b) planting can be done during any season, (c) local availability of supply, and (d) locally adapted landraces growing in the pasture. Soil stolonizing is a common method for establishing bermudagrass roadsides (Huffine et al., 1974).

SEEDING RATE

Seeding rates are those figures listed in most turf textbooks that tell you how many pounds of seed to plant per unit area of lawn (Table 7.3). For example, a typical seeding rate for bermudagrass might be 1 to 3 lb per 1000 ft^2 (5 to 15 g/m^2). These figures have been developed over the years by seat-of-the-pants observations by turf experts and practitioners (Brede and Duich, 1980). Here's how they might be determined: Let's say I planted a bermudagrass lawn at a 2 pound seeding rate and it produces an acceptable-looking turf. That figure would be recorded and would become the recommended standard.

In recent years, scientific research has been brought to bear on seeding rate. Research has shown that seeding rates can have a potent, long lasting impact on turf. Density differences induced by seeding rate can persist for four years or more after planting (Brede and Duich, 1982; Rossi and Meyer, 1995). Thus, seeding rates are not a transient effect. It can affect the growth

Table 7.2. Conversion factors for vegetative planting. These conversion factors can also be applied to grasses other than the ones listed here. For example, fine-textured grasses (e.g., seashore paspalum) would use rates similar to those of bermudagrass. These conversion factors do not account for wastage. It's a good idea to allow 5% wastage from fine-textured grasses, and 10% wastage on the coarser ones. Data are derived from unpublished research by Wayne Huffine, 1982.

Grass species	English			Metric		
Any	1 yd^2 of sod	=	1296 1-in. plugs	1 m^2 of sod	=	1600 2.5-cm plugs
Any	1 yd^2 of sod	=	324 2-in. plugs	1 m^2 of sod	=	400 5-cm plugs
Any	1 yd^2 of sod	=	81 4-in. plugs	1 m^2 of sod	=	100 10-cm plugs
Any	Plugs on 1-ft centers	=	1000 plugs per 1000 ft^2	Plugs on 0.3-m centers	=	108,000 plugs per ha
Any	Plugs on 6-in. centers	=	4500 plugs per 1000 ft^2	Plugs on 15-cm centers	=	484,000 plugs per ha
Bermudagrass or zoysiagrass	1 yd^2 of sod	=	2000 to 4000 sprigs	1 m^2 of sod	=	2200 to 4400 sprigs
Centipedegrass or St. Augustinegrass	1 yd^2 of sod	=	500 to 1000 sprigs	1 m^2 of sod	=	550 to 1100 sprigs
Bermudagrass	Sprigs per bushel	=	2000	Sprigs per m^3	=	56,000
Zoysiagrass	Sprigs per bushel	=	3000	Sprigs per m^3	=	85,000
Centipedegrass or St. Augustinegrass	Sprigs per bushel	=	500	Sprigs per m^3	=	14,000

Table 7.2. Continued.

Grass species	English			Metric		
Bermudagrass	Stolons on 12-in. centers	=	½ bushel per 1000 ft^2	Stolons on 0.3-m centers	=	2 m^3 per ha
Bermudagrass	Stolons on 8-in. centers	=	1 bushel per 1000 ft^2	Stolons on 20-cm centers	=	4 m^3 per ha
Bermudagrass	Stolons on 6-in. centers	=	2 bushels per 1000 ft^2	Stolons on 15-cm centers	=	8 m^3 per ha
Bermudagrass	Stolons on 4-in. centers	=	4½ bushels per 1000 ft^2	Stolons on 10-cm centers	=	17 m^3 per ha
Bermudagrass	Broadcast on greens and topdressed	=	10 bushels per 1000 ft^2	Broadcast on greens and topdressed	=	38 m^3 per ha
Bermudagrass	Broadcast on tees and topdressed	=	5 bushels per 1000 ft^2	Broadcast on tees and topdressed	=	19 m^3 per ha
Bermudagrass	Broadcast on sports fields and topdressed	=	3 bushels per 1000 ft^2	Broadcast on sports fields and topdressed	=	11 m^3 per ha
Centipedegrass or St. Augustinegrass	Stolons on 12-in. centers	=	3 bushels per 1000 ft^2	Stolons on 0.3-m centers	=	11 m^3 per ha
Centipedegrass or St. Augustinegrass	Stolons on 10-in. centers	=	6 bushels per 1000 ft^2	Stolons on 25-cm centers	=	23 m^3 per ha
Centipedegrass or St. Augustinegrass	Stolons on 8-in. centers	=	9 bushels per 1000 ft^2	Stolons on 20-cm centers	=	34 m^3 per ha
Centipedegrass or St. Augustinegrass	Stolons on 6-in. centers	=	12 bushels per 1000 ft^2	Stolons on 15-cm centers	=	45 m^3 per ha

Table 7.3. Seeding rates and seed counts of the traditional and lower maintenance turfgrass species. "Turf" seeding rates of the unconventional grasses are listed in the Appendix.

Grass Species	Seeding Rate		Seed Count	
	lb/1000 ft²	g/m²	per lb	per gram
Warm-season grasses				
Bahia grass	6–8	30–40	166,000	366
Bermudagrass (hulled)	1–3	5–15	1,787,000	3940
Buffalograss (burs)	4–8	20–40	50,000	110
Broad leaf carpet grass	1–3	5–15	1,200,000	2600
Narrow leaf carpet grass	1–3	5–15	1,250,000	2700
Centipede grass	0.5–6	2.5–30	404,000	900
Kikuyu grass	2–4	10–20	150,000	330
Seashore paspalum	n/a	n/a	n/a	n/a
St. Augustinegrass	2–3	10–15	307,000	670
Zoysia japonica	2–3	10–15	1,369,000	3000
Zoysia matrella	n/a	n/a	n/a	n/a
Zoysia tenuifolia	n/a	n/a	n/a	n/a
Cool-season grasses				
Alkaligrass, distans	1–3	5–15	1,200,000	2600
Colonial bentgrass	1–2	5–10	8,723,000	19,200
Creeping bentgrass	1–2	5–10	7,890,000	17,400
Highland bentgrass	1–2	5–10	5,742,000	12,600
Velvet bentgrass	1–2	5–10	11,800,000	26,000
Canada bluegrass	1–3	5–15	2,495,000	5500
Kentucky bluegrass	2–3	10–15	1,000,000	2200
Roughstalk bluegrass	1–3	5–15	2,540,000	5600
Supine bluegrass	0.5–2	2.5–10	2,000,000	4400
Chewings fescue	3.5–6	17.5–30	546,000	1200
Hard fescue	4–8	20–40	590,000	1300
Sheep fescue	4–8	20–40	680,000	1500
Slender creeping fescue	4–6	20–30	546,000	1200
Strong creeping red fescue	4–6	20–30	546,000	1200
Tall fescue	6–15	30–75	227,000	500
Perennial ryegrass	4–8	20–40	227,000	500
Redtop	1–2	5–10	4,990,000	11,000

n/a – Data not available, or the species does not commonly reproduce by seed.

and the health of the turf for years to come (Rossi and Millett, 1996).

A typical consequence of seeding rate is shoot density. If you sow 1000 seeds per square foot and 75% of them germinate, you'll have 750 shoots per square foot. Doubling or halving that rate would proportionately change the shoot density.

But seeding rate also has many nonobvious impacts. As plant density increases, shoots become smaller, root systems tinier, and leaves and plants more crushed into a tighter space (Brede, 1991b). Denser plants have narrower leaves, more slender shoots, and fewer green leaves. Leaves from one shoot will shade and overlap the leaves of others and compete with them for sunlight.

Parasitic fungi have a particular affinity for overly dense grass stands. For one thing, fungi can jump from plant to plant via overlapping leaves. Once they've found their new prey, the tiny light-starved plants are easy targets. It's not surprising that densely seeded stands have significantly more disease problems than sparser stands.

But low seeding rates are not the complete answer either. Turf that's seeded below its optimal rate can suffer from significant weed inva-

Seeding Rates to Use When Mixing Turfgrasses

When mixing two or more species together, the question comes up: Which rate do you use if two grasses have different recommended seeding rates? Should you use the higher rate or the lower?

The answer is to use the seeding rate of the component that makes up the *majority* of the mixture. For example, if a specification calls for a 90:10 mix of tall fescue and Kentucky bluegrass, use the tall fescue seeding rate of about 8 lb per 1000 ft^2 (40 g/m^2) rather than the lower bluegrass rate of 2 lb.

To gauge how much seed to add to the mix, first convert the mixture percentages to decimals. Then multiply 8 lb *x* 0.9 = 7.2 lb per 1000 ft^2 for the tall fescue (36 g/m^2). And use 8 lb *x* 0.1 = 0.8 lb per 1000 ft^2 for the bluegrass (4 g/m^2).

sion (Brede and Duich, 1981). A dense, vigorous stand of grass is one of the most effective deterrents against weeds. Dense grass shades the soil surface. Dense grass roots compete with emerging weed seedlings for moisture and nutrients, stopping opportunistic weeds dead in their tracks. Without a dense enough turf, the stand is vulnerable to weed invasion.

When to deviate from recommended seeding rates

There are some legitimate reasons to stray from recommended seeding rates. Listed below are practical examples of when it's advisable to stretch the recommendations one way or another:

Seed size. Turfgrasses differ in their seed size. A pound of turfgrass seed may contain from 200,000 seeds for tall fescue to 10,000,000 seeds for bentgrass (a range of 4400 to 22,000 seed/g) (Table 7.3). Seeding rate recommendations have been developed to try to compensate for species differences in seed count.

Varieties within a species can also differ significantly in seed count. For example, Kentucky bluegrass varieties have been shown to vary from 850,000 seed per lb for "Birka" to 2,000,000 seed per lb for "Merion" (1874 to 4413 seeds per gram) (Christians et al., 1979). This difference can have an impact on planting rate, since the ultimate goal is to establish a desired number of live seedlings per unit of area. Technically, a variety with twice as many seeds per lb could be planted at *half* the seeding rate and still provide the desired number of seedlings per square foot. A large-seeded variety should be planted at the higher end of the recommended range. A small-seeded variety can be sown lighter, saving money.

Cutting height. Shorter cutting heights demand a higher seeding rate. For example, a 6 lb per 1000 ft^2 (30 g/m^2) seeding rate would be acceptable for tall fescue if you're planning to mow at 3 in. (7.5 cm), but 10 lb (50 g/m^2) of seed is better for an 1 1/4-in. (3 cm) cut. A rule of thumb is to roughly *double* the seeding rate for every *halving* of the cutting height (Brede, 1992a). This rule does not apply to close-cut putting green turf, which is all seeded at a set rate regardless of height.

Clean soil and patience. If you have a clean, weed-free soil plus a lot of patience, you can use a fraction of the normally recommended seeding rate. A sod grower who's grown the same bluegrass blend on their farm every year for the past 15 has probably cleaned up nearly all of the problem weeds. Because of this, the farmer may be able to use 1/2 or 1/4 the normal rate.

The tradeoff of course is slower establishment. Instead of being able to mow in the usual 3 to 4 weeks, it may take 6 to 8 weeks to fill. But since weeds aren't a concern (we're assuming a weed-free soil here), the lower rate is tolerable.

Dirty soil and no patience. Another example: A golf course superintendent might need a *higher* than normal seeding rate when interplanting bent or other grasses into a *Poa annua* fairway. Higher rates would compete more effectively against preexisting weeds. Higher rates swing the competition toward the desirable grass and away from the pool of weed seed in the soil.

A poor seedbed. Don't even *think* of using a higher seeding rate to compensate for sloppy planting. Heavier rates cannot make up for inadequate soil preparation. The stand ends up looking like scattered tufts of extremely dense grass. Ugly.

Soil stabilization. In areas where erosion is expected, a higher seeding rate can help stabilize the soil. Higher seeding rates can take the place of undesirable companion crops or annual grasses. Mulches are an even better solution to erosion, with a lot fewer side-effects (Dudeck et al., 1967) (see section on mulches later in this chapter).

Vista, prairie, and meadow turf. Turf that's not subject to traffic and mowing can be seeded at dramatically lower rates than lawn turf. The sacrifice, of course, is a prolonged establishment period—often a year or two—and considerably more initial weed invasion (Schuman et al., 1985). If these difficulties are tolerable, seeding rates can be decreased by 90% or more.

For example, a species that's planted for mowed turf at 2 lb of seed per 1000 ft^2 (10 g/m^2) can be sown at 2 lb *per acre* for vista turf (0.2 g/m^2). Weeds during establishment can be controlled by mowing or chopping instead of herbicides (see Chapter 12 for more herbicide-saving tips).

High seed prices. Price can be a powerful determining factor in seeding rate decisions. Some low maintenance grasses are hand-collected from the wilds, commanding a high price compared to farm-raised seed. It is not unusual for wildland seed to cost *10 to 100 times more* than traditional turf seed. As a result, people have looked for ways of using lower seeding rates for these unconventional grasses.

Mixing is one option for moderating price. In mixtures, low maintenance grasses will still contribute to the diversity of the stand, even if they only comprise a fraction of the mix. By combining them with cheaper grasses, though, their extreme cost is moderated.

Lower seeding rates are also used with grasses that yield very little seed. Seed prices of centipedegrass, zoysiagrass, and St. Augustinegrass are relatively expensive because yields are low. Reduced seeding rates can be used to compensate for price.

Adjusting for seed quality. Textbooks list seeding rates as a range: For example, 1 to 3 lb per 1000 ft^2. Have you ever wondered why a range is given rather than just one rate, say 2 lb? The range is a way of compensating for differences in **seed quality**. If you have a seedlot with a lot of inert or chaff, you'd want to seed at the higher 3 lb rate. If, on the other hand, you have a top quality lot, you can seed at the lower end of the range (Table 7.3).

Sometimes the lowest priced product is not the best *value*. Here's an example: Let's say you're offered two seedlots. One lot has 85% purity, 80% germination and sells for 90¢ per lb. The other has 98% purity, 85% germination, and sells for $1.05 per lb. (Both 85/80 and 98/85 are standard grades for grass seed.) Which lot is the better buy?

The better buy is the one that gives you the most *viable seed* at the cheapest price. Seed that doesn't germinate is essentially just filler and costs you extra in shipping.

To figure which lot is cheaper, you need to determine the price per pound of **Pure-Live Seed (PLS)** by dividing the price per pound by the purity and germination:

PLS Formula

$$\frac{\text{price per lb}}{\text{purity} \times \text{germ}} = \frac{\text{\$ per lb of}}{\text{pure - live seed}}$$

Lot A

$$\frac{90¢\text{ per lb}}{0.85 \times 0.80} = \frac{\$1.32\text{ per lb of}}{\text{pure - live seed}}$$

Lot B — Cheaper

$$\frac{\$1.05\text{ per lb}}{0.98 \times 0.85} = \frac{\$1.26\text{ per lb of}}{\text{pure - live seed}}$$

Lot B, the higher quality, higher priced lot, is actually cheaper to plant when you consider the pure-live seed you're getting.

Estimating the seeding rates of untested species

Few of the unconventional grasses listed in the Appendix have been tested for their optimum seeding rates for turf. The recommendations that do exist for these grasses are based on forage or reclamation rates. And as explained above, a stand sown to an extremely low meadow seeding rate will never develop the density needed to withstand regular mowing and traffic. Some general guidelines are needed to help approximate the seeding rate of unconventional grasses.

Prairie seeding rates. Dan Ogle, plant materials specialist for the USDA in Boise, Idaho, developed a handy system for prairie and vista turf based on seed size. It works like this: Larger seeded grasses should be sown at *fewer* seed per square foot than smaller seeded grasses.

That's backward to the system described earlier (see section, *Adjusting for seed quality*). But vista and prairie plantings are a special case, where large seeds are better suited for establishing under adverse soil conditions. Larger seeded grasses have more seeding vigor, due to the greater quantity of stored carbohydrate energy, and can be sown at a lower square foot rate.

Ogle recommends:

- *For large-seeded grasses* (fewer than 500,000 seed per lb or 1100 per gram)—20 to 30 pure-live seed per ft^2 (200 to 300 PLS per m^2).
- *For medium-seeded grasses* (500,000 to 750,000 seed per lb or 1100 to 1600 per gram)—40+ pure-live seed per ft^2 (430+ PLS per m^2).
- *For small-seeded grasses* (more than 750,000 seed per lb or 1600 per gram)—50+ pure-live seed per ft^2 (540+ PLS per m^2).

Ogle's guidelines provide a good starting point for sowing meadow, prairie, or vista turf. The number of seed per lb (or gram) can be found in the Appendix. The total quantity of seed required for a project can be calculated from the following equation (adapted from Brede and Duich, 1980). Grams and m^2 can be substituted for lb and ft^2.

$$\text{Total lb of seed needed} = \frac{(\text{desired count of seedlings}/\text{ft}^2) \times (\text{ft}^2\text{ of turf area})}{(\#\text{ seeds}/\text{lb}) \times (\%\text{ germination*}) \times (\%\text{ purity*})}$$

**Seedlot quality, expressed as decimal equivalents (e.g., 90% would equal 0.90)*

Estimating "turf seeding rates" for unconventional grasses. If you plan to subject your low maintenance grass to mowing and traffic, it should be planted at higher seeding rates—those recommended for turf. It needs the higher rate to develop the necessary "body" to support a mower and foot traffic, and to resist weeds and clumpiness.

To approximate a "turf seeding rate" for unconventional grasses, I developed the prediction equation shown in Figure 7.5. The equation works by taking the number of seeds per pound of the traditional turfgrass species and plotting them against their normal seeding rates. The relationship between seed size and seeding rate turns out to be a logarithmic curve. As it turns out, 90% of the variation in seeding rate can be explained by seed size alone.

Next, I used seed counts from the unconventional grasses in this same prediction equation

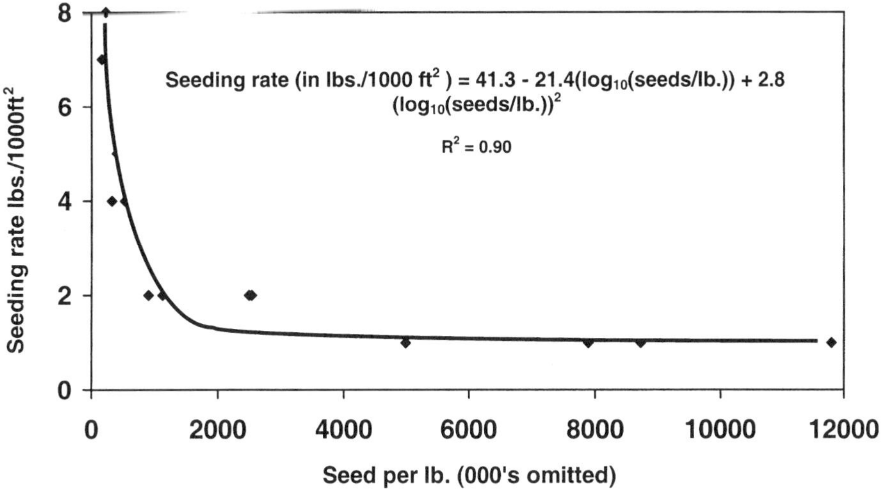

Figure 7.5. Turfgrass seeding rates can be estimated from the number of seeds per lb they possess. This graph was derived by plotting the number of seeds/lb versus the recommended seeding rates of the traditional turfgrass species. Regression analysis was used to best fit a line to the data, accounting for 90% of the variation in the relationship. This equation makes it possible to appropriate a seeding rate for unconventional grasses—ones that have not been previously tested for turf sowings (i.e., the species listed in Chapter 4). This equation was used for determining the "turf seeding rate" for the species listed in the Appendix.

(Figure 7.5) to determine their estimated *turf* seeding rate. These are the seeding rates you'll find listed in the Appendix for the unconventional grasses. These rates should serve as a starting point for planting unconventional grasses as mowed turf, until research takes place to prove otherwise.

Mulch

A turf stand is at its most vulnerable to runoff and erosion during the first few weeks after planting. A brief afternoon thundershower can carve gullies in unprotected soil, requiring extensive soil replacement and replanting. And as if that isn't enough, the eroded silt can add sediment to local lakes and rivers. The sediment can also contain pollutants and pesticides that wash away (Nus, 1993).

Mulching is a way to fight seedbed erosion. Mulching serves two prime functions:

- *It prevents soil erosion*—The mulch rather than the soil absorbs the impact of a falling raindrop.
- *It retains moisture, keeping the seedlings moist and cool between waterings*—As a result, the seedlings don't dry out as readily.

The erosion-reducing feature of mulch is a direct function of its depth. A heavier layer protects the soil better than a thinner one. But there *is* a point of diminishing returns. Too much mulch can smother the seedlings (Dudeck et al., 1967). The ideal depth is a compromise between erosion control, seedling growth, and cost. A 1/4 to 1/2 in. (6 to 12 mm) blanket is optimal for wood fiber mulch, whereas 1 to 2 in. (25 to 50 mm) is recommended for straw.

Mulches come in several forms, most of them organic. Organic mulches are ideal because they decompose and disappear over time, and don't need to be raked away. Mulch that hangs around too long can retard establishment.

Virtually any mulch is better than none. Studies by Mark Carroll, University of Maryland turf researcher, have shown all mulches he tested reduced soil loss by 90% over unprotected soil (Nus, 1993). A good mulch was nearly as effective as sodding for preventing erosion. Over 1.8 tons of topsoil per acre (4 tonnes/ha) eroded from bare soil, versus 0.2 tons (0.4 tonnes/ha) from mulched plots.

Although mulches are designed to retain soil moisture around seedlings, they may or may not reduce the actual watering load. In terms of *volume* of water used, the mulch itself may not cut water use during establishment. Research on horticultural crops at Texas A&M University has shown that—on a square foot basis—mulched plants used the same amount of water as unmulched plants (Anonymous, 1993d). A possible interpretation is that the mulch intercepts irrigation water, allowing some of it to evaporate before it reaches the plant. In the Texas study, the most efficient "mulch" was mature turf. A sod cover used 3.5 fl. oz. per ft^2 (1 L/m^2) *less* water than plants grown on bare soil.

Mulches are generally used with *seeded* stands. With vegetative plantings, mulches are uncommon but not out of the question. On erosive sites, a light mulch applied over sprigs is sometimes worth the extra trouble.

Some of the more common mulching materials (Dudeck et al., 1967; Kay, 1976; Nus, 1993) are:

- *Straw*—Straw is the dried stems remaining after a cereal crop is harvested. It is sold in small rectangular bales or larger round ones. Clean straw should be specified, free of weed and crop seed. Straw is applied manually to a seedbed or with a straw blower.
- *Hay*—Hay is a less desirable mulch than straw because of the leaf matter and seed present. Hay is produced for livestock feed and contains a lot of green vegetation. It should be used only if other mulches are unavailable, since it makes an inferior mulch.
- *Wood cellulose*—Wood fiber mulch is a by-product of the timber industry. It is applied through a hydromulching machine. Wood cellulose has become the mainstay of the hydroseeding industry.
- *Wood, jute, or coconut mats*—Strands of organic fiber bound together by string or nylon mesh form a mat that can be rolled out like carpet. Mats are useful for protecting ditches and waterways from extreme erosion. Trouble is, mats can hang around too long, impeding the turf's growth. But for extreme erosion situations, they can't be beat.
- *Paper netting*—Rolls of paper held together with netting are not highly effective as a mulch. Their inexpensive price compared to fiber mat mulches is their main drawing card.
- *Polyethylene plastic sheet*—Clear film is useful for germinating warm-season grasses under cool weather conditions. The heat generated from the greenhouse effect can cook other grasses though (Gordon, 1986).
- *Nonwoven polyester*—Polyester blankets have been used for a variety of landscape purposes. These blankets, known as geotextiles, were developed as an asphalt underlayment for roads. They've also been used as mulches and as sand barriers in putting greens. As mulches, they protect the soil but inhibit seedling growth. They also have to be physically removed at some point, before the seedlings grow through the fabric.
- *Wood chips and sawdust*—Fresh sawdust makes a poor mulch material: During decomposition it gives off toxic by-products that injures grass. Its rapid breakdown by microbes sucks nutrients away from the grass. Composting the sawdust beforehand can remove much of this toxic effect.
- *Latex spray*—Latex mulch, which looks a lot like latex paint, is applied to soil through a spray rig or **proportioner**. The solution sinks into the soil and binds the surface soil particles together. After it dries, the soil appears unmulched, but the adhesive property of the latex holds in moisture while allowing seedlings to emerge. This type of mulch sees little use, even though it has many desirable features.
- *Asphalt*—Emulsifiable asphalt can be sprayed onto the soil like latex mulch. However, asphalt is better used as an adhesive, sprayed on top of straw or other mulches to tack them together and prevent tumbling in the wind.

- *Pelleted recycled paper*—Pennmulch® is a patented material made from recycled newspapers. It looks and functions like cellulose fiber mulch but is applied via dry fertilizer spreaders.
- *Seed-impregnated blankets*—Every few years some naïve entrepreneur reinvents the seed blanket: Seed imbedded into a roll-on blanket, applied in carpet fashion. Sometimes fertilizer or pesticide are added to the blanket as well. Unfortunately, seed blankets are usually too expensive except for spot repair. Most cost more per square foot than sod. Modern blanket variations have included low maintenance grasses and even wildflowers.

Coated seed

The next package of grass seed you buy may look radically different. Instead of the usual straw-brown seed, you might find a bagful of colorful pellets resembling minuscular Easter eggs. Welcome to the world of coated seed.

Coated seed can be described as a technology in search of a function. Coated seed was conceived in the 1930s by Germain's, a British seed house, for use on cereal grain (Kaufman, 1991). Widespread use of coatings did not flourish until the 1960s. Today many horticultural crops are coated, including nearly all of the commercial lettuce production.

Coating of turfgrass seed has lagged years behind other crops because, frankly, no one could think of a good reason to use coated grass seed. Furthermore, the cheap cost of grass seed couldn't bear the extra add-on cost of coating. Flower and vegetable seed—costing hundreds of dollars per lb—were more likely candidates.

With time, some benefits of coated turf seed were discovered. However, most of them are benefits to the *seed seller*. Only a few genuine agronomic enhancements have been found for the consumer. Today, a sizable portion of the proprietary seeded bermudagrass crop is coated. Coating is also popular in the perennial ryegrass overseeding market.

Some of the advantages and disadvantages of coated seed:

- *The coating material is a diluent*—Coating manufacturers call it a "carrier," but actually the coating serves as a way to dilute expensive grass seed with a cheap coating. It doesn't take a financial genius to figure who comes out ahead if you mix $5 per lb grass seed with 10 cent per lb diatomaceous earth, and then sell the product for $5 per lb.
- *Better "throwability"*—Coatings smooth the rough edges on seed, helping them flow better through seeding equipment. Small-seeded grasses like bentgrass are normally difficult to sow with spinner seeders—the dust-sized seeds just blow away in the wind. Coating gives each seed a uniform size and bulk for better dispersion.
- *A carrier for pesticides*—In theory, seed coated with a fungicide should stand a better chance of fending off seedling diseases than untreated seed. For the most part, field research has verified this theory as sound. In fact, some research has suggested that fungicide seed coatings are even more effective at preventing seedling damping off fungus than postplanting aerial sprays.
- *A carrier for fertilizers*—A young seedling with a tiny root system has a limited ability to forage for nutrients. Adding a fertilizer coating to grass seed was seen as a method to spoon-feed the developing seeding as it germinated. Unfortunately, little agronomic benefit has been seen from fertilizer coatings in field studies. The amount of fertilizer in the coating is actually too little to be of value. Adding more fertilizer leads to toxicity because of its close contact with the seed.
- *A carrier for microbials*—With legume seed, **bacterial inoculants** are routinely added to seed coatings. As the legume grows, the rhizobium microbes form nitrogen-fixing nodules on the legume roots. Back in the 1970s, nitrogen-fixing bacteria were tested on grass seed. The amount of fixed nitrogen was measurable in the laboratory, but in the field

there was too little N released by the microbes to be of value—approximately 1/10th lb nitrogen per 1000 ft^2 (0.5 g N/m^2). One bacterial product is still being marketed today for grass seed.

- *Water-absorbing polymers*—Certain expanding starches and polymers can absorb 100 to 1000 times their weight in water. Over the years, water-absorbing coatings have been tested with the idea of drawing moisture away from the soil toward the seed. Unfortunately when tested in the field, the benefit of the coating was minimal. In fact, the coating seemed to draw moisture *away* from the seed and toward the coating. Research on the unconventional grasses has been similar. Russian wildrye seed showed no benefits of water-absorbing coatings on germination (Berdahl and Baker, 1980).
- *A color for identification*—Consider blue seed. No, I don't mean Kentucky bluegrass. I mean seed that's sky blue. Could you ever confuse it with anything else? Colorants are a way of making seed more interesting and attractive, and a way to identify one's unique product. Pennington Seed Company has even trademarked a green color for its coated grass seed.

Getting seeds off to a faster start: Pregermination and priming

Pregermination and **priming** are two pretreatment methods for getting seed to sprout faster. Pregerminating (or **presoaking** as it's sometimes called) is a straightforward process: Seed is soaked in water for 1 to 2 days prior to planting. After treatment, the seed has already begun to sprout and is ready for immediate planting.

Sports field managers have experimented with pregermination for years. George Toma, famous grounds manager for several Super Bowls, lectures on his techniques for prewetting ryegrass seed to induce germination within 24 hours (Brede, 1989). Others have tried and refined this technique. I once spoke with a hydroseeder in Maryland who presoaks every pound of seed he plants. He feels that pretreatment gives him a gimmick over his competition—and in today's business world, he says, everyone needs a gimmick.

Priming is similar to pregermination in many ways. Priming differs from pregerminating in that a *limited* amount of water is fed to the seed (Brede, 1992c). With pregermination, the seed gets all the water it wants. Germination comes quickly with presoaked seed. With priming, however, seed is *readied* for germination but not actually germinated.

Seed priming is nothing new. It's a technique that's widely used in the vegetable industry but had never been attempted in turf until recent years.

Priming is a process that occurs naturally in the wilds. Consider this: Have you ever noticed that after a passing shower hits a new seedbed, weeds seem to germinate literally overnight? Answer: The weeds have been *primed* by the natural wetting and drying cycles in the soil. The soil constantly feeds small amounts of moisture to buried seed—not enough to germinate them, just enough to keep them primed. When sufficient rainfall arrives, the primed weed seed sprout immediately.

In priming, water uptake can be limited in a number of ways, even by adding salt or fertilizer to the water. It seems strange that merely adding salt will limit the water uptake, but it does work. This limited water allows the germination juices to course through the seed but does not permit full germination. As a result, primed seed can be stored for a period of time without harm. By contrast, pregerminated seed is a living, growing organism that you can't shut off. Any unplanted seed is wasted.

Like anything valuable, priming and pregermination cost extra money. The added expense is certainly acceptable for vegetables which commonly sell for hundreds of dollars per lb. Whether the added cost is justified for turf seed is debatable.

Benefits and drawbacks to pregermination and priming

Priming and pregermination are similar in many respects. The key difference is that pregerminated seed is planted wet, while primed seed can be dried back and planted through conventional planting equipment, like drop or whirlybird spreaders. Pregerminated seed must be planted through a hydroseeder.

Freshly primed or pregerminated seed is quite dramatic in the early stages of germination in the field. Pregermination typically cuts 1 to 2 days off the field germination time for every day of soaking. So, if a grass normally germinates in 7 days, and you soak it for 2 days, it will germinate in the field in about 3 to 5 days. With some practice (and nerves of steel), it's possible to trim the presoaking interval so closely that the seed begins sprouting in the field within hours of when it's planted. You will be able to see green fuzz the very next morning. But the margin for error is nil.

As a rule of thumb, priming *at best* cuts the field germination time in half. So if a crop normally sprouts in 14 days (example: bluegrass), it will emerge 7 days quicker when primed. That's assuming, of course, that the primed seed is fresh. The priming effect dissipates with storage: the 7 quicker days become 6 and so on.

Al Dudeck at the University of Florida (Brede, 1989) and other researchers have found that adding a small amount of growth hormone to the presoaking solution helps jump-start the pregermination process. Seed soaked in gibberellic acid (GA) solution at 1 fl oz of GA per 75 gal water (10 mL/100 L) germinated three days faster than seed soaked in plain water. Gibberellic acid is available through the greenhouse supply business. Addition of a surfactant (wetting agent) to the presoaking solution reportedly has the opposite effect. It stunts germination and should be avoided (Detzel, 1994).

It's easy to become disillusioned with priming and pregermination after a few weeks. Six weeks after planting, it's nearly impossible to tell primed turf from unprimed. Nature is a great equalizer. Untreated seedlings catch up quickly (Brede, 1989).

The major benefit of seed pretreatment comes when temperatures are adverse. Karl Danneberger and his associates at Ohio State University (Danneberger et al., 1992) found that priming of perennial ryegrass was most helpful when temperatures were too cool or too warm. He concluded that although priming "enhanced initial germination rate and seedling root growth, it did not do so under prolonged favorable conditions. The promotive effects were more beneficial when seeds were exposed to less favorable germination conditions."

Priming and pregermination can benefit low maintenance turfgrasses and alter their competition with weeds during establishment. Stuart Hardegree, range scientist with the USDA in Boise, found that primed bluebunch wheatgrass, thickspike wheatgrass, and sheep fescue all competed more effectively against downy bromegrass, an aggressive winter annual weed, than untreated seed (Hardegree, 1994).

Jack Fry and his associates at Kansas State University improved the germination of buffalograss burs by presoaking (Fry et al., 1993). Presoaking resulted in 30% more buffalograss seedlings 2 weeks after planting. But pretreated seed reached 100% ground cover only one week before untreated seed. Earlier germination is still beneficial, though, in competing with emerging weeds.

TURF RENOVATION

Starting Over Is Easier Than Battling Maintenance Concerns

Walter called the other day to ask yet another lawn question. Walter is an old pal of mine from high school days. Years ago, he started his own lawn care business out of the back of his pickup truck. Ever since, whenever Walter's small but growing business faces a new agronomic challenge, I'll get a call from my old friend again.

"I'm getting too many lawns that just aren't responding anymore," Walter said with disgust. "I up the fertilizer rate, and I get lawn diseases. But if I don't fertilize, the lawns look awful, and the weeds take over." I knew something was bugging my old friend, but over the phone I couldn't tell just what.

"What kind of grass are you dealing with?" I inquired.

"Mainly old grass," he said.

"Old grass?"

Optimizing Pregermination and Priming

- *Temperature*—Pregermination and priming are usually done at temperatures between 70 and 80°F (21 to 27°C) for cool-season grasses and 80 to 90°F (27 to 32°C) for warm-seasons. Some studies have shown that alternating warm/cool, day/night temperatures add to the pretreatment effect (Brede, 1989).
- *Light*—Light aids any seed pretreatment. Seed pretreatment does not absolutely require light, but it's better with than without. Only a brief exposure to light (1 hour or less) is required. Red light is most beneficial. Fluorescent and mercury vapor light are least beneficial.
- *Air*—Exposure to oxygen is an essential ingredient in seed pretreatment. There's a natural mechanism in seed that plunges it into dormancy when conditions are too wet. Aeration or agitation can help overcome this obstacle.
- *Handling and storage*—Pregerminated seed, as stated earlier, does not store. If it's not planted immediately, it germinates and dies. Refrigeration is a last-ditch way to save pregerminated seed a few extra days. Primed seed, on the other hand, can be stored under cool conditions for a month or two.
- *Seedlot*—Every seedlot of every variety is different. For example, I once primed a fresh seedlot of "Destiny" Kentucky bluegrass alongside an older lot. I found that the fresh lot was germinating in the priming solution while the older lot was still treating. It would be nice if there a screening tool for individual seedlots that could determine their ideal pretreatment period. Using blended seedlots—several seedlots blended together—may help even things out.
- *Length of priming period*—For Kentucky bluegrass, I found that 5-day priming is about optimal for most seedlots. Weaker lots benefit from a 7-day prime. Priming for too brief a period of time will give little if any priming effect to the seed. Priming for too long will allow the seed to germinate in the priming solution—effectively a ruined lot unless it's planted immediately.
- *Inhibitors*—As seed germinates, it gives off waste products. The water solution can turn a murky brown or orange after a day of soaking. That's not from dirt—that's the inhibitors being given off by the seed. For successful seed pretreatment, change the water when it turns turbid.
- *Priming in water alone*—Rather than drown the seed in a bucket of water, this method of priming involves dampening the seed with just a minimal amount of moisture (see sidebar on do-it-yourself priming). The reason this method works is that it adheres to the basic concept of priming: *limited* water is fed to the seed, not enough for full germination to take place.
- *Drying seed after priming*—With seed priming, the seed can be dried back before planting. High temperature air (above 85°F [30°C]) can rapidly dry the seed, but the heat can effectively strip away all priming effect. Ideally treated seed should be dried with 60°F air (15°C). My research has found that the priming effect is negated by drying seed below a 12% moisture content. That's about the same dryness as untreated seed straight from the bag. Other researchers have found no detrimental effect from drying primed seed to 8% moisture.

Do-It-Yourself Seed Priming

Seed priming can be a complicated process. Priming is a method of fooling the seed into thinking it's in a nice, moist soil somewhere, and that it can begin the biological process of waking up. Priming overcomes many of the inherent dormancy mechanisms in seed. These mechanisms have evolved over the eons to prevent seed from germinating when soil conditions are not quite right.

To get seed to forego its dormancy mechanisms, we must lull it into believing it's in soil under ideal germination conditions. When we prime seed, anything we do to simulate near perfect germination conditions will enhance the effect.

One technique that seems to work well with home-brew priming is to dampen the seed with a limited quantity of water (8 parts water to 10 parts seed; or 5 gal. of water for a 50-lb bag of seed). Then spread a layer of grass seed onto a plastic sheet or concrete slab. Turn the seed periodically with a shovel, possibly several times a day. After 5 to 7 days, dry it in the sun for several hours. When dry, the primed seed can be planted through conventional drills or spreaders.

Another simple priming technique involves a sack. Priming can be done right in the same woven polybags seed is sold in. One Michigan company, Liquid Sod, Inc., sells specialized priming bags resembling gunny sacks that are tailor-made for home-brew priming (Brede, 1989). To prime, dampen the seed, mix thoroughly, and put it back into the polybag or priming sack. Allow free water to drip away from the damp seed. After priming, sun dry as before.

I've found that a successful technique for "sack" priming is to ventilate the seed by sticking an air hose into the bag. A normal air compressor hose works fine for this purpose as long as the air is filtered with an oil trap and the flow rate is slow. Check the temperature of the compressor air after it has run for a while. Sometimes air compressors pump blazingly hot air.

As it turned out, old grass was Walter's term for lawns of nondescript background and species—probably dating back to the 1940s or 1950s—lawns that now consisted of a hodgepodge of textures and colors. Keeping such a collection of plants happy was becoming a losing battle. His attempts to mend the problem with pesticides and fertilizers were failing. The existing grass lacked the vigor and disease resistance to fight its own battles.

Although Walter's company was strictly a spray operation, I suggested to him that he consider **renovation** as a solution. Lawn renovation is a way of introducing an improved grass into a lawn without tillage—preferably a lawn variety with added vigor and disease resistance to help in his war against weeds and fungi.

Lawn renovation can be done in a number of ways: some are relatively painless while others are costly and dramatic. Lawn renovation entails planting new grass in place of old. *How* you go about doing it differentiates the methods. **Overseeding**, the most painless method, involves drilling seed into live sod. Other approaches involve killing the old turf or removing it altogether.

"But I don't know anything about seed. I'm a spray man," moaned Walter. "And besides, how am I going to know which grass to put where?"

I explained that the choice of grass depends on where you're located, how attractive you want it to be, and how much you want to pay for upkeep. No one grass can suffice for all situations. That's why there're over a hundred grass seed varieties on the market.

"Over a hundred!" he exclaimed.

I could tell it was time to get down to specifics.

Reasons to Renovate

Up until about 1975 there was little incentive to renovate turf. Most of the grasses available at

Benefits of Overseeding

- Replaces older, inferior varieties with genetically superior ones
- Provides a smoother, more uniform playing surface
- Increases plant density
- Provides better competition against weeds without resorting to chemicals
- Repairs injury and thinning from hard summers, cold winters, or disease outbreak
- Allows you to broaden the genetic base of your turf by adding addition grasses
- Can be used to introduce endophyte-enhanced grasses for natural, biological pest control

that point were no better than the aging lawns themselves. Renovation offered little real benefit.

But since that time, a plethora of exciting, new cultivars have hit the market. Take for example, perennial ryegrass. With ryegrass—a popular renovation grass—a new generation of improvement comes every 4 to 5 years on the average. That means every few years it makes sense to add the benefits of the latest generation of grasses to your lawn. New varieties offer better insect and disease resistance, darker color with less fertilizer, slower vertical growth for reduced mowing, and improved turf performance with less overall maintenance. The real question seems to be: Why *wouldn't* you renovate?

People assume grass is eternal. And, yes, turf is indeed a perennial crop that doesn't need to be replanted each year. On the other hand, with continual varietal improvements offering more for less, it makes sense to renovate as a routine part of turf maintenance. Some form of renovation should be practiced every 5 to 10 years as superior varieties become available (Cook, 1990; Powell, 1984).

Another good reason to renovate relates to disease. When a new turf variety is first released by breeders, it has a "honeymoon" period in which it is relatively immune to disease attack. Then suddenly, after a decade or so of widespread use, a fungus strain mutates and cracks the grass' defenses. It goes from resistant to susceptible in short order.

This phenomenon hit "Merion" Kentucky bluegrass in the 1960s. For ten years after Merion was released, it was highly resistant to leaf spot and stripe smut diseases. Later as Merion was planted on countless lawns and golf courses, a fungus strain finally conquered its defenses and Merion became riddled with disease. The same has taken place with other varieties since.

TECHNIQUES FOR STARTING OVER

Renovation techniques range from the benign to the extreme. The method you choose depends on the condition of the turf: Does it just need to be perked up, or is it a disaster case? Four methods are described below.

Overseeding

Simply put, **overseeding** is the process of planting new grass into existing turf. The "over" in overseeding means that the new grass is planted "over the top" of the old. You'll also hear it called **seed topdressing** (as in, dressing seed over the top) or **sod seeding**.

Overseeding is the least invasive method of renovation. The existing grass is not killed, so it is possible (though not advisable) to continuously play the turf throughout the grow-in period. Turf is taken out of "play" the shortest amount of time—usually for only a few weeks. This is a big advantage for golf courses, sports fields, and home lawns where it may be impractical to completely close the turf during renovation (Minner, 1989; Watson, 1989).

Simply scattering seed over the top of turf is not a successful way to renovate. Seed still needs to be *planted,* even in renovation. Seed broadcast over the top of turf may light on leaves or thatch. It seldom finds its way to the soil. And unless there's direct contact between seed and

Necrotic Ring Spot: A Case Where Overseeding—Rather Than Chemicals—Solved a Problem

Necrotic ring spot is a tough disease to control by conventional means. Necrotic ring spot is caused by *Leptosphaeria korrae,* an aggressive root-eating fungus that shows little discrimination among bluegrass, bentgrass, bermudagrass, or fine fescue. A lawn infected with this soil-resident disease is marred by huge, circular, sunken patches that increase in volume over time. Fungicides provide only partial control of the disease. Eradication can take up to three years of expensive sprays.

Research by Dick Smiley, plant pathologist at Oregon State University's Pendleton research station, suggests that overseeding can be used as a nonchemical cure for necrotic ring spot.

"The perennial ryegrasses and tall fescues are susceptible to *Leptosphaeria* in the laboratory, but I've never seen necrotic ring spot hit them in the field. I advocate overseeding as the way to go in cultural necrotic ring spot control," says Smiley.

In Smiley's New York State field trials, he found that ryegrasses and tall fescues suffered blackened roots when exposed to the necrotic ring spot fungus in the lab. But for some reason, the fungus does not kill them as it did other grasses.

"They get black roots, but by god they survive! They come through some real tough conditions and they recover." He feels this recovery ability leads to the high level of resistance among ryegrass and tall fescue.

Kentucky bluegrass is another story. Taken as a whole, Kentucky bluegrass is highly susceptible to necrotic ring spot. But taken on an individual variety basis, there is hope. Certain bluegrass varieties show remarkable resistance to necrotic ring spot. Smiley published a series of papers in the American Phytopathological Society's Biological and Cultural Tests journal describing his findings on bluegrass resistance to necrotic ring spot.

"I truly believe there is varietal resistance in Kentucky bluegrass," he says. And recent data from the US National Turfgrass Evaluation Program back him up. Varieties ranged from 100% killed by the fungus to 100% alive.

Overseeding incorporates new attributes into old turf. In this case, overseeding with perennial ryegrass, tall fescue, or a resistant bluegrass variety remedied a malady that would otherwise require years of expensive chemical treatment.

soil, the seedling won't persist. The key point in case you missed it is: *Seeds grow only in soil.*

Vertical mowing (also called **dethatching, thatching, verticutting, power raking**) and **aerifying** (also called **aerating, punching, coring, core aerification**) are methods for opening up turf to let the overseeded grass contact the soil (see Chapter 8 for mechanical details). In addition to opening the turf, these methods thin the stand to reduce competition between the tough, older plants and the tender, emerging seedlings (for more on competition, see the section below on *Overseeding Summary*).

Depending on the quantity of thatch present, you may need to dethatch or aerify with more than one pass, to get the seed into contact with soil. On a thatchy stand, it may take 4 or 5 passes with the equipment before the thatch is open enough to accept seed. Between passes, excess thatch should be raked up and carted off. Don't be surprised if a typical home lawn generates several pickup truckloads of duff (see Figure 7.6).

In recent years, a device known as a **sod seeder** has become popular with folks who renovate for a living. This unit combines a thatcher and seeder into one. Vertically whirling blades slit the turf. Small metal disks open the slits and drop in seeds. A press-bar firms the overseeded turf. All this occurs with one pass of the machine. Combina-

Figure 7.6. The first step in overseeding is to thin the lawn with a vertical mower to open up channels for seedling establishment. Vertical mowing (shown here) or core aerification can punch holes in the turf and bring a small amount of soil to the surface (top left photo, going clockwise). Expect to bring up a lot of vegetation and duff during renovation. This material—resembling mattress stuffing—should be raked or vacuumed away (photo 2; photo credit, Art Wick). The *depth* of vertical mowing is governed by the quantity of thatch present. If the turf has a dense thatch, the vertical mower should be set deeper to rid the excess thatch (photo 3). An all-in-one overseeding machine can be purchased in lawn (photo 4) or tractor-mounted sizes (photo 5). These combination units save time by combining several steps into one.

tion overseeders are available in tractor-mounted and hand-pushed models (see Figure 7.6).

In addition to bringing up thatch, the dethatcher or aerifier will also bring soil to the surface. This small quantity of soil aids seedling establishment. Seed is typically broadcast over the surface and incorporated into the soil by a rake or drag mat. Commercial metal drag mats are available for this purpose, or you can fashion your own out of a section of chain-link fence, an old upside-down rug, a wooden shipping pallet, or a railroad tie chained perpendicularly behind a tractor.

After spreading the seed, it's important to rely on the same time-tested establishment techniques described for planting a bare seedbed, including starter fertilizer, rolling, and frequent, light watering (described earlier in this chapter). You won't need a mulch, though. The duff remaining after vertical mowing provides adequate mulch for the young seedlings.

Within a few weeks, the new seedlings will begin poking through. Care for them as you would a bare-seedbed planting until they reach 6 to 8 weeks of age.

And be sure to follow your normal mowing schedule. Mowing helps prevent the existing grass from getting too tall and shading the seedlings. Some people even mow a little closer during overseeding, to stress the existing plants and allow light to reach the seedlings. Walk-behind mowers and even triplex units can be safely run on overseeded turf. Tractor-pulled gang units cause abrasion and stand loss, though.

Winter overseeding of dormant warm-season turf

Yearly winter overseeding is not what one normally considers "low maintenance turf." The annual practice of planting a winter grass is both time-consuming and expensive. But like any other practice, it can stand to benefit from low maintenance refinements.

Winter overseeding is technically not renovation. However, because the procedures are nearly identical, I've included winter overseeding here in this chapter. Many of the tips and techniques of winter overseeding are directly applicable to renovation of permanent turf.

It has become common practice in many warmer areas (typically Zone 4, Chapter 5) to overseed dormant warm-season turf with a cool-season grass each fall. Winter overseeding is used in many facets of the turf industry, notably golf courses, sports fields, and home lawns. If you're new to winter overseeding, you may question why anyone would want to go to all the trouble and expense of planting a new turf every year only to have it fade away in the spring. The purpose is to enhance durability and color during winter when the warm-season turf would be dormant brown and easily trampled. Winter overseeding is a necessity on warm-season sites with heavy wintertime play.

The cool-season grass used in winter overseeding is usually a *perennial* species. But in this case, it's treated like an annual crop. In the spring, the cool-season grass fades away as the warm-season turf breaks dormancy.

Preparing for overseeding. Adequate preparation is important when overseeding because, essentially, you're about to plant a whole new turf stand. Malfunctioning equipment, irrigation problems, or late seed delivery can spell disaster. Taking a thorough inventory of supplies, seed, replacement parts, and labor beforehand will help avoid problems later.

A practice run is a good idea. Some golf courses do a dry run by overseeding the practice green. This allows training new workers, checking equipment, and working bugs out of the system.

The calendar date chosen for overseeding is critical. If you seed too early, the warm-season turf will outcompete the seedlings. If you plant too late, the seedlings will be sluggish and will not fully develop before winter.

In autumn when nighttime temperatures start dipping into the 60s or high 50s °F (12 to 17°C), the weather is right for overseeding. This usually occurs 2 to 3 weeks before the first frost date in the fall, though it varies from area to area.

Planting the seed. A couple of days before overseeding, turn off your irrigation system and allow the turf to dry down. Some turf managers use a herbicide or a plant growth regulator to slow the growth of the warm-season grass, but it's not required.

Vertical mowing is the key to successful overseeding—getting seed into physical contact with soil. Vertical mowing removes excess duff and opens slits for germinating the overseeded grass. Vertical mowing distributes a small amount of soil on top of the thatch and allows the seed to germinate in soil, not somewhere up in the canopy.

Bermudagrass turf can generally tolerate vertical mowing $^1/_4$-in. (5 mm) deep into the root zone, whereas zoysia is more sensitive and should be vertically mowed as shallow as possible. Vertical mowing too vigorously can reduce spring recuperation of the grass.

Next, scalp the turf with a low mower setting. Catch and remove excess duff and clippings.

Seeding rate depends on the area being planted. Typical overseeding rates are 1.5x to 2x higher than for permanent turf (Table 7.3). These rates are needed for quick coverage and a fine leaf texture. Because of the high rates, seedling damping-off can be a concern, particularly in humid climates. When damping off strikes, be ready for quick action. Contact or systemic fungicides are available for a rapid knockdown of the disease. Seed can also be purchased precoated with a fungicide effective against pythium damping off (see section in this chapter on *Coated Seed*). Minimizing nighttime watering will also help cut down on disease.

Seeding crisscross in two directions is one way to avoid skips, which can be quite glaring. Plant half your seed in a north-south direction, for example, and seed the other half east-west. A few turf managers plant half their quantity of seed, allow time for the seed to germinate, and later come in and overseed the rest. This technique may be useful in areas with unpredictable fall storms as a hedge against washouts. The disadvantage of doing a split seeding is that seed at the second planting date will germinate up in the foliage and not down at soil level. Moreover, the optimal date for one of the two plantings is compromised. Thus, most turf managers shy away from split-date plantings.

The same basic steps of turf establishment outlined earlier in this chapter apply to overseeding, including starter fertilizer, rolling, and light watering. In lieu of rolling, many sports facilities use a drag mat to incorporate the seed.

An alternative overseeding procedure involves a combination of seeding and topdressing with *no* vertical mowing. Spread the grass seed directly onto scalped (closely cropped) turf. Apply a *thin* layer of soil (or sand) topdressing on top of the seed to cover it. Drag the topdressing gingerly; too much dragging will distribute the seed unevenly. Brushing or watering is preferable. Then, treat it as you would any new planting.

Spring transition. In the spring as the warm-season grass begins to wake up, the overseeded grass fades away—or at least that's the way it's supposed to happen. With good transition management, though, it is possible to have full recovery of the warm-season grass and a dieback of the overseeded grass.

You can anticipate spring recovery by monitoring soil temperature. When soil temperatures reach the mid 60s °F (18°C), emergence is not far away. Irrigation prior to emergence is beneficial, since drought can weaken the emerging warm-season grass. After emergence the reverse becomes true. Reduce irrigation to near drought stress after the warm-season grass is up and growing to competitively favor it over the ryegrass and help speed transition.

As you near the point of bermudagrass emergence, begin lowering the cutting height. Continue fertilizer applications through this period, since fertilizer will make the ryegrass grow taller (to stress it more) and will spur the emerging warm-season.

Record your successes and failures. It's a long time from one season to the next and memories fade. Through the overseeding process, take notes of things to try next year. Note successes as well as failures. A debriefing session with your crew can get ideas on paper that would otherwise be forgotten. A good set of notes can serve as a useful scheduling guide for next year's overseeding.

Renovation

Overseeding and **renovation** are similar processes for rebuilding a stand of turf, with one principal difference: With overseeding, seed is introduced into a growing stand of grass without killing the existing stand. Overseeding *supplements* the existing stand with a better grass. Renovation is a more complete replacement of the turf than overseeding. With renovation, the existing turf is killed with herbicide. Perennial weed problems may still remain with overseeding. But with renovation, all vegetation is killed and left in place to serve as a seedbed for the new stand.

Why would you renovate turf as opposed to overseeding? To answer that question, I've listed three practical examples below. See if you can choose which method—*overseeding* or *renovation*—would be more appropriate. The correct answers appear in the footnote[1]:

1. Your turf is thin with a lot of bare ground showing. It is uniform in appearance but yellowish in color. Each spring and summer, disease reduces the stand even further.
2. Your turf is a conglomeration of coarse textured bunch grasses, fine bladed creepers, and an occasional noxious weed. It grows like hay when you try to green it up with fertilizer.
3. Your turf is no place for croquet. The uneven ground surface is pitted and heaving. You've had to shoot two of your polo horses who've twisted and broken ankles on it.

Renovation can be done anytime during the growing season. The best time to renovate depends on which grass you're using: Cool-season grasses are best established in late summer to early fall. With warm-season grasses, early summer is preferred, to allow ample time for establishment before cooler temperatures arrive.

Start renovation with the application of a nonselective, nonresidual, systemic herbicide (Roundup®, Finale®, or similar) to kill the existing grass (Cook, 1990). Soil fumigants (e.g., methyl bromide) have been used in putting green renovation, but their application is highly specialized and controversial; it's best to get an outside contractor to help. Contact herbicides that don't translocate to roots (Paraquat®, for example) work poorly for renovation, allowing grasses and weeds to recover from rootstocks.

Herbicides function best when applied to actively growing plants with ample green tissue. For maximum kill, irrigate the turf up until the time of spraying and beyond. Of course, don't irrigate on the day you spray or you'll wash off the herbicide. But irrigation is important before and after spraying, especially in arid areas or during drought. Drought stressed plants don't take up foliar herbicides.

Tough perennial weeds and grasses such as fine fescue or bermudagrass may require more than one herbicide treatment for complete kill. A good plan is to spray, wait a week, and treat again.

Seeding rates. Wait the label-prescribed length of time for the herbicide to work before scalping and thatching the turf. Remove debris and apply seed as described for overseeding. From this point on, the processes of **overseeding**, **winter overseeding**, and **renovation** converge. Planting procedures and aftercare are identical. The only difference is seeding rate. Winter overseeding uses high seeding rates to provide quick coverage and a fine texture. Renovation requires the same basic seeding rates used for a permanent planting on a bare seedbed (see Table 7.3). Overseeding into an existing stand of turf (without killing off the turf) is best suited to a slightly higher seeding rate, perhaps 1 to 2 lb (5 to 10 g) above normal rates. For example, Kentucky bluegrass which is normally sown at 2 to 3 lb of seed per 1000 ft^2 (10–15 g/m^2) would be overseeded at 3 to 4 lb (15–20 g/m^2). Field survival of overseeded grass is around 50%. A slightly higher seeding rate is used to compensate.

[1] Question 1: If the turf needs improvement, and it doesn't have permanent weed problems, overseeding is your best choice. Question 2: Renovation (killing the stand with herbicide and replanting) is the best bet for controlling preexisting coarse grass problems. Question 3: Reconstruction is your best answer. (Reconstruction is covered in the next section.)

Reconstruction

Overseeding and renovation remedy the vast majority of problem turfs. Sometimes, though, the deficits are so severe that merely changing the grass will not solve them. Obstacles such as a bumpy lawn surface or poor internal drainage can only be rectified by rebuilding the turf from the ground up.

Reconstruction should be a last resort. A prime credo of low maintenance is to take the path of least resistance. Tilling up an old turf and replanting it entails major surgery. It may take *more* time and effort to reestablish a turf than it did to plant it in the first place. Why? The dilemma with reconstruction is: What do you do with the old sod? Turf just a few years old can accumulate a substantial thatch. Tilling the thatch carves it into pieces but doesn't get rid of it. The mounds of remaining sod pieces make reestablishing a smooth seedbed a real challenge.

Several methods have been tried for dealing with leftover sod:

- *Mold-board plowing*—A deep, clean plow can flip the sod on its back, burying the thatch at plow depth. However, maneuvering a plow in the tight spaces of lawns and parks, around trees and buildings, and between sprinkler heads is generally impossible. It's also devastating to tree roots.
- *Rototilling*—In theory, a rototiller should be able to shred thatch into a fine mulch and blend it into the soil for replanting. But in practice that never happens. A rototiller rips sod into odd-sized chunks, creating an unbelievably lumpy planting bed. And the more you try to rake it smooth, the more new sod clumps you snag and bring to the surface.
- *Stripping the sod*—A sod cutter machine can be used to remove the old sod. After cutting, the sod can be windrowed with a tractor and blade and carted off with a bucket loader. Though this method requires several pieces of equipment, it provides the neatest cleanup of old sod. It's also the best way to reconstruct turf if you've got an in-ground irrigation system. (By the way, be sure to flag all sprinkler heads beforehand to avoid hitting them with equipment.)
- *Burying the sod under a layer of soil*—An alternative to stripping the old sod is to leave it in place and bury it beneath topsoil. New topsoil can be dumped and bladed over the sod, distributing an even layer for reestablishing grass. The old sod—sandwiched between layers of soil—decomposes over time. On poorly drained soils, the sod sandwich may inhibit water percolation. But after a year or so, the old sod should rot away.

Just as with renovation, a systemic herbicide is usually applied to the turf prior to reconstruction to rid the stand of existing grasses and weeds. Even if the old sod is stripped and removed, rootstocks can remain to reinvade the new turf.

Reconstruction is risky around trees and shrubs. Major tillage under the dripline of trees kills about half of them. Some are killed immediately, others fade years later. Even spreading topsoil onto the ground under trees is no guarantee of success. It can smother tree roots and distress the trees. Perhaps the best alternative under trees is to strip the sod with a sod cutter, smooth the surface with a drag (no tillage), and replant.

OVERSEEDING SUMMARY

A typical grass seedling during overseeding faces a greater than 50% chance of infant mortality. Fewer than half will make it to maturity. With smaller seeded grasses, this figure is much higher. Most never survive.

Successful overseeding depends on giving seedlings a break. Anything you can do to favor the young seedlings will aid their chances for success. It's not at all unusual to have a total establishment failure. Worse yet, you may have opened the stand for additional weed invasion (see *Bentgrass/annual bluegrass mixtures*, Chapter 6).

Some factors known to aid overseeded grasses are:

- Overseed at the optimal time of year for the grass you're planting.
- Thin the existing stand as much as possible with multiple passes of the renovation equipment. Anything that you can do to disturb the existing sod benefits the seedlings. Of course completely killing the sod with herbicide prior to overseeding is best. But if that's not on your agenda, try scalping, heavily verticutting, or aerifying just prior to seeding. This action will weaken the sod and give the seedlings their best shot at success.
- Plant vigorous grasses, preferably large seeded ones. Choose a vigorous variety and seedlot. A weak or unadapted variety is a poor competitor in the seedbed and in the mature stand. Likewise, a weak seedlot with low germination—even of a good variety—will establish poorly. Well adapted and well tested varieties are your best bet for success.
- Keep the stand mowed (perhaps closer than normal) during reestablishment to minimize shading.
- Regularly feed light applications of quick-release fertilizer to the young seedlings.
- Switch from deep infrequent watering to frequent, shallow watering during grow-in. And don't give up too soon—young overseeded seedlings take weeks longer to mature than grass on a bare soil bed. Sod-sown seedlings seem to be able to "hang on" for a couple of months in a state of simple existence. Perhaps they're waiting for their break to grow and establish.
- Some turf managers have reported success using preplant applications of growth regulators or herbicides to slow the existing turf. Joe DiPaola, turf specialist with Novartis, recommends "applying Primo growth regulator one to five days before overseeding to slow turf growth, giving the new seed a better chance to germinate and get establish."
- The species of sod into which you're planting is basically irrelevant to the success of your operation. In a series of experiments I ran, it didn't seem to matter which sod I planted into, survival was the same. The seed species being *planted* made all the difference. Perennial ryegrass was easiest to overseed, followed (in order) by tall fescue, strong creeping red fescue, bermudagrass, Kentucky bluegrass, creeping bentgrass, and zoysia. If anything, there was a slight tendency for likes to repel: For example, existing ryegrass sod was the toughest competitor against young ryegrass seedlings.

Chapter 8

Turf Soils

We demand a lot from our soil. We rely on soil to furnish the water and nutrients grass needs to grow, including some elements we don't even supply as fertilizer. We expect soil to bear the weight of foot traffic, even though trampling squashes the air out of the rootzone. And we expect soil to denature the chemicals we administer—pesticides and fertilizers—to prevent them from leaching into our drinking water supply (Watschke, 1991).

As Chapter 1 (Figure 1.5) emphasizes, the two key ingredients in the success or failure of a low maintenance turf are (1) the grass variety, and (2) the soil beneath. All other aspects of turf management—mowing, pesticides, watering, etc.—are icing on the cake. If there's something awry with your soil, no amount of watering or fertilizing will ever make it right. A favorable soil is at the root of low maintenance turf.

Soil problems are never simple to correct. Repair can involve a lot of digging, coring, thatching, or addition of amendments. It's a lot easier to fix soil problems *before* you plant than after. Modifying a turf stand after it's established is a lot trickier, especially if you're trying to keep the turf in service during the repair process. But it *can* be done. And you're better off doing something, rather than throwing away time and money trying to maintain an unmanageable stand.

This chapter deals with the vital topic of turf soils: How to test them, how to improve them, and how to fix problems and reduce your maintenance (Table 8.1).

THATCH

Have you ever noticed that the deepest, richest soils in the world are prairie soils? Grass is a phenomenal soil builder. It continuously generates organic matter that cycles into the soil through growth and decay. The fertile, black soils of the U.S. Midwest are a testament to eons of grass.

This miraculous soil-building character of grass does have its downside though: Thatch buildup. Thatch is the accumulation of dead and decaying **biomass** sandwiched between the grass plant and the soil. When unchecked, thatch can accumulate to depths of 6 in. (15 cm) or more, to the point where the grass roots are dwelling in thatch rather than soil (Charbonneau, 1994).

What is thatch?

Thatch forms from decaying crowns and stems—tissues high in lignin, cellulose, and hemicellulose. Contrary to popular opinion, grass clippings do not cause thatch (Shoulders, 1982). Clippings are made mostly of water and carbohydrates that are easily broken down. The misconception about clippings causing thatch undoubtedly stems from the relationship between thatch and fertilizer. If you up your fertilizer rate, you're rewarded with substantially more clipping, and at the same time, more thatch. But that doesn't mean the clippings are *causing* the thatch. Along with topgrowth, other plant parts are being stimulated as well, causing thatch to pile up. With fertilizer come more stems and crowns, hence, more thatch (Soper et al., 1988). It's the added stems and crowns that are causing the thatch, not the added clippings. (Here's another abuse of the cause-and-effect law: "Ninety-eight percent of criminals reportedly drank milk as children. Therefore, milk causes criminal behavior.")

Table 8.1. The causes and cures of common soil-related problems. For detailed information, refer to the page number listed on the right.

Problem	Causes	Effects on the Grass	Cures	See Page
Compaction	• Equipment and foot traffic, especially when the soil is wet • Soil high in silt and clay	• Reduced rooting • Thinning • Weed competition • More disease and stress	• Aerification • Soil modification • Redistribute traffic patterns • Turf pavers • Balloon tires	199–202
Dry spots	• Hydrophobic coatings on soil particles • Poorly tilled or mixed soil • Buried rocks or other debris • Excessive thatch • Sandy soil	• Drying in irregular patches • Higher maintenance due to hand-watering of dry spots	• Aerification and topdressing • Wetting agents • Careful water management	189,238, 239
Erosive soil	• Light soil texture • Steep slope	• Poor establishment • Soil erosion losses	• Mulches • Sod-forming grasses • Surface contouring	Chapter 7
Expansive clay	• Montmorillonite clays that swell when wet	• These "self-tilling" soils can disrupt the smooth playing surface of turf • Soil cracking when dry • Poor water penetration	• Careful water management • Adding drainage • Soil modification	192
Low organic matter content	• Subsoil • Infertile soil	• Moisture problems • Slow growth • Compaction • Poor nutrient retention	• Addition of compost, peat, or topsoil	193
Low water-holding capacity	• Sandy or gravely soil • Shallow topsoil	• Quickly drought stressed • Nutrients pass rapidly through soil profile	• Addition of compost, peat, or topsoil	193
pH – too acid	• Acidic parent material • High rainfall • Acid fertilizer	• Thinning • Weed competition • Disease problems • Nutrient deficiencies	• Addition of lime • Switch to alkaline or neutral fertilizer	202–206
pH – too alkaline	• Alkaline parent material • Low rainfall • Alkaline irrigation water	• Thinning • Weed competition • Nutrient deficiencies	• Addition of sulfur • Use of acid fertilizer	202–206
Poor water infiltration	• Compaction • Layering	• Poor wear tolerance • Shallow rooting	• Aerification • Spiking and slicing	199–202

	• High clay content • Excessive thatch buildup	• Drought susceptible • Moss and algae competition • Ponding	• Surface contouring • Installation of subsurface drainage • Soil modification	
Salt	• Salty parent material • Low rainfall • Salty irrigation water • Groundwater intrusion • High salt fertilizers • Salt applied to adjacent roadways	• Thinning • Weed competition • Increased irrigation requirement • Purpling • Wilt	• Irrigate to flush salt through the soil profile • Gypsum • Add a salt tolerant grass to the turf • Use of low-salt, organic fertilizer • Use of nontoxic ice-removal products	206–208
Soil layering	• Naturally occurring hard or clay pan • Poor construction	• Slow drainage • Surface ponding • Similar consequences to poor water infiltration (above) • Black layer	• Aerification and topdressing • Deep-tine aerification • Reconstruction • Addition of subsurface drainage	192, 200, 201
Texture – too much clay	• High clay parent material	• Easily compacted • Poor water drainage	• Modification with sand, compost, or topsoil • Addition of subsurface drainage	193
Texture – too much sand or gravel	• High sand/gravel parent material	• Droughty • Poor nutrient retention	• Modification with compost or topsoil	193, 211
Thatch	• Excessive fertilizer and water • Thatch-producing grass species	• Mower bouncing and scalping • Poor drought tolerance • Additional insect and disease problems	• Aerification • Topdressing • Dethatching with a vertical mower • Use of nonthatching varieties • Cut your maintenance	185–192
Wear	• Heavy play • Poorly distributed traffic patterns • Heavy maintenance equipment	• Abrasion • Thinning • Compaction	• Increase water and fertilizer rate • Switch to a wear tolerant grass • Turf pavers • Redistribute traffic patterns • Use paved paths to confine traffic	194–199

Lignin is a large polymer molecule thought to be responsible for thatch. Lignin occurs in woody plants as well as grass. Next to cellulose, it is one of the most abundant plant molecules on earth. Some species devote up to 25% of their molecular energies generating lignin (Lederboer and Skogley, 1967).

Lignin functions as the structural backbone of grass stems. It gives them strength and stiffness. Chemical analysis reveals that turf thatch is high in lignin (Lederboer and Skogley, 1967). Lignin resists bacterial breakdown for two reasons: (1) its long-chain polymers are too big for bacteria to "get into their mouth," and (2) the breakdown products of lignin are toxic to bacteria. Bacteria attempting to munch lignin are left with a sour taste. Hence, thatch persists.

Balancing buildup and breakdown

Reed Funk, turf professor at Rutgers University, several years ago pointed out to his students an interesting concept of thatch. Funk had a bluegrass turf at his New Jersey research farm that over the years had developed a swollen 3-in. thatch (7.5 cm). He killed half the sod with herbicide and left the other half growing. Nine months later, thatch in the killed half had melted away to bare soil. Meanwhile, thatch in the living half was still just as thick. The question arises: Why did the thatch disappear? And what can we learn from this to aid in thatch control?

Thatch management is a process of juggling inputs and outputs. If the rate of production exceeds the rate of breakdown, thatch accumulates (Figure 8.1). In Funk's example, the thatch *input* rate was turned off when the sod was killed. It took 9 months for the existing thatch to decompose to nothing. Once thatch production is throttled back, breakdown doesn't take long. Management practices that affect the production rate or breakdown rate will alter the rate of buildup. It *is* possible to get thatch under control. For the most part, lowering maintenance is the answer.

Factors that regulate thatch buildup:

- *Nitrogen fertilizer*—The main culprit in thatch buildup is overfertilization (Shoulders, 1982). Cut the fertilizer rate and thatch accumulation stops; simple as that.
- *Irrigation*—Researchers disagree on the exact interplay between irrigation and thatch (Duckworth, 1995). However, most feel that overwatering contributes to thatch buildup (Charbonneau, 1994). The underlying concept seems to be: If you create a boggy, undesirable, anaerobic environment for the microorganisms that degrade thatch, they won't work as hard, and thatch will amass.
- *Thatch-prone grasses*—Grasses with creeping stems pile up thatch faster than

Figure 8.1. Over time, the level of thatch rises through the continual process of soil building. In this photo, the elevation of a sprinkler box remained constant while the thatch layer around it grew increasingly taller.

Thatch: Evil Menace or Environmental Friend?

Why is thatch bad?

1. Thatch causes water problems
   - Once thatch dries out it is difficult to rewet
   - Thatch repels water
   - Localized dry spots are frequently associated with thatch
   - In a thick thatch, the grass root system may be confined to the thatch layer and not the soil, limiting its ability to ferret for water
   - Thatch reduces water infiltration into soil
2. Thatch prevents pesticides and fertilizers from reaching their targets
   - Some insecticides bind to thatch, preventing them from washing to where insects are feeding
   - Pesticides are degraded more quickly in thatch than in soil
   - Phosphorus and other immobile fertilizer elements remain in the thatch and never migrate into the soil where deficiencies may be occurring
   - Nitrogen fertilizer applied to thatch may volatilize (evaporate into the air) more readily than when applied to soil
3. Thatch acts as a safe haven for insects and disease organisms
   - Most pathogenic fungi are saprophytes for much of their life cycle, living off rotting organic matter; thatch provides a secondary food source for them
   - The physical confines of thatch offers an ideal environment for insects to lay their eggs and raise their young
4. Thatch causes mowing problems
   - A dense thatch causes scalping and mower bounce
   - Scalped turf is prone to weed invasion
5. Thatch decreases heat and cold tolerance
   - With excessive thatch, the crowns of the grass plant are growing high above the sheltering effect of the soil; soil acts as a temperature buffer, keeping turf cool in summer and warm in winter
   - Thatchy turf is subject to winterkill and summer heat stress

Why is thatch beneficial?

1. Thatch absorbs and degrades pesticides and fertilizers
   - A study led by Charles Mancino (Mancino et al., 1993) found that thatch contained 40 to 1600 times as many bacteria, 500 to 600 times as many fungi, and up to 100 times as many actinomycetes organisms as soil; these microorganisms are vital in pesticide decay
   - Water leaching out of a thatch layer can meet or exceed drinking water standards for purity, due to the water-purifying properties of thatch and its cadre of microbes (Watschke, 1991)
2. Thatch acts as a cushion
   - Research by Trey Rogers and Don Waddington (Rogers and Waddington, 1992) showed that turf with a thatch exerted 17% less *G*-force on a falling athlete, compared with turf without a thatch; thatch, more than the grass itself, was responsible for the cushioning effect
   - A thatch can cushion the grinding of grass crowns against abrasive soil particles caused by traffic and mowers

How much thatch is too much?

1. Thatch thicker than 1 in. (25 mm) can cause negative effects
2. Thatch thinner than 1/2 in. (12 mm) is too thin to offer much cushion
3. Most researchers agree that thatch 1/2 to 3/4 in. thick (12 to 19 mm) is about optimal
4. Close-cut turf is less forgiving of thatch buildup than higher cut turf

bunch-type grasses. Zoysia, strong creeping red fescue, creeping bentgrass, and certain Kentucky bluegrass varieties are prone to thatch. "Touchdown," a vigorous bluegrass variety, has been shown to accumulate thatch at nearly twice the rate as "Rugby" (Shearman et al., 1983). Perennial ryegrass and tall fescue (bunch grasses) rarely thatch, even when heavily fertilized (Shoulders and Hall, 1983).

- *Pesticide side effects*—Pesticides often do more than just kill the target organism. Frequently they affect **nontarget organisms**. For example, certain fungicides (benomyl) and insecticides (diazinon, carbaryl, ethoprop, and bendiocarb) have been shown to kill 76 to 99% of earthworms (Potter, 1991). Earthworms aid in thatch breakdown. Pesticides also affect beneficial bacteria and fungi that decompose thatch. Pesticide-treated turf will usually have a thicker thatch than untreated turf.
- *Surfactant side effects*—One of the consequences of thatch is dry spots. Thatch sheds water like a duck and is hard to rewet due to its waxy, organic coat. Some turf managers have fought dry spots with **surfactants** (also called **wetting agents**), chemicals that help water molecules adhere to an oily surface. Trouble is, surfactants themselves have been shown to contribute to thatch buildup (Shoulders and Hall, 1983), creating a vicious cycle.
- *Cutting height*—One study in Nebraska noted that thatch piled up 50% faster when the cutting height was doubled (Shoulders and Hall, 1983). Although there were a lot of complicating issues in the study, the main point seems to be: The more plant mass you induce, the more thatch builds up. This finding is contrary to the popular belief that close-cropped turf is particularly thatch-prone. That confusion is due to the confounding of high maintenance with low cut. If maintenance levels (water, fertilizer, pesticides) are held constant, a higher cut turf will accumulate thatch faster.
- *pH control*—Almost everything living is acidic. Living things are filled with all sorts of acids: nucleic acids, amino acids, and so on. The pH of thatch can often become more acid than the underlying soil. Veteran soil scientist Norm Hummel cites an example: "I had a situation where a guy was having soil problems. The pH of his soil was 7.4. The pH right up at the surface of the thatch was 3.8 or 4, almost like battery acid. And he had a pretty hefty thatch accumulation. It was a difficult thing for him to swallow when his soil pH was 7.4, and I was telling him to add lime." Light, annual applications of lime have been shown to speed thatch decomposition (Shoulders and Hall, 1983), even if the pH of the underlying soil is normal or even alkaline.
- *Coring, vertical mowing, and soil topdressing*—Thatch can be counteracted by physical control measures, described below.

Thatch control

Vertical mowing. **Vertical mowing** (dethatching) is the direct approach to control thatch. With vertical mowing, thatch is combed and removed from the turf, hopefully without damaging the grass plants. Vertical mowing can bring up copious quantities of thatch (see Figure 7.6). It's a lot of work, but through brute force the thatch problem is rectified.

David Duckworth, turf researcher at Oregon State University, offers some practical observations from a thatch-control study he performed (Duckworth, 1995). He initiated a "mechanical thatch control trial in April 1994 on a mature mixture of 'Merit' Kentucky bluegrass and 'Koket' chewings fescue. Thatch depth prior to dethatching was in excess of 1.5 in. (4 cm).

"Injury from dethatching treatments was generally greater from the flail blade machine (with hinged blades) than from the solid (nonhinged) blade machine. In plots dethatched by flail or solid blade devices, much of the debris removed was brown understory material. After cleaning this material out, the turf looked cleaner and darker green. There also seemed to be at least a short-term shift toward Kentucky bluegrass."

To be effective against thatch, vertical mowing has to be ruthless. Unfortunately when you're done, the turf has been thinned considerably from the operation. Light vertical mowing and thatch removal can be done at any time of the year. Heavy dethatching, however, should be reserved for periods just prior to vigorous growth. Otherwise, the turf will remain open, damaged, and subject to weed invasion. Additional fertilizer and water aid healing. I've seen a turf nearly die after heavy vertical mowing, when it didn't receive a comeback shot of water and fertilizer afterward.

Coring. **Core aerification**—as opposed to vertical mowing or dethatching—is an *indirect* approach to thatch control. Coring itself does little to remove thatch. Only a small plug of thatch is brought up with each core. The principal effect of coring is to distribute a fine layer of soil on top of the thatch. Thatch sprinkled with soil decomposes quickly. Gardeners will recall this concept from composting. Compost piles are built from alternate layers of organic matter and topsoil (Minnich and Hunt, 1979). Organic matter decomposes rapidly when mixed with soil.

Coring is perhaps the best, least invasive way to keep thatch in check. In Duckworth's study, coring was less disfiguring than other mechanical thatch remedies. "The coring machine caused the least damage," he says.

Topdressing with topsoil or a sand/soil mix also works to control thatch. Topdressing, like coring, distributes a layer of soil on top of the thatch to speed its breakdown by giving microbes a better growing environment.

Biological thatch control

Twenty-some years ago, when I was a fledgling assistant golf course superintendent, a salesman handed my boss a sample of a "revolutionary" new product that promised biological thatch control. The label on the bag described the contents as "bacteria, fungi, and enzymes known to digest thatch."

"What a deal!," I thought. "Our thatch problems are over."

My boss, bless his heart, was ready to purchase enough product to treat 100 acres when I suggested we first test the material to see if it really worked. I applied the product to a particularly thatchy bentgrass collar, and waited. I guess I was expecting the surface to subside away like a sinkhole. But it didn't. A year later I took cores of the treated area and an adjacent untreated check to measure thatch depth. The net result: No difference.

The lack of response from this early product has been followed by a generally similar lack of response from later biological products. Perhaps the lack of effectiveness stems from the fact that there are already plenty of organisms in the thatch. There's really no need for more. What the organisms need is a better growing environment, something coring and topdressing help to create.

Research results. Ever since my early experiences, many new bio-thatch-control products have been developed. Results have been mixed yet promising. Here are the findings of a few researchers:

Rich Cooper, turf researcher at the University of Massachusetts, tested four biological thatch control agents versus coring, vertical mowing, and lime application (Cooper, 1990). For the first 3 years of the study, there were no effects of any of the biological products on thatch depth. In year 4, one treatment distinguished itself.

"Thatch measurement during Fall 1989 revealed that Lawn Restore® had produced a slight, but statistically significant, reduction in thatch depth. This reduction was so slight that we were skeptical and so we sampled the study one final time during April 1990. This sampling confirmed that Lawn Restore® did indeed significantly reduce thatch (by 1/4 in. [6 mm]) compared to all other treatments," wrote Cooper.

A study by Bridgett Ruemmele and Noel Jackson at the University of Rhode Island (Ruemmele and Jackson, 1993) failed to detect the differences Cooper had noticed. In fact, Lawn Restore® produced a slightly *thicker* thatch (1 mm) than the untreated control. Sustane® and a couple of compost products showed minor, yet statistically measurable, thatch reductions. Studies at Rutgers University in New Jersey (Thompson et al., 1994) and the University of Arizona in Tucson (Mancino et al., 1993) reached similar conclusions. The organic products either had a neutral or slightly beneficial effect in thatch reduction.

Most organic dethatching products used in the university trials contain some fertilizer value. Typically they're rated as a 4-2-0 or 8-2-4 fertilizer. In controlled research studies, they're usually compared against an equivalent dose of N, P, and K fast-release fertilizer. Under this scenario, the organic dethatching products fall somewhere intermediate between a fast-release fertilizer and the unfertilized check, in terms of their dethatching ability. Even though they *reduce* thatch more than a fast-release fertilizer of equal value, they produce *more* thatch than unfertilized turf.

The reason organic, manure, and compost products are effective at reducing thatch may be the same reason soil topdressing works. Both methods bolster the growing medium and nutrient supply available to thatch-devouring bacteria and fungi. There seems to be no "secret formula" in biological thatch control. It's simply a matter of giving the existing thatch-eating organisms what they want: a better place to live.

SOIL MODIFICATION

It's easy to say: If you're not happy with your soil, change it. But changing or modifying soil is a big job—a job that should be attempted only if the present soil is uninhabitable for turf. To replace just the top 6 in. of soil in one acre requires moving 2,000,000 lb! No small task.

Radical soil modification—the kind that involves a complete replacement of existing soil—in practice takes place only with ultra-high-value turfs, such as bowling greens, grass tennis courts, or golf course putting greens and tees. Other than that, most soil modification entails just the addition of a small amount of topsoil or compost over the existing grade. Anything else is too expensive for the majority of sites.

What is topsoil?

Topsoil is a valuable commodity. It contains the structure and nutrients necessary to foster continuing turf growth. It is conserved, stockpiled, and redistributed during construction, so that it doesn't get buried beneath subsoil.

But what exactly is topsoil? Why is it so much better than subsoil? And what if anything can be substituted for topsoil if it's unavailable?

Topsoil has several things going for it that subsoil lacks. Of course, soils vary incredibly from location to location, and one person's subsoil might be better than another's topsoil. But in general, topsoil has several attributes:

- *More organic matter content*—The higher organic content in topsoil results from decomposing plant and animal residues.
- *Less clay*—Over time, clay particles flush out of topsoil, down into the subsoil.
- *Better soil structure*—More organic matter in topsoil means more channels for water to flow and roots to penetrate.
- *Higher nutrient content*—Decomposing organic matter in topsoil gives off nutrients, just like a controlled-release fertilizer.
- *Fewer problems with layering, hardpans, and rocks*—Subsoils are sometimes poor conductors of water due to mechanical impediments.

How much topsoil is necessary?

Adding or replacing topsoil is expensive. I'm sure more than one landscape contractor has contemplated the question of how much topsoil is *really* necessary—especially when it has to be trucked in, at the cost of thousands of dollars.

The benefits of topsoil replacement are apparent even under low maintenance conditions. In a trial of low maintenance grasses in New Mexico, crested wheatgrass produced 10 times the ground cover where topsoil was added, as opposed to straight subsoil (Gifford, 1984). The response of other low maintenance grasses was similar: More topsoil, better performance.

The general rule-of-thumb for topsoil replacement is that a 4 to 6 in. (10 to 15 cm) layer is optimum. This figure has become the industry standard. If for some reason 4 to 6 in. isn't available, adding *any* amount of topsoil is better than none.

Of course, with topsoil addition, after a while you'll reach a point of diminishing returns: Adding another inch or two more will provide less additional value. Research on disturbed sites has indicated that the point of diminishing returns occurs somewhere between 7 and 15 in. (200 to 400 mm) (Mielke and Schepers, 1986; Schuman et al., 1985). Greater depths—even over adverse subsoil—show no added benefit to low or high maintenance turf.

What is sand?

I know this question seems overly simple. But I'm always surprised by the number of turf managers and homeowners who think that sand is something you find at the beach. Sand is actually a *size*.

Soil particles come in various sizes, from clay (the smallest), to silt, to sand, and finally to gravel. The relative differences among these particles become apparent when they're compared with something you can see and touch. Table 8.3 graphically illustrates sand, silt, and clay-size particles from a human perspective.

A typical soil is a conglomeration of sand, silt, and clay in varied proportions. Beach sand might have *predominantly* sand-sized particles, but it also might contain 10 or 20% silt. The silt goes unnoticed because its particles are wedged between the larger sand particles, the same way poker chips might wedge between a crate of basketballs (see Table 8.3). When it comes to acting as a turf rootzone, though, that 10 to 20% silt can have a major impact, plugging up such things as water percolation and nutrient flow. The silt particles clog the water channels in between the sand grains.

Sand makes an ideal turf growing medium because it's virtually incompressible. Sand forms a **skeleton structure**, allowing water flow and root penetration through the large pores and channels (Waddington et al., 1974). No amount of compression will ever force sand to compact. Silt and clay soils, on the other hand, are highly prone to compaction (see the following section on *Compaction*).

Sand is important to soil modification. It adds drainage and compaction resistance to heavy soils (Figure 8.2).

Soil requires the addition of more than 50% sand before there is a noticeable improvement in water flow and compaction resistance (Waddington et al., 1974). More recent findings indicate that nearly 80% sand may be required before a significant benefit results. Simply adding 5 or 10% sand will have no impact.

Are there alternatives to topsoil?

For some turf sites, topsoil is unavailable or prohibitively expensive. Fortunately, in recent years new options have appeared for soil modification (Table 8.2). One of the best options is compost.

"For landscapers and grounds managers looking for ways to improve marginal or poor soils, compost may be the best deal around," says Pete Landschoot, Penn State University turf extension specialist. "In many cases, compost production sites are located near areas of intensive turf use and provide readily-available and inexpensive sources of organic matter. In many cases, compost is cheaper than topsoil."

Compost can be used as a soil amendment prior to turf establishment. It can also be topdressed onto existing turf to add organic matter and nutrients. Compost benefits both clay and sandy soils. On clay soils, compost increases air and water permeability, enhances soil aggregation and water channels, reduces surface crusting and compaction, and furnishes nutrients. On sandy soils, the organic matter in compost increases water and nutrient retention, increases microbial activity, and supplies mineral elements. Overall, composts can provide quicker establishment, better turf density and color, improved root development, and less dependency on fertilizer and irrigation (Landschoot and McNitt, 1994). In some locales, compost is available just for the asking, or at a nominal fee.

Landschoot cautions that all composts are not alike. "Composts are made from many different sources, including municipal solid waste (garbage), leaves and grass clippings (yard trimmings), sewage sludge (biosolids), animal manure, paper by-products, and food wastes, just to name a few. Depending on the source and how it is processed, composts may vary substantially," he says. Desirable characteristics of compost are summarized in Table 8.4.

Application rate. Compost is generally added to soil preplanting in a 1 to 2 in. (2.5 to 5 cm) layer placed atop the ground and tilled in to a 4-to-6-in. depth (10 to 15 cm). When applying compost, be sure to thoroughly mix the compost with soil to avoid layering. A 1-in. (2.5 cm) layer is recommended for marginally good soils, whereas 2 in. is better for sand, clay, or subsoils low in organic matter (Landschoot and McNitt, 1994).

A 1-in. depth would equate to 3.1 cubic yards of compost per 1000 ft^2 (250 m^3/ha). To raise the soil organic matter content by 2% requires different amounts of compost, depending on the soil type (Darrah, 1994):

Soil type*	Cubic yards of compost required per 1000 ft^2	Cubic meters of compost per ha
Sandy	2.9	238
Loam	2.2	180
Clay	1.9	156

(*Assumptions: Calculated for compost that contains 60% organic matter, a bulk density of 800 lb/yd^3, 30% moisture, and incorporated to a 6-in. depth.)

Compost can also be topdressed onto living turf to add fertilizer value and organic matter (Chapter 9 discusses using compost as fertilizer). Usually a layer of 1/2 in. (1 cm) is the maximum for a single application.

WEAR

Wear is a phenomenon distinctly different from soil compaction. Of course, both go hand in hand most of the time: Where there's wear, there's compaction. Not always, though. Wear can take place on sandy soils and modified rootzone mixes that are impervious to compaction.

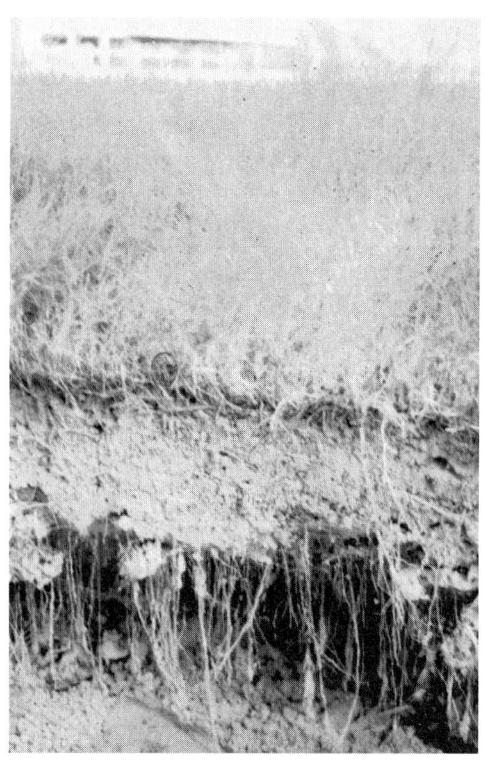

Figure 8.2. Soil modification helps to minimize the effects of compaction. In this "Tifway" bermudagrass rootzone at the Jockey Club of Hong Kong, the soil was replaced with a layer of sand and peat. The long roots are a testimony to the compaction resistance of such a rootzone, especially when you consider the daily pounding this turf receives from a stable of thoroughbreds.

Table 8.2. Common products used for amending turfgrass soils.

	Organic products
Composted yard waste	• Sometimes available from municipalities at no cost • Typical fertilizer value: 1-0.2-0.5 • May contain unacceptably high ash or soil content • Short (6 month) residual in soil
Spent mushroom manure	• High in nitrogen and potash, often over 2% • Alkaline pH, useful for counteracting acid soil • Free of weed seed
Composted manure	• High nitrogen content (around 2%) • Nitrogen may be quickly available • Good water-holding ability • May contain noxious weed seed if not fully composted
Composted rice hulls and other agricultural wastes	• Lower nutrient-holding ability than other composts • Increases soil porosity • Excellent longevity in soil, up to 10 years
Paper mill by-products	• Typically 2% nitrogen • Can contain soluble salts • Carbon-to-nitrogen ratio can be high, drawing N away from the soil
Brewery by-products	• Typically 2% nitrogen • Much of the nitrogen is quickly available
Composted sawdust, ground tree bark, and wood wastes	• Low water and nutrient-holding ability • Can be toxic if not fully composted • May alter soil pH • Carbon-to-nitrogen ratio can be very high, robbing soil of N
Tree leaves	• Decompose rapidly • No detrimental effects were observed from topdressing up to 100 lb/1000 ft^2 (470 g/m^2) of hardwood leaves into existing turf • Adds organic matter • Soil pH, phosphorus, and potassium levels are unaffected • Best applied when leaves are dry and shredded
Sewage sludge	• Heat-treated ("activated") sludge is used as a fertilizer (see Chapter 9) • Composted sludges can be used as a soil amendment • May be high in heavy metals or salt, depending upon source • A typical dried sludge might have a fertilizer value of 4-1-1 • Odor
Reed-sedge peat	• Excellent longevity • Good water and nutrient-holding capacity • pH is usually more neutral than sphagnum peat
Sphagnum moss peat	• Excellent water- and nutrient-holding capacity • Moderate longevity, depending on the state of decomposition • pH of 4 to 5 is typical
	Inorganic products
Sand	• Incompactable—useful for amending compacted soils • Poor water- and nutrient-holding ability
Calcined clay	• Better water-holding capacity than sand • Increases soil pore space • Wear and abrasion can break it down into clay over 10 to 20 years
Polymers	• Improves water-holding capacity of coarse textured soil • May reduce compaction by their swell-shrink action
Crumb rubber	• Beneficial for high-wear sites like athletic fields • Best if topdressed onto existing turf • No proved toxic effects to the soil or plant • Helps recycle a waste product that presently clogs landfills

Table 8.3. A visual analogy of submillimeter soil particles: If the particles of very coarse sand were as big as an 8-ft beach ball (2.4 m), clay particles would be the size of oatmeal. Analogy idea was borrowed from Charles White (1982).

Soil Particle	Particle Size Range (mm)	Analogy
Very coarse sand	1 to 2	8-ft beach ball
Coarse sand	0.5 to 1	4-ft beach ball
Medium sand	0.25 to 0.5	Medicine ball
Fine sand	0.1 to 0.25	Basketball
Very fine sand	0.05 to 0.1	Softball
Silt	0.002 to 0.05	Poker chips
Clay	less than 0.002	Oatmeal

Technically speaking, wear is the abrasion to turf caused by foot and vehicular traffic that results in thinning. In essence, the turf is worn out like a rug.

Worn-out turf is not something you have to live with. There are options to conquer foot-weary turfgrass. The most obvious solution—which almost goes without saying—is to redirect and redistribute traffic patterns (Figure 8.3). While this solution works wonders for golf course cart paths, it is certainly wasted advice for football fields.

The turf paver

Several years ago someone invented an ingenious device for dealing with high wear areas: The **turf paver**. Since that time, turf pavers have been manufactured from a variety of materials, including concrete block, rigid plastic, plastic mesh, and even a carpet-like product resembling Astroturf®.

A turf paver is implanted into the soil prior to turf establishment. The vertical fins of the paver absorb the wear and tear, protecting the sensitive grass crowns. Turf pavers have found their way into the source books of a number of landscape architects, who have used them for creating attractive grassed parking lots and driveways.

Research on pavers has validated their worth, provided of course they are correctly installed (Figure 8.4). A study by long-time wear researcher Bob Shearman (Shearman et al., 1980) showed that concrete pavers, "improve turfgrass wear tolerance and recuperative rate." Sensitive, easily damaged grass species were the ones helped the most.

The only drawback Shearman found to the paver was reduced winter survival of perennial ryegrass and tall fescue—two species that are marginally winter-hardy at his site in Nebraska. Evidently the concrete block in close proximity to the grass pulls warmth away during the wintertime.

The key to success with pavers is correct installation. To install a grass paver, first level and firm the soil grade. Then lay the pavers on the surface. Soil is filled into the paver's holes up to and *just below* the top of the paver. A common mistake is to fill soil clear to the top. When this happens,

Table 8.4. Guidelines for choosing a good compost material for turf soil modification. Composts can be applied as topdressing (surface application) or mixed and tilled with the soil (soil incorporation) prior to establishment. Composts originate from many different organic sources–not all of them are favorable for turf. It's best to check out the specifications of a particular compost before you buy. Table was adapted from an article on composts by Pete Landschoot and Andy McNitt (1994).

Desirable physical properties of "good" composts	
Color	Brown to black
Particle size (for surface application)	1/4 to 3/8 in. (6 to 10 mm)
Particle size (for incorporation into soil)	1/4 to 1/2 in. (6 to 12 mm)
Odor	Smells earthy or musty, not like ammonia or rotten eggs
State of decomposition	Individual pieces of organic matter should not be recognizable as leaves, stems, etc.
Moisture content	30 to 50%
Organic matter content	At least 25%
Ash content (inorganic matter)	Less than 75%
Desirable chemical properties	
Carbon-to-nitrogen ratio	30:1 or lower
Nitrogen content	0.4 to 3%
Phosphate (P_2O_5) content	0.2 to 1.5%
Potash (K_2O) content	0.4 to 1.5%
pH	6 to 8
Freedom from undesirable substances	
	• Rocks and stones • Silt and clay • Large particles • Heavy metals • Weed seed • Soluble salts

Figure 8.3. Up close, the symptoms of wear mimic a host of other turf ailments–they appear as a general thinning of the stand. Wear is diagnosed by examining *where* it occurs, such as at the end of a golf course cart path, shown here. In many cases wear can be prevented by rerouting traffic before symptoms appear.

Figure 8.4. The **turf paver** was invented to prevent grass from being trampled. Pavers work by absorbing the weight and wear of foot traffic and vehicles, sparing the tender grass crowns. For "moderate" wear situations, such as a bike rack area (shown in this photo), the paver works exceptionally well. However, it fails under continuous abrasion, like on a daily-use car parking lot.

the grass crown is not protected from abrasion, and the paver offers no advantage. Along the same lines, grasses that produce thatch actually raise up their own crowns over time, putting them into contact with traffic and defeating the purpose of the paver. Bunch grasses seem to work best, because they don't generate thatch.

Other ways to fight wear

Grass pavers are a costly but effective way to combat wear. They've found use throughout the turf industry in areas where turf has been perennially worn away. But grass pavers are not the solution for all sites. They obviously don't work for sports fields or other sites where player injury is a factor. Instead, simple cultural adjustments can be used to remedy the majority of wear effects:

- *Warm/cool-season grass*—Warm-season turfgrasses are generally more wear tolerant than cool-seasons (Hall, 1995). Switching from a cool-season grass to a warm-season one, where appropriate, will improve wear performance. The drawback of warm-season grasses is that during the winter dormant period they offer little if any wear protection. Supplementing the stand with winter overseeding can boost winter wear tolerance.
- *Turfgrass species*—Grasses vary remarkably in wear tolerance. One Nebraska study found that Kentucky bluegrass, tall fescue, and perennial ryegrass were more wear tolerant than chewings fescue and "Fairway" crested wheatgrass (Shearman et al., 1980). A study in England (Canaway and Baker, 1993) found significant differences among grasses in their traction ability, which is somewhat similar to wear tolerance. Their conclusions came from a pounding wear test that simulated soccer-type wear on a soil-based field: **Grasses with very high traction (*desirable*)**—Kentucky bluegrass, annual bluegrass; **high traction**—perennial ryegrass, chewings fescue, strong creeping red fescue; **medium traction**—turf-type timothy; **low traction (*undesirable*)**—tall fescue, colonial bentgrass.
- *Turfgrass variety*—Wear tolerance in a turf variety is tied to its (1) vigor, and (2) adaptation to the site. Dense, vigorous, well-adapted varieties will tolerate traffic better than others. Dave Minner, turf researcher at Iowa State University, recommends "Sydsport," "Trenton," "Wabash," "Glade," and "A-34" Kentucky bluegrass, and "Diplomat," "SR4000," "Gator," "Ovation," and "Prelude" perennial ryegrass, which all happen to be dense, vigorous varieties, well-adapted to the Iowa location where Minner's trials were run (Minner et al., 1993).

- *Mowing height*—A mowing height at the high end of the recommended range will add wear tolerance.
- *Irrigation*—Perpetually wet turf is more prone to damage from scuffing, slippage, and compaction (Roche, 1993). Back off on the water, but not to the point of drought—drought-stressed turf is easily worn out too.
- *Nitrogen fertilization*—Heavily-trafficked turf requires 30 to 40% more nitrogen to regrow foliage worn away by traffic (Hall, 1995). But don't go to extremes. You *can* get too much of a good thing (Carroll and Petrovic, 1991). "If you exceed the amount that turf needs, you have a tendency to get succulent, watery tissues that are susceptible to traffic injury and stress," says Shearman.
- *Potassium fertilization*—Potassium, applied during the growing season, increases wear tolerance. On high-wear sports fields, added nitrogen should be coupled with added potassium. Potassium is known to make turf resistant to a number of environmental stresses (Liu et al., 1996).

SOIL COMPACTION

You have to admire University of Georgia turf researcher Bob Carrow. Carrow has devoted much of his academic career to the study of turfgrass soil compaction, a subject few other scientists have taken more than a cursory stab at (Carrow, 1992). Over the years Carrow has gotten used to the typical reaction of most turf managers to the subject: "Yeah, I know what causes compaction. And, yeah, I know what I have to do about it." Most folks know that traffic causes compaction, and core aerification corrects it.

But the complacency on the part of turf managers hasn't phased the tenacious Carrow, who has single-handedly researched the myriad of causes and ramifications of compaction. For example, Carrow's research discovered that compacted turf requires up to 50% more water (Roche, 1993). "The grower often finds it necessary to irrigate [compacted turf] with low quantities of water on a frequent basis, which greatly increases evaporational losses. Therefore, total water use actually becomes greater under compacted conditions," he says.

Compacted turf is less vigorous and competitive overall, which can lead to increased need for herbicides and fungicides to help fight its battles. Bruce Clark and his associates at Rutgers University (Clark et al., 1995) uncovered a tie-in between compaction and a common turf affliction. They found that summer patch disease severity was 79% greater in compacted turf, as compared to an aerified control. That means relieving compaction could help cut fungicide dependency substantially. Spring aerification—before the disease hits—proved more effective than fall. Eliminating compaction can be a great shortcut to lower maintenance.

Core aerification has one frequently overlooked attribute: Punching holes causes a rapid drying effect. Coring exposes the soil volume to air, ventilating it, and quickly allowing evaporation to dry the turf. Some turf managers have used this drying effect just prior to an expected disease outbreak to alter the moisture status of turf. The drying creates an inhospitable home for disease organisms. Aerification-drying can be used as a cultural method of disease prevention, in place of pesticides. Of course, if the drying goes to extreme, it can dehydrate the turf. Judicious monitoring is recommended.

Some people are reluctant to aerify because they feel it will destroy the preemergence herbicide barrier they've applied. Preemergence herbicides are applied in the springtime for control of annual grassy weeds, usually just prior to the optimum time for aerification. Recent research at Michigan State University indicates little or no negative effect occurs from coring on the efficacy of preemergence herbicides. Therefore, your crabgrass herbicide shouldn't deter you from aerating.

Curing compaction

Soil modification is the only permanent cure for soil compaction. All other methods—coring, slicing, etc.—are only temporary measures. They relieve compaction today, but in another 6 or 12 months the turf will need it again. Which brings up a good point: *The proactive aerification program*. Rather than curing soil compaction after it happens, it's far better to anticipate compaction and remedy it *before* it harms the turf. Routine aerification can be planned between football games, golf tournaments, cemetery funerals, or similar events. The programmed approach prevents soil compaction from ever getting so bad that turf performance suffers.

Compaction is usually most acute at the soil surface, becoming progressively less severe deeper down (Roche, 1993). That's why aerification of the top 3 to 4 in. (7 to 10 cm) is usually sufficient to relieve the majority of compaction symptoms.

Recently, new technology has been developed for deep profile aerification, down to 1 ft (0.3 m) or more. Deep aerification is useful for obliterating soil layering or as a way to relieve compaction deep in the soil. These deep-soil aerifiers are available in a number of formats, including slicers, hollow and solid tine coring units, and even deep drills. Studies by Carrow and his associates (Wiecko et al., 1993) have found that root growth in the lower profile (1 to 2 ft deep [20 to 60 cm]) can be increased by up to 41% by deep drilling. They found up to 120% better rooting with deep slicing, and up to 38% better rooting with deep hollow-tine aerification. Turf growth and soil water extraction in the lower profile were also improved. For heavy-play turf sites, deep profile aerification may be well worth the expense.

Equipment for compaction control

Not all soil cultivation devices are created equal when it comes to correcting compaction. Some are aimed more at the temporary relief of water infiltration problems than at relieving compaction. In the long run they can actually result in *more* compaction.

Here is a survey of typical machines and their strengths and weaknesses:

- *Hollow-tine core aerifier*—The old, mainstay **core aerifier** punches holes and removes soil cores by means of hollow tines mounted on a rotating cam shaft. Mechanically this type of machine is a maintenance nightmare—there are hundreds of moving parts. But it is unparalleled in punching a clean, deep, accurate hole with minimal gouging.
- *Spoon aerifier*—**Spoon aerifiers** work like hollow-tine units, in that they extract a core of soil and drop it on the surface. But with a spoon aerifier, the spoons are mounted on a rolling wheel that pokes the turf as it rolls. Spoon aerifiers are the typical homeowner or landscaper unit. The mechanical simplicity of this machine makes up for the rather ragged core it pulls.
- *Barrel-mounted spoons*—A modification of the spoon aerifier has spoons mounted on the outside of a rolling barrel. As the unit rolls across the turf—usually towed behind a lawn tractor—the soil plugs pop into the barrel and are carted off. This unit gets rid of all of the messy plugs from the lawn. But remember, those messy plugs are what aid in thatch breakdown (see section above on *Thatch*).
- *Solid-tine aerifier*—A **solid-tine aerifier** punches holes but removes nothing. It is best suited to high sand or sand-modified soils, because while it's punching holes, it's actually compacting the soil at the bottom and sides of the holes. A solid-tine aerifier increases water infiltration but does little for compaction. One particular solid-tine aerifier model features a wobbling shaft mount, so that the tines twist and turn as they roll across the turf. This wobbling action churns the soil and opens more air channels than a conventional solid-tine aerifier. The down side of this method is more surface scaring.
- *Slicers and pin-spiking units*—**Slicers** and **spikers** are designed with one thing in mind: Increased water penetration. These devices slit a channel in the thatch to improve water flow. Like the solid-tine

How to Tell: Is Your Soil Compacted?

Wherever there's foot traffic, heavy mowers, or vehicles running across turf, there's bound to be soil compaction. Few soils are naturally immune to compaction. Only sandy soils or specially modified rootzone mixes are truly resistant. Most soils—particularly those high in clay—compact over time into a dense, impervious, concrete-like mass.

Viewed from our aboveground perspective, about the only telltale sign of soil compaction is thin turf. And there are virtually a million problems other than compaction that can cause thinning. So how do you know if your soil is compacted? And how can you avoid unnecessary remedial action if your soil isn't really compacted?

Four things to look for if you suspect compaction are:

- *Traffic patterns*—Compaction is rarely uniform. It occurs in strips of particularly heavy use. If the turf is thin along a pathway where foot traffic is concentrated, assume soil compaction is the culprit.
- *Slow water infiltration*—Compaction clogs pores, preventing water from flowing into soil. If you're noticing puddling where none existed before, compaction may be the cause. A good test for infiltration is to run a garden hose onto the suspected area and see how long it takes for the water to sink in.
- *Indicator weeds*—Compaction comes with its own entourage of weeds. Certain weeds—knotweed, annual bluegrass, goosegrass, and clover—are indicators of compaction (Shearman et al., 1983). Roots of these plants are fine-tuned to persist in compacted soil under oxygen-deprived conditions. It's not that they "prefer" compaction; they're just better suited to tolerate it than turfgrass.
- *The knife test*—A pocket knife is a useful tool for assessing compaction. A pocket knife stuck down into soil gives a tactile reading of compaction. If it takes a lot of force to push in a knife, your soil is probably compacted. (Or you may have just hit a rock, in which case you should try again.) You can "calibrate" your knife by first seeing what it feels like to poke uncompacted soil. Find an out-of-the-way spot that receives little traffic. Compare the knife force of the uncompacted spot with a compacted one. With a little practice, you'll be able to read turf soil compaction.
- *Penetrometers*—**Penetrometers** are preferred by turf managers who like numbers. A penetrometer measures in Newtons the resistance force encountered as you push a probe into the soil. Pocket-size penetrometers are available for sale from the larger supply houses.

aerifier, they do nothing for compaction.

- *Deep soil aerifiers*—A number of ultra-deep aerifiers have hit the market in recent years. Their various configurations are mentioned above. Some service companies make a living performing custom work using these machines. That way, the turf facility doesn't get saddled with the large price tag of the machine, for only occasional use.
- *Water injection*—The Toro Company has designed a proprietary machine for injecting pulses of extremely high pressure water into turf to penetrate and fracture compaction. The advantage of water injection is its nearly zero disturbance to the grass surface, even on put-

ting greens. Initial research data indicates the device may supplement but not replace core aerifiers.

- *Vertical mowers*—A vertical mower is better suited to dethatching or sod seeding than to controlling compaction. If set deeply enough, it might reduce surface compaction by a minor amount. Try to penetrate deeper than about 1/2 in. (12 mm), though, and the engine will stall.

Tips for preventing soil compaction

You are *not* powerless to prevent soil compaction from happening. Many people feel resigned that compaction is bound to occur, and there's nothing they can do about it. But there is. Listed below are tips for averting soil compaction before it starts:

- *Soil modification*—Even partial modification is better than none. Consider adding compost to the soil to improve its physical and chemical properties (see section above on *Soil Modification*).
- *Install additional drainage*—Wet soil compacts more easily than dry (see Figure 8.5). Adding surface contouring and subsurface drainpipe will help channel water away from easily compacted, high-wear areas (Roche, 1993).
- *Gypsum*—For years, gypsum was recommended as a cure for compaction (Peacock, 1986). Trouble is, it doesn't work. Gypsum has no compaction-relieving ability—unless you happen to have a certain unique, high salt, high pH, sodic soil. **Sodic soils** are rare and confined primarily to arid regions. On such soils, the calcium in gypsum bumps sodium off the soil's cation exchange complex and flushes it out, ultimately improving water flow. Unfortunately, gypsum doesn't work that way with any other soils.
- *Chemical additives*—Chemical soil conditioners, water-absorbing polymers (Uhring, 1993), and wetting agents have been used for correcting water flow problems associated with compaction. When considering chemical additives, take some advice from your aspirin bottle: "For temporary relief only. Use only as directed." Chemical additives offer no long-term remedies for compaction. At best they give a temporary "fix" for water infiltration.
- *Alternate your mowing patterns*—Each time you mow, use a slightly different mowing pattern. Yes, I know you like those stripes. But by varying your pattern, you'll redistribute the mower's weight each time.
- *Switch to "balloon" tires*—Big balloon tires are available for most turf tractors and large mowing units. Balloon tires help reduce compaction by spreading the tractor's weight over a wider area. The weight per square inch is reduced to the point where you can accidentally run over your foot without harm.
- *Restrict traffic when it's raining*—Most compaction takes place when the soil is wet.

SOIL pH

pH is overrated. The pH of soil indicates whether it's acid, alkaline, or neutral. An ideal target pH for growing turfgrass is between 6 and 6.5. However, turfgrasses can grow just over a wide range of pH—from 5.0 and 9.0—with few deleterious effects.

A common misconception is that pH is toxic. We all have learned of the deleterious effects of drinking concentrated sulfuric acid from watching Saturday morning cartoons as kids. But from a plant's point of view, pH operates a little bit differently in soil.

Guy McKee, plant physiologist at Penn State University (long since deceased), once ran a classic experiment on the effect of pH on plants. I was a young graduate student at the time, observing the experiment as I walked by each day. McKee grew plants in a soilless, hydroponic solution to take away ions that can interfere in soil. With water culture, he could tailor nutrients and pH to his satisfaction.

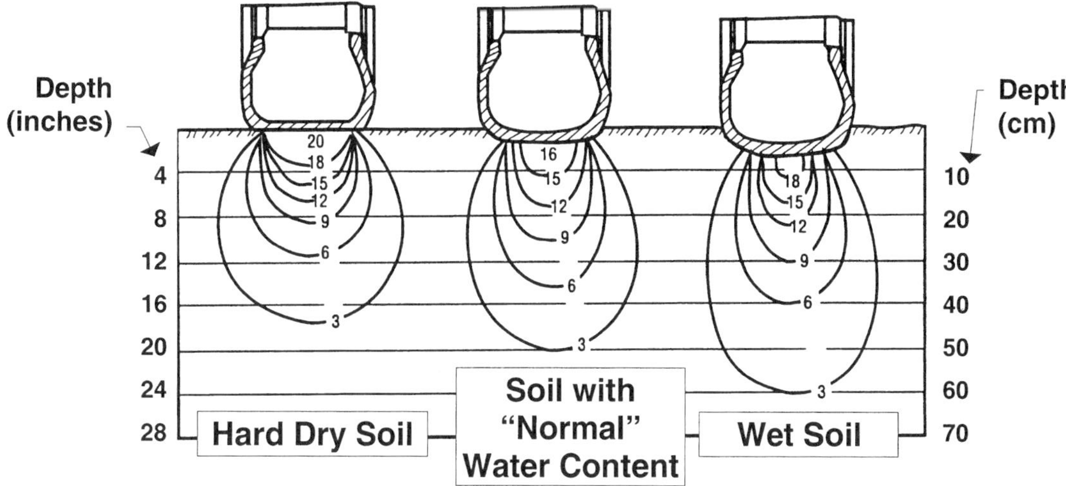

Figure 8.5. Soil compaction (in pounds per inch^2) created from driving a vehicle over soil with varying moisture. Wet soils are more prone to compaction than dry soils. The compacting effect from a typical tractor tire can extend 2 feet (60 cm) into the soil. Data were from an article by Thomas Hoffmann (1994). *Assumptions:* Tire size 11-28, load 1650 lb, tire inflation pressure 12 psi (83 kPa).

Remarkably, he found that when given balanced nutrition, plants could grow over an incredible pH range. They survived over a pH range from 2 (nearly battery acid) to 12.

McKee explained that pH itself is not toxic to plants. But in soil, pH can cause certain elements to *become* toxic or unavailable. Soil pHs below 4 are damaging to plants because aluminum switches into a highly available, rather nasty form. At high pHs, calcium becomes dominant and competes with other nutrients for uptake. But as long as your soil pH is in the 5 to 9 range: *Don't worry.*

Correcting soil pH

Soils with low pH can be adjusted by the addition of ground agricultural limestone. Dolomitic lime, if available, is a better solution because it supplies a balance of magnesium and calcium. Lime recommendations are provided in Table 8.5 for typical sand, loam, and clay soils. However, it's always better to run a soil test to determine the exact lime requirement, based on the buffering capacity of your soil.

Correction of *high* pH soils is more difficult. Elemental sulfur can be applied to acidify the soil and lower pH. However, with pHs above 8, the sulfur requirement may be prohibitively high. Perhaps a better idea is to try to live with the high pH, as long as it's not getting any worse. High pH induces deficiencies in heavy-metal micronutrients, particularly with centipedegrass and other warm-season grasses. These deficiencies can be anticipated and treated using foliar applications of micronutrient solution. Applying micronutrients to the *soil* will not work. Micronutrients are probably in ample supply in the soil already. The problem is that they are not getting to the plant because of the prohibitive pH.

Acidifying fertilizers can be used to moderate a slightly alkaline soil pH. Ammonium salt fertilizer has the greatest acidifying power in turf soil, followed by urea and sulfur-coated urea (Thompson et al., 1993). Ureaform, methylene urea, calcium nitrate, and potassium nitrate are neutral in their pH effect. Potassium nitrate tends to raise pH.

Soil pH also affects organisms other than the grass. Soil bacteria grow poorly below a pH of 5.0. Years ago, the prevalent thinking was that fungi—particularly the pathogenic ones—were unfazed by low pH. People believed the low pH benefited the disease fungi at the expense of the bacteria that competed with them. To-

Table 8.5. Effect of several common soil pH values on turfgrass growth. Adverse pH ties up soil nutrients, mineralizing them, and making them unavailable to the plant for uptake. Application of agricultural limestone can be used to raise pH; elemental sulfur can be used to lower it.

Soil pH Value	Occurrence	Best Adapted Grasses	Nutrient Deficiencies	Ground Limestone Needed to Correct pH[a]			Elemental Sulfur Needed to Correct pH[b]		
				Sandy	Loam	Clay	Sandy	Loam	Clay
4	Rare	Centipedegrass, bermuda, zoysia, deer tongue, weeping lovegrass	Nitrogen, phosphorus, potasium, calcium, magnesium, some metals	90 (4400)	140 (6800)	200 (9800)	0	0	0
5	Common in high rainfall areas	Most turfgrasses	Phosphorus	75 (3700)	125 (6100)	175 (8500)	0	0	0
6	Optimal pH for turf	All turfgrasses	None	25 (1200)	50 (2400)	60 (2900)	0	0	0
7	Calcarious soils in humid regions	All turfgrasses	None	0	0	0	0	0	0
8	Soils in arid regions	Buffalograss and other prairie species	Phosphorus, boron, iron, and other metals	0	0	0	10 (500)	20 (980)	40 (1900)
9	Rare	Blue grama, buffalograss, and other low maintenance species	Nitrogen, iron, and other metals	0	0	0	20 (980)	40 (1900)	80 (3900)

[a] lb per 1000 ft^2 of ground agricultural limestone ($CaCO_3$) needed to raise the pH to 6.5–7.0 (kg/ha in parentheses).

[b] lb per 1000 ft^2 of elemental sulfur (S_8) (kg/ha in parentheses). Rates over 10 lb per 1000 ft^2 (500 kg/ha) can be toxic to grass if applied as a single application; applications should be split over time. If aluminum sulfate is used in place of elemental sulfur, double the rate listed for elemental sulfur.

Frequently Asked Questions about Soil Testing

Q: How often should I test my soil?
A: Every 2 to 3 years.

Q: Can soil tests be taken too often?
A: Yes. For example, lime application takes 6 to 12 months before the soil pH adjusts. If you take another soil test before 12 months is up, you might be fooled into thinking the first application was ineffective and be tempted to reapply. Nutrient levels change slowly in soil. The only exception is sandy soils.

Q: When I send my soil sample to the lab, should I include the thatch?
A: Many farm labs at state universities routinely sieve off stones and thatch from soil samples. For them, it would make no difference whether you included the thatch or not. But if your thatch is sizable, I recommend sending it to a lab that specializes in turf soil testing. Request that the thatch be included in the test. They will grind the thatch and include it in the analysis.

Q: Should I dry the soil sample before I mail it to the lab?
A: No. Wetting or drying the soil sample can alter its readings. Send it as you found it in the field.

Q: I sent the same soil sample to two different labs and got back radically different recommendations. Which should I follow?
A: You're not alone. When Tom Turner, turf extension professor at the University of Maryland, sent the same soil to 7 labs, he got back lime recommendations ranging from 0 to 165 lb per 1000 ft^2, phosphate recommendations from 0.9 to 6 lb per 1000 ft^2, and potash recommendations from 1 to 7 lb per 1000 ft^2 (Turner, 1978). Soil labs use different handling procedures and wet chemistry techniques. It's best to pick a lab that you trust and stick with them, rather than jumping around. That way, you'll be able to spot *trends* in nutrient levels over time.

Q: I have one soil test that presents results in ppm, another in lb/acre, a third in meq per 100 grams, and a fourth in percent base saturation. Can I ever compare results?
A: Believe it or not, you *can* compare results. But it requires some calculation. I suggest you consult a soil textbook to get the lowdown on how to inter-convert. It's a little complicated, but it can be done.

Q: My soil test says the pH is 5.0 and that I should apply 800 lb/acre of lime. My neighbor's test reads pH 5.5 and recommends 1000 lb of lime. Is something goofy in the lab?
A: Probably not. Soils differ in **buffering capacity**—the resistance to pH change. If your soil is sandier, for instance, it may not require as much lime to move the pH. Check the buffer pH in your test report.

Q: Is a soil probe a good tool for taking a soil test?
A: It can work in a pinch. But with a soil probe, the tendency is to take a sample too deeply. For turf soils, a 4-in. (10 cm) depth is plenty. Sampling deeper can give you misleadingly low readings.

Q: How do I decide how many samples to send to the lab?
A: Take one sample for every unique soil zone. For example, a golf course might sample each green, tee, and fairway separately. For a home lawn, you might want two samples: One from the front and one from the back. On a sports field, send one sample from the high-wear center zone, and a second from the perimeter.

Q: Will one plug suffice?
A: No. Sample 10 to 15 plugs, scattered from throughout the turf. Combine and mix them in a plastic (not metal) bucket. Re-

move just enough blended soil to fill the sample bag. Don't include leaves or stems with the sample. Roots are okay, though.

Q: What's the best time of year to soil test?
A: The best time to soil test is when the local farmers aren't. If you submit a sample during a lab's slack time, it may be processed in a matter of days rather than weeks. Many turf managers sample during the winter months. If you sample repeatedly over years, it's important to stay consistent in the time of year you sample. Nutrient availability is subject to seasonal swings from temperature, moisture, and other factors. Sampling at the same time every year ensures uniform results.

Q: According to my soil test report, my boron is way out of whack. Should I be concerned?
A: Soil tests sometime analyze more than we need to know. Depending on where you submit the test, you might get back readings for all sorts of elements, even ones plants don't even use. Unless you're dealing with a highly specialized soil—a sand or peat soil, a modified sand mix, or a saline, high pH, or sodic soil—I'd consider most micronutrient recommendations as a guide and not a rule. Although micronutrient deficiencies have been documented in turf, they are rare and their effects generally benign. Moreover, recommended ranges for micronutrients in turf soils have never been scientifically established. Most are "borrowed" from other crops. My advice is: Concentrate on P, K, S, Ca, Mg, and pH.

Q: Is it better to take tissue tests rather than soil tests?
A: Turf **tissue testing** is currently in vogue, fueled by a relatively new technique that doesn't require the usual wet chemistry. NIR technology analyzes nutrient levels in plant tissue by bouncing off an infrared beam. Some people argue that tissue testing is a more relevant analysis, since it gauges the actual nutrients in the plant, and not some ambiguous value in the soil. But tissue testing is not without its shortcomings: (1) "normal" readings for one grass species may not hold true for another, (2) nutrient content in turf leaves can fluctuate from day to day, whereas soil tests are more steady, and (3) nutrients within the plant can interact with one another. Compared to soil testing, tissue testing is probably a better method for analyzing nitrogen and the micronutrients. My advice is, though, to get a specialist to help you interpret your results.

day, it is known that nearly all soil organisms are inhibited by low pH. Even pathogenic fungi, such as the one responsible for summer patch disease, are suppressed by low pH (Thompson et al., 1993). Earthworms and other beneficial fauna are intolerant of low pH as well (Potter, 1991).

SALT

Salt is becoming an increasingly pervasive factor in turf management. In the past, salt affected turf only in arid or seashore locations. Today, salt problems are widespread, touching a growing segment of the turf industry (Figure 8.6). Salt problems can originate from:

- Preexisting salt deposits in the soil
- Overpumping of aquifers and rivers along the ocean, allowing intrusion of seawater
- Salt in the irrigation water
- Water recycling and the use of salty effluent water
- The use of deicers for snow and ice removal along roads and walks.

Salt effects on turf

Salt takes its toll subtly on turf. The first thing you may notice is premature wilt. It may take more irrigation water to keep turf from fading into blue-gray moisture stress than it did before. You may notice fewer clippings coming off the turf, signaling a declining vigor.

Reductions in shoot and root growth are an early indication of salt. These reductions may stem from direct toxicity from the salt. But more frequently, they originate from the displacement of nutrients by salt in the soil. The salt ions are bumping calcium, magnesium, and potassium off the soil's storage complex. Eventually the soil's nutrient storage becomes overwhelmed with salt.

As salinity builds up, leaf tip burn and stand loss occur. Finally, with a high enough salt concentration in the rootzone, the plants collapse and die.

Chapters 2 through 4 list the turfgrass species with salt tolerance. If you're experiencing salt troubles, consider switching to a more salt-tolerant grass. Turfgrasses like "Emerald" zoysiagrass, "Tifway" bermuda, or seashore paspalum tolerate eight times more salt than "Jamestown" chewings fescue and "Sabre" roughstalk bluegrass (Dudeck, 1994). Furthermore, there are even profound salt differences among varieties of the same species (Ahti et al., 1980; Horst and Dunning, 1989).

Where does salt come from?

Nearly all supplies of fresh water contain some salt, albeit in small concentrations. Rainwater is free of salt. But as rainwater trickles through soil and rock on its way to the ocean, it picks up quantities of ancient salt. Eventually this salt is deposited in the ocean, which acts as a giant worldwide reservoir of soluble salt.

Salty soil originates in the opposite direction. In arid regions, precipitation is so sparse that the net flow of moisture in soil is in an *upward* direction—moisture from the groundwater rises through soil capillaries to the surface, bringing salt along for the ride. As water evaporates away at the soil surface, it leaves a salty crust.

This concept of salt buildup provides insights into ways to get rid of salt: If salt accumulates by water rising up in the soil, then salt can be purged by washing it back down. This soil-rinsing concept has been successfully used in reclamation of salty ground throughout the world. Water is applied to feed the plant and wash away the salt.

Here's an example of how it works: Let's say your turf is evaporating 1 in. of water a week. To irrigate *and* wash away the salt, you'd need to apply more than 1 in. of water per week. If you apply less than 1 in., soil water will regain its upward flow and salt will again begin depositing at the surface.

But don't apply too much extra water or you'll end up flushing the salt clear into the aquifer.

Figure 8.6. Salt can strike where you least expect it. In this photo at Wesleyan College, salt used for parking lot ice removal was killing the grass. Salt can originate from a number of sources in a turf environment, including existing salt deposits in the soil, overpumping of aquifers, salty irrigation water, or the use of deicers for snow and ice removal.

Just apply enough extra water to purge salt from the *rootzone*. Managing turf in a salty environment can mean higher maintenance overall—not just in added water, but additional fertilization and aerification.

Measuring saltiness

Most salt that affects turf is plain old table salt—sodium chloride (NaCl). But depending where you live, sodium chloride may not be the main salt plaguing your turf. Baking soda (sodium bicarbonate), Epsom salt (magnesium sulfate), gypsum (calcium sulfate), and salty fertilizer (ammonium sulfate, etc.) can also cause salt problems.

Saltiness is measured in the lab by means of electrical conductivity (Figure 8.7). You may remember from high school chemistry that pure water itself is a poor conductor of electricity. When you add salt, water becomes a conductor. The more salt you add the more it conducts. Scientists use this phenomenon to estimate the quantity of salt in soil or irrigation water. It's a lot cheaper and faster than other chemical tests.

Electrical conductivity (EC) meters are available for use in or out of the laboratory. You'll also hear them called **salt bridges**. EC meters are quite affordable. There are even inexpensive pocket models available for under $100. If you suspect salt problems, get one and test it yourself.

Irrigation water is easy to test: Just stick the sensor into a glass of water. Readings up to 0.75 dS/m are suitable for use as irrigation water. Readings from 0.75 to 2.25 dS/m require the use of salt-tolerant turf species. Above 2.25 dS/m, you should consider another water source.

Getting an accurate soil reading is a bit tougher. Conductivity meters need water to work. If you add water to the soil to wet it, you're diluting the salt concentration and will get a misleadingly low reading. The best method involves a **saturated paste extract**, wherein the salt concentration is read at field capacity.

Units of measure. In the past, soil labs reported salt concentration in terms of electrical conduction—millimhos per centimeter. A **mho** is the inverse of an **ohm**, the electrical unit of resistance (note how they're cleverly spelled backwards). Today, soil labs report EC by its politically correct format of deciSemens per meter (dS/m). Fortunately the units directly equate to the older mhos: 1 dS/m equals 1 mmho/cm.

Some laboratories express salt concentration in terms of parts per million (ppm) of chloride. This is done because chloride is a concern in human drinking water supplies. To convert chloride ppm into dS/m or mmho/cm, laboratories use a fudge factor, based on a typical salt. But as stated above, salts come in various flavors. The fudge factor for one salt is not the same as for another. When you're having your soil tested in a laboratory, request a direct EC reading rather than the less accurate chloride ppm.

Figure 8.7. Saltiness of soil or irrigation water is measured by its electrical conductivity (EC). A conductance meter gauges the flow of electricity across a sample, providing a direct readout of saltiness. Many turf managers in salt-prone areas own their own salt bridges, and take periodic readings to help spot increasing trends. Inexpensive, pocket-sized models are available for under $100.

Chapter 9

Using Less Fertilizer

Mrs. Fernstead got pretty upset when I told her I wasn't going to fertilize her yard as planned. For my final two summers of high school I mowed and tended Mrs. F's lawn, helping me pay my way through girlfriends. Every kid in the neighborhood wanted to mow Mrs. Fernstead's lawn—she paid a whopping $5 a week. By 1971 standards, that was a lot of money. But they quickly learned that if you wanted those big bucks, you had to do it *her* way.

"Whatta ya mean you're not going to fertilize it," she spit. "Isn't that what I'm paying you for?"

"Yes ma'am, but it really doesn't need it. I mean, its plenty green. And it looks okay. And the last time I fertilized it, it grew so much I couldn't keep up with the mowing," I tried to explain.

"Lawns need to be fed," she retorted. "If you don't feed them they'll die out. Would you like it if your mama gave you no food?"

I thought for a moment, shrugged, and tottered off to the shed for the fertilizer spreader.

Thus ended my first confrontation with the radical profertilizer establishment. To this day, Mrs. Fernstead probably has the best fed lawn in the neighborhood. It undoubtedly has never shown a single symptom of nutrient deficiency. And it may never have suffered any ill effects from excessive fertilizer, other than a few extra trips to the clippings pile for my many successors.

But after all these years I still ask myself, "did it really need all that fertilizer?"

FEED ME

What plants eat

Plants are the original "live-off-the-land" creatures. Plants predate animals in history by millions of years. Back before the cavemen, before the dinosaurs, and, yes, even before the cockroaches, there were plants.

Unlike animals, plants do not live by consuming other organisms. They are fully capable of inhabiting a barren piece of ground, relying on no other creature, living or dead, for food.

Plants absorb everything they need for growth from the air, from water, and from dissolved minerals in the soil. They don't need vitamins. They don't need proteins. Unlike humans, plants manufacture every key organic ingredient they need to survive.

Most of a plant's bulk weight is water. Carbon absorbed from the air makes up its structural backbone. The rest—just a few percent of its weight—are the mineral elements we call fertilizer.

Most of the minerals a plant needs it obtains from dissolved rock. Plants evolved with a "needs" list nearly identical to the composition of the earth's crust. Nitrogen is the key exception, as discussed later. Soil and rock contain nitrogen (N), phosphorus (P), potassium (K), sulfur (S), calcium (Ca), magnesium (Mg), iron (Fe), manganese (Mn), molybdenum (Mo), copper (Cu), boron (B), zinc (Zn), chlorine (Cl), sodium (Na), and silicon (Si)—all essential elements a plant needs. Cobalt (Co), vanadium (V), and iodine (I) are required by some plant species, but apparently not turfgrasses. N, P, K, S, Ca, and Mg are called the **macronutrients**, because they're required in the greatest quantity. Others are termed **micronutrients**.

A useful chemical phenomenon known as **equilibrium** assures that the plant's supply of nutrients is constantly replenished. As a plant

Q&A: Cutting Fertilizer Use

Norm Hummel has spent a lifetime studying turf fertilizers. During his graduate school days, Hummel embarked on a project few researchers attempt: He evaluated breakdown rates of turf fertilizers by sifting through thatch searching for fertilizer pellets. The tedium of this type of project prevents most scientists from studying fertilizer breakdown rates under actual field conditions. Not Hummel.

Later as an extension specialist for universities in Iowa and New York, Hummel developed one of the premier Integrated Pest Management (IPM) programs in the United States for turfgrass. In 1995, he abandoned academia to devote full time to his growing company (Hummel & Associates) which analyzes soils for golf courses. His consulting business takes him around the world of turf. Hummel's research and experiences offer insight into techniques for reducing fertilizer use.

Q: Can fertilizer rates be reduced without harming the turf? What kind of bad things might happen?

Hummel: I don't think there's any doubt that a lot of turfs are being overfertilized. Homeowners that are on one of those 5-times-a-year fertilizer programs probably would be better off with half the nitrogen. The turf might not be as lush throughout the year. Other than that, it should be fine. In terms of an athletic field, you'll see less recovery from injury and probably more weeds from less fertilizer.

Q: Can switching to a low maintenance grass species save fertilizer?

Hummel: It all depends what your expectations are. I mean, if you want a buffalograss lawn to look nice you've got to fertilize it. And it will respond to nitrogen. I don't think it's automatic that you can assume you're going to use less fertilizer just because you've got a low maintenance grass species. You're still in control of the fertilizer bag.

Q: Do you favor a programmed approach to fertilizing, or fertilizing "as needed?"

Hummel: I think a program serves as a "guide" for identifying what the nutrient needs are. From a soil test, for example, you can target however many lb of N, P, and K you want to use and when to apply them. But I think any program is just that: It should serve only as a guide. As weather conditions and use of an area change through the course of the year, some fine-tuning is necessary.

Q: Do you know of any tricks for getting turf to thicken up, without producing a lot of unnecessary topgrowth?

Hummel: I think there's some evidence that late-season fertilization does this to some degree. You apply fertilizer during a time when the turf is not rapidly growing. That trick only works on cool-season grasses, not warm seasons. If better color is your goal, you can supplement with iron. This gives you color without the topgrowth. Research work by Tom Fermanian (at the University of Illinois) showed that with iron, you can cut summer fertilization in half and still maintain at least as good quality. Also, some of the new plant growth regulators (PGRs) enhance color and reduce mowing requirement. Homeowners could take advantage of PGRs if they were offered as a lawn service. You could use PGRs in conjunction with a reduced fertilizer rate. I don't have a good sense of whether it would be a third less or a quarter less fertilizer. Maybe some of the PGR companies would know.

Q: You mentioned late fall fertilization. The concept has come under fire lately because of the risk of nutrient runoff from frozen soil or nutrient leaching when the plant isn't actively growing. Are the benefits of late fall fertilization being offset by the risks?

Hummel: Certainly, in some areas this is true. In areas where the soils are prone to leaching, I don't recommend it. On Long Island (New York), for example, we don't recommend it. There are fertilizer sources available, though, that can be used in a late fall fertilization program, that provide significant agronomic benefit with little risk of leaching: IBDU or the methylene ureas, for example. The methylene ureas are less water-soluble than ordinary urea and other water-soluble nitrogen sources. The larger molecules are not as mobile in a downward direction in the soil. We've gotten pretty decent responses out of sulfur-coated urea in late-season application, but nothing like IBDU or methylene urea.

Q: Are the natural organic fertilizers (for example, sewage sludge) the way to go for the environmentally conscious turf manager?

Hummel: There are advantages of a natural organic source as compared to a synthetic source. For one, some organics have been shown to have benefits in terms of disease suppression. I'm not quite sure how this happens, but it does. It may be from the metals in some organic fertilizers acting as fungicides. Another advantage might be the amount of organic matter delivered to the turf. With natural organics, the nutrient levels are so low that it takes a lot of organic matter to deliver a small amount of nutrient. If you use an organic fertilizer continuously over time, there might be some agronomic benefits like improved aggregation or aggregate stability of the soil. But there's no scientific documentation of that. Another advantage of natural organics is their nutrient release pattern. In a temperate climate, the natural organics probably have a better summer release pattern than something like ureaform. They're more uniform and even, more like IBDU. There're no spikes of nutrient release at the wrong time, for the most part. The big disadvantage of natural organics is their low nutrient content—the amount of material required to deliver a desired nutrient per acre. It takes a lot of bulk and a lot of shipping to get the job done.

Q: Are slow-release fertilizers always the way to go?

Hummel: One of the downsides of the slow-release fertilizers is that you have no control over nutrient availability because of the physical and biological activities required for release. If someone's in a situation where they really want to maintain control of nutrients, they can't obtain that control with the slow-release fertilizers—for example, on an athletic field where you need to "push" the field at certain times and not others. Certainly on golf courses, having predictability of nutrient release is pretty critical in some areas.

draws nutrients from the soil water, more minerals are induced to dissolve and take their place. Unfortunately, the rate of mineral release never quite keeps up with the absorption rate of a dense stand of grass. Demand outstrips the supply. That's where fertilizer comes in. Fertilizer supplies the necessary nutrients to make up this deficit. Without fertilizer, the grass population would shrink to a sparse few tufts that could persist on the equilibrium release rate.

Another helpful chemical phenomenon is known as **electrostatic attraction.** Electrostatic attraction helps keep the dissolved soil minerals from washing away. Individual mineral molecules are electrically held by clay and organic matter particles. It's the same phenomenon that allows balloons to stick to the wall after you rub them on your sweater. The mineral molecules adhere to the soil particles and are held there until needed by the plant. Soil mineralogists refer to this storage capacity as the **cation exchange capacity** or **CEC**.

Cation exchange capacity varies from soil to soil. Sandy soils tend to have a small cation exchange capacity and hence poor nutrient storing capability. Soils rich in clay or organic matter have higher capacity. This subtle difference in soils dictates how we fertilize: Sandy soils—with little storage capacity—should be fertilized in small, frequent increments (Marion, 1991). Too much fertilizer applied in one application will rinse clear through. Clay soils and rich, organic soils can absorb and retain more fertilizer and don't need to be fertilized as often.

The least common denominator

Human beings consume mass quantities of foodstuffs through a large opening known as a mouth. A whole array of complex molecules can be absorbed, from amino acids and carbohydrates to nachos and deep-fried pork rinds. Absorbing and utilizing these large, complex molecules saves us a lot of energy. We don't need to synthesize them from scratch. It's a trick animals evolved which plants lack.

Plants, of course, have no mouth. They rely on nutrient uptake straight through their "skin." Only very small, simple molecules can be absorbed through the epidermis of roots and shoots. *Some* complex molecules can traverse a plant's epidermis—herbicides for example—but the quantities are minute.

Contrary to popular belief, plants cannot absorb usable quantities of organic molecules from the soil. Complex organics from composts, humus, seaweed extract, or other natural sources must first be broken into simpler molecules before they can be absorbed by plants. The prevalent form of nutrient taken up by plants is a single mineral molecule bonded to an oxygen or hydrogen molecule. Nitrate (NO_3^-, NO_2^-) and ammonium (NH_4^+) molecules are the sole nitrogen sources absorbed by plants. A few elements—K, Mg, Ca, Fe, Zn, Cu, Mn, and Cl—are absorbed in an even simpler form: as naked, unpaired ions. Anything bigger and the plant chokes.

Here's an example of how a fertilizer works: Let's say you fertilize your lawn with **bone meal**, a natural organic product rich in calcium and phosphorus. Before your grass can absorb the nutrients from that bone meal, several things have to happen. In other words, the grass roots can't just suck in small bone slivers and use them.

First, the bone meal has to come into contact with water. Without water, fertilizers stay pretty much intact. Water allows microorganisms—fungi and bacteria—to grow and use the bone meal as *their* food source. As they grow the microbes digest the complex organic molecules and spit out simpler molecules such as carbon dioxide, calcium, and phosphate as their by-products. Only then can plants absorb fertilizer molecules from the soil. An application of bone meal can take a year or more for complete digestion by microbes, all the while giving off a steady stream of simple molecules for the grass to eat.

And unless the microbes are *active*, the plant receives nothing. During droughts, in winter, or after the application of microbial-inhibiting pesticides, the digestion capacity of soil microbes is diminished. Nutrient release is most rapid during the warm summer months, particularly when ample moisture is available. That's the time when microbes are most active. Nutrients during those times are spinning off at a fever pitch.

Not now, dear, I have a headache

The rate and timing in which nutrients are set free is called the **release rate** of a fertilizer. Different fertilizers have different release rates (Figure 9.1) (Duble, 1995). Inorganic fertilizers release immediately. Natural organic, synthetic, and coated fertilizers provide timed feeding (Table 9.1). With **slow-release fertilizers**, nutrients are distributed slowly over time rather than as one big burst of fertilizer elements.

Sometimes nutrients release when you *least* want them. An unexpected release may add to your mowing. At other times it can have far more serious consequences.

Many turf diseases are triggered by excessive fertilizer (Cook, 1994a; Rieke, 1994). Devastating diseases such as pythium and brown patch are far more severe in well fertilized turf (Figure 9.2) (Watkins, 1994). The added fertilizer induces a denser, more succulent growth in the grass, making it easy prey for the fungus. Under favorable weather conditions, large portions of turf can be lost in a single epidemic.

Natural and synthetic organic fertilizers depend on microbial action for release. When tem-

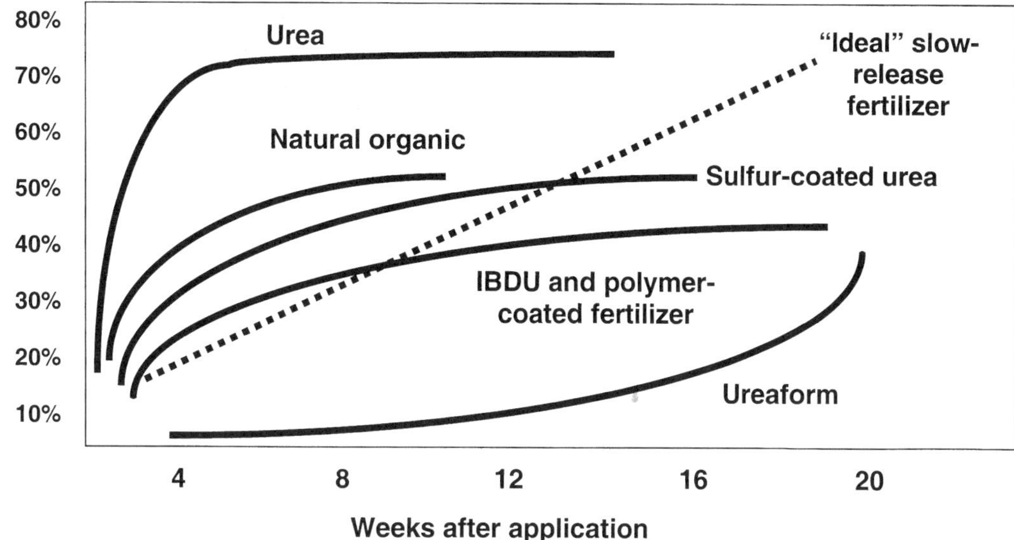

Figure 9.1. Nitrogen fertilizers vary widely in their release patterns. Slow-release fertilizers provide a steady, timed feeding, with small amounts of N delivered over time as the grass needs it. The "ideal" fertilizer would provide a uniform feeding throughout the growing season. In actuality, most products release their fertilizer elements too quickly, too slowly, or at the wrong time. That's why fertilizer products are blended, combining several components together to give a fast initial response and controlled feeding thereafter. Graph was adapted from Dick Duble (1995).

peratures are warm and the soil is moist, microbes are active, supplying great quantities of nutrients to the plant. Unfortunately, this is also the time when we *least* want heavy feeding. The added nutrient load can trigger disease outbreaks (Marion, 1991).

That's why many golf courses and sports facilities rely on a diverse regiment of natural organic, synthetic, coated, and inorganic fertilizers to tailor the soil's nutrient levels throughout the year. They don't rely on a single fertilizer product to do it all.

During midsummer, grasses are best kept a little hungry. A low fertility midsummer diet helps minimize disease potential (Figure 9.2). After temperatures cool, added fertilizer aids in root development and bolsters stress recovery.

Nitrogen is the primary culprit in disease stimulation. Other elements tend to have the opposite effect on disease. Sulfur, calcium, manganese, phosphorus, and even silicon can be used as effective fungicide substitutes (Buchanan, 1979; Clarke et al., 1996; Dorer et al., 1995; Uriarte and Bowman, 1996). Their application helps curb disease outbreaks without resorting to pesticides. Potassium, applied *before* a disease outbreak, has also been shown to diminish disease, theoretically by strengthening the plant's natural defenses (Buchanan, 1979; Carroll and Petrovic, 1991).

WHAT IS LAWN FERTILIZER?

Mrs. Fernstead (the lady I mentioned in the introduction to this chapter) and others like her firmly believe in fertilizing their lawns only with products labeled "lawn food." They fertilize their gardens with "garden food," their orchids with "orchid food," and so on. Have you ever wondered what would happen if you accidentally fertilized your lawn with orchid food, for example?

Actually, nothing happens. Nothing out of the ordinary, that is. All plant fertilizers are basically the same in that they contain N, P, and K in varying levels, and possibly other elements. You might see a lawn fertilizer with a 12-4-6 ratio of **Nitrogen-Phosphate-Potash** on the bag. Other

Table 9.1. Classes of fertilizers used for turf. No one fertilizer is perfect. Each has its own set of advantages and disadvantages that must be considered when selecting the right product for the job.

Fertilizer	What is it?	Examples	Advantages	Disadvantages
Natural organic	Vegetable, animal, or human waste products, recycled into fertilizers. Composting or descenting is sometimes necessary to make the product usable. Inorganic nutrients may be added to bolster the fertilizer value.	• Activated, composted, or dried sewage sludge • Ashes • Blood meal • Bone or hoof meal • Brewery grain • Castor pomace • Cocoa shell meal • Corn gluten meal • Cottonseed meal • Dried or composted manure • Feather meal • Fish or crab meal • Humates • Guano • Leaf compost • Leather tankage • Seaweed extract • Soybean meal	• Low potential for leaf burn • Recycles otherwise unusable waste products • Slow-release feeding • Generally pH neutral (exceptions: bone meal decreases soil acidity; dried blood increases it) • Low salt value • Organic matter contributes to the growth of earthworms, insects, and microorganisms • Negligible leaching potential • Usually contains desirable microelements as well as NPK • May have disease suppressive properties • May improve soil structure and porosity over time	• Low in nutrient value, which translates to additional bulk for trucking and spreading • May contain undesirable impurities, such as heavy metals, soil, weed seed, etc.—check the fine print • Nutrient release is dependent upon weather—warm, moist weather triggers release, which may be the wrong time • Often natural organics are "short" on one or more nutrients, unless they're added artificially • Can produce an unpleasant odor after application • Sluggish initial fertilizer response • Full release of ingredients may take more than a year • Some products, such as bone meal, may have been artificially processed or treated to enhance their potency • Higher cost per active nutrient than other fertilizers • Sometimes are dusty or difficult to handle

Synthetic organic	Organic (carbon-containing) fertilizers that are synthesized from petroleum products and minerals. They release their nutrient elements in a timed-release fashion when the long-chained molecules break down into simpler molecules	• Chelates • Cyanamid • Flowable ureaform (methylene urea and related products) • IBDU • Urea • Ureaform	• High nutrient content • A desired release pattern can be obtained by tailoring the chemistry and chain-length • Many offer timed feeding • Water solubility dictates release—natural organics, by contrast, are governed by microbes, which tend to release nutrients at exactly the wrong time when pathogenic microbes are also active • Medium water solubility means less leaching and runoff • Low potential for leaf burn • Easy application through dry spreaders or hose applicators	• Urea—the exception in this group—is a fast-release product with high burn, volatilization, and leaching potential • These are generally 1-nutrient products—they must be blended with other products for a balanced feeding • Release is virtually nil when soils are cold or dry • Generally more expensive per nutrient than coated products
Directly mined fertilizers	Minerals mined from the earth with little or no alteration from their original form	• Apatite and rock phosphate • Borax • Elemental sulfur • Granite dust • Gypsum • Limestone and dolomite • Potash feldspars and sulfates • Pyrites • Sodium nitrate • Sylvite (KCl)	• A "second best" in environmental friendliness to natural organics—approved by certain environmental groups • Generally safe handling • May offer timed feeding • Some products contain more than one nutrient element	• Nutrients may take a year or more to release • Low nutrient content means added handling costs • Handling and spreading may be impeded by dustiness, clumping, and clogging

Table 9.1. Classes of fertilizers used for turf. No one fertilizer is perfect. Each has its own set of advantages and disadvantages that must be considered when selecting the right product for the job (continued).

Fertilizer	What is it?	Examples	Advantages	Disadvantages
Coated fertilizers	Fast-release fertilizers that have been coated to slow their release. Plastics, polymers, resins, and sulfur have been used to encapsulate granules and control feeding	• Plastic-coated fertilizer • Polymer-coated fertilizer • Resin-coated fertilizer • Sulfur-coated urea	• Highly controllable feeding—a mixture of particle sizes and coating thicknesses can offer just about any release pattern you'd like • Nutrients in addition to nitrogen can be coated to provide timed feeding • Sulfur-coated urea contributes S, a desirable plant nutrient • Easy flow and handling for spreading • Minimal leaching and volatilization	• Traffic, mowing, or abrasion can trigger premature release • May have a high salt or acid value • Earlier formulations of coated fertilizers created a polka-dot turf, as individual particles released and produced a green dot
Inorganic fertilizers	Mined products that have been treated with sulfuric acid or other reactants to produce a higher nutrient content	• Ammonium nitrate • Ammonium sulfate • Calcium nitrate • Diammonium phosphate • Iron sulfate • MagAmP (magnesium ammonium phosphate) • Potassium sulfate • Triple superphosphate	• High in fertilizer potency • Quick greening and remedy of nutrient deficiencies • Short-duration feeding—useful for situations where you intentionally want nutrient levels to drop, such as right before a stress period • Provides feeding when soil temperatures are too cold for slow-release products—ammonium sulfate is the best for this situation • Can be dissolved in water for a drench or spray application • Lowest cost per unit of nutrient	• Higher leaching losses • Fire and explosion hazard—especially ammonium nitrate • Tends to attract water from the air, making the product sticky and hard to spread, limiting shelf life • Saltiness can burn foliage if it's not watered in • May be acidifying to the soil • Feeds the turf for only about 3 to 6 weeks—more labor and more applications are required than for timed-release products • Can be a skin and eye irritant to the applicator

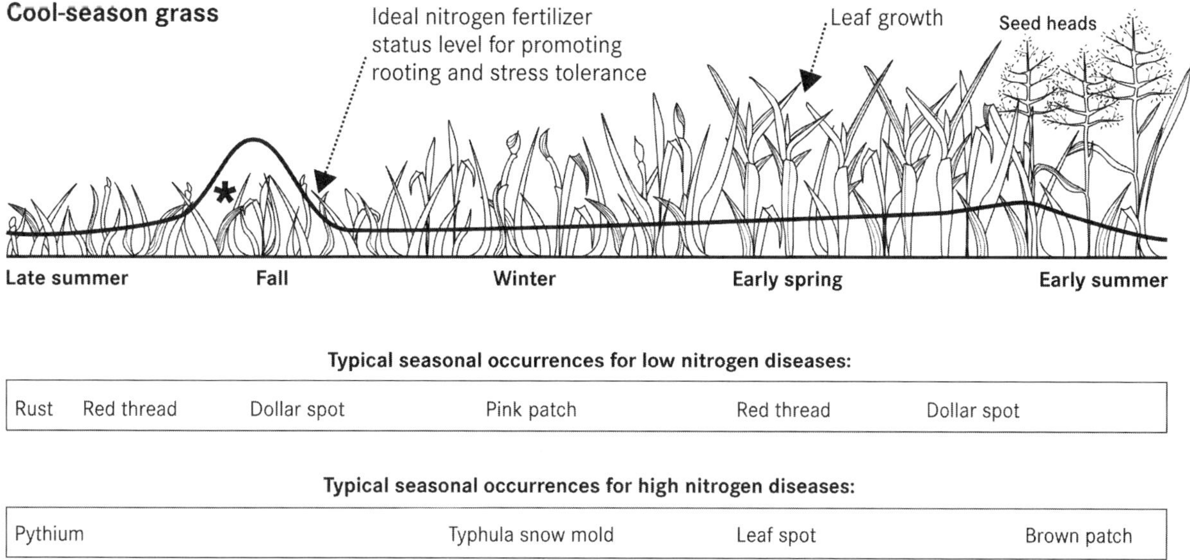

Typical seasonal occurrences for low nitrogen diseases:

Rust	Red thread	Dollar spot	Pink patch	Red thread	Dollar spot

Typical seasonal occurrences for high nitrogen diseases:

Pythium	Typhula snow mold	Leaf spot	Brown patch

*** Best time to fertilize**

Warm-season grass

Seed heads

Late summer **Fall** **Winter** **Early spring** **Early summer**

Figure 9.2. Fertilizing turf at the wrong time can backfire. Grasses go through a natural life cycle which begins shortly after flowering (see text). The plants grow and gain reserves, culminating in the production of seedheads, usually in midsummer. Even mowed grass that never appears to shoot seedheads still goes through this obligate cycle each year. Fertilization should be timed to take best advantage of this natural growth cycle, not fight it. Applying fertilizer at the *wrong* time makes plants excessively growthy and vulnerable to disease attack.

times the ratio might read 18-10-10, and yet it's still called lawn food. The element ratios and numbers seem as diverse as the companies that manufacture them. But strangely enough, they're all called lawn food. How can this be?

The answer is that there is actually no definition of lawn food. Turfgrass plants in your lawn, tomato plants in your garden, or orchids in a pot all use the same simple molecules described earlier. And while it's true that certain ratios are more favorable toward flowering or fruit-set than others, the fact remains that basically *any* fertilizer can serve as lawn food. In a pinch, garden food makes a adequate substitute for lawn food. And it usually costs less too. But before you use the reverse—lawn food in your garden—make sure it doesn't say "weed & feed."

The ideal lawn food

Years ago, someone developed a brilliant idea for turf fertilizers. To formulate the best ratio of

N-P-K, they analyzed the existing nutrient levels in turf clippings. After all, they reasoned, if that's what makes up clippings, it must be the ideal ratio to use for fertilization. The ratio they discovered came remarkably close to the typical 15-5-10 fertilizer commonly in use at the time. Ever since, this 3:1:2 ratio has stuck, becoming a turfgrass icon (Beard, 1995a). Whether it's 12-4-6 or 18-5-9, all turf fertilizers since that time have had the same basic ratio of nitrogen-phosphate-potash.

This line of reasoning has slowly changed as people have considered cutting their fertilizer usage (Sartain, 1994). Phosphorus is a prime example. Phosphate—the middle number in N-P-K—is immobile in the soil. Once it's applied it stays put. It does not wash away or vaporize like nitrogen does. Therefore the question arises: Why do we keep applying P?

If your soil test indicates adequate levels of P, K, Ca, and Mg, there is *no need* to keep applying them time and again (Brede, 1994a; Marion, 1991). Once the soil has been brought to sufficiency levels of these elements, you can switch to an inexpensive, nitrogen-only fertilizer. Forget the fancy lawn fertilizers. All it needs is N.

Well maybe you're not ready to go cold turkey on the other elements just yet. If not, at least consider cutting back on your **complete fertilizer** to once a year (a complete fertilizer contains all three numbers, N+P+K). Then use a nitrogen-only product such as a 38-0-0, for the rest of your fertilizing needs. The switch will be painless, it will save you money, and your turf will look just as attractive as before. And you'll be applying fewer unneeded nutrients into the environment.

Timed-release fertilizer

One of the original definitions of a "turf fertilizer" was a fertilizer with a slow, steady feeding over time. Farm and garden fertilizer, by contrast, is generally inorganically based, releasing all their fertilizing power in a single burst.

Over time the turf fertilizer market has become increasingly price-driven, and the level of slow-release fertilizer in most homeowner products has plummeted. A few turf fertilizers now being promoted to homeowners contain too little timed-release fertilizer to be of value. They're essentially indistinguishable from garden fertilizer.

Nitrogen is the key ingredient in a timed-release fertilizer. It doesn't matter if the other nutrients become active instantaneously, as long as nitrogen is metered out slowly. (In recent years some fertilizer manufacturers have encapsulated potassium and other elements to provide slow feeding of these as well, sometimes with positive results.)

Nitrogen, as explained in Chapter 8, is the key limiting factor to most turfgrasses. Though scientists have documented all kinds of mineral deficiencies in grass, most are rare. In all my years in the turf business, I can count on one hand the number of lawns I've seen with a true nutrient deficiency *other* than nitrogen. When they do occur, these deficiencies are generally found on infertile sandy or gravelly soils, during cold or wet periods, with quirky grasses such as centipedegrass, or on soils with a wacky pH (Butler and Fry, 1987).

The ideal turf fertilizer. If the ideal slow-release fertilizer did exist, it could be applied in a single shot. Enough fertilizer could be dumped on the lawn to supply its nutrient needs for a full year. It would slowly dispense perhaps $^1/_2$ lb of active nitrogen to the turf per 1000 ft^2 (2.5 g/m^2) every month during the growing season. And the discharge rate would never unexpectedly skyrocket during warm, wet weather. The plant's ability to absorb fertilizer would never be overwhelmed by the available supply. Topgrowth and disease would never be overstimulated.

Unfortunately the ideal turf fertilizer does not exist. No fertilizer provides perfectly timed feeding. Coated polymer fertilizers probably come the closest to ideal (Table 9.1), but their technology is still not flawless.

If you're an alert reader, you may have already formulated a brainstorm alternative to the slow-release fertilizer: The once-a-month feeding. Wouldn't it be easier to apply a small amount of fertilizer once a month rather than formulate a complex once-a-year timed-release product? In a word: Yes.

Many golf course superintendents, as a matter of fact, supply monthly *or even weekly* feeding to their turf, furnishing exactly what the grass needs, when it needs it. In doing so, they assume total control over the plant's growth, throttling back diseases and nutrient leaching (Koski, 1994). As a stress period approaches, they merely drop the fertilizer rate.

The trade-off of course is time and labor. It's hard enough for most people to remember to feed their lawns once a year, let alone once a month. But from the perspective of the grass, it really doesn't know or care how you meter its fertilizer, as long as it receives a steady dose on a regular basis.

Fast-release fertilizers can be used for lawns if you fertilize monthly or weekly. Fast-release products discharge their ingredients immediately, dissipating within weeks. A light application of fast-release fertilizer once a month will provide steady feeding, similar to a single timed-release application.

What a turf fertilizer should be

A turf fertilizer should have at least one-third of its nitrogen in a slowly available form. Read the fine print on the bag. It should read something like this: "35% of the nitrogen is water-insoluble." **Water-insoluble nitrogen (WIN)** is another name for slow-release N. If your fertilizer contains only 3% WIN, the label may call it a turf fertilizer, but it really isn't. It's no different than a farm or garden fertilizer. Some commercial-grade turf fertilizers contain up to 100% slow-release nitrogen, for truly timed feeding.

ORGANIC FERTILIZERS

Natural organic fertilizers have long remained a popular product for lawns. These products were the *original* lawn fertilizers from centuries ago. Today their popularity has gained, due in part to the *other* benefits derived from organic products (see Table 9.1 for examples) (Doyle, 1991).

Caution: Not all products that call themselves "organic" or "natural" are in fact either. The consumer should beware. Many natural organic products in their raw form lack one key fertilizer element—perhaps K might be nearly zero. Manufacturers compensate by adding inorganic sources to make their fertilizers "complete." Some natural organic fertilizers are actually blends of several ingredients (Heckman et al., 1994; Hummel, 1994), only one of which may be natural.

A few natural organics have less-than-desirable qualities. Though I'm not an animal-rights activist, I still get squeamish at the thought of applying **blood meal**—a natural organic fertilizer made of dried animal blood—to my lawn.

Other natural organics may contain unwanted contaminants. Composted **sewage sludge** may carry heavy metals such as cadmium. These metals, which originate from industrial sources that also feed the sewer system, prevent use of these natural organics on gardens, due to their human toxicity. But the government has deemed them "safe" for lawns. (Incidentally, the miraculous disease-curing properties espoused for natural organics can often be traced to heavy metal contaminants, which themselves make effective fungicides) (Fidanza and Dernoeden, 1996b).

An oxymoron in the fertilizer biz is the **synthetic organic** fertilizer. These fertilizers are sometimes sold with a big "ORGANIC" and a very small "synthetic" on the label. You may recall from chemistry class that **organic** simply means "carbon-containing." Synthetic organics are carbon-containing fertilizers synthesized from air and petroleum products. These products contain long-chain carbon compounds with embedded nitrogen molecules. Bacteria and oxidation break down the molecules, freeing nitrogen for the plants. But if you're looking for a truly organic product in the traditional sense, these are not for you.

TIMING IS EVERYTHING

It's easy to make the mistake of thinking of a lawn like it's an inanimate rug or carpet. Indoors there's wall-to-wall carpet; outdoors there's fence-to-fence turfgrass. But grass is alive. It's important to remember that lawns are really a vast collection of individual growing plants. And while those grass plants may look pretty much stagnant throughout the year, they are actually in constant flux, obeying an age-old call of nature. Successful turf managers keep the individual turf plant in mind in everything they do, instead of thinking of grass as a green rug.

Nature's cycle of grass

Although grass plants look static throughout the year, they're actually undergoing some pretty dramatic metabolic changes, which directly impact how they should be fed. The annual cycle of a perennial lawngrass begins in midsummer when new grass plants bud from older ones (Figure 9.2). These new plants won't become visible until late summer or early fall. As the young plants grow, they plunge roots and rhizomes deep into the soil to help survive oncoming cold temperatures. Grass plants initiate little new foliage in the fall, far less than in the spring. Their emphasis during early fall is putting down roots. The reason this occurs is that the soil is warmer than the air in the autumn, and grasses—being "cold-blooded"—put their growth where the warmth is.

After the season's first frost, warm-season grasses turn brown. In the spring they'll recover using reserves stored in rhizomes and crowns. Cool-season grasses often remain green all winter, even under snow. Their metabolism is slow but steady.

The first primordial grass flowers begin forming during winter, tucked quietly away, down among the grass sheaths. Yes, even in lawns that never blossom, there are tiny flowers that form. It'll take months of growth before the flowers pop out of the sheath.

In the spring the grass plant bursts into action. Grasses put on a tremendous flush of foliage during the late spring months. They're attempting to increase their photosynthetic surface to help fuel seed production. This makes for a tough time for anyone trying to keep the grass mowed. It seems like the grass needs cutting every other day.

You really notice this growth on unmown roadside turf. In a matter of weeks, the turf balloons from a carpet into a hayfield. All this growth is a reflection of the reproductive process. You notice the same phenomenon in wheat or barley. Grasses remain low-growing until they make their final surge toward flowering.

By late spring the first seedheads appear. The grass flower pushes up inside the sheath "tube" and pops out at the top of the stand. Some grasses are more prone to seedheads in the turf than others. Nearly all do it to one extent or another. The tough, wiry heads of ryegrass or bermudagrass can evade even the sharpest reel mower.

During flowering season, a majority of what you're mowing is actually seed stalks, not leaves. The turf takes on an upright, stubble-like appearance. It becomes vulnerable to a different set of disease problems as growth shifts from vegetative to reproductive. Leaf spot, rust, and stripe smut attack unexpectedly.

Then within days, flowering is finished. The grass generates new buds and the cycle begins again.

Timing your fertilizer to nature's cycle

Turfgrasses are more receptive to fertilization at certain phases of their growth cycle than others (Figure 9.2). By correctly timing the application you can encourage the grass to become deeply rooted, rather than encouraging it to produce hay. The choice is yours. If you feed grass when it's generating new buds and putting down roots, it'll generate *more* buds and put down *more* roots. If you fertilize it while it's ballooning foliage and shooting seed stalks, it will balloon even *more* foliage and shoot *more* stalks. Timing is the key.

Research results. To illustrate this point, Nick Christians and his colleagues, Richard Moore and Mike Agnew at Iowa State University (Moore et al., 1996), tested three fertilization programs on a Kentucky bluegrass lawn. Their treatments were designed to mimic typical fertilization programs offered by lawn care services. Timings, rates, and products were analogous to what the local lawn spray services were offering (Table 9.2).

The prime result from this study was rooting. The "late fall" program stimulated rooting better than the others. Late fall fertilization of "Vantage" Kentucky bluegrass gave 25% better rooting than "heavy spring" feeding, and 33% better rooting than the "balanced spring & fall" program. A similar trend was noted in other grasses they tested. The researchers also discovered a 6 to 18% increase in clippings with use of urea—a quick-release fertilizer—compared to the timed-release sources of methylene urea, methylol urea, and ureaform (more about urea later).

Table 9.2. Application treatments used in a fertilizer experiment at Iowa State University. Applications were based on "typical" lawn care programs in Iowa. Results showed that the "late fall" treatment significantly boosted rooting compared to the other two programs (see text).

	April	May	August	September	November
	– Nitrogen fertilizer applied per month in lb N/1000 ft^2 (g/m^2) –				
"Heavy spring"	1/2 lb (2.4 g)	1 1/2 lb (7.3 g)	1 lb (4.8 g)	1 lb (4.8 g)	none
"Balanced, spring & fall"	1 lb (4.8 g)	1 lb (4.8 g)	1 lb (4.8 g)	1 lb (4.8 g)	none
"Late fall"	1/2 lb (2.4 g)	3/4 lb (3.7 g)	3/4 lb (3.7 g)	1 lb (4.8 g)	1 lb (4.8 g)

Results from this study and others like it (Carrow, 1982; Dunn et al., 1993; Henry, 1991) give direction to anyone trying to cut their fertilizer usage. The key element is *timing*. When reducing your fertilization from 3 or more applications per year, to 2, to 1 or even fewer, timing of the application becomes critical.

Consider this question: If you were to fertilize only once a year, when would be the best time? For a cool-season grass, the optimal timing is early to mid-fall when the grass is budding new shoots and generating new roots. Fall fertilization helps grasses to naturally outgrow low-N diseases such as red thread and dollar spot, without the need for curative pesticides (Figure 9.2). Cold or alpine areas are an exception to this rule. Areas with a brief growing season benefit from spring or summer feeding. The season is simply too short for fall fertilization.

Warm-season grasses respond best when a single shot of fertilizer is timed to coincide with spring emergence (Henry, 1991). Warm-season grasses in the spring must regrow the foliage of an entire lawn in just a matter of weeks. A fertility boost during emergence gives it the food it needs. Of course, as explained earlier, this greenup shot of fertilizer may contribute to increased clippings. If clipping reduction is your goal, a midsummer shot would be preferable.

When is *not* a good time to fertilize? Fertilizing grasses during flowering only aggravates topgrowth and mowing, and exacerbates reproductive diseases. For cool-season grasses, fertilization in early to midsummer is a bad idea. Fertilizing during warm, wet weather predisposes turf to devastating pythium or brown patch attack, as mentioned earlier. Fertilizing warm-season grasses right before fall dormancy is also not a great idea. Though fall fertilization can make the grass green up sooner in the spring, it can also predispose it to additional winter injury.

Winter is generally a poor time to fertilize—not from the perspective of the grass, but from a concern of fertilizer efficiency and runoff. Fertilizer in winter is not readily absorbed by the grass and is prone to washing.

FERTILIZING THE UNCONVENTIONAL TURFGRASSES

Most of the discussion in this chapter has centered around the traditional turf species (grasses like bermudagrass and bluegrass). The unconventional grasses (Chapter 4) have their own peculiar fertilizer needs that should be taken into account before designing a fertility program.

Any grass—conventional or otherwise—has a point of diminishing returns when it comes to fertility. As fertility rates climb high enough, a *reduction* in quality inevitably occurs. This reduction may stem from higher disease or insect incidence. Or it might result from the grass being forced to produce foliage so fast that it no longer looks plush and attractive—it looks coarse and stemmy. In either event, all grasses eventually succumb at heavy enough rates.

The unconventional turfgrasses are efficient miners when it comes to extracting nutrients from the soil. After all, these grasses are popular for restoration of infertile, nonmaintained sites such as strip mines. Arid rangelands and prairies are often planted to these grasses, with no addition of water or fertilizer whatsoever.

As a whole, the unconventional turfgrasses tend to be rather unresponsive to fertilizer compared to traditional grasses like Kentucky bluegrass and bermudagrass (Neal et al., 1993). Small improvements in quality are gained by fertilization, but not to the extent seen in other grasses (Figure 9.3).

This does not imply that unconventional turfgrasses should not be fertilized at all. They *do* respond. However, their rates and frequencies of application are generally lower than for traditional turf species (Johnson and Carrow, 1988).

Tom Platt, grass specialist at Washington State University (Platt, 1996), found that beardless, crested, intermediate, and pubescent wheatgrasses all responded positively to fertilization. They responded so well, in fact, that they were still showing favorable effects from one shot of fertilizer up to four years later. Every variety Platt tested showed positive responses from a single 4.5 lb N/1000 ft^2 (22 g/m^2) application well into the third year of the trial.

Unconventional grasses do respond favorably to *some* fertilizer, but overload when given too much. High fertilization on native rangegrasses has even been shown to shift the stand population away from grass and toward the weeds. Weeds, it seems, appreciate lots of fertilizer (Dunn et al., 1993; Neal et al., 1993).

MINIMIZING FERTILIZER ESCAPE INTO THE ENVIRONMENT

Many people today are concerned with pollution of ground and surface waters with agricultural fertilizers and chemicals. Eutrophication and algae bloom in lakes and streams are one of the more visible results of fertilizer escape. But fertilizer migration into drinking water supplies can have a far more serious consequence (Figure 9.6).

Nitrogen is a prime concern in fertilizer movement. With the exception of nitrogen and per-

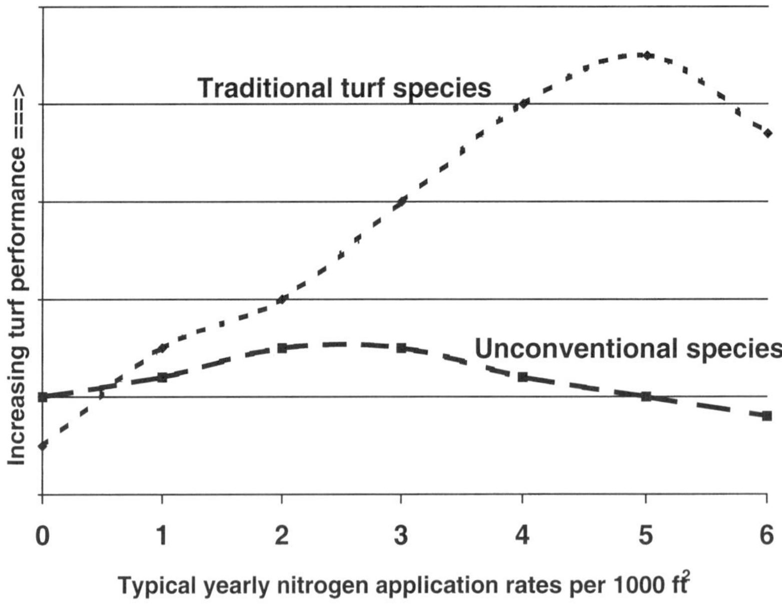

Figure 9.3. The traditional turfgrasses such as bluegrass and bermudagrass perform much differently than the unconventional, low maintenance species when the level of fertilization is raised. Unconventional grasses may provide a more acceptable cover at low or zero levels of fertilizer. But at higher rates, the traditional grasses form a nicer looking turf. They also tend to have a higher point of diminishing returns—the point at which added fertilizer starts to cause a drop in quality. All grasses when fertilized too heavily will eventually grow too thick and succulent, opening them up for disease and scalp. These graph curves are what you'll *typically* encounter with these grasses and are not based on research data. (*Metric conversion*: 5 lb of N per 1000 ft^2 = 25 g/m^2).

Step by Step: How to Drive a Fertilizer Spreader like a Pro

Most people assume that if you can drive a car, you can push a fertilizer spreader. Well, you might be able to *operate* a spreader, but using it to distribute a perfectly uniform coating of fertilizer or pesticide across a rolling turf surface is easier said than done (Figures 9.4 and 9.5).

The instruction manual that comes with most fertilizer spreaders gives you only a cursory idea of how the device operates. Directions are usually aimed at how *their* particular model works, assuming you've been fertilizing lawns all your life. At best, it gives you a sense of security while you're painting obnoxious green spirals across your lawn.

A lot can be learned about operating a fertilizer spreader by how the pros do it—those folks who fertilize some of the most visible turf real estate in the world: Ball parks and golf greens. One skip or spill on the 18th green at Augusta National might send an otherwise competent technician packing. There's little room for error when the television cameras are watching.

Here are some tips on how the pros do it, so that you too can become a Michelangelo at painting your turf uniformly green with fertilizer:

1. **Supplies you'll need:**
   - Twenty or more wire surveyors' flags, available at larger hardware stores. Choose brightly colored flags on a 1-ft ($^1/_3$ m) wire stem. If all you can find are taller flags, cut them to 1 ft with wire cutters. Buy two separate colors if you can find them.
   - A broom and dustpan.
   - A scale and bucket for calibration.

2. **Wait for good conditions:**
   - For best results, the grass should be dry and freshly mowed. Any piles of clippings should be dispersed.
   - Wind plays havoc with spreaders. A breeze stronger than 7 to 10 mph (12 to 17 kph) will distort the application pattern and streak the turf. Fortunately even perennially windy areas like West Texas usually have one time of day with still air: Winds generally diminish right around sunset. Sunrise is also a quiet time. Drop spreaders can operate in gustier winds than spinner spreaders.
   - Some turf professionals prefer to fertilize when there's a light dew on the grass. Dew allows you to monitor your wheel tracks, to make sure they're straight and parallel.

3. **Determine your spreader's pattern:**
   - Locate a clean, dry, level concrete surface such as a driveway.
   - Set the spreader on the initial setting suggested on the fertilizer bag. If there isn't one, then set it at midrange on the dial until you've determine a better value through **calibration**.
   - Close the spreader's gate by pulling back on the handle until it snaps shut.
   - Fill the hopper half full with fertilizer.
   - Take a test drive by opening the spreader's gate and walking forward about 5 steady paces.
   - Using a tape measure or by pacing with your feet, measure the width of application and record.
   - If you're using a drop-type spreader, the application width will be *less* than that of the wheel base. Keep this fact in mind when applying fertilizer—you'll have to overlap the wheel tracks by several inches for complete coverage.
   - If it's a spinner spreader, it will throw several feet beyond its wheel base. Most spreaders preferentially throw further on one side than the other, depending on the direction the disk spins. Record the distance on each side. Bear in mind that a few granules will be hurled 10 ft or more. Judge the effective spread width

by where the granules begin to rapidly diffuse. Your succeeding passes should merge together to create a uniform blanket. For a hand-pushed spinner spreader, the typical application width might be 2 to 3 paces (6 to 8 ft).

- Sweep up the fertilizer from a measured area. Weigh it to determine the actual rate of application, based on the measured area. If it's too heavy or too light, adjust the spreader's dial accordingly. Repeat the process until the desired application rate is found.

4. **Set your flags:**
   - Choose a straight edge such as a driveway or fence as your starting point.
   - Place flags on two opposite sides of the lawn. Space them apart using the effective spreader width you determined earlier: If your spreader throws a swath 3 paces across, plant the flags 3 paces apart. These flags will be your guide for walking and aiming. You'll want to point your spreader directly at the opposing flag as you walk.
   - Start your first flag 1/2 the normal spread distance away from the driveway, etc. For example, if your application width is 3 paces, begin your first flag 1 1/2 paces in.
   - If you have two flag colors, alternate the two colors so that color pairs match across the lawn.

5. **Ready, set, spread:**
   - *Important*: A common mistake people make is to start applying fertilizer before reaching "walking speed." If you open your spreader and then step forward, out comes a big glob of fertilizer, frying your turf. Instead, begin walking and *then* open the gate. Admittedly this takes practice. Try it with an empty spreader until you have the timing right.
   - Use this same advice at the end of your pass. The spreader should be shut off *before* you finish your last pace.
   - Keep a steady walking pace. Don't decelerate at the end of your pass.
   - Never, but never, keep the spreader running as you round the corner for the next stripe. A triple rate of fertilizer will be applied as you swing around.
   - As you round the bend for the next pass, pull the flag. That way you'll never head toward the wrong flag by mistake. Alternating flag colors also minimizes goofs.
   - Of course, if you're opening and closing properly, you should be left with a fertilizer "skip" beyond the flags. This is remedied by a final "header" or "cleanup" pass right along the flags, perpendicular to the other passes.

6. **Tips to remember:**
   - Premium turf sites use a fail-safe method for avoiding streaks: They apply fertilizer at 1/2 rate, then switch the flags and apply a crisscross pattern. That way, any omissions are masked by the later pass.
   - The speed you walk when fertilizing is irrelevant, provided you're *consistent* and your spreader is calibrated. The setting recommendations listed on the fertilizer bag are for a "typical" person walking briskly. It's a good idea to recalibrate for every person who operates a spreader, and for every product you use. With a spinner spreader, how fast you walk affects the application rate *and* width. Consistency is the key.
   - Don't run a fertilizer spreader in reverse. The application rate and pattern will be skewed.
   - Some fertilizer products such as ag limestone, certain minerals, and natural organics are too dusty to be applied with a spinner spreader. A drop spreader is required. Spinner spreaders do best with uniform, moderately sized granules. Even fertilizers with a range of granule sizes are poorly applied by spinner spreaders.

- Most spinner spreaders throw further on one side than the other. For best coverage, some turf professionals alternate the distance between flags as they place them: For example, 3 paces then 2 paces, then 3 paces then 2, and so on. Be sure to use a matching pattern on the other set of flags.
- Fill your spreader on a solid surface, not on your lawn. A spill on concrete can be swept up. Spillage on turf causes a long-term brown spot.
- Some turf pros use mower stripes to help gauge their application. It helps keep the passes straight and minimizes skipping.

7. **After you fertilize:**
   - Water the grass immediately after fertilizing. Watering rinses fertilizer off the leaves and into the soil, minimizing foliar burning and volatilization losses (i.e., fertilizer "evaporation"). Only a light application of water is needed. Too heavy an application will wash the fertilizer away.
   - Coated fertilizers should be watered in before the next mowing. Otherwise, mowing will chop the granules and immediately discharge the fertilizer, sometimes with disastrous results.
   - Many weed-and-feed products require that you water *before* fertilizing and not afterward. The goal is to have the turf damp so that the granules stick, aiding in weed control. Check the product label for details.
   - Sweep errant fertilizer off pavement and patios. Many fertilizers permanently stain concrete. Fertilizer on pavement can also pose a surface-runoff threat.
   - Rinse your spreader with water inside and out after use. Fertilizers are notoriously high in salt and can rust metal workings in short order.

Figures 9.4 and 9.5. Fertilizer burn (r.) and failure to overlap (l.) are common fertilizing mistakes that can be traced to poor technique. Fertilizer burn and streaking can be avoided by careful filling and turning of the spreader. Shutting off the spreader *before* the end of a pass helps avoid overapplication that can occur as the spreader swings around. Application skips can be minimized by the flagging technique described in the sidebar.

Figure 9.6. Won Kim of the Korean Turfgrass Research Institute uses a modified bathtub to gauge fertilizer and pesticide escape from turf. Kim monitors the outflow of percolate water from the tub. Research from Kim and other scientists has shown that, with good management, the water leaching beneath a turf stand can meet or exceed current standards for drinking water.

haps phosphorous, the other elements are comparatively benign from an escape standpoint. Nitrate (NO_3^-) is the primary form of nitrogen pollution. The ammonium (NH_4^+) form of nitrogen is less of a nuisance because it is positively charged and readily sticks to the soil's cation exchange complex and resists leaching.

Excessive nitrates in drinking water can lead to a rare but serious malady known as **methemoglobinemia** or blue-baby syndrome (Gold et al., 1990). Infants lack the strong stomach acids needed to prevent growth of certain bacteria in their digestive tracts. Bacteria in their gut convert nitrate to nitrite which diminishes the oxygen-carrying capacity of the hemoglobin in their blood. Oxygen starvation, brain damage, and even suffocation are possible (Gallant, 1994). If diagnosed early, the condition is readily reversible with antibiotics and diet. The United States government has set a limit of 10 ppm of nitrate in drinking water as the maximum safe level for human consumption. Healthy adults can tolerate more than this level. Infants can't.

Nitrogen is not entirely bad however. Humans require a certain amount of nitrogen in their everyday diet. Adult humans need an average daily intake of 13 grams of nitrogen. Dietary nitrogen is derived from green, leafy vegetables such as spinach, celery, and lettuce. Meats are sometimes fortified with nitrates and nitrites, giving them a rosy pink color. Although 78% of the air we breath is nitrogen gas, we get none of our essential nitrogen from this source. Atmospheric nitrogen gas is essentially inert and unusable by nearly all living organisms (see Chapter 1 for a discussion on nitrogen fixation).

Where does the nitrogen go?

Lawns, parks, and golf courses are the most visible users of fertilizer in most people's environs. Every spring millions of homeowners make the annual ritual of mindlessly dousing their lawns with plant food, with little thought to where it will all end up.

A flurry of scientific studies in recent years has helped answer the question, "Where does this fertilizer go?" Curiously, this research was funded not by concerned environmental groups, but by the U.S. Golf Association. The balance of this chapter is devoted to discussing these research findings, and pointing out steps that can be used to minimize fertilizer runoff and leaching from turf sites.

The most obvious and direct way to limit the escape of turf fertilizers into the environment is to *use less fertilizer* (Hipp and Knowles, 1993; Hull et al., 1993). The fewer fertilizers we apply to turfgrass, the fewer there'll be to migrate elsewhere. In one study involving seven golf courses, researchers found that fertilizer levels could be diminished by 35% without a noticeable loss in playing quality (McCarty et al., 1990).

But perhaps a more important issue than using less fertilizer, is to use it responsibly. Even a small quantity of fertilizer, thrown carelessly or applied at the wrong season, can escape and become a pollutant. It doesn't take a big lawn to cause big problems. On the flip side, a turf facility that applies fertilizers wisely can cut nutrient loss to essentially nil by careful product selection, application, and timing (Table 9.3).

Worst-case scenario

Some turfs are more prone to nutrient escape than others. Probably the turf that would be *most* susceptible to leaching and runoff loss is a newly seeded golf course putting green (Figure 9.7). A new putting green has several factors working against it:

- *Greens are constructed typically from 85 to 100% sand.* Water rapidly percolates through sand, carrying with it any dissolved nutrients.
- *New greens have few grass roots for absorbing nutrients.* They also have a minimal microbial complement for retaining fertilizer.
- *Putting greens contain no clay and little organic matter* to adhere fertilizer molecules.
- *New greens must be irrigated frequently* to keep the tiny grass seedlings alive.

Therefore, a newly constructed putting green is probably the *best* place to test for nutrient escape.

Dick Duble and his associates at Texas A&M University (Brown et al., 1977) tested fertilizer escape on a newly constructed putting green. As expected, they found significantly higher leaching losses than had been documented for other kinds of turf. During the first few weeks after establishment, nitrogen in the percolating water ran as high as 300 ppm—thirty times higher than the recommended safe drinking water level. This nitrate loss was not only a health hazard, but it represented a significant loss of nutrients for the turf. Twenty-two percent of the applied nitrogen washed away in the first three weeks alone. Ammonium nitrate fertilizer was the offender.

When Duble switched from ammonium nitrate to a slow-release source of fertilizer, nitrate leaching stopped. He concluded: "When organic or slow-release forms of fertilizers, including IBDU, ureaform, and sewage sludge (Milorganite) were applied, the concentrations of nitrate found in the leachate were always low and the water met EPA standards of drinking water."

In a related putting green study (Gonzalez-Carrascosa et al., 1995), Michigan researchers found that the *rate* of fertilization also governs leaching. As long as their fertilizer rate *per application* was held to a maximum of 1 lb N per 1000 ft^2 (5 g/m^2), leaching losses were negligible. Higher rates applied to a new seedbed in a single shot caused measurable leaching.

Figure 9.7. A new seedbed: One of the situations most prone to fertilizer leaching. Newly planted turf has several things going against it that makes it vulnerable to nutrient escape (see text). Slow-release fertilizers and limited dosages can trim nutrient loss to a minimum during this critical time.

Figure 9.8. One of the most painless ways of conserving fertilizer is to drop your fertilizer rate as your turf matures. Young turf requires high doses of fertilizer to aid its coverage. Later as the turf matures and forms a thatch, turf becomes more capable of "self-feeding"—the steady breakdown of thatch and soil organic matter recycles nutrients back to the grass. The statistics used for the graph are actual fertilization rates used by Dove Canyon Country Club in California during grow-in. The astute superintendent at this golf course reduced fertilization each year, all while maintaining an acceptable level of playing quality. (*Metric:* 10 lb of N per 1000 ft^2 = 50 g/m^2.)

Table 9.3. Tips for using less fertilizer.

Cut your fertilizer...	• Plant greener grass. Overseed your pale, fertilizer-starved turf with a darker green variety. Newer turf varieties are several shades darker green than older varieties, requiring less fertilizer to keep them attractive. • Never apply more fertilizer in one application than your turf can use—especially nitrogen. Turf can absorb a *maximum* of 1 lb of fast-release nitrogen per 1000 ft^2 (5 g/m^2) in a single application. Giving it more than that wastes fertilizer. Slow-release fertilizers can be safely applied at up to 3 lb N per 1000 ft^2 (15 g/m^2) in a single application without harm. Their timed release spreads out feeding over a longer period. • Don't create a phosphorus mine in your soil. Phosphorus is an immobile element in the soil, which means is stays put and doesn't wash away. Over time, P levels can build up. If your turf soil test indicates adequate P levels, consider a 30-0-6 or similar fertilizer without phosphorus. • Zoysiagrass, centipedegrass, carpetgrass, and fine fescue are noted for their low fertilizer requirements. These grasses persist with little or no added nutrients. • Slow-release fertilizers are more *efficient* at feeding turf than water-soluble, quick release fertilizers. Less fertilizer leaches, less vaporizes, more reaches the plant. • Fertilize your turf with iron. Iron quickly greens up pale turf without overstimulating topgrowth like N-P-K does. Moreover, the application rates for iron are about 5% of what they are for N-P-K. • Consider the *timing* of your fertilizer application. With grass, timing is sometimes more important than rate. Putting fertilizer down when the grass can't use it wastes product. Cool-season grasses use fertilizer efficiently in early fall, warm-seasons in spring.

- Turf in shade may need less fertilizer than in sun. Heavy fertilization in shade induces grass to become upright and leggy. Try a half-rate in the shade. Monitor the turf, though, to make sure the trees are not robbing fertilizer from the turf, turning it pale. Research has shown that a majority of tree feeder roots are intermingled with grass roots.
- Untrafficked vista turfs can be sown with 10% clover seed to add the nitrogen-fixing ability of the legume. White clover adds as much as 2 lb of actual nitrogen per 1000 ft^2 per year (10 g N/m^2/year) to the turf, from N it obtains from the air (Wheeler et al., 1957).
- Less fertilizer sometimes means fewer disease problems. Brown patch (*Rhizoctonia solani*), fusarium patch (*Microdochium nivale*), gray snow mold (*Typhula* spp.), leaf spot (*Drechslera poae*), necrotic ring spot (*Leptospaeria korrae*), powdery mildew (*Erysiphe graminis*), pythium blight (*Pythium aphanidermatum*), and yellow tuft (*Sclerophthora macrospora*) are known to be reduced by lower N (Cook, 1994a).

In a pinch...

- For a quick greenup treatment of lawns, try a dilute solution of household ammonia mixed with water. Apply 1 qt. of ammonia per 1000 ft^2 of lawn (1 L/15 m^2).
- Ordinary chemistry-set litmus paper can be used for checking soil pH. It's particularly handy for checking the pH of thatch, which varies considerably from inch to inch. Compare the color change against a suitable pH chart. The soil or thatch should be dampened before measuring.
- Fertilizer can be used as a valuable means of weed control (see Chapter 12 for more tips). Dropping the N rate to zero in an Oklahoma study prevented encroachment of volunteer bermudagrass into a tall fescue turf (Brede, 1992a). Increasing nitrogen rates from zero up to 1 lb N per 1000 ft^2 per year (5 g/m^2) on Kentucky bluegrass and perennial ryegrass turf reduced weedy clover cover down to negligible levels (Neal et al., 1993). Doubling the N rate from 2 to 4 lb per 1000 ft^2 (10 to 20 g/m^2) in "K-31" tall fescue turf in Georgia cut crabgrass infestation from 31% down to 5% (Johnson, n.d.). Monthly applications of iron sulfate reduced dandelion, clover, slender speedwell, and lawn daisy from 20% down to a trace (Kavanagh et al., 1982).
- Forget those hose-end fertilizer applicators intended for homeowners. They apply too little N-P-K fertilizer to be of value for turf. They are better suited to applying chelated iron for a quick greenup.

Know your turf...

- An inexpensive soil test can save big money on fertilizer. A typical university soil analysis costs about as much as one bag of fertilizer. But it can save you from applying unneeded nutrients.
- Alan Hayes, golf course superintendent at Topeka's Public Course, uses paint-store color chips to document his turf's fertility level. He brings home different color chips from a local paint store and compares them against the hue of his turf. Later, when the turf grows hungry, he can contrast the clippings with his "good turf" reference sample.
- A large turf area may be comprised of many soil types. Sandier soils need lighter, more frequent fertilization than heavy soils. Adjust accordingly.

Get to the root of your problem...

- Find out what's really bugging your turf. Is it nutrient deficiency? Or could it be a disease or insect causing the discoloration? Cure the pest problem first. Afterward, you might use a shot of quick-release fertilizer to green the turf back up.
- Soils with an adverse pH can tie up nutrients. Fertilizer becomes unavailable or mineralized into rock before it ever reaches the plant. A relatively inexpensive lime or sulfur application (depending on pH) will correct the imbalance and ensure maximum fertilizer efficiency.

Table 9.3. Tips for using less fertilizer (continued).

Get to the root of your problem... (continued)	• Check your thatch. If it's too thick, it may be preventing nutrients from reaching the soil. Core aerification punches holes in the thatch and directs fertilizer into the soil (see Chapter 8 for coring information).
Save time...	• Rotary or spinner spreaders are more time-efficient than drop-type fertilizer spreaders. They cover a wider swath and their diffuse banding helps hide skips. • Use **fertigation** to fertilize while you water. Liquid fertilizer injectors are available to fit most in-ground sprinkling systems. A proportioning pump injects fertilizer solution into the irrigation pipes as you water. Inexpensive injectors that use fertilizer pellets are less effective. Liquid-injection models cost more, but are more reliable. The down side of fertigation is that it's only as good as your irrigation system. Sprinklers with skewed application patterns will distribute nutrients unevenly too. Fertigation also harms certain metallic pipe and pump parts. • Green while you brown. Some turf pesticides leave a residual brown cast on the turf. Add urea fertilizer to your spray tank as you're applying pesticides to green the turf back up. Because it's a foliar application, only a few ounces of fertilizer are needed for a big kick. Consult the pesticide label to make sure the product is compatible with fertilizer in the spray tank. Some aren't.
Be more precise...	• If your fertilizer spreader isn't calibrated, you may be applying too much fertilizer. The recommended spreader settings on the backs of fertilizer bags are only approximate guidelines. Ask yourself: Would the fertilizer manufacturer err on the high side of the recommendation or low? • To calibrate your spreader, weigh up, say, 10 lb of fertilizer. Then measure how many square feet of lawn is covered when you spread those 10 lb. Multiply the 10 lb times the percent nitrogen in the fertilizer (for 18-3-6 multiply by 0.18) and divide by the square footage (in 1000 ft^2 units) to obtain the actual nitrogen application rate. • Buy a catch pan. Manufacturers of commercial turf equipment sell calibration pans for drop spreaders. These inexpensive pans ride underneath the spreader, catching the fertilizer as you roll over a test area. Weigh the fertilizer caught over a 1000 ft^2 area and you have your application rate. • Keep good records of fertilizer application. Know how many lb of fertilizer have been applied to each zone or area. That way, there's less chance of double-application because someone "forgot" what was fertilized and what wasn't.
Don't bag it...	• Research has shown that returning clippings saves the equivalent of 2 lb of actual nitrogen per 1000 ft^2 every year. For a typical 5000 ft^2 home lawn, that's the equivalent of 100 lb of 10-4-6 fertilizer each year. In addition to saving fertilizer, clipping recycling reduces bagging and disposal costs. An estimated 40% of trash entering landfills in summer is yard waste. More details are presented in Chapter 11. • A mulching mower will help recycle those clippings. Contrary to popular belief, clippings do not cause thatch buildup.
Fertilize older turf less...	• Mature turf needs far less fertilizer than young turf. For the first 3 years after establishing a new lawn, expect to use *half* the amount of fertilizer progressively each year (see Figure 9.8). Nutrients and organic matter accumulate with time, necessitating fewer applications.
Do your environmental bit...	• Never permit fertilizers to be thrown into surface water or onto a paved area where runoff may occur. Avoid fertilizing grass drainage channels. Switch to a drop spreader near environmentally sensitive areas to distribute fertilizers only where you want them.

- Build berms or buffer strips adjacent to surface waters to prevent and trap fertilizer runoff. As a bare minimum, leave a 5 to 10 ft (2 to 3 m) unmowed grass buffer strip around all bodies of water.
- There is one season of the year when turfgrasses are not actively growing, when fertilization poses a distinct runoff threat: Wintertime. Wayne Kussow at the University of Wisconsin–Madison (1995a, 1995b) researched wintertime fertilizer runoff and discovered that 82% of the total nitrogen and 96% of the total phosphorus that runs off turf sites in surface water in a given year, does so when the ground is frozen. Frozen soil does not allow water or fertilizer to infiltrate. Eventually the water ponds up and runs off, carrying with it any fertilizers still on the surface.
- Redirect drainage pipes away from lakes and streams. Vent them instead into a grass swale; the turf will filter and remove nutrients and pesticides.
- Irrigate lightly and frequently—in contrast to the deep, infrequent watering suggested in Chapter 10—in areas prone to runoff. Lighter watering also minimizes leaching. Light, frequent watering on slopes is a must.
- Skip fertilization altogether during winter or during periods of heavy rain, when runoff or leaching could be excessive. Quick-release, water-soluble fertilizers are the worst choice during these times.
- Clean up spills. Spilled fertilizer can damage turf and potentially can wash away into surface or groundwater. A tank vacuum works best for cleaning up granular fertilizer spilled into turf.
- Be watchful of runoff and leaching during the critical period: the first 2 days after fertilizer application. In a fertilizer fate study performed at the University of California in Davis (1989), Daniel Bowman concluded, "essentially all of the applied N was depleted by 48 hours. Absorption by the turf is largely responsible for the disappearance, although the role of microorganisms in the rapid immobilization of N may be significant."
- Plant absorbent grass varieties. Research has shown that certain grass varieties absorb nutrients more efficiently than others. "Eclipse" and "Able I" Kentucky bluegrass were found to have significantly less nitrate in their soil water than "Liberty," "Blacksburg," "Trenton," "Kenblue," and "Bristol." "Repel" and "Ranger" perennial ryegrass were more efficient absorbers than "Manhattan" and "Linn." "Jaguar" and "Rebel II" tall fescue were more efficient than "Falcon" and "Apache" (Liu et al., 1993). The research suggests that dense, vigorous varieties are better sponges for absorbing nutrients than older, weaker varieties.
- It's always a good idea to verify that products with an environmental name truly live up to their reputation. In a Rhode Island study (Koehler et al., 1982, Gold et al., 1990), one of the fertilizers with an environmental-sounding name, *Earthgro Lawn Food,* leached just as much nitrate as soluble urea. The 5-2-2 Earthgro product was manufactured from composted manure, a natural organic source. Yet in spite of its "natural" origins, it was a leaching hazard.

Learn to live with less...

- Grasses have survived just fine, thank you, before mankind ever started cultivating them. Who was fertilizing them eons ago, eh? Grasses persist with much less fertilizer than we give them. Fertilizer should be provided only to compensate for damage from wear and tear.
- Lower your standards. Accept a turf that is not vibrantly green all the time, as long as it is reasonably attractive and thick enough to keep out weeds.
- Remember: Turf uses only as much fertilizer as you give it.

Chapter 10

Conserving Water

We've all seen it before: Lawn sprinklers running in the rain. Underground sprinklers, obeying the electronic call of a distant timer somewhere, are performing a normal water cycle, oblivious to the fact that there's a downpour in progress. To many people, this is the epitome of waste—abusing a scarce natural resource when, for pete's sake, it's raining! For this reason alone, it's easy to see why turfgrass earns the reputation for being a gluttonous consumer of water.

By some accounts, 40 to 50% of the water used by a typical American residence goes to outdoor use (Stroud, 1987). And while turfgrass draws a considerable fraction of that outdoor water, it is also shared among a variety of tasks: gardening, shrubbery and flower irrigation, pool maintenance, car washing, etc. An estimated 30% of urban water on the U.S. East Coast is expended on lawn irrigation, rising to 60% in the arid West (Bormann et al., 1993). To irrigate a typical 5000-ft^2 lawn (540 m^2) just once, wetting it to a soil depth of 4 to 6 in. (10 to 15 cm) requires 1875 gallons of water (7090 L) (Roberts and Roberts, 1993). Over the period of a year, a typical single-family residence in the West might expend 90,000 gallons (340 kL) for landscaping watering (Stroud, 1987).

When drought hits, turf—the most visible abuser of water—is usually the first to be curtailed. Often water restrictions strike overnight without notice.

"Right here in Griffin [Georgia], officials just came out one day and told us to quit watering lawns," says University of Georgia turf professor, Bob Carrow, talking about a particular summer drought. "They gave us no previous indications that they were going to restrict watering. Some areas had total watering restrictions, while others were every-other-day or once-a-week. This really did affect lawns as the summer went on, particularly the cool-season lawns" (Brede, 1987).

But few people are willing to give up their plush lawns for a landscape of gravel, stones, and cactus. The Xeriscape® landscaping concept, though promoted for over a decade, has failed to make inroads into the typical American lawn (see Chapter 1 for Xeriscape® details). Most people still water and tend to their lawns much as they did before the whole minimal-watering hubbub arose.

Yet a lot can be done to trim turf watering, aside from converting your turf to a dust bowl of stones and cacti. Lawns can be *trained* to demand less water. The fundamental precept of this process is building a solid base for good drought tolerance. As I outlined in Chapter 1, this process entails a systematic, step-by-step plan, to prepare your grass for withstanding the rigors of reduced moisture. It includes:

- Ensuring that the turf is growing in a deep, moisture-retentive soil—or if fertile soil is unavailable, that the existing soil has been supplemented with a rich organic compost source
- Using grass species and varieties that are not only adapted to your area, but are capable of weathering drought
- Employing other waterwise tips as cataloged in Table 10.1.

Table 10.1. Tips for conserving water.

Spring training...	• Yes, grass can be trained to demand less water. Avoid the temptation to be the first on your block to run your irrigation in the spring. In fact, see how long you can go into the summer without watering. In the Eastern United States, it should be possible to delay your first watering until around the 4th of July, most years. That'll train your grass' roots to plummet into the ground in search of H_2O. • Of course, grass training does involve a risk factor. Todd Williams, president of RBI Maintenance Company in Littleton, Colorado, (Williams, 1994) explains: "If we are to water infrequently, the margin for error decreases if things go wrong when we are training the grass. In the process of tuning a system to minimize overwatered spots, we will, of course, stress the underwatered spots. If our clients are aware of the benefits of intensive water management in both cost savings and overall health of the landscape, they usually are more than willing to work with us on the additional costs of labor it takes to achieve it." • **Deficit irrigation** is the process of irrigating turf with less water than an open pail of water evaporates in the same period of time. Most turfgrasses can thrive at 80% of net evaporation with no visible loss of quality. Bermudagrass, zoysiagrass, buffalograss, and sheep fescue can easily survive on 60% of net evaporation without loss of quality. (See Figure 10.2 for an explanation of deficit irrigation and calculating water use based on open-pan evaporation).
Adjust your sprinkling to save water...	• Change your watering as the weather changes. A week of cool, damp weather in midsummer can save you 50% on your water bill—but only if you reset your sprinklers accordingly for that week. Some modern irrigation equipment offers a tie-in between weather sensors and sprinkler timers. Irrigation cycles are automatically regulated according to wind speed, sunlight, humidity, and rainfall (see section, *High Tech Irrigation*). • As a bare minimum, install a rain cutoff switch on your sprinkler system. A simple $40 relay cancels irrigation when rain falls. More sophisticated systems use rain gauges or moisture sensing blocks inserted in the soil, to cancel irrigation only after sufficient precipitation falls. • Watering less often can benefit the turf. Switching from a 4x-per-week to a 2x-per-week watering cycle had negligible effect on turf performance in a University of California–Riverside study (Richie et al., 1995). In both situations, the same quantity of water was applied *per week*. Paradoxically, turf watered twice weekly tended to have moister soil overall, versus turf sprinkled 4x-per-week. • If you have the choice of running your sprinklers once a day for 10 minutes or twice a day for 5 minutes, choose the latter. Many electronic timers offer the option of multiple water cycles. Choosing two shorter cycles as opposed to one longer one will allow better infiltration with less puddling and runoff. • Match your sprinkler's application rate to fit the soil's **infiltration rate**. Applying water faster than the soil can absorb it results in ponding, evaporation, runoff, and waste. *Rule of thumb:* Sandy soils infiltrate 2 in. (50 mm) of water per hour, loamy soils 1/2 in. (12 mm), and clay soils 1/5 in. (5 mm). • Choose sprinkler heads with interchangeable nozzles. That way, you'll be able to retrofit the head with a smaller orifice if needed. It takes only 2 minutes to pop on a smaller nozzle to reduce water application to a particularly wet area. After nozzle changing, though, check the sprinkler's throw, to be sure it's overlapping surrounding heads. • Contrary to popular belief, you can safely water turf at anytime of the day without "burning" it. Some people avoid afternoon watering because they believe it'll burn the turf. Though no burning occurs, afternoon is in fact the worst time of day to water from an efficiency standpoint—up to 60% of applied water evaporates before reaching the roots. Wastage can be even higher in

desert areas. Watering is most efficient when temperature and wind speed are lowest—generally between 4 and 6 A.M.

- Avoid evening watering. Evening watering leaves moisture on the grass blades for hours on end, enabling the spread of pathogenic fungi. Michael Fidanza and Pete Dernoeden at the University of Maryland (Fidanza and Dernoeden, 1996a) saw brown patch disease severity jump by as much as 50% when they switched from a 5 A.M. to a 10 P.M. watering.

Determine if it's really thirsty...

- Rather than watering on a set schedule, check the turf for signs of moisture stress before watering. Water-stressed turf will easily "footprint," because of the lack of turgidity in the plant. It turns purplish or bluish in irregular, circular spots, particularly late in the day. That's your clue to get out the hose.
- A soil probe, available from many ag supply houses, can be used to pull soil cores from the lawn to check for moisture. Probing is also handy for telling when to stop irrigating. Apply enough water to wet only the top 4 to 8 in. (10 to 20 cm) of soil.

Demand better uniformity...

- An irrigation system with spotty coverage is a water hog. It forces you to use more water to compensate for the less-watered spots. You end up over-applying water just to keep certain dry areas damp. Improving sprinkler uniformity can easily save 10 to 25% on your water bill.
- Recruit Charlie the Tuna to check your sprinkler's uniformity (Hawes, 1996). Place empty tuna tins across the lawn and observe the variation in water delivery from place to place. Repeat the test on a windy day to see if coverage is similar. A ruler dipped in the cans after a normal water cycle will give you a reading of coverage. If measurements vary by more than 1/4 in. (6 mm), sprinkler realignment is needed.
- Certain sprinkler layout designs are more uniform and efficient than others. A **triangular arrangement** of sprinkler heads across the turf is more effective than a single-row or a rectangular design. More uniformity means less over-application. A triangular design may be a bit more expensive initially, but it pays for itself in better coverage and efficiency.
- Contrary to popular belief, a lawn sprinkler should not throw water *halfway* to the next sprinkler head, it should throw the *whole* way. Sprinklers are engineered for 100% overlap. With less overlap, uniformity suffers, particularly in the wind. Up to 130% overlap may be needed on windy or hilly sites.
- Water pressure plays havoc with sprinkler uniformity. Insufficient pressure can result from too-small irrigation pipe, too many heads on one line, or line pressure that fluctuates during the day. On the flip side, excessive pressure can cause misting and wind-loss of applied water. When designing your irrigation system, be sure to measure the actual line pressure at the time of day you intend to water. It is difficult and expensive to correct irrigation design defects *after* they're in the ground.
- Something as simple as checking your sprinkler heads for levelness can save water. Tilted heads spray too much water in one direction. Leveling is easier if you use **three-elbowed swing joints** between the source pipe and head. These allow tilting a head in all three dimensions. Sprinklers on slopes generally should be oriented parallel with the slope—within reason, of course. Special sprinkler designs are required for really steep slopes.

Plant a less thirsty turf...

- Pick the right grass for your location. Pushing a grass beyond its normal range of adaptation will waste water. Choose a grass well suited to local conditions (see Chapter 5 for grass selection tips).
- Does grass color affect water use? Everyone knows that lighter-colored fabric is cooler and more comfortable to wear in the summer. But does the same concept apply to grass? Do lighter shades of grass use less water? Turf scientists have debated this question for years. In actuality, it appears that darker

Table 10.1. Tips for conserving water (continued).

Plant a less thirsty turf... (continued)	colored grasses may actually be *more* water efficient than lighter ones. Green color in plants stems from chlorophyll, the energy substance. Darker grasses tend to have more chlorophyll and tend to be more aggressive and vigorous, foraging effectively in search of water. Their added vigor offsets any heating deficits. • Some researchers have found a link between drought tolerance and endophyte infection. Endophytes are beneficial fungi intentionally introduced into varieties of tall fescue and perennial ryegrass to bolster insect resistance (see Chapter 12 for details). Researchers theorize that endophytes may have the ability to quell a grass' thirst for water (Carrow, 1996). • Bermudagrass—a C_4 warm-season grass—uses about 20% less water than Kentucky bluegrass—a C_3 cool-season grass (Feldhake et al., 1983). The difference in water use relates to the physiological difference between C_3 and C_4 grasses (explained in Chapters 1 and 2). Where adapted, warm-season grasses should be used preferentially over cool-season grasses for maximum moisture efficiency. • Turf species, ranked in order of decreasing drought tolerance by Ali Harivandi and Vic Gibeault of the University of California (Harivandi and Gibeault, 1990), are: Kikuyugrass, bermudagrass, seashore paspalum, St. Augustinegrass, zoysiagrass, tall fescue, fine fescue, Kentucky bluegrass, perennial ryegrass, colonial bentgrass, and creeping bentgrass. Species were evaluated on their rooting depth and drought recuperative potential.
Management practices affect water use...	• Turf scientist Bruce Augustin believes that pesticides can add extra stress to a turf through phytotoxicity. Herbicides, he says, can have a root-pruning effect, even though there may be no visible damage to the stand. During a drought, even minor rooting or physiological changes can be detrimental. According to Augustin, "pesticides should never be applied on a preventive basis" during a drought (Brede, 1988a). • Contrary to popular belief, closer-cut turf consumes less—*not more*—irrigation water. In one study, bentgrass used half the water when the cutting height was lowered from 1 in. (2.5 cm) to 1/4 in. (0.7 cm) (Kneebone et al., 1992). Bear in mind, though, that closer-cut turf will also have shorter roots. Thus closely mown turf can't tolerate a delayed or missed watering without discoloration and damage. Using closer cutting for water efficiency works best in desert climates (see section, *Two Breeds of Drought*). • Experts agree that the optimal water efficiency of turfgrass species is obtained at or near the grass' optimum cutting height (see Chapter 11 for recommended mowing heights). • Mow less frequently to conserve moisture. In one study where mowing frequency was increased from twice a week to 6 times a week, water use shot up 41% (Kneebone et al., 1992). There are practical limits, however, to conserving water with fewer mowings. Grass allowed to grow too tall will also waste water (see above tip on mowing height). • In theory, a sharp mower blade should be able to trim a grass blade with less injury and fraying, resulting in better water conservation. Frayed ends expose more leaf tissue to evaporation, compared with a clean scissor cut. In practice, however, the reverse holds true (Kneebone et al., 1992). A dull mower blade weakens the stand and thins it. And because there are fewer healthy plants to consume water, the frayed stand actually uses less water overall. Still, for healthy, attractive turf, a sharp blade is the best advice. • Core aerification improves turf growth and water infiltration. It can also encourage deeper rooting. Bob Carrow, turf soils researcher at the University of Georgia, found 33 to 71% better deep-soil (20 to 60 cm) water extraction from

grass plants as a result of deep aerification (Carrow, 1992). Aerification works the other way around on water-use rate. Aerified turf generally uses more water, because aerification makes plants and roots more vigorous. Carrow found 28 to 96% higher water use in aerified plots, compared to the compacted control.

Correct other stresses...

- An errant soil pH can stunt rooting and limit the soil volume available to the grass for moisture capture. Keep soil pH within the 5.5 to 7.5 range.
- Insects or diseases that gnaw away at roots can impair a turf's drought tolerance, causing it to waste water. Nematodes can be menacing to roots—particularly in mild climates or sandy soils. These minute pinworms live by attaching themselves to roots and sucking juices. Eliminating these pests will trim water use.
- Thatch thicker than 3/4 in. (19 mm) can diminish drought hardiness by forcing roots to grow in decomposing vegetation rather than soil. Thatch dries out readily and is extremely hard to rewet. Water runs through dry thatch like water off a duck's back.
- A deeper, richer topsoil holds more water than a thin, infertile, or sandy soil. Adding additional topsoil during construction, or incorporating compost—either during construction or onto existing turf—improves water retention.

Prepare to repair...

- A great deal of irrigation water can be saved by switching to a different watering strategy: Instead of watering your turf endlessly through the summer to keep it green, allow it to go naturally dormant. Then in early fall, revive the grass with a wake-up splash of water. Repair any summer damage with a light yearly overseeding (see Chapter 7 for renovation tips).

Fine tune your fertilizer for better water efficiency...

- Contrary to popular belief, banning fertilizer is not the answer to water efficiency. Turf maintained with moderate annual applications of fertilizer is more water efficient than unfertilized turf (Petrovic and Baikan, 1996).
- Potassium fertilizer makes turf tougher—better able to withstand a range of environmental stresses, including drought. Annual applications of potash at 2 to 4 lb per 1000 ft^2 (10 to 20 K_2O g/m^2) increased water-use efficiency by 19 to 45% in one New York trial (Petrovic and Baikan, 1996).
- Nitrogen fertilizer makes turf softer, more succulent, and more growthy. For optimal water conservation, turf maintained with lighter nitrogen applications used less water in several studies (Devitt et al., 1992). Applying "adequate" to heavy nitrogen fertilizer caused 10 to 13% more water use in one study (Kneebone et al., 1992). Zero nitrogen fertilization is not the answer for optimal water efficiency, though, because nitrogen applied in metered quantities has been shown to benefit root development and water extraction from the soil (Stout et al., 1991).

Improve your irrigation system...

- Set up separate sprinkler zones for slopes and level areas. Water infiltration on slopes is a fraction of that of level turf. The best solution for slopes is irrigation with a solid-state programmable timer, capable of watering in several short bursts rather than one long soaking. The result is better infiltration, less runoff.
- Does your property have a prevailing wind? An added row of sprinklers on the upwind side will improve coverage on windy days.
- Shaded turf uses up to 50% less water than sunny areas. Does your irrigation system have separate controls for shade and sun areas? The shady sprinkler heads can run for half the time as the sun heads.
- Salt in irrigation water makes water less effective. Turf irrigated with even slightly salty water requires more water overall. Salt can also diminish rooting, making turf prematurely prone to wilt. Effluent (reclaimed or recycled) water, commonly used to irrigate turf in desert areas, may contain levels of salt.
- Wear dictates water use. Research at the University of California–Riverside, has shown that untrafficked turf consumes up to 80% less water than heavily worn

Table 10.1. Tips for conserving water (continued).

Improve your irrigation system... (continued)	turf (Anonymous, 1990). "In areas receiving little or no wear, there is no need for irrigation regimes that support recuperative ability from heavy foot traffic," says Vic Gibeault, director of the UCR project. "We have shown that irrigation water can drop to 20% of normal for these grasses, and they still look green, have a uniform appearance, and have adequate ground cover in nonuse areas." Even a busy sports complex or golf course has perhaps half of its grounds in minimally trafficked turf. These areas could be irrigated with separate controllers to slice water use by half.
Resist temptation...	• Automatic irrigation systems make it easier than ever to abuse water. With a manual watering system, the work of hauling hoses and dodging sprinklers encourages good water stewardship. After all, who wants to go through all that trouble if it's not essential? With automatic sprinklers, it's only a push of the button. Use water wisely when you convert to an automated system. • Turf is actually an efficient water user, even compared to desert ground covers. Dale DeVitt, University of Nevada soil scientist, says, "The temptation might be to replace turfgrass with a green, desert ground cover like myoporum. That would be a mistake. Recent research in Las Vegas has demonstrated that myoporum uses over 30% more water than high maintenance bermudagrass" (Morris and Devitt, 1995).
Conserve water during planting...	• Trying to conserve water during turf establishment is usually a bad idea. Skimping on water during grow-in can mean spotty establishment and prolonged fill. Over time you may end up expending more water to compensate. There are, however, a few useful techniques for trimming moisture while you plant: • Plant when seasonal moisture is available. A.J. Powell, turf professor at the University of Kentucky, was able to establish bermudagrass sprigs without any watering by early spring planting (Powell and Tapp, 1989). He timed planting to coincide with a normally damp period. • Where irrigation is unavailable, deeper plantings can help. Seed or sprigs planted a little deeper than normal can bring the roots into contact with subsurface moisture (Powell and Tapp, 1989). Establishment time is longer, though, and certain species can run out of steam before reaching the surface—so there are practical limits to this technique. But it helps bring up a stand when water isn't handy. • Better design begets better water efficiency. Avoid narrow grass "islands" next to curbs and streets. These pint-size grass patches waste water. Sprinkler overthrow dampens surrounding concrete. Scrutinize all turf strips that serve no apparent function.
Conserve water with chemistry...	• **Wetting agents** (commonly known as detergents or surfactants) have been shown to reduce overall water use. Wetting agents are applied by mixing with water and spraying. For the first two days after application, wetting agents actually *increase* water use. But then for the next 3 to 4 weeks, treated turf uses less water than untreated (Shearman, 1990). • Remedy localized dry spots. Localized dry spots are caused by hydrophobic (water repelling) films on mineral particles. Certain soil fungi are known to play a role in this spotting. And as explained in the spare tire example (see text: The Importance of Solving Soil Problems), dry spots dictate the level of irrigation for the whole turf surface. Wetting agents can be doused onto these spots to improve infiltration and moisture retention. Hand watering of individual dry spots also helps. • Plant growth regulators (PGRs) are sedatives for your lawn. They slow the overall growth, resulting in fewer clippings. PGRs have a side effect of reducing

water consumption by 11 to 29%, depending on rate and kind (Shearman, 1990). (Chapter 11 discusses using PGRs for reduced mowing).

- There's no strong evidence that polyacramide gels instill better water efficiency to turf. These water-absorbing gels are typically amended into soil to a depth of 12 to 18 in. (30 to 45 cm) to hold and retain moisture. At best, results have been mixed.
- Controlling lawn weeds can help trim watering by a small degree. Weeds such as clover use up to 50% more water than lawngrass (Fry and Butler, 1989a). Most lawn weeds can be banished with selective herbicides.
- Camouflage dormant turf with a colorant. Commercially available green dyes can give dormant turf a live appearance. This technique has become popular among realtors, who use it to green up lawns around a vacant house they're selling. Depending on the weather, colorants can last up to 10 weeks.
- **Antitranspirants** have been used to reduce transplant shock on woody ornamentals. These materials work by sealing or closing the leaves' **stomates**—the tiny air-vent pores on plant leaves. Documentation on whether these products also work for grasses is lacking (Beard, 1985b), though a few studies have shown promise (Stahnke and Beard, 1982).

THE IMPORTANCE OF SOLVING SOIL PROBLEMS

A detective story. Years ago when I was a fledgling assistant golf course superintendent, I learned the importance of solving soil problems to reduce water demand. The golf course I maintained was irrigated manually using old-fashioned, hand-operated valves. It took a crew of two most of the night to water all 27 holes, including greens, tees, and fairways (see a photo of the course, Figure 10.1, right).

The greens were watered on standard 15-minute settings. Each green would puddle if given more than 15 minutes at one shot. All 27 greens were treated alike, except for green #6. Unless green #6 received *two* 15-minute shots of water each night, it would start developing a large brown spot near the center. With twice the water, though, that green was usually wet and sloppy. But without it, the middle part would brown out and die.

During one particularly hot summer, the large brown ring began forming on #6 right on cue. The grass began wilting in a circular patch roughly 3 to 4 ft across. Theories abounded as to its cause, from fusarium ring spot to pythium root dieback, to localized dry spot. Plant samples couriered to the state disease lab revealed traces of three different pathogens in the sod—three suspects, but no smoking gun.

My pet theory was fairy ring. My boss disagreed. So I waited until one day when he was out of town at a superintendent's meeting to verify my hypothesis. I knew that fairy ring could be diagnosed by taking a soil core and examining it for a dense, white mycelium and musty smell—the calling card of fairy ring.

With no one looking, I plunged a long, metal soil probe into the ring. Instantly it sprang back up. I did it again—same response.

Ten minutes later I stood there on the green proud as punch. Next to me was a 3-ft deep chasm with a line of golfers waiting to play through. I had finally solved the brown-spot mystery. On the green rested a tractor tire I had excavated. Evidently the contractors who built the course abandoned it years earlier. It laid entombed 8 in. below the green's surface.

When my boss returned later that day, he wasn't as excited about the tire as I was. I had solved the mystery of the strange brown ring. But as my boss reminded me, I still had a 3-ft crevasse in green #6 to repair before dark.

Implications. This story illustrates an important concept about turf soils and water conservation: Turfgrass is irrigated to keep the spot with the *shallowest* soil moist. A droughty area as small as a tractor tire can *double* the watering requirements on the whole rest of the turf surface. The late Jacky Butler, renowned Colorado turf-water

Figure 10.1. Managing drought in the arid desert (l.) is far different than managing it in a normally moist region where occasional summer dry spells occur (r.). Grasses with a high water-use efficiency are best in desert climates. In moist climates, spring root training is a valuable tool for encouraging grasses to become water wise.

researcher, summed it up best many years ago when he said: "The presence of one small dry spot often calls for the activation of the whole [irrigation] system. And it seems that virtually no turfsman will work on improving distribution if simply more water will solve the problem."

A lesson can be learned from my tire experience: Get out there and plunge soil probes into those dry spots whenever moisture stress first occurs. You might find a spare tire. Or you might find something as simple as a rock. But at least you'll be able to rectify those isolated dry spots and cut down on your water bill.

Uniform irrigation and uniform soil are the two keys to water conservation. Good construction practices, such as stockpiling and redistributing of topsoil, are vital for consistent moisture retention across a turf. Yet even after construction, it's still possible to repair droughty areas and reduce watering by conquering those mysterious brown spots.

TWO BREEDS OF DROUGHT

Most turf textbooks, when discussing turfgrass drought and irrigation, lump together all forms of drought and discuss them interchangeably. One pat answer is offered for all situations—a mistake that can lead to confusion and skepticism.

The fact is, all droughts are not alike. Droughts in the desert are a much different animal than droughts in a moist, humid climate. And their management and handling are different too. In the desert, essentially *all* of the water a turf receives is supplied through the irrigation system. California golf course superintendent Ron Hostick comments: "Here in the desert, we regard rainfall as a nuisance and not a blessing. We're so used to it not raining, that when it does rain, it throws our whole management into a tizzy."

Bob Carrow, noted turf-soil researcher at the University of Georgia, found that water axioms developed in the desert don't necessarily apply to the humid conditions in Georgia. In a scholarly publication on the subject (Carrow, 1995), Carrow concluded: "Under humid environments, ranking grasses for drought resistance based on relative evapotranspiration does not correlate well with field observations of drought resistance based on wilt and leaf firing." In other words, the irrigation formulas developed by desert researchers do not apply to the performance differences Carrow sees under humid conditions in Georgia.

A normally moist climate with *occasional* dry spells (like Georgia) has droughts that behave differently than droughts in the desert. A moist climate would be one with an annual precipitation of typically 30 in. (750 mm) or more. For the most part, 30 in. of rainfall should be able to sustain turf. The problem is *distribution*—whether the rain falls in timely enough intervals to keep the grass green. In normally moist North Carolina, for example, only 1 in 4 residences ever water their lawns (Bormann et al., 1993). The other 3 rely on nature to eventually fill the moisture void on its own.

Drought management in a moist, humid climate

Spring training for grasses. In moist climates, turf receives basically all the water it needs for survival from natural rainfall. It's only during occasional lapses in precipitation that it requires irrigation. Summer droughts may be an annual affair, when evaporation exceeds precipitation due to hot weather. Rainfall may not be spaced evenly enough to keep the turf from turning brown. However in these regions, irrigation is the exception, not the rule.

A vital drought strategy in a moist climate is **root training**. Roots can be trained to plummet as deeply into the soil as possible to extract moisture from the greatest possible volume of soil. Consider this: Grass plants that have a 2-ft root system can tap into *twice* as much available soil water as plants with 1-ft roots. Rooting depth is paramount for surviving drought and minimizing irrigation.

Roots are trained by purposely letting the lawn dry out. In the spring, try to resist firing up your sprinklers as long as you can. East of the Mississippi, it should be possible in most years to abstain until the 4th of July, if you can overlook an occasional spring blemish. The natural cycles of wetting and drying train the roots to extend and ferret for moisture.

Grasses need to be *pressured* into expending their resources on roots—they'd much rather grow leaves instead. You may have to sacrifice a little beauty during training season, but the grass will be tougher for it. Think of it like Army boot camp for grass.

Summer drought. Later when summer drought hits, waterings should be deep and infrequent. Once-a-week watering is a good target to shoot for, although twice-a-week may be more realistic. Allow the turf to dry out between waterings. Watch for **footprinting** or purplish wilted spots to appear before turning on the sprinklers (see Table 10.1). Then as you water, moisten the soil to a depth of 6 to 8 in. (15–20 cm) to replenish the soil's reservoir.

Grasses beat the drought with a number of different mechanisms, as discussed in the sidebar. A single strategy does not serve all needs of all grasses. Some grasses may be very tolerant of drought and may perform admirably when water is scarce, but when water is plentiful, they might be quite wasteful. Drought *tolerance* is the strategy to choose when dealing with drought in a moist, humid climate—not necessarily *water-use efficiency*. The reverse is true in the desert as I'll explain below. There, you want a grass that sips water slowly.

Drought management in the desert

Root training in the desert is virtually a waste of time. Irrigation—not rainfall—supplies the grass' prime source of moisture. So it doesn't matter whether the roots are short or long. About the only advantage of deeper roots would be as a safety cushion in case of a missed watering cycle or stuck sprinkler head.

Deep watering in the desert can even be counterproductive. Deep watering can place the moisture *below* the level where the roots can get it. Although some of the water might still trickle back to the surface from the wicking action that occurs in desert soils, most is lost forever. Deep watering can even flush fertilizers, pesticides, and soil salts into the drinking water aquifer.

In the desert, turf dormancy should be treated with more alarm than in a moister climate. In a moist climate like the U.S. East Coast, dormancy is acceptable, even recommended. But things are different in the desert. Turf has a finite capacity to recover from drought dormancy. And while grass can readily recover from one episode, the desert is capable of dishing out *multiple* dormancy episodes every year. When pushed into dormancy too often, grass never recovers.

A balancing act. Efficient desert irrigation is a delicate balancing act between water *lost* and water *added*. Think of it like your car's gas tank:

You fill up your car's gas tank when it gets low just like you fill up your topsoil with water.

After the gas has been used, the tank runs low. When refilled, only as much gas should be added as was expended, and no more. Otherwise, the excess runs out of the tank and down the street. In the desert, it's important to match inputs and outputs for optimal water efficiency. Applying too much water in one application is wasteful.

An open pan of water is useful as a gauge of evaporation in the desert. Though it sounds hokey, this method has become a standard of the irrigation industry over time (see Figure 10.2 for an explanation of open-pan evaporation).

Turf can persist on far less water than evaporates from an open pan of water. Drought-hardy grasses thrive with minimal loss of quality on the replacement of only 50 to 75% of open-pan water evaporation. That means if 1 in. of water evaporates from an open pan, you'd apply 1/2 in. of water to the turf. And while you might presume the soil would eventually run dry using this calculation, it doesn't happen. The formula works because a turf surface evaporates less water overall than an open pan.

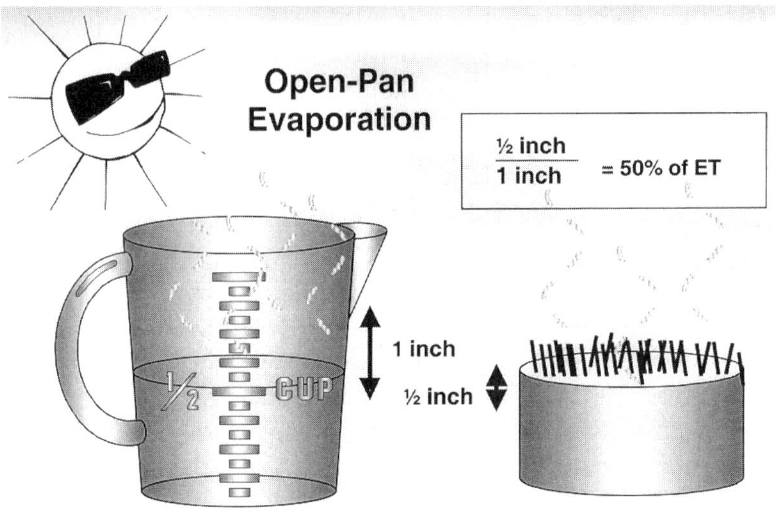

Figure 10.2. Open-pan evaporation has become an industry standard for metering irrigation water. Here's how it works: Let's say on August 1 you put a bucket of water outside. One week later on August 8, you check the water level and find it's now 1 in. below the rim. That means the open pan evaporated 1 in. of water during that week. During a milder week—perhaps in early spring—that same pail might evaporate less than 1/4 in. of water. That's why open-pan evaporation is a good gauge for actual water evaporation for a given period. Most turfgrasses can survive on far *less* water than evaporates from an open pan. In fact, many can persist on 75% or even 50% of open-pan evaporation without loss of quality (see text). In the above illustration, if the open-pan evaporation was 1 in., and 1/2 in. of replacement watering was supplied, then the effective irrigation rate would be "50% of ET." The U.S. Weather Service recommends a standardized metal pan inserted into the ground for measuring open-pan evaporation. A more user-friendly option is shown in Figure 10.3. University of Colorado turf researcher, Tony Koski, demonstrates a water-evaporation meter designed for turf. This device keeps a running tally of water need, based on evaporation from a simulated surface.

Figure 10.3. Colorado State University turf researcher Tony Koski demonstrates a simple evapotranspiration gauge, the *ETgage*, marketed by C&M Meteorological Supply. For more information, contact their web site at *http://www.pcisys.net/~c-m.met.supply/index.htm.* (This photo is not an endorsement for the product by Koski or the University.)

WATERWISE GRASSES

It's your choice

Can something as simple as changing grasses save water? Will replanting your turf to a water-thrifty grass species really trim your water bill? The answer to this question is an unequivocal: Yes, *but.* Changing to a water-efficient grass has the *potential* to lower your water use. The rest is up to you. After all, if you don't reset the timers on your sprinklers after changing grasses, your turf will still use the same amount of water.

David Staats, a former graduate student at Colorado State University's Horticulture Department, did a research study that puts this concept into perspective. He concluded: "The fact that Kentucky bluegrass maintained good quality at the 50% evapotranspiration rate [of irrigation] substantiates the belief that the reason Kentucky bluegrass lawns are large consumers of water may be due to overwatering, poor soil preparation prior to planting, or some other microclimate problem" (Staats and Klett, 1992). One simple fact cannot be overemphasized: Turfgrasses are only as water frugal as the person with their finger on the sprinkler button.

Saving money on your utility bill is not the only reason to conserve water. Reduced irrigation—or more specifically, *smarter* irrigation—has many side-benefits for turf (see Table 10.2).

Research findings

Over the past decade literally hundreds of research papers have been published on turfgrass water use. Some of the first initial studies were brief and simple—perhaps too simple. In these early studies, researchers grew grasses in pots in a greenhouse. After the grasses were established, the researchers cut off the water supply and watched which ones died first.

While this research provided some interesting glimpses into water-use differences among grasses, it obviously didn't answer all the questions. For one thing, a normally deep-rooted grass would have no advantage in such a trial—the pot was only so deep. As a result, many of these earlier trials related poorly to real-world drought conditions.

In later studies, the endurance trial was moved from the greenhouse to the field, making use of more natural growing conditions. Jim Beard, Robert Green, Sam Sifers, and Mother Nature all cooperated one year for such a field study at Texas A&M University in College Station (Beard, 1992b). An exceptionally long Texas drought of 158 days stressed turfgrasses to their bitter end, just as in the greenhouse pot studies. Except in this case, the plants were growing under normal turf conditions. Adding to the severity, the researchers grew the grasses on sand (which retains very little moisture) and with no irrigation whatsoever.

The Texas researchers found a startling number of grasses that withstood the torturous drought. The bermudagrasses faired virtually unscathed, followed by zoysiagrass and Kentucky bluegrass. Centipedegrass and St. Augustinegrass were intermediate.

Perhaps even more striking was the finding of immense *cultivar* differences in drought resistance. They discovered that two varieties of the same species could perform radically different in drought. Beard concluded: "These data emphasize that when selecting water-conserving turfgrasses, it is important to specify the cultivar as well as the species" (Beard, 1992b).

Modern research

More recent research projects have employed increasingly sophisticated technology. One such study at the experiment station in Dallas, Texas, used a **linear-gradient sprinkler system** (Engleke et al., 1996). This system was specially designed to put out a gradient of irrigation across a piece of land, from saturation on one end to bone dry on the other. The researchers simply striped varieties across the gradient and watched where they withered over time (Figure 10.4).

Results revealed vast differences in water requirements among turfgrasses. "Tifway" bermudagrass had the best drought stamina, petering out between 3 and 18% of open-pan evaporation. "Prairie" buffalograss survived on 3 to 11% of open-pan evaporation, and "Nortam" St. Augustinegrass, 5 to 20%. "Meyer" zoysiagrass and "Rebel II" tall fescue had higher water re-

Table 10.2. Benefits of conserving water.

Better wear tolerance...	• Optimal wear tolerance of turf occurs when the soil is neither too-wet nor too-dry (Butler, date not specified). Turf grown under perpetually damp conditions lacks a substantive root system. Overwatering promotes soft, succulent growth—rather than the tougher, hardened tissue of slightly underwatered turf. • Optimal wear tolerance occurs at a point slightly drier than the point of optimal leaf growth.
Fewer weeds...	• Large and smooth crabgrass, yellow and creeping wood sorrel, dallisgrass, annual and rough bluegrass, velvetgrass, yellow and purple nutsedge, common and mouse-ear chickweed, moss, and algae are weeds more prevalent in overwatered conditions (Colbaugh and Elmore, 1985). • Excessive moisture also promotes the seed germination of knotweed, goosegrass, buckhorn plantain, dandelion, and white clover—weeds that later persist even when conditions turn drier (McAfee, 1996). • U.S. Golf Association Green Section Director Jim Snow says, "Although it would be unrealistic to expect to eliminate annual bluegrass from a golf course, one of the keys to successfully suppressing *Poa annua* is certainly careful irrigation. There is one basic rule to follow: Irrigate only as necessary to keep the desirable grasses alive" (Snow, 1979).
Fewer diseases and insects...	• Overwatering is one of the prime triggers of disease. Excessive irrigation, particularly on steamy summer nights, can incite rapid disease growth (Hagan, 1996). • Pythium blight, brown patch, dollar spot, and take-all patch are among the diseases favored by wet leaves and saturated soils (Hagan, 1996). • One type of watering, however, has been shown to cut down on disease. A brief, predawn irrigation—known as **syringing**—flushes dew and nutrient-rich guttation from the plant. Syringing is a bona fide tool for minimizing disease without pesticides (see Chapter 12). • Moderation is the rule when shutting off water to control diseases. Some diseases become more active in drier soil: Rust, melting out, red thread, and root-feeding nematodes prefer drier soils (Couch, 1997; Hagan, 1996). • Moisture is necessary for the maturation of most turf insects (Colbaugh and Elmore, 1985). Perennially damp turf ensures insect survival through the different developmental stages of growth. Less moisture disrupts their life cycles.
Fewer clippings...	• Vegetative topgrowth can be limited by restricting available moisture. Giving turf slightly less water than it wants will produce fewer clippings. • Dormant turf produces no clippings at all. Many turf species are capable of withstanding a period of drought dormancy each year with full recovery (Hook et al., 1992). • Scientists in North Wales have discovered a mutant grass strain that stays bright green even while dormant. They are attempting to breed it into existing turfgrasses to develop varieties that go dormant without loss of color. Stay tuned. • Mowing is easier when the turf is a little dry. Most mowers do a better job—producing fewer clumps and less shredding—when the grass blades aren't damp. Mowers also can leave wheel marks and streaks if the soil is too wet (see Chapter 11 for more mowing tips).
Better fertilizer and pesticide efficiency...	• Irrigation water can rinse foliar chemicals off the grass and into the soil where they're wasted. Nonsystemic fungicides, insecticides, and herbicides work only when they evenly coat grass blades. • Foliar fertilizers—notably chelated micronutrients (see Chapter 9)—must remain

on the foliage to be absorbed. These specialty fertilizers rely on leaf uptake and are essentially deactivated when washed into the soil by too much water.

- Excessive irrigation can cause fertilizers and pesticides to become pollutants. Products may rinse clear through the soil profile and into the groundwater. Or surface ponding can occur, carrying chemicals away into nearby lakes and streams.

Less wastage from over-throw...

- Even the best designed irrigation system can put water where you don't want it—on the sidewalk, on fences and buildings, along a driveway. Aside from making these surfaces slippery and hazardous when wet, water overspray can leave unsightly lime deposits over time.
- Typical out-of-court settlements for someone slipping on a wet, slimy sidewalk and breaking their hip currently runs about $200,000 (Baetz, 1988).

Less thatch...

- Wet, waterlogged soil can cause excessive thatch buildup. The microbes that degrade thatch grow best when conditions are neither too wet nor too dry.

Figure 10.4. The Texas A&M experiment station at Dallas uses a linear-gradient sprinkler system to test the drought tolerance of turfgrasses. The specialized system applies a continuous gradient of moisture across the ground, from moist at one end to dry at the other. The "dry" end of the system is in the foreground of this photo.

quirements, in the 22 to 49% range. Even under sparsely sprinkled conditions, Tifway, Prairie, and Meyer hung on to a robust 75 to 93% ground coverage, while Nortam and Rebel II covered only 15 to 20% of the ground.

One of the most elaborate outdoor turf water studies ever conducted was at the University of California's South Coast Field Station in Irvine (Gibeault et al., 1990). This experiment, headed by project leader Vic Gibeault, was a feat of engineering, combining computers, irrigation clocks, sprinklers, moisture sensors, and an integrated weather station. This experiment helped answer many lingering questions on drought resistance of turfgrasses and how they compare against low maintenance alternative plants (Table 10.3).

The experiment was conducted over three growing seasons. After sifting through the mountains of data, Gibeault found that cool-season turfgrasses were capable of withstanding a 20% cutback in watering with negligible ill effects on performance (Figure 10.6). "There was no significant difference in cool-season grass performance between the 100% and 80% [irrigation] regimes," he concluded. Gibeault used "100%" to indicate the watering practices of a typical California lawn.

Stressing the cool-season grasses still further—below 80% irrigation—caused problems. "More

Evaluating Drought in Grasses

Turf researchers evaluate drought performance of grasses in a variety of ways. In national test trials, a 1 to 9 rating scale is used. A rating value of 9 indicates perfect resistance to drought, whereas a 1 would be a variety that readily succumbs.

Grasses use different strategies to respond to drought. Their various strategies are quantified by jargon terms you'll hear bantered about by scientists:

- **Wilt resistance** is a rating score used by researchers for tallying the combined effects of **drought hardiness** and **drought avoidance**. Drought hardiness is strategy plants evolved for withstanding drought, by use of special biological or physiological adaptations. Their internal chemistry and genetics are fine-tuned for bearing dehydration without permanent harm to the plant. Warm-season, C_4 grasses, for example, possess a type of photosynthesis with better water-use efficiency. Drought hardiness is only successful for surviving short-term drought. Longer duration droughts tax even the most hardy plant. Drought avoidance is a nebulous-sounding term implying that some plants have the ability to move to avoid drought. Obviously plants can't move. They *avoid* drought by having deeper roots, more root hairs, waxy or hairy leaves, fewer leaf pores, slower leaf regrowth after mowing, or an adaptation like leaf rolling or folding to shut down evaporation. The one thing all drought avoidance mechanisms share in common is: They help *shield* the inside of the plant from dehydration.

  Wilt first appears as a purplish cast. Wilted grass readily "footprints"—the lack of turgidity in the plant prevents it from springing back after footsteps. Some varieties resist wilt better than others due to their superior genetics or root systems.
- **Drought dormancy** ratings assess a variety's ability to withstand the temptation to go dormant (Figure 10.5). Higher scores indicate less dormancy. One of the strategies used by low maintenance grasses is to go drought dormant at the first hint of stress. Although this works well as a survival strategy on the open prairie, on a lawn or golf course this ability backfires, leading to excessive irrigation just to keep the grass cosmetically green. As a result, turf researchers reward varieties that resist going dormant with higher scores. Sometimes drought dormancy is also called **drought escape**—another rather nebulous term. **Drought tolerance** combines both drought escape and drought hardiness

Figure 10.5. Turf researchers use their own jargon when discussing drought. **Drought dormancy** ratings assess the ability of a grass to avoid going dormant during a drought. These plots at Fairwood Farms near Washington, DC, show striking differences in drought dormancy among varieties.

into one term. **Drought resistance** is an even more generalized term, encompassing all possible strategies of withstanding drought.

- **Drought recovery** ratings assess a grass' ability to bounce back following dormancy. It is advantageous to have a grass that wakes up quickly from drought. There's an obvious connection between drought dormancy and drought recovery. Varieties that jump into dormancy quickly also rebound faster.

weed activity, disease activity (i.e., fusarium blight on Kentucky bluegrass), and reduced recuperative potential could be expected with cool-season turfgrasses irrigated at less water," he concluded (Gibeault, 1987).

Warm-season turfgrass species fared far better than cool-seasons at reduced irrigation (Table 10.3). "Santa Ana" and "common" bermudagrass topped the roster of 27 grasses and ground covers in low moisture tolerance. Bermudagrass maintained a respectable performance right down to 20% of evapotranspiration—*that's one-fifth of what a typical lawn is irrigated!*

"Adalayd" seashore paspalum (called "Excalibre" in Australia) had drought performance similar to bermudagrass. Bermuda and paspalum weathered an incredible 40% cut in irrigation without even a dip in performance (Gibeault, 1987).

As a lark, Gibeault tested two species of saltbush alongside the grasses. Saltbush is a scraggly, salt-loving, desert forb. He found that even this dryland bush could not top bermudagrass and paspalum in water conservation. Other forbs faired even worse. Clover, trefoil, and yarrow showed declining performance at watering levels that left bermudagrass unscathed (Table 10.3).

Prairiegrasses—wheatgrass, grama, buffalograss, and ricegrass—had moderate to poor performance in Gibeault's test. Buffalograss performed best, though its drought resistance was challenged by one traditional cool-season grass, "Alta" tall fescue.

In summary, the traditional turfgrass species have tremendous potential to survive—even thrive—under restricted moisture levels. Attractive turfgrasses like bermudagrass and paspalum beat out even bristly desert forbs like saltbush and stiff prairiegrasses like blue grama in water conservancy.

More than anything, these results throw the ball back into our court as caretakers of turf: Turfgrass is capable of withstanding reduced irrigation. It can survive unblemished on 80% of what we're now giving it. Some varieties can even persist on 20%. Now it's up to *us* to deliver it.

HIGH TECH IRRIGATION

It seems odd that by adding more sprinklers, more timers, and more sophisticated irrigation hardware you could actually conserve more water. It's strange but true. Sprinkler technology has come a long way from the days of rubber hoses and movable whirlybird heads. Metering out precise doses of irrigation water has moved into the realm of high tech science. After all, when you're trying to conserve water, there's a fine line between overwatering and dehydration. The goal is to give the grass plant exactly what it needs and no more. Accomplishing this goal over hundreds of acres of turf—and doing it uniformly—is an ongoing challenge to the irrigation engineer.

In this section I deal with some of the recent innovations in irrigation technology, and how they can be applied to save you water. Small adjustments in a sprinkling system can sometimes pay off in big bucks—it doesn't take a major system overhaul to save water.

Retirement community success story. Here's an actual success story of water savings: The Metropolitan Water District of Southern California, a utility serving 13 million customers, launched a water conservation program several years ago

Table 10.3. Vic Gibeault and his coworkers at the South Coast Field Station in Irvine, California, calculated the water demand of 27 turfgrasses and landscape alternatives (Gibeault et al., 1990). Plots were irrigated at 20, 40, and 60% of calculated evapotranspiration. Over the course of a year, plots in the 20% treatment received only 6.6 in. (168 mm) of water. The two other regimes received correspondingly more. The box color (see key below) relates to the combined quality and ground cover scores given by the researchers. White-colored boxes indicate *best* performance and persistence under restricted irrigation.

		Evapotranspiration (water provided vs. demand)		
Common name	**Latin name**	**20%**	**40%**	**60%**
'Santa Ana' bermudagrass	*Cynodon* spp.			
'Common' bermudagrass	*Cynodon dactylon*			
Glaucus saltbush	*Atriplex glaucus*			
Seashore paspalum	*Paspalum vaginatum*			
Australian saltbush	*A. semibaccata corta*			
Buffalograss	*Buchloe dactyloides*			
Sirosa phalaris	*Phalaris stenoptera*			
Blue grama	*Bouteloua gacilis*			
'Alta' tall fescue	*Festuca arundinacea*			
'Fresa' strawberry clover	*Trifolium fragilerum*			
Perla koleagrass	*Phalaris tuberosa* var. *hirtiglumus*			
'Brookston' tall fescue	*F. arundinacea*			
'Fairway' crested wheatgrass	*Agropyron desertorum*			
Birdsfoot trefoil	*Lotus corniculata*			
'El Toro' zoysiagrass	*Zoysia japonica*			
'Berber' orchardgrass	*Dactylis glomerata*			
O'Conner's legume	*T. fragilerum*			
Smooth bromegrass	*Bromus inermis*			
Crested wheatgrass	*A. cristatum*			
'Palestine' orchardgrass	*D. glomerata*			
Hard fescue	*F. ovina* var. *duriscula*			
Yarrow	*Archillea millefolium*			
Tall wheatgrass	*A. elongatum*			
Indian ricegrass	*Oryzopis hymenoides*			
'Fults' weeping alkaligrass	*Puccinellia distans*			
Lemmon alkaligrass	*P. lemmoni*			

Key	
	Excellent quality and ground coverage (scoring value of >20)
	Moderate (10 to 20)
	Fair (2 to 10)
	Little or no vegetation present (<2)

Figure 10.6. Turfgrasses at the South Coast Field Station in Irvine, California, were unblemished when irrigated at only 60% of normal. Some even remained green and produced an "acceptable" turf down to a 20% ET value.

targeted at major consumers of landscape water (Thornhill and Brown, 1987). One of their early pilot projects was a 700-acre retirement community, Leisure World of Laguna Hills, a facility with a hefty water bill. An irrigation audit was performed on the property beforehand, mapping the goal of better sprinkler coverage and minimized runoff. After changes to the sprinkling system were made, the retirement community enjoyed a water savings of 8 to 25%. And to top that off, they had fewer breakdowns and runoff problems as well. Program organizers estimate that their customers saved $250 to $500 in water bills for every $27 invested in the landscape audit process.

Consider low tech solutions first

Low tech solutions to improving irrigation efficiency may be less glamorous than their high tech counterparts, but they can pay off nonetheless. The goal of any water-conserving project should be (1) better sprinkler uniformity to provide even coverage, and (2) adjusting irrigation amount to match the weather conditions. It doesn't take expensive machinery to achieve these goals. Even the homeowner with a hose-end sprinkler can make improvements in water efficiency—as long as they're cognizant of these two prime objectives. Larger irrigators stand to benefit even more.

Listed below are several low-tech solutions for efficient watering. Other options are cataloged in Table 10.1.

- *Minimize overspray*—A typical sprinkler system wastes up to 15% of its water in overspray and wind drift (Sommerfeld, 1996). Overspray is water that lands beyond its intended boundaries and cannot be used by plants. Correcting this problem may be as simple as adding a line of part-circle heads along a boundary.
- *Check the water pressure at the sprinkler head*—Sprinklers are designed to operate within a given range of pressures. Many irrigation suppliers and some hardware stores sell pressure gauges designed to read pressure right at an operating head, without removing it from service. A small sampling tube is inserted into the water stream emitted from the nozzle, giving a direct readout of operating pressure. If pressure is low, there may be too many heads on one circuit. Correction may mean replacing the heads with lower pressure models, using fewer heads per set, or reducing nozzle size. Excessive pressure can also jeopardize uniformity. Excessive pressure contributes to drift and overspray. Sev-

eral strategies can be used if pressure is too high: Switching to a higher pressure head, running additional heads on the same line, or inserting a pressure regulator valve in the pipe.

- *Compensate for wind*—In perennially windy locations it may be necessary to use 30% more sprinkler heads to compensate for the wind's distorting effect. Sprinkler overlap should increase 10 to 30% in windy locations.
- *Uniform watering of slopes is always a challenge*—Slopes always seem to dry out prematurely, even while the bottom of the slope is sopping wet. The simple addition of a **check valve** in the pipe may help alleviate the problem. A check valve prevents water from flowing out the bottom sprinklers of a slope after the water cycle has ended. Properly installed, water will remain in the pipe so the pipe doesn't have to refill at the start of every watering cycle.
- *Don't irrigate in the rain*—For a $40 investment, a simple rain cutoff relay can stop your sprinkling system from running in the rain. As mentioned in the introduction to this chapter, nothing seems to anger a passerby more than watching sprinklers run in the rain. Mostly this is a public relations issue, since there may be a valid agronomic reason to irrigate even when it's raining. But irrigating in the middle of rainstorm gives the *appearance* of waste and indifference. "Most turfgrass growers, all the way down to the homeowner, should try to incorporate a rain-override device into their system. A contractor should recommend it to the client," says University of Georgia researcher Bob Carrow (Anonymous, 1989a). Recently equipment innovations offer better reliability in rain relays. Earlier models were easily fouled by leaves and debris.
- *Fix leaks*—It kind of goes without saying that repairing breaks, leaks, and stuck heads also reduces water loss.

High tech irrigation

Step into the irrigation control room of a large, modern golf or sports complex these days and you'll swear you're entering Cape Kennedy Space Center. Computer screens flash out last night's pump performance on a multicolored CRT display. Other monitors show weather maps downloaded directly from a geosynchronous satellite 22,000 miles overhead. Printers tally meteorological data from an on-site electronic weather station. Handheld radios relay impulses through the air to trigger the action of a single sprinkler out of thousands.

Irrigation today has met the computer age. And the only limit is the amount of money you wish to spend. With enough cash and the right hardware, anything is possible, right up to a fully integrated system that tracks the weather and adjusts each head's timing accordingly (Figure 10.7). Many systems even diagnose their own emergencies. If a pump fails or a pipe breaks, the computer senses the predicament, shuts down the system, and phones for help. With modern irrigation equipment, it's possible to conserve water right down to the razor's edge.

Of course not every piece of every manufacturer's equipment is top-notch. Some designs work better than others. In the balance of this chapter, I discuss some of the high tech gadgets available for conserving water. Several scenarios are presented, from budget systems right up to top-of-the-line setups using space-age technology.

Moisture sensors. **Remote sensing** is the science of determining the status of something at a distance. Government satellites that spy on Russia use remote sensing. Over the years, these satellites have provided a better estimate of the size of the Russian wheat crop than the Russians could tally from weighing their own truckloads. Nurses use remote sensing to take your body temperature by inserting an infrared thermometer in your ear. Reading body temperature by remote sensing is less invasive and uncomfortable than the old-fashioned mercury thermometer method.

Remote sensing is useful in irrigation technology because it gives a window into the in-

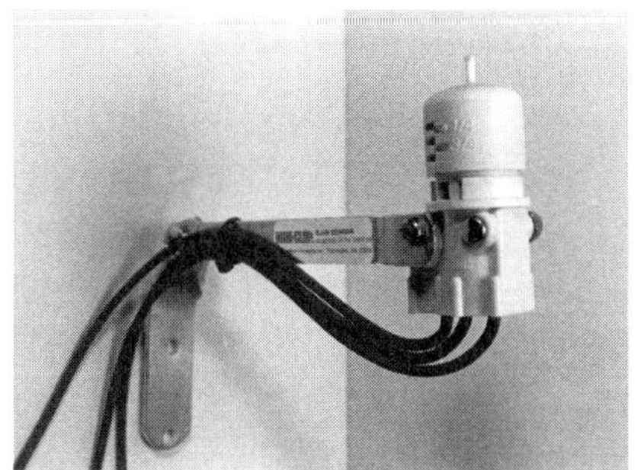

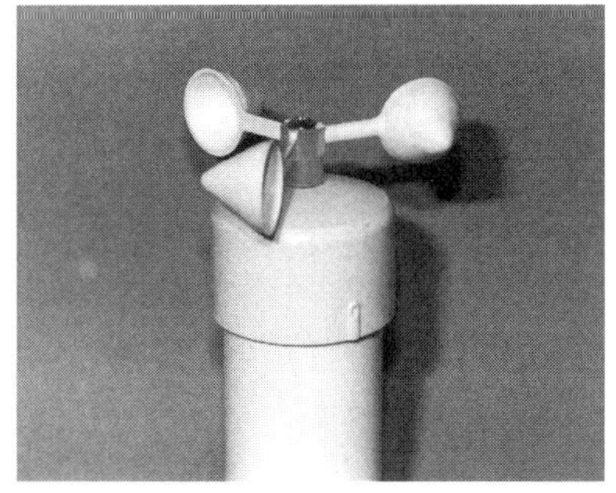

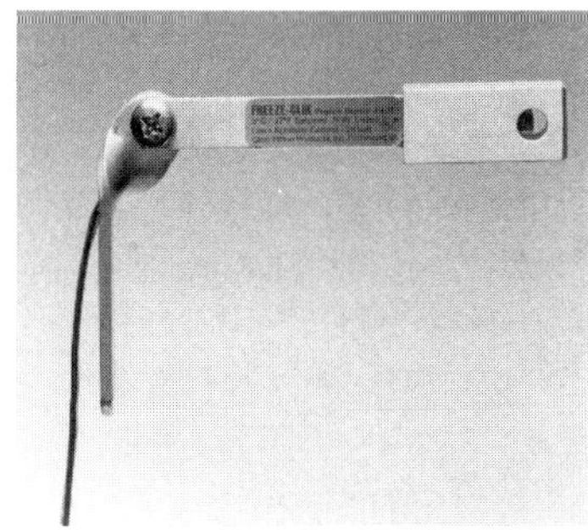

Figure 10.7. Irrigation shutoff devices have gone high tech. The Mini-Clik II rain sensor (l.) by the Glen-Hilton Co. is relatively immune to debris. It monitors rainfall with water-absorbing, hygroscopic disks. The Wind-Clik (center photo) senses high winds that may distort sprinkler patterns. It shuts off the system at wind speeds from 7 to 50 mph, user selectable. The Freeze-Clik (r.) senses freezing temperatures that may cause ice on walks or drives and suspends watering.

side of the grass plant. For total irrigation control, we need to know if things are adequately moist inside the grass tissue. Is water starting to run a little low or is everything hunky-dory? Water is wasted by irrigating when everything's satisfactory.

But how do you tell when turf is thirsty? There really aren't any good ways to step inside a grass plant to take its moisture reading directly.

Thus turf scientists and irrigation engineers must rely on remote sensing to estimate the water status inside a grass plant. Many different methods have been used over the years, including—as incredible as it may seem—the same type of infrared thermometry used by nurses.

Moisture sensors function in the same way as the rain cutoff relay discussed above: They shut off the sprinklers when moisture is sensed, except instead of monitoring raindrops falling from the sky, they monitor the water status nearer the plant, usually right in its rootzone. Because of this, moisture sensors tend to closely parallel the moisture status within the plant.

Types of sensors. Unfortunately, no one moisture sensor is perfect. The inexpensive ones tend to be short-lived. And the really accurate ones tend to be prohibitively expensive.

Some moisture sensors read out moisture status right on the face of the instrument. They rely on someone checking their display each day and manually adjusting sprinklers to match. More sophisticated sensors interconnect directly with the sprinkler control box, functioning as a relay to override the watering cycle.

Some moisture sensors have to be adjusted for a desired wetness level. They have a rheostat that lets you dial in the moisture level. To conserve water, you simply set the rheostat a little lower, to have the sprinklers kick on only when the soil gets really dry.

One factor that's even more critical than which moisture sensor you buy is: How you *install* the sensors. Inserting sensors in the turf right beside the maintenance shed is probably not a good idea. It's always best to get a representative moisture reading from an actual turf use area. This may involve some long extension cords. But at least it'll give you an accurate read of the turf in play.

Burying moisture sensors at the wrong depth can give you misleading readings. If buried too deeply, they're below the grass's rootzone. Buried too shallow and you risk damage from maintenance equipment (Figure 10.8). Another common mistake is to install sensors too close to a sprinkler head, fooling the controller into thinking the ground is wetter than it actually is.

Here are some tips for installing moisture sensors:

- *Install them directly within a turf use area, not somewhere off to the side*—Wires from remote-readout sensors can be routed underground to a handy valve box nearby

Typical Turfgrass Moisture Sensors

- *Moisture blocks*—Moisture blocks work by measuring the electrical resistance between two wires imbedded in gypsum or nylon. These blocks represent some of the oldest technology in the irrigation business. Their biggest advantage is cost. Gypsum blocks are inexpensive, but they need to be calibrated for each particular soil they're used in, to ensure they're providing accurate readings. They tend to function erratically in salty or wet soils. Unlike some other sensors, they can be left in the ground year-round. Their working life is a brief 1 to 4 years.
- *Tensiometers*—A tensiometer measures the *tension* between the soil water and a sample of pure water inside the probe. As the soil gets dry, it tries to pull water out of the probe, and the probe measures the physical tension or pulling force involved. Early tensiometers had a readout directly on the face of the instrument. Modern models have wires that can be routed to a nearby sprinkler controller. Because they contain water, tensiometers need to be removed or drained each winter in freezing climates.
- *Soil psychrometers*—**Psychrometers** are used by meteorologists to measure relative humidity. The same physics that measures humidity of air can be used to determine moisture content of soil. Psychrometers, like gypsum blocks, need to be calibrated. They also have difficulties in sandier soils. Psychrometers are more expensive to buy than gypsum blocks but tend to be more accurate.
- *Infrared thermometers*—Point-and-shoot infrared thermometers are finally making headway into the turf business at a reasonable price. Top quality models retail for over $1000, but budget models can be located for under $300. These devices look like a Star Wars phaser gun and work by taking an infrared snapshot of the foliage. Handheld, these meters can be toted from place to place as needed, and are not tied to one spot like other sensors are. A digital display on the back of the instrument reads out the temperature of the objects where the gun is pointed. An infrared thermometer is not really a moisture sensor—it determines moisture status indirectly. When leaves get too hot, it means the plants are running short of water and can't cool themselves properly. The infrared thermometer tells you the temperature of the leaf blades more accurately than can a hand touch. With a little practice, the versatility and portability of a infrared thermometer makes a valuable tool for irrigation scheduling.
- *Time-domain reflectometry (TDR)*—The most complicated and expensive type of moisture sensor is also the most accurate.

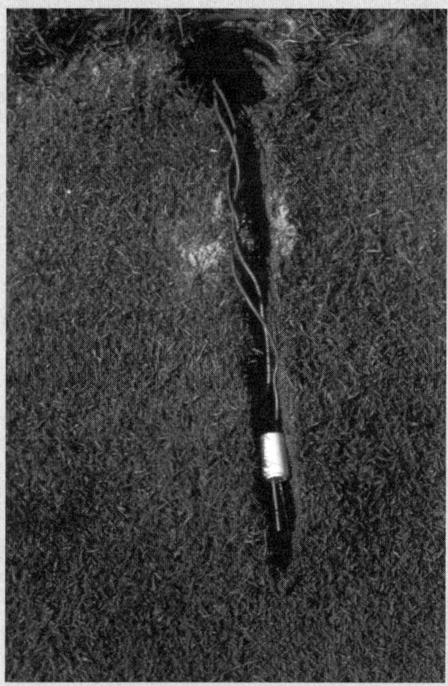

Figure 10.8. Moisture sensors should be installed within the grass's rootzone, so that the reading truly reflects the moisture status of the plant. This particular sensor was installed a little too shallow, making it vulnerable to damage from aerification equipment.

TDR is so accurate, in fact, that scientists use it as a standard to *calibrate* other types of sensors. TDR works by clocking how long radio waves take to travel across soil—radio waves take slightly longer to traverse wet soils than dry. The physics involved in TDR work over a broad range of soils. But it may be a few years before this technology becomes affordable to the average Joe.

- *Locate them halfway between sprinkler heads*
- *Bury them at a depth of 4 in. (10 cm)*—That's deep enough that you won't hit them with aerification equipment, but shallow enough that they're still within the rootzone.

Subsurface drip irrigation. Aboveground sprinklers all share one Achilles' heel: The water they throw into the air is prone to wind drift and evaporation. As a result, manufacturers for years have been trying to perfect the technology of **subsurface drip irrigation**. Subsurface drip irrigation is basically a leaky pipe that, when inserted into the sod, oozes irrigation water directly into the rootzone (Figure 10.9).

The concept is fundamentally sound: Water *will* be conserved if it is delivered directly to the rootzone without being subject to wind and evaporation. Underground drip also has the advantage of eliminating overspray of water onto curbs and sidewalks. Moreover, with underground drip, it is possible to irrigate turf while it's being played. That alone is no small bonus.

But the technology has proved vexing. For one thing, underground drip irrigation is more expensive per square foot than sprinkler technology. Secondly, monitoring and repair of the irrigation system is difficult if not impossible. If a pipe breaks, you may have brown grass before you realize it. And locating the break can be tedious.

Third, buried drip pipes have had a questionable history when it comes to endurance. The water-emitting pores in the pipe tend to become clogged with sediment or roots. Manufacturers have been slowly remedying these shortcomings over time. One company uses a root inhibitor chemical imbedded in the pipe to prevent grass roots from plugging the pores.

Subsurface drip irrigation has been finding its way into a number of vital turf functions. Slopes, parking lot islands, grass patios, and golf bunker faces benefit from this technology.

Vic Gibeault at the University of California–Riverside, tested subsurface drip irrigation as a potential water-conserving option. He employed the same large, controlled, field experiment described in the above section, *Modern Research*. However, results of the drip experiment fell short of expectations. The subsurface system did not deliver adequate watering. Turf performance was always better with aboveground sprinklers.

"Each of the cool-season species performed significantly better when irrigated by the sprinkler method. The subterranean system was apparently too deep and/or too widely spaced to provide adequate amounts of water," Gibeault concluded (Gibeault and Meyers, 1988).

Gibeault installed the system according to the manufacturer's specifications, using a 23-in. (58 cm) spacing and 8-in. (20 cm) depth. He speculated that the depth may have been excessive for many cool-season grasses.

The warm-season grasses also preferred aboveground sprinklers over the subsurface drip system. "Santa Ana" bermudagrass was the only exception. It performed equally well with either system. Gibeault speculated that the 5 1/2-ft deep (1.7 m) root system of the Santa Ana may have made the difference.

Integrated weather/irrigation systems. If the perfect irrigation system existed, it would check the weather forecast for you, poll the moisture status of the grass plant, and track potential evaporation for the coming day. And it would do all this before turning on the first sprinkler. Today engineers are coming startlingly close to developing the perfect system. Sprinklers are taking on a mind of their own.

Figure 10.9. Subsurface drip irrigation is basically just leaky plastic pipe. When buried into turf, it feeds the rootzone with the moisture it needs. Among its benefits, subsurface drip irrigation can be operated even while turf is being played upon.

At the heart of these advanced-generation systems is the solid-state irrigation controller. Early irrigation controllers were simply mechanical clocks. When the timer gears ground around to Station #1, electrical contacts would close and fire up sprinklers for the time dialed in on the tiny plastic knob. With mechanical clocks, accuracy was not always attainable. For example, perhaps Station #1 was set to come on at 5 A.M. but it didn't actually start until 5:20 A.M. Error was to be expected. And maybe it activated for the 10 minutes dialed on the knob, or maybe it ran for closer to 14. Whatever the case, the job got done.

But it wasn't efficient. A seemingly insignificant error of 14 minutes instead of 10 meant a 40% overapplication of water. Also, there was no easy way to readjust the system or scale it back on a dreary day when water demand was low. The sprinklers came on, rain or shine.

Today, piece by piece, irrigation controllers are becoming computerized. The master control unit has evolved into an accessory you plug into the back of your PC, just as you'd install a printer or modem. Once a day—or as often as needed—you adjust the settings by dialing up the controller on your PC and punching in a new value. On an overcast day, you might type "60%" onto the screen and magically all your sprinklers are reset to run for 60% of their normal time. On a parched, windy day, you might enter "120%." The master controller sends those signals to the satellite field controllers to readjust each and every timer.

Now comes the truly water-thrifty part: Integration of environmental data. By feeding input from moisture sensors into the controller, the controller can respond automatically to the moisture status of the grass—even when you're away for the weekend. If it's moist, the signal from the moisture sensor tells the controller to back off. It might reset all sprinklers for a 60% cycle—with no human intervention.

Even more exciting is when weather data—past, present, and future—can be fed into an irrigation controller. Some golf courses and pro sports fields now have their own on-site electronic weather stations. Relative humidity, sunlight intensity, rainfall, dew, temperature, open-pan evaporation, and wind speed are fed continuously into a computer. Based on the data, the computer calculates water use and adjusts irrigation accordingly. The computer crunches the data using complex formulas developed by irrigation scientists. The electronic eyes on the sky make minute-to-minute adjustments even as a large cloud passes overhead.

Are weather stations worth the investment? If you're a major user of irrigation water, they are. Weather stations hold the potential for tremendous savings. "If you can cut down on your water by 10, 15, or 20% because you're scheduling the irrigation better, and you have quality turf for a lot less water, then a weather station can pay for itself," says Carrow (Anonymous, 1989a).

Community irrigation scheduling. In California, Arizona, and Florida where water is limited, municipalities are taking the concept of weather-based irrigation scheduling to homeowners. California started its project in 1982 in an effort to conserve irrigation water in the state's fertile San Joaquin Valley (Thornhill and Brown, 1987). Since that time, the California Irrigation Management Information System (CIMIS) has grown to include urban landscape irrigation as well as farmland. The CIMIS system employs 52 weather stations (costing about $5000 each) operating across the state. Automated weather stations gather and process data continuously. Computers turn the data into irrigation recommendations.

Homeowners or turf managers equipped with a computer and phone modem can log into the CIMIS system and download data for their area. Casual users can rely on announcements of CIMIS readings made over TV and radio stations as part of their local weather report.

"Using real-time weather data, CIMIS is a basis for large-scale scheduling of irrigation," says John Van Dam, cooperative extension specialist at the University of California, who is involved in the CIMIS program (Van Dam, date not specified). "It gives both the time as well as the amount of water to be applied to answer a water user's three most pressing questions: (1) when to irrigate, (2) how much water to deplete from the soil, and (3) how to effectively replace that amount that has been depleted."

Through CIMIS and similar community programs, weather-based irrigation scheduling is becoming available to everyone. Basing irrigation on actual weather conditions and turf needs is a valuable tool for conserving water.

Chapter 11

Lighten Your Mowing

Mowing grass is a lot like paying taxes: It doesn't work to neglect them and hope they'll go away. Delay only causes taxes and clippings to pile up. And if you put them off long enough, both can become so massive they're virtually overwhelming.

With those delightful thoughts in mind, let me say that there is no *direct* way to reduce your mowing. You can't simply ignore it or decide today to mow less often. The grass just keeps on growing, with or without your help.

So, how *do* you reduce mowing? Is mowing frequency something the grass dictates and we have no control over?

The only proven way to reduce mowing is to limit the things that *induce* grass growth in the first place. Nitrogen fertilizer is the most obvious culprit. For every pound of nitrogen you spread on turf per 1000 ft^2 (5 g/m^2), you can expect to roughly *double* the amount of clippings you've got to deal with (Petrovic and Baikan, 1996). The more nitrogen you spread, the more you mow.

Fortunately, this relationship also works in reverse. Apply half the nitrogen, and you can expect to harvest about half the hay crop. But it takes time. The fertilizer you've been stockpiling in the soil may take weeks or months to dissipate. And until it does, it will continue to feed the grass and generate more clippings. Eventually, though, the rate should slack to something more manageable. When it does, you can use other tricks of the trade to keep your turf attractive. For example, did you know that applications of iron can darken the color of grass without generating clippings? Other conservation mowing tips are cataloged in Table 11.4. (See also Table 11.2 and Figures 11.3 and 11.4.)

Nitrogen is not the only means of regulating growth and mowing. There are a number of options open to the progressive turf manager or homeowner. Grass recycling, choosing the best height, picking appropriate mowers, plant growth regulators (PGRs), and a change of grass species are a few of the possibilities open to anyone weary of cutting grass. There *are* things you can do to reduce mowing. This chapter shows you how.

SELECTING THE RIGHT MOWER

Right-sizing for the job

Selecting the right size mower is the first step in managing your mowing. Choosing the wrong blade configuration or a mower too small for the task can waste labor and lead to excessive machine wear and fuel consumption. Right-sizing is the answer. Your equipment dealer can help you select the correct mower size to match your landscaping needs.

The choices of mowers today are virtually limitless. There are mowers to fill any landscape need, from small, hand-pushed garden models to gigantic tractor-powered, multigang units that can tackle 40 ft in a single swath. Even human-powered mowers (motorless) are making a comeback. Last year's production of push mowers topped a record set in 1945. Pushing a human-propelled reel mower burns 480 calories a hour, equal to tennis, downhill skiing, and low-impact aerobics.) Today's mowers offer a range of power options, including human-propelled, gasoline, diesel, propane, AC electric, battery operated, and recently even, solar powered. Cutter options extend from the precise scissor-trim action of the professional reel mower to flail units that chop

Types of Mowers

- *Reel mower*—Reel mowers produce a scissor-action cut between the rotating reel and the stationary **bedknife**. To keep them in top working shape, reel mowers require the same precision machining as a pair of dressmaker shears. Periodic grinding and honing (**backlapping**) keeps the gap between the bedknife and reel adjusted. A precisely set mower will crease one sheet of paper and cut two. Better reel mowers offer more blades per reel and a higher reel rotation speed. This translates into more snips per foot of turf. Top-of-the-line models can adjust reel speed independently of tire speed, to give the same quality of cut regardless of travel velocity.
- *Rotary mower*—The rotary mower is the workhorse of turf maintenance. Rotary mowers don't require the precision machining as reel mowers, though a sharp blade is still recommended. Rotary mowers feature a blade that whirls horizontally. With enough horsepower, rotary mowers can tackle taller turf and even brush. The **brush hog** mower is a trade name that has become synonymous with large, tractor-mounted rotaries, useful for low maintenance areas.
- *Mulching mower*—The mulching mower is an offshoot of the rotary mower, except its shoot has been taken off. Instead of blowing the clippings into a bag, the mulching mower grinds them—often with multiple blades—and filters them back into the turf. See text for more details.
- *Flail mower*—A flail mower cuts grass using whirling machete-like blades. The difference with a flail mower is that the blades are *hinged*, not fixed to the shaft like rotaries. Because of their hinge, flail mowers are forgiving when they hit something. Instead of the ricochet force acting against the machinery, the hinge takes the brunt. Flail mowers can have blades mounted horizontally or vertically on the shaft, depending on the model. Flail mowers do not deliver the same quality of cut as other mowers.
- *String trimmer*—String trimmers were conceived as a way to reduce hand trimming.

Figure 11.1. String trimmers have all but put an end to hand trimming. One operator can do the work of a team of manual trimmers—minimizing the backbreaking work of edge maintenance. Other techniques for reducing edge maintenance include: (a) installing a mulch strip along boundaries, (b) spraying a narrow band of nonselective herbicide to kill the grass, or (c) applying a strip of PGR.

A string trimmer is fundamentally the same as a small rotary mower, with nylon string in place of a blade (Figure 11.1). Nylon line is obviously safer to the operator, though it can cut through grass and even weeds. A feeding system is required to keep the line replenished, as it readily wears off during use. Better models feature a more reliable feed system that means less down time. Recently the string trimmer has grown larger, with some newer models big enough to tackle a full-size lawn or roadside.

- *Sickle bar*—Rarely do you see sickle bar mowers used these days. Sickle bar mowers were a carryover from farm operations, where they are used for harvest of grain and forage. When applied to turf, they find use only on low maintenance grounds like roadsides, where their inferior cutting quality can be tolerated. Unlike other mowers that chop grass repeatedly into segments, the sickle bar mower cuts it once and lets it drop. Heavy foliage can smother the remaining stand. The slow ground speed, relatively dangerous operation, and fairly high maintenance of the sickle bar has all but eliminated it from landscape maintenance.

grass with large, machete-like blades. There's even a mower without wheels that hovers on air, providing easier care of banks and slopes (Skorulski, 1996).

Quality of cut

The big difference between mowers is the quality of cut they produce. Some mowers precisely nip the grass blade while others hack away at it. Expect to pay a premium for units that give the finest cutting quality. Premium mowers also require the greatest outlay of periodic service to keep them in tip-top shape. It takes a qualified machinist to keep a putting-green reel mower in peak condition. An errant pebble sandwiched between the bedknife and the reel can send an expensive reel mower back to the shop for regrinding. That's why certain mower configurations are suited to fine turf while others are better for industrial and low maintenance turf.

In 1995, *Landscape Management* magazine surveyed turf managers in various segments of the business to learn their mower preferences (Anonymous, 1996c). It was no surprise that the riding reel mower was the most popular mower for golf, purchased that year by 53% of golf courses. With golf turf, cutting quality is at a premium. Reel mowers generally provide the highest quality cut, particularly under close mowing.

Lawn care operators and landscape contractors surveyed preferred the walk-behind rotary mower over other configurations. Only 2% of lawn care companies purchased a riding reel mower in that year. With lawn care, overall ruggedness and durability is demanded, more so than cutting quality. It's out of the question for a landscape mower to go back to the shop every time it encounters a pebble.

Grounds managers were evenly split in their preferences between walk-behind and riding rotary mowers. Grounds managers maintain parks, industrial grounds, cemeteries, roadsides, and schools.

Cutting height

Cutting height is the next obvious variable that dictates mower choice. Each mower configurations has its height where it gives the best cut. Reel mowers do their best work below 1 in. (2.5 cm) compared to other mowers. Other mowers tend to scalp and shred when set that low. Between 1 and 2 in. (2.5 to 5 cm), rotary and reel mowers are nearly matched in cutting quality, as long as the blades are kept sharp.

Research on mowers and cutting heights. In a research study at the University of Georgia (Johnson et al., 1987), B.J. Johnson and his cohorts Bob Carrow and Bob Burns looked at the cutting quality of the three primary mower configurations—reel, rotary, and flail. Height of cut ranged from 3/4 to 1 3/4 in. (1.9 to 4.4 cm) in this 3-year bermudagrass lawn study.

In the first year of their study, both the rotary and reel mowers produced identical cutting qualities. In the second year, the reel mower was slightly favored, while in the third year the rotary produced the better cut.

Thus cutting quality was a toss-up between the reel and rotary mowers, provided both mowers were well maintained and the cutting height was 3/4 in. or above. However, the reel mower was favored in terms of turf density. Turf mowed with the reel mower was 3 to 7% denser than turf mowed by the rotary. Exactly *how* the reel mower induced this greater density was unclear. Perhaps it was less damaging to the grass plants.

The flail mower in the Georgia study produced the poorest cut and lowest shoot density of the three mowers. The chopping action of the flail mower butchered the plants and thinned the turf. Johnson concluded: "On many low- to medium-maintenance sites, the grower may have the choice of using a rotary or a flail mower. In this study, choice of the flail mower resulted in substantially lower quality and shoot density. Thus, selection of a proper mower type can have a major influence on turf quality that a fertilization program will not alter."

Each mower design has a range of heights where it does best. Close cuts (1 in. or below) are best handled by reel mowers, with their precision manicured trim. The dominance of the rotary mower extends between 1 and perhaps 6 in. (2.5 to 15 cm) of cut. Above 6 in. (15 cm), the flail mower becomes the more practical mower design. A flail mower is built for general vegetation control. It is forgiving of heavy foliage, uneven ground, and the occasional rock.

Bigger is better. Let's face it, mowing is expensive. To mow a 1-acre home lawn for one season costs $462, according to a Cornell University economic analysis of mowing (Hummel, 1993). Their calculations were based on a 22-in. push mower, traveling 3 mph, using $7.00-per-hour labor.

Labor makes up the majority of mowing costs, equipment second. Labor gobbles up 60 to 90% of a typical turf facility's maintenance budget (Watschke, 1994). And a majority of that labor is for mowing (Hummel, 1993).

One solution to the high cost of labor is to buy bigger machines. Larger mowers demand a greater up-front outlay of dollars, but the savings can be recouped later in reduced labor costs. For example, in the 1-acre lawn mentioned above, switching from a 22-in. push mower to a 72-in. rider would cut the labor cost from $462 to $150 per year according to Cornell researchers—a substantial savings.

The downside of larger mowers is that they cause more wear and tear to the turf—especially when they turn. That's why some premium golf courses have returned to the walk-behind greens mower. Larger triplex riders wear out the grass on the "cleanup" pass around the perimeter of the green. Lightweight walk-behinds are gentler on the grass though more expensive on labor.

Selecting the right height. Cutting height is dictated by a turf's intended use. Sports turfs are customarily mowed shorter than utility turf. When choosing a grass, it's important to select one that's capable of withstanding the cutting height you intend to dish out (Figure 11.2).

Mowing is a stress to the grass plant. And the *closer* you mow, the more stressful it is. Certain grasses because of their physical attributes, are better suited to close mowing. The optimal and minimal cutting heights of traditional and low maintenance turfgrasses are listed in Table 11.1.

Several rules of nature govern the recommended mowing height of turfgrasses:

- *A grass that creeps horizontally can be mowed shorter than an upright, bunch-type one*—Stoloniferous grasses can be mowed closest, followed by rhizomatous, and finally bunchgrasses.
- *Grasses with narrower blades usually can be mowed closer than broad-bladed ones.*
- *Mowing a grass below its optimal height will thin it, opening it up for weed invasion.*
- *Close cut turf demands better mowers, more pesticides, more precise watering, and higher overall maintenance than higher cut turf.*
- *Turf cut **above** its optimal height is not trouble-free either*—Certain creeping

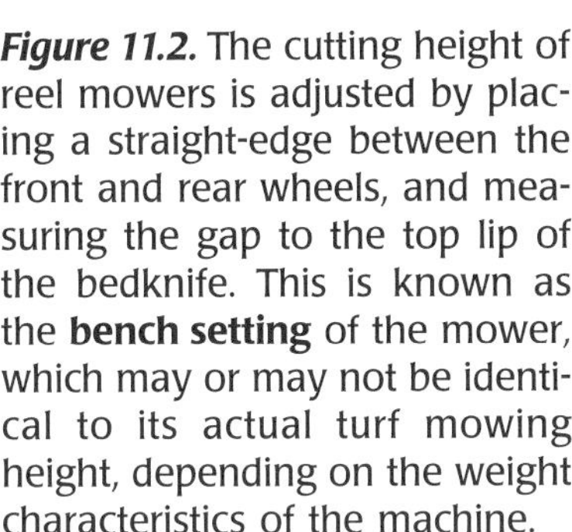

Figure 11.2. The cutting height of reel mowers is adjusted by placing a straight-edge between the front and rear wheels, and measuring the gap to the top lip of the bedknife. This is known as the **bench setting** of the mower, which may or may not be identical to its actual turf mowing height, depending on the weight characteristics of the machine.

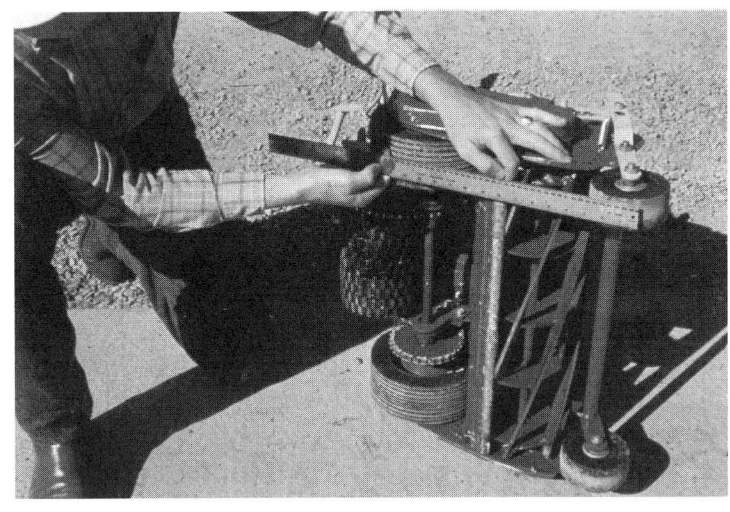

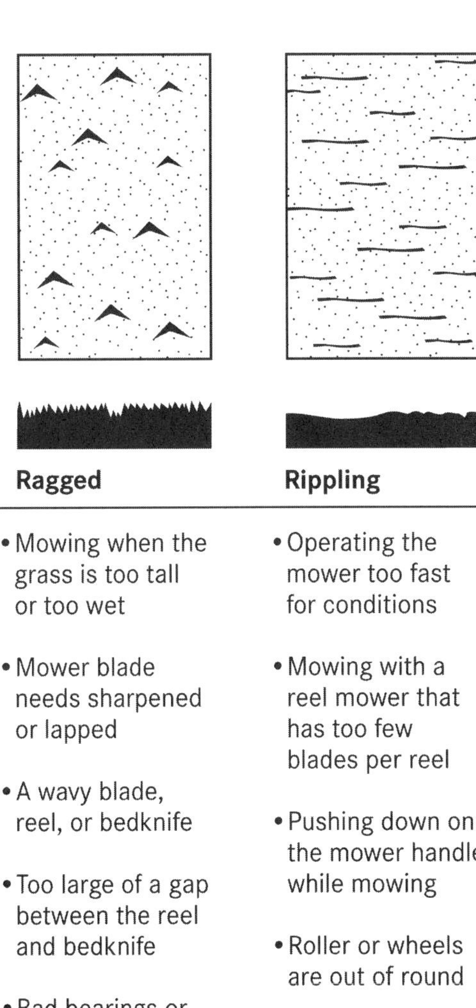

Symptoms	**Streaking**	**Strip cutting**	**Ragged**	**Rippling**
Causes	• Not overlapping between passes • A lip, gouge, or dull spot on the blade, reel, or bedknife • A sticking wheel or roller that's slipping and marking the turf	• High or low areas along the blade, reel, or bedknife • Loose mounting screws on the bedknife	• Mowing when the grass is too tall or too wet • Mower blade needs sharpened or lapped • A wavy blade, reel, or bedknife • Too large of a gap between the reel and bedknife • Bad bearings or radial play	• Operating the mower too fast for conditions • Mowing with a reel mower that has too few blades per reel • Pushing down on the mower handle while mowing • Roller or wheels are out of round • Bad bearings

Figure 11.3. Causes and cures for common mowing problems. Mowing problems can be diagnosed by examining the distinctive patterns left behind. Each pattern suggests a needed service remedy. This chart was adapted from a Jacobsen Manufacturing Co. training guide.

Table 11.1. Suggested mowing heights for turfgrass. The recommended mowing height depends on its intended use. Sports turf is usually mowed shorter than other turfs. Vista or low maintenance turf can be given a higher mowing height, and is often left unmowed entirely. The recommended heights—and especially the absolute minimum height—are strongly dependent on the variety specified. Elite varieties are usually better suited to close cut.

		High maintenance		Low maintenance		Best type of mower to use	
Grass species	**Absolute minimum height in. (cm)**	**Recommended height, in. (cm)**	**Recommended mowing frequency, days**	**Recommended height, in. (cm)**	**Recommended mowing frequency, days**	**Rotary**	**Reel**
Bermudagrass	3/16 (0.5)	1/2–1 (1.3–2.5)	3–5	1–4 (2.5–10)	5–14		✔
St. Augustinegrass	1 (2.5)	2-1/2–3-1/2 (6.3–8.8)	7–14	3–5 (7.5–13)	7–14	✔	
Zoysiagrass	1/2 (1.3)	1–2 (2.5–5)	5–10	2–3 (3–7.5)	10–14		✔
Carpetgrass	3/8 (1)	1–2 (2.5–5)	7–10	2–3 (3–7.5)	10–14	✔	
Centipedegrass	1 (2.5)	1-1/2–2 (3.8–5)	10–14	2–3 (3–7.5)	14–28	✔	
Buffalograss	3/4 (1.9)	1–2 (2.5–5)	10–14	2–4 (5–10)	14–28	✔	
Bahiagrass	2 (5)	3–4 (7.5–10)	7–10	3–6 (7.5–15)	10–14	✔	
Seashore paspalum	3/8 (0.9)	1/2–1-1/2 (1.3–3.8)	5–7	1–2 (2.5–5)	6–14		✔
Kikuyugrass	1/4 (0.6)	1/2–1-1/2 (1.3–3.8)	1–3	1–4 (2.5–10)	3–7		✔
Colonial bentgrass	3/8 (0.9)	1/2–1 (1.3–2.5)	1–3	2–3 (5–7.5)	5–7		✔
Creeping bentgrass	1/8 (0.3)	3/16–5/8 (0.5–1.6)	1–2	2–3 (5–7.5)	5–7		✔
Velvet bentgrass	1/8 (0.3)	3/16–5/8 (0.5–1.6)	1–2	2–3 (5–7.5)	5–7		✔
Highland bentgrass	5/8 (1.6)	3/4–1-1/2 (1.9–3.8)	2–5	2–4 (5–10)	7–14		✔
Redtop	1-1/2 (3.8)	2–3 (5–7.5)	7–10	3–4 (7.5–10)	10–14	✔	

Tall fescue	3/4 (1.9)	1–2-1/2 (2.5–6.4)	5–7	3–6 (7.5–15)	7–21	✔	
Sheep fescue	1-1/2 (3.8)	2–3 (5–7.5)	7–10	2-1/2–4 (6.3–10)	10–28	✔	
Strong creeping red fescue	1 (2.5)	1-1/2–2 (3.8–5)	5–7	2–6 (5–15)	7–21		✔
Chewings fescue	1/4 (0.6)	3/4–1-1/2 (1.9–3.8)	5–7	2–4 (5–10)	7–14		✔
Slender creeping fescue	1 (2.5)	1-1/2–2 (3.8–5)	5–7	2–4 (5–10)	7–21		✔
Hard fescue	1-1/2 (3.8)	2–3 (5–7.5)	7–10	2-1/2–6 (6.3–15)	10–28	✔	
Perennial ryegrass	3/8 (1)	3/4–2 (1.9–5)	4–7	2–4 (5–10)	7–10	✔	
Kentucky bluegrass	5/8 (1.6)	1–2-1/2 (2.5–6.3)	5–10	2–4 (5–10)	10–14		✔
Canada bluegrass	2 (5)	2-1/2–4 (6.3–10)	7–14	3–5 (7.5–13)	10–21	✔	
Supine bluegrass	1/2 (1.3)	3/4–2 (1.9–5)	5–7	1–3 (2.5–7.5)	7–10	✔	
Roughstalk bluegrass	1/2 (1.3)	3/4–1-1/2 (1.9–3.8)	5–7	1–3 (2.5–7.5)	7–10		✔
Alkaligrass	1-1/2 (3.8)	2–3 (5–7.5)	7–10	3–5 (7.5–4)	10–21	✔	
Low growing unconventional grasses (0 to 2 ft native height)	1-1/2 (3.8)	3–4 (7.5–10)	7–10	4–8 (10–20)	10–28	✔	
Medium growing unconventional grasses (3 to 4 ft native height)	3 (7.5)	4–6 (10–15)	7–10	6–12 (15–30)	10–28	✔	
Tall growing unconventional grasses (>5 ft native height)	6 (15)	10–18 (25–46)	14–21	12–24 (30–61)	21–28	✔	

Table 11.2. Safe mowing tips.

Mowing is serious business. According to Stacey Reuben Mesa of the Consumer Product Safety Commission, 76,133 people are injured every year in mower-related accidents. That figure includes professional turf operators, homeowners, and children. About a third of the injuries occur on riding mowers. The Commission reported 75 mower-related fatalities in 1991 (Rogers, 1994).

What to wear...	• Ankle-high steel-toed shoes with slip resistant soles • Full-length slacks • Safety glasses • Never wear shorts or go barefoot
Before you mow...	• Pick up all stones, sticks, wire, toys, and other debris • Know the mower's controls and how to shut it off in an emergency • Make sure all safety features are operational, including guards and cutoff switches • Keep children and pets at a safe distance • Adjust the mowing height on a solid surface by measuring the distance from the blade to the ground
Safe fueling...	• Shut off the engine before fueling • Never fill a hot mower with gasoline—let it cool down first • Move the mower off the grass before fueling—spilled fuel kills grass • Wipe up any spills before starting engine • No smoking
While mowing...	• Never mow after dark—be sure there's sufficient light for good visibility • Always push the mower rather than pull—if you slip while pulling a mower, your leg can slide underneath • Empty the grass catcher regularly, before its weight becomes excessive • Shut off the engine and remove the spark plug wire before working on the blade or unclogging the deck • Avoid mowing excessively wet turf—especially on slippery slopes • Shut off the engine before crossing gravel paths and driveways • Never leave a running mower unattended
Safe riding mower operation...	• Never carry passengers • Don't mow in a backward direction unless absolutely necessary—if you do, watch behind you the entire time • Observe traffic rules when crossing streets or mowing near roadways
Safe slope mowing...	• Riding mowers should mow directly up and down slopes, not crosswise • Shift to a lower gear before driving a riding mower downslope • Slopes steeper than 10% pose rollover problems • Before mowing an untested slope for the first time, check it out with the blade off—if you can't handle the mower, find another way to cut it • If you find yourself putting your foot aground to stabilize the mower, the slope is too steep to safely mow • Avoid sharp turns on slopes—when turning, disengage the blades first • Skip the grass catcher on slopes and rough terrain—it can unbalance your center of gravity • With a walk-behind mower, mow across the slope rather than up and down—that way if you slip, your legs won't end up under the deck

Figure 11.4. *Accurate diagnosis* is at the cornerstone of lowering your maintenance. Here are three common turf problems that look a lot alike, but require radically different remedies: Mower scalp (top) is easily mistaken for other ailments, such as leafspot disease (center) or drought (bottom). Quick, precise diagnosis of look-alike ailments like these can save you an unneeded pesticide application or irrigation cycle.

grasses become puffy or stemmy when mowed above their ideal height.

- *Most low maintenance grasses cannot tolerate frequent, close cutting*—They thin out and die if kept too short or mowed too often.
- *Some low maintenance grasses are mowed mainly to keep their protruding seedheads in check*—Sheep fescue, alpine bluegrass, zoysia, centipedegrass, and bahiagrass, for example. These short-growing grasses could remain unmowed forever, were it not for their untidy seedstalks.
- *Shaded turf benefits from a higher mowing height.*
- *Mowing turf too low probably ruins more lawns than any other maintenance practice* (Augustin, n.d.).

THE ONE-THIRD RULE OF MOWING

It's been said that in turfgrass management, there are probably 10 ways to do just about anything—and 8 of those ways will turn out just fine. In turfgrass culture there are very few "right ways" and "wrong ways" to do most things. There's not much that's black and white.

That's why **the one-third rule** comes as such as jolt. One of the first and only absolutes a newcomer to turf care learns is: *Never remove more than one-third of the grass leaf when mowing*. Removing more than one-third reportedly has all sorts of negative ramifications. You'll find the one-third rule listed boldly in nearly every turf textbook and extension fact sheet.

In a discipline like turf management that deals in shades of gray, an absolute like the one-third rule seems strangely out of place. For example, you can fertilize tomorrow rather than today and not much happens. You can water your turf with a super high tech sprinkler or with a watering can, and it doesn't know the difference. But you violate the one-third rule of mowing and....

And what? What happens if you violate the one-third rule?

Let's say you take a long three-day weekend only to come back and discover your 2-in. ryegrass is now 4-in. tall. Horrors! Mowing it back down to 2 in. would mean removing *one-*

half of the leaf surface, directly violating the one-third rule. What will become of the turf?

You probably already know the answer. You know what happens because you've already done that before, haven't you? The answer is: Nothing happens. The turf goes on growing as always. True, you might have trouble with clippings clogging the mower. But the grass itself quickly bounces back.

The scoop on the one-third rule. To tell you the truth, the one-third rule is actually more like a **one-third suggested guideline**. There's nothing absolute about it. And if you knew where the one-third rule originated, you'd probably snicker and wonder why everyone's been taking it so seriously all these years.

The one-third rule was born in a small greenhouse nearly 50 years ago in a study done by a U.S. Department of Agriculture soil scientist. The scientist used narrow wooden boxes with glass fronts to observe the growth of grass roots. The trial was aimed more at cattle defoliation than turf mowing. The grass was common pasture-type Kentucky bluegrass that was allowed to grow tall before the scientist hacked it back down to observed the root's response.

No, the affected grass plants didn't die when more than one-third of its leaves were cut. Even the roots didn't die. They just paused their growth for a time until more foliage was regenerated. Then they resumed their growth.

Over the years this simple study has been blown out of proportion: "Cut too much leaf surface and your grass will die." Nothing could be further from the truth.

Research reveals the truth. Joe DiPaola and his colleagues at North Carolina State University (Shepard et al., 1989) in 1986 repeated the defoliation study run years earlier by the USDA scientist. Instead this time, they conducted the trial in the field under natural growing conditions, rather than in cramped greenhouse boxes.

DiPaola selected 3 in. (7.6 cm) as the base mowing height for high maintenance tall fescue and 6 in. (15 cm) as his base for low maintenance fescue. Then he allowed the grass to grow 30, 50, 100, or 300% taller than the base height before mowing it back down. The 50% defoliation treatment fell smack on the maximum guideline of the one-third rule—higher percentages violated the rule by progressive amounts.

DiPaola found no significant negative effects of defoliation up to 100%. In other words, a fescue stand maintained at 3 in. could be grown to 6 in. tall before mowing, without serious consequences.

Beyond 100% defoliation, he started to see damage to the stand: "Stand reductions exceeded 20% when the turf was allowed to reach a height of 200 to 300% greater than the base cutting height before mowing." In other words, about 1 in every 5 grass shoots was killed by the mowing treatment.

Taller turf has a naturally lower plant density than close-cut turf, with fewer individual plants per square foot. By letting turf grow taller between cuttings, DiPaola was allowing it to revert to a naturally lower shoot density. That alone explains away some of the density reductions he observed in the taller turf.

Another drawback of letting your turf grow too tall is clippings. Piles of clippings can have an impact on turf quality. By whacking away too much foliage at one time, the quantity of clippings becomes immense. And unless they're removed, clippings can shade and smother the plants, thinning the stand.

Benefits of violating the one-third rule. With low maintenance turf, violating the one-third rule may not just be *acceptable*, at times it may even be *beneficial*. Letting grass grow taller between mowings is a bona fide way of throttling back growth.

Ken Diesburg, researcher at Southern Illinois University, chaired a regional mowing committee that studied the effect of clipping on low maintenance turfgrass (Diesburg, 1992). In the study's summary he wrote: "It is commonly stated that no more than one-third of the total canopy height should be removed in any single mowing to optimize turfgrass health. In reality, a good deal more than one-half the canopy height is often removed in low maintenance turf, usually after long periods between mowing. In fact, a little damage to the turf is sometimes preferred in order to slow down turfgrass growth rate, especially during the vigorous growth period during spring."

A replacement for the one-third rule. So what can we use in place of the one-third rule? What general guideline can be employed to govern mowing frequency?

How about **the plugged-up mower rule**: "If your mower plugs up when you're mowing, you let it grow too tall." This guideline makes more sense for the turf caretaker who's battling practical limitations of budget, equipment, labor, and weather. This guideline also allows added flexibility for managing low maintenance turf.

MOWING DIFFERENCES AMONG GRASS SPECIES

"While high maintenance is often necessary on sports turf and highly visible residential, commercial and industrial lawns, there are many other sites that could require as much as 50% less mowing if proper species and cultivars were established."

—James Willmott, Cornell University (NY)
Cooperative Extension Service
(Hummel, 1993)

Mowing the traditional turf species

One potential avenue of savings people seldom explore when it comes to mowing is switching grasses. A lower or slower growing grass may demand less mowing than a taller growing one.

Yes, switching grasses seems like a radical approach for a minor annoyance like mowing. And yes, the conversion process will be initially expensive. But like upgrading to a larger mower, the switch to a lower growing grass can pay for itself over time. The money you save from fewer mowings will help pay for the added investment.

But changing grasses is a good idea only if the savings are real. It's easy to be misled by flashy sales claims. It's important to ask yourself: Is there that much difference between grasses in the amount of clippings they generate to justify conversion?

Mowing studies. Results from a study by James Willmott of the Cooperative Extension Service in Monroe County, New York (Hummel, 1993), suggest that the conversion may indeed be worth the trouble. Willmott established a lawn trial in search of reduced mowing answers. He solicited low maintenance grass mixtures from several seed outlets across the state, looking for grasses specifically targeted at reduced mowing. Willmott grew the grasses like a lawn and tallied the clippings each produced over a growing season. He then plugged the totals into some cost-analysis formulas.

Shortly after planting it became clear to him that mixes containing ryegrass had very fast growth rates and required a lot of mowing. Tall fescues were also prolific producers of top-growth—even the so-called "dwarf" tall fescue varieties. Mixes containing ryegrass or tall fescue generated 90 to 270% more clippings than slower growing grasses (Table 11.3). That's nearly a *3-fold difference* in clippings, simply by choosing the right grass.

Plugging these findings into his economic equations, Willmott showed that a large turf facility could reap huge savings simply by switching grasses. The savings were compounded when he factored in the reduced fertilizer rates demanded by these same grasses.

"If mixes with the highest [mowing] frequency cost $150 per acre, the lowest would have cost about $50. Combined with a need for only about one-third of the fertilizer, the total savings would be about $120 per acre. If you were managing 100 acres, the total savings would add up to $12,000 a season," he says.

Willmott found that mixes containing Kentucky bluegrass or fine fescue produced the fewest overall clippings. Tall fescue and perennial ryegrass mixtures produced the most. Of course, substituting bluegrass or fine fescue for every turf situation would not be practical. There are sites where the wearability or drought tolerance of tall fescue or ryegrass would be more important than the additional mowing.

Listed below are findings from other research studies on mowing reduction that demonstrate clipping yield differences among the traditional turf species:

- It's been known for a long time that strong creeping red fescue produces far fewer clippings than Kentucky blue-

Table 11.3. Lawn mixtures differ widely in the amount of clippings they produce. These lawn mixtures, sold in New York State, are promoted as having reduced mowing requirement. Researchers at Cornell University (Hummel, 1993) found that mixtures containing perennial ryegrass produced the most clippings, tall fescue was intermediate, and Kentucky bluegrasses and fine fescues were low.

Mixture Trade Name	Perennial Ryegrass	Kentucky Bluegrass	Tall Fescue	Sheep Fescue	Chewings Fescue	Hard Fescue	Strong Creeping	Clippings lbs/A
Agriturf Safelawn/Crusader	SR4200 49.19%				SR5000 24.88%	SR3000 24.51%		332
Lesco Compact Dwarf Tall Fescue Blend			Trailblazer 39.82% Trailblazer II 29.93% Shortstop 29.85%					298
Agriturf Far Rough	Champion 19.81%	Touchdown 9.87%		Bighorn 29.26%		SR3000 39.59%		281
Pennington Drought Tolerant Bluegrass		Newport 43% KenBlue 43% Huntsville 9%						268
Agway-Prolawn Monroe County Low Maintenance Mix	Manhattan II 14.80%	Merit 14.85%			Koket 19.61%	Spartan 24.64% Aurora 24.44%		219
Scott's Perfect Choice For Shade		Bristol 15% Coventry 15%			Banner 30%	Brigade 40%		158
Lesco Fine Fescue Links Blend				9.77%	Shadow 19.79%	Spartan 29.76%	Shademaster 39.64%	147
Loft's Ecosystems Ecology Mix					Jamestown 19.60%	Crystal 39.20% Reliant 39.20%		87

grass. The late Bill Daniel in his turfgrass Ph.D. dissertation of 1950 discovered that red fescue produces 11,682 lb of clippings for every 16,244 lb produced by bluegrass—about 30% less (Daniel, 1950).

- A recent study in England showed that certain *varieties* of Kentucky bluegrass produce *more* clippings than even perennial ryegrass. "Unique," "Haga," and "Star" Kentucky bluegrasses each generated over 500 total millimeters of accumulated clipping length (20 in.) per year compared to 423 mm (16 in.) for two, low-growing European perennial ryegrasses (Newell et al., 1995). One ryegrass variety, "Elka," yielded the fewest clippings—only 329 accumulated mm (13 in.).
- Common-type varieties can be expected to produce *more* clippings than elite cultivars. This is a noteworthy paradox, because common varieties are often targeted by seed sellers at the low maintenance end of the market. In a Rhode Island study, Haibo Liu (Liu et al., 1996) found big differences in clipping yield between common and elite varieties. "Kenblue," a common Kentucky bluegrass variety, produced 70% more clippings than elite "Blacksburg." "Linn," a common perennial ryegrass, produced 50% more clippings than "Tara," "KY-31," a common tall fescue, produced 13% more clippings than "Apache."
- An 11-week study of cumulative mowing at Turf Seed, Inc., Hubbard, Oregon, found that elite cultivars of tall fescue produced half the clippings as common. KY-31 yielded 16,478 lb of clippings per acre, versus 8,264 lb for "Silverado," a lower growing cultivar. The same trend was noted in the perennial ryegrasses, with elite varieties yielding about 1/3 fewer clippings than others.
- Among the warm-season grasses, data are more scarce. One Florida study found that mowing St. Augustinegrass required about half as much horsepower as mowing bermudagrass or bahiagrass (Fluck and Busey, 1988).

Mowing the unconventional turf species

For the most part, the unconventional turfgrasses all suffer from one common malady: Topgrowth. There are exceptions, as I'll explain below. But in general, you can plan to mow an unconventional turf as often as or even *more often* than an equivalent traditional turfgrass. It's one of those trade-offs you make to gain other benefits, such as drought tolerance.

Many of the unconventional grasses are bunch grasses. Bunch grasses are noted for their proclivities in piling up foliage. On top of that, few unconventional species have been bred for improved low growth. One of the first things a turf breeder does to refine a grass is to make it less growthy. Shorter plants and slower growth translates directly into a more attractive lawn.

Mowing research. Here's a typical example of the growthiness of some of the unconventional grasses: In the British study (Newell et al., 1995) mentioned above—the study that compared the topgrowth inches of varieties—the researchers painstakingly found that tufted hairgrass, an unconventional low maintenance grass, produced *twice* the length of clippings as "Fortuna" Kentucky bluegrass. That would mean you'd have to mow your tufted hairgrass lawn twice as often. That's a lot of extra mowing.

Unlike the traditional turfgrasses that get denser when mowed, the unconventional grasses are often thinned or killed by close, frequent mowing. Grass researcher Jerry Jung and his associates at Penn State University's Pasture Lab (Jung et al., 1974) observed this phenomenon firsthand on several grasses they tested. In a low maintenance mowing trial, they found that Kentucky bluegrass and tall fescue *improved* in quality when mowed more often. Stand density improved as mowing frequency increased from three to eight cuts per year. Orchardgrass and timothy also responded to mowing, with better persistence on plots mowed more often. Reed canarygrass and smooth bromegrass, on the other hand, survived best when mowed *less* often. The more they were cut, the less they per-

Table 11.4. Tips for reducing your mowing and stretching your maintenance dollar.

Back off on the nitrogen fertilizer...	• Nitrogen is the prime nutrient that *causes* clippings. More N equals more mowing–it's as simple as that. In one New York study, the quantity of clippings more than doubled when nitrogen fertility of Kentucky bluegrass went from zero to 1 lb N per 1000 ft^2 (5 g/m^2). Clippings piled up even faster with creeping bentgrass, increasing 138% with 2 lb N, 666% with 4 lb N, and 866% with 6 lb N per 1000 ft^2, versus unfertilized turf (Petrovic et al., 1994). That's an increase of almost *nine times.* • Turf that receives little traffic needs less fertilizer. You can fertilizer out-of-play areas about half as much as high-wear areas. Less fertilizer will mean less mowing in these areas (see Chapter 9 for more mowing tips). • Want better color but not the clippings that go with it? Try fertilizing with iron instead of conventional N-P-K fertilizer. Iron—available as iron sulfate or chelated iron—turns the grass darker green without speeding up growth. Iron applications also have the side benefit of weed control. In one study, monthly applications of iron sulfate showed no adverse effects to the turf but reduced dandelion, clover, slender speedwell, and lawn daisy from 20% down to a trace (Kavanagh et al., 1982).
Adjust your fertilizer type...	• Slow-release nitrogen fertilizers generally produce fewer clippings than an equal dose of fast-release product. Grass receives timed feeding from slow-release fertilizer, rather than one large burst (Heckman et al., 1994; Toews et al., 1996; Hull et al., 1993). • Natural organic products may be easier on the clippings than their synthetic counterparts. In an Alberta, Canada, study using equal rates of nitrogen, Milorganite (a natural organic product made from sewage sludge) induced 506 grams of total clippings per plot over a growing season, compared to 1945 grams for Nutralene (Toews et al., 1996). The difference may be traced in part to the slower nutrient discharge of natural organics; they sometimes require more than a year for full availability.
Mow at the right time...	• Mowing when turf is too wet can lead to clumping and a generally bad trim job. Mowers work best when grass is dry. • Avoid mid-afternoon mowing when turf is under heat or moisture stress. On hot summer afternoons, turf may be wilted. Mowing will disfigure or even kill stressed grass. • Early morning mowing is a proven disease-fighting weapon. Morning mowing strips away dew and helps stop the spread of fungus. It's been shown to reduce dollar spot disease (Williams et al., 1996). • Early morning mowing is a bad idea when the turf is frosty. Frosted blades crack off like icicles, causing damaged brown streaks where wheels or feet tread. • Choosing *when* to apply fertilizer may be even more important than the *amount* you apply, in terms of stimulating clippings. As part of his master's thesis, U.S. Golf Association Green Section Director Jim Snow found a big difference between spring and fall application: "Fertilizer treatments during the spring months produced a large increase in dry weight shoot production. During the fall months there was little or no increase in production" (1976). His research was on Kentucky bluegrass turf in New York state.
Mowing myths...	• Recycling clippings does not lead to thatch buildup. Several studies have shown *no effect* of clipping return on thatch buildup. One study revealed a modest 3% increase in thatch from clipping recycling (Soper et al., 1988), but attributed the increase to the added nutrients that grasscycling returns to the turf. • Collecting clippings doesn't reduce disease. A Kentucky study found that removing bentgrass clippings did not diminish dollar spot disease (Williams et

al., 1996). A Rhode Island study even showed *increased* dollar spot and leaf spot disease where clipping were removed versus where they were returned (Ruemmele et al., 1993). And a Texas study found fewer–not more–disease spores where clippings were returned. "We counted fewer *Bipolaris* and *Dreschslera* spores in bermudagrass mowed weekly with the mulching mower. We suspect that the mulched clippings were rapidly broken down by decay organisms. This rapid decay may have been too fast for disease populations to build up," says project leader, Phil Colbaugh (1990).

- Closer cutting does not necessarily make turf more disease prone. Over the years, golf superintendents have noted pythium disease occurring first on higher-cut aprons of greens long before it hits the green itself. Brown patch was once though to be a disease of close-cut turf. Recent results show differently. In the first year of a 2-year study in Kentucky, brown patch incidence was greater at a 4-in. (10 cm) cut than at 3/4 or 2 1/2 in. (1.9 or 6.3 cm). But in year 2, the reverse was true (Vincelli et al., 1995). These findings suggest that environmental factors may play more of a role than cutting height in disease development.
- Turf does not require spring scalping. In some areas of the country, homeowners and turf managers ritualistically scalp their lawns each spring. This labor-intensive operation generates bushels of unnecessary yard waste. Although spring scalping may offer a slight advantage to warm-season lawns, making them green up a week earlier, the slight advantage does not outweight the drawbacks. Cool-season grasses can even be injured by spring scalping. In Idaho, I tried scalping a perennial ryegrass turf in March, only to have a late cold snap freeze out the stressed turf.

Get the height right...

- Data from Jim Beard (1995b) at the International Sports Turf Institute, reveal a near straight-line relationship between mowing height and root weight. Root weight was cut in half with every halving of the cutting height. "Under nonirrigated conditions or where your capability to irrigate is unreliable, you should strive for a deep extensive root system capable of drawing moisture from as great a portion of the soil as possible. The best way to do this is to elevate the mowing height," Beard advises.
- Changing cutting heights during the growing season may actually have a beneficial effect on turf. Some turf managers raise their cutting height as turf enters a period of stress. Although certain researchers disagree, one study in New York (Baikan et al., 1992) found that turf resized from 1 to 3 in. or from 3 to 1 in. had better quality and used less water than turf maintained unchanged at either 1 or 3 in. (2.5 or 7.5 cm).
- Raising the mowing height before the onset of winter has been shown to add insulation to warm-season turf. The extra foliage helps buffer the sensitive grass crowns against harsh winter temperatures (Brunneau et al., 1990).
- Higher-cut turf produces fewer overall clippings than close-cut turf. University of Georgia researcher, Robert Burns (1976), found that tall fescue maintained at 1/2 or 1 in. (1.3 or 2.5 cm) produced more total clippings than fescue maintained at 1 1/2 or 2 in. (4 or 5 cm). The effect persisted for only the first year of a 4-year experiment, however. Thereafter, clipping quantities were similar.
- It's sad to say that many homeowners never readjust the height of their mowers from the original factory setting. And often, the factory height is set too high or too low for the grass being cut.

Do your environmental bit...

- Follow the manufacturer's guidelines for periodic maintenance: Tune-ups, replacing filters, changing oil, using the right gas-oil mix, and scraping clippings from underneath the deck help a mower run cleaner.
- Avoid gasoline spills when fueling equipment. Spilled gasoline is a major cause of hydrocarbon air pollution. A funnel or spout with an auto-stop can prevent overfilling a gas tank.

Table 11.4. Tips for reducing your mowing and stretching your maintenance dollar (continued).

Do your environmental bit... (continued)	• Many mowers have an air-relief valve on the gas tank's cap that can fail over time, sprinkling gasoline down the side of the mower as it bounces over terrain. Replace faulty caps immediately, and avoid fueling the mower's tank all the way to the brim. • Retire and recycle old equipment. Modern mowers and trimmers are fitted with air-pollution devices like those on cars, for cleaner burning. • Mowing grass that's wet, heavily fertilized, or too tall causes excessive gasoline consumption (Fluck et al., 1988). • Keeping the mower blade sharp can help save fuel. Studies in Nebraska show that a mower with a sharp blade requires 22% less gasoline than one with a dull blade (Bruneau et al., 1990). • On the positive side, a survey by Landscape Management magazine (Roche, 1995) indicates that turf managers are receptive to doing their environmental role for responsible mowing. Eighty-one percent of golf course superintendents polled said they would pay an additional 10% in purchase price for a quieter, lower-polluting mower.
Don't bag it...	• Mowing turf with a recycling mower turns it darker green than when mowed with a bagger. A New Jersey study showed a 17 to 26% color benefit from recycling (Keckman et al., 1994). The greatest gains in color were on leaner, less fertilized turfs. • Dry grass clippings have the same nutrient value as a 4-1-3 organic fertilizer. They release their nutrients slowly, just like a slow-release turf fertilizer (Bruneau et al., 1990). • Clipping recycling seems to aid in moisture conservation, particularly in lower maintenance turf. Researchers at Colorado State University (Wilhelm et al., 1993) found that under low water conditions, clipping return reduced plant stress. Under wetter conditions, though, it had no effect. The scientists speculate that returned clippings may act like a water-conserving mulch. • In a Connecticut study, earthworm counts were greater where clippings were returned (Dest, 1992). Water infiltration was also improved in clippings-returned plots compared to clippings-removed plots. • Grasscycling appears to be a natural method of weed control. In one California lawn study, turf mowed with a recycling mower had 43 to 74% fewer dandelions than turf clipped with a traditional bagger (Harivandi et al., 1996). Bear in mind, though, that recycling may also recycle weed seed back into the turf. If weeds are setting seed, a bag mower collects and discards them, while a recycling mower redeposits them. • Modern recycling mowers more efficiently purée clipping than their earlier predecessors. If you haven't tried a recycling mower lately, they deserve a second look.
Give your grass a sedative...	• Plant growth regulators (PGRs) work like Valium for your turf. PGRs counteract the hormones responsible for leaf elongation. In addition to reduced mowing, PGRs have other desirable benefits: • Turf soil in a Rhode Island study (Pennucci, 1986) was 4 to 8% more moist where PGRs had been applied. The effect lasted for 5 weeks with mefluidide—even longer with paclobutrazol and flurprimidol. Researchers speculated the effect was caused by PGRs slowing the grass's growth and water consumption. • Many PGRs are also powerful seedhead inhibitors. Grass seedheads can be even taller and more objectionable than the leaves. Eliminating seedheads may reduce or even eliminate the need for mowing of low maintenance areas, such as roadside rights-of-way.

Save time while you trim...

- Toro's Mow & Feed® mower eliminates one time-consuming step toward a beautiful, green lawn. This unique mower has a piggyback granular fertilizer spreader, to fertilize and mow in one pass. According to company literature, "Toro's exclusive AccuFeed® system and infinite flow rate adjustment apply just the right amount of fertilizer to your lawn precisely where you mow."
- Save time by applying PGRs as you mow: Doug Montgomery, Oklahoma State University extension assistant, experimented with injecting PGRs directly into the deck of an operating mower (Lucas et al., 1986). The idea was to mow the turf, all the while treating it with PGR so it didn't need to be mowed again so soon. The injection system actually worked, as long as a recycling mower was used. A side-discharge mower tended to blow the PGR out the shoot and into the operator's face.
- Ideally, turf should be mowed often enough that clipping piles never form. But with low maintenance turf, piles are bound to happen. Clipping piles can be damaging to turf if allowed to remain, eventually bleaching or smothering the grass underneath. Clipping piles form from mowing grass that's too wet or too tall, or mowing with too fast a ground speed. Sometimes a second mow of the area will help disperse the piles. Blowers, vacuums, and rakes can be used to physically remove them. Some turf managers drag a hose between two trucksters to disperse piles. Golf superintendents use a fiberglass whip or a quick syringe cycle of irrigation to clear piles left on putting surfaces.

Mowing new lawns...

- Don't wait too long to begin mowing newly planted turf. Ideally, new turf should be cut shortly after its blades exceed the intended mowing height. However, in practice, this is not always possible. The seedbed must firm up enough to support the weight of the mower and operator. Mowing when the ground is too soft will rut and ruin a new stand.
- Frequent mowing during grow-in signals the grass to begin its horizontal growth (i.e., filling in) rather than vertical growth (clippings). The grass picks up on these physiological clues.
- Mowing is a great, natural control for weeds. Many of the weeds that sprout along with a new lawn can be chopped off and destroyed without pesticides. The trick is to let them elongate a few inches taller than the turf. Then, hack them down with mowing. Many never recover.

Don't be a speed demon...

- Riding mowers today offer the option of separate controls for ground speed and blade RPMs. It's possible to keep blade RPM's constant while varying travel speed according to conditions. Wetter or taller grass cuts best with a slower ground speed but a constant blade.
- Close-cut turf should be mowed slower than higher-cut turf. Hold the blade RPMs constant while you adjust the travel speed downward. Consult the mower's service manual for options.

Advanced mower technology...?

- Poulan/Weed Eater has introduced a solar-powered mowing robot (Anonymous, 1994a). The $2000 lawn robot, which looks more like a garbage can lid than a mower, is powered by photovoltaic cells spread across its back. It meanders freely across a lawn, limited by a thin wire buried around the lawn's perimeter. The unit snips the grass using three, 1-inch, triangular steel blades. An alarm sounds if someone absconds with your $2000 investment.
- *Popular Science* magazine popularized a curious mowing variation in one of its 1960s editions: Lawn mowing without an operator. A self-propelled rotary mower was tethered to a stake hammered into the center of a lawn. As the mower traveled unattended, the tether would wind around the stake, directing the mower on an inward spiral—all while the homeowner sipped iced tea on the patio. I've tried this trick, and while it works well if the grass is not too tall or wet, a watchful eye is needed in case the stake gives way or the mower strays.

sisted. Low maintenance prairiegrasses like big bluestem, indiangrass, and switchgrass, never persisted beyond the first season of frequent mowing.

When shopping through the catalog of unconventional grasses in the Appendix, pay attention to the **natural height** of grasses. Taller mature heights indicate faster vertical growth, more clippings, and the tendency for injury from mowing. Grasses with a natural height of 2 ft (60 cm) or less have the slowest growth rate, least clippings, and the best chance of surviving turf conditions.

GRASSCYCLING:

"Don't haul off those clippings–return them to the turf!"

I can recall my usual summer job in high school: mowing neighbors' yards for spending money. They all wanted me to use a grass catcher when I mowed, which I abhorred because it caused me significant mental distress walking back and forth to the clipping pile:

ME: "Why do I have to pick up these clippings? Can't I just leave them lay?"

CUSTOMER: "No, they make the yard look ugly."

ME: "No they don't."

CUSTOMER: "Yes they do."

Of course, it's clear to see why I didn't end up with a career in the lawn care industry.

But today, scientific research is vindicating my teenage impulses in the realm of clipping removal. Clipping removal is no longer in vogue.

Grasscycling is a clever name for simply returning clippings to the turf, rather than hauling them away to the dump. As it turns out, clipping recycling is not only beneficial to the environment, it is also good for the turf (as I'll explain in the following section).

Yard trash comprises 20% of the municipal waste deposited in landfills, soaring to an incredible 50% in summer (Colbaugh, 1990). Domestic yard waste contains an estimated 40% grass clippings, according to the Waste Management Division of the Michigan Department of Natural Resources (Gilstrap, 1995). The remainder is tree leaves (40%) and brush (20%). In Plano, Texas, a town of 80,000 population, over 700 tons of grass clippings are disposed of in landfills each week (Landschoot, 1991).

As a result, landfills are filling at a record pace, prompting legislators to ban yard waste entirely from some public landfills. To date, 10 states and the District of Columbia have joined the bandwagon, enacting laws that restrict yard waste from landfills. Eight other states have bans ready to go into effect. Twenty-four states have established reduced yard waste goals, and seven others have significant voluntary recycling programs. Only Alaska has yet to mount a yard waste recycling effort (Welterlen, 1992).

Bonuses from grasscycling

Aiding your local landfill is not the only benefit of grasscycling, although this alone would certainly justify its use. Grasscycling also offers:

- Less work
- Better turf quality (Haley et al., 1985)
- Reduced reliance on fertilizer (Heckman and Hill, 1993; Landschoot, 1991)
- And it even remedies certain turf diseases (Ruemmele and Jackson, 1993).

Less work. Catching, bagging, and hauling clippings takes a lot of extra effort compared with just letting them lay. I discovered that myself as a teenage lawn boy. By some estimates, mowing time is cut by 38% with grasscycling, compared with bagging (Roche, 1994). One Florida study recorded a 50% reduction in mowing time and a 50% reduction in fuel consumption from grasscycling (Rodier, 1994). Along with less work, there is also less expense involved in traveling back and forth to the landfill, less equipment wear and tear—particularly on the bag side of the mower—and of course, no landfill tipping fees.

In a study of 147 homeowners in Fort Worth, Texas (Marting, 1991), who were asked to convert from catching to recycling clippings, initially the homeowners found themselves mowing more often. Their frequency of mowing jumped from 4.1 to 5.4 mows per month as they tried to compensate for the added clippings on their lawns. But because they weren't bagging, their

Grasscycling: Questions and Answers

Q: Are recycling mowers more expensive?
A: Yes. Larger engines, refined decks, and multiple blades add to cost. Entry level homeowner units by Toro, Honda, Snapper, and John Deere are typically priced between $400 and $600—slightly more than what you'd pay for an equivalent conventional mower (Anonymous, 1991b).

Q: Are kits for converting a conventional mower to a recycling mower worth the expense?
A: *Consumer Reports* magazine evaluated several popular recycling mowers, and conventional mowers fitted with recycling conversion kits (Anonymous, 1991b). They concluded that the mowers designed specifically for grasscycling produced the better cut. The retrofit kits tended to clump and clog.

Q: With recycling mowers, do you have to mow more often?
A: Not necessarily (Roche, 1994). Modern recycling units provide an adequate trim job even on high grass. Older units did not.

Q: Do you have to fertilize differently with grasscycling?
A: Yes. If you've been hauling away clippings in the past, you can expect to fertilize about half. Grasscycling returns nutrients to the soil (see text).

Q: Can you mow when the grass is wet?
A: Newer higher powered recycling mowers do an admirable job under wet conditions. But if given the choice, you're still better off waiting until things dry out.

Q: Do recycling mowers travel slower than regular mowers?
A: Generally, yes (Rodier, 1994).

Q: Does grasscycling cause thatch?
A: Research studies have concluded that grasscycling causes no additional thatch buildup, or at most promotes a millimeter-sized increase (Welterlen, 1992). Clippings contain 90% water. After the water evaporates, the remaining solid tissue breaks down quickly into a desirable slow-release fertilizer. Recycling mowers have been shown to produce *less* thatch than an equivalent side-discharge mower with clippings returned (Haley et al., 1985).

Q: Do recycling mowers contribute to weeds?
A: In theory, yes. In practice, probably not. Technically, any mower that returns the clippings to the turf will also recycle any weed seeds that happen to be there. Weed seed are returned to the turf rather than being carted away. But because a recycling mower

Figure 11.5. When you catch and cart away clippings, you're throwing away a valuable source of organic plant nutrients. Once dry, clippings have a fertilizer value equal in potency to many natural organic fertilizers. Studies have shown that you can cut your fertilization rate in half just by recycling clippings back into the turf, instead of carting them away.

returns nutrient-rich clippings—a valuable source of free fertilizer—the turf tends to be denser and exclude weeds better. Bill Hagan, grasscycling researcher at the University of California (Cline, 1993a) reports: "We planted weed seeds four different times since the research began a year ago, and as yet have had absolutely no infestation of weeds in the grasscycling plots."

Q: Do recycling mowers cause disease problems?
A: A Texas A&M study says no (Colbaugh, 1990). In fact, recycling may even cut down on diseases (Ruemmele and Jackson, 1993).

Q: Do grass clippings damage a lawn?
A: Only if they lay in piles. Clippings finely chopped and evenly dispersed cause no noticeable damage (Marting, 1991; Soper et al., 1988).

Q: Are there any other benefits to clipping recycling?
A: Better water infiltration, more earthworms, reduced erosion (Dest, 1992)—to name a few.

time spent on *each mowing* dropped by 35 minutes. After six months of grasscycling, the homeowners had cut their yard work by an average of seven hours.

Free fertilizer. About half of the fertilizer applied to turf winds up in the clippings (Brauen et al., 1994; Snow, 1976; Wilhelm and Koski, 1993). No, I'm not talking about fertilizer pellets that occasionally get vacuumed up with the clippings. Fifty percent of the applied fertilizer elements are contained *inside* the tissue of clippings, as part of the grass leaf itself.

According to a 3-year study at Penn State University, 46 to 59% of the nitrogen applied to turf eventually ends up in the tissue of clippings (Landschoot, 1991). Other researchers have found even higher values. Thus, grasscycling represents a valuable source of *free fertilizer* (Figure 11.5). On a dry weight basis, clippings contain the equivalent fertilizer value equal to many natural organic fertilizers. Returning clippings—rather than hauling them off—recycles nutrients back to the soil. The recycled clippings break down slowly, releasing their nutrient elements back over time.

Grasscycling even works on *unfertilized* turf. A New Jersey study showed that unfertilized turf mowed with a recycling mower had a darker green color than turf with clippings removed. The darker green color was equivalent to a shot of 2 lb N per 1000 ft^2 fertilizer (10 g/m^2) (Heckman et al., 1994). Still more benefits of grasscycling are cataloged in Table 11.4.

Innovation in recycling mowers

Early recycling mowers a flop. The **recycling mower** (also called a **mulching mower**) first dawned on the consumer market in the 1970s, in response to landscape environmental concerns. Initially, mowing manufacturers were reluctant to jump into the recycling concept with both feet, not knowing whether it was a trend or a passing fad. As a result, they sold conversion kits for do-it-yourselfers to modify existing units into a recycling mower. These kits worked by sealing off the mower's discharge shoot, trapping the clippings inside rather than spewing them into a bag (Anonymous, 1991b). Some manufacturers still offer these conversion kits even today.

Early recycling mowers proved disappointing, because no provision was made for managing the airflow, chopping and rechopping the clippings, and distributing them back into the grass. Cut was uneven at best. And with heavy, wet grass, the mower would simply clog and stall.

Modern changes. By the twilight of the 1980s, manufacturers realized that grasscycling was not a passing craze, and they began building mowers designed specifically for grasscycling.

A recycling mower requires slightly more horsepower than a traditional mower. It takes more power to cut the grass not once, but repeatedly into tiny, easily dispersed segments. Traditional baggers use less energy because they cut grass once and simply toss it aside.

Faster blade speed is another innovation that made recycling mowers possible. The blade tips of most recycling mowers are twirling at an incredible 19,000 ft-per-second or 215 mph (350 kph). This speed is at the safety speed limit imposed by the American National Standards Institute (Nesbitt, 1994). Higher speeds, while beneficial to grasscycling, become increasingly risky to the operator.

The third innovation in modern recycling mower design was improvements in the deck. Baffles and special curved or angled blades direct the air flow to keep clippings buoyant in air until they are chopped fine enough to filter back into the turf.

A recent modification to recycling mowers is the use of multiple blades. Some high-end recycling mowers sport two—even three—whirling blades, all on the same shaft. Simpler models have a single Z-shaped blade, with dual high and low cutting surfaces. Of course, with more blades comes more sharpening and maintenance. Dull blades pulp the grass, sending it out in clumps. A finely honed blade pulverizes the grass into crumb-size bites.

The Toro Recycler® mower uses deflectors to guide clippings back to the blades for a second cutting. The Bolens mulching mower uses a two-step cutting blade, with a shorter blade down low and a longer blade above. The Bunton Eliminator® employs three distinct mowing chambers with six-edged fanlike blades. Is that high tech or what?

With all of these refinements in recycling mower technology, the question becomes: Why would anyone buy anything *other* than a recycling mower? Conventional bagging mowers are still cheaper than recycling mowers. But they offer few other advantages. Recycling mowers, with reduced labor costs, no disposal fees, and half the fertilizer requirement, are now poised to become the mowing standard of the turfgrass industry.

GROWTH REGULATION

PGRs have a slow beginning

Plant growth regulators (PGRs) got off to the same slow start as did recycling mowers. PGRs are chemical compounds that retard the growth of grass, resulting in less need for mowing. They regulate the growth of turf by counteracting one or more of the plant's natural growth substances.

PGRs were first conceived almost 50 years ago as a way to reduce turf mowing (Rossi, 1994). Just think of it: Spray your lawn with PGR and you won't have to mow it for the rest of the season. The concept sounded almost too good to be true.

Early PGRs a flop. Of course, nothing cools a hot trend faster than lack of performance. Just as the early recycling mowers suffered from inadequate engineering and overambitious promotion, early PGRs also failed to live up to expectations.

"The problem with PGRs in the past is that they've been a little unpredictable," says Dennis Shepard, PGR specialist at Louisiana State University (Harlow, 1994). "They worked better in some years than others. The response depended on the plant's health and the stage of growth."

Early PGRs worked by stopping cells from dividing. It stood to reason, if cells couldn't divide, the grass couldn't grow taller. Later PGRs centered their attack on **cell elongation** rather than division.

But like many chemical remedies, early PGRs suffered from a myriad of side-effects. **Phytotoxicity** or leaf burn was one. Early PGR formulations were hard on the grass, leaving it scarred and discolored. But phytotoxicity wasn't *all* bad. For certain situations, stunted yellowish grass was still preferable to jungle turf. Over time, PGRs earned a following among people who used them to manage hard-to-mow areas, such as steep hillsides and ditches, where an occasional scar or blemish could be easily overlooked.

Other drawbacks of early PGRs included root retardation, a restricted number of acceptable grasses, high cost, a short working lifespan, unregulated weed growth, and a curious whiplash growth after the application wore off. After the effect of the growth regulator diminished, the grass grew even faster than before. Researchers speculated that this whiplash growth represented photosynthesis energy stockpiled during the PGRs coverage period.

Yet in spite of their failings, early PGRs had one redeeming feature that enamored many a turf practitioner: They suppressed seedheads. When applied at the correct stage of growth, these chemicals could suppress seedheads by as much as 90% (Watschke, 1994). This was no minor accomplishment. Unmowed grass can sometimes be tolerated along roadsides, riparian areas, and untrafficked sites as long as the bushy seedheads are gone. Once the unsightly seedheads were eliminated, mowing of many areas could skipped entirely.

Seedhead suppression even caught the fancy of golf course superintendents who used PGRs to manage annual bluegrass fairways and greens. The seeding tendency of *Poa annua* makes for untidy golf play. The grass looks unkempt and the pollen gets on shoes and clothing. As these superintendents found out, seedheads could be eliminated by a single timely application of PGR.

But timing was paramount. Apply the product too early or too late, and it was ineffective. And there was no guarantee that applying it on the exact same day next year would work as before. Subtle differences in spring weather played havoc. Applications were most effective if timed to coincide with certain **bioindicators**, such as the blooming of forsythia or dandelion (Banko and Stefani, 1988). One high-tech manufacturer even developed a computerized weather monitor that buzzes on the exact spring day when PGR has the best chance for suppressing seedheads.

Modern PGRs

Today's PGRs offer new innovative chemistries, with fewer of the side-effects that dogged older products (Figure 11.6). Improvements include:

- Little or no root inhibition
- Less whiplash regrowth after the PGR wears off
- Little or no phytotoxicity (leaf burn)
- A broader range of turfgrasses controlled, including the warm-season species
- A tendency to turn the grass bluer in color
- Improvements in turf quality, rather than decreases
- Suppression or even eradication of certain weeds
- More reliability—fewer unexpected results
- Overall better, longer growth suppression

Dual-purpose herbicide/PGRs. Some herbicides have the side-effect of slowing the growth of grasses. Chemical entrepreneurs, quick to pick up on this valuable side-effect, began promot-

Pointers for Using PGRs

- With PGRs, a *uniform* spray application is essential. PGRs are notoriously unforgiving of rate—too heavy and you may burn the turf; too low and there's no retardation (Kopec, 1996). The older products were more critical of rate than the newer ones.
- Be aware that different grass species may need different rates of application. One rate does not work for all. Warm-season grasses usually require a higher dose. Check the label before you spray.
- Some PGRs *must* be irrigated afterward to be activated. Others are denatured if they are rinsed off the leaves by irrigation or rainfall (Banko and Stefani, 1988;

Gaussoin, 1994a). Consult the label on whether to water or not.

- PGRs work best with cool-season grasses when applied just prior to the spring flush of growth. Over 65% of cool-season clippings are normally generated during this spring period (DiPaolo, 1987). Apply PGRs on warm-season grasses just prior to the big summer flush.
- After spraying, wait 3 to 4 days and give the turf a "trim" mowing. A light trimming keeps the grass noticeably neater and less ragged.
- Avoid using nitrogen fertilizer to counteract the effects of PGR discoloration. Nitrogen fertilizer fights the effect of the PGR. Instead, use iron fertilizer to green the turf during PGR treatment.
- PGRs pay for themselves on hard-to-mow areas: Along fence rows, ditch banks, busy roadways, steep or rocky terrain, and at the base of trees, signs, and light poles. PGRs are a salvation for cemetery managers, who use them to avoid tedious trimming operations around gravestones.
- Newer PGRs can be used to improve the appearance of turf. They tend to enhance the color and performance, above and beyond the advantages of less mowing.
- Modern PGRs are even coming near the goal of season-long control—provided, of course, that you administer a few strategic mowings: "You can get vegetative and seedhead suppression for 12 weeks with four or five timely mowings," says University of Georgia turf specialist, B.J. Johnson (Harlow, 1994). Johnson found a 60 to 65% reduction in mowing by applying Primo® at full rate, followed later by a half rate.

PGR Don'ts:

- Don't apply PGRs to dormant or damaged turf. They "freeze" a turf in whatever state it's in—good or bad.
- Don't apply to stressed turf: Heat, drought, or cold stress. PGRs weaken a grass's ability to withstand stress.
- Don't apply to turf that has an active disease or insect problem. Turf cannot respond offensively to pests when it's under the regulation of a PGR.
- Don't use PGRs on high traffic areas. Unless turf can grow, it can't recover from wear and tear.
- Don't scalp the turf before application.

Figure 11.6. **Plant Growth Regulator** (PGR) studies like this one at Oregon State University, have shown that PGRs can eliminate 2 to 4 mowings in a single spray. Modern PGRs regulate leaf growth without all the undesirable side-effects of their early predecessors. Some products even make the turf less stemmy and more attractive. Others reduce seedhead formation.

ing their products for dual purpose: Weed control and growth regulation. Manufacturers liked this idea because they could resurrect new applications for older products, rather than develop and register entirely new chemicals for use as PGRs. Turf managers liked the idea because they received weed control in addition to slower growing grass.

Dedicated PGRs. Today's PGRs are no longer just for low maintenance. They are rapidly gaining a place on elegant turf. "I use PGRs to make my grass look better. I'm not so much concerned with mowing reduction. But PGR makes my grass greener and less stemmy," says one superintendent, overheard at a recent golf course convention.

Gone is the overt sensitivity to weather. Gone is the erratic, unpredictable performance. Modern PGRs reduce grass growth without all of the negative side-effects of their predecessors.

Chapter 12

Trim Your Pesticide Budget

There's a trend starting among progressive turf managers: Managing turf with fewer pesticides. And it's easy to see why this trend is gaining momentum. Success stories like the one at Cornell University's golf course are helping to spread the word:

"We put out a simple demonstration a few years ago at the University golf course on their unirrigated *Poa* fairways. We did a total renovation and overseeded with a blend of three improved perennial ryes," says Norm Hummel, a soil scientist in private practice who served for several years as turf extension director for New York State (Brede, 1992b). Hummel knew that by switching to better adapted grasses, he could control pests naturally, and cut pesticide use in future years.

"The differences we saw were unbelievable," he says. "We saw virtually no disease damage at all on the fairways, except for a little bit of brown patch. The adjacent [nonrenovated] fairways were devastated with summer patch and everything else. The turf quality of the renovated fairways was superb. So the next year the superintendent renovated four more fairways."

CURING THE CAUSE, NOT THE SYMPTOMS

Achieving the goal of less chemicals involves a change in direction and thought from the see-it-and-spray-it philosophies of yesteryear. At the core of any successful pesticide reduction program are five important credos:

- Accurately diagnosing the pest, so that the right control measures can be brought to bear
- Seeking out all pest control options—biological, cultural, chemical—not just one
- Managing and tolerating pests at low levels, rather than trying to eradicate them
- Relying on a curative approach to chemicals, rather than repetitive, preventive sprays
- Using chemicals responsibly, to avoid side effects, pest resistance, and pesticide escape into the environment

Some possible nonchemical measures would include improvements in the soil, fertilizer, mowing, or irrigation to create a better growing environment for the grass plant and a hardship for the pest. A typical control program might entail turf renovation, to install newer, pest-resistant varieties in place of older, weaker ones, as Hummel demonstrated.

A more unorthodox approach might include **biological pest control** measures. Biological controls pit one organism against another. These are safe, environmentally benign measures ranging from endophytes to exotic spray-on antagonistic organisms.

Of course, one of the quickest ways to save chemicals is simply by switching from a preventive to a curative pest control philosophy. Admittedly this will take more legwork and training on your part, to accurately diagnose the pest and

First the Bad News

Before I sell you on the myriad benefits of reducing chemicals, I'm first going to *unsell* you on the idea. Let me cut to the chase: Anyone who's grown accustomed to the picture-perfect control of lawn pests from chemical pesticides is bound to find alternative control methods somewhat unsettling. Cultural and biological control measures offer—at best—perhaps 50 to 80% control of a target pest, rarely the 100% effectiveness we're accustomed to with pesticides. Every single insect or weed in the lawn will not be eliminated with these alternative procedures.

The second bit of bad news is that you will have to gain more knowledge, experience, and confidence than with old-fashioned preventive spray programs. Instead of spraying when the calendar says July 1st, you must wait and watch the turf for signs of illness. When those first signals show up, you've got to be ready to rapidly diagnose the culprit and take appropriate curative action.

And if that weren't enough, here's one more concept you've got to embrace: The idea that you'll need to live with some "minor quantities" of pests around at all times. The word *eradication* doesn't apply here. Instead, the key word is *management*. The idea is to *manage* pests at a low but acceptable level.

Admittedly this idea makes some people nervous. They acquaint it with having a lit match in a room full of gasoline: Eventually if you've got the pest around, something's going to blow up!

determine if pest levels justify treatment. But as Hummel explains, "stressing a curative approach rather than preventive usually cuts down on chemical use."

GETTING TO THE ROOT OF YOUR PEST PROBLEM

Laurie Broccolo runs a lawn and tree service company in upstate New York (Domangue, 1994). For the past 16 years her firm has provided a full-service lawn care package, covering fertilization and pest control. Her company makes five scheduled trips to each of her client's lawns annually unless a history of problems dictates more. Broccolo's business is a success story for reduced chemical use.

In the past, Broccolo's company routinely made blanket applications of pesticides for grub and weed control to clients' lawns. During her first year on a reduced chemical program, she cut her use of broadleaf herbicide to 30% of what it was. The second year she trimmed it even further.

"We took a stand of spot-treating for weeds instead of a blanket application," she says. "We lost a few customers. You have to lower their expectations, tell them you might miss something here or there. But most customers were fine about it as long as the lawn overall looked good."

Broccolo reduced the acreage treated for white grub to 21% of before by spot-spraying just the high grub areas. During the first year of the program, she saved $6500 versus a blanket application. "That's a lot for a small company," she says. Over the next two years, she trimmed it even further—to $9000 and finally to $15,000 savings.

Admittedly, the grubs did occasionally get the upper hand. And she had to reseed a few areas where grub damage was severe. But the repair work took only three man-hours—not a bad trade-off, considering the money saved on chemicals.

Spot treatment alone won't work without careful monitoring. Through her monitoring she learned the typical hangouts of grubs and where to target applications:

Figure 12.1. Pest diagnosis requires careful examination of the turf to figure out where pests are and where they aren't. Areas with high pest numbers are treated. Areas with low numbers are not. Untreated areas are monitored for future flare-ups.

- Shady areas had fewer grubs than sunny areas
- Older lawns tended to have fewer grubs than new construction
- Sloping lawns were particularly grub-prone
- Lawns with a medium-thick thatch ($^{1}/_{2}$ to 1 in. [13 to 25 mm]) had the most grubs
- Front yards had more grubs than back yards.

Once her technicians learned these hot spots, they were able to treat just the potential problem areas. In the end, they ended up treating 82% less lawn area. "That shows it's worth the time to look and sample before deciding to treat," she says (Figure 12.1).

Diagnostic tools

Accurate diagnosis is the cornerstone of any reduced chemical pest-control program. Misdiagnosis means wasted time and money.

To get started in diagnosing your pest problems, you'll need a few simple diagnostic tools. Some of them you probably already have. An attentive set of eyes is the main ingredient. Other helpful equipment includes:

- 10x hand lens
- Pocket knife
- Soil probe
- Collection vials
- Tweezers and scalpel
- Field pest identification books
- Golf course cup cutter (optional)
- 1 to 2 gallons of dilute detergent solution or pyrethrin solution (see Table 12.3)
- Empty coffee can with both ends removed
- Insect traps, such as sticky tape, pheromone attractants, or pitfall traps (optional)
- Microscope and microscope slides (optional)

Yes, microscopic diagnosis of turf diseases is *not* out of the question even for the average-Joe turf manager, says Pat Sanders, retired turf pathologist at Penn State University. For years Sanders has traveled the country teaching turf managers how to use a microscope to identify diseases. Perhaps hundreds of golf course maintenance shops now sport microscopes thanks to her efforts (Landschoot, 1990).

High-tech pest detection. Dave Cassat, golf course superintendent at Baltimore's Pine Ridge Golf Course, has gone high-tech when it comes to diagnosing and forecasting pest outbreaks. He purchased a PestCaster environmental monitoring station (Neogen Corp.) that continuously monitors humidity, precipitation, and air and ground temperature at the course. The device looks and works like a sophisticated weather station. But inside is an electronic weather computer, continuously analyzing incoming data for signs of disease-prone weather.

Built into the onboard computer are software programs that predict the onset of turf disease, based on weather models developed by university scientists. It's like having a university scientist on site, monitoring your weather conditions for the onset of disease. Their observations, data, and reasoning are compressed directly onto the microchip.

Present microchips can predict anthracnose, brown patch, and pythium blight—three of the most devastating turf diseases. It can even forecast the formation of grass seedheads to guide the application of plant growth regulators in the spring (see Chapter 11 for PGR details).

One July, Cassat had some tense moments with his PestCaster. While neighboring golf superintendents were all starting to treat for summer disease, Cassat's weather unit told him to wait. By waiting until the threshold was reached, he ended up making his chemical application when it did the most good. He saved money and the course looked great.

Cassat also uses diagnostic strips for disease detection to supplement the results from his PestCaster. Reveal Detection Kits (also by Neogen) are based on the same monoclonal antibody technology used in home pregnancy tests. To use the kit, you grind a diseased sample of grass, dip it in extraction solution, add drops of five different treatment solutions, and then check for a color change.

Cassat has some sage advice for other turf managers considering a reduced chemical program: "Stop thinking about it and do it. It saves money and it benefits the environment. And because part of our work is managing the environment, it's our duty to be leaders in developing these practices" (Leslie, 1991).

The diagnostic process

Back in the early days of turf pesticides, you could apply a single treatment of a toxic, long-residual, heavy-metal pesticide and control not only weeds, but also several insects and diseases to boot. And the control of pests from this one application lasted all season long and sometimes into the next.

But those days are gone. Today's pesticides are sharply focused, often right down to a single pest species. Most modern pesticides are short residual—they're gone from the environment in a matter of days or even hours. These new products require the applicator to have skilled knowledge of turf pests and be able to diagnose them right down to the species level.

The diagnostic process becomes second nature after a while. For experienced turf managers, the following summary of how to diagnose pest problems will be a review. But for the first-timer just beginning a pest-control program, these steps can set you on a logical path to solving your lawn problems.

Start with a brown spot. There are a plethora of problems that can leave a brown spot on turf—some of them physical, some environmental, others infectious. Before treating *any* brown spot, you need to get to the root of the problem. This will involve getting down on your hands and knees and excavating a chunk of sod. Few turf problems can be diagnosed from a standing position.

Most brown spots reveal their secrets around the perimeter of the spot—in the area where green blades are turning brown. It's there you're likely to find the smoking gun.

Here are some typical causes of brown spots on turf, adapted from a paper by Kay Sicheneder of Michigan State University. Going through this list will help hone your skills for diagnosing turf pests:

- *Mower injury*—Dull or poorly adjusted blades can sometimes cause suspicious brown spots on turf. Check for a slightly lower cutting height on the spot, or ripping or tearing of blade tips (see Figure 11.3).
- *Dry spots*—Dry spots come from many causes: nonuniform sprinklers, buried rocks, tree roots, thatch, and soil fungi. The quickest way to identify dry spots—and to tell them apart from more serious illnesses—is to simply sink a knife or soil probe into the spot and check the moisture status.

- *Summer dieback*—Grasses like annual and roughstalk bluegrass are programmed by nature to go brown in summer. Fine fescues also do this to some extent. Annual ryegrass, which is often mixed with desirable grasses in homeowner seed blends (see Table 6.4), dies out soon after it flowers in early summer. Diagnosing summer dieback requires examination of the dying grass to check its species identity.
- *Foliar burn from chemicals, gasoline, or oil*—Gasoline evaporates soon after it's spilled and leaves no tell-tale signs. Other spills can be identified by their residue. The *pattern* of kill is usually the give-away. Spillage is rarely in neat, circular spots but as scattered, irregular patches across the lawn. Look for signs where the spillage was tracked on tires, creating a repeating spot pattern as the wheel rolled.
- *Fertilizer burn*—Even experienced applicators spill fertilizer now and then. Spills of granular fertilizer can be diagnosed by residual particles left in the lawn—also by where the spots occur (where the spreader was filled). Spills of liquid fertilizer leave no residue, but can be diagnosed by the rapid, vibrant-green growth stimulation at the edge of the spot.
- *Pesticide phytotoxicity*—Pesticide toxicity is an example of being your own worst enemy—applying a product that injures or scalds the turf. Perhaps the rate was too high or the application timing coincided with a particularly stressful period. Even innocuous products can discolor turf when applied during drought or heat stress. Symptoms can range from a slight discoloration to total kill. More than one turf manager has experienced the agony of an unwitting employee spraying Roundup® by mistake and killing an entire lawn.
- *Dog injury*—This one's easy: Check for a dog (Figure 12.2).
- *Insect damage*—Birds often give us the first indication of an insect infestation. Birds, skunks, and moles feed on turf insects, leaving scattered pock marks that sometimes can be more damaging than the insects themselves. Some insects do not attract birds. They are diagnosed by noticing yellow, wilted patches of turf, and then probing them for insects. Diagnostic solutions, baits, and traps can aid in insect detection, when you can't find them by probing alone.
- *Fungal diseases*—Fungal disease symptoms involve such a wide variety of patterns and colors that it isn't possible to describe them all in one sentence. All foliar diseases do have one thing in common: Leaf lesions. If you closely examine the perimeter of the brown spot,

Figure 12.2. A mysterious brown spot can arise from different sources: Mower damage, droughty spots, summer dieback of plants, burn from chemicals or fuels, or pest invasions (see text). Each source produces a very similar blemish. That's why it's important to get to the root cause of the brown spot to ensure it won't reoccur. In this case, the offending "pest" was a friendly dog.

you'll see new lesions forming on green leaves. The shape, size, and color of these lesions can tip you off to the pathogen.

- *Nematode infestation*—Nematodes are hard to diagnose because (a) they can't be seen by the naked eye, and (b) even experts disagree on the numbers and types of nematodes that cause damage (Dernoeden, 1993). Nematodes are microscopic pinworms that attach themselves to roots, primarily in warm, sandy soils. The aboveground symptom is a general yellowing with no distinct leaf lesions. Nematodes are diagnosed by extracting a core of soil and sending it to a lab for extraction and counting. Send it to a *disease* lab and not an *entomology* lab—strangely enough, pathologists group these worms in with fungi, not bugs.

Seeking outside help

Even educated turf managers sometimes need outside help to diagnose a particularly baffling problem. There are literally hundreds of puzzling diseases and insects out there that can strike turf. Most turf facilities experience no more than five or ten pests in a given year. But sometimes a rare bug or fungus comes along—and it has to choose *your* turf. That's the time to call for assistance.

Another appropriate time to seek outside help in diagnosis is when the outbreak is so serious that your job is threatened. I've seen pythium blight hit one of the premier golf courses in Oklahoma so hard that the jobs of the course's superintendents were in jeopardy. The superintendents brought in a series of experts (including me) to help diagnose the problem. Eventually the owners realized it was natural catastrophe and not a management mistake that led to the flare-up.

The diagnostic lab. Let's face it, experts are expensive. For diagnosis of weeds, insects, and diseases, however, there is a reasonably priced alternative for getting expert help: Send a sample to a diagnostic lab for analysis. Some state universities analyze pest samples for merely a processing fee. Other universities and private labs charge up to $75 per sample (Dernoeden, 1993). In return, they'll examine the sample and tell you the causal agent (Figure 12.3).

There's a lot you can do to make the diagnosis quicker and more accurate. When you choose to send a sample to a lab specialist, *you* become the eyes and ears of the expert. You—more than they—know the peculiarities of the pest and the damage it caused. The lab's job more than anything is to *confirm your hunch*. This simple point cannot be overemphasized. If you have a hunch, tell them what it is. Some people play cat-and-mouse, seeing if they can stump the expert. This helps no one.

So, how can you make the lab specialist's job easier? What can you give them to ensure an accurate diagnosis?

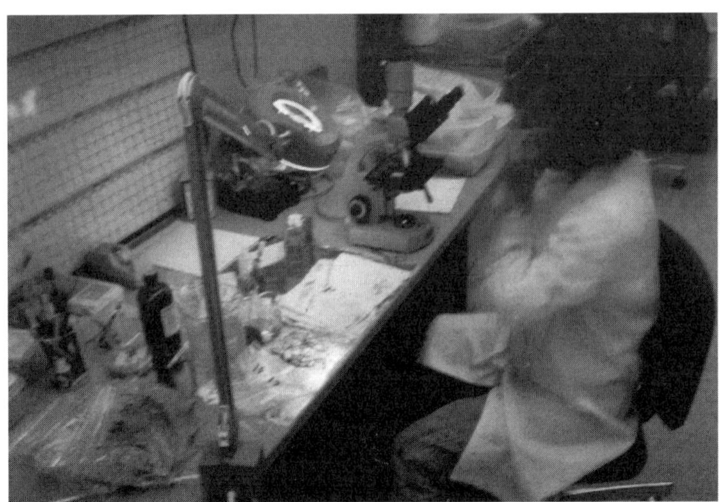

Figure 12.3. Diagnostic laboratories are an excellent source of outside advice on tough pest problems. But believe it or not, many of the diagnosticians at these labs are not *turf* experts. Most of the time they are specialists on a particular strain of fungus or on fruit trees, etc. Therefore, it's vital that you give them all the information they need to understand your problem.

Here are important points to write down and relay to the lab along with the sample:

- *Take a Polaroid*—Give them a look at the damage. One close-up and one overall shot can go a long way toward diagnosis. Pathologists can diagnose some pests from symptoms alone.
- *List all the symptoms*—Describe the patches: Color, thinning, widespread, localized? Does it look water-soaked, dried, scorched? Have you noticed any insects or fungal mycelium?
- *Area affected*—What's the turf used for? Golf course fairway, soccer field, home lawn? Sun, shade, wet, dry, compacted? Do other lawns nearby show symptoms?
- *Development*—When did you first notice it? How did it start? What's the weather been like? Did it occur in the same exact spot last year?
- *Culture*—Have you changed your management lately in any way? Have you aerated or topdressed recently? What fertilizers were used on the area? Are there any imbalances on your soil test report?
- *Grass species*—What grass species and variety are you growing?
- *Curative treatments*—What pesticides and cultural practices have you tried already? Was the sample you sent to the lab treated with pesticide?

Sending a sample. You might want to check ahead of time before you mail your specimen, to make sure the particular lab specialist is in town. A simple phone call to the lab beforehand can assure a faster turnaround.

Ship the sample overnight express so it arrives fresh. And don't send it so it arrives on Friday afternoon or over the weekend. After two or three days of sitting in a closed box, whatever was killing your grass will have polished off the specimen.

If you plan to send a sample to the lab for disease analysis, you will want to sample from an area that hasn't been treated with fungicide. Should the pathologist need to culture the fungus for identification, no fungi will grow out if the sample has been fungicide treated.

Collect the sample from the fringe of the blighted area, not from the central dead part (Figure 12.4). It's important to get some green matter in the sample. A golf course cup cutter works particularly well for extracting a clean specimen. When packaging, hold the soil in place with aluminum foil so the grass doesn't arrive slathered with dirt.

Put the sample in a paper or plastic bag. I've found that refrigerator zipper bags designed for vegetables (they have pinholes in them) work particularly well for keeping plants fresh during transit. Place your notes and photos in a *separate* plastic bag, or stick them to the outside of the box. Notes left inside the bag with the soil become unreadable.

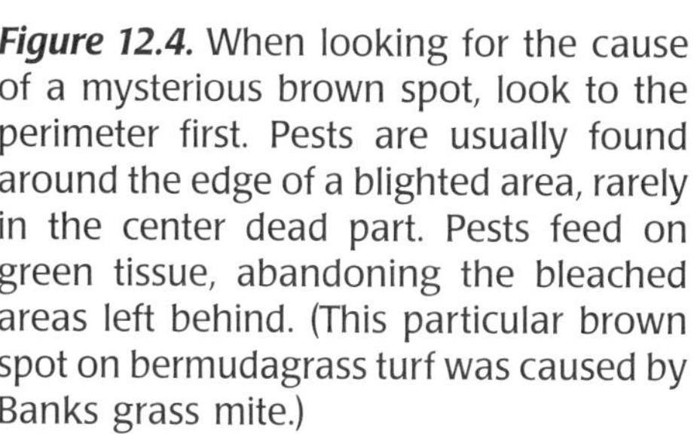

Figure 12.4. When looking for the cause of a mysterious brown spot, look to the perimeter first. Pests are usually found around the edge of a blighted area, rarely in the center dead part. Pests feed on green tissue, abandoning the bleached areas left behind. (This particular brown spot on bermudagrass turf was caused by Banks grass mite.)

Collecting insects and weeds is more straightforward. A vial or plastic bag will suffice. For nematode analysis, collect 15 to 20 soil cores to a depth of 3 in. (7.5 cm) across the affected area. Accumulate a total of 1 pint ($^1/_2$ L) of soil. You might also want to collect another sample from a nonblighted area, to compare nematode numbers with what a "healthy" area represents.

For soil, use a sturdy plastic bag—never use paper bags. Collect the soil after a rain or irrigation cycle when the soil is moist. *Never* water a specimen before mailing—for nematodes or otherwise. And avoid the temptation to throw a few ice cubes in the box as well.

With good prearrangements with the lab, you'll know the diagnosis within 48 hours. Disease analyses may take longer if the pathologist has to culture the organism. If time is of the essence, you might ask for the expert's "best guess."

Interpreting the diagnosis. Discuss treatment options with the specialist. If it's a major outbreak, you'll need to select the treatment that gives you the quickest knockdown of the pest. Cultural controls may have to wait until the emergency is over.

Keep one practical consideration in mind when interpreting your diagnosis: Specialists almost *always* find something. That's what they're paid for, to find potential pests. Rarely will they tell you they've come up empty-handed.

Other times you might get more diagnosis than you've bargained for. Once when I sent a sample to the lab, it came back with a diagnosis of leafspot, dollar spot, and pythium. It was up to me—in consultation with the specialist—to figure out which of those three suspects was really causing my turf problems.

CULTURAL PEST CONTROL

The idea behind cultural pest control is to improve the growth of turfgrass so that it resists pests naturally by its own vigor. It's been said many times that the best defense against pests is a good, thick turf. Think of your grass in these human terms: People who are vigorous, well nourished, and otherwise healthy are better able to fend off disease and sickness than someone who is stressed, poorly fed, and living in cramped, squalid conditions.

If we give grass the growing conditions it needs, it will survive and flourish. If we give it less than ideal conditions, we can expect escalating problems with pests. Chemical controls are a "Band-Aid" to treat grass ills. They don't remedy the underlying cause.

Variety selection, good soil, timely fertilization, irrigation, and *mowing* are the "big five" of cultural controls (see Figure 1.5). Many pest problems can be remedied just by adjusting these five. For example, suppose we're fertilizing too heavily, bringing on disease from the lush grass the fertilizer produces. Subtle changes in fertilizer makeup, rate, timing, or NPK ratio can be employed to cut disease severity, all while keeping visual appeal constant.

Examples of successful cultural controls:

- *Mowing*—Close mowing stresses turf, making it more susceptible to disease and insects. Turf mowed either below or above its optimum runs the risk of weeds outcompeting the grass at those heights. For example, at extremely low cut, algae and moss can become a serious nuisance, whereas they're rarely a concern in taller turf.
- *Grass variety and species*—The most economical way to combat pests is to tap into the natural resistance of improved turf varieties. Genetic resistance can be used to combat nearly every turf pest, with the possible exception of nematodes, ground pearl insects, mole cricket, and some warm-weather blighting fungi. In general, seed or sprigs of advanced, pest-resistant varieties cost *no more to buy* than seed of susceptible varieties. The only added expense is the time it takes to seek out these improved types.
- *Timely irrigation*—Precise metering of watering is possible with today's sophisticated electronic irrigation systems. The element of human error is removed: No longer is irrigation dependent upon someone remembering to turn off and on the manual valves. Irrigation can be

applied at just the right time and in just the right quantity to keep the grass healthy and vigorous, but not soak it to the point of waste. Overwatering is one of the fastest ways to incite pest problems.

- *Fertilization*—Fertilizer has a profound effect on turf. Apply too much and diseases go rampant. Apply too little and the turf can't keep up with weeds. *What* you apply and *when* you apply it, are equally as important as the quantity applied. Timed-release fertilizer products give gentle feeding over time, without the disruptive burst of soluble fertilizers.
- *Thatch control*—In a survey of golf course superintendents in Iowa, 87% reported they use some form of thatch removal to control pests (Agnew and Lewis, 1993). Thatch is beneficial for resiliency and wear resistance of turf. But too much thatch serves as a safe harbor for pests and a poor rooting medium for grasses.
- *Core cultivation*—Walking and driving on turf compacts the soil, forcing out tiny air bubbles and making the soil generally inhospitable to roots. Reducing soil compaction by core cultivation is an important tool for minimizing compaction stress and heading off future pests.
- *Topdressing*—Applying a thin layer of topsoil, compost, or sand-soil mix on top of grass can help control disease. Jim Wilkinson (1994) and other researchers have found that applying compost to turf suppresses brown patch, dollar spot, necrotic ring spot, pythium blight, pythium root rot, red thread, and typhula blight. Researchers speculate that topdressing contributes microbes that attack pathogenic fungi, while furnishing a richer, more favorable growing medium for grass roots. Topdressing is also one of the most effective methods of breaking down thatch.
- *Optimizing air flow*—Good air flow is crucial in humid climates to evaporate excess dew and moisture from grass blades. Free moisture on leaves serves as a breeding ground for fungi. Tree pruning is one way to open a suffocating environment to a cool breeze. Golf course superintendents in the southeastern United States have even resorted to electric fans to keep the air flowing and keep their putting greens cool.
- *Improving soil drainage*—High clay soils drain poorly. Rainfall and irrigation water saturate these soils, turning them into a sticky goo. Soil modification (the incorporation of sand or compost) and the installation of subsurface drain pipe helps siphon away excessive moisture, so the grass doesn't grow webbed feet (see Chapter 8 for soil modification ideas).
- *Biostimulants*—**Biostimulants** are products that somehow enhance the growth of grass. Biostimulants come in either dry or liquid forms, depending on the product. Although they contain natural or man-made chemicals, biostimulants are generally not considered to be pesticides. As such, they do not fall under the jurisdiction of government regulation for efficacy and safety. And unlike pesticides which are tightly scrutinized, biostimulants carry no governmental guarantee that they'll work and won't harm the grass. For years, turf experts considered biostimulants to be "snake oils"—products of mysterious origin that promise to do almost unbelievable miracles. Dick Schmidt, Virginia Polytechnic University turf researcher, has reversed the opinion of many by doing peer-review scientific studies of biostimulants and finding genuine benefits. The composition of biostimulants is extremely diverse. Many start with a base of processed seaweed and add microbes, plant hormones, wetting agent, iron, fertilizer, nitrogen-fixing bacteria, and even human vitamins (Hall, 1994). This conglomeration of ingredients functions to turn grass greener and denser, although skeptics still attribute the change to the added fertilizer elements.

BIOLOGICAL PEST CONTROL

Biologicals are a powerful weapon. The grim specter of biological warfare loomed in January of 1991 as President George Bush prepared to send troops of the multinational force against the invading Iraqi army in Kuwait. Intelligence sources knew that Saddam Hussein had been stockpiling biological weapons for possible use in the impending Gulf war. Deadly infectious agents such as anthrax and bubonic plague were cultured in weapons laboratories for delivery to the warfront. Americans held their collective breath wondering whether these heinous weapons of mass destruction would be unleashed on our troops.

Without a doubt, biological agents are a potent, powerful weapon. To many, they represent the ultimate in destructive firepower. Curious as it may seem, these agents of war are actually benign to the environment. Biological agents kill enemy troops while leaving buildings, aircraft, armaments, and even livestock standing—characteristics that have endeared biological weapons to legions of military dictators the world over. Unlike chemical agents which take time to degrade in the environment, biological agents dissipate almost instantaneously in the absence of a host. Plagues that can cripple a human population are harmless to the rest of ecology. Biological agents are narrowly focused to paralyze only a single organism—in the case of biological weapons of war, the target organism is us.

Pest vs. pest. It may seem macabre to compare biological warfare to **biological pest control**, but the two have striking similarities. Biological warfare is a way to kill invading armies of troops. Biological pest control is a way to infect invading armies of *pests* with their own natural plagues. Even the smallest insect, nematode, or fungus has itself an even smaller pest or disease that weakens and kills it. Biological pest control agents are:

- all natural
- safe to the environment
- safe to humans and pets
- highly specific in their control, often affecting just a single pest species.

Unlike biological warfare weapons, biological pest control agents are *safe to humans*. Only the target pest is affected. No residue remains in the environment that can cause pollution or harm beneficial organisms.

Biological pest control agents operate in several different ways (Table 12.1). Not all agents directly kill their hosts. Other modes of action are:

- Treatments may affect just a certain phase of the pest's life cycle, such as the nymph stage of an insect. Feeding adults may be unfazed but their ability to reproduce is interrupted. With controls such as these, *timing* of application is essential, to bring the agent and pest into contact at just the right moment.
- Control organisms may compete for food with the pest. Many fungal pests live as **saprophytes** during the off-season, devouring decaying litter and organic material to stay alive until conditions are ripe. Biological control organisms can be introduced that are more effective foragers of organic litter than pathogens, and they may literally overrun them. Composts, for instance, contain billions of these foraging organisms.
- Biological control organisms may secrete an antibiotic that renders the pest defenseless. Antibiotics may directly kill the pest, they may alter its natural life cycle, or they can simply leave a bad taste in the pest's mouth, causing it to graze elsewhere.

Biological pest control agents get their start from nature. Researchers do not *create* biological pest control agents, they *find* them. In the case of Japanese beetles, scientists began their search by testing natural beetle populations for signs of illness. Japanese beetle is an introduced insect pest that damages turf, ornamental, and crop plantings throughout much of the United States.

When scientists found a prospective parasite of Japanese beetle, they isolated and cultured it. After growing the parasite into sizable numbers,

Table 12.1. Biological pest control agents. Biological controls are remarkably safe to humans, safe to the environment, and newer products have control levels approaching chemical pesticides (Georgis and Poinar, 1994; Vavrek, 1990).

Biological control agents	Organism species	Commercial product	Pests controlled	Handling and application
Endophyte fungi	*Neotyphodium* (ex-*Acremonium*)	Endophyte enhanced turf varieties	Sod webworm, bluegrass billbug, Argentine stem weevil, southern armyworm, chinch bug, and possibly dollar spot disease	Endophytes are introduced to turf by overseeding with high endophyte varieties. There is no way to spray them on. Shelf life of infected seed is 6 to 9 months, unless seed is kept under cool, dry conditions.
Predator nematodes	*Steinernema carpocapsae* *S. glaseri* *S. scapterisci* *S. riobravis*	*Biosafe*®, *Exhibit*®, *Sanoplant*® *Vector*®*-WG* *Proact* *Vector*®*-MC*	Japanese beetle, mole cricket, masked chafer, cutworm, white grub, plant parasitic ring, sting, and root knot nematode	Limited shelf life. Watering is needed before and after application. Nematodes survive for 60 minutes on plants when applied during the day, but can persist for 10 hours applied at night. Fall is the best time for application. The nematodes work by injecting *Xenorhabdus* bacteria into the insect, causing death in 24 to 72 hours. Control potential is 90% of commercial insecticides.
Beneficial insects	Ants, rove beetle (*Staphylinidae*), big-eyed bug, ground beetle (*Carabidae*), spiders, ladybird beetle (*Coccinellidae*), predatory mites	Supplies of these beneficial insects can be purchased from specialty houses. Garden suppliers charge 10x the price of specialty suppliers.	Sod webworm, chinch bug, aphid, mealybug, spider mite	These naturally occurring insects have a role in regulating pest insect populations. Insecticides that harm these beneficial insects can be expected to increase pest populations. The effectiveness of beneficial insects when purchased and introduced onto a lawn are negligible, as they tend to stray.
Bacterial antagonists	*Pseudomonas* and *Enterobacter* species	Bio Releaf B+	Dollar spot, pythium blight, fusarium patch, take-all patch disease, downy bromegrass	Certain strains of bacteria are effective at outcompeting pathogens for nutrients and growth factors. Others may produce antibiotics. Effectiveness varies with the strain of bacteria. Selected isolates can provide 50 to 90% of the control of chemical fungicides.

Table 12.1. Biological pest control agents. Biological controls are remarkably safe to humans, safe to the environment, and newer products have control levels approaching chemical pesticides (Georgis and Poinar, 1994; Vavrek, 1990) (continued).

Biological control agents	Organism species	Commercial product	Pests controlled	Handling and application
Bt	*Bacillus thuringiensis* (various subspecies and varieties)	Bactur®, Pactospeine®, Caterpillar Killer®, Dipel®, Futura™, Javelin®, SOK-Bt™, Thuricide®, Topside™, Tribactur™, Worm Attack®, Bactimos®, Mosquito Attack®, Skeetal™, Teknar®, Vectobac®, M-One®, Trident®, Doom®, Condor®, Troy BT®, Mattch, MVPII, Japidemic™, Milky Spore Disease™, Grub Attack®, M-Press™, XenTari®, Steward™	Mosquito larvae, black fly, fungus gnat, Japanese beetle larvae, Oriental beetle, armyworm, cutworm, sod webworm and other lawn grubs	The success claimed for Bt on turf insects is questionable. Entomologist Dan Potter of the University of Kentucky says, "basically they don't work." Control is very slow acting and the infection does not persist in turf. Ohio State University entomologist Harry Niemczyk recently reported 96% control of Japanese beetle grub with a new Bt isolate, M-Press™. Certain Bt strains are more effective on certain insects—be sure to check the label. Bacteria in the Bt group develop a large crystal of antibiotic Bt in their cell. Biotechnologists have introduced the blueprint for this crystal into cotton, soybean, and other crop plants, so that Bt is expressed as the plant grows. It's only a matter of time until someone tries the same on turfgrasses.

Fungal antagonists	*Trichoderma, Laetisaria, Pennicillium, Sporidesmium, Talaromyces, Verticilium* species	A commercial product from a new company, TGT, is expected soon.	Brown patch, pythium blight, southern blight, take-all patch	Shelf life is 1 to 2 years. Effectiveness is regulated by the level of organic matter, nutrients and pH in the soil, temperature, and moisture. Best applied with soil temperatures 55 to 60°F (12 to 15°C). Banner, Rubigan, and triazole fungicides can reduce their effective-
ness.				*Trichoderma* and *Sporidesmium* appear to parasitize pathogenic fungi. Selected isolates can provide up to 90% of the control as chemical fungicides.
Compost topdressing	A myriad of naturally occurring soil organisms	Typical products: *Ringer Compost Plus* and *Greens Restore, Sustane*, composted	Dollar spot, brown patch, gray snow mold, red thread,	As little as 10 lb of compost per 1000 ft^2 (50 g/m^2) can suppress dollar spot, brown patch, gray snow mold, red thread. Other diseases require heavier
or		sludge, spent mushroom	pythium blight,	continuous applications for success.
Only		compost, leaf compost (for more information on compost, see Chapter 8).	pythium root rot, necrotic ring spot, summer patch	*unsterilized* compost contains beneficial microbes.

they then had to verify its effectiveness. Potency was gauged by introducing the parasite into captive beetle populations. If the beetles were unharmed, it was back to the drawing board in search of another agent.

Trouble is, not all germs can be easily **inoculated**. It takes a lot of searching to find just the right one. Between the years 1920 and 1933, 49 different parasites and predators were introduced to control Japanese beetle populations. Few ever became established and none have had more than a minor impact on beetle populations (Potter, 1993).

Delivery to the pest. Even after finding the right parasite, researchers still have to find a reliable way to get it into contact with pest populations in the landscape. Most parasitic organisms cannot persist for long outside a host. To illustrate that point, let me return to the Gulf War example:

Weapons designers knew that if plague germs were scattered helter-skelter across the battlefield, their effectiveness would be nil. It took considerable design effort to figure a way to deliver doses of biological agents to the warfront to infect enemy troops. If the projectile strayed from its target, the germ cloud would drift harmlessly away. If it discharged over scattered troops, the chances of a **secondary infection**—one person passing the infection to another—would be slim, since there would be little chance for interpersonal contact. Biological agents depend upon **epidemic infection** to be successful. Infected individuals must pass the infection on to others before they expire. Otherwise, control is short-lived and ineffectual.

Makers of biological pest control agents face the same types of challenges as weapons manufacturers. Once a successful biological control agent is perfected, practical questions arise on how to deliver it to the pest in the landscape:

- How do you store and transport a live control organism from the manufacturing plant to the lawn without it dying enroute?
- How do you get the product into contact with the bug or fungus, especially if the pest is feeding several inches below the surface? How can you keep the control organism from drying out before it encounters its target?
- Will the product work when pest levels are low? Or will it work only when pests are in epidemic proportions?
- How do you apply the agent for maximum effectiveness? Sprays, powders, drenches? Are there certain environmental conditions that favor control?
- Will the infection be transmitted from bug to bug like an epidemic? Or will it affect only those few bugs it directly contacts?
- Is the control agent selective enough or does it damage populations of desirable organisms?
- Is the control as effective as chemicals are? Or does it just reduce pest populations by a few percent? Is the cost similar to conventional controls?

Issues like these challenge the developers of biological pest control agents. Of course their single biggest challenge is getting veteran pesticide users to switch to a new realm of pest control—one that brings with it its own peculiar concerns of storage, delivery, and effectiveness.

Turfgrass is a success story when it comes to biological pest control. In turf—perhaps more than in any other crop—biological control agents have been brought to bear against a number of pests. Turfgrass science has been at the forefront of many advancements. As a result, turf managers are now able to control and manage pest problems biologically that formerly required chemical interdiction (Tables 12.2–12.5).

Endophyte

By their very definition, endophytes are parasites on grass (Figure 12.5). But strange as it may seem, these are *good* parasites. Endophytes are a special class of fungus that live their lives solely within the body of a grass plant. The word endophyte derives from *endo* meaning inside and *phyte* meaning plant. These benign organisms spend their lives peacefully within the leaf veins of certain turfgrass varieties. Endophytes are a

Table 12.2. Trouble thresholds of common turf insects. Insect counts less than the figures listed here normally cause no discernible damage to turf. No treatment is needed until insect counts reach the levels listed. Sometimes untreated turf will recover on its own with no curative action. But after severe infestations, regrowth may take a growing season. These figures are based on an articles by Lee Hellmann (1992), Kevin Mathias (1994), Pete Dernoeden (1993), and Tom Watschke et al. (1994).

Turf species	Insect	Threshold (immature insects per ft^2)	Threshold (per m^2)	Other visual clues	Will the turf recover if not treated?
Kentucky bluegrass and fine fescue	Japanese beetle grub	6 to 10	65 to 108	Birds, skunks digging holes	Rare
	Masked chafer grub	8 to 15	108 to 161	Birds, skunks digging holes	Rare
	European chafer grub	10 to 15	108 to 161		Rare
	Asiatic garden beetle grub	18	194		Rare
	Sod webworm	4 to 6	43 to 65		Yes
	Billbug	6 to 8	65 to 108	Frass at base of plant	Yes
	Chinch bug	15 to 20	161 to 215		No
	Cutworm, armyworm	1 to 3	11 to 32		Yes
	Aphid	–	–	First sign of yellowing	No
Annual bluegrass and creeping bentgrass	Black turfgrass ataenius	30 to 40	323 to 430		Rare
	Skipper larvae	½ to 1	5 to 11		–
	Root knot nematode	–		100 to 800 per 250 cm^2 soil	Yes
Perennial ryegrass	Green June beetle grub	3 to 5	32 to 54	Birds, skunks digging holes	No
Tall fescue	Japanese beetle grub	8 to 15	108 to 161	Birds, skunks digging holes	Rare
	Masked chafer grub	8 to 15	108 to 161	Birds, skunks digging holes	Rare
Zoysiagrass	Billbug	6 to 8	65 to 108	Frass at base of plant	Yes

Table 12.3. Insect control tips: Pest management ideas for efficient control of turf insects with less reliance on insecticides.

Adjust your fertilizer...	• With certain insects, nitrogen fertilizer can be both the cause and the cure. Turf damage from root-feeding white grubs can be more severe with well fertilized turf. But *remedial* nitrogen fertilization is also needed to help the turf outgrow the damage (Crutchfield et al., 1995). • Boric acid can be used for ant control.
If you find something that works, change it...	• Turf insects can develop **resistance** to pesticides. Even if you find an insecticide that controls your turf insects, it's a good idea to occasionally switch to another product to prevent the buildup of resistant insects. Rotating among two or three products will minimize resistance. • When rotating insecticides, make sure you are switching between products of different chemistries, not just different trade names.
Adjust your watering...	• Insects need water too. Insects reproduce more prolifically in moist soil than in dry. Maintaining the soil a little on the dry side will keep many insects in check. • Spider mites can often be eliminated by irrigation alone (Cranshaw, 1995). Unlike most insects, they prefer things on the slightly drier side. • Know where your insects are. For control of leaf-feeding insects, insecticides must remain on the leaves and not be washed away into the thatch. • Dry soil drives grubs and other subsurface crawlers deeper in the soil in search of moisture. This makes chemical control of these pests more difficult. Grub insecticides work best if you preirrigate to bring insects to the surface before treating.
Know your bugs...	• Don't kill beneficial look-alike bugs. Big-eyed bugs, ground beetles, and parasitic wasps are often confused with harmful insects. These desirable bugs actually feed on dangerous turf insects and help reduce their numbers. • Disclose your bugs. Chinch bugs can be detected by sinking an open-ended coffee can into the lawn and filling it with water. Chinches float to the top. If you capture more than 15 to 20 bugs in one try, you've got an outbreak on your hands. • Dilute dish detergent or insecticidal pyrethrin can be used to force sod webworms to the surface for counting. Pyrethrin is available in many household insecticide balms, such as Raid®. Lightly water the solution into the grass and watch as the insects crawl out, irritated by the chemical. Tallies of more than 10 webworms per square foot spell trouble (Cranshaw, 1995). • For every insect, there is a particular time in its life cycle when it's most susceptible to insecticides. Treatments should coincide with peak periods of activity. Note that this may *not* be the period when the insects are most visible.
Control weeds to control insects...	• Berry Crutchfield and Dan Potter of the University of Kentucky (Crutchfield and Potter, 1995) have found that white clover, red clover, large crabgrass, annual bluegrass, buckhorn plantain, and dandelion are favorite foods of Japanese beetle and southern masked chafer grubs. Controlling these weeds, they found, helps reduce insects. "Our data are the first to show that either of these important pests will feed upon the roots of common lawn weeds," they wrote. Their findings dispel "the perception that weed-infested turf is less prone to grub problems."
Spot treat...	• Insects, more so than other pests, tend to occur in colonies or patches, rather than being evenly distributed across the whole turf. Instead of making a blanket treatment with insecticide, spot spray only those areas with significant insect numbers (see the success story of Laurie Broccolo in the text).

Other cultural controls...	• Chinch bugs not only suck moisture from grass blades, they deposit saliva that is toxic to grass. A mixture of insecticidal soap with a pinch of isopropyl alcohol will help eradicate this goo. The solution should be sprayed on the grass every few days until the bugs are gone. • Biological control measures pit one organism against another. Even tiny bugs themselves get attacked by even tinier parasites. You can control certain problem insects by treating them with natural parasites (see Table 12.1 for more information). • Insecticidal soap and even dishwashing detergent can be used against bees, wasps, hornets, aphids, and certain other turf insects. • Encourage flying predators such as birds and bats by placing bird and bat houses where insects are a problem. Some birds consume their weight in bugs every day. • Use **insect growth regulators** in place of insecticides when possible. These products are more specific to pest insects than general insecticides. • The cheapest, most effective control of turf insects is endophyte (see text and sidebar).

Table 12.4. Disease control tips: Pest management ideas for efficient control of turf diseases with less reliance on fungicides.

Manage disease with nitrogen fertility...	• Too much or too little nitrogen fertilizer can predispose turf to disease attack. With too much nitrogen, turf produces growthy, succulent leaves that are highly susceptible to blight diseases. With too little nitrogen, grass can't outgrow slow moving diseases such as rust. Turf pathologist Joe Vargas laments: "Unfortunately, as things are, a program of nitrogen fertilizer that alleviates one disease may worsen another" (Vargas, 1995). Moderation and good timing of fertilizer application are the answer. • Pythium blight, brown patch, gray leaf spot, stripe smut, microdochium patch, and typhula snow mold are worsened by high nitrogen. • Dollar spot, rust, red thread, anthracnose, necrotic ring spot, take-all patch, summer patch, melting-out, and leaf spot diseases are more severe at low nitrogen levels. • Slow-release nitrogen fertilizers are generally less risky on disease than fast release sources. In two University of Maryland studies, brown patch, summer patch, necrotic ring spot, and dollar spot disease were lower when fertilized with slow-release fertilizer than when fertilized with an equivalent dose of fast-release (Dernoeden, 1991; Fidanza and Dernoeden, 1996a). • Ammonium sulfate fertilizer is an effective cultural control for take-all patch disease. A study at North Carolina State University found 33 to 42% less take-all patch where ammonium sulfate was applied, compared to an equal rate of composted sewage sludge (Clarke et al., 1996). The researchers attribute the reduction to the acidifying effect of the ammonium sulfate. Take-all patch, they theorize, hates acid soil. Spring dead spot and Fusarium patch disease are also controlled by ammonium sulfate (Dernoeden, 1991). • Experts disagree on the benefits of natural organic fertilizers on disease. Benefits show up in some trials but not all. The discrepancy may be tied to microbes supplied in the fertilizer itself. Some natural organic composts contain a host of beneficial microbes. Others are essentially sterile. Supplied microbes can compete with or even kill disease organisms (see text).

Table 12.4. Disease control tips: Pest management ideas for efficient control of turf diseases with less reliance on fungicides (continued).

Use other nutrients to control disease...	• Maintaining favorable potash (K) levels in the soil helps combat red thread, Fusarium patch, brown patch, leaf spot, and dollar spot (Buchanan, 1979). • Researchers at North Carolina State University (Dorer et al., 1995) discovered that foliar sprays of phosphorous or manganese could be used to control brown patch disease, through not as thoroughly as commercial fungicides. • In a separate study, NC State (Uriarte and Bowman, 1996) researchers learned that brown patch could be reduced 10 to 20% with potassium silicate fertilizer applied at $^1/_2$ lb per 1000 ft^2 (2.5 g/m^2). Dollar spot disease was also reduced 10%. • Bill Walmsley, agronomist at New Zealand's Sports Turf Institute (Walmsley, 1996), discovered that potassium carbonate fertilizer could be used to control basidiomycete fairy rings in turf. He found best results by applying the fertilizer in spring or early summer when rings first appear. The product is applied twice, spaced a week apart, at 1.8 lb per 1000 ft^2 (9 g/m^2) each time. It needs to be watered in to prevent foliar burn from the salty fertilizer. Walmsley also observed reductions in Rhizoctonia brown patch disease from the treatment.
Adjust your watering to discourage disease...	• Afternoon watering is the least efficient time to irrigate in terms of *water efficiency*—the lowest amount of water actually reaches the roots due to evaporation. However, afternoon irrigation cools the plant and helps it through midday stress, reducing disease (Vargas, 1995). • The worst time to irrigate from a *disease standpoint* is in the evening. "This wets the turfgrass plant and debris (mat and thatch) and allows foliar pathogens to germinate, grow and infect all night, since normally very little drying takes place before sunrise," says Michigan State University pathologist Joe Vargas (1995). • Controlled studies have shown that morning watering consistently reduces brown patch disease versus evening watering (Fidanza and Dernoeden, 1993, 1996a). • Most turf diseases are discouraged by infrequent, deep watering. The notable exceptions: necrotic ring spot and fairy ring (Dernoeden, 1991). The ring symptoms produced by these soil-inhabiting fungi can be masked by consistent watering, though the pathogen itself is not destroyed.
Learn what diseases are telling you...	• Pythium blight alerts you to drainage problems in the soil. Aerification or installation of subsurface drainage pipes will help correct the underlying problem inciting the disease. Brown patch and typhula blight are also fueled by poor drainage. • Microdochium patch, powdery mildew, brown patch, and gray leaf spot indicate an air flow problem: Trees or buildings are interfering with the flow of fresh air and the removal of humidity. Judicious tree pruning can help open the air flow and reduce disease. • Locate an **indicator area** on your property—a place where disease first occurs, long before it spreads to other areas. With close observation, you'll find that diseases strike first in the same general area each year. By observing your indicator areas, you'll know when to spray and when not. The use of indicator areas is important in the switch from preventive to curative pest management.
Don't be your own worst enemy...	• Fumigation—the sterilization of soil by a nonselective fumigant such as methyl bromide—can later predispose turf to disease (Clarke et al., 1996). Though fumigation kills off pathogenic fungi, it also kills antagonistic flora. It sets up the turf for rapid disease outbreaks for the first 2 or 3 years of growth, until soil organisms later balance out. Additions of (nonsterilized) compost can help speed the equilibrium process and damped flare-ups.

Know your families...

- Fungicides come in three basic families of chemistry: benzimidazoles, dicarboximides, and sterol inhibitors. "If a fungus becomes resistant to one fungicide in a group, it will automatically be resistant to the other members of the group even if you have never used those products," advises Gail Schumann, plant pathologist at the University of Massachusetts (Schumann, 1995). Schumann recommends rotating or alternating between different families to prevent or delay the buildup of resistance.
- Don't apply **systemic fungicides** when the turf or pest is dormant. Systemic fungicides need to be taken into the tissue of grasses. They're only effective if the grass is actively growing. **Contact fungicides** are products that remain on the leaf surface and do not enter the plant. They can be used on dormant (or actively growing) turf.

Think curative...

- Considerable pesticide can be saved by switching from a preventive treatment program to a curative one. Instead of applying pesticides in hopes of heading off disease problems, switch to a curative approach of treating only active problems. Not all disease (or insect or weed) problems occur every single year. By taking a wait-and-see attitude, you'll save pesticides, time, and money.
- The trade-off of course is: You must know how to identify your pests. You've got to be able to quickly spot and accurately diagnose potential problems. A faulty diagnosis can lead to an ineffectual cure. Early stages of dollar spot disease, for example, can often be confused with pythium blight—a much more serious ailment. A trigger-happy applicator might be tempted to jump the gun and spray a pythium fungicide, which would be useless against dollar spot.

Other cultural controls...

- Always use resistant varieties. There are turf varieties that resist nearly every known turf disease, partially if not totally. And seed or sprigs of resistant varieties generally cost no more to buy than those of susceptible varieties.
- Morning mowing can be used to control disease. Mowing removes moisture from grass leaves. A golf course study at the University of Kentucky found an 80% reduction in dollar spot disease by morning mowing (Williams et al., 1995). Other methods of dew removal, such as dragging a hose or rolling the turf with a sponge-covered roller, were not as effective as mowing. **Syringing** (sprinkling with a short blast of irrigation) or spraying **surfactant** (wetting agent) also helped cut disease severity, but were not as effectively as mowing.
- If snow mold is a problem, do what you can to prevent turf from going into winter while tall and succulent. In the autumn continue mowing until growth stops. Apply fertilizer no later than 6 weeks before dormancy.
- Other winter tips: Use snow fencing and windbreak plantings to prevent formation of large drifts. Avoid snow compaction by keeping snowmobiles and other equipment off turf areas. As snow melts in spring, rake matted diseased areas to encourage rapid drying and regrowth.
- Use surfactants, stickers, and extenders to increase the effectiveness of your fungicide, and to reduce the amount of active ingredient needed.

Table 12.5. Weed control tips: Pest management ideas for efficient control of turf weeds with less reliance on herbicides.

Cultural rule #1...	• The best deterrent for weeds is a good, thick turf. • Any management practice that invigorates the turf will generally discourage weeds.
Use fertilizer to control weeds...	• Elevating soil phosphate above deficiency levels has been shown to be an effective cultural control for both crabgrass and dandelion (Huffine, 1980). • Don't fertilize warm-season turf right before it goes dormant in the fall. The added fertilizer only spurs the growth of winter annual weeds. In a study of autumn zoysia fertilization at the University of Missouri (Dunn et al., 1993), project leader John Dunn concluded: "Any small benefit in fall color and spring greenup of zoysiagrass with fall fertilization in the Midwest transition zone was mitigated by the increasing weed populations." • Roy Goss, emeritus professor at Washington State University, discovered that applications of sulfur can suppress *Poa annua* weed populations in mixed bentgrass turf (Buchanan, 1979). Sulfur lowers soil pH, making *Poa annua* less competitive with acid-tolerant bentgrass. Sulfur should be used cautiously on sandier soils because it can lead to development of **black layer**—a root strangling soil layer. • Applications of iron sulfate fertilizer have been shown to reduce or eliminate algae, moss, clover, slender speedwell, dandelion, and lawn daisy (Kavanagh and Cormican, 1982). • Nitrogen fertilizer can help minimize weeds in the legume family (Neal et al., 1993). Clover and other legumes are competitive only when a turf is at lower nitrogen fertility levels. Legumes manufacture their own fixed nitrogen from the air (see Chapter 10 for details). Adding nitrogen deprives them of this competitive advantage. • Dropping the N rate in an Oklahoma study prevented encroachment of volunteer bermudagrass into a tall fescue turf (Brede, 1992a). • Doubling the N rate from 2 to 4 lb per 1000 ft^2 (10 to 20 g/m^2) in tall fescue turf in Georgia cut crabgrass infestation from 31% down to 5% (Johnson, date not specified). • Changing the nitrogen form from nitrate to ammonium decreased shoot density and root weight of *Poa annua* in a "Penncross" bentgrass putting green (Eggens and Wright, 1985).
Sprayer pointers...	• Many herbicides (and other pesticides) are affected by the pH of the spray water. Check the pH of your tap water with an inexpensive test strip, a pocket pH meter, or by sending a sample to the lab. The herbicide label will guide you to the best water pHs. • Beware of mixing fertilizer in the spray tank with your herbicide—it may undesirably alter the pH of the spray solution. Although fertilizer in the spray tank can help mask the browning effects of herbicide on turf, the addition of fertilizer may make the herbicide less effective by altering the water pH. The same goes for adding fertilizer with insecticides or other pesticides. • Combining two pesticides in the spray tank is a way to save time when spraying. Unfortunately, not all pesticides are compatible with each other. And because of the vast number of possible combinations, there are no guides available to point the way. To determine pesticide compatibility, mix small portions of the two chemicals with water in a glass jar. Shake, and watch for sedimentation and clumping. If the solution resembles oatmeal or Jell-O, they're incompatible. • When mixing pesticides in a spray tank, add them in the right order. Charles Darrah of CLC Labs (Roche, 1997) recommends this sequence: Water first, then water-dispersible granules, wettable powders, flowables, fertilizers salts (agitate them as they're added), water-soluble liquids, and finally, emulsifiable concentrates.

- Hang a hand spray bottle of diluted herbicide solution on your mower to spot treat weeds as you mow. It avoids the need to treat the whole turf for just a few scattered problem weeds.

Observe bioindicators...

- **Bioindicators** are plants—usually woody ornamentals—that bloom at the same time as important natural deadlines, such as the right time to apply herbicides or insecticides. For example, application of preemergence crabgrass herbicides is most effective when timed to coincide with the end of forsythia blooming. Goosegrass preemergence herbicides should be applied as the lilac blossoms open. Flowering shrubs are remarkably reliable indicators of cumulative weather and temperature. They are far better predictors of year-to-year weed, insect, and disease activity than a simple calendar.
- Pay close attention to **indicator weeds**—weeds that suggest an underlying soil deficiency. Red sorrel indicates acid pH. Annual bluegrass, sedge, alligatorweed, moss, and algae indicate excessive moisture. Prostrate knotweed and goosegrass indicate compaction.
- The presence of weeds may imply that the grass you planted is not the right choice for your particular location. If weeds are continually a problem, the grass may not be tough enough to fight them. Choosing a better adapted species or cultivar can help (see Chapter 5 for selection tips).

Maximize the herbicide's effectiveness...

- Broadleaf turf weeds like dandelion are more easily controlled in the fall than the following spring (McCarty, 1994). Weeds get tougher and woodier as they mature, making them more resistant to herbicide. Young weeds are easier to control and a lower herbicide rate will suffice. A fall application requires *half* the herbicide rate needed in the spring.
- Herbicide applications should be coordinated with soil temperature. For example, ester herbicide formulations work with soil temperatures 45°F (7°C) and above. Salt formulations work best at soil temperatures above 55°F (13°C) (Lefton, 1996).
- **Adjuvents** are products that make pesticides work better. Some products help spread the herbicide more evenly over the plant's leaves, while others help stick it tighter to foliage.
- Check your local weather forecast before spraying. A postemergence herbicide is less effective if it rains before the chemical has had a chance to dry on the foliage. Preemergence herbicides, on the other hand, need to be watered in to be activated.
- In the plant world, **herbicide resistance** is not as common as resistance to fungicides or insecticides. But it's not unheard of either. Herbicide resistance is when a weed mutates to a form untouchable by the herbicide. Ever since the first case of herbicide resistance was reported in the late 1960s, more than 100 weed species have been identified with resistance to 14 families of herbicide (Morishita et al., 1994). As a rule of thumb, it's always a good idea to alternate between two or more products in different herbicide families to prevent the buildup of resistance.

Choose a natural alternative...

- Nick Christians, turf professor at Iowa State University (Christians, 1993), discovered that corn gluten meal acts as an effective preemergence herbicide for annual grassy weeds. Christians achieved 95% crabgrass control by applying gluten meal at 100 lb per 1000 ft^2 (495 g/m^2). The gluten meal doubles as a natural organic slow-release fertilizer, containing 10% N by weight.

Use a lower rate...

- University of Georgia weed researcher B.J. Johnson (1995), discovered that for control of crabgrass or goosegrass, a *decreasing* rate of preemergence herbicide can be used with each successive year of application. In year 1 he recommends a full rate of product, in year 2 a half rate, and in year 3 (and beyond) a quarter rate. The reason this trick works is because the turf itself becomes denser and resists weeds better each following year.

Table 12.5. Weed control tips: Pest management ideas for efficient control of turf weeds with less reliance on herbicides (continued).

	• B.J. Johnson (1996) also discovered that preemergence herbicide rates for large crabgrass can be reduced 50 to 67% by the addition of a postemergence herbicide after weeds emerge. He obtained a satisfactory 85% control for 8 full weeks with a 1/3 rate of preemergence herbicide, when it was followed by a full-rate of postemergence herbicide such as fenoxaprop or MSMA. In general, preemergence products tend to be more expensive and hang around longer in the environment than their postemergence counterparts. Thus, this technique is environmentally beneficial and it saves money. • Billy Huskins, superintendent of the Rivers Edge Golf Club in Fayetteville, GA, has an intriguingly simple method for reducing pesticide use. "Basically you should always use the lower rate," he says, referring to the range of rates listed on most pesticide labels. A typical label might recommend you spray a product at 1 to 2 lb per acre. Huskins always chooses the lower figure. Doing so has rewarded him with 10% less pesticide use than neighboring golf courses (Anonymous, 1996a).
Mow your weeds away...	• Let mowing rather than spraying rid your newly planted turf of weeds. Many weeds emerging with a new turf will simply mow away, without the need for spraying. • Mowing height has a profound effect on weed invasion. In a study of smooth crabgrass invasion, Pete Dernoeden and his colleagues (Dernoeden et al., 1992) found that a higher cutting height was an effective deterrent. Turf mowed at 3 1/2 in. (8.8 cm) resisted crabgrass invasion much better than turf cut at 1 1/4 or 2 1/4 in. (3.2 and 5.5 cm). "High mowing (8.8 cm) was of greater importance than N-level or herbicides in reducing smooth crabgrass encroachment and maintaining tall fescue cover," he concluded. • When lawn weeds are actively setting seed, collect the grass clippings as you mow. That way, you'll be vacuuming up the weed seed and preventing new plants from starting. Be cautious if you compost those clippings, since they'll be chocked full of new weeds. Research has shown that clipping collection is particularly useful for *Poa annua* control on golf courses. *Poa annua* seeds are collected in grass catchers and carted away, rather than sowing next year's crop of weeds. • Broadleaf weeds in turf can sometimes be controlled by vertical mowing in a crisscross direction. The vertical mower snips off all the weed's leaves and lateral stems, leaving just a bare stump. Golf superintendents use this technique for ridding putting greens of chickweed and other spreading weeds, without the need for spraying. • Taller growing weeds can sometimes be destroyed by temporarily lowering the cutting height. Weeds such as pigweed and lambsquarters, which grow uninhibited in taller turf, are destroyed by closer cutting. Of course, a closer cut will also bring its own cadre of weeds—annual bluegrass, chickweed, and moss prosper as cutting height is lowered.
Other cultural controls...	• Weeds can be tracked from one area to another by clinging to the mower deck. Avoid transferring weeds by hosing the mower with water between sites. Creeping bentgrass and other aggressive stoloniferous plants can be relocated simply by clippings. Pieces of cut stolon can propagate to places they're not supposed to be. • Turf weeds can be controlled by incinerating them where they're growing. Spot treatment with a propane flame can be used to sizzle and destroy individual weeds. Sales brochures for the Primus-Sievert Homeowner Flaming Device state that "weeds are killed effectively and conveniently without the need to crawl on the ground or use environmentally dangerous chemicals." One university researcher has even tested the *selectivity* of weed flamers—the ability to control weeds within live turf while leaving the turf only partially singed (Desjardins et al., 1995).

turf manager's most effective biological control weapon against many turf pests.

Endophytes were first recognized about 30 years ago by New Zealand pasture researchers studying a livestock disease known as Fescue Foot or Ryegrass Staggers. Something in the tall fescue, they reasoned, was contributing to this debilitating cattle ailment, since cattle rapidly recover when removed from a fescue ration. Researchers discovered that the fungus *Neotyphodium* (formerly called *Acremonium* or *Epicloe*) was living within the veins of infected plants, causing the cattle symptoms.

The remarkable thing about endophytes is that they are parasites that cause no apparent harm to their host plants. In fact, there is a mutually *beneficial* relationship between the fungus and grass—a type of **symbiosis**. The grass nourishes the fungus with energy compounds it creates from photosynthesis, while the fungus offers protective antibiotic chemicals to the grass. These antibiotics are toxic to animals that derive their sole diet from grass.

Endophyte antibiotics are also toxic to insects. Sod webworm, bluegrass billbug, Argentine stem weevil, southern armyworm, and chinch bugs are killed when they feed on infected grass. The endophyte gives the grass natural biological insect control, without the need for commercial pesticides.

The best thing about endophytes is that they don't have to be repeatedly inoculated, like some other biological agents. Once endophyte is within a grass plant, it's there for life. Endophytes readily spread into new shoots as your lawn grows, providing enduring pest control over the life of the turf. But they only spread from mother to daughter shoots of the same plant. They never spread across the lawn from plant to plant like infectious fungi do.

Endophytes are introduced into turf by planting or overseeding with high endophyte varieties. Unlike other forms of biological control, endophytes do not come in a sprayable form. To get endophytes into plants, grass breeders have to painstakingly inject the fungus with a hypodermic into each individual seedling. It's a laborious process that can only be performed on a limited number of breeder plants. There is no other known way to introduce endophytes into turf.

Many claims have been made about the power of endophytes, ranging from insect control, to disease control, better vigor, lower water use, and so on. Some of these claims have been substantiated by research, others originate from observation only. It's easy to jump to the conclusion that a plant has better drought tolerance when in fact it's the endophyte removing the insects that normally nibble away at its roots, that is causing the effect. Reed Funk, Bruce Clark, and Jennifer Johnson-Cicalese at Rutgers University (Funk et al., 1989) were unable to find differences in water use, evapotranspiration, plant canopy temperature, heat tolerance, or wilting from the presence or absence of endophyte alone.

Reports of disease resistance by endophytes are also heavily debated. Suichang Sun (Clarke et al., 1994) documented one example of endophyte control of dollar spot disease on strong creeping red fescue. Other researchers studying endophytes have come up empty-handed. University of Georgia plant pathologist Lee Burpee offers a reason why: "There have been some people who have suggested that endophyte plays a role [in disease control], but in many cases they haven't used **clonal** [plant] material. They'd maybe use one variety that has high endophyte and one that has low. Then of course you get into problems with varietal differences, besides the endophyte differences. There's really been no good clear-cut evidence that you get more or less disease—at least with brown patch anyway—with the endophyte versus no endophyte."

Even if the impact of endophytes on disease and water use eventually turns out to be minimal, endophyte's benefits in insect control is still a significant leap forward in pest management. To date, no reports of resistance to endophyte antibiotics have surfaced. Resistance is a real concern with many commercial pesticides, as pests mutate into resistant forms that can grow in spite of a pesticide. The reason endophytes have been spared may trace to the wide array of products produced by these microscopic chemical factories. But just to be on the safe side, endophyte technologists are presently searching the world for new sources of endophyte to ensure that the

Endophytes: Questions and Answers

Q: Do endophytes harm the grass plant?

A: Endophytes cause no injury or disease to turfgrasses. The only known "disease" is a curious symptom that occasionally shows up in seed production fields, never turf. Certain strains of endophytes are known to induce a seed production disease known as **choke**, but this disease affects only seedheads and does not affect mowed turf. Plant breeders minimize the effects of this disease by avoiding these problem strains.

Q: Are the endophyte toxins poisonous to children or pets who take a munch of infected grass?

A: The level of toxin in endophyte-infected grass is so low that it is harmless to children and pets. Endophytes only harm animals that derive their *sole* diet from infected plants. Walking barefoot on infected turf is also harmless.

Q: Do the toxins in endophyte grass wash away into the surface or groundwater?

A: No. The toxins are confined to inside the grass plant.

Q: How long will the endophyte live in my turf?

A: An endophyte will live in your lawn as long as the lawn itself lives. The endophyte passes from mother to daughter plant as the grass divides and thickens. It has no finite lifespan in turf.

Q: Do fungicides applied to the turf kill the endophyte?

A: Generally not. However, repeated heavy doses of systemic fungicide have been shown to diminish endophyte populations in turf.

Q: How long will endophytes stay viable in grass seed?

A: Endophytes are living entities, and care must be taken to ensure their viability when handling seed. Always buy fresh seed. Seed stored for longer than 9 to 12 months will loose endophyte viability. If possible, store seed under cool, dry conditions. Endophytes will remain viable in seed for up to 18 months if stored at 42°F (5°C).

Q: Can I inoculate my existing turf with endophyte?

A: No. There is no way to inoculate existing turf with endophyte. The only way to add endophyte is in a laboratory, plant by plant. Plant breeders do this while developing new varieties. The best way to add endophytes to existing turf is to *overseed* your turf with endophyte-containing varieties. Eventually the endophyte varieties will

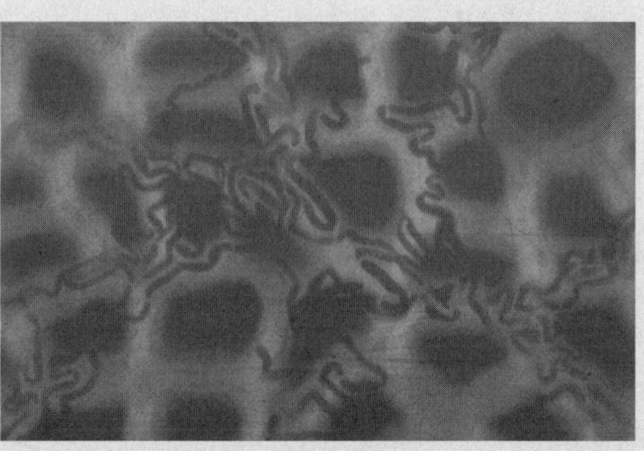

Figure 12.5. An **endophyte** is a microscopic fungus that resides inside a grass plant, snaking its way between cells. In exchange for its home, the endophyte gives off protectant chemicals that guard the grass against attack from certain insects. The endophyte fungus in this photo appears as the "spaghetti-looking" lines in between the round cells of a grass seed.

dominate by outcompeting the older, weaker plants.

Q: Do all turfgrasses contain endophyte?
A: No. Turf species and varieties vary widely in endophyte level. Kentucky bluegrass and creeping bentgrass never contain endophyte. Fescue and ryegrass may or may not contain it, depending upon variety. Some perennial ryegrass and tall fescue varieties contain high levels of endophyte. Others contain none. The informed buyer should beware.

Q: Why isn't the endophyte level listed on the bag of grass seed?
A: Plant breeders endeavor to instill a high level of endophyte in grass varieties. But seed farming, cleaning, handling, storage, shipping, and planting can affect the level of endophyte in the final turf. Storing seed for a month in a hot steamy warehouse can diminish the endophyte content considerably. That's why you're always best to use fresh seed, to get the highest level of endophyte possible. And that's why the exact level isn't listed on the label.

Q: Will I see the benefits of endophyte on my turf right away?
A: Probably not. Endophytes are like an insurance policy. They protect against future damage by insects and some other pests. But unless insects strike, you won't notice a difference.

Q: Where should I plant endophyte grasses?
A: The best use of high endophyte grasses is on turf sites facing restricted use of pesticides. The natural pest killers in high endophyte grass will decrease the need for commercial pesticide products. *All* turf projects stand to benefit from endophytes, including golf courses, sports fields, home lawns, parks, highway rights-of-way, and cemeteries.

varieties of tomorrow will be just as powerful against pests as today's.

Researchers are also attempting to move endophytes into turf species that don't normally contain one. Right now, endophytes are confined to only the ryegrasses and fescues. Never before have endophytes been reported in other common turf species.

A recent breakthrough by researcher Suichang Sun has succeeded in locating and inoculating the world's first Kentucky bluegrass endophyte. Some technical questions still remain be ironed out before the bluegrass endophyte is brought to the market, though with luck, Sun is hoping to have seed production of his new endophyte-enhanced bluegrass soon.

CHEMICAL CONTROL

Before I discuss pesticide use on turf, let me first review the list of what everybody already "knows" about pesticides:

- *Everybody "knows"* that turf management today is not nearly as good for the soil, plants, or consumers as the type of management practiced 100 years ago,
- *Everybody "knows"* that anything developed by a scientist or made or refined in a factory could not possibly be natural, and therefore must be bad,
- *Everybody "knows"* that anything with chemicals in it is bad,
- *Everybody "knows"* that synthetic chemicals are far more toxic than natural chemicals,
- *Everybody "knows"* that pesticide use on turf is comparatively huge, and is on the rise,
- *Everybody "knows"* that scientists or government regulators who disagree with what *everybody "knows,"* are in cahoots with the big chemical companies and should be shunned.

Everybody it seems has their minds made up on the subject of pesticides. You're either for them or against. You either see them as the salvation of our generation or as evil incarnate. And there's probably little I can do to convince you to change that belief one way or another.

But I feel it's important to moderate the extreme views on both poles of the pesticide issue. On the extreme propesticide side, there are people who reach for the pesticide bottle whenever they see a single insect or disease. Rather than confirm the identity of the pest, they'll apply two or three different pesticides at once "just to be sure." While there is nothing legally wrong with this approach, it does waste money and add unnecessary chemicals to the landscape. Golf courses, because of their high visibility, often get blamed for overapplication of pesticides. But I believe there are probably more untrained, unlicensed homeowners that fall into this category of overappliers than career turf professionals.

Then on the other side of the issue is the extreme antipesticide crowd. Some extremists go so far as to promote the complete abolishment of pesticides from the world, with little thought to the consequences of starvation and pestilence.

William Luellen, journal editor for the American Society of Agronomy who is credited with several of the wry *"everybody knows"* lines above (Luellen, 1996), discovered how thoroughly the popular aversion to chemicals permeates our society. One day he walked into a garden store and inquired about the chemical makeup of a particular brand of fertilizer. "Oh, it doesn't have chemicals," replied the clerk, "it's all natural."

Agricultural chemicals are seen by many people as dangerous, insidious, baby-killing, water-poisoning, and just plain uncool. Luellen believes that conventional wisdom about ag chemicals has been taken out of the hands of scientists and placed in the hands of spin doctors. "Politicians, network new anchors and reporters, radio talk show hosts, and TV and movie celebrities have ready access to the media, can talk convincingly, and have little or no credible opposition. So the scientifically illiterate public believes them," he says.

Of course it doesn't help when one scientist disagrees with another: (Cut to the videotape)—First you see a scientist talking about a big breakthrough in the lab. Then you see a second scientist saying the first one is full of cabbage. It's no wonder the viewing public grows cynical. But this is the nature of scientific debate. Scientists are *supposed* to question each other's findings. And journalists are *supposed* to show both sides of the issue. It's unfortunate that the general outcome is a distrust for anyone in a lab coat.

I believe moderation is the best answer in the pesticide debate. Wise use of pesticides can ensure good control of pests, while minimizing undesirable environmental impacts. Cultural and biological methods can supplement and even replace chemical application in many instances. But a total ban on ag pesticides would be devastating for the world's surging population.

In the remainder of this chapter, I'm going to discuss two important issues in pesticide management: Pesticide side effects and pesticide escape. For those of you who want more information on chemicals, I will refer you to the books on the market from this publisher on Integrated Pest Management. If you're looking for chemical recommendations for curing a specific pest problem, I would suggest a resource like *Grounds Maintenance* magazine. Pesticides change every year as new products and applications are added and older ones fall by the wayside. *Grounds Maintenance* annually publishes the most comprehensive, up-to-date listing of current turf pesticides available anywhere. Subscriptions to this magazine are free of charge to career turf managers (write to P.O. Box 12930, Overland Park, KS 66282-2930). Current chemical recommendations are also available on-line on the internet, using Cornell University's information server at *http://cce.cornell.edu/*.

Pesticide side effects

Picture a fish bowl containing two fish, a couple of plants, sand, gravel, and rocks. Introducing a chemical into this fish bowl would have fairly predictable results, biologically speaking. There aren't that many variables to confound the action of the introduced element.

Now picture that same chemical introduced into a large ocean. Because of the vastness of the

Concerns about Pesticides

Q: Do turf pesticides cause cancer?

A: Tests using high doses of turf pesticides on lab animals have shown that certain turf pesticides can induce cancer. The level of pesticide used in these tests is so high that it is nearly at toxic levels to the animal—many times higher than any applicator would encounter. Actually about half of *all* chemicals—natural or synthetic—induce cancer in lab animals. Even half of all chemicals found in nature can induce cancer at high doses. That's no endorsement to use pesticides haphazardly. It helps, though, to view the issue in balance.

Q: Aren't synthetic pesticide chemicals more harmful than natural chemicals?

A: Most people don't know that plants themselves produce natural protectant chemicals, similar to pesticides. According to Bruce Ames, professor of biochemistry at the University of California at Berkeley, we eat 10,000 times more of these natural pesticides in our diet than our consumption of synthetic pesticides.

Q: Why are medicines good and pesticides bad?

A: This may be hard to swallow, but some of the medicines we humans use are actually the exact same chemicals we spray as pesticides. Joe Vargas, professor of botany and plant pathology at Michigan State University, regularly lectures on the connection between medicines and pesticides. Mycotin® or myconasol, a popular athlete's foot medicine and jock itch, is actually the same active ingredient used to treat turf diseases. Lindane, a product used against turf spider mites, finds use as a medicine to kill human body lice. You'll also find lindane in your pet's flee collar. A popular over-the-counter sore throat remedy containing phenol, actually makes a potent herbicide against broadleaf weeds.

Q: Is turf pesticide use escalating?

A: Turf pesticide use has increased over the decades. Recent reports suggest the rate may be slowing. Furthermore, with the advent of biotechnology, advanced sciences promise to trim pesticide use even further. But even today, individuals can choose to use less pesticide, simply by adopting an attitude of lower maintenance. Park managers in Canada decreased their pesticide use 49% over the last five years through a concerted effort of alternative pest control methods (Anonymous, 1995c).

Q: Where is the greatest risk of pesticide exposure to humans?

A: Contrary to popular opinion, the greatest risk of pesticide exposure is not to the baby sitting on previously treated grass, or even to the cat who nibbles leaves. Studies show that the person who *mixes* the chemicals into the spray tank receives the greatest exposure, and should thus take the most safety precautions.

Q: Can applying too many pesticides harm the grass?

A: Applying pesticides at *above* their label rates can and does cause discoloration or phytotoxicity to turf. Excessive rates may even *kill* a lawn. But rates within label guidelines are generally safe to the grass, even if used frequently. Zac Reicher and Clark Throssell, researchers at Purdue University, made repeated fungicide treatments to turf and discovered only minor negative effects—the turf yielded slightly more clippings, turned a little darker green, and had a minor decrease in visual quality where treated (Reicher and Throssell, 1997). A word of caution, though: Repeated pesticide use can lead to **resistance**—the pest mutates into a pesticide-resistant form which is impervious to the chemical. Rotating your applications among several active ingredients is one way to slow the buildup of resistance.

environment and the plethora of species present, the chemical's behavior would be nearly unpredictable. It would be impossible to visualize all the possible ramifications a chemical would have on the legions of organisms encountered in a huge body of water. The outcome would be totally unknown.

Many people, when they apply a pesticide, envision the effect of one chemical on one pest. They think of their turf like a fish bowl. In reality, however, applying pesticides to turf is more like the ocean analogy. In a single fistful of thatch there are literally billions of living organisms—some good, some bad—all competing and interacting with one another. Every chemical we add to this system flips the biological apple cart one way or another.

One example of this unpredictability happened to Dick Smiley, plant pathologist at Oregon State University's Pendleton station. While on staff at Cornell University, Smiley noticed a huge buildup of mites in his plots following a routine fungicide application.

"We were using benomyl one season," says Smiley, "and we observed a fantastic mite population only where benomyl was being used. You know, it was in regular, rectangular blocks and in every replicate of those blocks."

Smiley, like many who have observed similar strange phenomena of turf pesticides, was at a loss to explain the population explosion. "I don't know what the mechanism might have been. It probably knocked down the predator mites."

The predator mites Smiley mentions are mites that feed on turf parasitic mites, helping keep their population in check. Once unleashed from their foe, the turf mites went berserk.

"The following season where there was a thinning of the turf, there was a greater heat buildup and the mite population evidently just exploded. There was just no doubt about the truism that the benomyl somehow induced a tremendous mite buildup in that turfgrass," he says.

Many other people have noticed these oddball side effects of turf pesticides. Most of the time there are no side effects at all. Turf pesticides produce no side effects perhaps 99% of the time. But every now and then, like a will-o'-the-wisp, strange things happen.

Nailing down these transient phenomena into scientific terms has proved frustrating for researchers. Although scientists like Smiley may note their occurrence in a single trial, researchers rarely can duplicate their findings a second time. When repeated, most such experiments come up negative. And to get published in a respected scientific journal, researchers need two years of positive data.

Some people have speculated that the big chemical companies may be quietly hushing research in this area, preventing results like Smiley's from coming to light. Pat Sanders, retired plant pathologist from Penn State University, disagrees: "No, I don't think it's because of the chemical companies. I think it's because progress in this area is so slow, so unrewarding, so frustrating. Researchers don't like to beat their heads on walls eternally. The system demands that eventually you do something—eventually you take something in your hand and say this is what I have produced. You can't always do that with this area. I mean, a lot of people have tried it for a while, but, you know, for a while."

University of Maryland's Pete Dernoeden has been one of the few researchers to land a scientific article on pesticide side effects (Dernoeden, 1992). In a three-year study, Dernoeden found significant *increases* in stripe smut disease from the use of thiram. The increases were significant in two of the three years. That was enough to convince fellow scientists to agree to publication. Dernoeden's article concluded: "Enhancement of nontarget diseases by fungicide use is attributed to offsetting a delicate balance between microbial antagonists and pathogens in the turfgrass ecosystem. These effects are likely to be caused by a complex interaction of plant genotype, environmental conditions, cultural practices, soil and rhizosphere pH, soil and thatch microorganisms, and probably other unknown factors."

Another possible explanation of these unexplained side-effects is what I'll call the "bounce-back" effect (Figure 12.6). Here's how it works: Let's say I spray half my lawn with fungicide to control an oncoming disease outbreak, leaving the other half untreated. As the disease epidemic progresses, the treated half remains green and

Figure 12.6. No, the signs in this photo are not reversed. This is an example of the type of "bounce-back" side effect that turf pesticides can have. In this photo from Penn State University, colonial bentgrass was sprayed repeatedly for dollar spot (r.), leaving the left half untreated (no fungicide). Later after the chemicals wore off, dollar spot preferentially struck the treated half over the untreated (see text for an explanation of the "bounce-back" effect).

vigorous, while the untreated half crumbles from the illness. If the epidemic is strong enough, the foliage in the untreated half may wither nearly to the ground.

Later as the epidemic passes, the untreated half bounces back, regenerating robust leaves and stems from the base of the plant. The treated half, however, has all along remained dense. This density, however, predisposes it to later damage after the protective pesticide wears off. An insect or disease that comes along would prefer the half that was thick and plush—the previously treated half—rather than the thin but regenerating untreated half. Thus to the observer, the treated half now appears to be *more* susceptible to pests than the untreated half.

What to do? Becoming aware of the potential for pesticide side effects is in itself a big step forward in prevention. For if a person anticipates the possibility of these strange phenomena, they may not come as such a surprise.

Smiley carries this thought one step further: "If a person knew what these side effects were, they could make a better selection among materials on the market. They would have a better perspective of the overall management costs on a year-to-year basis, rather than just season-to-season."

Until more knowledge is amassed on which products induce side effects and which don't, there are some general guidelines to help avoid these mysterious occurrences:

- Seek out pesticides that have *fewer* rather than more controlled pests listed on the label. A narrow-spectrum product has less chance of affecting nontarget organisms than a broad-spectrum kill-all.
- Never apply the same pesticide twice in a row. Alternate between two or three pesticides for a given pest, preferably ones with different active ingredients. Note that some pesticides with different trade names are made from the same active ingredient chemistry. These products would act identically in a turf ecosystem.
- If you're considering treating an area that's never been treated before, think again. After all, if an area has made it to this point without chemicals, it can make it now. Introducing a pesticide into a virgin ecosystem will throw a monkey wrench into the natural gears, albeit minor.
- Use a curative rather than preventive approach to pest control. Smiley: "I personally don't like to see totally preventive programs being utilized because they use way too much chemical. As quickly as [today's chemicals] get control of many diseases, I like to have them wait and see until the disease actually starts to occur the first time to make an application. And then hold off a while until it starts to come back before making another."

- If you're already experiencing what you think are pesticide side effects, you might try switching to a shorter residual product. Short-residual products give fewer weeks of pest control and have to be applied more often than long-lived ones. But their impact on the ecosystem is shorter lived as well. Penn State's Sanders believes a turf manager must understand "that controlling the disease is an infinitesimal part of the effect you're creating when you put fungicides down—especially ones that hang around forever and ever—the ones whose effect is felt for months, even years after they're down." Short-residual products control the pest and quickly dissipate from the environment.
- When applying pesticides, always leave an untreated check area somewhere. That way, you'll have a gauge of whether pesticide side effects are occurring. If you treat every square foot from fence to fence, you'll never know what your chemicals are doing to the ecosystem underfoot.
- Use systemic products sparingly. Systemic pesticides are taken up inside plants and other organisms. Inside, they have the opportunity to wreak havoc with the metabolism and physiology of the organism. Many people have seen the common bluish-green color that certain pesticides turn grass—that's the pesticide monkeying with the plant's physiology. Contact pesticides don't enter the plant. They reside on the *outside* of plants and don't interfere with growth processes.
- Minimize pesticide applications when turf is under stress. Heat and drought stress can make an ordinarily benign pesticide hot. And its effects may not be felt until months later. In one Tennessee study, agronomist Lloyd Callahan (1972) concluded: "Herbicides, applied months earlier, can and often do seriously weaken turf and predispose it to easy disease attacks during periods when the grass is under physical and/or environmental stress." Callahan emphasizes the "danger of consecutive annual herbicide treatments" on pest problems later on.

Pesticide escape

No matter how remote or isolated your turf facility is, it still has neighbors. A park or golf course located far removed from population centers is still connected to them by a number of branches. Your golf course may share a common drinking water aquifer with a distant community. A stream running through your park may drain into a river serving a downstream city. Or people walking across your pesticide-treated grounds may launder their clothes along with their family's.

No matter how distant your turf site may be, it is still connected to the community at large. And along with this connection comes the possibility of unwanted pesticide migration off-site. As good stewards of the land, it's up to us to do our part to minimize the impact of pesticides on neighbors and clients.

Fortunately there are some guidelines you can follow to reduce or eliminate pesticide escape, without resorting to a ban on pesticides. Below, are special situations where pesticides should be used *cautiously* or not at all, due to their tendency to escape into the environment:

- *Newly planted turf*—Before a young turf fills in and establishes a thatch, it is more prone to leaching and runoff losses. It takes about six months for seeded or sprigged turf to become dense enough to limit pesticide movement. Newly *sodded* turf does not suffer from this deficiency, however. It is fully capable of retaining and denaturing pesticides shortly after installation.
- *Slopes*—Slopes are particularly problematic for pesticide runoff. The steeper the slope, the greater the chance for runoff. South or west-facing slopes are more subject to photodecomposition and volatilization of pesticides, due to their higher light intensities.

- *Sandy soil*—Deep, sandy soils are prone to leaching. Water—and any suspended chemicals—flows readily through sand. Sandy soils are sometimes artificially created to serve as the base for a golf course putting green or all-weather sports field. These structures should be maintained lightly with pesticides until the turf has had a chance to develop a thatch and root system.
- *Soils with low organic matter content*—Organic matter and clay absorb and retain considerable quantities of pesticides and fertilizers. Soils low in organic retain little pesticide, allowing it to rinse through. A soil test indicating less than 2% organic matter content might signal trouble. Fortunately, soil organic matter tends to accumulate over time in a turf stand, as roots and shoots decay. It can also be bolstered by topdressings of compost or topsoil.
- *Wet weather*—Applying pesticide to damp foliage increases the risk of escape, because the chemical cannot adhere to the plant. Pay heed to the weather forecast. Heavy rain shortly after spraying can exaggerate leaching and runoff. Heavy irrigation can have the same effect. On the other end of the moisture spectrum, dry soils may pose a different problem: Prolonged persistence. Microbes need moisture to operate. In dry soils, microbes shut down and pesticides can persist longer than normal.
- *Wind*—High winds and low humidity aggravate drift and volatilization, during and after pesticide application.
- *High water table*—Perennially moist soils with a high water table can be prone to leaching. That's why Florida, with its high water tables, was the site of nearly all of the positive turf pesticide detections in U.S. groundwater, according to an EPA study. In certain areas, water tables may fluctuate throughout the year. Avoid or minimize pesticide applications during times of high water.
- *Winter*—Microbial decay of pesticides is linked to temperature. Higher temperatures stimulate microbes to break down chemicals faster. The optimal soil temperature for microbial breakdown is 77 to 95°F (25 to 35°C). Breakdown in cold or frozen soils is near nil, and pesticides can persist far longer than normal. Moreover, frozen soils are prone to surface runoff, because infiltration becomes blocked by ice.
- *Close proximity to bodies of water*—Good agronomic practice dictates leaving an untreated buffer strip around all lakes and streams as a barrier against pesticide escape.

Appendix

A Catalog of Unconventional Grasses

Many of the grasses listed in this table have been used in the past for reduced maintenance turf. Some have been employed along roadsides or as utility turf, while a few have even found applications on golf course fairways. Modern breeders have already set their sights on some of these species, producing experimental cultivars in various stages of development. Other grasses listed here are more speculative–they've shown the raw talent for low maintenance turf but have yet to be "discovered." By listing them here, I hope to create interest in their potential for turf application.

Key

Seed cost	$	*Inexpensive* – less than $1 per lb
	$$	*Moderate* – $1 to $5 per lb
	$$$	*Expensive* – $5 to $20 per lb
	$$$$	*Very expensive* – more than $20 per lb
Seed availability	✪	*Excellent* – readily available "off the shelf" as a commodity
	☆	*Moderate* – generally available but spot shortages can limit supply
	✧	*Fair* – seed is relatively scarce or is grown and harvested only on demand
	❍	*Poor* – seed is either unavailable or is hand harvested from the wild
Mowing and shade tolerance	✪	*Excellent*
	☆	*Moderate*
	✧	*Fair*
	❍	*Poor or no tolerance*
Wetland, salt, and alkalinity tolerance	👍	*Tolerant*
	👎	*Intolerant*
Ornamental/turf value	T	Suited for turf only; little ornamental value
	T/O	Adapted for both turf and ornamental purposes
	O	Best when used as an ornamental; usually intolerant of mowing
Bloom month		This is the month of the year when seedheads are apparent. (In the Southern Hemisphere, add or subtract 6 to find the correct month.)
Adapted zones		The six zones listed here correspond to the zone maps in Chapter 5.

Interpreting the Data in the Species Tables (Appendix)

- *Common name.* Grasses sometimes have more than one common name. I presented the most frequently referenced common name here, based on agronomic literature in the United States.

  Confusion takes place when two different grasses share the same common name. *Buchloe dactyloides,* for instance, is called buffalograss in the United States, while in Australia *Stenotaphrum secundatum* is called buffalograss. That's why it's important to consult the scientific or Latin name to make sure you've got the right grass. Synonyms are listed as "Other Common Names."
- *Scientific name.* A grass may have many common names, but it has only one scientific name. Scientific names—also called Latin names—are comprised of a first and last name, along with an authority. The first name is the **genus**; the last name is the **species**. That's backward to our English system of naming people, where the family name appears last. Two species of the same genus usually share many of the same characteristics and perform somewhat alike. Botanists classify plants into a genus based on their flower and internal characteristics more than their agronomics and management, though.

  Gardening books generally omit the final part of the scientific name: The **authority**. A scientific name is not complete without an authority listed. The authority is the person who first identified (or correctly identified) the species. Usually their name is abbreviated: "L.," for instance, stands for the ubiquitous 18th-century botanist, Carl Linnaeus, who roamed the land naming every plant in sight. The authority's name is also used for resolving disputes about a species. Scientists can look up the authority's original paper for verification.

  Contrary to what one might believe, Latin names are not cast in stone. Botanists change the names as they learn more about plants. Recently many of the *Agropyrons* were renamed to more accurately reflect their family ties. Unfortunately it takes a long time before this information trickles down to the rest of us. There is still a lot of confusion and misnaming of species in the trade. You may want to refer to the "Other Scientific Names" for assistance, which lists obsolete Latin names.
- *Varieties.* Varieties go in and out of vogue. Not all of the varieties listed here are available in a given year. But this list should serve as a starting point.

  Some varieties may be vegetatively propagated (sprigged or plugged) while others are seeded. Generally **variegated** (striped) ornamental varieties are established vegetatively.

  A few species (notably the forage grasses) have too many varieties to list them all here. I limited them to perhaps 15 of the more popular ones.
- *Plant height.* Plant height of a mature, unmowed, flowering grass plant was rounded to the nearest foot. This height reflects the height of mature seed stalks. The height of the leaves is usually less.

  Plant heights vary from one location to another. Fertile soils, adequate moisture, full sun, and a long growing season increase plant height. Use these height numbers for comparison purposes only. The height figures listed here are on the "robust" side; normally they are less.
- *Precipitation requirement.* This statistic is the minimum annual rainfall required to sustain a grass (assuming you're not irrigating). The minimum precipitation figure is determined by growing a grass under various rainfall zones and seeing where it survives. The precipitation statistic is somewhat subjective, based on the individual preferences of the researcher who took the data. For some obscure grasses, the researcher may have panned the grass because it grew too short—a disadvantage in the eyes of a forage specialist.

Also, mowing may not have been factored into the equation. Mowed grasses generally require more water to survive than unmowed grasses. No one knows exactly how much more (Gernert, 1936).

The precipitation figure also does not take into account seedling establishment. Turf establishment is vastly improved by judicious seedling irrigation. Even on sites that will eventually be unwatered, irrigation during establishment is beneficial. Without seedling irrigation, establishment may take one or more growing seasons to complete.

- ***Seeding rate.*** The seeding rate listed is the number of pounds of seed typically planted per 1000 ft^2 of lawn (grams per square meter). These figures are for *solid turf plantings*. They were derived from a unique equation described in Chapter 7. If you're going to use these grasses for soil stabilization or unmowed vista turf and don't care about the density of the stand, you can typically use one-tenth the seeding rate recommended here (Harlan et al., 1952).
- ***Ornamental value.*** Some grasses are beautiful when in bloom, with brightly colored plumes standing above brilliant foliage. Other grasses are rather dull and olive green. I suppose any grass could be used for ornamental purposes. After all, beauty is in the eye of the beholder. But some grasses are just naturally prettier than others—especially when in bloom. The grasses noted with ornamental value are useful for unmowed or infrequently mowed conditions, where the plant can form a tuft and develop showy seedheads.
- ***Flowering time.*** Nearly all grasses flower at one time or another. The flowers might be large and attractive or inconspicuous and nestled down in the foliage.

  The flowering month listed in the table is for grasses grown in the Northern Hemisphere. The flowering month indicates when seedheads are typically in bloom. In the Southern Hemisphere add or subtract 6 to get the correct flowering month.

  In climates lacking a distinct winter season (i.e., the tropics), flowering of many grasses can be indiscriminate. Flowering often coincides with the onset of the rainy season, for instance. Or grasses may just flower off and on throughout the year.

  Some cool-season grasses such as annual bluegrass are **indeterminate**, meaning they flower throughout the season regardless of weather. For indeterminate grasses, the month with the *most* flowering is listed in the table.
- ***Zone of adaptation.*** The zones listed here refer to the **zone maps** in Chapter 5. They *do not* correspond to the USDA zone maps (although similarities exist).

  For some of the more obscure grasses, the zone of adaptation and/or the mature plant height were extrapolated from botanical descriptions. These grasses may in fact turn out to have a broader range than what's listed here. But at least it's a starting point.
- ***Missing data.*** You've probably noticed data missing in the species table. For certain grasses, agronomic statistics as elementary as the number of seeds per pound or the flowering date have not been recorded in the literature. Rather than make up these figures, I left them blank. Perhaps these omissions will point the way toward future research work.

  I've included a few oddball grasses in the species table in hopes of motivating future entrepreneurs, researchers, and breeders toward the possibility of new low maintenance species with turf potential. My research on hundreds of grasses has indicated some with a strong potential for successful turf use.

Crested wheatgrass
Agropyron cristatum (L.) Gaertn.

Native to North America	Unmowed Height ft (m)	Cool- or Warm-Season	Growth Habit	Seed Count x000 per lb (kg)	"Turf" Seeding Rate lb/M (g/m^2)	Minimum Precipitation in. (mm)	Seed Cost	Seed Availability	Mowing Tolerance	Shade Tolerance	Wetland Tolerance	Salt Tolerance	Alkalinity Tolerance	Ornamental/ Turf Uses	Bloom Season	Adapted Zones
Exotic	2 ft (0.6)	Cool	Bunch	192 (422)	7 lb (36)	10 (254)	$	✪	☆	✪	👎	👍	👎	T/O	6	16

Varieties: Ephraim, Fairway, Hycrest, Kirk, Parkway, Ruff, Szarvasi 55

Comments: "Fairway" cultivar has turf potential. Credited with salvaging the Dust Bowl in the 1930s. Early spring growth. Rapid, vigorous establishment, ample seed yield, and favorable turf characteristics. Turf cultivars are being bred at Utah State University. Notable resistance to salinity, but substantially less than tall wheatgrass. The cultivars "Hycrest," "Parkway," and "Ruff" are an interspecific hybrid with *A. desertorum*. The species has been shown to dominate low maintenance stands and biologically-suppress noxious weeds. Has been used on golf fairways and lawns in arid environments.

References: Alderson and Sharp, 1994; Anonymous, 1993c; Asay and Jensen, 1996; Chapman, 1992; Spackeen, 1993; Stubbendieck et al., 1991; Troeh et al., 1991; Voigt and Haley, 1990; Wiesner and Brown, 1984

Standard crested wheatgrass
Agropyron desertorum (Fisch.) Schult.

Native to North America	Unmowed Height ft (m)	Cool- or Warm-Season	Growth Habit	Seed Count x000 per lb (kg)	"Turf" Seeding Rate lb/M (g/m^2)	Minimum Precipitation in. (mm)	Seed Cost	Seed Availability	Mowing Tolerance	Shade Tolerance	Wetland Tolerance	Salt Tolerance	Alkalinity Tolerance	Ornamental/ Turf Uses	Bloom Season	Adapted Zones
Exotic	3 ft (0.9)	Cool	Bunch	175 (385)	8 lb (38)	9 (228)	$	✪	☆	✪	👎	👎	👎	T	6	16

Former Latin names: *A. cristatum* spp. *desertorum*

Varieties: Nordan, Summit

Comments: A taller growing subspecies of regular crested wheatgrass. Not as turf adapted, except for low maintenance mixtures. Cold, drought, and shade tolerant. Early spring greenup.

References: Alderson and Sharp, 1994; Asay and Jensen, 1996; Olson and Anderson, 1994; Spackeen, 1993

Siberian wheatgrass
Agropyron fragile (Roth) P Candargy spp. *sibiricum* (Willd.) Melderis

Native to North America	Unmowed Height ft (m)	Cool- or Warm-Season	Growth Habit	Seed Count x000 per lb (kg)	"Turf" Seeding Rate lb/M (g/m^2)	Minimum Precipitation in. (mm)	Seed Cost	Seed Availability	Mowing Tolerance	Shade Tolerance	Wetland Tolerance	Salt Tolerance	Alkalinity Tolerance	Ornamental/ Turf Uses	Bloom Season	Adapted Zones
Exotic	2 ft (0.6)	Cool	Bunch	170 (374)	8 lb (38)	6 (152)	$$	✪	☆	☆	👎	👎	👎	T	?	16

Former Latin names: *A. sibiricum, A. cristatum* spp. *fragile*

Other common names: Siberian crested wheatgrass

Varieties: P-27

Comments: More drought hardy than crested wheatgrass but less "turfy." Suited to fine, dry soils. Extremely winter-hardy.

References: Alderson and Sharp, 1994; Asay and Jensen, 1996; Spackeen, 1993; Tutin et al., 1980

Sand couch
Agropyron junceum (L.) Beauv.

Native to North America	Unmowed Height ft (m)	Cool- or Warm-Season	Growth Habit	Seed Count x000 per lb (kg)	"Turf" Seeding Rate lb/M (g/m^2)	Minimum Precipitation in. (mm)	Seed Cost	Seed Availability	Mowing Tolerance	Shade Tolerance	Wetland Tolerance	Salt Tolerance	Alkalinity Tolerance	Ornamental/ Turf Uses	Bloom Season	Adapted Zones
Exotic	2 ft (0.6)	Cool	Rhiz.	? (?)	? lb (?)	? (?)	$$$$	❍	✪	☆	👍	👍	👎	O	6	123 6

Former Latin names: *Triticum junceum*

Comments: Dune/seashore grass. Fine, bluish green foliage.

References: Oakes, 1990

Idaho bentgrass
Agrostis idahoensis Nash.

Native to North America	Unmowed Height ft (m)	Cool- or Warm-Season	Growth Habit	Seed Count x000 per lb (kg)	"Turf" Seeding Rate lb/M (g/m^2)	Minimum Precipitation in. (mm)	Seed Cost	Seed Availability	Mowing Tolerance	Shade Tolerance	Wetland Tolerance	Salt Tolerance	Alkalinity Tolerance	Ornamental/ Turf Uses	Bloom Season	Adapted Zones
Native	1 ft (0.3)	Cool	Bunch	? (?)	? lb (?)	? (?)	$$	✪	✪	☆	👍	👎	👍	T/O	7	123 46

Former Latin names: *A. filiculmis*

Other common names: Idaho redtop

Varieties: GolfStar

Comments: U.S. native bentgrass found in nature along the Rocky Mountains from New Mexico to Fairbanks, Alaska. Slender and low growing. Tolerant of acid soil and heavy metals. Suited to mid to high elevation. Similar to *A. oregonensis*, but shorter. "GolfStar" variety tolerates mowing to $^{1}/_{2}$-in. (12 mm) as permanent turf, or to putting green heights for winter overseeding.

References: Correll and Correll, 1972; Cronquist et al., 1977; Hitchcock, 1951; Pojar and MacKinnon, 1994

Creeping foxtail
Alopecurus arundinaceus Poir.

Native to North America	Unmowed Height ft (m)	Cool- or Warm-Season	Growth Habit	Seed Count x000 per lb (kg)	"Turf" Seeding Rate lb/M (g/m^2)	Minimum Precipitation in. (mm)	Seed Cost	Seed Availability	Mowing Tolerance	Shade Tolerance	Wetland Tolerance	Salt Tolerance	Alkalinity Tolerance	Ornamental/ Turf Uses	Bloom Season	Adapted Zones
Exotic	3 ft (0.9)	Cool	Rhiz.	900 (1980)	3 lb (14)	25 (635)	$$	✪	☆	☆	👍	👍	👎	T	?	136

Former Latin names: *A. ventricosus*

Varieties: Garrison, Retain

Comments: Used for reclamation of erosion-prone stream banks. Submersion tolerant. Dense sod-former helps bind erosive soils.

References: Anonymous, 1995d; Hitchcock, 1951; Spackeen, 1993; Tutin et al., 1980

Meadow foxtail — *Alopecurus pratensis* L.

Native to North America	Unmowed Height ft (m)	Cool- or Warm-Season	Growth Habit	Seed Count x000 per lb (kg)	"Turf" Seeding Rate lb/M (g/m²)	Minimum Precipitation in. (mm)	Seed Cost	Seed Availability	Mowing Tolerance	Shade Tolerance	Wetland Tolerance	Salt Tolerance	Alkalinity Tolerance	Ornamental/ Turf Uses	Bloom Season	Adapted Zones
Exotic	2 ft (0.6)	Cool	Bunch	580 (1276)	4 lb (19)	20 (508)	$$	☆	☆	☆	👍	👎	👎	T/O	7	123 6

Other common names: Yellow foxtail, lamb's tail, common foxtail
Varieties: Alko, Aureo-variegatus, Aureus, Dan, Epic, Glaucus, Levocska, Lipex, Mountain, Vulpera, Wehrdaer Rhona
Comments: Prefers wet soils. Persistent on low pH soils. Light benefits seed germination. Not adapted for desert climates. Rust susceptible. Ornamental vegetative cultivars are available.
References: Anonymous, 1993c; Anonymous, 1996b; Greenlee and Fell, 1992; Grounds, 1979; Hooven and Hooven, 1995; Long, 1981; Oakes, 1990; OECD, 1996; Spackeen, 1993; Tutin et al., 1980; Young and Young, 1986

European beachgrass — *Ammophila arenaria* (L.) Link

Native to North America	Unmowed Height ft (m)	Cool- or Warm-Season	Growth Habit	Seed Count x000 per lb (kg)	"Turf" Seeding Rate lb/M (g/m²)	Minimum Precipitation in. (mm)	Seed Cost	Seed Availability	Mowing Tolerance	Shade Tolerance	Wetland Tolerance	Salt Tolerance	Alkalinity Tolerance	Ornamental/ Turf Uses	Bloom Season	Adapted Zones
Exotic	4 ft (1.2)	Cool	Rhiz.	114 (250)	9 lb (46)	? (?)	$$$$	❍	✧	☆	👍	👍	👎	O	8	12

Former Latin names: *Arundo arenaria*
Other common names: European beach rye, marram grass, dune grass
Comments: One of the bluest ornamental grasses. Not suited for long-term dune stabilization but as a temporary solution until other grasses take hold. Does best where sand is "accumulating" rather than stable. Seed is often sterile.
References: Alderson and Sharp, 1994; Dorris, 1993; Greenlee and Fell, 1992; Hughes et al., 1951; Oakes, 1990; Pojar and MacKinnon, 1994

American beachgrass — *Ammophila breviligulata* Fern.

Native to North America	Unmowed Height ft (m)	Cool- or Warm-Season	Growth Habit	Seed Count x000 per lb (kg)	"Turf" Seeding Rate lb/M (g/m²)	Minimum Precipitation in. (mm)	Seed Cost	Seed Availability	Mowing Tolerance	Shade Tolerance	Wetland Tolerance	Salt Tolerance	Alkalinity Tolerance	Ornamental/ Turf Uses	Bloom Season	Adapted Zones
Native	3 ft (0.9)	Cool	Rhiz.	? (?)	? lb (?)	? (?)	$$$$	❍	✧	☆	👍	👍	👎	O	8	123 4

Former Latin names: *A. champlainensis*
Other common names: Sand reed, psamma, marram
Varieties: Cape, Hatteras
Comments: Gray-green leaves. Limited seed availability—about 50 acres of U.S. seed production of the variety "Cape." Widely used as a sand-stabilizing grass.
References: Alderson and Sharp, 1994; Brown, 1979; Oakes, 1990; Reinhardt et al., 1989

Big bluestem — *Andropogon gerardi* Vitman

Native to North America	Unmowed Height ft (m)	Cool- or Warm-Season	Growth Habit	Seed Count x000 per lb (kg)	"Turf" Seeding Rate lb/M (g/m²)	Minimum Precipitation in. (mm)	Seed Cost	Seed Availability	Mowing Tolerance	Shade Tolerance	Wetland Tolerance	Salt Tolerance	Alkalinity Tolerance	Ornamental/ Turf Uses	Bloom Season	Adapted Zones
Native	5 ft (1.5)	Warm	Rhiz.	165 (363)	8 lb (39)	18 (457)	$$	✪	✧	❍	👎	👎	👍	T/O	8	134 5

Other common names: Popotillo gigante, turkeyfoot, turkey claw, beardgrass
Varieties: Bison, Bonilla, Champ, Kaw, Niagara, Pawnee, Roundtree, Sunnyview
Comments: Classic, tall prairie grass. Purple and yellow seedheads. Bluish green stems that turn purple in winter. Has 190,000 seed/lb when debearded. Mild, moist conditions for 2 weeks are required to initiate germination. Light and shallow planting also benefit establishment. Tolerates the usual herbicides of warm-season grasses.
References: Anonymous, 1995d; Anonymous, 1996b; Archer and Sellers, 1956; Brown, 1979; Oakes, 1990; Spackeen, 1993; Stubbendieck et al., 1991; Young and Young, 1986

Sand bluestem — *Andropogon hallii* Hack.

Native to North America	Unmowed Height ft (m)	Cool- or Warm-Season	Growth Habit	Seed Count x000 per lb (kg)	"Turf" Seeding Rate lb/M (g/m²)	Minimum Precipitation in. (mm)	Seed Cost	Seed Availability	Mowing Tolerance	Shade Tolerance	Wetland Tolerance	Salt Tolerance	Alkalinity Tolerance	Ornamental/ Turf Uses	Bloom Season	Adapted Zones
Native	6 ft (1.8)	Warm	Rhiz.	105 (231)	10 lb (48)	14 (355)	$$	✪	✧	❍	👎	👎	👎	T	7	134

Other common names: Hall's beardgrass
Varieties: Elida, Garden, Goldstrike, Woodward
Comments: A useful sod-forming grass for droughty soils in the arid zone. Prefers sandy, drier sites. Lighter in color than big bluestem. Mild, moist conditions for 2 weeks are required for germination. Sunlight and shallow planting benefits germination.
References: Alderson and Sharp, 1994; Anonymous, 1995a; Featherly, 1946; Spackeen, 1993; Wiesner and Brown, 1984; Young and Young, 1986

$ – Inexpensive; $$ – Moderate; $$$ – Expensive; $$$$ – Very expensive; ✪ – Excellent; ☆ – Moderate; ✧ – Fair; ❍ – Poor or no tolerance; 👍 – Tolerant; 👎 – Intolerant; T – *Turf;* T/O – *Turf and Ornamental;* O – *Ornamental*

Creeping bluestem
Andropogon stolonifer (Nash) Hitchc.

Native to North America	Unmowed Height ft (m)	Cool- or Warm-Season	Growth Habit	Seed Count x000 per lb (kg)	"Turf" Seeding Rate lb/M (g/m^2)	Minimum Precipitation in. (mm)	Seed Cost	Seed Availability	Mowing Tolerance	Shade Tolerance	Wetland Tolerance	Salt Tolerance	Alkalinity Tolerance	Ornamental/ Turf Uses	Bloom Season	Adapted Zones
Native	3 ft (0.9)	Warm	Rhiz.	? (?)	? lb (?)	? (?)	$$$$	❍	☆	✧	👎	👎	👎	T/O	8	5

Former Latin names: *Schizachyrium stoloniferum*
Comments: Low growing, soil-knitting grass that provides erosion control. Somewhat shade and acid soil tolerant.
References: Oakes, 1990

Sweet vernal grass
Anthoxanthum odoratum L.

Native to North America	Unmowed Height ft (m)	Cool- or Warm-Season	Growth Habit	Seed Count x000 per lb (kg)	"Turf" Seeding Rate lb/M (g/m^2)	Minimum Precipitation in. (mm)	Seed Cost	Seed Availability	Mowing Tolerance	Shade Tolerance	Wetland Tolerance	Salt Tolerance	Alkalinity Tolerance	Ornamental/ Turf Uses	Bloom Season	Adapted Zones
Exotic	2 ft (0.6)	Cool	Bunch	726 (1597)	3 lb (16)	? (?)	$$$	✧	✪	☆	👍	👎	👎	T/O	5	1234

Former Latin names: *Xanthonanthos odoratum*
Other common names: Flouve
Comments: Widely distributed wasteland grass, occasionally cultivated for turf. University of Rhode Island was developing turf cultivars. Yellow blossoms in early spring. Tolerates wide pH. Plants resemble redtop. Fragrant from coumarin when cut. Foliage is too bitter for wildlife. Tolerates traffic. Goes into summer dormancy and disappears by midsummer.
References: Anonymous, 1995a; Breakwell, 1923; Brown, 1979; Daniels, 1995; Francis, 1912; Grenlee and Fell, 1992; Hughes et al., 1951; Oakes, 1990; Pohl, 1968; Pojar and MacKinnon, 1994; Young and Young, 1986

Polargrass
Arctagrostis latifolia (R.Br.) Griseb.

Native to North America	Unmowed Height ft (m)	Cool- or Warm-Season	Growth Habit	Seed Count x000 per lb (kg)	"Turf" Seeding Rate lb/M (g/m^2)	Minimum Precipitation in. (mm)	Seed Cost	Seed Availability	Mowing Tolerance	Shade Tolerance	Wetland Tolerance	Salt Tolerance	Alkalinity Tolerance	Ornamental/ Turf Uses	Bloom Season	Adapted Zones
Native	1 ft (0.3)	Cool	Rhiz.	? (?)	? lb (?)	? (?)	$$$$	❍	✪	☆	👍	👎	👎	T	5	16

Varieties: Alyeska, Kenai
Comments: Alpine grass tolerant of extreme cold and drought. Dark color. Low growing.
References: Alderson and Sharp, 1994

Tall oatgrass
Arrhenatherum elatius (L.) J.&K. Presl

Native to North America	Unmowed Height ft (m)	Cool- or Warm-Season	Growth Habit	Seed Count x000 per lb (kg)	"Turf" Seeding Rate lb/M (g/m^2)	Minimum Precipitation in. (mm)	Seed Cost	Seed Availability	Mowing Tolerance	Shade Tolerance	Wetland Tolerance	Salt Tolerance	Alkalinity Tolerance	Ornamental/ Turf Uses	Bloom Season	Adapted Zones
Exotic	3 ft (0.9)	Cool	Bunch	150 (330)	8 lb (41)	14 (355)	$$$$	✧	✧	☆	👍	👍	👎	T	8	123

Former Latin names: *A. elatius bulbosum*
Other common names: Meadow oatgrass, bulbous oat grass, false oat grass, onion couch
Varieties: Arel 41, Arone, Deal, Gala, Grano, Levocsky, Odenwalder, Roznovsky, SK-5, Sora, Tualatin, Wena, Wiwena, Variegatum (ssp. *Bulbosum*)
Comments: Classic seashore sand-stabilizing grass. Dark green foliage. Good winter performance. Light yellow panicles. Seed glumes can be dehulled to aid in planting and germination. Seed germinates readily and vigorously with no dormancy. Seed supplies are hard to locate, though. Susceptible to rust.
References: Alderson and Sharp, 1994; Anonymous, 1993c; Anonymous, 1993f; Beard, 1988; Bernstein, 1958; Greenlee and Fell, 1992; Grounds, 1979; Hitchcock, 1951; Hubbard, 1984; Leasure et al., 1994; OECD, 1996; Reinhardt et al., 1989

Caucasian bluestem
Bothriochloa caucasica (Trin.) C.E. Hubbard

Native to North America	Unmowed Height ft (m)	Cool- or Warm-Season	Growth Habit	Seed Count x000 per lb (kg)	"Turf" Seeding Rate lb/M (g/m^2)	Minimum Precipitation in. (mm)	Seed Cost	Seed Availability	Mowing Tolerance	Shade Tolerance	Wetland Tolerance	Salt Tolerance	Alkalinity Tolerance	Ornamental/ Turf Uses	Bloom Season	Adapted Zones
Exotic	4 ft (1.2)	Warm	Bunch	1072 (2358)	2 lb (12)	16 (406)	$$	☆	✧	❍	👎	👎	👎	O	7	134

Former Latin names: *Andropogon caucasicus, A. intermedius caucasius, Sorghum caucasicum*
Varieties: Caucasian, KG-40
Comments: Good heat and drought tolerance. Seed quality is a problem. Seedlots typically have less than 30% PLS. Strongly pink to purplish seedheads. Useful in prairie mixtures.
References: Alderson and Sharp, 1994; Grounds, 1979; Tutin et al., 1980; Wasser, 1982

Yellow bluestem
Bothriochloa ischaemum (L.) Keng

Native to North America	Unmowed Height ft (m)	Cool- or Warm-Season	Growth Habit	Seed Count x000 per lb (kg)	"Turf" Seeding Rate lb/M (g/m^2)	Minimum Precipitation in. (mm)	Seed Cost	Seed Availability	Mowing Tolerance	Shade Tolerance	Wetland Tolerance	Salt Tolerance	Alkalinity Tolerance	Ornamental/ Turf Uses	Bloom Season	Adapted Zones
Exotic	4 ft (1.2)	Warm	Bunch	1400 (3080)	2 lb (10)	15 (381)	$$	☆	✧	❍	👎	👎	👎	T/O	7	345

Former Latin names: *Andropogon ischaemum*
Other common names: Old world bluestem, Turkestan bluestem, King Ranch bluestem, yellow beardgrass
Varieties: El Kan, Ganada, King Ranch, Plains, WW-Iron Master, WW-Spar
Comments: Vigorous prairiegrass. Prefers dry, fine textured soils. Two botanical varieties exist: *ischaemum* and *songarica*, of which "King Ranch" belongs to the latter. The other cultivars listed are variety ischaemum. Yellow bluestem derives its names from its blue foliage and yellow heads.
References: Alderson and Sharp, 1994; Anonymous, 1996b; Skerman and Riveros, 1990; Tutin et al., 1980

Native to North America	Unmowed Height ft (m)	Cool- or Warm-Season	Growth Habit	Seed Count x000 per lb (kg)	"Turf" Seeding Rate lb/M (g/m²)	Minimum Precipitation in. (mm)	Seed Cost	Seed Availability	Mowing Tolerance	Shade Tolerance	Wetland Tolerance	Salt Tolerance	Alkalinity Tolerance	Ornamental/ Turf Uses	Bloom Season	Adapted Zones

Red grass

Bothriochloa macra (Steudel) Blake

Native to North America	Unmowed Height ft (m)	Cool- or Warm-Season	Growth Habit	Seed Count x000 per lb (kg)	"Turf" Seeding Rate lb/M (g/m²)	Minimum Precipitation in. (mm)	Seed Cost	Seed Availability	Mowing Tolerance	Shade Tolerance	Wetland Tolerance	Salt Tolerance	Alkalinity Tolerance	Ornamental/ Turf Uses	Bloom Season	Adapted Zones
Exotic	2 ft (0.6)	Warm	Bunch	? (?)	? lb (?)	? (?)	$$$	✧	☆	✧	👎	👎	👎	T/O	7	345

Other common names: Redleg grass
Comments: Ornamental red-purple color to heads and stems. Tolerates zero fertilizer but responds if given more. Best when mowed above 2 in. (5 cm). Seed is produced in Australia.
References: Greenway, 1997

Creeping bluegrass

Bothriochloa pertusa (L.) A. Camus

Native to North America	Unmowed Height ft (m)	Cool- or Warm-Season	Growth Habit	Seed Count x000 per lb (kg)	"Turf" Seeding Rate lb/M (g/m²)	Minimum Precipitation in. (mm)	Seed Cost	Seed Availability	Mowing Tolerance	Shade Tolerance	Wetland Tolerance	Salt Tolerance	Alkalinity Tolerance	Ornamental/ Turf Uses	Bloom Season	Adapted Zones
Exotic	ft ( )	Warm	Stolon	? (?)	? lb (?)	? (?)	$$$$	✪	☆	❍	👎	👎	👎	T/O	8	345

Former Latin names: *Andropogon pertusus, Dichanthium pertusum, Holcus pertusus*
Other common names: Hurricane grass, pitted-bluestem, Indian couch grass, comegueyana, bowen grass
Varieties: Dawson
Comments: Introduced grass from South Africa. Cultivated as an informal lawngrass in Queensland, Australia, where it is known locally as "Dawson" creeping lawngrass.
References: Greenway, 1997; Tothill and Hacker, 1983

Silver beardgrass

Bothriochloa saccharoides (Sw.) Rydb.

Native to North America	Unmowed Height ft (m)	Cool- or Warm-Season	Growth Habit	Seed Count x000 per lb (kg)	"Turf" Seeding Rate lb/M (g/m²)	Minimum Precipitation in. (mm)	Seed Cost	Seed Availability	Mowing Tolerance	Shade Tolerance	Wetland Tolerance	Salt Tolerance	Alkalinity Tolerance	Ornamental/ Turf Uses	Bloom Season	Adapted Zones
Native	3 ft (0.9)	Warm	Bunch	? (?)	? lb (?)	? (?)	$$$	✧	✪	✧	👎	👍	👍	T/O	7	345

Former Latin names: *Andropogon saccharoides, A. argenteus*
Other common names: Silver bluestem, beardgrass, popotillo plateado
Comments: A dual turf and ornamental grass. Attractive, white puffy seedheads. Smooth, blue-green foliage. Can escape cultivation and become a weed, particularly in bermudagrass turf. Begins growing in spring when temperatures reach 75°F (21 to 24°C). Flowers emerge 3 to 4 weeks later.
References: Darke, 1994; Greenlee and Fell, 1992; Olson and Anderson, 1994; Pohl, 1968; Stubbendieck et al., 1991

Sideoats grama

Bouteloua curtipendula (Michx.) Torr.

Native to North America	Unmowed Height ft (m)	Cool- or Warm-Season	Growth Habit	Seed Count x000 per lb (kg)	"Turf" Seeding Rate lb/M (g/m²)	Minimum Precipitation in. (mm)	Seed Cost	Seed Availability	Mowing Tolerance	Shade Tolerance	Wetland Tolerance	Salt Tolerance	Alkalinity Tolerance	Ornamental/ Turf Uses	Bloom Season	Adapted Zones
Native	2 ft (0.6)	Warm	Rhiz.	191 (420)	7 lb (36)	14 (355)	$$	☆	☆	❍	👎	👍	👍	T/O	8	134

Former Latin names: *B. oligostachya, Chloris curtipendula*
Other common names: Banderilla, tall grama, mesquite grass
Varieties: Butte, El Reno, Haskell, Killdeer, Niner, Pierre, Premier, Trailway, Vaughn
Comments: Less drought hardy than blue grama and not as mow tolerant. Prefers well-drained sites. Unique, ornamental seedheads. Good seed germination, no dormancy. Early greenup for a warm-season grass.
References: Anonymous, 1988; Anonymous, 1993c; Anonymous, 1995d; Brown, 1979; Oakes, 1990; Pair, 1994; Portz, 1986; Spackeen, 1993; Stubbendieck et al., 1991; Young and Young, 1986

Black grama

Bouteloua eriopoda (Torr.) Torr.

Native to North America	Unmowed Height ft (m)	Cool- or Warm-Season	Growth Habit	Seed Count x000 per lb (kg)	"Turf" Seeding Rate lb/M (g/m²)	Minimum Precipitation in. (mm)	Seed Cost	Seed Availability	Mowing Tolerance	Shade Tolerance	Wetland Tolerance	Salt Tolerance	Alkalinity Tolerance	Ornamental/ Turf Uses	Bloom Season	Adapted Zones
Native	2 ft (0.6)	Warm	Stolon	1335 (2937)	2 lb (10)	9 (228)	$$	☆	✧	❍	👎	👎	👎	T	7	34

Other common names: Navajita negra
Varieties: Nogal
Comments: Very drought hardy desert grass. Palatable to wildlife. Seed is hard to locate and suffers from low viability. Slow spring growth, waiting until ample moisture is available. Desirable forage for desert wildlife.
References: Alderson and Sharp, 1994; Anonymous, 1988; Archer and Sellers, 1956; Stubbendieck et al., 1991; Young and Young, 1986

$** – *Inexpensive;* **$$** – *Moderate;* **$$$** – *Expensive;* **$$$$ – *Very expensive;* ✪ – *Excellent;* ☆ – *Moderate;* ✧ – *Fair;* ❍ – *Poor or no tolerance;* 👍 – *Tolerant;* 👎 – *Intolerant;* T – *Turf;* T/O – *Turf and Ornamental;* O – *Ornamental*

Blue grama
Bouteloua gracilis (Willd. ex Kunth) Lag. ex Griffiths

Native to North America	Unmowed Height ft (m)	Cool- or Warm-Season	Growth Habit	Seed Count x000 per lb (kg)	"Turf" Seeding Rate lb/M (g/m^2)	Minimum Precipitation in. (mm)	Seed Cost	Seed Availability	Mowing Tolerance	Shade Tolerance	Wetland Tolerance	Salt Tolerance	Alkalinity Tolerance	Ornamental/ Turf Uses	Bloom Season	Adapted Zones
Native	2 ft (0.6)	Warm	Bunch	897 (1973)	3 lb (14)	12 (304)	$$	☆	☆	❍	👎	👍	👎	T/O	8	1345

Other common names: Mosquito grass, navajita azul
Varieties: Alma, Bad River, Hachita, Lovington
Comments: Grama has been used for years as a lawngrass in arid regions. Highly drought resistant. Slow seed germination and low purity. Not as salt tolerant as bermudagrass or zoysia. Produces a stemmy, blue turf. Tolerates mowing but best if mowed above 3 in. (7.5 cm). Dormant during dry summers. Improved turf cultivars being bred at Colorado State University. Long stand life.
References: Alderson and Sharp, 1994; Anonymous, 1995d; Anonymous, 1996b; Harivandi, 1993; Pair, 1994; Reinhardt et al., 1989; Spackeen, 1993; Stubbendieck et al., 1991; Wasser, 1982; Wiesner and Brown, 1984; Young and Young, 1986

Signal grass
Brachiaria decumbens Stapf

Native to North America	Unmowed Height ft (m)	Cool- or Warm-Season	Growth Habit	Seed Count x000 per lb (kg)	"Turf" Seeding Rate lb/M (g/m^2)	Minimum Precipitation in. (mm)	Seed Cost	Seed Availability	Mowing Tolerance	Shade Tolerance	Wetland Tolerance	Salt Tolerance	Alkalinity Tolerance	Ornamental/ Turf Uses	Bloom Season	Adapted Zones
Exotic	2 ft (0.6)	Warm	Stolon	1000 (2200)	3 lb (13)	60 (1524)	$$$$	❍	☆	☆	👍	👎	👎	T	5	5

Other common names: Suriname grass, Kenya sheep grass
Varieties: Basilisk, Reyan #3
Comments: Fairly drought and shade tolerant, but prefers moist, humid, tropical regions. Dense growth suppresses weeds. An obligate aposporous apomict (clones itself through seed). Excellent on low fertility soils.
References: Anonymous, 1993c; de Guzman, 1984; Judd, 1979; McIvor and Chen, 1985; Skerman and Riveros, 1990; Wu et al., 1992

Tor grass
Brachypodium pinnatum (L.) Beauv.

Native to North America	Unmowed Height ft (m)	Cool- or Warm-Season	Growth Habit	Seed Count x000 per lb (kg)	"Turf" Seeding Rate lb/M (g/m^2)	Minimum Precipitation in. (mm)	Seed Cost	Seed Availability	Mowing Tolerance	Shade Tolerance	Wetland Tolerance	Salt Tolerance	Alkalinity Tolerance	Ornamental/ Turf Uses	Bloom Season	Adapted Zones
Exotic	3 ft (0.9)	Cool	Rhiz.	? (?)	? lb (?)	? (?)	$$$$	❍	✪	☆	👎	👎	👍	T	6	12346

Other common names: Chalk false-brome, heath false-brome
Comments: Perhaps the best of the *Brachypodium* species for turf. Tolerant of heat, cold, drought, low fertility. Survives to 62 degrees North latitude. Good seed productivity and germination. An erect bunch grass with light green to yellow-green foliage.
References: Darke, 1994; Hitchcock, 1951; Hubbard, 1984; Tutin et al., 1980; Wu and Harivandi, 1988

Smooth brome
Bromus inermis Leyss.

Native to North America	Unmowed Height ft (m)	Cool- or Warm-Season	Growth Habit	Seed Count x000 per lb (kg)	"Turf" Seeding Rate lb/M (g/m^2)	Minimum Precipitation in. (mm)	Seed Cost	Seed Availability	Mowing Tolerance	Shade Tolerance	Wetland Tolerance	Salt Tolerance	Alkalinity Tolerance	Ornamental/ Turf Uses	Bloom Season	Adapted Zones
Exotic	3 ft (0.9)	Cool	Rhiz.	143 (314)	8 lb (42)	16 (406)	$	✪	☆	☆	👍	👍	👎	T	7	1236

Other common names: Hungarian brome
Varieties: Achenbach, Badger, Barton, Baylor, Bromar, Lincoln, Manchar, Polar, (others)
Comments: Vigorous grass, useful for wildlife cover and feed. Needs fertile, moist soil. Seed germinates readily with no dormancy problems. Tolerant of regular mowing over 6 in. (15 cm).
References: Bernstein, 1958; Oakes, 1990; Spackeen, 1993; Wiesner and Brown, 1984; Young and Young, 1986

Meadow brome
Bromus riparius Renmann

Native to North America	Unmowed Height ft (m)	Cool- or Warm-Season	Growth Habit	Seed Count x000 per lb (kg)	"Turf" Seeding Rate lb/M (g/m^2)	Minimum Precipitation in. (mm)	Seed Cost	Seed Availability	Mowing Tolerance	Shade Tolerance	Wetland Tolerance	Salt Tolerance	Alkalinity Tolerance	Ornamental/ Turf Uses	Bloom Season	Adapted Zones
Exotic	2 ft (0.6)	Cool	Rhiz.	140 (308)	8 lb (42)	16 (406)	$$	✪	✧	☆	👍	👎	👎	T	6	1236

Former Latin names: *B. biebersteinii, B. fibrosus, B. erectus*
Varieties: Budapest, Fleet, Paddock, Regar
Comments: Ideal for stabilizing streambanks and rocky slopes. Seed germinates readily with no dormancy problems. Prefers moist soil over dry.
References: Alderson and Sharp, 1994; Anonymous, 1995d; Anonymous, 1996b; OECD, 1996; Spackeen, 1993; Tutin et al., 1980; Young and Young, 1986

Bluejoint reedgrass

Calamagrostis canadensis (Michx.) Beauv.

Native to North America	Unmowed Height ft (m)	Cool- or Warm-Season	Growth Habit	Seed Count x000 per lb (kg)	"Turf" Seeding Rate lb/M (g/m²)	Minimum Precipitation in. (mm)	Seed Cost	Seed Availability	Mowing Tolerance	Shade Tolerance	Wetland Tolerance	Salt Tolerance	Alkalinity Tolerance	Ornamental/ Turf Uses	Bloom Season	Adapted Zones
Native	4 ft (1.2)	Cool	Rhiz.	2270 (4994)	1 lb (7)	? (?)	$$$	☆	☆	✪	👍	👍	👎	T/O	7	1236

Other common names: Marsh reed grass, foin bleu, Canadian bluejoint
Varieties: Sourdough
Comments: Useful on wet sites, acid soils, slopes, shade, and mid-elevations. Widely adapted. Aggressive. Mildly shade tolerant. Silver-green showy seedheads persist into early autumn as a golden brown. Seed germination requires cool, moist conditions, sunlight. Tolerates high calcium soils and rocky areas. Resembles redtop. Forms large patches in temperate bogs. Cold tolerant to Arctic Circle. Not traffic tolerant.
References: Anonymous, 1993b; Brown, 1979; Campbell et al., 1956; Hitchcock, 1951; Oakes, 1990; Pojar and MacKinnon, 1994; Rhoades and Klein, 1993; Spackeen, 1993; Young and Young, 1986

Prairie sandreed

Calamovilfa longifolia (Hook.) Scribn.

Native to North America	Unmowed Height ft (m)	Cool- or Warm-Season	Growth Habit	Seed Count x000 per lb (kg)	"Turf" Seeding Rate lb/M (g/m²)	Minimum Precipitation in. (mm)	Seed Cost	Seed Availability	Mowing Tolerance	Shade Tolerance	Wetland Tolerance	Salt Tolerance	Alkalinity Tolerance	Ornamental/ Turf Uses	Bloom Season	Adapted Zones
Native	4 ft (1.2)	Warm	Rhiz.	273 (600)	6 lb (30)	12 (304)	$$	☆	☆	❍	👎	👎	👎	T/O	8	1236

Other common names: Prairie sandgrass
Varieties: Bowman, Goshen, Pronghorn
Comments: Adapted for dune stabilization. Coarse, woody. Slow seedling establishment. Deeply rooted to 5 ft (1.5 m) but with most roots in the top 18 in. (45 cm). Greens up in late spring and stays green until frost.
References: Alderson and Sharp, 1994; Anonymous, 1995d; Anonymous, 1996b; Campbell et al., 1956; Long, 1981; Olson and Anderson, 1994; Pair, 1994; Spackeen, 1993; Stubbendieck et al., 1991; Wasser, 1982; Wiesner and Brown, 1984

Wild oats

Chasmanthium latifolium (Michx.) Yates

Native to North America	Unmowed Height ft (m)	Cool- or Warm-Season	Growth Habit	Seed Count x000 per lb (kg)	"Turf" Seeding Rate lb/M (g/m²)	Minimum Precipitation in. (mm)	Seed Cost	Seed Availability	Mowing Tolerance	Shade Tolerance	Wetland Tolerance	Salt Tolerance	Alkalinity Tolerance	Ornamental/ Turf Uses	Bloom Season	Adapted Zones
Native	3 ft (0.9)	Cool	Rhiz.	94 (206)	10 lb (50)	? (?)	$$$$	❍	❍	✪	👍	👍	👎	O	7	1234

Former Latin names: *Uniola latifolia*
Other common names: Northern sea oats, river oats, broadleaf chasmanthium, inland sea oats, spangle grass
Comments: Attractive, ornamental, drooping, oat-like seedheads which turn bronze in fall. Medium textured, light green leaves, turning green/buff/yellow in fall. Shade tolerant. Greens up in early spring. Stems erect with lance-shaped, alternate, glossy leaves. Lodges severely in winter.
References: Daniels, 1995; Darke, 1994; Hughes et al., 1951; Leasure et al., 1994; Oakes, 1990; Reinhardt et al., 1989; Stubbendieck et al., 1991; Woods, 1992

Rhodes grass

Chloris gayana Kunth

Native to North America	Unmowed Height ft (m)	Cool- or Warm-Season	Growth Habit	Seed Count x000 per lb (kg)	"Turf" Seeding Rate lb/M (g/m²)	Minimum Precipitation in. (mm)	Seed Cost	Seed Availability	Mowing Tolerance	Shade Tolerance	Wetland Tolerance	Salt Tolerance	Alkalinity Tolerance	Ornamental/ Turf Uses	Bloom Season	Adapted Zones
Exotic	4 ft (1.2)	Warm	Stolon	1712 (3766)	2 lb (8)	23 (584)	$$	☆	☆	❍	👎	👍	👍	T/O	7	5

Other common names: Mpwapwa rhodes
Varieties: Bell, Boma, Callide, Capital, Elmba, Fine cut, Hatsunatsu, Masaba, Mbarara, Nemkat, Pokot, Samford, Topcut
Comments: Aggressive, tall growing tropical grass with poor winter-hardiness. Not as drought tolerant as buffel grass. pH tolerant to 4.0. Short-day flowering.
References: Alderson and Sharp, 1994; Anonymous, 1979; Anonymous, 1993c; Archer and Sellers, 1956; Boonman, 1993; Brown et al., 1986; Humphreys, 1979; Judd, 1979; Musser, 1950; Oakes, 1990; OECD, 1996; Skerman and Riveros, 1990

Purple pampas grass

Cortaderia jubata (Lemoine) Stapf

Native to North America	Unmowed Height ft (m)	Cool- or Warm-Season	Growth Habit	Seed Count x000 per lb (kg)	"Turf" Seeding Rate lb/M (g/m²)	Minimum Precipitation in. (mm)	Seed Cost	Seed Availability	Mowing Tolerance	Shade Tolerance	Wetland Tolerance	Salt Tolerance	Alkalinity Tolerance	Ornamental/ Turf Uses	Bloom Season	Adapted Zones
Exotic	10 ft (3)	Cool	Bunch	? (?)	? lb (?)	? (?)	$$$$	❍	❍	❍	👎	👎	👎	O	9	45

Former Latin names: *C. quila, C. rudiuscula*
Other common names: Pink pampas grass
Comments: Showy ornamental, produces variable offspring through seed. Seed has short viability. Colored plants should be vegetatively propagated. Aggressive. Reseeds itself in mild climates. Flower spikes break off in the wind. Razor sharp foliage. Hardy to 20°F (–7°C).
References: Darke, 1994; Greenlee and Fell, 1992

$ – Inexpensive; $$ – Moderate; $$$ – Expensive; $$$$ – Very expensive; ✪ – Excellent; ☆ – Moderate; ✧ – Fair; ❍ – Poor or no tolerance; 👍 – Tolerant; 👎 – Intolerant; T – Turf; T/O – Turf and Ornamental; O – Ornamental

Pampas grass
Cortaderia selloana (Schult.) Aschers. and Graebn.

Native to North America	Unmowed Height ft (m)	Cool- or Warm-Season	Growth Habit	Seed Count x000 per lb (kg)	"Turf" Seeding Rate lb/M (g/m²)	Minimum Precipitation in. (mm)	Seed Cost	Seed Availability	Mowing Tolerance	Shade Tolerance	Wetland Tolerance	Salt Tolerance	Alkalinity Tolerance	Ornamental/ Turf Uses	Bloom Season	Adapted Zones
Exotic	10 ft (3)	Warm	Bunch	? (?)	? lb (?)	? (?)	$$$$	✧	❍	❍	👎	👎	👎	O	8	45

Former Latin names: *C. argentea, C. rosea, C. rubra, Arundo selloana*
Varieties: Argenteum, Carnea (pink), Elegans (white), Gold Band, Monstrosa, Pumila, Silver Commet, Silver Stripe, Sunningdale Silver, Sun Stripe, (others)
Comments: Classic over-used ornamental grass. Cultivars are vegetatively propagated, but a limited quantity of common seed is available. "Pumila" is a dwarf cultivar, only 4 to 6 ft tall (1.5 to 2 m).
References: Darke, 1994; Greenlee and Fell, 1992; Oakes, 1990; Woods, 1992

Giant bermudagrass
Cynodon dactylon (L.) Persoon var. aridus

Native to North America	Unmowed Height ft (m)	Cool- or Warm-Season	Growth Habit	Seed Count x000 per lb (kg)	"Turf" Seeding Rate lb/M (g/m²)	Minimum Precipitation in. (mm)	Seed Cost	Seed Availability	Mowing Tolerance	Shade Tolerance	Wetland Tolerance	Salt Tolerance	Alkalinity Tolerance	Ornamental/ Turf Uses	Bloom Season	Adapted Zones
Native	3 ft (0.9)	Warm	Rz/St	1338 (2943)	2 lb (10)	10 (254)	$$	✪	☆	❍	👍	👍	👍	T	5	45

Former Latin names: *C. aridus*
Other common names: Star grass
Varieties: NK-37
Comments: Taller growing and more aggressive than turf bermuda. Some seedlots may have poor germination. Light and alternating temperatures benefit germination. A contaminant in many seedlots of turf bermudagrass, and has even been known to intercross, producing intergrade offspring.
References: Anonymous, 1979; Anonymous, 1995b; Hanson, 1959; Hitchcock, 1951; Skerman and Riveros, 1990; Spackeen, 1993; Yaklich et al., 1984; Young and Young, 1986

Crested dog's-tail
Cynosurus cristatus L.

Native to North America	Unmowed Height ft (m)	Cool- or Warm-Season	Growth Habit	Seed Count x000 per lb (kg)	"Turf" Seeding Rate lb/M (g/m²)	Minimum Precipitation in. (mm)	Seed Cost	Seed Availability	Mowing Tolerance	Shade Tolerance	Wetland Tolerance	Salt Tolerance	Alkalinity Tolerance	Ornamental/ Turf Uses	Bloom Season	Adapted Zones
Exotic	2 ft (0.6)	Cool	Bunch	960 (2112)	3 lb (13)	? (?)	$$$$	❍	✪	☆	👍	👎	👎	T	6	12

Varieties: Grasslands Aspiring, Roznovska, Southland
Comments: Upright, stemmy grass, similar in appearance to perennial ryegrass. Used as mowed turf in Europe. Introduced onto occasional Midwestern (U.S.) golf courses in the early 1900s. Can be included in wildflower meadow or sports turf mixtures. Fair/poor wear tolerance. Tolerates low fertility soils and some shade.
References: Anonymous, 1993c; Breakwell, 1923; Crampton, 1961; Darke, 1994; House and Underwood, 1996; Hubbard, 1984; Oakes, 1990

Orchardgrass
Dactylis glomerata L.

Native to North America	Unmowed Height ft (m)	Cool- or Warm-Season	Growth Habit	Seed Count x000 per lb (kg)	"Turf" Seeding Rate lb/M (g/m²)	Minimum Precipitation in. (mm)	Seed Cost	Seed Availability	Mowing Tolerance	Shade Tolerance	Wetland Tolerance	Salt Tolerance	Alkalinity Tolerance	Ornamental/ Turf Uses	Bloom Season	Adapted Zones
Exotic	4 ft (1.2)	Cool	Bunch	487 (1071)	4 lb (21)	18 (457)	$	✪	☆	☆	👍	👍	👎	T	5	1234

Other common names: Cocksfoot
Varieties: Aberystwyth S.26, Baraula, Bartego, Bartyle, Barviva, Berber, Cambria, Currie, Dorise, Latar, Mobite, Modac, Paiute, Peraivia, Pizza, Porto, Potomac, Saborto, Shinyo, (others)
Comments: Leafy, coarse grass bred for forage, not turf. Highly productive for wildlife graze. Variegated, vegetative cultivar available. Some experimental turf varieties have been developed in Europe but with limited commercial success.
References: Bernstein, 1958; Greenlee and Fell, 1992; Hubbard, 1984; Oakes, 1990; Spackeen, 1993; Young and Young, 1986

Wallaby grass
Danthonia semiannularis (Labill.) R. Br.

Native to North America	Unmowed Height ft (m)	Cool- or Warm-Season	Growth Habit	Seed Count x000 per lb (kg)	"Turf" Seeding Rate lb/M (g/m²)	Minimum Precipitation in. (mm)	Seed Cost	Seed Availability	Mowing Tolerance	Shade Tolerance	Wetland Tolerance	Salt Tolerance	Alkalinity Tolerance	Ornamental/ Turf Uses	Bloom Season	Adapted Zones
Exotic	1 ft (0.3)	Cool	Bunch	? (?)	? lb (?)	? (?)	$$$	☆	☆	☆	👎	👎	👎	T/O	7	345

Varieties: Tarana, Bundarra
Comments: Classic low maintenance grass of Australia. Tolerant of frost, drought, and low fertility. Pale straw brown bristly seedheads and stems. Fine leaves with light gray color. Best mowed infrequently at $1^1/_2$ in. or above (3 cm). Not wear tolerant.
References: Greenway, 1997; Tothill and Hacker, 1983

Tufted hair grass
Deschampsia caespitosa (L.) Beauv.

Native to North America	Unmowed Height ft (m)	Cool- or Warm-Season	Growth Habit	Seed Count x000 per lb (kg)	"Turf" Seeding Rate lb/M (g/m²)	Minimum Precipitation in. (mm)	Seed Cost	Seed Availability	Mowing Tolerance	Shade Tolerance	Wetland Tolerance	Salt Tolerance	Alkalinity Tolerance	Ornamental/ Turf Uses	Bloom Season	Adapted Zones
Native	2 ft (0.6)	Cool	Bunch	2500 (5500)	1 lb (6)	20 (508)	$$$	☆	✪	✪	👍	👍	👍	T/O	6	12346

Former Latin names: *Dichanthium caricosum, Aira caespitosa, D. caricosum* Complex
Other common names: Salt-and-pepper grass, fairy wand
Varieties: Bronzeschleier, Fairy's Joke (vivipara), Goldstaub (vegetative), Holciformis, Nortran, Norcoast (ssp. *beringensis*), Peru Creek
Comments: Attractive ornamental grass with a purplish seedhead. Prefers moist soils. Good shade, high/low pH tolerance. Performs poorly in hot climates. Seedheads remain in place well into winter. Useful as mowed turf if not clipped too short. Resembles tall fescue when mowed. Turf cultivars are being developed.
References: Alderson and Sharp, 1994; Greenlee and Fell, 1992; Grounds, 1979; Reinhardt et al., 1989; Smith and Smith, 1996; Spackeen, 1993; Stubbendieck et al., 1991

Deer tongue grass
Dichanthelium clandestrinum (L.) Gould

Native to North America	Unmowed Height ft (m)	Cool- or Warm-Season	Growth Habit	Seed Count x000 per lb (kg)	"Turf" Seeding Rate lb/M (g/m²)	Minimum Precipitation in. (mm)	Seed Cost	Seed Availability	Mowing Tolerance	Shade Tolerance	Wetland Tolerance	Salt Tolerance	Alkalinity Tolerance	Ornamental/ Turf Uses	Bloom Season	Adapted Zones
Native	3 ft (0.9)	Warm	Rhiz.	? (?)	? lb (?)	? (?)	$$$	☆	☆	☆	👍	👎	👎	T/O	7	1234

Former Latin names: *Panicum clandestinum*
Varieties: Tioga
Comments: Curious-looking soil-stabilizing grass. One of the most tolerant grasses to acid pH (down to 3.8). Seedhead is a small, panicle that rapidly fades. Unique, ornamental, spade-shaped blades borne on brownish purple, extremely hairy stems. Suffers in hot, dry climates.
References: Alderson and Sharp, 1994; Featherly, 1946; Greenlee and Fell, 1992; Oakes, 1990

Arizona cottontop
Digitaria californica (Benth.) Henr.

Native to North America	Unmowed Height ft (m)	Cool- or Warm-Season	Growth Habit	Seed Count x000 per lb (kg)	"Turf" Seeding Rate lb/M (g/m²)	Minimum Precipitation in. (mm)	Seed Cost	Seed Availability	Mowing Tolerance	Shade Tolerance	Wetland Tolerance	Salt Tolerance	Alkalinity Tolerance	Ornamental/ Turf Uses	Bloom Season	Adapted Zones
Native	2 ft (0.6)	Warm	Bunch	1090 (2398)	2 lb (12)	7 (177)	$$$	☆	✪	❍	👎	👎	👎	O	7	5

Former Latin names: *Trichachne californica*
Other common names: California cottontop, zacate punta blanca
Comments: Drought hardy ornamental grass. Plants are erect, fuzzy, and often purplish. Seed set is good. Light, fluffy seed is favored by wildlife.
References: Alderson and Sharp, 1994; Anonymous, 1993f; Henrard, 1950; Munshower, 1994; Spackeen, 1993; Stubbendieck et al., 1991

Serangoon grass
Digitaria didactyla Willd.

Native to North America	Unmowed Height ft (m)	Cool- or Warm-Season	Growth Habit	Seed Count x000 per lb (kg)	"Turf" Seeding Rate lb/M (g/m²)	Minimum Precipitation in. (mm)	Seed Cost	Seed Availability	Mowing Tolerance	Shade Tolerance	Wetland Tolerance	Salt Tolerance	Alkalinity Tolerance	Ornamental/ Turf Uses	Bloom Season	Adapted Zones
Exotic	2 ft (0.6)	Warm	Stolon	? (?)	? lb (?)	28 (711)	$$$	✧	✪	❍	👎	👎	👎	T	5	45

Former Latin names: *Cynodon incompletus, Panicum gracile, P. subtile, P. didactylum, P. becorne*
Other common names: Australian blue couch
Comments: Withstands close mowing, reportedly even better than bermudagrass. Resistant to wear and drought. Attractive blue-green leaf color. Susceptible to dollar spot and chlorosis. Ideal for sandy, moist soils. A popular lawngrass in Queensland, Australia. Limited quantities of seed are produced with typical seed specs: 60% germination, 97% purity. Prefers frost-free, coastal locations.
References: Beard, 1991; Bor, 1960; Burbridge, 1966; Henrard, 1950; Rotar, 1968; Skerman and Riveros, 1990

Pangola grass
Digitaria eriantha Steud.

Native to North America	Unmowed Height ft (m)	Cool- or Warm-Season	Growth Habit	Seed Count x000 per lb (kg)	"Turf" Seeding Rate lb/M (g/m²)	Minimum Precipitation in. (mm)	Seed Cost	Seed Availability	Mowing Tolerance	Shade Tolerance	Wetland Tolerance	Salt Tolerance	Alkalinity Tolerance	Ornamental/ Turf Uses	Bloom Season	Adapted Zones
Exotic	3 ft (0.9)	Warm	Rz/St	1099 (2417)	2 lb (12)	26 (660)	$$$$	❍	☆	❍	👍	👍	👎	T	6	45

Former Latin names: *D. altissima, D. decumbens, D. pentzii*
Other common names: Woolly finger grass, digitgrass
Varieties: Leesburg No. 5, Mealani, Pangola, Slenderstem, Taiwan, Transvala
Comments: Drought resistant tropical grass, useful in erosion control. Light green, hardy to 30 degrees North latitude. A sterile aneuploid (mixed up chromosome number) with flowers that bear no seed. Vegetatively propagated. A dwarf selection exists in Hawaii which is adaptable to mowing.
References: Alderson and Sharp, 1994; Henrard, 1950; Humphreys, 1979; Price, 1972; Rotar, 1968; Skerman and Riveros, 1990; Zinn, 1997

$ – Inexpensive; $$ – Moderate; $$$ – Expensive; $$$$ – Very expensive; ✪ – Excellent; ☆ – Moderate; ✧ – Fair; ❍ – Poor or no tolerance; 👍 – Tolerant; 👎 – Intolerant; T – Turf; T/O – Turf and Ornamental; O – Ornamental

Inland saltgrass
Distichlis spicata (L.) Green

Native to North America	Unmowed Height ft (m)	Cool- or Warm-Season	Growth Habit	Seed Count x000 per lb (kg)	"Turf" Seeding Rate lb/M (g/m²)	Minimum Precipitation in. (mm)	Seed Cost	Seed Availability	Mowing Tolerance	Shade Tolerance	Wetland Tolerance	Salt Tolerance	Alkalinity Tolerance	Ornamental/ Turf Uses	Bloom Season	Adapted Zones
Native	2 ft (0.6)	Warm	Rhiz.	518 (1139)	4 lb (20)	? (?)	$$	✧	✪	☽	👍	👍	👍	T/O	8	12345

Former Latin names: *Uniola spicata*
Other common names: Salt grass, spike grass, alkali grass, seashore saltgrass
Comments: Seashore grass, widely adapted to wet sand or marshy salt plains. Seed germination is limited, occurring best at 50/105°F night/day (10/40°C) temperatures. Forms a dense mat of foliage. Separate male and female plants, with female flowers being wider than males. Slow growing. Greens up early in the spring and remains green well into autumn.
References: Brown, 1979; Hitchcock, 1951; Oakes, 1990; Stubbendieck et al., 1991; Young and Young, 1986

Desert saltgrass
Distichlis stricta (Torr.) Rydb.

Native to North America	Unmowed Height ft (m)	Cool- or Warm-Season	Growth Habit	Seed Count x000 per lb (kg)	"Turf" Seeding Rate lb/M (g/m²)	Minimum Precipitation in. (mm)	Seed Cost	Seed Availability	Mowing Tolerance	Shade Tolerance	Wetland Tolerance	Salt Tolerance	Alkalinity Tolerance	Ornamental/ Turf Uses	Bloom Season	Adapted Zones
Native	1 ft (0.3)	Warm	Rhiz.	520 (1144)	4 lb (20)	8 (203)	$$$	☆	☆	☽	👍	👍	👍	T	7	123 456

Other common names: Inland saltgrass, alkaligrass
Comments: Tough desert grass widely tolerant of climate. Tolerates sandy soil, surface salt to 0.6%, and subsurface salt to 2%. Known to grow in pure seawater. Male and female flowers are borne on separate plants. Male flowers are larger and deeper yellow. Good traffic tolerance. Sporadic commercial seed availability.
References: Anonymous, 1993b; Campbell et al., 1956; Hitchcock, 1951; Sours, 1985; Spackeen, 1993

Canada wildrye
Elymus canadensis L.

Native to North America	Unmowed Height ft (m)	Cool- or Warm-Season	Growth Habit	Seed Count x000 per lb (kg)	"Turf" Seeding Rate lb/M (g/m²)	Minimum Precipitation in. (mm)	Seed Cost	Seed Availability	Mowing Tolerance	Shade Tolerance	Wetland Tolerance	Salt Tolerance	Alkalinity Tolerance	Ornamental/ Turf Uses	Bloom Season	Adapted Zones
Native	4 ft (1.2)	Cool	Bunch	115 (253)	9 lb (46)	12 (304)	$$$	☆	✧	☆	👍	👍	👎	O	7	1236

Other common names: Prairie wildrye, cnteno silvestre, nodding wildrye
Varieties: Mandan 419
Comments: A useful grass for soil stabilization under adverse conditions. Widely adapted to a range of soils. Quick establishment. Sunlight, moisture, and cool soil favor seed germination. "Mandan" is shorter growing, with more leaves and better persistence than common.
References: Alderson and Sharp, 1994; Anonymous, 1988; Anonymous, 1993b; Bernstein, 1958; Long, 1981; Oakes, 1990; Spackeen, 1993; Stubbendieck et al., 1991; Young and Young, 1986

Dahurian wildrye
Elymus dahuricus Turcz. ex Griseb.

Native to North America	Unmowed Height ft (m)	Cool- or Warm-Season	Growth Habit	Seed Count x000 per lb (kg)	"Turf" Seeding Rate lb/M (g/m²)	Minimum Precipitation in. (mm)	Seed Cost	Seed Availability	Mowing Tolerance	Shade Tolerance	Wetland Tolerance	Salt Tolerance	Alkalinity Tolerance	Ornamental/ Turf Uses	Bloom Season	Adapted Zones
Exotic	2 ft (0.6)	Cool	Bunch	108 (237)	9 lb (47)	? (?)	$$	☆	✧	☆	👎	👍	👍	T	7	1236

Varieties: Arthur, Chabei, James
Comments: Loose, erect, short-lived perennial. Cold and drought tolerant. Quick germination and good first-year establishment but seldom persists beyond 3 years. May reseed itself. Excellent seedling vigor. Similar to Siberian wildrye but with more erect spikes.
References: Alderson and Sharp, 1994; Anonymous, 1996b; Wu et al., 1992

Bottlebrush squirreltail
Elymus elymoides (Raf.) Swezey

Native to North America	Unmowed Height ft (m)	Cool- or Warm-Season	Growth Habit	Seed Count x000 per lb (kg)	"Turf" Seeding Rate lb/M (g/m²)	Minimum Precipitation in. (mm)	Seed Cost	Seed Availability	Mowing Tolerance	Shade Tolerance	Wetland Tolerance	Salt Tolerance	Alkalinity Tolerance	Ornamental/ Turf Uses	Bloom Season	Adapted Zones
Native	1 ft (0.3)	Cool	Bunch	192 (422)	7 lb (36)	6 (152)	$$$	☆	☆	☆	👎	👎	👎	T/O	6	1236

Former Latin names: *Sitanion hystrix*
Other common names: Zacate trigillo
Comments: Dual-purpose grass for arid prairies or ornamental beds. Tolerant of drought and shallow soil. Short-growing, short-lived plants. Summer dormant. Seed germinates readily with no dormancy problems. Greens up early in spring. May flower twice a year if moisture is favorable. Seed spikes resemble bottlebrushes, as its name implies.
References: Alderson and Sharp, 1994; Cronquist et al., 1977; Schaff, 1994; Spackeen, 1993; Stubbendieck et al., 1991

Blue wildrye

Elymus glaucus Buckl.

Native to North America	Unmowed Height ft (m)	Cool- or Warm-Season	Growth Habit	Seed Count x000 per lb (kg)	"Turf" Seeding Rate lb/M (g/m²)	Minimum Precipitation in. (mm)	Seed Cost	Seed Availability	Mowing Tolerance	Shade Tolerance	Wetland Tolerance	Salt Tolerance	Alkalinity Tolerance	Ornamental/ Turf Uses	Bloom Season	Adapted Zones
Native	3 ft (0.9)	Cool	Bunch	110 (242)	9 lb (47)	13 (330)	$$$	✧	✪	✪	👎	👍	👎	O	6	1236

Former Latin names: *E. americanus*
Other common names: Blue limegrass, lymegrass
Varieties: Anderson, Arlington, Berkeley Hills, Mariposa, Ramaley (vegetative), Stanislaus 2000 & 5000
Comments: Aggressive, invasive, short-lived perennial. Attractive blue color. Shade tolerant. Seed germinates readily with no dormancy problems. Plants go dormant in the summer in dry climates. Hardy to 5000 ft elevation (1500 m).
References: Asay and Jensen, 1996; Carlson, 1991; Cronquist et al., 1977; Oakes, 1990; Pair, 1994; Spackeen, 1993; Young and Young, 1986

Streambank wheatgrass

Elymus lanceolatus (Scribn. & J.G. Sm.) Gould ssp. *lanceolatus*

Native to North America	Unmowed Height ft (m)	Cool- or Warm-Season	Growth Habit	Seed Count x000 per lb (kg)	"Turf" Seeding Rate lb/M (g/m²)	Minimum Precipitation in. (mm)	Seed Cost	Seed Availability	Mowing Tolerance	Shade Tolerance	Wetland Tolerance	Salt Tolerance	Alkalinity Tolerance	Ornamental/ Turf Uses	Bloom Season	Adapted Zones
Native	2 ft (0.6)	Cool	Rhiz.	160 (352)	8 lb (39)	8 (203)	$$	☆	☆	☆	👎	👎	👍	T/O	6	1236

Former Latin names: *Agropyron dasystachyum, A. riparium, Elytrigia dasystachyam*
Other common names: Thickspike wheatgrass, Northern wheatgrass, downy wheatgrass
Varieties: Critana, Sodar, Thickspike
Comments: A drought tolerant, low growing, range species with some turf adaptation. Looks similar to western wheatgrass but is more drought resistant. Unclipped seedheads attract songbirds. *Wawawaiensis*, a subspecies, is called Snake River wheatgrass. Certain varieties are better adapted to ground cover while others are better for clipping. "Sodar" is 30% shorter and produces half the clippings as other varieties. It has been used on roadsides, golf roughs, and arid lawns. Diseases and frequent mowing may thin stands.
References: Alderson and Sharp, 1994; Anonymous, 1988; Anonymous, 1993e; Asay and Jensen, 1996; Campbell et al., 1956; Spackeen, 1993; Wasser, 1982; Wiesner and Brown, 1984

Slender wheatgrass

Elymus trachycaulus (Link) Gould ex Shinners

Native to North America	Unmowed Height ft (m)	Cool- or Warm-Season	Growth Habit	Seed Count x000 per lb (kg)	"Turf" Seeding Rate lb/M (g/m²)	Minimum Precipitation in. (mm)	Seed Cost	Seed Availability	Mowing Tolerance	Shade Tolerance	Wetland Tolerance	Salt Tolerance	Alkalinity Tolerance	Ornamental/ Turf Uses	Bloom Season	Adapted Zones
Native	2 ft (0.6)	Cool	Bunch	136 (299)	9 lb (43)	16 (406)	$	✪	✧	☆	👎	👍	👍	T/O	6	1236

Former Latin names: *Agropyron trachycaulum* var. *glaucum, A. trachycaulum var. typicum, A. dasystachyum*
Other common names: Agropiro delgado
Varieties: Adanac, Elbee, Highlander, Primar, Pryor, Revenue, San Luis
Comments: Short-lived perennial. Performs best the first 3 to 4 years. Moderate drought, elevation, and flooding tolerance. Holds the distinction of being the first North American native grass to be used in reclamation. Excellent seed yield, with large, good quality seed. Easy to establish, given 2 years. Purplish spiky seedheads. Better suited to moister climates than dry prairies. Susceptible to billbug. "Revenue" is salt tolerant, whereas "Highlander" variety is not. Slender wheatgrass is similar in salt tolerance to Russian wildrye but inferior to tall wheatgrass.
References: Alderson and Sharp, 1994; Anonymous, 1988; Anonymous, 1993e; Anonymous, 1996b; Archer and Sellers, 1956; Asay and Jensen, 1996; Campbell et al., 1956; OECD, 1996; Schaff, 1994; Spackeen, 1993; Stubbendieck et al., 1991; Weisner and Brown, 1984

Virginia wildrye

Elymus virginicus L.

Native to North America	Unmowed Height ft (m)	Cool- or Warm-Season	Growth Habit	Seed Count x000 per lb (kg)	"Turf" Seeding Rate lb/M (g/m²)	Minimum Precipitation in. (mm)	Seed Cost	Seed Availability	Mowing Tolerance	Shade Tolerance	Wetland Tolerance	Salt Tolerance	Alkalinity Tolerance	Ornamental/ Turf Uses	Bloom Season	Adapted Zones
Native	3 ft (0.9)	Cool	Bunch	75 (165)	11 lb (56)	? (?)	$$$	✧	✪	☆	👍	👎	👎	T/O	7	12346

Former Latin names: *Hordeum virginicum*
Other common names: Terrell grass
Varieties: O'Ma'Ha
Comments: Attractive ornamental grass useful in far roughs of golf courses in most areas of the world. Colorful winter foliage, dark green summer foliage. Erect stems and limp leaves turn an interesting brown. Plants are extremely variable in form, from light to dark green, from fine to coarse and stemmy.
References: Anonymous, 1993b; Anonymous, 1996b; Archer and Sellers, 1956; Campbell et al., 1956; Oakes, 1990; Pair, 1994

$ – Inexpensive; $$ – Moderate; $$$ – Expensive; $$$$ – Very expensive; ✪ – Excellent; ☆ – Moderate; ✧ – Fair; ❍ – Poor or no tolerance; 👍 – Tolerant; 👎 – Intolerant; T – *Turf;* T/O – *Turf and Ornamental;* O – *Ornamental*

Native to North America	Unmowed Height ft (m)	Cool- or Warm-Season	Growth Habit	Seed Count x000 per lb (kg)	"Turf" Seeding Rate lb/M (g/m²)	Minimum Precipitation in. (mm)	Seed Cost	Seed Availability	Mowing Tolerance	Shade Tolerance	Wetland Tolerance	Salt Tolerance	Alkalinity Tolerance	Ornamental/ Turf Uses	Bloom Season	Adapted Zones

Intermediate wheatgrass

Elytrigia intermedia (Host) Nevski

Exotic	3 ft (0.9)	Cool	Rhiz.	79 (173)	11 lb (54)	15 (381)	$	✪	✧	☆	👎	👍	👍	T	7	16

Former Latin names: *Thinopyrum intermedium, Agropyron intermedium, A. trichophorum*
Other common names: Pubescent wheatgrass, intermediate pubescent wheatgrass
Varieties: Amur, Chief, Clarke, Greenar, Greenleaf, Luna, Mandan 759, Manska, Nebraska 50, Oahe, Reliant, Rush, Slate, Tegmar, Topar, Trigo
Comments: Not as mowing tolerant as crested wheatgrass. Prefers moist, fine soils. Good seedling vigor. Blue-green foliage. Flooding tolerant. Flowers later than other wheatgrasses. Older cultivars were weak yielders and nonpersistent, a trait overcome in newer releases. "Montana 2" is a durum wheat x intermediate wheatgrass hybrid with 3x larger seed, useful for wildlife. "Tegmar" is a lower growing variety, useful for low maintenance turf.
References: Alderson and Sharp, 1994; Anonymous, 1988; Anonymous, 1996b; Asay and Jensen, 1996; Spackeen, 1993; Troeh et al., 1991; Wiesner and Brown, 1984

Boer lovegrass

Eragrostis curvula (Schrad.) Nees. var. conferta Stapf

Exotic	3 ft (0.9)	Warm	Bunch	3000 (6600)	1 lb (6)	12 (304)	$$	☆	☆	❍	👎	👎	👎	T/O	5	45

Former Latin names: *E. chloromelas*
Varieties: Catalina, OTA-S
Comments: More drought tolerant than weeping lovegrass but lacks cold tolerance. Develops chlorosis on alkaline soils. Sunlight and shallow planting benefit seed germination.
References: Alderson and Sharp, 1994; Humphrey, 1970; Tutin et al., 1980; Young and Young, 1986

Weeping lovegrass

Eragrostis curvula (Schrad.) Nees.

Exotic	3 ft (0.9)	Warm	Bunch	1463 (3218)	2 lb (10)	17 (431)	$$	✪	✧	❍	👎	👍	👎	O	7	345

Former Latin names: *Poa curvula*
Other common names: Zacate horon, African lovegrass
Varieties: Consol, Ermelo, Morpa
Comments: Weeping lovegrass has become the gold standard of cascading grasses on slopes, and if anything, has been overutilized for that purpose. Medium-green, fine bladed foliage, turning light to dark green by autumn. Retains slender seedless stalks into early winter. Acid soil tolerant. Sunlight benefits seed germination. Starts growing in mid to late spring. Relatively poor wildlife feed but good cover. Tolerates mowing as turf as long as it's above 6 in. (15 cm).
References: Anonymous, 1993c; Anonymous, 1995b; Archer and Sellers, 1956; Chapman, 1992; Cronquist et al., 1977; Darke, 1994; Oakes, 1990; Skerman and Riveros, 1990; Spackeen, 1993; Stubbendieck et al., 1991; Troeh et al., 1991

Plains lovegrass

Eragrostis intermedia Hitchc.

Native	2 ft (0.6)	Warm	Bunch	3500 (7700)	1 lb (5)	11 (279)	$$$	☆	✪	❍	👎	👎	👎	O	5	4

Comments: Shorter-growing ornamental for dry, low humidity sites. Tall gray to bronze-tipped spikes, turning reddish in alkaline soils.
References: Spackeen, 1993; Tutin et al., 1980

Lehmann lovegrass

Eragrostis lehmanniana Nees.

Exotic	2 ft (0.6)	Warm	Rz/St	4245 (9339)	1 lb (5)	12 (304)	$$	☆	☆	❍	👎	👍	👍	T	?	5

Varieties: A-68, Cochise (hybrid), Kuivato, Puhuima
Comments: A low maintenance grass for drier sites. Shorter growing than weeping lovegrass. Seed germinates readily with no dormancy problems. Ideal germination temperature 60 to 100°F (14 to 36°C). Its creeping habit makes for better erosion control than weeping lovegrass.
References: Archer and Sellers, 1956

Sand lovegrass
Eragrostis trichodes (Nutt.) Wood

Native to North America	Unmowed Height ft (m)	Cool- or Warm-Season	Growth Habit	Seed Count x000 per lb (kg)	"Turf" Seeding Rate lb/M (g/m^2)	Minimum Precipitation in. (mm)	Seed Cost	Seed Availability	Mowing Tolerance	Shade Tolerance	Wetland Tolerance	Salt Tolerance	Alkalinity Tolerance	Ornamental/ Turf Uses	Bloom Season	Adapted Zones
Native	3 ft (0.9)	Warm	Bunch	1779 (3913)	2 lb (8)	12 (304)	$$	☆	✧	❍	👎	👎	👎	O	6	34

Varieties: Bend, Mason, Nebraska 27

Comments: Wispy pink seedheads. Drought hardy and persistent. pH tolerant down to 4.0. Cool, moist conditions for 6 weeks needed for germination. Will tolerate moist, sandy soils. Greens up as much as 2 weeks earlier than other warm-season grasses.

References: Anonymous, 1995d; Archer and Sellers, 1956; Spackeen, 1993; Stubbendieck et al., 1991; Troeh et al., 1991; Woods, 1992; Young and Young, 1986

Atherstone lovegrass
Eragrostis trichophora Coss. & Dur.

Native to North America	Unmowed Height ft (m)	Cool- or Warm-Season	Growth Habit	Seed Count x000 per lb (kg)	"Turf" Seeding Rate lb/M (g/m^2)	Minimum Precipitation in. (mm)	Seed Cost	Seed Availability	Mowing Tolerance	Shade Tolerance	Wetland Tolerance	Salt Tolerance	Alkalinity Tolerance	Ornamental/ Turf Uses	Bloom Season	Adapted Zones
Exotic	3 ft (0.9)	Warm	Stolon	? (?)	? lb (?)	10 (254)	$$	☆	✪	❍	👎	👎	👎	T	?	345

Former Latin names: *E. atherstonii*

Varieties: Cochise (hybrid)

Comments: A finer leafed alternative to weeping lovegrass. Some ecotypes have stolons but most are bunch-type. Larger, more vigorous plants than Lehmann or weeping lovegrass, but with the same weeping habit. Good seedling vigor and cold tolerance.

References: Alderson and Sharp, 1994; Spackeen, 1993

Arizona fescue
Festuca arizonica Vasey

Native to North America	Unmowed Height ft (m)	Cool- or Warm-Season	Growth Habit	Seed Count x000 per lb (kg)	"Turf" Seeding Rate lb/M (g/m^2)	Minimum Precipitation in. (mm)	Seed Cost	Seed Availability	Mowing Tolerance	Shade Tolerance	Wetland Tolerance	Salt Tolerance	Alkalinity Tolerance	Ornamental/ Turf Uses	Bloom Season	Adapted Zones
Native	2 ft (0.6)	Cool	Bunch	550 (1210)	4 lb (20)	14 (355)	$$	☆	☆	✪	👎	👎	👎	T	7	1346

Other common names: Pinegrass

Comments: Tolerates shallow, dry soils, and shade. Similar to *F. idahoensis*. Low yielder. Intolerant of traffic. Useful in mixtures. Has been over-promoted because of its ready seed supplies.

References: Anonymous, 1988; Anonymous, 1995d; Brown et al., 1986; Cronquist et al., 1977; Hitchcock, 1951; Humphrey, 1970; Spackeen, 1993

California fescue
Festuca californica Vasey.

Native to North America	Unmowed Height ft (m)	Cool- or Warm-Season	Growth Habit	Seed Count x000 per lb (kg)	"Turf" Seeding Rate lb/M (g/m^2)	Minimum Precipitation in. (mm)	Seed Cost	Seed Availability	Mowing Tolerance	Shade Tolerance	Wetland Tolerance	Salt Tolerance	Alkalinity Tolerance	Ornamental/ Turf Uses	Bloom Season	Adapted Zones
Native	2 ft (0.6)	Cool	Bunch	? (?)	? lb (?)	? (?)	$$	☆	☆	☆	👎	👎	👎	T/O	5	45

Varieties: Salmon Creek

Comments: Shade tolerant ornamental. Thrives in dry soil. Bluish foliage turns purplish to brown after frost.

References: Daniels, 1995; Greenlee and Fell, 1992; Hitchcock, 1951; Schaff, 1994

Hair fescue
Festuca capillata Lam.

Native to North America	Unmowed Height ft (m)	Cool- or Warm-Season	Growth Habit	Seed Count x000 per lb (kg)	"Turf" Seeding Rate lb/M (g/m^2)	Minimum Precipitation in. (mm)	Seed Cost	Seed Availability	Mowing Tolerance	Shade Tolerance	Wetland Tolerance	Salt Tolerance	Alkalinity Tolerance	Ornamental/ Turf Uses	Bloom Season	Adapted Zones
Exotic	1 ft (0.3)	Cool	Rhiz.	1452 (3194)	2 lb (10)	? (?)	$$$	❍	✪	☆	👎	👎	👎	T/O	6	12

Former Latin names: *F. tenuifolia*

Comments: Finer textured than sheep fescue. Good drought and wear tolerance. Excellent adaptation to mowing but produces a brownish colored turf.

References: Darke, 1994; Hubbard, 1984; Hughes et al., 1951; Oakes, 1990; Pohl, 1968

Slender fescue
Festuca filiformis Pourret

Native to North America	Unmowed Height ft (m)	Cool- or Warm-Season	Growth Habit	Seed Count x000 per lb (kg)	"Turf" Seeding Rate lb/M (g/m^2)	Minimum Precipitation in. (mm)	Seed Cost	Seed Availability	Mowing Tolerance	Shade Tolerance	Wetland Tolerance	Salt Tolerance	Alkalinity Tolerance	Ornamental/ Turf Uses	Bloom Season	Adapted Zones
Exotic	1 ft (0.3)	Cool	Bunch	? (?)	? lb (?)	? (?)	$$	☆	✪	✪	👎	👎	👎	T	6	1234

Former Latin names: *F. ovina var. tenuifolia, F. tenuifolia*

Varieties: Barok

Comments: A fescue species with desirable low maintenance turf adaptation. Fine, delicate, hairlike leaves. Shade and drought tolerant. Previously classed as sheep fescue. Tolerates poor, dry soils and moderate to high traffic.

References: Alderson and Sharp, 1994

$ – *Inexpensive;* $$ – *Moderate;* $$$ – *Expensive;* $$$$ – *Very expensive;* ✪ – *Excellent;* ☆ – *Moderate;* ✧ – *Fair;*
❍ – *Poor or no tolerance;* 👍 – *Tolerant;* 👎 – *Intolerant;* T – *Turf;* T/O – *Turf and Ornamental;* O – *Ornamental*

Blue fescue

Festuca glauca Vill. non Lam.

Native to North America	Unmowed Height ft (m)	Cool- or Warm-Season	Growth Habit	Seed Count x000 per lb (kg)	"Turf" Seeding Rate lb/M (g/m²)	Minimum Precipitation in. (mm)	Seed Cost	Seed Availability	Mowing Tolerance	Shade Tolerance	Wetland Tolerance	Salt Tolerance	Alkalinity Tolerance	Ornamental/ Turf Uses	Bloom Season	Adapted Zones
Exotic	1 ft (0.3)	Cool	Bunch	? (?)	? lb (?)	? (?)	$$	✪	✪	✪	👎	👎	👎	T/O	6	123

Former Latin names: *F. ovina var. glauca*
Other common names: Gray fescue
Varieties: Aprilgruen, Azurit, Blaufink, Bllaufuchs, Blauglut, Blausilber, Daeumling, Elija Blue, Fruhlingsblau, Glaucantha, Harz, Kentucky Blue, Meerblau, Palatinat, Seeigel, Soehrenwald, Solling, Superba
Comments: Similar to (or possibly indistinguishable from) sheep fescue. Disease prone in warm-humid climates. Generally will not tolerate full sun, dry soil. Labor intensive as spaced plantings. Stouter, later maturing flowers than red fescue. Waxy, ornamental, bluish green, needle-like leaves. Vegetative cultivars such as "Elija Blue" need to be cloned to retain their color.
References: Darke, 1994

Idaho fescue

Festuca idahoensis Elmer

Native to North America	Unmowed Height ft (m)	Cool- or Warm-Season	Growth Habit	Seed Count x000 per lb (kg)	"Turf" Seeding Rate lb/M (g/m²)	Minimum Precipitation in. (mm)	Seed Cost	Seed Availability	Mowing Tolerance	Shade Tolerance	Wetland Tolerance	Salt Tolerance	Alkalinity Tolerance	Ornamental/ Turf Uses	Bloom Season	Adapted Zones
Native	2 ft (0.6)	Cool	Bunch	450 (990)	4 lb (22)	12 (304)	$$	☆	✪	☆	👎	👎	👍	T/O	5	126

Other common names: Blue bunchgrass
Varieties: Joseph, Nezpurs
Comments: Slow to establish—may take years to fill. Seed yield and germination are poor. Deep rooted. Tolerates poor soils, extreme drought, and higher elevation. Closely related to sheep fescue and may intercross. Very fine textured and useful in mixtures with turf fescues.
References: Alderson and Sharp, 1994; Campbell et al., 1956; Carlson, 1991; Cronquist et al., 1977; Munshower, 1994; Schaff, 1994; Spackeen, 1993; Stubbendieck et al., 1991; Young and Young, 1986

Western fescue

Festuca occidentalis Hook.

Native to North America	Unmowed Height ft (m)	Cool- or Warm-Season	Growth Habit	Seed Count x000 per lb (kg)	"Turf" Seeding Rate lb/M (g/m²)	Minimum Precipitation in. (mm)	Seed Cost	Seed Availability	Mowing Tolerance	Shade Tolerance	Wetland Tolerance	Salt Tolerance	Alkalinity Tolerance	Ornamental/ Turf Uses	Bloom Season	Adapted Zones
Native	3 ft (0.9)	Cool	Bunch	? (?)	? lb (?)	? (?)	$$$	✧	☆	☆	👎	👍	👍	T/O	6	1236

Varieties: PI-518819
Comments: Short, tufted, dryland grass. Looks similar to hard fescue. Drooping panicles have long (4 to 10 mm), slender, showy whiskers. Best at low to mid-elevations.
References: Carlson, 1991; Hitchcock, 1951; Pohl, 1968; Pojar and MacKinnon, 1994

Meadow fescue

Festuca pratensis Huds.

Native to North America	Unmowed Height ft (m)	Cool- or Warm-Season	Growth Habit	Seed Count x000 per lb (kg)	"Turf" Seeding Rate lb/M (g/m²)	Minimum Precipitation in. (mm)	Seed Cost	Seed Availability	Mowing Tolerance	Shade Tolerance	Wetland Tolerance	Salt Tolerance	Alkalinity Tolerance	Ornamental/ Turf Uses	Bloom Season	Adapted Zones
Exotic	3 ft (0.9)	Cool	Bunch	229 (503)	7 lb (33)	? (?)	$$	☆	☆	☆	👍	👍	👎	T	6	123

Former Latin names: *F. elatior*
Varieties: Altesse, Barbarossa, Barkas, Barmondo, Bartran, Bartura, Belimo, Benfesta, Bundy, Comtessa, Darimo, Ensign, First, Mimer, Pegaso, Remko, Rossa, Stella, Swift, Trader, Wendelmoed, (others)
Comments: Moderately cold and drought hardy. Similar to tall fescue in turf appearance. Certain ecotypes are adapted to mowed turf. European breeders have developed experimental cultivars with limited success. Good drought tolerance under mowing.
References: Alderson and Sharp, 1994; Anonymous, 1993c; Anonymous, 1995d; Archer and Sellers, 1956; Bernstein, 1958; Jones, 1992

American mannagrass

Glyceria grandis S. Wats.

Native to North America	Unmowed Height ft (m)	Cool- or Warm-Season	Growth Habit	Seed Count x000 per lb (kg)	"Turf" Seeding Rate lb/M (g/m²)	Minimum Precipitation in. (mm)	Seed Cost	Seed Availability	Mowing Tolerance	Shade Tolerance	Wetland Tolerance	Salt Tolerance	Alkalinity Tolerance	Ornamental/ Turf Uses	Bloom Season	Adapted Zones
Native	4 ft (1.2)	Cool	Rhiz.	? (?)	? lb (?)	? (?)	$$$	✧	✧	☆	👍	👎	👎	O	7	12346

Former Latin names: *Panicularia americana, Poa aquatica*
Other common names: Reed mannagrass, reed meadow grass, tall manna grass
Comments: Useful as a pond-edge grass, along marshes, streambanks. Broad, whitish to purple, pyramid-shaped seedheads up to 2 ft tall (0.6 m). Broad basal leaves.
References: Anonymous, 1993f; Anonymous, 1995a; Brown, 1979; Campbell et al., 1956; Cronquist et al., 1977; Hitchcock, 1951; Powers, 1995; Rhoades and Klein, 1993

Manna grass

Glyceria maxima (Hartm.) Holmb.

Native to North America	Unmowed Height ft (m)	Cool- or Warm-Season	Growth Habit	Seed Count x000 per lb (kg)	"Turf" Seeding Rate lb/M (g/m²)	Minimum Precipitation in. (mm)	Seed Cost	Seed Availability	Mowing Tolerance	Shade Tolerance	Wetland Tolerance	Salt Tolerance	Alkalinity Tolerance	Ornamental/ Turf Uses	Bloom Season	Adapted Zones
Exotic	6 ft (1.8)	Cool	Rz/St	? (?)	? lb (?)	? (?)	$$$$	❍	✪	☆	👍	👍	👎	O	7	13

Other common names: Reed sweet-grass
Varieties: Pallida, Variegata
Comments: Strongly rhizomatous. Grows even in shallow water. Variegated vegetative variety available.
References: Hubbard, 1984; Oakes, 1990; Reinhardt et al., 1989

Fowl manna grass
Glyceria striata (Lam.) Hitchc.

Native to North America	Unmowed Height ft (m)	Cool- or Warm-Season	Growth Habit	Seed Count x000 per lb (kg)	"Turf" Seeding Rate lb/M (g/m²)	Minimum Precipitation in. (mm)	Seed Cost	Seed Availability	Mowing Tolerance	Shade Tolerance	Wetland Tolerance	Salt Tolerance	Alkalinity Tolerance	Ornamental/ Turf Uses	Bloom Season	Adapted Zones
Native	3 ft (0.9)	Cool	Rhiz.	2880 (6336)	1 lb (6)	? (?)	$$$	☆	✪	☆	👍	👍	👎	O	6	12346

Former Latin names: *Poa nervata, Panicularia nervata stricta*
Other common names: Fowl meadow grass
Comments: Very widely adapted grass, suited to most climates. Tolerates standing water. Useful in streambank erosion control. Interesting purplish seed spikes. Has smaller flower clusters than other Glycerias.
References: Anonymous, 1993b; Anonymous, 1995a; Brown, 1979; Correll and Correll, 1972; Cronquist et al., 1977; Diboll, 1996; Hitchcock, 1951

Blue oatgrass
Helictotrichon sempervirens (Vill.) Pilg.

Native to North America	Unmowed Height ft (m)	Cool- or Warm-Season	Growth Habit	Seed Count x000 per lb (kg)	"Turf" Seeding Rate lb/M (g/m²)	Minimum Precipitation in. (mm)	Seed Cost	Seed Availability	Mowing Tolerance	Shade Tolerance	Wetland Tolerance	Salt Tolerance	Alkalinity Tolerance	Ornamental/ Turf Uses	Bloom Season	Adapted Zones
Exotic	4 ft (1.2)	Cool	Bunch	150 (330)	8 lb (41)	? (?)	$$$$	❍	✪	☆	👍	👎	👎	O	6	1234

Former Latin names: *Avena sempervirens, A. striata*
Other common names: Ornamental oats
Varieties: Glauca, Saphirsprudel
Comments: Stiff, blue foliage. May go dormant in hot summers. Inconspicuous flowers. Rust susceptible. May get root rot in poorly drained soils.
References: Bluemel, 1995; Greenlee and Fell, 1992; Grounds, 1979; Leasure et al., 1994; Oakes, 1990; Reinhardt et al., 1989; Simon, 1988; Woods, 1992

Limpo grass
Hemarthria altissima (Poir.) Stapf & C.E. Hubbard

Native to North America	Unmowed Height ft (m)	Cool- or Warm-Season	Growth Habit	Seed Count x000 per lb (kg)	"Turf" Seeding Rate lb/M (g/m²)	Minimum Precipitation in. (mm)	Seed Cost	Seed Availability	Mowing Tolerance	Shade Tolerance	Wetland Tolerance	Salt Tolerance	Alkalinity Tolerance	Ornamental/ Turf Uses	Bloom Season	Adapted Zones
Exotic	3 ft (0.9)	Warm	Rz/St	? (?)	? lb (?)	60 (1524)	$$$$	❍	☆	❍	👍	👎	👎	O	7	5

Other common names: Red vlei grass, rooikweek, swamp couch, halt grass
Varieties: Bigalta, Floralta, Greenalta, Redalta
Comments: Very growthy. Adapted to wetlands. Propagation by sprigging, since seed availability is poor. Beautiful red color in dry season. Will not tolerate extended drought.
References: Alderson and Sharp, 1994; Oakes, 1990; Skerman and Riveros, 1990; Zinn, 1997

Sweetgrass
Hierochloe odorata (L.) Beauv.

Native to North America	Unmowed Height ft (m)	Cool- or Warm-Season	Growth Habit	Seed Count x000 per lb (kg)	"Turf" Seeding Rate lb/M (g/m²)	Minimum Precipitation in. (mm)	Seed Cost	Seed Availability	Mowing Tolerance	Shade Tolerance	Wetland Tolerance	Salt Tolerance	Alkalinity Tolerance	Ornamental/ Turf Uses	Bloom Season	Adapted Zones
Native	2 ft (0.6)	Cool	Rhiz.	? (?)	? lb (?)	? (?)	$$$$	✧	☆	☆	👍	👍	👎	T/O	5	12346

Former Latin names: *H. nashii, Holcus odoratus*
Other common names: Vanilla grass, holy grass, seneca grass, common sweetgrass
Comments: Interesting aromatic grass used by native Americans for weaving baskets. Pleasant fragrance when clipped. Coumarin is the chemical responsible for fragrance. *Hierochloe* means "holy grass," used in religious festivals. Tulip-shaped, golden-yellow panicles. Awnless seed. Useful grass in controlling water erosion. Limited seed quantities are harvested in Europe. Turf adaptation.
References: Anonymous, 1996b; Campbell et al., 1956; Cronquist et al., 1977; Hitchcock, 1951; Oakes, 1990; Olson and Anderson, 1994; Pohl, 1968; Pojar and MacKinnon, 1994; Powers, 1995

Curly mesquite
Hilaria belangeri (Steud.) Nash

Native to North America	Unmowed Height ft (m)	Cool- or Warm-Season	Growth Habit	Seed Count x000 per lb (kg)	"Turf" Seeding Rate lb/M (g/m²)	Minimum Precipitation in. (mm)	Seed Cost	Seed Availability	Mowing Tolerance	Shade Tolerance	Wetland Tolerance	Salt Tolerance	Alkalinity Tolerance	Ornamental/ Turf Uses	Bloom Season	Adapted Zones
Native	1 ft (0.3)	Warm	Stolon	269 (591)	6 lb (30)	14 (355)	$$$$	❍	✪	✧	👎	👍	👎	T	5	5

Other common names: Toboso menudo
Comments: Very drought hardy desert grass. Prefers neutral pH. Not shade tolerant. Resembles buffalograss. Begins growth late in spring. Short growth habit, generally less than a foot (30 cm). Seed availability is scarce. Some seed is hand collected from nature. An incomplete, USGA-sponsored breeding program at University of Arizona developed turf-type plants.
References: Brown et al., 1986; Humphrey, 1970; Pohl, 1968; Stubbendieck et al., 1991

$** – *Inexpensive;* **$$** – *Moderate;* **$$$** – *Expensive;* **$$$$ – *Very expensive;* ✪ – *Excellent;* ☆ – *Moderate;* ✧ – *Fair;*
❍ – *Poor or no tolerance;* 👍 – *Tolerant;* 👎 – *Intolerant;* T – *Turf;* T/O – *Turf and Ornamental;* O – *Ornamental*

Galleta grass
Hilaria jamesii (Torr.) Benth.

Native to North America	Unmowed Height ft (m)	Cool- or Warm-Season	Growth Habit	Seed Count x000 per lb (kg)	"Turf" Seeding Rate lb/M (g/m²)	Minimum Precipitation in. (mm)	Seed Cost	Seed Availability	Mowing Tolerance	Shade Tolerance	Wetland Tolerance	Salt Tolerance	Alkalinity Tolerance	Ornamental/ Turf Uses	Bloom Season	Adapted Zones
Native	1 ft (0.3)	Warm	Rhiz.	470 (1034)	4 lb (22)	8 (203)	$$$	☆	☆	❍	👎	👍	👍	T	5	4

Former Latin names: *H. sericea*
Varieties: Viva
Comments: Tolerant of drought, heavy traffic, and mowing, as long as it's above 4 in. (10 cm). Good seed germination from native ecotypes, although some commercial seed has low PLS. Coarse, stemmy rhizomes. May enter a strong summer dormancy. Superior drought tolerance.
References: Alderson and Sharp, 1994; Cronquist et al., 1977; Featherly, 1946; Long, 1981; Olson and Anderson, 1994; Spackeen, 1993; Stubbendieck et al., 1991; Wasser, 1982; Young and Young, 1986

Big galleta
Hilaria rigida (Thurb.) Benth. ex Scribn.

Native to North America	Unmowed Height ft (m)	Cool- or Warm-Season	Growth Habit	Seed Count x000 per lb (kg)	"Turf" Seeding Rate lb/M (g/m²)	Minimum Precipitation in. (mm)	Seed Cost	Seed Availability	Mowing Tolerance	Shade Tolerance	Wetland Tolerance	Salt Tolerance	Alkalinity Tolerance	Ornamental/ Turf Uses	Bloom Season	Adapted Zones
Native	2 ft (0.6)	Warm	Rhiz.	33 (72)	15 lb (77)	5 (127)	$$$	☆	✧	❍	👎	👍	👍	T	4	45

Comments: Coarse, woody, dryland bunchgrass. Can survive some of the driest deserts of any grass.
References: Brown et al., 1986; Carlson, 1991; Hitchcock, 1951; Long, 1981

Soft grass
Holcus mollis Schreb.

Native to North America	Unmowed Height ft (m)	Cool- or Warm-Season	Growth Habit	Seed Count x000 per lb (kg)	"Turf" Seeding Rate lb/M (g/m²)	Minimum Precipitation in. (mm)	Seed Cost	Seed Availability	Mowing Tolerance	Shade Tolerance	Wetland Tolerance	Salt Tolerance	Alkalinity Tolerance	Ornamental/ Turf Uses	Bloom Season	Adapted Zones
Exotic	2 ft (0.6)	Cool	Rhiz.	? (?)	? lb (?)	? (?)	$$$$	❍	☆	✪	👍	👎	👎	T/O	6	123

Former Latin names: *Aira mollis*
Other common names: Creeping softgrass, wood softgrass, velvetgrass
Varieties: Albo-variegatus, Variegatus
Comments: Mat-forming ornamental grass with a strong rhizome habit. More shade tolerant than *H. lanatus*. Gray-green, slightly hairy leaves are 1/2-in. wide (1 cm). Tolerant of acid soils. Useful and attractive in wildflower mixes. Too aggressive to be used in a formal garden.
References: Darke, 1994; Oakes, 1990; Rhoades and Klein, 1993

Meadow barley
Hordeum brachyantherum Nevski.

Native to North America	Unmowed Height ft (m)	Cool- or Warm-Season	Growth Habit	Seed Count x000 per lb (kg)	"Turf" Seeding Rate lb/M (g/m²)	Minimum Precipitation in. (mm)	Seed Cost	Seed Availability	Mowing Tolerance	Shade Tolerance	Wetland Tolerance	Salt Tolerance	Alkalinity Tolerance	Ornamental/ Turf Uses	Bloom Season	Adapted Zones
Native	2 ft (0.6)	Cool	Bunch	? (?)	? lb (?)	? (?)	$$$	☆	✪	☆	👍	👍	👍	O	6	12346

Former Latin names: *H. boreale, H. nodosum*
Comments: Fast growing, short-lived perennial. Wide adaptation.
References: Cronquist et al., 1977; Hitchcock, 1951; Schaff, 1994

Squirrel's tail grass
Hordeum jubatum L.

Native to North America	Unmowed Height ft (m)	Cool- or Warm-Season	Growth Habit	Seed Count x000 per lb (kg)	"Turf" Seeding Rate lb/M (g/m²)	Minimum Precipitation in. (mm)	Seed Cost	Seed Availability	Mowing Tolerance	Shade Tolerance	Wetland Tolerance	Salt Tolerance	Alkalinity Tolerance	Ornamental/ Turf Uses	Bloom Season	Adapted Zones
Native	2 ft (0.6)	Cool	Bunch	? (?)	? lb (?)	? (?)	$$$	✧	☆	☆	👍	👍	👎	T/O	6	12346

Other common names: Foxtail barley, squirreltail grass, wild barley
Comments: An interesting ornamental grass with long awned, barley-like seedheads. Short-lived perennial. Can become invasive. Considered a noxious weed by some farmers, as the bristles can pierce animals' tongues. Green to purple flowers. Prefers moist, well drained soil in full sun. Huge flower spikes are easily damaged by wind, rain.
References: Brown, 1979; Campbell et al., 1956; Cronquist et al., 1977; Greenlee and Fell, 1992; Hitchcock, 1951; Reinhardt et al., 1989

Cogon
Imperata cylindrica (L.) Beauv.

Native to North America	Unmowed Height ft (m)	Cool- or Warm-Season	Growth Habit	Seed Count x000 per lb (kg)	"Turf" Seeding Rate lb/M (g/m²)	Minimum Precipitation in. (mm)	Seed Cost	Seed Availability	Mowing Tolerance	Shade Tolerance	Wetland Tolerance	Salt Tolerance	Alkalinity Tolerance	Ornamental/ Turf Uses	Bloom Season	Adapted Zones
Exotic	2 ft (0.6)	Warm	Rhiz.	? (?)	? lb (?)	10 (254)	$$$$	❍	✧	☆	👎	👍	👎	O	7	12345

Former Latin names: *I. cylindrica* var. *rubra*
Other common names: Japanese bloodgrass, alang-alang, gi, sword grass, kunai, lalang, blady, chigaya, fushigechigaya
Varieties: Red Baron
Comments: Common tropical grass throughout Thailand, the Philippines, Indonesia, and Papua New Guinea. Acid soil and drought tolerant. Useful for reclamation of waste areas. "Red Baron" (vegetative) cultivar has stunning, red foliage in late summer. Rarely flowers in temperate climates and is slow growing. Native form of plant is highly invasive in warmer areas. Rhizomes are eaten raw to remedy chest colds by children in Lesotho.
References: Chapman, 1992; Daniels, 1995; Darke, 1994; de Guzman, 1984; Greenlee and Fell, 1992; Ivory and Siregar, 1984; Leasure et al., 1994; McIvor and Chen, 1985; Oakes, 1990; Skerman and Riveros, 1990

Prairie june grass
Koeleria cristata (L.) Pers.

Native to North America	Unmowed Height ft (m)	Cool- or Warm-Season	Growth Habit	Seed Count x000 per lb (kg)	"Turf" Seeding Rate lb/M (g/m^2)	Minimum Precipitation in. (mm)	Seed Cost	Seed Availability	Mowing Tolerance	Shade Tolerance	Wetland Tolerance	Salt Tolerance	Alkalinity Tolerance	Ornamental/ Turf Uses	Bloom Season	Adapted Zones
Native	2 ft (0.6)	Cool	Bunch	2250 (4950)	1 lb (7)	12 (304)	$$$	☆	✪	☆	👎	👎	👍	T/O	5	12346

Former Latin names: *K. nitida, K. gracilis*
Other common names: Koeler's grass
Comments: Widely adapted. Thrives in dry or sandy soils. Early spring greenup. Difficult to establish. This species is often confused with crested hairgrass.
References: Anonymous, 1996b; Carlson, 1991; Humphrey, 1970; Oakes, 1990; Spackeen, 1993; Wiesner and Brown, 1984

Crested hair grass
Koeleria macrantha (Ledeb.) J.A. Schultes

Native to North America	Unmowed Height ft (m)	Cool- or Warm-Season	Growth Habit	Seed Count x000 per lb (kg)	"Turf" Seeding Rate lb/M (g/m^2)	Minimum Precipitation in. (mm)	Seed Cost	Seed Availability	Mowing Tolerance	Shade Tolerance	Wetland Tolerance	Salt Tolerance	Alkalinity Tolerance	Ornamental/ Turf Uses	Bloom Season	Adapted Zones
Native	1 ft (0.3)	Cool	Bunch	? (?)	? lb (?)	? (?)	$$$	☆	✪	☆	👎	👎	👎	T/O	5	123

Former Latin names: *K. cristata*
Other common names: Prairie junegrass
Varieties: Barkoel
Comments: Widely distributed in nature but best suited to Zone 2 for turf. Favorable winter color, but not as winter-hardy as Kentucky bluegrass. May be short-lived in fertile soil. Well adapted to dry, rocky, infertile soils. Traffic tender. "Barkoel," an improved cultivar from Europe, offers high density for turf purposes. Adapted from roadsides to golf fairways.
References: Alderson and Sharp, 1994; Anonymous, 1996b; Reinhardt et al., 1989; Rhoades and Klein, 1993

Rice cutgrass
Leersia oryzoides (L.) Swartz

Native to North America	Unmowed Height ft (m)	Cool- or Warm-Season	Growth Habit	Seed Count x000 per lb (kg)	"Turf" Seeding Rate lb/M (g/m^2)	Minimum Precipitation in. (mm)	Seed Cost	Seed Availability	Mowing Tolerance	Shade Tolerance	Wetland Tolerance	Salt Tolerance	Alkalinity Tolerance	Ornamental/ Turf Uses	Bloom Season	Adapted Zones
Native	4 ft (1.2)	Cool	Rhiz.	? (?)	? lb (?)	? (?)	$$$	☆	✪	☆	👍	👍	👎	T	8	12346

Former Latin names: *Homalocenchrus virginicus*
Other common names: Rice grass
Comments: Widely adapted to wet sites throughout the world as a soil-stabilizing grass. Requires little care after establishment. Provides food and shelter for birds.
References: Anonymous, 1993b; Anonymous, 1993f; Hubbard, 1984; Rhoades and Klein, 1993

Altai wildrye
Leymus angustus (Trin.) Pilger

Native to North America	Unmowed Height ft (m)	Cool- or Warm-Season	Growth Habit	Seed Count x000 per lb (kg)	"Turf" Seeding Rate lb/M (g/m^2)	Minimum Precipitation in. (mm)	Seed Cost	Seed Availability	Mowing Tolerance	Shade Tolerance	Wetland Tolerance	Salt Tolerance	Alkalinity Tolerance	Ornamental/ Turf Uses	Bloom Season	Adapted Zones
Exotic	3 ft (0.9)	Cool	Rhiz.	581 (1278)	4 lb (19)	14 (355)	$$	☆	✪	☆	👎	👍	👍	O	?	126

Former Latin names: *Elymus angustus, Aneurolepidium angustum, Leymus karelinii*
Other common names: Altai ryegrass
Varieties: Eejay, Pearl, Prairieland
Comments: Seedlings are slow to establish. Low seed yields make for an irregular supply. Well suited to heavy clay soils. Very deeply rooted, to 14 ft (4.3 m). Leaves stay erect, protruding through snow in winter with fairly attractive seed spikes.
References: Alderson and Sharp, 1994; Anonymous, 1996b; AOSCA, 1996; Spackeen, 1993; Tutin et al., 1980; Walton, 1983

Beach wildrye
Leymus arenarius (L.) Hochst.

Native to North America	Unmowed Height ft (m)	Cool- or Warm-Season	Growth Habit	Seed Count x000 per lb (kg)	"Turf" Seeding Rate lb/M (g/m^2)	Minimum Precipitation in. (mm)	Seed Cost	Seed Availability	Mowing Tolerance	Shade Tolerance	Wetland Tolerance	Salt Tolerance	Alkalinity Tolerance	Ornamental/ Turf Uses	Bloom Season	Adapted Zones
Exotic	4 ft (1.2)	Cool	Rhiz.	? (?)	? lb (?)	? (?)	$$$$	❍	✧	☆	👎	👍	👎	O	6	123 456

Former Latin names: *Elymus arenarius*
Other common names: European dune grass, blue lyme grass, sand wildrye, sea lyme
Varieties: Reeve
Comments: Valuable for dune stabilization the world over. Attractive blue-gray foliage and gray flowers. Beautiful blue (glaucus) color reproduces unevenly through seed. Similar in appearance to *L. mollis.* Vegetatively propagated.
References: Alderson and Sharp, 1994; Darke, 1994; Greenlee and Fell, 1992; Woods, 1992

$ – Inexpensive; $$ – Moderate; $$$ – Expensive; $$$$ – Very expensive; ✪ – Excellent; ☆ – Moderate; ✧ – Fair; ❍ – Poor or no tolerance; 👍 – Tolerant; 👎 – Intolerant; T – *Turf;* T/O – *Turf and Ornamental;* O – *Ornamental*

Basin wildrye

Leymus cinereus (Scribn. & Merr.) A. Love

Native to North America	Unmowed Height ft (m)	Cool- or Warm-Season	Growth Habit	Seed Count x000 per lb (kg)	"Turf" Seeding Rate lb/M (g/m²)	Minimum Precipitation in. (mm)	Seed Cost	Seed Availability	Mowing Tolerance	Shade Tolerance	Wetland Tolerance	Salt Tolerance	Alkalinity Tolerance	Ornamental/ Turf Uses	Bloom Season	Adapted Zones
Native	6 ft (1.8)	Cool	Bunch	130 (286)	9 lb (44)	8 (203)	$$	☆	☆	☆	👍	👍	👍	T/O	7	126

Former Latin names: *Elymus cinereus*
Other common names: Great basin wildrye, giant wildrye
Varieties: Magnar, Trailhead
Comments: Attractive ornamental grass with a distinctive blue color. Drought tolerant, good soil binder. Poor seed yielder due to low seed fill. Seed germinates moderately well but seedling survival can be an issue. An important reclamation species for disturbed ground.
References: Alderson and Sharp, 1994; Spackeen, 1993; Stubbendieck et al., 1991; Tutin et al., 1980; Wasser, 1982; Young and Young, 1986

American dunegrass

Leymus mollis (Trin.) Hara

Native to North America	Unmowed Height ft (m)	Cool- or Warm-Season	Growth Habit	Seed Count x000 per lb (kg)	"Turf" Seeding Rate lb/M (g/m²)	Minimum Precipitation in. (mm)	Seed Cost	Seed Availability	Mowing Tolerance	Shade Tolerance	Wetland Tolerance	Salt Tolerance	Alkalinity Tolerance	Ornamental/ Turf Uses	Bloom Season	Adapted Zones
Native	4 ft (1.2)	Cool	Rhiz.	? (?)	? lb (?)	? (?)	$$$$	❍	✪	☆	👎	👎	👎	O	?	12346

Former Latin names: *Elymus mollis*
Varieties: Benson
Comments: Useful grass for wind and water erosion control. Stabilizes blowing sand. Generally sprig propagated.
References: Alderson and Sharp, 1994; Darke, 1994

Mammoth wildrye

Leymus racemosus (Lam.) Tzvelev

Native to North America	Unmowed Height ft (m)	Cool- or Warm-Season	Growth Habit	Seed Count x000 per lb (kg)	"Turf" Seeding Rate lb/M (g/m²)	Minimum Precipitation in. (mm)	Seed Cost	Seed Availability	Mowing Tolerance	Shade Tolerance	Wetland Tolerance	Salt Tolerance	Alkalinity Tolerance	Ornamental/ Turf Uses	Bloom Season	Adapted Zones
Exotic	6 ft (1.8)	Cool	Rhiz.	100 (220)	10 lb (49)	7 (177)	$$	☆	☆	☆	👎	👍	👎	O	?	136

Former Latin names: *Elymus giganteus, E. racemosus, E. glaucus*
Other common names: Volga wildrye, Siberian wildrye, giant blue wildrye
Varieties: Volga, Glaucus
Comments: Useful for stabilization of dunes, rocky slopes. Spreading rhizomes may be invasive into other plantings. Produces variable plant forms from seed. Blue-gray, 1.5-cm-wide leaves.
References: Alderson and Sharp, 1994; Darke, 1994; Greenlee and Fell, 1992; Spackeen, 1993; Tutin et al., 1980; Woods, 1992

Beardless wildrye

Leymus triticoides (Buckl.) Pilger

Native to North America	Unmowed Height ft (m)	Cool- or Warm-Season	Growth Habit	Seed Count x000 per lb (kg)	"Turf" Seeding Rate lb/M (g/m²)	Minimum Precipitation in. (mm)	Seed Cost	Seed Availability	Mowing Tolerance	Shade Tolerance	Wetland Tolerance	Salt Tolerance	Alkalinity Tolerance	Ornamental/ Turf Uses	Bloom Season	Adapted Zones
Native	6 ft (1.8)	Cool	Rhiz.	137 (301)	8 lb (42)	18 (457)	$$	☆	☆	☆	👍	👍	👍	O	7	1236

Former Latin names: *Elymus triticoides*
Other common names: Bearded wildrye
Varieties: Gray Dawn, Rio, Shoshone
Comments: A tall, background grass that prefers moist sites. Useful in controlling stream erosion. Can be dormant-seeded right before first frost, emerging in spring. Seed germinates readily with no dormancy. Brown to gray winter color. Bearded wildrye is considered a variant of this species.
References: Alderson and Sharp, 1994; Anonymous, 1988; Archer and Sellers, 1956; Smith and Smith, 1996; Spackeen, 1993; Wiesner and Brown, 1984; Young and Young, 1986

Weeping grass

Microlaena stipoides var. stipoides (Labill.) R. Br.

Native to North America	Unmowed Height ft (m)	Cool- or Warm-Season	Growth Habit	Seed Count x000 per lb (kg)	"Turf" Seeding Rate lb/M (g/m²)	Minimum Precipitation in. (mm)	Seed Cost	Seed Availability	Mowing Tolerance	Shade Tolerance	Wetland Tolerance	Salt Tolerance	Alkalinity Tolerance	Ornamental/ Turf Uses	Bloom Season	Adapted Zones
Exotic	1 ft (0.3)	Cool	Rhiz.	? (?)	? lb (?)	? (?)	$$	☆	☆	☆	👎	👎	👎	T/O	6	1234

Former Latin names: *Ehrharta stipoides*
Varieties: Griffin, Shannon, Wakefield
Comments: Native Australian grass resembling fine fescue. Likes low fertility, a mulched seedbed, and shallow sowing. Can be mowed as close as 1 in. (2.5 cm). Tolerates treflan and pendimethalin preemergence herbicides at sowing. A slow germinator, so seedbed preparation is essential. Olive-green leaf color with brownish cast. "Griffin" variety was bred for turf in Australia.
References: Greenway, 1997; Tothill and Hacker, 1983

Silver banner grass
Miscanthus sacchariflorus (Maxim.) Hack.

Native to North America	Unmowed Height ft (m)	Cool- or Warm-Season	Growth Habit	Seed Count x000 per lb (kg)	"Turf" Seeding Rate lb/M (g/m²)	Minimum Precipitation in. (mm)	Seed Cost	Seed Availability	Mowing Tolerance	Shade Tolerance	Wetland Tolerance	Salt Tolerance	Alkalinity Tolerance	Ornamental/ Turf Uses	Bloom Season	Adapted Zones
Exotic	7 ft (2.1)	Warm	Rhiz.	? (?)	? lb (?)	? (?)	$$$$	❍	❍	❍	👍	👎	👎	O	8	345

Former Latin names: *M. saccharifera, Imperata sacchariflora*
Other common names: Eulalia grass, amur silver grass
Varieties: Aureus, Robustus, Variegatus
Comments: Vigorous, erect, deciduous perennial with interesting orange fall color. Cone-shaped, silvery white/red/purplish panicles. Panicle more silky than *M. sinensis*. Grows poorly in a Mediterranean climate.
References: Darke, 1994; Greenlee and Fell, 1992; Grounds, 1979; Reinhardt et al., 1989

Eulalia
Miscanthus sinensis Anderss.

Native to North America	Unmowed Height ft (m)	Cool- or Warm-Season	Growth Habit	Seed Count x000 per lb (kg)	"Turf" Seeding Rate lb/M (g/m²)	Minimum Precipitation in. (mm)	Seed Cost	Seed Availability	Mowing Tolerance	Shade Tolerance	Wetland Tolerance	Salt Tolerance	Alkalinity Tolerance	Ornamental/ Turf Uses	Bloom Season	Adapted Zones
Exotic	8 ft (2.4)	Warm	Bunch	? (?)	? lb (?)	? (?)	$$$$	❍	❍	❍	👍	👎	👎	O	9	1234

Former Latin names: *Eulalia japonica, Saccharum japonicum*
Other common names: Chinese silver grass, Japanese silver grass
Varieties: Adagio, Arabesque, Autumn Light, Cabaret, Cosmopolitan, Emerald Shadow, Goldfeder, Gracillimus, Graziella, Malepartus, Morning Light, Purpurascens, Silberfeder, Stricus, Variegatus, Yaku Jima, Zebrinus
Comments: Classic, tall, clump-forming, ornamental grass. Some plants have purple or copper foliage, others have variegated leaves. In colder climates, flowers do not appear until as late as November. Too many vegetative cultivars to list here.
References: Greenlee and Fell, 1992; Grounds, 1979; Reinhardt et al., 1989; Woods, 1992

Moor grass
Molinia caerulea (L.) Moench.

Native to North America	Unmowed Height ft (m)	Cool- or Warm-Season	Growth Habit	Seed Count x000 per lb (kg)	"Turf" Seeding Rate lb/M (g/m²)	Minimum Precipitation in. (mm)	Seed Cost	Seed Availability	Mowing Tolerance	Shade Tolerance	Wetland Tolerance	Salt Tolerance	Alkalinity Tolerance	Ornamental/ Turf Uses	Bloom Season	Adapted Zones
Exotic	4 ft (1.2)	Cool	Bunch	? (?)	? lb (?)	? (?)	$$$$	❍	☆	☆	👍	👎	👎	T/O	7	123

Former Latin names: *Festuca caerulea, Aira caerulea, Melica caerulea*
Other common names: Purple moorgrass, flying bent, purple mellic, blue moor grass
Varieties: Aureo-variegata, Bergfreund, Dauerstrahl, Edith Buksaus, Heidebraut, Karl Foerster, Moorflamme, Moorhexe, Nana-Variegata, Strahlenquelle, Skyracer, Staefa, Transparent, Windspiel, Variegata
Comments: A reed-like native of damp areas. Possesses tough cord-like roots. Blue-green foliage, turning yellow by autumn. Prefers acid soil. Very slow growing, sometimes taking years to fill in. A good ground cover. Delicate brown-purple-to-olive, translucent heads.
References: Ellefson et al., 1992; Grounds, 1979; Hitchcock, 1951; Hooven and Hooven, 1995; Oakes, 1990; Reinhardt et al., 1989; Sutton, 1938; Tutin et al., 1980

Spike muhly
Muhlenbergia wrightii Vasey ex Coult.

Native to North America	Unmowed Height ft (m)	Cool- or Warm-Season	Growth Habit	Seed Count x000 per lb (kg)	"Turf" Seeding Rate lb/M (g/m²)	Minimum Precipitation in. (mm)	Seed Cost	Seed Availability	Mowing Tolerance	Shade Tolerance	Wetland Tolerance	Salt Tolerance	Alkalinity Tolerance	Ornamental/ Turf Uses	Bloom Season	Adapted Zones
Native	2 ft (0.6)	Warm	Bunch	1635 (3597)	2 lb (9)	15 (381)	$$$	☆	☆	✧	👎	👎	👎	T	7	345

Former Latin names: *M. coloradensis*
Varieties: El Vado
Comments: Tolerant of shade, elevation, and drought. Short growing but rather intolerant of mowing.
References: Alderson and Sharp, 1994; Anonymous, 1988; Anonymous, 1995d; Cronquist et al., 1977; Spackeen, 1993

Green needlegrass
Nassella viridula (Trin.) Barkworth

Native to North America	Unmowed Height ft (m)	Cool- or Warm-Season	Growth Habit	Seed Count x000 per lb (kg)	"Turf" Seeding Rate lb/M (g/m²)	Minimum Precipitation in. (mm)	Seed Cost	Seed Availability	Mowing Tolerance	Shade Tolerance	Wetland Tolerance	Salt Tolerance	Alkalinity Tolerance	Ornamental/ Turf Uses	Bloom Season	Adapted Zones
Native	3 ft (0.9)	Cool	Bunch	181 (398)	7 lb (37)	12 (304)	$$	☆	❍	☆	👍	👎	👍	T	6	16

Former Latin names: *Stipa viridula*
Other common names: Feather bunchgrass
Varieties: Lodorm, Green Stipa
Comments: Deeply rooted rangegrass with excellent drought tolerance. Good winter, early spring green color. Seed requires acid treatment and aging for best germination. Attractive needle-like seedheads, characteristic of all the needlegrasses.
References: Alderson and Sharp, 1994; Archer and Sellers, 1956; Spackeen, 1993; U.S. Soil Conservation Service, 1982; Wasser, 1982; Wiesner and Brown, 1984

$** – *Inexpensive;* **$$** – *Moderate;* **$$$** – *Expensive;* **$$$$ – *Very expensive;* ✪ – *Excellent;* ☆ – *Moderate;* ✧ – *Fair;* ❍ – *Poor or no tolerance;* 👍 – *Tolerant;* 👎 – *Intolerant;* T – *Turf;* T/O – *Turf and Ornamental;* O – *Ornamental*

Indian ricegrass
Oryzopsis hymenoides (Roem. & Schult.) Ricker ex Piper

Native to North America	Unmowed Height ft (m)	Cool- or Warm-Season	Growth Habit	Seed Count x000 per lb (kg)	"Turf" Seeding Rate lb/M (g/m^2)	Minimum Precipitation in. (mm)	Seed Cost	Seed Availability	Mowing Tolerance	Shade Tolerance	Wetland Tolerance	Salt Tolerance	Alkalinity Tolerance	Ornamental/ Turf Uses	Bloom Season	Adapted Zones
Native	2 ft (0.6)	Cool	Bunch	235 (517)	6 lb (32)	6 (152)	$$	☆	☆	☆	👎	👎	👍	T	6	12346

Varieties: Immigrant, Nezpar, Paloma, Rimrock

Comments: Desert grass adapted to dry, sandy soils. Branching seedheads and rice-like seed provide valuable food for birds. Seeds are largely self-dormant without sulfuric acid or mechanical scarification treatment. However, they will germinate without it if you're patient enough. In arid environments, plant goes dormant in early summer, after seed set. Seed was used by various Indian tribes for flour.

References: Alderson and Sharp, 1994; Anonymous, 1988; AOSCA, 1996; Archer and Sellers, 1956; Cronquist et al., 1977; Humphrey, 1970; Spackeen, 1993; Stubbendieck et al., 1991; Young and Young, 1986

Coastal panicgrass
Panicum amarum Elliot

Native to North America	Unmowed Height ft (m)	Cool- or Warm-Season	Growth Habit	Seed Count x000 per lb (kg)	"Turf" Seeding Rate lb/M (g/m^2)	Minimum Precipitation in. (mm)	Seed Cost	Seed Availability	Mowing Tolerance	Shade Tolerance	Wetland Tolerance	Salt Tolerance	Alkalinity Tolerance	Ornamental/ Turf Uses	Bloom Season	Adapted Zones
Native	6 ft (1.8)	Warm	Rhiz.	? (?)	? lb (?)	? (?)	$$$$	❍	✧	✧	👎	👎	👎	T	7	1234

Former Latin names: *P. amarulum*

Other common names: Kisosi

Varieties: Atlantic

Comments: Bluish, leafy stems. Useful for dune stabilization. Poor shade tolerance. Scarce seed due to only 2 acres of US seed production of "Atlantic." Tolerant of droughty, sandy, infertile soils.

References: Alderson and Sharp, 1994; Anonymous, 1993h; AOSCA, 1996

Klein grass
Panicum coloratum L.

Native to North America	Unmowed Height ft (m)	Cool- or Warm-Season	Growth Habit	Seed Count x000 per lb (kg)	"Turf" Seeding Rate lb/M (g/m^2)	Minimum Precipitation in. (mm)	Seed Cost	Seed Availability	Mowing Tolerance	Shade Tolerance	Wetland Tolerance	Salt Tolerance	Alkalinity Tolerance	Ornamental/ Turf Uses	Bloom Season	Adapted Zones
Exotic	3 ft (0.9)	Warm	Stolon	490 (1078)	4 lb (21)	12 (304)	$$	☆	✪	❍	👍	👎	👎	T	?	45

Other common names: Buffalo panic, coloured guinea, small buffalograss, keria

Varieties: Bushman Mine, OKPC-1, Selection 75, Solai, Tamidori, Tayutaka, Verde

Comments: A robust, growthy grass with good drought and humidity tolerance. Provides seed and cover for birds. Seed requires scarification for good germination. A long-day flowering habit in tropical zones.

References: Alderson and Sharp, 1994; Anonymous, 1979; Anonymous, 1993c; Anonymous, 1995d; Humphreys, 1979; Skerman and Riveros, 1990; Spackeen, 1993; Wiesner and Brown, 1984

Panicum
Panicum laxum Sw.

Native to North America	Unmowed Height ft (m)	Cool- or Warm-Season	Growth Habit	Seed Count x000 per lb (kg)	"Turf" Seeding Rate lb/M (g/m^2)	Minimum Precipitation in. (mm)	Seed Cost	Seed Availability	Mowing Tolerance	Shade Tolerance	Wetland Tolerance	Salt Tolerance	Alkalinity Tolerance	Ornamental/ Turf Uses	Bloom Season	Adapted Zones
Exotic	3 ft (0.9)	Warm	Bunch	? (?)	? lb (?)	? (?)	$$$	✧	✪	✪	👍	👎	👎	T	?	45

Varieties: Shadegro

Comments: One of the only shade grasses adapted to the humid tropics. Optimal seed germination occurs at 100°F (39°C). A rare warm-season grass with C_3 photosynthesis. "Shadegro" variety was bred for turf in tropical Australia.

Vine mesquite
Panicum obtusum H.B.K.

Native to North America	Unmowed Height ft (m)	Cool- or Warm-Season	Growth Habit	Seed Count x000 per lb (kg)	"Turf" Seeding Rate lb/M (g/m^2)	Minimum Precipitation in. (mm)	Seed Cost	Seed Availability	Mowing Tolerance	Shade Tolerance	Wetland Tolerance	Salt Tolerance	Alkalinity Tolerance	Ornamental/ Turf Uses	Bloom Season	Adapted Zones
Native	2 ft (0.6)	Warm	Stolon	145 (319)	8 lb (41)	12 (304)	$$$	☆	☆	❍	👍	👎	👎	T	8	4

Other common names: Zacate guia

Comments: A true wetland grass. Good soil binding on damp, erosive sites. Stolons to 6 ft (2 m), sometimes with rhizomes. Germinates best at 50/90°F (10/32°C) alternating temperatures. Acid scarification of seed aids germination. Greens up in early spring.

References: Cronquist et al., 1977; Featherly, 1946; Spackeen, 1993; Stubbendieck et al., 1991; Young and Young, 1986

Torpedo grass
Panicum repens L.

Native to North America	Unmowed Height ft (m)	Cool- or Warm-Season	Growth Habit	Seed Count x000 per lb (kg)	"Turf" Seeding Rate lb/M (g/m^2)	Minimum Precipitation in. (mm)	Seed Cost	Seed Availability	Mowing Tolerance	Shade Tolerance	Wetland Tolerance	Salt Tolerance	Alkalinity Tolerance	Ornamental/ Turf Uses	Bloom Season	Adapted Zones
Exotic	2 ft (0.6)	Warm	Rhiz.	510 (1122)	4 lb (21)	20 (508)	$$$$	❍	☆	❍	👍	👍	👎	T	?	5

Other common names: Cheno, limanato, creeping panicum, couch panicum, panic rampant, muran

Comments: A useful sand/shore-binding grass. Gets its name from the young shoots covered by leaf sheaths, resembling a torpedo. Prefers wet soils. Can become invasive. Seed production is poor. Has been used as a "volunteer" low maintenance turf in tropical regions.

References: Anonymous, 1979; Hitchcock, 1951; Skerman and Riveros, 1990

Switchgrass *Panicum virgatum* L.

Native to North America	Unmowed Height ft (m)	Cool- or Warm-Season	Growth Habit	Seed Count x000 per lb (kg)	"Turf" Seeding Rate lb/M (g/m^2)	Minimum Precipitation in. (mm)	Seed Cost	Seed Availability	Mowing Tolerance	Shade Tolerance	Wetland Tolerance	Salt Tolerance	Alkalinity Tolerance	Ornamental/ Turf Uses	Bloom Season	Adapted Zones
Native	5 ft (1.5)	Warm	Rhiz.	382 (840)	5 lb (25)	18 (457)	$$	✪	✧	❍	👍	👍	👎	T/O	8	1345

Other common names: Prairie switchgrass
Varieties: Alamo, Blackwell, Caddo, Cave-in-rock, Dacotah, Forestburg, Haense Herms, Grenville, Heavy Metal, Kanlow, Nebraska-28, Pathfinder, Shelter, Summer, Trailblazer, Rehbraun, Squaw
Comments: Classic prairiegrass useful for recreating a tallgrass prairie appearance. Prefers fairly moist soil. Seedheads are useful for wildlife. Feathery green to pink flowers. Acid soil tolerant. Grows primarily in clumps, often with reddish-purple bases. Red and tall switchgrass are vegetatively propagated variants. "Haense Herms" cultivar has red foliage and is vegetatively propagated.
References: Anonymous, 1993b; Anonymous, 1995d; Chapman, 1992; Darke, 1994; Leasure et al., 1994; Oakes, 1990; Spackeen, 1993; Stubbendieck et al., 1991; Troeh et al., 1991; Wiesner and Brown, 1984

Western wheatgrass *Pascopyrum smithii* (Rydb.) A. Love

Native to North America	Unmowed Height ft (m)	Cool- or Warm-Season	Growth Habit	Seed Count x000 per lb (kg)	"Turf" Seeding Rate lb/M (g/m^2)	Minimum Precipitation in. (mm)	Seed Cost	Seed Availability	Mowing Tolerance	Shade Tolerance	Wetland Tolerance	Salt Tolerance	Alkalinity Tolerance	Ornamental/ Turf Uses	Bloom Season	Adapted Zones
Native	2 ft (0.6)	Cool	Rhiz.	107 (235)	10 lb (48)	10 (254)	$$	✪	☆	☆	👍	👍	👍	T/O	7	1236

Former Latin names: *Agropyron smithii, Elytrigia smithii, Elymus smithii*
Other common names: Bluejoint, agropiro del oeste, Wyoming wheatgrass, Colorado wheatgrass, bluestem wheatgrass
Varieties: Arriba, Barton, Flintlock, Mandan 456, Rodan, Rosanna, Walsh
Comments: Sluggish germination from seed dormancy problems, requiring 2 to 3 years to form a full stand. Deep rooted. Green in winter. Wildlife graze on seedheads. Prefers heavy, fine-textured soils on flood plains. Very resistant of alkali and saline soils, compared with other wheatgrasses. Survives heavy clay (adobe) soils. May be aggressive in mixtures with crested wheatgrass, especially under mowing. Water-use efficiency is about half that of blue grama and significantly lower than crested or intermediate wheatgrass.
References: Alderson and Sharp, 1994; Anonymous, 1988; Anonymous, 1993e; Anonymous, 1995d; Asay and Jensen, 1996; Daniels, 1995; Spackeen, 1993; Stubbendieck et al., 1991; Wasser, 1982; Wiesner and Brown, 1984; Young and Young, 1986

Dallis grass *Paspalum dilatatum* Poir.

Native to North America	Unmowed Height ft (m)	Cool- or Warm-Season	Growth Habit	Seed Count x000 per lb (kg)	"Turf" Seeding Rate lb/M (g/m^2)	Minimum Precipitation in. (mm)	Seed Cost	Seed Availability	Mowing Tolerance	Shade Tolerance	Wetland Tolerance	Salt Tolerance	Alkalinity Tolerance	Ornamental/ Turf Uses	Bloom Season	Adapted Zones
Exotic	3 ft (0.9)	Warm	Rhiz.	220 (484)	7 lb (34)	30 (762)	$$	✧	✪	❍	👍	👍	👎	T	7	45

Other common names: Dalis, knot grass, water grass
Varieties: Grasslands Raki, Prostrate
Comments: A turf weed that can be cultivated as a low maintenance lawn. Resembles bahiagrass when mowed. Slow seed germination due to dormancy. Sunlight and shallow planting benefit germination. Prefers fertile soils. Not persistent on light soils or high elevation. Not highly drought hardy. A long-day flowering habit in tropical zones. Tolerates frequent mowing as low as 1 in. (2.5 cm).
References: Alderson and Sharp, 1994; Anonymous, 1993c; Anonymous, 1995b; Archer and Sellers, 1956; Bernstein, 1958; Breakwell, 1923; Darke, 1994; Humphreys, 1979; Judd, 1979; Stubbendieck et al., 1991; Wasser, 1982; Young and Young, 1986

Fountain grass *Pennisetum alopecuroides* (L.) Spreng.

Native to North America	Unmowed Height ft (m)	Cool- or Warm-Season	Growth Habit	Seed Count x000 per lb (kg)	"Turf" Seeding Rate lb/M (g/m^2)	Minimum Precipitation in. (mm)	Seed Cost	Seed Availability	Mowing Tolerance	Shade Tolerance	Wetland Tolerance	Salt Tolerance	Alkalinity Tolerance	Ornamental/ Turf Uses	Bloom Season	Adapted Zones
Exotic	4 ft (1.2)	Warm	Bunch	? (?)	? lb (?)	? (?)	$$$$	❍	✧	✧	👍	👎	👎	O	7	1234

Former Latin names: *P. japonicum. P. caudatum*
Other common names: Australian fountain grass
Varieties: Cassian, Caudatum, Hameln, Little Bunny, Moudry, National Arboretum, Paul's Giant, Weserbergland, (others)
Comments: Tall ornamental grass with stiff, white, bottlebrush-like flowers. Becomes stemmy and brown after 5 years growth. Benefits from yearly rejuvenation (see text). Grows at pond's edge, provided soil is well drained. Not drought tolerant in arid environments. Tolerates a wide range of soils. Purple vegetative variants are available.
References: Darke, 1994; Leasure et al., 1994; Reinhardt et al., 1989; Woods, 1992

$ – Inexpensive; $$ – Moderate; $$$ – Expensive; $$$$ – Very expensive; ✪ – Excellent; ☆ – Moderate; ✧ – Fair; ❍ – Poor or no tolerance; 👍 – Tolerant; 👎 – Intolerant; T – Turf; T/O – Turf and Ornamental; O – Ornamental

Buffel grass

Pennisetum ciliare (L.) Link

Native to North America	Unmowed Height ft (m)	Cool- or Warm-Season	Growth Habit	Seed Count x000 per lb (kg)	"Turf" Seeding Rate lb/M (g/m^2)	Minimum Precipitation in. (mm)	Seed Cost	Seed Availability	Mowing Tolerance	Shade Tolerance	Wetland Tolerance	Salt Tolerance	Alkalinity Tolerance	Ornamental/ Turf Uses	Bloom Season	Adapted Zones
Exotic	3 ft (0.9)	Warm	Rhiz.	440 (968)	5 lb (23)	11 (279)	$$	☆	☆	❍	👎	👎	👎	T	5	5

Former Latin names: *Cenchrus ciliaris*
Other common names: Zacate buffel, African foxtail, dhaman grass, anjan grass, koluk katai
Varieties: American, Biloela, Blue, Boorara, Higgins, Llano, Molopo, Nunbank, Nueces, Tarewinnebar
Comments: Dryland grass. No tolerance of flooding or cold. When cut, grass smells like molasses. Ecotypes vary in germination. Light and well-packed soil enhances germination. Blooms indiscriminately (day neutral). Obligate apomict (clones itself through seed).
References: Alderson and Sharp, 1994; Anonymous, 1979; Anonymous, 1994b; Humphreys, 1979; Munshower, 1994; Oakes, 1990; Skerman and Riveros, 1990; Spackeen, 1993; Stubbendieck et al., 1991; Young and Young, 1986

Flaccid grass

Pennisetum flaccidum Griseb.

Native to North America	Unmowed Height ft (m)	Cool- or Warm-Season	Growth Habit	Seed Count x000 per lb (kg)	"Turf" Seeding Rate lb/M (g/m^2)	Minimum Precipitation in. (mm)	Seed Cost	Seed Availability	Mowing Tolerance	Shade Tolerance	Wetland Tolerance	Salt Tolerance	Alkalinity Tolerance	Ornamental/ Turf Uses	Bloom Season	Adapted Zones
Exotic	6 ft (1.8)	Warm	Rhiz.	? (?)	? lb (?)	? (?)	$$$$	❍	☆	❍	👎	👎	👎	T/O	8	45

Former Latin names: *P. incomptum*
Other common names: Meadow pennisetum
Varieties: Carostan
Comments: Vigorous foragegrass that can tolerate occasion clipping to 1 in. (2.5 cm). Bright, straw color when dormant and unmowed.
References: Alderson and Sharp, 1994; Greenlee and Fell, 1992; Pair, 1994; Woods, 1992

Oriental fountain grass

Pennisetum orientale L.

Native to North America	Unmowed Height ft (m)	Cool- or Warm-Season	Growth Habit	Seed Count x000 per lb (kg)	"Turf" Seeding Rate lb/M (g/m^2)	Minimum Precipitation in. (mm)	Seed Cost	Seed Availability	Mowing Tolerance	Shade Tolerance	Wetland Tolerance	Salt Tolerance	Alkalinity Tolerance	Ornamental/ Turf Uses	Bloom Season	Adapted Zones
Exotic	2 ft (0.6)	Warm	Rhiz.	? (?)	? lb (?)	? (?)	$$$$	❍	☆	✧	👎	👎	👎	O	7	45

Other common names: Hardy oriental fountain grass
Varieties: Triflorum (botanical variety)
Comments: Ornamental bunchgrass that produces masses of whitish-pink, foxtail flowers. Gray-green foliage. Propagates from seed, but slowly. Not an aggressive spreader. Needs supplemental water in arid environments. Grows in clumps with decumbent (horizontal-growing) stems.
References: Darke, 1994; Oakes, 1990; Reinhardt et al., 1989; Woods, 1992

Napier grass

Pennisetum purpureum Schumach.

Native to North America	Unmowed Height ft (m)	Cool- or Warm-Season	Growth Habit	Seed Count x000 per lb (kg)	"Turf" Seeding Rate lb/M (g/m^2)	Minimum Precipitation in. (mm)	Seed Cost	Seed Availability	Mowing Tolerance	Shade Tolerance	Wetland Tolerance	Salt Tolerance	Alkalinity Tolerance	Ornamental/ Turf Uses	Bloom Season	Adapted Zones
Exotic	10 ft (3)	Warm	Bunch	1402 (3084)	2 lb (10)	40 (1016)	$$$$	❍	✧	❍	👎	👎	👎	T	?	5

Other common names: Elephant grass, Uganda grass, gigante, mufu
Varieties: Banagrass, Capricorn, Chadi, Costa Rica 532, Gold Coast, Merkeron, Mott, Tift N75
Comments: Vegetatively propagated due to low seed germination. Drought tolerant but prefers moist, fertile soil. Grows from 10 degrees North latitude to 20 degrees South latitude. Tolerates elevation to 5500 ft (1600 m) in the tropics. Robust, cane-like growth.
References: Alderson and Sharp, 1994; Anonymous, 1979; Archer and Sellers, 1956; Breakwell, 1923; de Guzman, 1984; Judd, 1979; Skerman and Riveros, 1990; Tutin et al., 1980

Fountain grass

Pennisetum ruppelii Steud.

Native to North America	Unmowed Height ft (m)	Cool- or Warm-Season	Growth Habit	Seed Count x000 per lb (kg)	"Turf" Seeding Rate lb/M (g/m^2)	Minimum Precipitation in. (mm)	Seed Cost	Seed Availability	Mowing Tolerance	Shade Tolerance	Wetland Tolerance	Salt Tolerance	Alkalinity Tolerance	Ornamental/ Turf Uses	Bloom Season	Adapted Zones
Exotic	3 ft (0.9)	Warm	Bunch	450 (990)	4 lb (22)	12 (304)	$$$$	❍	✧	❍	👍	👎	👎	O	8	12345

Comments: Beautiful purplish plumes. Annual in colder climates. Long lived in warm climates. Similar to *P. setaceum*.
References: Aonymous, 1994b; Hubbard, 1984; Schaff, 1994; Spackeen, 1993

Feather top

Pennisetum villosum R.Br.

Native to North America	Unmowed Height ft (m)	Cool- or Warm-Season	Growth Habit	Seed Count x000 per lb (kg)	"Turf" Seeding Rate lb/M (g/m^2)	Minimum Precipitation in. (mm)	Seed Cost	Seed Availability	Mowing Tolerance	Shade Tolerance	Wetland Tolerance	Salt Tolerance	Alkalinity Tolerance	Ornamental/ Turf Uses	Bloom Season	Adapted Zones
Exotic	2 ft (0.6)	Warm	Rhiz.	? (?)	? lb (?)	30 (762)	$$$$	❍	☆	❍	👎	👎	👎	O	8	5

Other common names: White-flowering fountaingrass, long-styled feather grass, tender fountain grass
Comments: Short growing ornamental, producing heads at a height of 1 ft (30 cm). Greenish-white, cottony seedheads, turning tawny brown with age. An annual in cool climates. Easily reseeds itself in warm environments.
References: Darke, 1994; Greenlee and Fell, 1992; Reinhardt et al., 1989; Schaff, 1994; Skerman and Riveros, 1990

Harding grass

Phalaris aquatica L.

Native to North America	Unmowed Height ft (m)	Cool- or Warm-Season	Growth Habit	Seed Count x000 per lb (kg)	"Turf" Seeding Rate lb/M (g/m²)	Minimum Precipitation in. (mm)	Seed Cost	Seed Availability	Mowing Tolerance	Shade Tolerance	Wetland Tolerance	Salt Tolerance	Alkalinity Tolerance	Ornamental/ Turf Uses	Bloom Season	Adapted Zones
Exotic	5 ft (1.5)	Cool	Rhiz.	355 (781)	5 lb (26)	16 (406)	$$	☆	✧	☆	👎	👍	👎	T	5	45

Former Latin names: *P. tuberosa, P. stenoptera, P. nodosa*
Other common names: Koleagrass, towomba canary grass
Varieties: Au Oasis, Australian, Castelar INTA, Estanzuela Urunday, Holdfast, Maru, Perla, Sirocco, Sirolan, Sirosa, Siro Seedmaster, Tresur Tala, Uneta, Wintergreen
Comments: Tall, coarse textured foragegrass. Withstands low fertility and drought. Resembles reed canarygrass. Stays green through winter. Well adapted to Mediterranean climates.
References: Alderson and Sharp, 1994; Anonymous, 1993c; Archer and Sellers, 1956; Brown et al., 1986; OECD, 1996; Stubbendieck et al., 1991; Troeh et al., 1991; Tutin et al., 1980; U.S. Soil Conservation Service, 1982

Reed canarygrass

Phalaris arundinacea L.

Native to North America	Unmowed Height ft (m)	Cool- or Warm-Season	Growth Habit	Seed Count x000 per lb (kg)	"Turf" Seeding Rate lb/M (g/m²)	Minimum Precipitation in. (mm)	Seed Cost	Seed Availability	Mowing Tolerance	Shade Tolerance	Wetland Tolerance	Salt Tolerance	Alkalinity Tolerance	Ornamental/ Turf Uses	Bloom Season	Adapted Zones
Native	4 ft (1.2)	Cool	Rhiz.	538 (1183)	4 lb (20)	16 (406)	$$	✪	✧	☆	👍	👍	👎	O	5	12346

Former Latin names: *Typhoides arundinacea, Digraphis arundinacea, Baldingera arundinacea*
Other common names: Ribbon grass, roseau, gardeners' grass, reed grass
Varieties: Bellevue, Castor, Dwarf Garters, Feesey's Form, Grove, Ioreed, Keszthelyi 52, Lara, Luteo-Picta, Motycha, Palaton, Peti, Rival, Szarvasi 50 & 60, Tricolor, Vantage, Venture, (others)
Comments: Tough, vigorous, pond-edge grass, tolerant of periodically wet soil. pH tolerant down to 4.0. Cool, moist conditions and well aerated soil enhance germination. Vegetative cultivars "Picta" and "Feesey" are variegated.
References: Alderson and Sharp, 1994; Anonymous, 1993f; Bernstein, 1958; Darke, 1994; Greenlee and Fell, 1992; Grounds, 1979; Leasure et al., 1994; Oakes, 1990; OECD, 1996; Troeh et al., 1991; Wiesner and Brown, 1984

Timothy

Phleum pratense L.

Native to North America	Unmowed Height ft (m)	Cool- or Warm-Season	Growth Habit	Seed Count x000 per lb (kg)	"Turf" Seeding Rate lb/M (g/m²)	Minimum Precipitation in. (mm)	Seed Cost	Seed Availability	Mowing Tolerance	Shade Tolerance	Wetland Tolerance	Salt Tolerance	Alkalinity Tolerance	Ornamental/ Turf Uses	Bloom Season	Adapted Zones
Exotic	3 ft (0.9)	Cool	Bunch	1519 (3341)	2 lb (9)	16 (406)	$	✪	☆	☆	👎	👎	👍	T/O	7	1236

Former Latin names: *P. nodosum, P. pratense* var. *nodosum*
Other common names: Cat's tail, meadow cat's tail
Varieties: Aberystwyth S.48, Barliza, Barmidi, Barmoti, Barnee, Barvanti, Climax, Farol, Goliath, Heidemij, Intenso, Melora, Motim, Olympia, Scots, Thibet, Tiller, (others)
Comments: Vigorous foragegrass with interesting purplish green, bottlebrush seedheads. Poor heat, drought, and wear tolerance. Tolerates bog conditions through much of the colder regions of the world. Creeps by weak rhizomes. Turf cultivars are available in Europe with enhanced tiller density. *P. bertolonii* (formerly *P. nodosum*) is a small-leafed subspecies. Produces fewer, smaller heads in hot climates.
References: Archer and Sellers, 1956; Darke, 1994; House and Underwood, 1996; Oakes, 1990; Spackeen, 1993; Stubbendieck et al., 1991; Young and Young, 1986

Smilo grass

Piptatherum miliaceum (L.) Coss.

Native to North America	Unmowed Height ft (m)	Cool- or Warm-Season	Growth Habit	Seed Count x000 per lb (kg)	"Turf" Seeding Rate lb/M (g/m²)	Minimum Precipitation in. (mm)	Seed Cost	Seed Availability	Mowing Tolerance	Shade Tolerance	Wetland Tolerance	Salt Tolerance	Alkalinity Tolerance	Ornamental/ Turf Uses	Bloom Season	Adapted Zones
Exotic	4 ft (1.2)	Cool	Bunch	884 (1944)	3 lb (14)	16 (406)	$$	☆	☆	☆	👎	👎	👎	T/O	5	234

Former Latin names: *P. multiflorum, Urachne parvifolia, Oryzopsis miliacea*
Other common names: Rice grass
Varieties: Smilo
Comments: Stout, vigorous, erect grass with a decumbent base. Adapted to a Mediterranean climate, where it may naturalize and escape. Wide soil tolerance. Greens up in spring when moisture is available and goes dormant in dry summers and cold winters.
References: Alderson and Sharp, 1994; Brown et al., 1986; Greenlee and Fell, 1992; Grounds, 1979; Hitchcock, 1951; Stubbendieck et al., 1991; Tutin et al., 1980

***$* – *Inexpensive;* *$$* – *Moderate;* *$$$* – *Expensive;* *$$$$* – *Very expensive;* ✪ – *Excellent;* ☆ – *Moderate;* ✧ – *Fair;*
❍ – *Poor or no tolerance;* 👍 – *Tolerant;* 👎 – *Intolerant;* T – *Turf;* T/O – *Turf and Ornamental;* O – *Ornamental*

Alpine bluegrass

Poa alpina L.

Native to North America	Unmowed Height ft (m)	Cool- or Warm-Season	Growth Habit	Seed Count x000 per lb (kg)	"Turf" Seeding Rate lb/M (g/m^2)	Minimum Precipitation in. (mm)	Seed Cost	Seed Availability	Mowing Tolerance	Shade Tolerance	Wetland Tolerance	Salt Tolerance	Alkalinity Tolerance	Ornamental/ Turf Uses	Bloom Season	Adapted Zones
Native	1 ft (0.3)	Cool	Bunch	1000 (2200)	3 lb (13)	20 (508)	$$$	☆	✪	☆	👎	👎	👎	T	5	16

Former Latin names: *P. alpina var. minor*
Other common names: Alpine meadow grass
Varieties: Gruening, Matterhorn, Vivipara
Comments: Very low growing alpine grass, only 4 to 6 in. at maturity (10 to 15 cm). Rust susceptible. Tolerant of drought and acid soils. Avoids drought by going dormant. Tolerant of most Kentucky bluegrass herbicides. Can be maintained as a lawn without any mowing (see text).
References: Alderson and Sharp, 1994; Greenlee and Fell, 1992; Oakes, 1990; Smith and Smith, 1996; Spackeen, 1993

Big bluegrass

Poa ampla Merr.

Native to North America	Unmowed Height ft (m)	Cool- or Warm-Season	Growth Habit	Seed Count x000 per lb (kg)	"Turf" Seeding Rate lb/M (g/m^2)	Minimum Precipitation in. (mm)	Seed Cost	Seed Availability	Mowing Tolerance	Shade Tolerance	Wetland Tolerance	Salt Tolerance	Alkalinity Tolerance	Ornamental/ Turf Uses	Bloom Season	Adapted Zones
Native	2 ft (0.6)	Cool	Bunch	882 (1940)	3 lb (14)	12 (304)	$$	☆	☆	☆	👎	👎	👍	T	5	16

Former Latin names: *P. laeviculmis, P. confusa, P. truncata*
Varieties: Service, Sherman
Comments: Vigorous, upright bluegrass species with a very early spring growth. Blue-green color. Tolerates moist or dry soil. Low seedling vigor results in slow establishment, often requiring more than one growing season where unirrigated. Can be used in low maintenance mixtures with other *Poas.*
References: Cronquist et al., 1977; Hitchcock, 1951; Jones, 1992; Spackeen, 1993; Wasser, 1982

Annual bluegrass

Poa annua L.

Native to North America	Unmowed Height ft (m)	Cool- or Warm-Season	Growth Habit	Seed Count x000 per lb (kg)	"Turf" Seeding Rate lb/M (g/m^2)	Minimum Precipitation in. (mm)	Seed Cost	Seed Availability	Mowing Tolerance	Shade Tolerance	Wetland Tolerance	Salt Tolerance	Alkalinity Tolerance	Ornamental/ Turf Uses	Bloom Season	Adapted Zones
Exotic	1 ft (0.3)	Cool	Bunch	1196 (2631)	2 lb (11)	? (?)	$$	✧	✪	☆	👍	👎	👎	T	5	12346

Other common names: Annual meadowgrass, wintergrass, low speargrass, six-weeks grass
Varieties: DW-184
Comments: Limited quantities of common annual bluegrass seed are sold each year, but seed is of an annual ecotype that does not persist beyond midsummer. Yellow-green in color. Perennial ecotypes rapidly breed themselves in turf to tolerate close mowing. Perennial "reptans" varieties are being bred by the University of Minnesota. Penn State University is developing putting green cultivars.
References: Anonymous, 1995a; Brown, 1979; Hubbard, 1984; Hughes et al., 1951; Tutin et al., 1980

Texas bluegrass

Poa arachnifera Torr.

Native to North America	Unmowed Height ft (m)	Cool- or Warm-Season	Growth Habit	Seed Count x000 per lb (kg)	"Turf" Seeding Rate lb/M (g/m^2)	Minimum Precipitation in. (mm)	Seed Cost	Seed Availability	Mowing Tolerance	Shade Tolerance	Wetland Tolerance	Salt Tolerance	Alkalinity Tolerance	Ornamental/ Turf Uses	Bloom Season	Adapted Zones
Native	2 ft (0.6)	Cool	Rhiz.	1847 (4063)	2 lb (8)	? (?)	$$$	✧	✪	☆	👎	👎	👎	T	5	1234

Variety: Reveille
Comments: Occasionally cultivated as turf or pasture. Puffy, cottony seed is nearly impossible to plant except by hydroseeding. A seedlot with 65% PLS is considered "good." Texas A&M University is developing turf-type hybrids with Kentucky bluegrass.
References: Harlan et al., 1952; Hitchcock, 1951

Canby bluegrass

Poa canbyi (Scribn.) Piper

Native to North America	Unmowed Height ft (m)	Cool- or Warm-Season	Growth Habit	Seed Count x000 per lb (kg)	"Turf" Seeding Rate lb/M (g/m^2)	Minimum Precipitation in. (mm)	Seed Cost	Seed Availability	Mowing Tolerance	Shade Tolerance	Wetland Tolerance	Salt Tolerance	Alkalinity Tolerance	Ornamental/ Turf Uses	Bloom Season	Adapted Zones
Native	2 ft (0.6)	Cool	Bunch	926 (2037)	3 lb (14)	10 (254)	$$	☆	☆	☆	👍	👍	👍	T	5	16

Former Latin names: *P. tenuifolia, P. laevis, Glyceria canbyi*
Varieties: Canbar
Comments: Very early spring greenup, but poor summer endurance. Turf adaptation, particularly in low maintenance bluegrass mixtures. Purplish white leaf colors. Drought tolerant, but avoids drought by going dormant. Erratic seed yielder. Relatively shallow rooted. Slender leaves and stems. Susceptible to disease in high humidity areas.
References: Campbell et al., 1956; Cronquist et al., 1977; Munshower, 1994; Spackeen, 1993

Upland bluegrass

Poa glauca Vahl ssp. glaucantha (Gauldin) Lindm.

Native to North America	Unmowed Height ft (m)	Cool- or Warm-Season	Growth Habit	Seed Count x000 per lb (kg)	"Turf" Seeding Rate lb/M (g/m^2)	Minimum Precipitation in. (mm)	Seed Cost	Seed Availability	Mowing Tolerance	Shade Tolerance	Wetland Tolerance	Salt Tolerance	Alkalinity Tolerance	Ornamental/ Turf Uses	Bloom Season	Adapted Zones
Exotic	1 ft (0.3)	Cool	Bunch	2500 (5500)	1 lb (6)	? (?)	$$$	☆	☆	☆	👎	👎	👎	T/O	7	16

Former Latin names: *Glaucous bluegrass, P. glaucantha*
Other common names: Greenland bluegrass
Varieties: Draylar, Tundra
Comments: Tufted, wiry grass with dark blue-green blades, sometimes with a strong whitish (glaucus) cast. Short enough that it can be maintained without mowing. May exhibit summer dormancy in drier climates.
References: Alderson and Sharp, 1994; Oakes, 1990; U.S. Soil Conservation Service, 1982

Wood meadowgrass
Poa nemoralis L.

Native to North America	Unmowed Height ft (m)	Cool- or Warm-Season	Growth Habit	Seed Count x000 per lb (kg)	"Turf" Seeding Rate lb/M (g/m²)	Minimum Precipitation in. (mm)	Seed Cost	Seed Availability	Mowing Tolerance	Shade Tolerance	Wetland Tolerance	Salt Tolerance	Alkalinity Tolerance	Ornamental/ Turf Uses	Bloom Season	Adapted Zones
Exotic	2 ft (0.6)	Cool	Bunch	3350 (7370)	1 lb (5)	? (?)	$$$$	❍	✧	✪	👎	👎	👎	T/O	6	1236

Former Latin names: *Agrostis alba*
Other common names: Wood bluegrass
Varieties: Barnemo, Dekora, Enhary, Novombra, Pallas, Shadow (Dekora CZE)
Comments: Shade, cold tolerant relative of Kentucky bluegrass. Not as attractive as Kentucky bluegrass when mowed, but requires little maintenance. Elegant, airy seedheads. Erect, clumpy, and somewhat spreading. Summer dormant in hot, arid environments. Mowing sensitive.
References: Alderson and Sharp, 1994; Anonymous, 1993c; Breakwell, 1923; Darke, 1994; Hubbard, 1984; Jones, 1992; Oakes, 1990; OECD, 1996

Foul bluegrass
Poa palustris L.

Native to North America	Unmowed Height ft (m)	Cool- or Warm-Season	Growth Habit	Seed Count x000 per lb (kg)	"Turf" Seeding Rate lb/M (g/m²)	Minimum Precipitation in. (mm)	Seed Cost	Seed Availability	Mowing Tolerance	Shade Tolerance	Wetland Tolerance	Salt Tolerance	Alkalinity Tolerance	Ornamental/ Turf Uses	Bloom Season	Adapted Zones
Native	4 ft (1.2)	Cool	Bunch	? (?)	? lb (?)	? (?)	$$	✧	☆	☆	👍	👎	👎	T/O	6	12

Other common names: Swamp meadow grass
Varieties: Bono, Roznovska
Comments: Short-lived perennial bluegrass, similar to *P. trivialis*. Valuable for wetlands. Has been cultivated for pastures in Britain since 1814. Heads are yellowish green to purple, turning golden brown at maturity.
References: Anonymous, 1995a; Hubbard, 1984; OECD, 1996

Sandberg bluegrass
Poa sandbergii Vassey

Native to North America	Unmowed Height ft (m)	Cool- or Warm-Season	Growth Habit	Seed Count x000 per lb (kg)	"Turf" Seeding Rate lb/M (g/m²)	Minimum Precipitation in. (mm)	Seed Cost	Seed Availability	Mowing Tolerance	Shade Tolerance	Wetland Tolerance	Salt Tolerance	Alkalinity Tolerance	Ornamental/ Turf Uses	Bloom Season	Adapted Zones
Native	1 ft (0.3)	Cool	Bunch	925 (2035)	3 lb (14)	8 (203)	$$$	☆	☆	☆	👎	👎	👎	T	4	16

Former Latin names: *P. secunda, P. andina, P. incurva*
Other common names: Little bluegrass
Comments: Similar to Canby bluegrass and in fact may be identical. Tolerant of poor soil, drought, and cold. Good soil binder. Ecotypes vary in germination rate, but overall, seeds germinate well with no dormancy problems. Greens up early in spring and then goes dormant in summer.
References: Anonymous, 1988; Archer and Sellers, 1956; Cronquist et al., 1977; Munshower, 1994; Spackeen, 1993; Stubbendieck et al., 1991; Wasser, 1982; Young and Young, 1986

Russian wildrye
Psathyrostachys juncea (Fisch.) Nevshi

Native to North America	Unmowed Height ft (m)	Cool- or Warm-Season	Growth Habit	Seed Count x000 per lb (kg)	"Turf" Seeding Rate lb/M (g/m²)	Minimum Precipitation in. (mm)	Seed Cost	Seed Availability	Mowing Tolerance	Shade Tolerance	Wetland Tolerance	Salt Tolerance	Alkalinity Tolerance	Ornamental/ Turf Uses	Bloom Season	Adapted Zones
Exotic	4 ft (1.2)	Cool	Bunch	187 (411)	7 lb (36)	8 (203)	$$	☆	☆	✪	👍	👍	👍	O	6	126

Former Latin names: *Elymus junceus*
Varieties: Bozoiski-Select, Cabree, Idaho 100, Mankota, Mayak, Piper, Sawki, Swift, Tetracan, Vinall
Comments: Striking, bushy ornamental rangegrass. Drought, elevation tolerant. Some shade tolerance. Slow to establish. Moist, cold conditions benefit seed germination. A good seedbed is critical for establishment; 80 to 90% of failures trace to too-deep planting.
References: Alderson and Sharp, 1994; Anonymous, 1988; Archer and Sellers, 1956; Spackeen, 1993; Wasser, 1982; Wiesner and Brown, 1984; Young and Young, 1986

Beardless wheatgrass
Pseudoroegneria spicata (Pursh) A. Love

Native to North America	Unmowed Height ft (m)	Cool- or Warm-Season	Growth Habit	Seed Count x000 per lb (kg)	"Turf" Seeding Rate lb/M (g/m²)	Minimum Precipitation in. (mm)	Seed Cost	Seed Availability	Mowing Tolerance	Shade Tolerance	Wetland Tolerance	Salt Tolerance	Alkalinity Tolerance	Ornamental/ Turf Uses	Bloom Season	Adapted Zones
Native	2 ft (0.6)	Cool	Rhiz.	117 (257)	9 lb (46)	8 (203)	$$	☆	✧	☆	👎	👎	👎	T/O	7	124

Former Latin names: *Agropyron inerme*
Other common names: Beardless bluebunch
Varieties: Whitmar, Newhy
Comments: Similar in appearance to slender wheatgrass but more leafy. A relatively low seed yielder. "Newhy" RS wheatgrass is an interspecific hybrid with *Elytrigia repens* var. repens. Tolerant of salinity, alkalinity, and drought down to 13 in. (330 mm) of annual rainfall. Doesn't tolerate wet soils. Subspecies *"inermis"* is hairless.
References: Alderson and Sharp, 1994; Asay and Jensen, 1996; Smith and Smith, 1996; Spackeen, 1993; Tutin et al., 1980; Wasser, 1982

$ – Inexpensive; $$ – Moderate; $$$ – Expensive; $$$$ – Very expensive; ✪ – Excellent; ☆ – Moderate; ✧ – Fair; ❍ – Poor or no tolerance; 👍 – Tolerant; 👎 – Intolerant; T – *Turf;* T/O – *Turf and Ornamental;* O – *Ornamental*

Bluebunch wheatgrass

Pseudoroegneria spicata ssp. *spicata* (Pursh) A. Love

Native to North America	Unmowed Height ft (m)	Cool- or Warm-Season	Growth Habit	Seed Count x000 per lb (kg)	"Turf" Seeding Rate lb/M (g/m^2)	Minimum Precipitation in. (mm)	Seed Cost	Seed Availability	Mowing Tolerance	Shade Tolerance	Wetland Tolerance	Salt Tolerance	Alkalinity Tolerance	Ornamental/ Turf Uses	Bloom Season	Adapted Zones
Native	4 ft (1.2)	Cool	Bunch	95 (209)	10 lb (50)	8 (203)	$$	☆	✧	☆	👎	👎	👎	T/O	7	123

Former Latin names: *Agropyron spicatum, Elytrigia spicata*
Other common names: Big bunchgrass, Snake River wheatgrass
Varieties: Goldar, Secar
Comments: One of several wheatgrasses recently reclassed into a separate species. Tolerates slopes, elevation, and poor soil. Does well on coarse-textured soils or deep well-drained loams. Weakened by constant mowing, particularly when flowering. Responds favorably to fertilization. Seed germinates readily with no dormancy problems. Ideal germination temperature is 70°F (21°C). Ecotypes vary in germination ability. Reliable seed yielder with steady supply.
References: Alderson and Sharp, 1994; Anonymous, 1988; Archer and Sellers, 1956; Asay and Jensen, 1996; Hughes et al., 1951; Spackeen, 1993; Stubbendieck et al., 1991; Tutin et al., 1980; Wasser, 1982; Young and Young, 1986

Nuttal alkaligrass

Puccinellia airoides (Nutt.) Wats. and Coult.

Native to North America	Unmowed Height ft (m)	Cool- or Warm-Season	Growth Habit	Seed Count x000 per lb (kg)	"Turf" Seeding Rate lb/M (g/m^2)	Minimum Precipitation in. (mm)	Seed Cost	Seed Availability	Mowing Tolerance	Shade Tolerance	Wetland Tolerance	Salt Tolerance	Alkalinity Tolerance	Ornamental/ Turf Uses	Bloom Season	Adapted Zones
Native	2 ft (0.6)	Cool	Bunch	2789 (6135)	1 lb (6)	14 (355)	$$	☆	☆	☆	👍	👍	👍	T	6	1236

Former Latin names: *P. nuttalliana*
Other common names: Zawadke alkali, Nuttall's alkali
Varieties: Quill
Comments: Tolerant to flooding, poor drainage, and alkaline soils. Smooth, yellow-green foliage.
References: Anonymous, 1996b; Crampton, 1961; Hitchcock, 1951; Pohl, 1968; Spackeen, 1993

Lemmons alkaligrass

Puccinellia lemmoni (Vasey) Scribn.

Native to North America	Unmowed Height ft (m)	Cool- or Warm-Season	Growth Habit	Seed Count x000 per lb (kg)	"Turf" Seeding Rate lb/M (g/m^2)	Minimum Precipitation in. (mm)	Seed Cost	Seed Availability	Mowing Tolerance	Shade Tolerance	Wetland Tolerance	Salt Tolerance	Alkalinity Tolerance	Ornamental/ Turf Uses	Bloom Season	Adapted Zones
Native	1 ft (0.3)	Cool	Bunch	1027 (2259)	3 lb (13)	? (?)	$$	☆	☆	☆	👎	👍	👍	T	6	12

Former Latin names: *P. rubida*
Comments: Prefers moist soils. Has problems with sluggish seed germination. Cool, moist conditions favor germination.
References: Cronquist et al., 1977; Hitchcock, 1951; Sours, 1985; Wu and Harivandi, 1988; Young and Young, 1986

Blowout grass

Redfieldia flexuosa (Thurb.) Vasey

Native to North America	Unmowed Height ft (m)	Cool- or Warm-Season	Growth Habit	Seed Count x000 per lb (kg)	"Turf" Seeding Rate lb/M (g/m^2)	Minimum Precipitation in. (mm)	Seed Cost	Seed Availability	Mowing Tolerance	Shade Tolerance	Wetland Tolerance	Salt Tolerance	Alkalinity Tolerance	Ornamental/ Turf Uses	Bloom Season	Adapted Zones
Native	3 ft (0.9)	Cool	Rhiz.	263 (578)	6 lb (30)	8 (203)	$$$	☆	✧	☆	👍	👎	👎	T/O	7	13

Former Latin names: *Graphephorum flexosum*
Other common names: Sandgrass
Comments: Sand stabilizing grass, of little feeding value for wildlife. Grows in colonies primarily in the short-grass prairie region. Flowers well into autumn. Stems erect, coarse, tough, hairless. Large open panicle bloom.
References: Brown et al., 1986; Carlson, 1991; Cronquist et al., 1977; Hitchcock, 1951; Hughes et al., 1951; Sours, 1985

Natal grass

Rhynchelytrum repens (Willd.) C.E. Hubbard

Native to North America	Unmowed Height ft (m)	Cool- or Warm-Season	Growth Habit	Seed Count x000 per lb (kg)	"Turf" Seeding Rate lb/M (g/m^2)	Minimum Precipitation in. (mm)	Seed Cost	Seed Availability	Mowing Tolerance	Shade Tolerance	Wetland Tolerance	Salt Tolerance	Alkalinity Tolerance	Ornamental/ Turf Uses	Bloom Season	Adapted Zones
Exotic	3 ft (0.9)	Warm	Bunch	200 (440)	7 lb (35)	6 (152)	$$$	☆	☆	❍	👍	👎	👎	T/O	7	45

Former Latin names: *R. roseum, Tricholaena rosea, T. repens*
Other common names: Champagne grass, ruby grass
Comments: Valuable ornamental grass with showy, attractive pink, fluffy seedheads with reddish, long, silky hairs. Short-lived perennial. Naturally invasive in mild climates and may escape cultivation.
References: Darke, 1994; Ellefson et al., 1992; Greenlee and Fell, 1992; Judd, 1979; Oakes, 1990; Pair, 1994; Schaff, 1994; Spackeen, 1993

Plume grass
Saccharum ravennae (L.) L.

Native to North America	Unmowed Height ft (m)	Cool- or Warm-Season	Growth Habit	Seed Count x000 per lb (kg)	"Turf" Seeding Rate lb/M (g/m²)	Minimum Precipitation in. (mm)	Seed Cost	Seed Availability	Mowing Tolerance	Shade Tolerance	Wetland Tolerance	Salt Tolerance	Alkalinity Tolerance	Ornamental/ Turf Uses	Bloom Season	Adapted Zones
Exotic	12 ft (3.6)	Warm	Bunch	? (?)	? lb (?)	? (?)	$$$$	❍	❍	❍	👍	👎	👎	O	9	12345

Former Latin names: *Erianthus ravennae*
Other common names: Ravennae grass, hardy pampas grass, silver plume
Varieties: Purpurascens
Comments: Substitute for pampas grass (*Cortaderia*) for colder climates. Silver-bronze showy flowers. Robust, smooth medium-green stems turning brown by autumn with hints of purple, orange, and yellow. Plants stand into winter but plumes deteriorate.
References: Darke, 1994; Leasure et al., 1994; Pohl, 1968; Reinhardt et al., 1989; Woods, 1992

Little bluestem
Schizachyrium scoparium (Michx.) Nash

Native to North America	Unmowed Height ft (m)	Cool- or Warm-Season	Growth Habit	Seed Count x000 per lb (kg)	"Turf" Seeding Rate lb/M (g/m²)	Minimum Precipitation in. (mm)	Seed Cost	Seed Availability	Mowing Tolerance	Shade Tolerance	Wetland Tolerance	Salt Tolerance	Alkalinity Tolerance	Ornamental/ Turf Uses	Bloom Season	Adapted Zones
Native	4 ft (1.2)	Warm	Bunch	254 (558)	6 lb (31)	14 (355)	$$	☆	✧	❍	👎	👎	👎	T/O	8	1345

Former Latin names: *Andropogon scoparius*
Other common names: Prairie beardgrass, broom sedge, bunchgrass, zacate colorado
Varieties: Aldous, Badlands, Blaze, Camper, Cimarron, Littorale, Pastura
Comments: Classic rangegrass of the shortgrass prairie. Blue-green foliage, turning red/orange/purple in autumn to red by winter. Retains leaves and color through winter. Tufted, leafy, greenish white stems. Greens early in spring for a warm-season grass. Fluffy, zigzag seedheads ripen in late fall to buff color. Tolerant of drought and mowing above 3 in. (7.5 cm).
References: Anonymous, 1995d; Anonymous, 1996b; Darke, 1994; Greenlee and Fell, 1992; Spackeen, 1993; Stubbendieck et al., 1991; Wiesner and Brown, 1984

Autumn moor grass
Sesleria autumnalis (Scop.) Schultz

Native to North America	Unmowed Height ft (m)	Cool- or Warm-Season	Growth Habit	Seed Count x000 per lb (kg)	"Turf" Seeding Rate lb/M (g/m²)	Minimum Precipitation in. (mm)	Seed Cost	Seed Availability	Mowing Tolerance	Shade Tolerance	Wetland Tolerance	Salt Tolerance	Alkalinity Tolerance	Ornamental/ Turf Uses	Bloom Season	Adapted Zones
Exotic	2 ft (0.6)	Cool	Bunch	? (?)	? lb (?)	? (?)	$$$$	❍	☆	✪	👍	👎	👍	T/O	6	1234

Former Latin names: *S. elongata, S. caerulea*
Other common names: Blue moor grass
Comments: Curled, dark green, narrow (4 mm) leaves, with bluish-white underneath. Silver-white flowers. Shade and drought tolerant. Tolerates limited traffic. Competes well in the shade against tree roots.
References: Daniels, 1995; Greenlee and Fell, 1992; Hooven and Hooven, 1995; Reinhardt et al., 1989; Tutin et al., 1980; Woods, 1992

Plains bristlegrass
Setaria macrostachya H.B.K.

Native to North America	Unmowed Height ft (m)	Cool- or Warm-Season	Growth Habit	Seed Count x000 per lb (kg)	"Turf" Seeding Rate lb/M (g/m²)	Minimum Precipitation in. (mm)	Seed Cost	Seed Availability	Mowing Tolerance	Shade Tolerance	Wetland Tolerance	Salt Tolerance	Alkalinity Tolerance	Ornamental/ Turf Uses	Bloom Season	Adapted Zones
Native	3 ft (0.9)	Warm	Bunch	305 (671)	6 lb (28)	12 (304)	$$	☆	✧	❍	👎	👎	👎	T/O	5	345

Former Latin names: *S. leucopila*
Other common names: Zacate tempranero
Comments: Adapted to drier sites and higher elevation. Seed is valuable for attracting birds and other wildlife to naturalized areas. Seed germination is enhanced by acid scarification and alternating (45/80°F, 7/27°C) temperatures. Greens up in mid to late spring.
References: Archer and Sellers, 1956; Featherly, 1946; Pair, 1994; Pohl, 1968; Spackeen, 1993; Stubbendieck et al., 1991; Young and Young, 1986

Palm grass
Seteria palmifolia (Koen.) Stapf.

Native to North America	Unmowed Height ft (m)	Cool- or Warm-Season	Growth Habit	Seed Count x000 per lb (kg)	"Turf" Seeding Rate lb/M (g/m²)	Minimum Precipitation in. (mm)	Seed Cost	Seed Availability	Mowing Tolerance	Shade Tolerance	Wetland Tolerance	Salt Tolerance	Alkalinity Tolerance	Ornamental/ Turf Uses	Bloom Season	Adapted Zones
Exotic	7 ft (2.1)	Warm	Bunch	? (?)	? lb (?)	? (?)	$$$$	❍	☆	✧	👍	👍	👎	T/O	5	345

Former Latin names: *Panicum palmaefolium, P. nervosum, P. neurodes, P. plicatum, Chamaeraphis palmifolia*
Varieties: Variegata
Comments: Tall growing ornamental. Withstands some mowing. Widely distributed in Jamaica and India. Shade tolerant. Coarse blades of medium green color, with a distinct weeping habit. Winter tender.
References: Bor, 1960; Greenlee and Fell, 1992; Hitchcock, 1951; Oakes, 1990; Rominger, 1962

$ – Inexpensive; $$ – Moderate; $$$ – Expensive; $$$$ – Very expensive; ✪ – Excellent; ☆ – Moderate; ✧ – Fair; ❍ – Poor or no tolerance; 👍 – Tolerant; 👎 – Intolerant; T – *Turf;* T/O – *Turf and Ornamental;* O – *Ornamental*

Indiangrass
Sorghastrum nutans (L.) Nash

Native to North America	Unmowed Height ft (m)	Cool- or Warm-Season	Growth Habit	Seed Count x000 per lb (kg)	"Turf" Seeding Rate lb/M (g/m^2)	Minimum Precipitation in. (mm)	Seed Cost	Seed Availability	Mowing Tolerance	Shade Tolerance	Wetland Tolerance	Salt Tolerance	Alkalinity Tolerance	Ornamental/ Turf Uses	Bloom Season	Adapted Zones
Native	5 ft (1.5)	Warm	Rhiz.	170 (374)	8 lb (38)	14 (355)	$$	☆	❍	❍	👎	👍	👎	T/O	8	1345

Former Latin names: *S. avenaceum, Chrysopogon nutans*
Other common names: Yellow indiangrass, gold beard grass, zacate indio
Varieties: Cheyenne, Holt, Llano, Lometa, Nebraska 54, Osage, Oto, Rumsey, Sioux Blue, Tejas, Tomahawk
Comments: Beautiful ornamental prairiegrass with rather undistinguished foliage, but showy, medium-sized white plumes. Rather intolerant of clipping. Classic tallgrass prairie plant. Medium spring greenup rate. Relatively slow establishment.
References: Anonymous, 1995d; Greenlee and Fell, 1992; Spackeen, 1993; Stubbendieck et al., 1991; Woods, 1992

Smooth cordgrass
Spartina alternifora Loisel.

Native to North America	Unmowed Height ft (m)	Cool- or Warm-Season	Growth Habit	Seed Count x000 per lb (kg)	"Turf" Seeding Rate lb/M (g/m^2)	Minimum Precipitation in. (mm)	Seed Cost	Seed Availability	Mowing Tolerance	Shade Tolerance	Wetland Tolerance	Salt Tolerance	Alkalinity Tolerance	Ornamental/ Turf Uses	Bloom Season	Adapted Zones
Native	7 ft (2.1)	Warm	Rhiz.	? (?)	? lb (?)	? (?)	$$$$	❍	❍	☆	👍	👍	👎	T	8	345

Former Latin names: *Dactylis maritima*
Other common names: Saltwater cord grass
Varieties: Aureo-marginata, Bayshore, Vermilion
Comments: Vegetatively propagated soil-binding grass that will grow in straight saltwater. Variegated varieties are available.
References: Alderson and Sharp, 1994; Oakes, 1990

Saltmeadow cordgrass
Spartina patens (Ait.) Muhl.

Native to North America	Unmowed Height ft (m)	Cool- or Warm-Season	Growth Habit	Seed Count x000 per lb (kg)	"Turf" Seeding Rate lb/M (g/m^2)	Minimum Precipitation in. (mm)	Seed Cost	Seed Availability	Mowing Tolerance	Shade Tolerance	Wetland Tolerance	Salt Tolerance	Alkalinity Tolerance	Ornamental/ Turf Uses	Bloom Season	Adapted Zones
Native	2 ft (0.6)	Warm	Rhiz.	? (?)	? lb (?)	? (?)	$$$$	❍	☆	✧	👍	👍	👎	T	7	345

Other common names: Highwater grass, muscotte, marshhay cordgrass
Varieties: Avalon, Flageo
Comments: Useful for revegetating salt flats along ocean shores. Vegetatively propagated. Can be invasive on moist, fertile soils. Creeps and roots along drooping stems. Purple, scaly flowers. Tolerates a daily flooding of seawater. Generally poor for wildlife, except muskrats. Green through the winter.
References: Alderson and Sharp, 1994; Brown, 1979; Oakes, 1990

Prairie cordgrass
Spartina pectinata Link

Native to North America	Unmowed Height ft (m)	Cool- or Warm-Season	Growth Habit	Seed Count x000 per lb (kg)	"Turf" Seeding Rate lb/M (g/m^2)	Minimum Precipitation in. (mm)	Seed Cost	Seed Availability	Mowing Tolerance	Shade Tolerance	Wetland Tolerance	Salt Tolerance	Alkalinity Tolerance	Ornamental/ Turf Uses	Bloom Season	Adapted Zones
Native	6 ft (1.8)	Warm	Rhiz.	? (?)	? lb (?)	? (?)	$$$$	✧	✧	☆	👍	👍	👎	O	7	12346

Former Latin names: *S. michauxiana*
Other common names: Freshwater cordgrass, marsh grass, slough grass, tall marshgrass
Varieties: Aureo-marginata (variegated)
Comments: Adapted from prairies to bogs. Shiny saw-edged leaves with yellow edges. Grows via thick, scaly rootstocks with dense, wide, rough-edged, basal foliage. Interesting seed spikes made up of 40 paired spikelets on one side of spike, with bristly awns.
References: Anonymous, 1993b; Anonymous, 1995d; Campbell et al., 1956; Greenlee and Fell, 1992; Leasure et al., 1994; Oakes, 1990; Pair, 1994; Pohl, 1968; Reinhardt et al., 1989; Stubbendieck et al., 1991; Woods, 1992

Alkali sacaton
Sporobolus airoides (Torr.) Torr.

Native to North America	Unmowed Height ft (m)	Cool- or Warm-Season	Growth Habit	Seed Count x000 per lb (kg)	"Turf" Seeding Rate lb/M (g/m^2)	Minimum Precipitation in. (mm)	Seed Cost	Seed Availability	Mowing Tolerance	Shade Tolerance	Wetland Tolerance	Salt Tolerance	Alkalinity Tolerance	Ornamental/ Turf Uses	Bloom Season	Adapted Zones
Native	3 ft (0.9)	Warm	Bunch	1758 (3867)	2 lb (8)	8 (203)	$$$	☆	☆	❍	👍	👍	👍	T	6	134

Former Latin names: *Agrostis airoides, S. wrightii*
Other common names: Bunchgrass, tussock grass, alkali dropseed, zacaton alcalino
Varieties: Salado, Saltalk, Salty, Wilcox
Comments: Coarse bunchgrass, well suited to extremely adverse conditions, such as salt, alkali, drought, or flooding. Good germination even in poor soil. Germinates best at 80 to 90°F (25 to 32°C). Can survive being watered with seawater. Gray-green stemmy, almost woody foliage with pinkish, open panicles, turning golden brown by fall. Flowers have cloud-like appearance in mass. Useful pond-edge plant and for wildlife habitat. Little wildlife value, except for cover. Heat, drought tolerant.
References: Alderson and Sharp, 1994; Allison et al., 1954; Anonymous, 1995d; AOSCA, 1996; Brown et al., 1986; Cronquist et al., 1977; Daniels, 1995; Hitchcock, 1951; Long, 1981; Spackeen, 1993; Stubbendieck et al., 1991; Wasser, 1982

Sand dropseed
Sporobolus cryptandrus (Torr.) Gray

Native to North America	Unmowed Height ft (m)	Cool- or Warm-Season	Growth Habit	Seed Count x000 per lb (kg)	"Turf" Seeding Rate lb/M (g/m²)	Minimum Precipitation in. (mm)	Seed Cost	Seed Availability	Mowing Tolerance	Shade Tolerance	Wetland Tolerance	Salt Tolerance	Alkalinity Tolerance	Ornamental/ Turf Uses	Bloom Season	Adapted Zones
Native	3 ft (0.9)	Warm	Rhiz.	5470 (12034)	1 lb (4)	10 (254)	$$	☆	☆	❍	👎	👍	👎	T	7	12346

Other common names: Zacaton

Comments: Erosion controlling grass for droughty sites. Somewhat tolerant of mowing. Sunlight and cool, moist conditions favor seed germination. Aged seed germinates faster than fresh seed. Grows well on rocky, silty soils.

References: Anonymous, 1988; Anonymous, 1995d; Humphrey, 1970; Musser, 1950; Spackeen, 1993; Stubbendieck et al., 1991; Wiesner and Brown, 1984; Young and Young, 1986

Giant dropseed
Sporobolus giganteus Nash.

Native to North America	Unmowed Height ft (m)	Cool- or Warm-Season	Growth Habit	Seed Count x000 per lb (kg)	"Turf" Seeding Rate lb/M (g/m²)	Minimum Precipitation in. (mm)	Seed Cost	Seed Availability	Mowing Tolerance	Shade Tolerance	Wetland Tolerance	Salt Tolerance	Alkalinity Tolerance	Ornamental/ Turf Uses	Bloom Season	Adapted Zones
Native	6 ft (1.8)	Warm	Bunch	1723 (3790)	2 lb (8)	12 (304)	$$	☆	✧	❍	👎	👎	👍	T	6	45

Comments: Tall, dune-stabilizing, desert grass. Large, narrow seed spikes.

References: Cronquist et al., 1977; Hitchcock, 1951; Spackeen, 1993

Prairie dropseed
Sporobolus heterolepis (A. Gray) A. Gray

Native to North America	Unmowed Height ft (m)	Cool- or Warm-Season	Growth Habit	Seed Count x000 per lb (kg)	"Turf" Seeding Rate lb/M (g/m²)	Minimum Precipitation in. (mm)	Seed Cost	Seed Availability	Mowing Tolerance	Shade Tolerance	Wetland Tolerance	Salt Tolerance	Alkalinity Tolerance	Ornamental/ Turf Uses	Bloom Season	Adapted Zones
Native	3 ft (0.9)	Warm	Bunch	224 (492)	7 lb (33)	? (?)	$$$$	✧	☆	❍	👎	👎	👎	T/O	9	1236

Other common names: Northern dropseed

Comments: Tufted, erect, slender rangegrass, with gold fall color, turning creamy brown by winter. Fairly slow growing. Fine textured, arching leaves. Useful on arid prairie sites.

References: Daniels, 1995; Diboll, 1996; Greenlee and Fell; Hitchcock, 1951; Oakes, 1990; Powers, 1995

Salt marsh grass
Sporobolus virginicus (L.) Kunth.

Native to North America	Unmowed Height ft (m)	Cool- or Warm-Season	Growth Habit	Seed Count x000 per lb (kg)	"Turf" Seeding Rate lb/M (g/m²)	Minimum Precipitation in. (mm)	Seed Cost	Seed Availability	Mowing Tolerance	Shade Tolerance	Wetland Tolerance	Salt Tolerance	Alkalinity Tolerance	Ornamental/ Turf Uses	Bloom Season	Adapted Zones
Native	1 ft (0.3)	Warm	Rhiz.	? (?)	? lb (?)	? (?)	$$$$	❍	✧	❍	👍	👍	👎	T	?	45

Other common names: Beach drop seed, seashore rush grass, saltwater couch

Comments: Marshgrass with potential for low maintenance turf. Tolerant of salt and occasional standing water to 2 in. (5 cm). Excellent shore stabilizing grass.

References: Marcum and Murdoch, 1991; Skerman and Riveros, 1990

Needle and thread
Stipa comata Trin. & Rupr.

Native to North America	Unmowed Height ft (m)	Cool- or Warm-Season	Growth Habit	Seed Count x000 per lb (kg)	"Turf" Seeding Rate lb/M (g/m²)	Minimum Precipitation in. (mm)	Seed Cost	Seed Availability	Mowing Tolerance	Shade Tolerance	Wetland Tolerance	Salt Tolerance	Alkalinity Tolerance	Ornamental/ Turf Uses	Bloom Season	Adapted Zones
Native	4 ft (1.2)	Cool	Bunch	115 (253)	9 lb (46)	10 (254)	$$$	☆	✧	☆	👎	👎	👎	O	7	1346

Former Latin names: *S. capillata, S. juncea*

Other common names: Speargrass, feather grass

Comments: Rangegrass species with curious tan seedheads have long, tangled, sharp spikes that can scratch. Very drought tolerant. Deeply rooted to 3 ft (1 m). Huge awns (seed whiskers) up to 4 in. (10 cm).

References: Anonymous, 1988; Campbell et al., 1956; Cronquist et al., 1977; Greenlee and Fell, 1992; Oakes, 1990; Spackeen, 1993; Stubbendieck et al., 1991; Young and Young, 1986

Letterman needlegrass
Stipa lettermani Vasey.

Native to North America	Unmowed Height ft (m)	Cool- or Warm-Season	Growth Habit	Seed Count x000 per lb (kg)	"Turf" Seeding Rate lb/M (g/m²)	Minimum Precipitation in. (mm)	Seed Cost	Seed Availability	Mowing Tolerance	Shade Tolerance	Wetland Tolerance	Salt Tolerance	Alkalinity Tolerance	Ornamental/ Turf Uses	Bloom Season	Adapted Zones
Native	2 ft (0.6)	Cool	Bunch	150 (330)	8 lb (41)	18 (457)	$$$	☆	✪	☆	👎	👎	👎	T	7	126

Comments: High elevation grass. Resembles *S. nelsonii*, but is shorter growing. Good seed germination with no dormancy difficulties.

References: Cronquist et al., 1977; Hitchcock, 1951; Spackeen, 1993; Young and Young, 1986

Columbia needlegrass
Stipa nelsonii Scribn.

Native to North America	Unmowed Height ft (m)	Cool- or Warm-Season	Growth Habit	Seed Count x000 per lb (kg)	"Turf" Seeding Rate lb/M (g/m²)	Minimum Precipitation in. (mm)	Seed Cost	Seed Availability	Mowing Tolerance	Shade Tolerance	Wetland Tolerance	Salt Tolerance	Alkalinity Tolerance	Ornamental/ Turf Uses	Bloom Season	Adapted Zones
Native	2 ft (0.6)	Cool	Bunch	150 (330)	8 lb (41)	12 (304)	$$$	☆	✧	☆	👎	👎	👍	O	6	12346

Former Latin names: *S. columbiana, S. viridula, S. williamsii*

Other common names: Subalpine needlegrass

Comments: Primarily an alpine species with broad lowland adaptation. Poor seed germination, requiring cool, moist conditions for emergence. But once germinated, it has good seedling vigor. Very deeply rooted, to 10 ft (3 m). Needle-like awns to 2 in. (5 cm).

References: Alderson and Sharp, 1994; Anonymous, 1993c; Campbell et al., 1956; Cronquist et al., 1977; Spackeen, 1993; Stubbendieck et al., 1991; Wasser, 1982; Young and Young, 1986

$** – *Inexpensive;* **$$** – *Moderate;* **$$$** – *Expensive;* **$$$$ – *Very expensive;* ✪ – *Excellent;* ☆ – *Moderate;* ✧ – *Fair;* ❍ – *Poor or no tolerance;* 👍 – *Tolerant;* 👎 – *Intolerant;* T – *Turf;* T/O – *Turf and Ornamental;* O – *Ornamental*

New Mexico needlegrass — *Stipa neomexicana* (Thurb.) Scribn.

Native to North America	Unmowed Height ft (m)	Cool- or Warm-Season	Growth Habit	Seed Count x000 per lb (kg)	"Turf" Seeding Rate lb/M (g/m²)	Minimum Precipitation in. (mm)	Seed Cost	Seed Availability	Mowing Tolerance	Shade Tolerance	Wetland Tolerance	Salt Tolerance	Alkalinity Tolerance	Ornamental/ Turf Uses	Bloom Season	Adapted Zones
Native	2 ft (0.6)	Cool	Bunch	70 (154)	11 lb (57)	10 (254)	$$$	☆	✪	☆	👎	👎	👎	O	6	45

Former Latin names: *S. pannata*
Other common names: Feather grass
Comments: Very drought tolerant desert grass. Attractive, wispy seedheads with long awns.
References: Cronquist et al., 1977; Featherly, 1946; Hitchcock, 1951; Olson and Anderson, 1994; Spackeen, 1993

Purple needlegrass — *Stipa pulchra* Hitchc.

Native to North America	Unmowed Height ft (m)	Cool- or Warm-Season	Growth Habit	Seed Count x000 per lb (kg)	"Turf" Seeding Rate lb/M (g/m²)	Minimum Precipitation in. (mm)	Seed Cost	Seed Availability	Mowing Tolerance	Shade Tolerance	Wetland Tolerance	Salt Tolerance	Alkalinity Tolerance	Ornamental/ Turf Uses	Bloom Season	Adapted Zones
Native	3 ft (0.9)	Cool	Bunch	115 (253)	9 lb (46)	? (?)	$$$	☆	☆	✧	👎	👎	👎	T/O	6	345

Comments: Drought tolerant, coastal, Mediterranean grass. Good seed germination with no dormancy. Immense, drooping whiskers on panicles. Effective for ground cover or erosion control. Naturalizes, but is not invasive. Vegetative propagation is difficult and seed is expensive.
References: Greenlee and Fell, 1992; Hitchcock, 1951; Schaff, 1994; Stubbendieck et al., 1991; Young and Young, 1986

Porcupine grass — *Stipa spartea* Trin.

Native to North America	Unmowed Height ft (m)	Cool- or Warm-Season	Growth Habit	Seed Count x000 per lb (kg)	"Turf" Seeding Rate lb/M (g/m²)	Minimum Precipitation in. (mm)	Seed Cost	Seed Availability	Mowing Tolerance	Shade Tolerance	Wetland Tolerance	Salt Tolerance	Alkalinity Tolerance	Ornamental/ Turf Uses	Bloom Season	Adapted Zones
Native	3 ft (0.9)	Cool	Bunch	? (?)	? lb (?)	? (?)	$$$$	☆	✪	☆	👎	👎	👎	O	6	13

Former Latin names: *S. robusta*
Other common names: Needlegrass
Comments: Unique, twisted seedhead with long awns. Readily self-sows.
References: Hitchcock, 1951; Oakes, 1990; Pohl, 1968; Powers, 1995

Desert needlegrass — *Stipa speciosa* Trin. and Rupr.

Native to North America	Unmowed Height ft (m)	Cool- or Warm-Season	Growth Habit	Seed Count x000 per lb (kg)	"Turf" Seeding Rate lb/M (g/m²)	Minimum Precipitation in. (mm)	Seed Cost	Seed Availability	Mowing Tolerance	Shade Tolerance	Wetland Tolerance	Salt Tolerance	Alkalinity Tolerance	Ornamental/ Turf Uses	Bloom Season	Adapted Zones
Native	2 ft (0.6)	Cool	Bunch	150 (330)	8 lb (41)	8 (203)	$$$	☆	✪	☆	👎	👎	👎	O	5	345

Former Latin names: *S. californica, S. humilis*
Comments: Attractive, hardy desert grass. Survives in arid, mountainous regions. Long-lived. Good seed germination with no dormancy. Tolerates mowing as long as it's above 3 in. (7.5 cm).
References: Cronquist et al., 1977; Hitchcock, 1951; Schaff, 1994; Spackeen, 1993; Young and Young, 1986

Kangaroo grass — *Themeda triandra* Forssk.

Native to North America	Unmowed Height ft (m)	Cool- or Warm-Season	Growth Habit	Seed Count x000 per lb (kg)	"Turf" Seeding Rate lb/M (g/m²)	Minimum Precipitation in. (mm)	Seed Cost	Seed Availability	Mowing Tolerance	Shade Tolerance	Wetland Tolerance	Salt Tolerance	Alkalinity Tolerance	Ornamental/ Turf Uses	Bloom Season	Adapted Zones
Exotic	3 ft (0.9)	Warm	Bunch	? (?)	? lb (?)	? (?)	$$$	☆	✧	❍	👎	👎	👎	T/O	5	345

Former Latin names: *Anthistiria imberbis, T. forskalii, T. imberbis*
Other common names: Red-oat grass
Comments: Light green bunchgrass with reddish-brown tinge on older leaves. Responds well to fertilizer, but may be outcompeted by weeds. Best mowed minimally and above 2 in. (5 cm). Some seed available from Australia.
References: Greenway, 1997; Tothill and Hacker, 1983

Tall wheatgrass — *Thinopyrum ponticum* (Podp.) Liu and Wang

Native to North America	Unmowed Height ft (m)	Cool- or Warm-Season	Growth Habit	Seed Count x000 per lb (kg)	"Turf" Seeding Rate lb/M (g/m²)	Minimum Precipitation in. (mm)	Seed Cost	Seed Availability	Mowing Tolerance	Shade Tolerance	Wetland Tolerance	Salt Tolerance	Alkalinity Tolerance	Ornamental/ Turf Uses	Bloom Season	Adapted Zones
Exotic	5 ft (1.5)	Cool	Bunch	75 (165)	11 lb (56)	14 (355)	$	✪	✧	✪	👎	👍	👍	T/O	7	16

Former Latin names: *Agropyron elongatum, Elymus elongatus, Elytrigia elongata, Elytrigia pontica*
Varieties: Alkar, Jose, Largo, Orbit, Platte, Tyrrell
Comments: As its name implies, this is a tall, coarse prairiegrass. It is useful as a natural windbreak or snow fence. Somewhat drought tolerant but prefers moist soil. Shade tolerant. Strongly blue colored under alkali or drought stress. According to some accounts, tall wheatgrass is the most tolerant of any cultivated grass to saline or alkaline soils. "Alkar" cultivar is particularly resistant to alkali. Large seeds, good seedling vigor, and a steady seed supply make for ready establishment. Remains green 6 weeks longer into summer than other wheatgrasses. Provides excellent nesting and cover for birds. Mowing below 8 in. (20 cm) causes thinning.
References: Alderson and Sharp, 1994; Anonymous, 1993c; Asay and Jensen, 1996; Spackeen, 1993; Wasser, 1982; Wiesner and Brown, 1984

Native to North America	Unmowed Height ft (m)	Cool- or Warm-Season	Growth Habit	Seed Count x000 per lb (kg)	"Turf" Seeding Rate lb/M (g/m^2)	Minimum Precipitation in. (mm)	Seed Cost	Seed Availability	Mowing Tolerance	Shade Tolerance	Wetland Tolerance	Salt Tolerance	Alkalinity Tolerance	Ornamental/ Turf Uses	Bloom Season	Adapted Zones

Eastern gamagrass

Tripsacum dactyloides (L.) L.

Native to North America	Unmowed Height ft (m)	Cool- or Warm-Season	Growth Habit	Seed Count x000 per lb (kg)	"Turf" Seeding Rate lb/M (g/m^2)	Minimum Precipitation in. (mm)	Seed Cost	Seed Availability	Mowing Tolerance	Shade Tolerance	Wetland Tolerance	Salt Tolerance	Alkalinity Tolerance	Ornamental/ Turf Uses	Bloom Season	Adapted Zones
Native	7 ft (2.1)	Warm	Rhiz.	7200 (15840)	1 lb (4)	39 (990)	$$	☆	❍	❍	👍	👍	👎	O	7	345

Other common names: Sesame grass, finger grass, fakahatchee
Varieties: Iuka IV, K-24, Pete
Comments: Originally widespread grass of the American tallgrass prairie, but heavy grazing killed it out. Provides cover and seed for wildlife. Repeated clipping severely weakens stand. Wide corn-like leaves. Has been known to hybridize with corn in the wild. Has separate male and female flowers. An interesting, persistent background grass for ornamental plantings.
References: Alderson and Sharp, 1994; AOSCA, 1996; Brown, 1979; Oakes, 1990; Pohl, 1968; Skerman and Riveros, 1990; Stubbendieck et al., 1991; Tutin et al., 1980; U.S. Soil Conservation Service, 1982

Sea oats

Uniola paniculata L.

Native to North America	Unmowed Height ft (m)	Cool- or Warm-Season	Growth Habit	Seed Count x000 per lb (kg)	"Turf" Seeding Rate lb/M (g/m^2)	Minimum Precipitation in. (mm)	Seed Cost	Seed Availability	Mowing Tolerance	Shade Tolerance	Wetland Tolerance	Salt Tolerance	Alkalinity Tolerance	Ornamental/ Turf Uses	Bloom Season	Adapted Zones
Native	7 ft (2.1)	Cool	Rhiz.	? (?)	? lb (?)	? (?)	$$$$	❍	❍	✧	👍	👍	👎	O	7	345

Other common names: Spike grass, North American sea oats, seaside oats
Comments: Excellent for dune stabilization. Seed spikes are constantly present. Generally established vegetatively. Provides animal habitat. Tolerates windy, salty, coastal climates. Drought tolerant, but goes dormant in dry weather. May be legally protected in some areas as an endangered species.
References: Darke, 1994; Greenlee and Fell, 1992

Vetiver grass

Vetiveria zizanoides (L.) Nash.

Native to North America	Unmowed Height ft (m)	Cool- or Warm-Season	Growth Habit	Seed Count x000 per lb (kg)	"Turf" Seeding Rate lb/M (g/m^2)	Minimum Precipitation in. (mm)	Seed Cost	Seed Availability	Mowing Tolerance	Shade Tolerance	Wetland Tolerance	Salt Tolerance	Alkalinity Tolerance	Ornamental/ Turf Uses	Bloom Season	Adapted Zones
Exotic	8 ft (2.4)	Warm	Bunch	? (?)	? lb (?)	20 (508)	$$$$	❍	☆	✧	👍	👍	👎	O	8	5

Former Latin names: *Andropogon muricatus, Phalaris zizaniodes, V. odorata, V. arundinacea, Vetiver zizanioides*
Other common names: Khus khus grass, Khas khas
Comments: Useful as a hedge or screen in the tropics. Adapted to rocky soils. Tolerates windy, coastal conditions. Used best where temperatures below freezing are rare. Foliage is fragrant when wet. Roots are an ingredient in curry, khasu-khasu, and perfumes.
References: Anonymous, 1993h; Boonman, 1993; Bor, 1960; Chapman, 1992; Darke, 1994; Greenlee and Fell, 1992; Oakes, 1990; Skerman and Riveros, 1990

Seashore zoysia grass

Zoysia sinica Hance.

Native to North America	Unmowed Height ft (m)	Cool- or Warm-Season	Growth Habit	Seed Count x000 per lb (kg)	"Turf" Seeding Rate lb/M (g/m^2)	Minimum Precipitation in. (mm)	Seed Cost	Seed Availability	Mowing Tolerance	Shade Tolerance	Wetland Tolerance	Salt Tolerance	Alkalinity Tolerance	Ornamental/ Turf Uses	Bloom Season	Adapted Zones
Exotic	1 ft (0.3)	Warm	Rz/St	? (?)	? lb (?)	? (?)	$$$	☆	✪	❍	👍	👍	👎	T	7	12345

Varieties: J-14
Comments: Characteristics similar to *Z. japonica*, but with larger seed and better seed germination. More salt tolerant than *Z. japonica*. Able to grow in near-seawater saltiness. "Cathay J-14" variety has improved turf characteristics, resembling "Meyer" zoysia.
References: Christians and Engleke, 1994

$** – *Inexpensive;* **$$** – *Moderate;* **$$$** – *Expensive;* **$$$$ – *Very expensive;* ✪ – *Excellent;* ☆ – *Moderate;* ✧ – *Fair;* ❍ – *Poor or no tolerance;* 👍 – *Tolerant;* 👎 – *Intolerant;* T – *Turf;* T/O – *Turf and Ornamental;* O – *Ornamental*

References

Agnew, M. and D. Lewis. 1993. A Survey of Pesticides Used on Iowa Golf Courses in 1990. Iowa Coop. Ext. Serv. FG-460.

Ahti, K., A. Moustafa, and H. Kaerwer. 1980. Tolerance of turfgrass cultivars to salt. In *Proc. 3rd Int. Turfgrass Res. Conf.*, ASA, Madison, WI.

Albrecht, W. 1993. Turfgrass Water Use in Northern Arizona. Ext. Bull. No. 93-05, Arboretum at Flagstaff, AZ.

Alderson, J. and W.C. Sharp. 1994. Grass Varieties in the United States. USDA SCS Ag. Handbook No. 170.

Allison, L.E. et al. 1954. Saline and alkali soils. In L.A. Richards, Ed. USDA Agric. Handbook No. 60.

Anonymous. 1979. A Zambian Handbook of Pasture and Fodder Crops. Food and Ag. Organiz. of the UN, Rome, Italy.

Anonymous. 1981. Native grasses no better or worse than introduced. *Idaho Farmer-Stockman.* May 7, p. 16.

Anonymous. 1986. *Landscape Contractors Magazine.* July, pp. 13–14.

Anonymous. 1988. Plant Materials Handbook. Office of Surface Mining Reclamation and Enforcement. SCS Plant Materials Center.

Anonymous. 1989a. Minimizing summer water stress on turfgrass. *Landscape & Irrig.* June, pp. 86–95.

Anonymous. 1989b. What has a lawn done for you lately? *Turfgrass Environment.* Am. Sod Producers Assoc., summer.

Anonymous. 1990. Researchers advocate turfgrass selection theory. *Lawn & Landscape Maint.* Mar., p. 6.

Anonymous. 1991a. Fescue turf can be conserving. *Southwest Lawn & Landscape.* May, pp. 6–7.

Anonymous. 1991b. Mulching mowers: clean and green. *Consumer Reports.* June, pp. 408–413.

Anonymous. 1992a. *National Gardening Survey 1991–1992.* Nat'l. Gardening Assoc., Burlington, VT.

Anonymous. 1992b. Pesticide and Nutrient Fate. 1992 Environmental Res. Summary. U.S. Golf Assoc. Green Sec., Far Hills, NJ.

Anonymous. 1993a. Conserving water. *J. Envir. Turfgrass.* 5(1):10.

Anonymous. 1993b. FS Turfgrass Handbook (catalog). Growmark, Inc., Bloomington, IL.

Anonymous. 1993c. OECD Schemes for the Varietal Certification of Seed Moving in International Trade. OECD, Paris, France.

Anonymous. 1993d. Researching maintenance: Mulching. *Grounds Maint.* July, p. 1.

Anonymous. 1993e. Seed facts. *Prairie Landscape Mag.* May/June, p. 11.

Anonymous. 1993f. The Best Single Source, Reclamation/Native Grasses (catalog). Davenport Seed Co., Davenport, WA.

Anonymous. 1993g. Turfgrass sod and seed installation. *J. Envir. Turfgrass* 4(1):11.

Anonymous. 1993h. *Vetiver Grass, a Thin Green Line Against Erosion.* National Academy Press, Washington, DC.

Anonymous. 1994a. A mower for George Jetson. *Popular Sci.* June, p. 52.

Anonymous. 1994b. Hapuna golf course. *Turf & Landscape Press.* p. 1–6.

Anonymous. 1994c. Keys to survival for range grass: Heavy seed and deep sprouting. *Seeds & Crops.* Feb. p. 17.

Anonymous. 1995a. Ernst Crownvetch Farms, Conservation Plants & Seeds (catalog). Meadville, PA.

Anonymous. 1995b. Kaufman Seeds (catalog). Ashdown, AR.

Anonymous. 1995c. Pesticide use declining. *Landmark Mag.* Oct./Nov., p. 9.

Anonymous. 1995d. Sharp Bros. Seed Co. (catalog). Greeley, CO.

Anonymous. 1995e. Turfgrass is the Low Maintenance Landscape Option. Turfgrass Bulletin. Nebraska Turfgrass Foundation., Hastings, NE, summer, p. 9.

Anonymous. 1996a. Low chemical use good for turf and super. *Crittenden Golf* 5(4):T1/9-T15/39.

Anonymous. 1996b. Native Plant and Seed Sources for the Northern Great Plains. USDA-NRCS, Bismarck, ND.

Anonymous. 1996c. What they're saying out there. *Landscape Mgmt.* July, pp. 24–28.

AOSCA. 1996. Acres Applied for Certification in 1996 by Seed Certification Agencies. Assoc. of Official Seed Certifying Agencies, Mississippi State, MS.

Archer, S.G. and C.E. Sellers. 1956. *The American Grass Book.* University of Oklahoma Press, Norman, OK.

Asay, K.H. and K.B. Jensen. 1996. Wheatgrasses. In *Cool-Season Forage Grasses,* ASA monograph No. 34, Madison, WI.

Augustin, B.J. n.d. Mowing southern lawns requires proper height, frequency. *LESCO News,* Rocky River, OH.

Baetz, R.L. 1988. Xeriscapes wilt without teamwork. *Amer. Nurseryman.* June 1, pp. 46–51.

Baikan, B.B. and A.M. Petrovic. 1992. Effect of seasonal mowing heights on water used, root growth and quality of Kentucky bluegrass. *Agron. Abstr.* p. 7.

Baird, J.H. 1995. Evaluation of Best Management Practices to Protect Surface Water Quality from Pesticides and Fertilizers Applied to Bermudagrass Fairways. U.S. Golf Association Research Summary, Far Hills, NJ.

Banko and Stefani. 1988. PGRs: a tool to manage mowing. *Landscape Mgmt.* Oct., p. 54.

Beard, J.B. 1985a. An assessment of water use by turfgrass. In *Turfgrass Water Conservation,* V.A. Gibeault and S.T. Cockerham, Eds. University of California Cooperative Extension Service publ. 21405.

Beard, J.B. 1985b. Turfgrass water conservation strategies. *Proc. Michigan Turfgrass Conf.,* East Lansing, MI, pp. 124–135.

Beard, J.B. 1986. Temperature stress hardiness of perennial ryegrass. *Grounds Maint.* Apr., pp. 84–86.

Beard, J.B. 1988. Checklist of water conservation strategies. *Grounds Maint.* Apr., pp. IR-6-18.

Beard, J.B. 1991. *A Manual on Malaysian Golf Course Turf Construction, Establishment and Maintenance.* Beard Books, College Station, TX.

Beard, J.B. 1992a. Trees or turf? *Grounds Maint.* Oct., pp. 13–68.

Beard, J.B. 1992b. Turfgrass selection and management to achieve maximum water conservation. *Proc. Michigan Turfgrass Conf.* pp. 161–167.

Beard, J.B. 1993. Even tan or brown lawns benefit the environment. *J. Envir. Turfgrass* 5(1):6–7.

Beard, J.B. 1995a. A balancing act. *Grounds Maint.* Oct., pp. 25–29.

Beard, J.B. 1995b. Mowing practices for conserving water. *Grounds Maint.* Jan., pp. C2–C4.

Beard, J.B. and K.S. Kim. 1989. Low-water-use turfgrasses. *U.S. Golf Association Green Section Rec.* Jan./Feb., p. 12–13.

Beard, J.B. and R.L. Green. 1994. The role of turfgrasses in environmental protection and their benefits to humans. *J. Environ. Qual.* 23:452–460.

Berdahl, J.D. and R.E. Baker. 1980. Germination and emergence of Russian wildrye seeds coated with hydrophilic materials. *Agron. J.* 73:85–90.

Bernstein, L. 1958. Salt Tolerance of Grasses and Forage Legumes. USDA Agric. Info. Bull. No. 194.

Blake, C.T. 1982. Turfgrasses and Shade. North Carolina Coop. Ext. Serv. Turf Memo No. 12.

Bluemel, K. 1995. Wholesale Nursery Catalogue (catalog), Baldwin, MD.

Boonman, J.G. 1993. *East Africa's Grasses and Fodders: Their Ecology and Husbandry.* Kluwer Academic Publishers, Boston, MA.

Booth, D.T. 1995. Native-plant propagation in the northern plains and Rocky Mountains. *Agron. Abstr.* p. 143.

Bor, N.L. 1960. *The Grasses of Burma, Ceylon, India, and Pakistan.* Pergamon Press, New York.

Borland, D.F. and J.D. Butler. 1982. Buffalograss—A "new" turfgrass for golf courses? *U.S. Golf Association Green Sec. Rec.* Sept./Oct., p. 6–8.

Bormann, F.H., D. Balmori, and G.T. Geballe. 1993. *Redesigning the American Lawn.* Yale Univ. Press, New Haven, CT.

Bowman, D.C., J.L. Paul, W.B. Davis, and S.H. Nelson. 1989. Rapid depletion of nitrogen applied to Kentucky bluegrass turf. *J. Amer. Soc. Hort. Sci.* 114:229–233.

Brammer, R. and J. Rondon. 1982. Buffalograss. *NatureScape,* July, pp. 31–32.

Branham, B. 1989. 1988 turf weed control, PGR, and management studies: II. Turfgrass performance under low maintenance. *Proc. 59th Annual Michigan Turfgrass Conf.,* East Lansing, MI, pp. 4–5.

Branham, B.E., R.N. Calhoun, M. Collins, and D.S. Douches. 1995. 1994 Turf weed control and management research. *65th Annual Mich. Turfgrass Conf. Proc.,* East Lansing, MI, p. 24–26.

Brauen, S.E., G.K. Stahnke, W.J. Johnston, J.E. Chapman, and C.G. Cogger. 1994. Quantification and fate of nitrogen from amended and pure sand putting green profiles. *Agron. Abstr.* p. 189.

Breakwell, E. 1923. The Grasses and Fodder Plants of New South Wales. Deptartment of Agriculture, NSW, Australia.

Brede, A.D. 1984a. Establishment characteristics of Kentucky bluegrass—Perennial ryegrass turf mixtures as affected by seeding rate and ratio. *Agron. J.* 76:875–879.

Brede, A.D. 1984b. Initial mowing of Kentucky bluegrass—Perennial ryegrass seedling turf mixtures. *Agron. J.* 76:711–714.

Brede, A.D. 1987. Recovering from 1986. *Amer. Lawn Applicator* 8(5):37–47.

Brede, A.D. 1988a. Drought Recovery '88. Grass Clippings. Jacklin Seed, Post Falls, ID.

Brede, A.D. 1988b. Establishment clipping of tall fescue and companion annual ryegrass. *Agron. J.* 80:27–30.
Brede, A.D. 1989. Seed priming. *Grounds Maint.* Apr., pp. 42–46.
Brede, A.D. 1991a. Field apparatus for testing allelopathy of annual bluegrass on creeping bentgrass. *Crop Sci.* 31, pp. 1372–1374.
Brede, A.D. 1991b. Interaction of management factors on dollar spot disease severity in tall fescue turf. *HortSci.* 26, pp. 1391–1392.
Brede, A.D. 1992a. Cultural factors for minimizing bermudagrass invasion into tall fescue turf. *Agron. J.* 84, pp. 919–922.
Brede, A.D. 1992b. IPM. *Landmark Mag.* 4(3), pp. 24.
Brede, A.D. 1992c. Limited water seed priming. *SportsTurf.* Sept., pp. 18–20.
Brede, A.D. 1993a. Tall fescue/Kentucky bluegrass mixtures: Effect of seeding rate, ratio, and cultivar on establishment characteristics. In R.N. Carrow, N.E. Christians, and R.C. Shearman, Eds. *ITRC Journal* 7, pp. 1005A–1005G.
Brede, A.D. 1993b. The Turfgrass Technical Manual (catalog). Jacklin Seed, Post Falls, ID.
Brede, A.D. 1994a. Maintaining turf with less fertilizer. *Prairie Landscape.* June/July, pp. 28–30.
Brede, A.D. 1994b. Turfgrass mixtures: The importance of a bluegrass base. *Lawn & Landscape Maint.* Apr., pp. 102–105.
Brede, A.D. and J.M. Duich. 1980. Moderate seeding rate best for new Kentucky bluegrasses. *Sci. in Agric.* 27(4), p. 10.
Brede, A.D. and J.M. Duich. 1981. Annual bluegrass encroachment affected by Kentucky bluegrass seeding rate. *NE Weed Sci. Soc. Proc.* 35, pp. 307–311.
Brede, A.D. and J.M. Duich. 1982. Cultivar and seeding rate effects on several physical characteristics of Kentucky bluegrass turf. *Agron. J.* 74, pp. 865–870.
Brown, D. et al. 1986. Reclamation and Vegetative Restoration of Problem Soils and Disturbed Lands. Noyes Data Corp., Park Ridge, NJ.
Brown, K.W., R.L. Duble, and J.C. Thomas. 1977. Nitrogen losses from golf greens. *U.S. Golf Association Green Sec. Rec.* Jan., pp. 5–7.
Brown, L. 1979. *Grasses, An Identification Guide.* Houghton Mifflin Co., Boston, MA.
Bruneau, Art and Joe Dipaola. 1990. Good mowing practices can aid you, the turf and the environment. *N. Carolina Turfgrass* 8(3), pp. 17–19.
Buchanan, W.G. 1979. Nutrients affect color and vigor of turfgrasses. *U.S. Golf Assoc. Green Sec. Rec.* pp. 18–20.
Burbidge, N.T. 1966. *Australian Grasses.* Angus and Robertson Publishers, Sydney, NSW, Australia.
Burns, R.E. 1976. Tall fescue as affected by mowing height. *Agron. J.* 68, pp. 274–276.
Burt, M.G. and N.E. Christians. 1990. Morphological and growth characteristics of low- and high-maintenance Kentucky bluegrass cultivars. *Crop Sci.* 30, pp. 1239–1243.
Butler, J.D. {date not specified}. Water and Salt Problems in Turfgrass Production (mimeo). Colorado State Univeristy, Ft. Collins, CO.
Butler, J.D. and J.D. Fry. 1987. Growing Turf with Less. Rutgers Turfgrass Proc., NJ AES, pp. 1–4.
Callahan, L.M. 1972. The real culprit behind turf disease. *Golf Superintendent.* May, pp. 13–16.
Campbell, J.B., K.F. Best, and A.C. Budd. 1956. 99 Range Forage Plants of the Canadian Prairies. Publ. 964. Canada Department of Agriculture, Ottawa, Ontario, Canada.
Campbell, R. and B. Rogers. 1996. Selecting a site for a new golf course—Avoid the death of a dream! *Landmark* 7(1), pp. 4–25.
Canaway, P.M. and S.W. Baker. 1993. Soil and turf properties governing playing quality. In R.N. Carrow, N.E. Christians, and R.C. Shearman, Eds. *ITRC J.* 7, Intertec Publishers, Overland Park, KS.
Carlson, J.R. 1991. Grass cultivar development at SCS plant materials centers in western states. In D.A. Sleper, Ed. *Proc. 31st Grass Breeders Work Planning Conf.*, Columbia, MO.
Carroll, M.J. and A.M. Petrovic. 1991. Wear tolerance of Kentucky bluegrass and creeping bentgrass following nitrogen and potassium application. *Hort. Sci.* 26, pp. 851–853.
Carrow, R.N. 1982. Efficient use of nitrogen fertilizer. *Grounds Maint.* July, pp. 10–18.
Carrow, R.N. 1992. Development of Cultivation Programs on Turfgrass to Reduce Water Use and Improve Turf Quality (progress rep.). University of Georgia, Griffin, GA.
Carrow, R.N. 1995. Drought resistance aspects of turfgrasses in the Southeast: Evapotranspiration and crop coefficients. *Crop Sci.* 35, pp. 1685–1690.
Carrow, R.N. 1996. Drought avoidance characteristics of diverse tall fescue cultivars. *Crop Sci.* 36, pp. 371–377.
Casnoff, D.M. and J.B Beard. 1986. Comparative rooting of warm season turfgrasses. *Grounds Maint.*, Sept., p. 64.
Catling, P.M., A.R. McElroy, and K.W. Spicer. 1994. Potential forage value of some eastern Canadian sedges *(Cyperaceae: Carex)*. *J. Range Mgmt.* 47, pp. 226–230.
Chambliss, C.G. 1991. Bahiagrass. University of Florida Institute of Food and Agricultural Science SS-AGR-36.
Chapman, G.P. (Ed.). 1992. *Grass Evolution and Domestication.* Cambridge University Press, London, England.

Charbonneau, P. 1994. Thatch—Causes and control. *Turf & Recreation.* Jan./Feb., pp. 24–25.

Chen, Yue-lan, J.L. Eggens, T. Hsiang, J.C. Hall, and K. Carey. 1996. Stress response of single and multiple cultivar populations of turfgrass species. *The GTI Advisor* 1(2), p. •:6.

Christians, N. 1989a. Kentucky bluegrass for low-maintenance areas. *Grounds Maint.*, Aug., pp. 49–96.

Christians, N.E. 1989b. Results of High- and Low-Maintenance Kentucky Bluegrass Regional Cultivar Trials—1988: II. Low-Maintenance, Non-Irrigated Trial. 1989 Iowa Turfgrass Res. Rep., Iowa State University, Ames, IA.

Christians, N.E. 1993. The use of corn gluten meal as a natural preemergence weed control in turf. In R.N. Carrow, N.E. Christians, and R.C. Shearman, Eds. *ITRC J.* 7, Intertec Publ., Overland Park, KS.

Christians, N.E. and M.C. Engelke. 1994. Choosing the right grass to fit the environment. In *IPM for Turf and Ornamentals.* A.R. Leslie, Ed. CRC Press, Boca Raton, FL.

Christians, N.E. and M.G. Burt. 1989. Growth and Morphological Characterization Study of Low- and High-Maintenance Kentucky Bluegrass Cultivars. 1989 Iowa Turfgrass Res. Rep., Iowa State University, Ames, IA.

Christians, N.E., J.F. Wilkinson, and D.P. Martin. 1979. Variations in the number of seeds per unit weight among turfgrass cultivars. *Agron. J.* 71, pp. 415–418.

Clark, B.B., David Thompson, Jim Murphy, and Pradip Majumdar. 1995. Development of an integrated summer patch control program for fine turf areas. pp. 18–19. In *Proc. 4th Ann. Rutgers Turf. Symp.* Jan. 5–6, New Brunswick, NJ.

Clarke, B.B., D.R. Huff, D. A. Smith, C.R. Funk, and Suichang Sun. 1994. Enhanced resistance to dollar spot in endophyte-infected fine fescues. *Agron. Abstr.* p. 187.

Clarke, B.B., J.A. Murphy, and P. Majumdar. 1996. Impact of selected fungicides and nitrogen sources on the development of take-all patch in bentgrass. *Agron. Abstr.* p. 151.

Cline, H. 1993a. No weeds, less nitrogen with grasscycling. *Western Turf Mgmt.* Oct., pp. 12–13.

Cline, H. 1993b. OSU evaluating ecology lawn mixes. *Western Turf Mgmt.* Nov./Dec., p. 6.

Cline, H. 1995. New PGA West course will be friendly for everyone. *Western Turf & Landscape Press.* June, pp. 7–9.

Cockerham, S.T. and J.A. Van Dam. 1992. Turfgrass management operations. In D.V. Waddington, R.N. Carrow, and R.C. Shearman, Eds. *Turfgrass. Agron. Monograph 32,* ASA, Madison, WI.

Colbaugh, P.F. 1990. Recycle clippings. *Grounds Maint.* May, pp. 11–13.

Colbaugh, P.F. and C.L. Elmore. 1985. Influence of water on pest activity. In V.A. Gibeault and S.T. Cockerham, Eds. *Turfgrass Water Conservation,* University of California Cooperative Extension Service publ. 21405.

Connolly, J.C. 1995. The history of the putting green. *Golf Course News.* Feb./Mar./April/May issues.

Cook, T. 1990. Strategies for turfgrass renovation. *44th Northwest Turfgrass Conf. Proc.*, pp. 52–57.

Cook, T. 1994a. Fertilizer effects on turfgrass disease. *48th NW Turfgrass Conference,* Gleneden Beach, OR, pp. 10–15.

Cook, T. 1994b. Low maintenance turf? *The Turf Line News,* W. Canada Turfgrass Association Conference 114, pp. 44–47.

Cooper, R.J. 1990. Biological Thatch Reduction. University of Massachusetts Turfgrass Field Day Rep., Amherst, MA.

Coppens, Y. 1994. East side story: The origin of mankind. *Sci. Amer.* 270(5), p. 88.

Correll, D.S. and H.B. Correll. 1972. *Aquatic and Wetland Plants of the Southwestern United States.* Vol. 1. Stanford University Press, Stanford, CA.

Couch, H.B. 1997. Relationship of Management Practices to the Incidence and Severity of Turfgrass Diseases. Department of Plant Path., Virginia Tech, Blacksburg, VA.

Crampton, B. 1961. Range Plants—A Laboratory Manual. Department of Agronomy, University of California, Davis, CA.

Cranshaw, W. 1995. Insect control in cool-season turf. *Landscape Mgmt.* Apr., pp. 30–36.

Cronquist, A., A.H. Holmgren, N.H. Holmgren, J.L. Reveal, and P.K. Holmgren. 1977. *Intermountain Flora.* Columbia University Press, New York.

Crutchfield, B.A. and D.A. Potter. 1995. Feeding of Japanese beetle and southern masked chafer grubs on lawn weeds. *Crop Sci.* 35, pp. 1681–1684.

Crutchfield, B.A., D.A. Potter, and A.J. Powell. 1995. Irrigation and nitrogen fertilization effects on white grub injury to Kentucky bluegrass and tall fescue turf. *Crop Sci.* 35, pp. 1122–1126.

Cuany, R.L. 1982. The high altitude revegetation committee. In *Proc. High Altitude Revegetation Workshop* No. 5. Water Resources Res. Inst., CSU, Ft. Collins, CO.

Cudney, D., J.A. Downer, V.A. Gibeault, J. M. Henry, and J.S. Reints. 1994. Low-impact management of kikuyugrass in cool-season turf. *Calif. Fairways.* Jan./Feb., p. 20.

Dale, D. 1993. Turfgrass reduces Arizona utility bills. *Western Turf Mgmt.* April, p. 14.

Daniel, W.H. 1950. The effect of varying soil moisture, fertilization, and height of cutting on the quality of turf. Ph.D. diss. Michigan State University, East Lansing, MI.

Daniels, Stevie. 1995. *The Wild Lawn Handbook, Alternatives to the Traditional Front Lawn.* Macmillan, New York.

Danneberger, T.K., M.B. McDonald, C.A. Geron, and P. Kumari. 1992. Rate of germination and seedling growth of perennial ryegrass seed following osmoconditioning. *Hort. Sci.* 27, pp. 28–30.

Darke, Rick (Ed.). 1994. *Manual of Grasses.* Timber Press, Portland, OR.

Darrah III, Charles. 1994. Superior soils. *Lawn & Landscape Maint.* May, pp. 67–71.

de Guzman Jr., M.R. 1984. Pasture research and development in the Philippines. In *Asian Pastures.* Food & Fert. Tech. Center, Ag. Bldg, Taiwan, ROC.

Dernoeden, P.H. 1991. Cultural management of turfgrass diseases. *Agron. Abstr.* p. 174.

Dernoeden, P.H. 1992. The side effects of fungicides. *Golf Course Mgmt.* July, pp. 88–110.

Dernoeden, P.H. 1993. Collecting and shipping diseased turfgrass samples. *Golf Course Mgmt.* Nov., pp. 56–58.

Dernoeden, P.H., M. Carroll, and J.M. Krouse. 1992. Crabgrass encroachment in tall fescue as influenced by mowing, nitrogen, and herbicides. *Agron. Abstr.* p. 167.

Dernoeden, P.H., M.J. Carroll, and J.M. Krouse. 1994. Mowing of three fescue species for low-maintenance turf sites. *Crop Sci.* 34, pp. 1645–1649.

Desjardins, Y., M. Laganiere, and G. Allard. 1995. Control of annual bluegrass in Kentucky bluegrass sod with propane flame burners. *Agron. Abstr.* p. 152.

Dest, W.M. 1992. 1990 NE-169 Annual Rep., Univ. Conn. AES, Storrs, CT.

Detzel, T. 1994. Speed seed outpaces pregermination and limited priming. *SportsTurf.* Feb., pp. 18–21.

Devitt, D.A., D.S. Neuman, D.C. Bowman, and R.L. Morris. 1995. Comparative water use of turfgrasses and ornamental trees in an arid environment. *J. Turfgrass Mgmt.* 1(2), pp. 47–63.

Devitt, D.A., R.L. Morris, and D.C. Bowman. 1992. Evapotranspiration, crop coefficients, and leaching fractions of irrigated desert turfgrass systems. *Agron. J.* 84, pp. 717–723.

Diboll, Neil. 1996. Prairie Nursery (catalog), Westfield, WI.

Diesburg, K.L. and H.L. Portz. 1993. Zoysiagrass from seed. *Golf Course Mgmt.* May, pp. 102–106.

Diesburg, Ken. 1992. Low Input Sustainable Turf (LIST). Rep. to summer NCR-10 meeting, Ohio State University, Columbus, OH.

DiPaola, J.M. 1987. Plant growth regulators. *Lawn Servicing.* Mar., pp. 18–22.

DiPaola, J.M. 1994. Turfgrass management in shady areas of lawns. *Landscape Mgmt.* Feb., p. 54.

Domangue, M. 1994. Monitoring grubs reduced area treated with pesticide. *Northern Turf Mgmt.* Jan., p. 9.

Dorer, S.P., C.H. Peacock, L.T. Lucas, and D.C. Bowman. 1995. The effect of nutrients present in a fungicide combination on summer bentgrass decline. *Agron. Abstr.* p. 147.

Dorris, L. 1993. Problem solving with grasses gone wild. *Landscape Design.* Feb., pp. 8–13.

Doyle, J.M. 1991. Fertilizers. *Landscape Mgmt.* Oct., pp. 10–12.

Duble, R. 1995. Developing a turfgrass fertilization program. *Texas Turfgrass.* Texas Turfgrass Association, Fall, pp. 11–21.

Duckworth, David. 1995. Thatch Study. Oregon State University field day booklet, Corvallis, OR, p. 4.

Dudeck, A.E. 1994. Growing turf under saline conditions. *Grounds Maint.* Jan., pp. G10–G13.

Dudeck, A.E., N.P. Swanson, and A.R. Dedrick. 1967. Mulches for Grass Establishment on Steep Construction Slopes. Highway Res. Rec. 206, Highway Res. Board, Washington, DC.

Duncan, R.R. 1996. Seashore paspalum: The next-generation turf for golf courses. *Golf Course Mgmt.* Apr., pp. 49–51.

Dunn, J.H., D.D. Minner, B.F. Fresenburg, and S.S. Bughrara. 1993. Fall fertilization of zoysiagrass. In R.N. Carrow, N.E. Christians, and R.C. Shearman, Ed. *ITRC J.* 7, Intertec Publ., Overland Park, KS.

Dunn, J.H., D.D. Minner, B.F. Fresenburg, and S.S. Bughrara. 1994. Bermudagrass and cool-season turfgrass mixtures: Response to simulated traffic. *Agron. J.* 86, pp. 10–16.

Eggens, J.L. and C.P.M. Wright. 1985. Nitrogen effects on monostands and polystands of annual bluegrass and creeping bentgrass. *HortSci.* 20, pp. 109–110.

Ellefson, C.L., T. L. Stephens, and D. Welsh. 1992. *Xeriscape Gardening.* Macmillan, New York.

Engelke, M.C., Y. Qian, and I. Yamamoto. 1996. Evaluation of five turfgrasses under linear gradient irrigation. *Agron. Abstr.* p. 147.

Engleke, M.C. and J.J. Murray. 1982. Zoysiagrass Exploration in the Orient. Trip Rep. to USDA, Texas A&M University, Dallas, TX.

Featherly, H.I. 1946. Manual of the grasses of Oklahoma. *Okla. Ag. & Mech. College Bull.* 43(21).

Feldhake, C.M., R.E. Danielson, and J.D. Butler. 1983. Turfgrass evapotranspiration: I. Factors influencing rate in urban environments. *Agron. J.* 75, p. 824.

Fidanza, M.A. and P.H. Dernoeden. 1993. Influence of N-source, mowing height, and irrigation on brown patch severity. *Agron. Abstr.* p. 157.

Fidanza, M.A. and P.H. Dernoeden. 1996a. Brown patch severity in perennial ryegrass as influenced by irrigation, fungicide, and fertilizers. *Crop Sci.* 36, pp. 1631–1638.

Fidanza, M.A. and P.H. Dernoeden. 1996b. Influence of mowing height, nitrogen source, and iprodione on brown patch severity in perennial ryegrass. *Crop. Sci.* 36, pp. 1620–1630.

Fluck, R.C. and P. Busey. 1988. Energy for mowing turfgrass. *Trans. ASAE* 31, pp. 1304–1308.

Francis, M.E. 1912. *The Book of Grasses.* Doubleday, Page & Co., New York.

Fry, J.D. and J.D. Butler. 1989a. Evapotranspiration rates of turf weeds and ground covers. *Hort. Sci.* 24, pp. 73–75.

Fry, J.D. and J.D. Butler. 1989b. Responses of tall and hard fescue to deficit irrigation. *Crop Sci.* 29, pp. 1536–1541.

Fry, J.D. and J.D. Butler. 1989c. Water management during tall fescue establishment. *Hort. Sci.* 24, pp. 79–81.

Fry, J.D., W. Upham, and L. Leuthold. 1993. Seeding month and seed soaking affect buffalograss establishment. *Hort. Sci.* 28, pp. 902–903.

Funk, C.R., B.B. Clark, and J.M. Johnson-Cicalese. 1989. Role of endophytes in enhancing the performance of grasses used for conservation and turf. In *IPM for Turfgrass and Ornamentals,* U.S. EPA, Washington, DC, pp. 203–210.

Gallant, Adrien. 1994. Nitrogen transformation and movement in the environment. *Turf & Recreation.* Jan./Feb., pp. 6–9.

Garrot Jr., D.J. and C.F. Mancino. 1994. Consumptive water use of three intensively managed bermudagrasses growing under arid conditions. *Crop Sci.* 34, pp. 215–221.

Gaussoin, R. 1994a. Which PGR best for your turf? *Northern Turf Mgmt.* Feb., p. 16.

Gaussoin, R.E. 1994b. Choosing traffic-tolerant turfgrass varieties. *SportsTurf.* July, pp. 25–26

Georgis, R. and G.O. Poinar Jr. 1994. Nematodes as bioinsecticides in turf and ornamentals. In *IPM for Turf and Ornamentals.* A.R. Leslie, Ed. CRC Press, Boca Raton, FL.

Gernert, W.B. 1936. Native grass behavior as affected by periodic clipping. *J. Am. Soc. Agron.* 28, pp. 447–456.

Gibeault, V.A. 1987. Factors influencing water use. *Proc. NW Turfgrass Assoc.,* pp. 116–119.

Gibeault, V.A. and J.L. Meyers. 1988. Irrigation and water conservation. *Grounds Maint.* May, p. IR-8-17.

Gibeault, V.A. and M. Leanard. 1987. Strawberry clover and common bermudagrass combination turf for low maintenance and energy conservation. *Calif. Turfgrass Culture* 27(1), pp. 4–5.

Gibeault, V.A., R. Autio, S. Spaulding, and V.B. Youngner. 1980. Mixing turfgrasses controls Fusarium blight. *Calif. Turfgrass Culture* 30(2–4), pp. 9–11.

Gibeault, V.A., S. Cockerham, J.M. Henry, and J. Meyer. 1990. California turfgrass: Its use, water requirement and irrigation. *Calif. Turfgrass Culture* 39(2,3), pp. 1–9.

Gifford, C.L. 1984. Species Establishment for Reclamation Purposes on Four "Soils" in Northwestern New Mexico. Utah State University MS thesis, Logan, UT.

Gilstrap, D.M. 1995. Michigan bagging law. *Proc. Michigan Turfgrass Conf.,* East Lansing, MI, p. 191.

Gold, A.J., W.R. DeRagon, W.M. Sullivan, and J.L. Lemunyon. 1990. Nitrate-nitrogen losses to groundwater from rural and suburban land uses. *J. Soil and Water Conserv.* Mar./Apr., pp. 305–310.

Gonzalez-Carrascosa, R., B.E. Branham, and P.E. Rieke. 1995. Leaching of nitrates during establishment of creeping bentgrass on high sand soils. *Agron. Abstr.* p. 153.

Gordon, B. 1986. Korean common zoysiagrass for the transition zone. *Grounds Maint.* Apr., p. 88.

Gover, A.E., L.J. Kuhns, and G.T. Lyman. 1989. Evaluation of turfgrass varieties for roadside conditions. *Turfgrass Res. Results 1989,* Penn State, University Park, PA.

Green, R.L., S.I. Sifers, C.E. Atkins, and J.B Beard. 1991. Evapotranspiration rates of eleven zoysia genotypes. *Hort. Sci.* 26, pp. 264–266.

Greenlee, J. and D. Fell. 1992. *The Encyclopedia of Ornamental Grasses.* Rodale Press, Emmaus, PA.

Greenway, G. 1997. Heritage Seeds Native Turf Seed Guide (catalog). Melbourne, Australia.

Gross, C.M., J.S. Angle, R.L. Hill, and M.S. Welterlen. 1991. Runoff and sediment losses from tall fescue under simulated rainfall. *J. Environ. Qual.* 20, pp. 604–607.

Grounds, R. 1979. *Ornamental Grasses.* Van Nostrand Reinhold Co., New York.

Hagan, A.K. 1996. Irrigation and its impact on turfgrass diseases. *Golf Course Irrigation.* Sep./Oct., pp. 12–14.

Hair, M. 1993. Getting the boot. *Chicago Tribune* Home Sec. 15. Oct. 10, 1993, p. 8.

Haldane, E.S. 1934. *Scots Gardens in Old Times (1200–1800).* Alexander Maclehose & Co., London, England.

Haley, J.E., D.J. Wehner, T.W. Fermanian, and A.J. Turgeon. 1985. Comparison of conventional and mulching mowers for Kentucky bluegrass maintenance. *Hort. Sci.* 20, pp. 105–107.

Hall, R. 1994. Turf pros respond to biostimulants. *Landscape Mgmt.* Oct., pp. 8–9.

Hall, R. 1995. Perking up foot-weary turfgrass. *Landscape Mgmt.* May, p. 39.

Hanson, A.A. 1959. Grass Varieties in the United States. USDA ARS Agric. Handbook No. 170.

Hardegree, S.P. 1994. Matric priming increases germination rate of Great Basin perennial grasses. *Agron. J.* 86, pp. 289–293.

Harivandi, A. and L. Wu. 1995. Buffalograss — A promising drought-resistant turf for California. *Calif. Turfgrass Culture* 45(1–2), pp. 1–2.

Harivandi, A. 1993. Using reclaimed water for golf course irrigation. *Golf Course Mgmt.* July, pp. 28–38.

Harivandi, M.A. and V.A. Gibeault. 1990. Managing turfgrasses during drought. *Calif. Turfgrass Culture* 40(1–3), pp. 1–2.

Harivandi, M.A., J.D. Butler, and L. Wu. 1992. Salinity and turfgrass culture. In D.V. Waddington, R.N. Carrow, and R.C. Shearman, Eds. *Turfgrass. Agron. Monograph 32,* ASA, Madison, WI.

Harivandi, M.A., W.B. Hagan, and C.L. Elmore. 1996. The use of recycling mowers in grasscycling. *Calif. Turfgrass Culture* 46(1,2), pp. 4–6.

Harivandi, M.A., W. Davis, V.A. Gibeault, M. Henry, J.V. Dam, and L. Wu. 1984. Selecting the best turfgrass. *Calif. Turfgrass Culture* 34(4), pp. 17–18.

Harlan, J.R., W.C. Elder, and R.A. Chessmore. 1952. Seeding Rates of Grasses and Legumes. Forage Crops Leaflet No. 2, Jan., Oklahoma AES, Stillwater, OK.

Harlow, Susan. 1994. Plant growth regulators come into their own. *Turf West.* Jan.

Harper II, J.C. and P.J. Landschoot. 1991. Turfgrass Seed and Seed Mixtures. Pa. Coop. Ext. circ. 391.

Harper-Lore, B.L. 1995. When Native Plants Become Federal Policy. ASA meetings C-4 div., 30 Oct.

Hathaway, P.M. 1979. Kikuyugrass, like it or not it's here to stay. *Golf Course Mgmt.* Jan., pp. 44–46.

Hawes, Kay. 1996. Super savers. *Golf Course Mgmt.* Sept., pp. 44–70.

Heckman, J.R. and W.J. Hill. 1993. Mowing practice and turf color. *Rutgers Turfgrass Proc.,* pp. 21–23.

Heckman, J.R., H. Liu, and W.J. Hill. 1994. Impact of mowing practices and fertilizer sources on turfgrass quality. *Rutgers Turfgrass Proc.,* pp. 7–20.

Hellman, L. 1992. The ETs and ATs of pest-based spraying. *Grounds Maint.* Mar., pp. 74–80.

Henrard, J.T. 1950. Monograph of the genus *Digitaria.* Universitaire pers Leiden, Leiden, So. Africa.

Henry, M.J. 1991. To improve quality, fertilize zoysiagrass. *Grounds Maint.* 26(8), pp. 14–60.

Hipp, B.W. and T.C. Knowles. 1993. Nitrate pollution prevention in surface runoff from landscapes. *Texas Turfgrass Res. Rep.,* Texas A&M University, College Station, TX.

Hitchcock, A.S. 1951. Manual of the Grasses of the United States. USDA Misc. Publ. 200.

Hoffman, T.R. 1994. Compaction root of many problems. *Inland Farmer.* May. p. 18.

Hook, J.E., W.W. Hanna, and B.W. Maw. 1992. Quality and growth response of centipedegrass to extended drought. *Agron. J.* 84, pp. 606–612.

Hooven, N. and P. Hooven. 1995. Limerock Ornamental Grasses (catalog). Port Matilda, PA.

Horst, G.L. and N.B. Dunning. 1989. Germination and seedling growth of perennial ryegrasses in soluble salts. *J. Amer. Soc. Hort. Sci.* 114, pp. 338–342.

House, I. and K. Underwood. 1996. Standard Use Terms, Definitions, and General Turfgrass Information. Amenity Grass Marketing Association, Bourne, England.

Howard, S.W. and C.B. McConnell. 1989. Living mulches. *Proceedings of the 43rd NW Turfgrass Conference* 43, pp. 55–58.

Hubbard, C.E. 1984. *Grasses.* Penguin Books, Middlesex, England.

Huffine, W.W. 1980. The Effect of P Applications on Spring Greening and Crabgrass Encroachment of Merion Kentucky Bluegrass (mimeo). Oklahoma State University, Stillwater, OK.

Huffine, W.W., L.W. Reed, and C.E. Whitcomb. 1982. Selection, Establishment and Maintenance of Roadside Vegetation. Okla. ODOT project 77-05-3, Oklahoma State University, Stillwater, OK.

Huffine, W.W., L.W. Reed, and Fenton Gray. 1977. Roadside Erosion Control—Final Report. Oklahoma ODOT project 70-01-3, Oklahoma State University, Stillwater, OK.

Huffine, W.W., L.W. Reed, and G.W. Roach. 1974. Roadside Development and Erosion Control. Oklahoma AES Misc. publ. MP-93, Oklahoma State University, Stillwater, OK.

Hughes, H.D., M.E. Heath, and D.S. Metcalfe. 1951. *Forages, the Science of Grassland Agriculture.* Iowa State Press, Ames, IA.

Hull, R.J., H. Liu, and P.M. Groffman. 1993. Nitrogen Losses from Well Fertilized Turf. 62nd. Rhode Island Turfgrass Field Day, AES, Kingston, RI.

Hummel Jr., N.W. 1993. Selecting Turfgrass for Low Maintenance Sites. Cornell University Coop. Ext. *CUTT* 4(3), pp. 1–5.

Hummel Jr., N.W. 1994. Organic Lawn Care, The Facts and Fallacies. Cornell University Coop. Ext. *CUTT* 5(1), pp. 1–6.

Humphrey, R.R. 1970. *Arizona Range Grasses.* University of Arizona Press, Tucson, AZ.

Humphreys, L.R. 1979. Tropical Pasture Seed Production. Food & Agric. Org. of the United Nations, Rome, Italy.

Iory, D.A. and M.E. Siregar. 1984. Forage research in Indonesia: Past and present. In *Asian Pastures.* Food & Fert. Tech. Center, Ag. Bldg, Taiwan, ROC.

Johns, D. and J.B Beard. 1978. Use and establishment of *Zoysia tenuifolia. Texas Turfgrass Res. 1977–78.* PR-3490. College Station, TX.

Johnson, B.J. {date not specified}. Minimal Herbicide Usage for Summer Weed Control in Turfgrasses (mimeo). Ga. AES, Griffin, GA.

Johnson, B.J. 1995. Herbicide programs utilizing reduced rates for weed control in bermudagrass turf. *Agron. Abstr.* p. 145.

Johnson, B.J. 1996. Herbicide programs for large crabgrass control in tall fescue. *Agron. Abstr.* p. 138.

Johnson, B.J. and R.N. Carrow. 1988. Frequency of fertilizer applications and centipedegrass performance. *Agron. J.* 80, pp. 925–929.

Johnson, B.J., R.N. Carrow, and R.E. Burns. 1987. Bermudagrass turf response to mowing practices and fertilizer. *Agron. J.* 79, pp. 677–680.

Jones, Jr., M. 1993. The new turf wars. *Newsweek.* June 21, 1993, pp. 62–63.

Jones, L.L. 1992. Report of Acres Applied for Certification in 1992 by Seed Certification Agencies. Prod. Publ. No. 46, AOSCA, Raleigh, NC.

Judd, B.I. 1979. *Handbook of Tropical Forage Grasses.* Garland STPM Press, New York.

Jung, G.A., J.A. Balasko, F.L. Alt, and L.P. Stevens. 1974. Persistence and yield of 10 grasses in response to clipping frequency and applied nitrogen in the Allegheny highlands. *Agron. J.* 66, pp. 517–521.

Kaplan, R., S. Kaplan, and R.L. Ryan. 1998. *With People in Mind: Design and Management for Everyday Nature.* Island Press, Washington, DC.

Karnok, K.J. 1981. Shade tolerance. *Golf Course Mgmt.* Jan./Feb., pp. 62–68.

Kaufman, Glen. 1991. Seed coating: A tool for stand establishment; a stimulus to seed quality. *HortTechnology.* Oct./Dec., pp. 98–101.

Kavanagh, T. and T.P. Cormican. 1982. Sulfate of iron: New techniques with an old herbicide. Proc. 1982 Br. Crop. Protection Conf. Weeds, pp. 947–951.

Kay, B.L. 1976. Hydroseeding, Straw, and Chemicals for Erosion Control. Agron. Progress Rep. no. 77, Agron. and Range Sci. Dept., UCO. June, p. 14.

Keeley, S. and T. Koski. 1995. Drought Resistance of Kentucky Bluegrass Cultivars. WRCC-11 Rep., Tacoma, WA, June 11.

Khan, R.A., S.T. Cockerham, and V.A. Gibeault. 1995. Kikuyugrass (*Pennisetum clandestinum*) response to nitrogen fertilizer applications and sports traffic. *Agron. Abstr.* p. 149.

Kieffer, L. 1995. Uniting the turf industry won't be an easy task. *Florida Turf Digest* 13(1), p. 6.

Kinbacher, E.J., R.C. Shearman, T.P. Riordan, and D.E. Vanderkolk. 1981. Salt tolerance of turfgrass species and cultivars. *Agron. Abstr.* p. 88.

Kneebone, W.R. 1981. Water conservation research. *Golf Course Mgmt.* June, pp. 35–40.

Kneebone, W.R., D.M. Kopec, and C.F. Mancino. 1992. Water requirements and irrigation. In D.V. Waddington, R.N. Carrow, and R.C. Shearman, Eds. *Turfgrass. Agron. Monograph 32,* ASA, Madison, WI.

Koehler, F.A., F.J. Humenik, D.D. Johnson, J.M. Kreglow, R.P. Dressing, and R.P Maas. 1982. Best Management Practices for Agricultural Nonpoint Source Control. USDA Coop. Agree. 12-05-300-472, EPA and N. Carolina Ag. Ext. Serv.

Kopec, D.M. 1996. Plant growth regulators for turf. *Landscape & Irrig.* Mar.

Koski, T. 1994. Fertilization and water quality. *Colo. Green.* Fall, pp. 20–21.

Krick, T.M., J.C. Stier, J.N. Rogers III, and J.R. Crum. 1995. Sod establishment and maintenance procedures study for athletic turf in sand based rootzones. *65th Ann. Michigan Turf Conf. Proc.,* Jan. 17–19, Lansing, MI.

Kussow, W.R. 1995a. Soil disturbance effects on N and P losses from turf. *Agron. Abstr.* p. 157.

Kussow, W.R. 1995b. Soil disturbance effects on nutrient losses from turf. *Wisc. Turf Res.* Vol. XII, pp. 95–100.

Landschoot, P.J. 1990. Diseases of turfgrass. *Landscape Mgmt.* May, pp. 32–40.

Landschoot, P.J. 1991. Recycling Turfgrass Clippings. PA. Coop. Ext. publ. R5M494.

Landschoot, P.J. and Andrew McNitt. 1994. Using composts to improve turf performance. *Rutgers Turfgrass Proc.* New Brunswick, NJ, pp. 21–26.

Leasure, G., D. Simon, and R. Simon. 1994. Bluemount Nurseries, Inc. Ornamental Grasses (catalog). Baldwin, MD.

Lederboer, F.B. and C.R. Skogley. 1967. Investigations into the nature of thatch and methods for its decomposition. *Agron. J.* 59, pp. 320–323.

Lefton, J. 1996. Herbicide efficacy linked to weather. *Landscape Mgmt.* Jan., p. 25.

Leslie, A.R. 1991. An IPM program for turf. *Grounds Maint.* March, pp. 84–116.

Liu, H., R.J. Hull, and D.T. Duff. 1993. Comparing cultivars of three cool-season turfgrasses for nitrate uptake kinetics and nitrogen recovery in the field. In *ITRC J.* 7, Intertec Publ., Overland Park, KS.

Liu, Haibo, R.J. Hull, and D.T. Duff. 1996. Turfgrass phosphorus and potassium use efficiency. *Golf Course Mgmt.* Feb., pp. 51–53.

Long, S.G. 1981. *Characteristics of Plants Used in Western Reclamation.* 2nd ed. Environ. Res. & Tech., Ft. Collins, CO.

Lucas, M.D., D.P. Montgomery, and A.D. Brede. 1986. Mower-deck injection of pesticides in turf. *Proc. SWSS* 39, p. 128.

Luellen, W.R. 1996. Call for speculation in scientific writing. *Agron. News.* ASA, Madison, WI, May, pp. 7–8.

Lundell, D. 1994. A new turfgrass species, *Poa supina. Grounds Maint.* June, pp. 26–27.

Macik, J. 1987. Sports turf injuries—Are they avoidable? *Sports Turf Manag.* 3(1), p. 9.

Mancino, C.F., M. Barakat, and A. Maricic. 1993. Soil and thatch microbial populations in an 80% sand: 20% peat creeping bentgrass putting green. *Hort. Sci.* 28, pp. 189–191.

Marcum, K.K. and C.L. Murdoch. 1991. Salt tolerance of the coastal salt marsh grass *Sporobolus virginicus* (L.) Kunth. *Agron. Abstr.* p. 180.

Marion, P.W. 1991. Spring fertilization program helps turf survive drought. *Western Turf Mgmt.* Feb., p. 10.

Marting, S.H. 1991. Grasscycling: A solution for lawn and environment. *J. Environ. Turfgrass* 3(1), p. 6.

Mathias, J.K. 1994. Insect control, cool-season turf. *Landscape Mgmt.* Apr., pp. 38–39.

Matthews, P., M.D. McCarthy, Mark Young, and N.D. McWhirter. 1993. *The Guinness Book of Records 1993.* Bantam Books, New York.

McAfee, J.A. 1996. Irrigation scheduling for weed control. *Landscape & Irrigation.* Mar., pp. 64–65.

McCarty, L.B. 1994. Winter weed control in southern turf. *Grounds Maint.* Nov., pp. 28–33.

McCarty, L.B., D.W. Roberts, L.C. Miller, and J.A. Brittain. 1990. TIPS: An integrated plant management project for turf managers. *J. Agron. Educ.* 19, pp. 155–159.

McGinnies, W.J. and K.A. Crofts. 1986. Effects of N and P fertilizer placement on establishment of seeded species on redistributed mine topsoil. *J. Range Mgmt.* 39, p. 118.

McIver, T. 1992. Buffalograss roams beyond the plains. *Landscape Mgmt.* Mar., p. 74.

McIvor, J.G. and C.P. Chen. 1985. Tropical grasses: Their domestication and role in animal feeding systems. In G.J. Blair et al., Eds. *Forages in SE Asian and S. Pacific Agric.* ACIAR Proc. 19–23 Aug., Cisarua, Indonesia.

McKernan, D. and J. Ross. 1993. Low Maintenance Grass Trial. Prairie Turfgrass Research Centre Annual Rep. Olds, Alberta, Canada.

McKernan, D., J.B. Ross, J. Penrice, and G. Patzer. 1996. The Evaluation of Various Grasses Grown Under Low Maintenance Conditions, Medicine Hat and Lethbridge Trial. Prairie Turfgrass Research Centre Rep. Olds, Alberta, Canada.

McPoland, F. 1995. Office of the federal environmental executive; guidance for presidential memorandum. *Federal Register* 95-19795.

Meyer, W.A. 1993. Local Commercial Lawn Seed Trial. Pure Seed Testing, Inc., Hubbard, OR.

Mielke, L.N. and J.S. Schepers. 1986. Plant response to topsoil thickness on an eroded loess soil. *J. Soil Water Conserv.* 41(1), pp. 59–63.

Minner, D.D. 1989. Bermudagrass solutions for low-budget transition zone fields. *SportsTurf.* July, pp. 16–18.

Minner, D.D., J.H. Dunn, S.S. Bughrara, and B.S. Fresenburg. 1993. Traffic tolerance among cultivars of Kentucky bluegrass, tall fescue, and perennial ryegrass. p. 97. *ITRC J.* 7, Intertec Publishers, Overland Park, KS.

Minnich, J. and M. Hunt. 1979. *The Rodale Guide to Composting.* Rodale Press, Emmaus, PA.

Moore, R.W., N.E. Christians, and M.L. Agnew. 1996. Response of three Kentucky bluegrass cultivars to sprayable nitrogen fertilizer programs. *Crop Sci.* 36, pp. 1296–1301.

Morishita, D.W., C. Mallory-Smith, and D. Thill. 1994. Herbicide resistance. *Farm Chemicals.* Dec. pp. 96–97.

Morris, K.N. 1995a. Cool-Season Grass Response to Simulated Athletic Traffic. Turfgrass Res. Field Day, NTEP No. 95-13, USDA, Beltsville, MD.

Morris, K.N. 1995b. Management of the Zoysiagrass/Tall Fescue Mixture. Turfgrass Res. Field Day, NTEP No. 95-13, USDA, Beltsville, MD.

Morris, R.L. and D. Devitt. 1995. Considerations for designing for the desert. *SW Lawn & Landscape* 8(2), pp. 1–3.

Munshower, F.F. 1994. *Practical Handbook of Disturbed Land Revegetation.* Lewis Publishers, Boca Raton, FL.

Murphy, J.A. and D.E. Zaurov. 1994. Shoot and root growth response of perennial ryegrass to fertilizer placement depth. *Agron. J.* 86, pp. 828–832.

Murphy, J.A., R.F. Bara, W.K. Dickson, D.A. Smith, S. Sun, B.B. Clark, and C.R. Funk. 1993. Performance of Kentucky bluegrass cultivars and selections in New Jersey turf trials. *Rutgers Turfgrass Proc.* June, pp. 88–126.

Murray, J. 1985. Potential for breeding new zoysiagrasses. *26th Illinois Turfgrass Conference Proceedings,* Urbana, IL.

Musser, H.B. 1950. *Turf Management.* McGraw-Hill, New York.

Neal, J., A. Senesac, M. Macksel, and C. Morse. 1993. Weed Control in Turfgrass and Ornamentals. Cornell University Weed Sci. Res. Rep. no. 9.

Neal, J., A. Senesac, M. Macksel, and C. Morse. 1994a. Creeping bentgrass variety/mowing height comparison. In *Weed Control in Turfgrass and Ornamentals.* Cornell University Weed Sci. Res. Rep. 10, p. 52.

Neal, J., A. Senesac, M. Macksel, and C. Morse. 1994b. *Weed Control in Turfgrass and Ornamentals.* Cornell University Weed Sci. Res. Rep. No. 10.

Nesbitt, Scott. 1994. The new breed of mulching mowers. *Golf Course Mgmt.* Feb., pp. 106–118.

Newell, A.J., A.C. Jones, N. Blaudau, and E.J. Goodall. 1995. STRI Rep. to Turfgrass Breeders. STRI, Bingley, England.

Nikolai, T.A., P.E. Rieke, B.E. Branham, D.W. Lickfeldt, M.T. Saffel, and R.N. Calhoun. 1995. Mulching tree leaves into Kentucky bluegrass turf. *Agron. Abstr.* p. 152.

Nus, J. 1993. Erosion control. *Golf Course Mgmt.* Apr., pp. 106–116.

Oakes, A.J. 1990. *Ornamental Grasses and Grasslike Plants.* Van Nostrand Reinhold, New York.

OECD. 1996. OECD Schemes for the Varietal Certification of Seed Moving in International Trade. OECD, Paris.

Oldenburg, D. n.d. Green grass glimpses make better workers. *The Washington Post.*

Olson, I. and B. Anderson. 1994. Plants of the Southwest (catalog). Sante Fe, NM.

Pair, J.C. 1994. Ornamental Grasses at Botanica, the Wichita Fardens. Kansas Coop. Ext. Serv., Manhattan, KS.

Peacock, C.H. 1986. Can we cope with salty water? *U.S. Golf Assoc. Green Sec. Rec.*, July/Aug, pp. 6–7.

Pennucci, A. 1986. Fluctuations in soil moisture associated with growth retardant use on Kentucky bluegrass. *Proc. 14th Annual NE Weed Sci. Soc.*, pp. 122–125.

Petrovic, A.M. and B.B. Baikan. 1996. Water Conservation Techniques in Turfgrass. Cornell University *CUTT* 6(2), pp. 1–6.

Piersol, J.R. 1994. Bahia grass gets no respect. *Southern Golf.* Nov./Dec., p. 30.

Platt, Tom. 1996. Fertilizing Dryland Pastures. Ag. Horizons. Wash. State Univ. Coop. Ext. Serv. Nov., pp. 9–11.

Pohl, R.W. 1968. *How to Know the Grasses.* Wm. C. Brown, Co., Dubuque, IA.

Pojar, J. and A. MacKinnon, Eds. 1994. *Plants of the Pacific Northwest Coast, Washington, Oregon, British Columbia, & Alaska.* Lone Pine Publ., Edmonton, Alberta, Canada.

Portz, H.L. 1986. Low maintenance turfs. *Proc. 27th Illinois Turfgrass Conf.*, pp. 7–18.

Potter, D.A. 1991. Earthworms, thatch and pesticides. *U.S. Golf Assoc. Green Sec. Rec.* Oct., pp. 6–8.

Potter, D.A. 1993. Integrated insect management in turfgrasses: prospects and problems. In R.N. Carrow, N.E. Christians, and R.C. Shearman, Eds. *ITRC J.* 7, Intertec Publ., Overland Park, KS.

Powell, A.J. 1984. Renovating Kentucky Bluegrass & Fescue Lawns. Kentucky Coop. Ext. Serv. AGR-51.

Powell, A.J. and L.D. Tapp. 1989. Bermudagrass Esablishment Without Irrigation. Kentucky Turfgrass Res., University of Kentucky prog. rep. 328.

Powers, J.A. 1995. Prairie Ridge Nursery (catalog). Mt. Horeb, WI.

Price, V.J. 1972. A dwarf goes Hawaiian. *Soil Conserv.* 37(8), pp. 82–84.

Raikes, C., N.W. Lepp, and P.M. Canaway. 1996. The effect of dual species mixtures and monocultures on disease severity on winter sports turf. *J. Sports Turf Res. Inst.* 72, p. 67.

Ralowicz, A.E. 1991. Evaluation and breeding of *Hilaria belangeri* for turfgrass use. Ph.D. dissertation, University of Arizona, Tucson, AZ.

Rea, John. 1665. *Ceres and Pomona.* Richard Marriot, London, England.

Reicher, Z.J. and C.S. Throssell. 1997. Effect of repeated fungicide applications on creeping bentgrass turf. *Crop Sci.* 37, pp. 910–915.

Reinhardt, T.A., M. Reinhardt, and M. Moskowitz. 1989. *Ornamental Grass Gardening.* HP Books, Los Angeles, CA.

Rhoades, A.F. and W.M. Klein Jr. 1993. The vascular flora of Pennsylvania. American Philosophical Society, Philadelphia, PA.

Rice, E.L. 1984. *Allelopathy.* Academic Press, Inc., HBJ, New York.

Richardson, J.A. and M.E. Evans. 1986. Restoration of grassland after magnesian limestone quarrying. *J. Appl. Ecol.* 23, pp. 317–332.

Richie, W.E., R.L. Green, V.A. Gibeault, and R. Autio. 1995. Influence of irrigation scheduling: Cultivar and mowing height on tall fescue performance. *Agron. Abstr.* p. 146.

Rieke, P.E. 1994. Fertilization—fall and late fall style. NW Turfgrass Assoc. *Turfgrass Topics.* Fall, pp. 9–11.

Riordan, R. and P. Busey. 1993. Sustainable future landscapes. *Turf News [ASPA].* "Special Issue" 1993, pp. 8–12.

Riordan, T.P. 1994. The Buffalograss Story. Nebraska Turfgrass Foundation Bulletin, pp. 3–4.

Riordan, T.P., M. Manton, E.J. Kinbacher, and R.C. Shearman. 1979. Evaluation of Kentucky bluegrass under low maintenance conditions. *Agron. Abstr.* p. 123.

Riordan, T.P., S.A. de Shazer, J.M. Johnson-Cicalese, and R.C. Shearman. 1993. An overview of breeding and development of buffalograss for golf course turf. In R.N. Carrow et al., Eds. *ITRC J.* 7, Intertec Publ., Overland Park, KS.

Roberts, B.C. and E.C. Roberts. 1993. The Lawnscape, Our Most Intimate Experience with Ecology. The Lawn Inst., Pleasant Hill, TN.

Roche, J. 1993. Minimizing compaction on athletic fields, golf courses. *Landscape Mgmt.* Aug., pp. 24–30.

Roche, J. 1994. Mulching mowers: Saving the environment? *Landscape Mgmt.* Feb., p. 18.

Roche, J. 1995. Supers say they'd dole out extra dollars for low-pollution, low-noise equipment. *Landscape Mgmt.* May, p. 26G.

Roche, J. 1997. Getting the most out of your pesticide program. *Golf Course Turf & Irrig.* 5(2), pp. 12–13.

Rodier, R. 1994. Mulching mowers: Then and now. *Grounds Maint.* May, pp. 14–20.

Rogers III, J.N. and D.V. Waddington. 1992. Impact absorption characteristics of turf and soil surfaces. *Agron. J.* 84, pp. 203–209.

Rogers, M. 1994. Mowing safely. *Grounds Maint.* Jun., pp. 60–66.

Rominger, J.M. 1962. Taxonomy of *Seteria* (Gramineae) in North America. Illinois Biol. Monograph 29. University of Illinois Press, Urbana.

Rossi, F.S. 1994. Plant growth regulators in landscape management. *Northern Turf Mgmt.* Feb.

Rossi, F.S. and J. Meyer. 1995. Cultivar and seeding rate effects on stand population, leaf texture, annual bluegrass invasion and disease incidence in creeping bentgrass. *Wisc. Turf Res.* Vol. XII. Madison, WI.

Rossi, F.S. and S. Millett. 1996. Long-term consequences of seeding bentgrasses at high rates. *Golf Course Mgmt.* Oct., pp. 49–52.

Rotar, P.P. 1968. *Grasses of Hawaii.* University of Hawaii Press, Honolulu, HI.

Roybal, J. 1977. People's pasture lawn may be the answer for water-short times. *Rangeman's J.* 4(1), pp. 20–21.

Ruemmele, B.A. and N. Jackson. 1993. Effect of Organic and Inorganic Fertilizer and Biostimulant Applications on Health and Vigor of Turfgrasses. 62nd. Rhode Island Turfgrass Field Day Rep., Kingston, RI.

Ruemmele, B.A., M.C. Engelke, S.J. Morton, and R.H. White. 1993. Evaluating methods of establishment for warm-season turfgrasses. *ITRC J.* 7, Intertec Publ., Overland Park, KS.

Sadasivaiah, R.S. and J. Weijer. 1981. The utilization of native grass species for reclamation of disturbed land in the alpine and subalpine regions of Alberta In *Reclamation in Mountainous Areas.* Proc. 6th Ann. Meeting Can. Land Reclaim. Assoc.

Saha, D.C. and J.M. Johnson-Cicalese. 1988. Endophyte content of cultivars and selections entered in the 1987 National Tall Fescue Test. *Rutgers Turfgrass Proc.*, N. Brunswick, NJ, pp. 50–53.

Samudio, S.H. 1996. Whatever became of the improved seeded zoysia varieties? *Golf Course Mgmt.* Aug., pp. 57–60.

Sartain, J.B. 1994. Spring fertilization. *Landscape Mgmt.* Feb., pp. 50–51.

Schaff, V. 1994. Seed selection guide (catalog). S&S Seeds, Carpinteria, CA.

Schuman, G.E., E.M. Taylor, Jr., F. Rauzi, and B.A. Pinchak. 1985. Revegetation of mined land: Influence of topsoil depth and mulching method. *J. Soil Water Conserv.* 40(2), pp. 249–252.

Schumann, G.L. 1995. What's in a name? Important changes in turf fungicides. *SportsTurf.* Feb., p. 23.

Shank, B.F. 1991. Seed and sod selection: The Xeriscape controversy. *Landscape & Irrigation.* Sept., pp. 46–47.

Shearman, R.C. 1990. Cultural practice effects on turfgrass rooting and water use. *Proc. 44th NW Turfgrass Conf.*, pp. 5–8.

Shearman, R.C., A.H. Bruneau, E.J. Kinbacher, and T.P. Riordan. 1983. Thatch accumulation in Kentucky bluegrass cultivars and blends. *Hort. Sci.* 18, pp. 97–99.

Shearman, R.C., D.M. Bishop, A.H. Bruneau, and J.D. Furrer. 1983. Turfgrass Weed Identification and Control. Nebr. Coop. Ext. Serv. EC83-1241.

Shearman, R.C., E.J. Kinbacher, and T.P. Riordan. 1980. Turfgrass-paver complex for intensively trafficked areas. *Agron. J.* 72, pp. 372–374.

Shepard, D.P., J.M. Dipaola, and W.M. Lewis. 1989. Effects of clipping regime on turf quality and mowing requirement. *Agron. Abstr.* p. 165.

Shoulders, J.F. 1982. Thatch—A menace in turf management. *Virginia Tech Turf Topics.* Oct., pp. 5–6.

Shoulders, J.F. and J.R. Hall. 1983. Avoiding the 3 to 5 year thatch syndrome. *Amer. Lawn Applicator.* Oct., p. 4–7.

Simon, R.A. 1988. Using Ornamental Grasses in the Landscape. NY State Turfgrass Assoc. Bull. 128. Oct., pp. 1199–1201.

Skerman, P.J. and F. Riveros. 1990. Tropical Grasses. Food & Agric. Org. of the United Nations, Rome, Italy.

Skogley, C.R. 1984. Landscape manager's guide to fine fescues. *Weeds, Trees, and Turf.* Nov., pp. 48–92.

Skorulski, Jim. 1996. A float above the rest. *U.S. Golf Assoc. Green Sec. Rec.* 34(3), p. 8.

Smith Jr., S.R. and Stephani Smith, Eds. 1996. Native Grass Seed Production Manual. USDA Plant Materials Program, Bismark, ND.

Smith, S. 1975. Selecting a Lawngrass for Florida. Florida Coop. Ext. Serv. Ornamental Hort. fact sheet 4.

Snow, J.T. 1976. The influence of nitrogen rate and application frequency and clipping removal on nitrogen applied in a Kentucky bluegrass turf. MS thesis, Cornell University, Ithaca, NY.

Snow, J.T. 1979. Irrigation affects species predominance. *U.S. Golf Assoc. Green Sec. Rec.* Mar./Apr., pp. 21–22.

Sommerfeld, S. 1996. Sprinkler head replacement for water conservation. *Landscape & Irrig.* 20(3), 50–52.

Soper, D.Z., J.H. Dunn, D.D. Minner, and D.A. Sleper. 1988. Effects of clipping disposal, nitrogen, and growth retardants on thatch and tiller density in zoysiagrass. *Crop Sci.* 28, pp. 325–328.

Sours, J. 1985. Reclamation and Environmental Grasses (catalog). Jacklin Seed, Post Falls, ID.

Spackeen, S. 1993. Granite Seed (catalog). Lehi, UT.

Sprague, H.B. 1940. *Better Lawns.* The Am. Garden Guild. Doubleday, Doran & Co., Garden City, NY.

Staats, D. and J.E. Klett. 1992. How dry am I? *Colo. Green.* Summer, pp. 10–11.

Stahnke, G.K. and J.B Beard. 1982. An Assessment of Antitranspirants on Creeping Bentgrass and Bermudagrass Turfs. Texas Turfgrass Res. PR-4041, pp. 36–37.

Steinegger, D.H., R.C. Shearman, and D.E. Janssen. 1979. An Evaluation of Native and Exotic Grass Species for Ornamental Use in Nebraska. Nebr. AES publ. SB546.

Stetson, D.L., C.D. Sawyer, and W.M. Sullivan. 1993. Seasonal Variability of Grass Root Mass. 62nd. Rhode Island Turfgrass Field Day Rep., Kingston, RI.

Stout, W.L., J.A. Shaffer, G.A. Jung, T.E. Staley, and R.R. Hill, Jr. 1991. Nitrogen effects on soil water extraction by tall fescue in northern Appalachia. *J. Soil Water Conserv.* 46(2), pp. 150–153.

Stroud, T. 1987. Xeriscaping. Xeri-what? *Grounds Maint.* Apr., pp. 74–82.

Stubbendieck, J., S.L. Hatch, and C.H. Butterfield. 1991. *North American Range Plants,* 4th ed. University of Nebraska Press, Lincoln, NE.

Sutton, M.A.F. 1938. Sutton's Grass Advisory Station and Research Laboratory. Sutton & Sons, Royal Seed Establishment, Reading, England.

Thompson, D.C., B.B. Clark, J.R. Heckman, and J.A. Murphy. 1993. Influence of nitrogen source and soil pH on summer patch development in Kentucky bluegrass. *ITRC J.* 7, Intertec Publ., Overland Park, KS.

Thompson, D.C., J.A. Murphy, and B. Clark. 1994. Evaluation of Organic and Microbiological Products for the Ability to Reduce Thatch and Influence Turf Quality in a Bentgrass/Annual Bluegrass Golf Course Fairway. Rutgers University Res. Rep., N. Brunswick, NJ.

Thornhill, E.J. and Ron Brown. 1987. Testing new landscape water audits in California. *Amer. Nurseryman.* 15 Jan., pp. 98–100.

Toews, E. and J.B. Ross. 1996. Response of Kentucky Bluegrass/Fescue Turf to Various Nitrogen Fertilizers. PTRC annual rep., Prairie Turfgrass Res. Center, Olds, Alberta, Canada.

Tothill, J.C. and J.B. Hacker. 1983. *The Grasses of Southern Queensland.* University of Queensland Press. St. Lucia, Queensland, Australia.

Troeh, F.R., J.A. Hobbs, and R.L. Donahue. 1991. *Soil and Water Conservation.* 2nd ed. Prentice-Hall, Englewood Cliffs, NJ.

Turner, T.R. 1978. Soil testing for turfgrasses. *U.S. Golf Assoc. Green Sec. Rec.* May/June, pp. 6–8.

Tutin, T.G. et al. 1980. *Flora Europaea.* Vol. 5. Cambridge University Press, Cambridge, England.

Uhring, A. 1993. The good, the bad, and the reality of polymers. *Southern Golf.* May/June, pp. 30–31.

Uhring, Anne. 1995. Segregation: Is it a problem? *Southern Golf.* May/June, pp. 10–11.

Uriarte, R. and D. Bowman. 1996. The use of soluble silica in the protection of fungal diseases in turfgrass. *Agron. Abstr.* p. 151.

U.S. Golf Assoc. 1994. Golf Courses Benefit People and Wildlife. U.S. Golf Association, Far Hills, NJ.

U.S. Soil Conservation Service. 1982. Improved Plant Materials Cooperatively Released by SCS through December 1982. USDA SCS, Beltsville, MD.

Van Dam, J. {date not specified}. California Irrigation Management Information System. University of California Cooperative Extension Service (mimeo).

Vargas Jr., J.M. 1995. Discouraging diseases with cultural management. *SportsTurf.* June, pp. 20–23.

Vavrek, R.C. 1990. Beneficial turfgrass invertebrates. U.S. Golf Association Green Sec. Rec. Nov./Dec., pp. 7–9.

Vincelli, P., P.B. Burrus, and A.J. Powell Jr. 1995. Impact of Mowing Height and Nitrogen Fertility on Brown Patch on Tall Fescue, 1995. Kentucky Turfgrass Res., University of Kentucky Prog. Rep. 387, p. 85.

Voigt, T.B. and J.E. Haley. 1990. 1989 NCR-10 Regional Alternative Turfgrass Species Evaluation. Illinois Turfgrass Res. Rep., University of Illinois Hort. Series 51, pp. 26–31.

Waddington, D.V., T.L. Zimmerman, G.J. Shoop, L.T. Kardos, and J.M. Duich. 1974. Soil Modification for Turfgrass Areas. Pa. AES Prog. Rep. 337.

Wagner, T. 1994. *In Our Backyard: A Guide to Understanding Pollution and Its Effects.* Van Nostrand Reinhold, New York, NY.

Walmsley, B. 1996. Potassium carbonate controls fairy ring and other diseases. *NW Turfgrass Assoc.* newsletter. Summer, p. 23.

Walton, P.D. 1983. *Production and Management of Cultivated Forages.* Reston Publishing Co., Reston, VA.

Wasser, C.H. 1982. Ecology and Culture of Selected Species Useful in Revegetating Disturbed Lands in the West. U.S. Dept. Int., Fish Wildl. Serv. FWS/OBS-82/56.

Watkins, J.E. 1994. Nitrogen affects severity of turfgrass disease. *Northern Turf Mgmt.* Feb., pp. 24–25.

Watschke, T.L. 1991. Runoff and leachate from turf treated with fertilizers and pesticides. *N. Carolina Turfgrass* 9(2), pp. 28–29.

Watschke, T.L. 1994. PGRs on golf courses. *Grounds Maint.* Jan., pp. G4–G6.

Watschke, T.L., P.H. Dernoeden, and D.J. Shetlar. 1994. *Managing Turfgrass Pests.* Lewis Publishers, Boca Raton, FL.

Watson, J.R. 1989. Athletic field renovation. *SportsTurf.* Apr., pp. 25–26.

Weijer, J. 1989. And I will send grass in thy fields. *Recreation Canada.* Mar., p. 33.

Welterlen, M.S. 1992. Beat waste bans with mulching mowers. *Grounds Maint.* May, pp. 16–22.

Wheeler, W.A. and D.D. Hill. 1957. *Grassland Seeds.* Van Nostrand, New York.

Whitcomb, C.E. and E.C. Roberts. 1973. Competition between established tree roots and newly seeded Kentucky bluegrass. *Agron. J.* 65, 126–129.

White, C.B. 1982. Sand—The building block. *U.S. Golf Assoc. Green Sec. Rec.* Sep/Oct., pp. 1–5.

White, R.H., A.H. Bruneau, and T.J. Cowett. 1993. Drought resistance of diverse tall fescue cultivars. In R.N. Carrow, N.E. Christians, and R.C. Shearman, Eds. *ITRC J.* 7, Intertec Publishers, Overland Park, KS.

White, R.H., M.C. Engelke, S.J. Morton, and B.A. Ruemmele. 1993. Irrigation water requirement of zoysiagrass. In R.N. Carrow, N.E. Christians, and R.C. Shearman, Eds. *ITRC J.* 7, Intertec Publishers, Overland Park, KS.

Whitmore, Lynn. 1989. On the native trail. *Seed World.* Aug., pp. 12–16.

Wiecko, G., R.N. Carrow, and K.J. Karnok. 1993. Turfgrass cultivation methods: influence on soil physical, root/shoot, and water relationships. *ITRC J.* 7, Intertec Publ., Overland Park, KS.

Wiesner, L.E. and G.A. Brown. 1984. Selecting Species for Revegetation. Montana Agric. Exp. Stn. special rep. No. 3.

Wilhelm, S.J. and A.J. Koski. 1993. Effects of clipping return vs. clipping removal on Kentucky bluegrass turf. *Agron. Abstr.* p. 165.

Wilkinson, J.F. 1994. Applying compost to the golf course. *Golf Course Mgmt.* Mar., pp. 80–88.

Williams, D.W., A.J. Powell Jr., P. Vincelli, and C.T. Dougherty. 1995. Kentucky Turfgrass Res. 1994–1995. University of Kentucky Progress Rep. 387, pp. 92–100.

Williams, D.W., A.J. Powell Jr., P. Vincelli, and C.T. Dougherty. 1996. Dollar spot on bentgrass influenced by displacement of leaf surface moisture, nitrogen, and clipping removal. *Crop Sci.* 36, pp. 1304–1309.

Williams, T. 1994. Turfgrass irrigation management, minimizing waste, maximizing resources. *Colo. Green.* Fall, pp. 17–18.

Woods, C. 1992. *Encyclopedia of Perennials: A Gardener's Guide.* Facts on File, New York.

Wu, L. and M.A. Harivandi. 1988. In search of low-maintenance turf: several species show promise. *Calif. Ag.* Jan./Feb., pp. 16–17.

Wu, Y. et al. 1992. *Licensed Cultivars of Herbage Crops in China.* Beijing Ag. University Press, Beijing, China.

Yaklich, R.W. et al., Eds. 1984. Rules for testing seeds. *AOSA. J. Seed Tech.* 6(2), pp. 4–13.

Young, J.A. and C.G. Young. 1986. *Collecting, Processing, and Germinating Seeds of Wildland Plants.* Timber Press, Portland, OR.

Young, S., S. Kitchen, J. Armstrong, and V. Watson. 1995. AOSCA approves certification guidelines for wild land collected seed. *Seed World.* Jan., pp. 20–21.

Youngner, V.B. 1961. Observations on the ecology and morphology of *Pennisetum clandestinum. Phyton* 16, pp. 77–84.

Youngner, V.B., A.W. Marsh, R.A. Strohman, V.A. Gibeault, and S. Spalding. 1981. Water use and turf quality of warm-season and cool-season turfgrasses. *Calif. Turfgrass Culture* 31(3,4), pp. 1–4.

Zinn, S. 1997. Florida researchers test turf of the future. *Turf.* Aug., pp. A6–A16.

Index

C

E

Q

R

S

T

U

V

W